THE ROUTLEDGE COMPANION TO EMPLOYMENT RELATIONS

Comprising five thematic sections, this volume provides a critical, international and interdisciplinary exploration of employment relations. It examines the major subjects and emerging areas within the field, including essays on institutional theory, voice, new actors, precarious work and employment. Led by a well-respected team of editors, the contributors examine current knowledge and debates within each topic, offering cutting-edge analysis and reflection.

The Routledge Companion to Employment Relations is an extensive reference work that offers students and researchers an introduction to current scholarship in the longstanding discipline of employment relations. It will be an essential addition to library collections in business and management, law, economics, sociology and political economy.

Adrian Wilkinson is Professor and Director of the Centre for Work, Organisation and Wellbeing at Griffith University, Australia.

Tony Dundon is Professor of Human Resource Management and Employment Relations in the Work and Equalities Institute, Alliance Manchester Business School, The University of Manchester, UK.

Jimmy Donaghey is Professor of Industrial Relations at Warwick Business School, University of Warwick, UK.

Alexander J.S. Colvin is the Martin F. Scheinman Professor of Conflict Resolution and Associate Dean for Academic Affairs, Diversity, and Faculty Development at the ILR School, Cornell University, USA.

Routledge Companions in Business, Management and Accounting

Routledge Companions in Business, Management and Accounting are prestige reference works providing an overview of a whole subject area or sub-discipline. These books survey the state of the discipline including emerging and cutting-edge areas. Providing a comprehensive, up-to-date, definitive work of reference, Routledge Companions can be cited as an authoritative source on the subject.

A key aspect of these Routledge Companions is their international scope and relevance. Edited by an array of highly regarded scholars, these volumes also benefit from teams of contributors that reflect an international range of perspectives.

Individually, Routledge Companions in Business, Management and Accounting provide an impactful one-stop-shop resource for each theme covered. Collectively, they represent a comprehensive learning and research resource for researchers, postgraduate students and practitioners.

Published titles in this series include:

THE ROUTLEDGE COMPANION TO EMPLOYMENT RELATIONS

*Edited by Adrian Wilkinson, Tony Dundon,
Jimmy Donaghey and Alexander J.S. Colvin*

Routledge
Taylor & Francis Group

LONDON AND NEW YORK

First published 2018
by Routledge
4 Park Square, Milton Park, Abingdon, Oxon OX14 4RN
605 Third Avenue, New York, NY 10017

First issued in paperback 2022

Routledge is an imprint of the Taylor & Francis Group, an informa business

© 2018 selection and editorial matter, Adrian Wilkinson, Tony Dundon, Jimmy Donaghey and
Alexander J.S. Colvin; individual chapters, the contributors.

The right of Adrian Wilkinson, Tony Dundon, Jimmy Donaghey and Alexander J.S. Colvin to be identified
as the authors of the editorial material, and of the authors for their individual chapters, has been
asserted in accordance with sections 77 and 78 of the Copyright, Designs and Patents Act 1988.

Publisher's Note
The publisher has gone to great lengths to ensure the quality of this reprint but points out
that some imperfections in the original copies may be apparent.

British Library Cataloguing-in-Publication Data
A catalogue record for this book is available from the British Library

Library of Congress Cataloging-in-Publication Data
A catalog record for this book has been requested

Typeset in Bembo
by Out of House Publishing

ISBN 13: 978-1-03-247619-3 (pbk)
ISBN 13: 978-1-138-91117-8 (hbk)

DOI: 10.4324/9781315692968

CONTENTS

LIST OF FIGURES/TABLES

List of figures

List of tables

ABOUT THE EDITORS

Adrian Wilkinson is Professor and Director of the Centre for Work, Organisation and Wellbeing at Griffith University, Australia and Visiting Professor at Loughborough University in the UK. Adrian has authored, co-authored and edited 30 books and more than 160 articles in refereed journals. His books include *Understanding Work and Employment: Industrial Relations in Transition* (Oxford University Press, 2003); *The Sage Handbook of Human Resource Management* (Sage, 2009); *The Oxford Handbook of Organisational Participation* (OUP, 2010); *The Handbook of Work and Employment Relations* (Elgar, 2011); *New Directions in Employment Relations* (Palgrave, 2011); *The Handbook of Comparative Employment Relations* (Elgar, 2011); *The International Handbook of Labour Unions* (Elgar, 2011); *HRM at Work: People Management and Development, 5th edition* (CIPD, 2012); and *The Oxford Handbook of Employment Relations* (2014). He is a Fellow and Accredited Examiner of the Chartered Institute of Personnel and Development in the UK and a Fellow of the Australian Human Resource Institute. Adrian was appointed as a British Academy of Management Fellow in 2010. In 2011 he was elected as an Academician (now Fellow) of the Academy of Social Sciences in recognition of his contribution to the field. In 2012 he was shortlisted by *HR Magazine* for the award of HR's Most Influential International Thinker.

Tony Dundon is Professor of Human Resource Management and Employment Relations at Alliance Manchester Business School, The University of Manchester, UK. He is a Fellow of the Academy of Social Sciences (AcSS), a Fellow of the Chartered Institute of Personnel and Development (CIPD) and previously Editor-in-Chief of the *Human Resource Management Journal* (HRMJ) and former Chief Examiner: Employee Relations for the CIPD. He has published in a range of journals, including the *British Journal of Management, Human Relations, Work Employment & Society; International Journal of Human Resource Management* – among others. His other books include: *A Very Short, Fairly Interesting and Reasonably Cheap Book about Employment Relations* (2017, Sage); *Human Resource Management: Cases and Texts*, 5th edition (2017, Pearson); *Handbook of Research on Employee Voice* (2014, Edward Elgar); *Global Anti-Unionism* (2013, Palgrave); and *Understanding Employment Relations*, 2nd edition, (2011, McGraw-Hill).

Jimmy Donaghey is Professor in Industrial Relations at Warwick Business School, University of Warwick, UK and Adjunct Associate Professor at Monash University, Australia. Prior to joining Warwick, Jimmy worked at Queen's University Belfast, from where he also received his PhD, and the University of Ulster. His research focuses on social partnership and employee voice, alongside an emerging interest in the governance of labour in global supply chains. His most recent project is a British Academy/Society for the Advancement of Management Studies-funded project examining the response to the Rana Plaza disaster in apparel supply chains. He has published in journals such as the *British Journal of Industrial Relations*, *Human Resource Management*, *Human Relations*, *Work, Employment and Society* and *Economic and Industrial Democracy*. He is an Academic Fellow of the CIPD in the UK, member of the editorial board of the *British Journal of Management* and member of the Economic and Social Research Council Peer Review College.

Alexander J.S. Colvin is the Martin F. Scheinman Professor of Conflict Resolution at the ILR School, Cornell University. He is also the Associate Director of the Scheinman Institute on Conflict Resolution and Associate Editor of the *ILR Review*. His research and teaching focuses on employment dispute resolution, with a particular emphasis on procedures in non-union workplaces and the impact of the legal environment on organisations. His current research projects include an empirical investigation of the outcomes of employment arbitration and a cross-national study of labour and employment law change in the Anglo-American countries. Alex has published articles in journals such as *Industrial & Labor Relations Review*, *Industrial Relations*, *British Journal of Industrial Relations*, *Academy of Management Journal*, *Personnel Psychology*, *Relations Industrielles*, the *Journal of Empirical Legal Studies*, the *Ohio State Journal on Dispute Resolution* and the *Cornell Journal of Law & Public Policy*. His books include *An Introduction to Collective Bargaining and Industrial Relations; the Oxford Handbook of Conflict Management, Labor Relations in a Global World: An Introduction Focus on Emerging Countries* and *Arbitration Law*.

THE CONTRIBUTORS

Matthew M.C. Allen: Senior Lecturer in Organisation Studies, The University of Manchester

Mark Anner: Associate Professor of Labor and Employment Relations, and Political Science, Penn State University

Ariel C. Avgar: Associate Professor at the Industrial and Labor Relations School at Cornell University

Michael Barry: Professor of Employment Relations, Griffith University

Rose Batt: Alice Hanson Cook Professor of Women and Work, Industrial and Labor Relations School, Cornell University

María Jesús Belizón: Assisant Professor, University College, Dublin

Chiara Benassi, Lecturer in HRM, King's Business School, King's College London

Chris King-Chi Chan: Associate Professor, City University of Hong Kong

Paul F. Clark: Director and Professor of the School of Labor and Employment Relations, Penn State University

Alexander J.S. Colvin: Martin F. Scheinman Professor of Conflict Resolution at the Industrial and Labor Relations School, Cornell University

Niall Cullinane: Senior Lecturer in Management, Queen's University, Belfast

Pauline Dibben: Professor of Employment Relations, University of Sheffield

Michael Doherty: Professor of Law and Head of Law Department, Maynooth University, Ireland

Jimmy Donaghey: Professor of Industrial Relations, The University of Warwick

Tony Dundon: Professor of HRM and Employment Relations, University of Manchester

Lorenzo Frangi: Associate Professor of Employment Relations, University of Quebec, Montreal

Stephen Frenkel: Professor of Organization and Employment Relations, University of New South Wales

Katiuscia Galhera: PhD in Political Science at Campinas State University, Brazil; Professor, Federal University of Dourados Metropolitan Region (UFGD)

Michel Goyer: Senior Lecturer, Department of Management, University of Birmingham

Samanthi J. Gunawardana: Lecturer in Gender and Development in the Faculty of Arts, Monash University

Bill Harley: Professor, University of Melbourne. James Riady Chair of Asian Business

Brian Harney: Associate Professor in Strategic HRM at Dublin City University Business School

Yunbing He: PhD student, City University of Hong Kong

Robert Hebdon: Emeritus Professor, McGill University

Gail Hebson: Senior Lecturer in Human Resource Management, University of Manchester

Robert MacKenzie: Professor of Working Life Science, Karlstad University, Sweden

Samuel Mansell: Lecturer in Business Ethics, School of Management, University of St Andrews

Miguel Martínez Lucio: Professor of International HRM & Comparative Industrial Relations, University of Manchester

Sung-Chul Noh: Assistant Professor of HRM and Employment Relations, Saitama University, Japan

Greg Patmore: Emeritus Professor of Business and Labour History, The University of Sydney

Dionne Pohler: Assistant Professor, University of Toronto

Juliane Reinecke: Professor of International Management and Sustainability, King's College London

Jill Rubery: Professor of Comparative Employment Systems, University of Manchester

Peter Sheldon: Professor, School of Management and Industrial Relations Research Centre, University of New South Wales

Milena Tekeste: PhD student, School of Management, Royal Holloway College

Andrew Timming: Associate Professor of Human Resource Management, University of Western Australia Business School

Rocio Valdivielso del Real: Senior Lecturer in Management/Business at Liverpool Business School

Keith Whitfield: Professor of Human Resource Management and Economics, Cardiff University

Adrian Wilkinson: Professor of Employment Relations, Griffith University

Colin C. Williams: Professor of Public Policy, University of Sheffield

Paul Willman: Professor of Management, London School of Economics

Geoffrey Wood: Professor of International Business, University of Essex

Suhaer Yunus: Research Associate, Wales Institute of Social and Economic Research, Data and Methods, Cardiff University

General introduction

1

EMPLOYMENT RELATIONS

Older reflections and new horizons

*Adrian Wilkinson, Tony Dundon, Jimmy Donaghey
and Alexander J.S. Colvin*

Introduction

Almost everyone has an employment relationship of sorts, from the employed, traditional employee to the (so-called) independent contractor engaged in the 'gig economy'. The extent to which the study of work and employment remains central and relevant to the functioning of a modern economy is well established (Ackers and Wilkinson, 2003; BUIRA, 2008; Kaufman, 2004; Meardi; 2014, Wilkinson, Wood and Deeg, 2014). However, of equal importance is the scope and variability of the broader environmental and contextual changes to the nature of paid work and employment relations (ER) as a field of study. This volume seeks to produce an overview of these key trends to understand the nature and governance of work relations in the modern economy. We outline examples of both change and continuity within the area of employment relations.

Most people have an instinctive understanding of what they think employment relations is about. After all, most people have to work to earn a living. Almost every adult has had some direct and immediate experience of employment, which is shaped by the relations they have with others at their workplace, whether in a small or large firm, in a private or public sector organisation, or as a skilled or unskilled employee. However, employment contexts are also highly variable and so instinctive perceptions are changeable and can become biased: work may be secure or insecure, highly gendered or precarious and subject to different influences that change over time and space. A lot can depend on where you work and live, how you are managed and by whom, or the immediacy of the personal and social relations with those around you. The subject matter is thus not so instinctive or straightforward: sources of influence can be wide and varied, and evaluating human behaviours and people's intentions in a work setting can be extremely uneven and complicated.

Drawing on a long history of literature (Budd, 2004; Clegg, 1975; Commons, 1959; Dunlop, 1958; Edwards, 1986; Kaufman, 1993; Kelly, 1998), 'employment relations' is defined here as a field of study in *the regulation and governance of rules, rule-making processes, institutions, attendant behaviours of actors, and relevant outcomes such as co-operation, equity, performance and conflict in employment*. Two key underpinning concepts underlie this approach. First, at the heart of employment relations is understanding how such parties with different – sometimes competing, sometimes complementary – interests interact with each other and how wider societal context shapes this interaction. Central to this are the places of the owner, manager and the managed in relation to production: with industrialisation, to use Marxist terminology, capital owns the means of production (land, plant, machinery etc.) and uses labour to increase profits from those means of production, with managers directing labour in this pursuit. Thus, the interests of the various parties in the relationship may differ.

A second key issue building on this is the idea of the 'indeterminacy' of labour and the regulatory power of labour market institutions (Fox, 1974): both employers and employees have an enduring dependency on each other, yet at the same time also have divergent (even opposing) interests and objectives. Edwards (1986), in developing his concept of "structured antagonism", alludes to the dilemma that on the one hand managers need to control and regulate the work effort of employees, yet on the other hand, they also want to engender co-operative compliance, if not active engagement. In turn, employees have a vested interest in seeking higher wages, which would distribute private profit away from the employer, while also preferring to co-operate with employers for stable earnings and job security. The indeterminacy is thus a constant dynamic because the detailed capacity of employees to fulfil their work obligations and moderate earnings and effort has an element of uncertainty (Smith, 2006). Edwards (1990) explained such a dynamic as the degree of 'relative autonomy' of labour in terms of executing work tasks. This dynamic is heavily influenced by the institutional context in which it is set. Thus, a key theme of ER is the necessity of understanding the disciplinary perspectives and methodological influences upon which the study is based; these are covered in the first section of the book. Section Two includes a set of chapters that discuss actors, followed in Section Three by chapters reviewing how core ER processes are regulated. The final sections cover new and emerging issues within the field, along with a chapter considering the future of work and ER. The remainder of this chapter situates the contributions in this volume against the broad nature of the field.

Employment relations perspectives

Employment relations is best viewed as a 'field of study' rather than an academic discipline in its own right. In many ways, ER academics use theoretical perspectives to explain particular issues and empirical observations, while in disciplines like organisation studies, empirical phenomena are used to explain and develop particular theories. Whitfield (Chapter 10, this volume) makes the point that the methods employed by researchers draw upon their specific perspectives: for example economists are more likely to use surveys and be positivist while sociologists are more likely to use qualitative methods. Employment relations is rich and dynamic because of its multi-disciplinary nature, covering economics, sociology, psychology, history and law (among others). Contemporary developments include human resource management (HRM), labour process theory (LPT), organisational behaviour (OB) and institutionalism and neo-institutional contributions (Barry and Wilkinson, 2016; Thompson, 2013). Each of these disciplinary perspectives brings unique and varied contributions to the field of study.

Researchers in the UK and US in the 1950–60s tended to approach the subject as one that addressed a growing 'labour problem': that is with a rise in collective mobilisation and militancy, both academic debates and public policy addressed issues of voluntary regulation of market forces through the institution of collective bargaining and employment law. In other countries (e.g. in continental Europe) national traditions shaped various regulatory approaches, some of which followed a more statutory model of corporatist democracy, such as works councils and social pacts (Frege and Kelly, 2013; Schmitter, 1974; Streeck, 1992). Cullinane outlines in Chapter 2 of this volume how, with the benefit of hindsight, these earlier traditions seeking to promote the 'institution of liberal democracy' were misplaced. In subsequent decades, particularly in the Anglo-American world from the 1980s, a globalised neo-liberal paradigm weakened organised labour, witnessed a vast decline in manufacturing, elevated unregulated markets and espoused the financialisation of international capitalism (Crouch, 2000).

A key starting point in understanding the employment relationship is naturally the field of economics. The employment relationship is essentially one of exchange: workers sell their labour to employers through the labour market. However, this market as understood is significantly different from other markets due to the nature of the social relations contained within it. As such, economics is typically heterodox in the ER field, as economists seek to explain the role of labour market institutions and other external agencies on employment outcomes (Grimshaw and Rubery, 2008). Willman (Chapter 3, this volume) charts the historical turn from neoclassical to broader and heterodox interest among economists about employment and labour market institutions. Arguably, the neoclassical approach is founded on flawed assumptions because labour is viewed as a commodity in the same sense as other goods or services in competitive markets. This has been problematic for two reasons, as outlined by John Commons (1911, 1931, see also, Kaufman, 2006). First, there is no satisfactory theory of the firm that is capable of considering the indeterminacy of work relations, job tasks and interpersonal relations. In short, far too much is assumed to be *ceteris paribus*. Second, the hiring and firing of labour is viewed as a simplified transaction, rather than a human idiosyncratic dynamic. Neoclassical interpretations assume hiring contracts are final and definitive, with the parties having full market information and equal power when making transactions, whereas more political and heterodox interpretations recognise agency and hierarchy in shaping labour market functionality. A further twist is 'institutional economics' as an approach to capturing contracting transactions, such as voice and bargaining (Freeman and Medoff, 1984). The distinctive contribution here is that economics views efficiency and performance, not processes or power relations, as driving outcomes (see Willman, Chapter 3, this volume). To this end, institutional economics predicts that outcomes such as voice, collective organisation or conflict meditation have to produce efficiency gains specifically for the firm, not necessarily for employees, whereas other academic disciplines approach power and authority in very different ways.

While acknowledging that labour is a market-based transaction, though substantially different, a key institution supporting the maintenance of markets is that of law. For many legal scholars it is the contract of employment that is typically considered the alpha and omega of employment regulation. However, there are a number of flawed assumptions in treating the employment contract as the single or key central institution. For example the assumption that the actors enter a contract as equally powerful bargaining agents is problematic (Fox, 1966). Employees do not possess the same resources or power base as corporations when negotiating a contract, whether for pay or other work rules. Arguably, the nature of a wider regulatory dynamic is such that more complex, multiple sources of influence exist alongside or in addition to the law, such as institutional policy, collective agreements or even unilateral employer power (Inversi et al., 2017; Kochan, Katz and MacKersie, 1986; Streeck, 1992). Indeed, one doyen of legal ER scholarship argued that the contract of employment is little more than a 'figment' conceived only in the legal mind (Kahn-Freund, 1967), to which an independent trade union would be a more realistic and equitable force in redressing the imbalance of power in ER (Kahn-Freund, 1977, p. 10). Doherty (Chapter 4, this volume) charts the changing way the law and legal regulation has shifted over time, from, on the one hand, statute to a more reflexive and soft regulatory approach in many jurisdictions and, on the other hand, from collective to individual rights, which coincides with a decline in collective bargaining and unionisation.

Richard Hyman (2004) famously described the study of the employment relationship as being "ethnocentric" and embedded in the national system within which it was based. As such, employment relations are often heavily path dependant, with the development of mutually reinforcing institutions needing to be examined in historical context (Hall and Soskice, 2001). Patmore argues (Chapter 5, this volume) that historical perspectives in ER allow a deeper and more temporal understanding of change, theory and practice, which by default cannot be unravelled through the short-term studies found in, for example, economics or psychology. Measuring cause and effect between discrete variables (X, Y or Z), or among conflicting actors or complementary institutions, cannot assess futuristic change and it is historical analysis that shows so-called modern management practices (e.g. employee voice) have been tried many times under different guises (e.g. affective commitment, industrial democracy or worker partici-pation (see Wilkinson and Fay, 2011; Wilkinson, Wood and Deeg, 2014).

The study of work and labour has a long tradition in sociology, going back to the works of Marx and Durkheim. In particular, the focus of both of these was understanding the rela-tionship of work to wider societal issues but with vastly different prescriptions. In recent times, the sociological strain within employment relations has utilised critical forms of analysis about management and wider societal forces, typically from the labour process school of thought, building on the seminal work of Braverman (1974). In Chapter 6 Harley advances Wright-Mills' (1959) 'sociological imagination' lens as a particularly fruitful perspective. Sociology draws attention to various critical intersections: between organisational structures and processes (pay, voice, co-operation), history (changes over time, place and context), institutional behaviours (bargaining, the church, community, unions, employer agencies) and lived experiences of indi-viduals (including identities as workers, as women, etc.). In many ways, sociological perspectives draw attention to multiple 'levels' of analysis in ER, from the individual to the type of society in which employment is commodified and organised (Burawoy, 2008). In contrast to many other perspectives and approaches, sociological scholars have often had an 'activist' role in seeking to contribute to public policy and improve practice for the good of society as a whole, not neces-sarily just for the good of the firm or shareholders.

Economics, history, legal analysis and sociology all have a strong imprint on gender analysis of employment and the labour market. Gender has brought a unique perspective to the analysis of the employment relationship that unpacks key issues beyond a narrow gender focus. Hebson and Rubery (Chapter 7, this volume) highlight that as a perspective gender has made four distinctive contributions: it has broadened the analysis of the relationship to include a wider array of societal interaction; it has been at the forefront of the study of inequality at work; it has focused on how issues around the regulation of the workplace reproduces hierarchies; and it has brought a focus onto "doing gender" in the workplace. A key observation is that the gender perspective has opened up new areas of study, such as aesthetic labour, which go beyond a more narrow interpretation of gender.

One of the closest perspectives to employment relations is that of human resource man-agement (HRM). Arguably, the nomenclature distinctions drawn between HRM, personnel management and employee relations is the result of the gap left by the diminished interest in 'industrial' relations as a separate or distinct field of academic study (Storey and Sisson, 1993). For some, the HRM perspective is connected to, or is an extension of, employment relations, seeing the field as evolving to incorporate the regulation and management of employment drawing on multiple perspectives such as economics, psychology, the law or sociology (Boxall and Purcell, 2011; Wilkinson et al., 2017). Indeed, many HRM professors and scholars, espe-cially in the UK, started life as employment (or industrial) relations academics (see Ackers and Wilkinson, 2003). Harney et al. (Chapter 8, this volume) draw out some key points of difference as well as embedded connections with employment relations. As an approach to managing employment, HRM draws on different theoretical and philosophical antecedents. While the origins of HRM are unclear, it is generally accepted that the term emerged in the USA in the early 1980s, with a distinct unitarist underpinning that employees and managers have shared goals and interests (Guest, 1987). To some extent the differences between the two revolve around whether HRM is viewed as 'soft' or 'hard'. The former accentuates the '*human*' (interested in employee commitment, voice, nurturing talent and plurality of values), while the latter emphasises people as a '*resource*' (who are easily and readily disposable).

Related to the historical turns in the field is the evolution of institutional approaches, which draws heavily on the comparative politics literature. Institutionalism is less a perspective than an approach that utilises political science, economics (classical and heterodox), business systems theory and sociology. Much analysis draws on broader patterns of capitalism, such as Varieties of Capitalism (VoC) literatures contrasting liberal and coordinated business models (Hall and Soskice, 2001). Analysis often extrapolates workplace issues to international narratives about isomorphic pressures for change and business system developments (Morgan, 2007). The institutionalist school is much more nuanced than simplified liberal versus coordinated market explanations. Allen and Wood (Chapter 9, this volume) draw attention to three neo-institutional approaches incorporating formal and hierarchical views. These may be narrow in defining institutions as somehow separate and distinct entities, rather than connected or complementary within and across international boundaries (Wilkinson and Wood, 2017). Of further utility to employment relations is the intersection of institutions with actors and the way relationships, sources of power and influence intermix. Some institutionalists argue for state regulation (Streeck and Thelen, 2005; Thelen, 2012) to promote rights or institutional advantage (e.g. training or skills), while others assess the way firms and multinationals obtain competitive advantage from exercising influence over political decision-makers, resulting in gains from outcomes that may include outsourced jobs, weakened labour and lowered wages through precarious employment through global supply networks (Jessop, 2012; Taylor et al., 2013). Institutional approaches, while often eclectic and embedded in multiple other socio-economic paradigms, offer fruitful analyses about possible ER issues that draw on international patterns of change (see Allen and Wood, Chapter 9, this volume).

Realising the subject of employment relations as a field of study that encompasses multi-disciplinary perspectives and occurs at multiple levels – workplace, sector, societal and global – is only a starting point. Who is involved in employment relations, how actors influence one another and ER processes and outcomes is another part of the specification.

Actors

As outlined above, the role of interests has been central to the study of the employment relationships. As such, the role of actors – the parties who make up the employment relationship – has long occupied analytical focus in the field. Indeed, one of the key debates in many of the disciplinary paradigms summarised above is to what degree agency deals with and modifies substantive issues in the employment relationship, or whether institutions and structural arrangements for rule-making remain more dominant in shaping employment relations outcomes. The main actors typically include: the state and related government agencies, including the judiciary; owners and managers, and their respective collective organisations such as employer associations and professional institutes; and employees and their representative institutions such as trade unions and collective professional associations. Given the decline in trade union membership since the mid-1980s, interest in other non-government organisations (NGOs) has occupied a role in ER (Heery et al., 2012). These actor groups include the likes of citizens advice advocacy, local community coalitions and mobilisations for ethnic minority workers outside the boundaries of the workplace (Heery et al., 2014; Holgate, 2009)

Of all the actors associated with employment relations, the state is undoubtedly the most powerful in singular resource and mobilisation terms (Crouch, 1993). Despite many predicting its decline in the context of neo-liberalism, the state maintains the ability to shape ER both directly and indirectly (Howell, 2005; Meardi et al., 2016). Indeed, it is the state that occupies a forceful role in being the only party that can directly change the 'rules of the game' through statutory legislation, whether that legislation is in support of worker rights or to weaken unions, or to promote a more business-friendly economic environment. Nonetheless, as Martínez Lucio and McKenzie note (Chapter 11, this volume), the politicisation of the state and its unique agencies (e.g. the police, military) can be more complex. Over time different political trajectories of the state have changed according to the shifting influences of vested-interest parties: unitarist ideologies underpinning employer or market interests, while alternative pluralist (or Marxist) state ideologies may promote a regulatory focus towards collective bargaining or union legitimisation. While much neoliberal discourse focuses on "de-regulation", a key point made has been that what has been re-experienced is actually re-regulation, with states shifting their attention onto curbing the ability of parties, particularly labour, to act (Jessop, 1995; Standing, 1997).

This shift in the focus of the state has had profound implications for all actors, but particularly for trade unions. The environment for unions has changed significantly since Freeman and Medoff (1984) put forward their two faces of unionism: monopoly power and voice. Marginson (2015) highlights that state support for the decentralisation of pay bargaining played an important role in the decline of collective bargaining and unions in the UK. In Chapter 12 (this volume), Clark charts the rise and decline of trade unions through an Anglo-American lens. Of note is how ER approaches the study of trade unionism, with interest in union government and formation, strategy and decision-making, external regulation and economic influence. Clark reviews several theories to explain the changing landscape for unionisation, including global economic shifts and displacement of domestic manufacturing with multinational supply chains and cheaper sources of labour. Ultimately, Clark finishes on an upbeat note that despite decline, unions are needed but that new forms and strategies may be required. Clark's analysis also connects with the politicisation of the state considered by Martínez-Lucio and McKenzie (Chapter 11, this volume), showing how political motivations of government can exert coercive change: for example President Ronald Reagan's sacking of 17,000 striking US federal air traffic controllers in 1981 and replacement of them with a strike-busting work force, or Margaret Thatcher's defeat of the National Union of Mineworkers (NUM) in the UK in 1984–1985.

The issues related to managerial prerogative, power and the role of multinational enterprises are taken up in the next two chapters (Sheldon about managers as actors in Chapter 13, and in Chapter 14 multinational employers are considered by Belizón). Offe and Wiesenthal (1980) presented a rather simplified approach to employers by arguing that the interests of employers are relatively easily united as they are all seeking to increase profit. Sheldon highlights that such an approach is overly simplistic in the context of intensified competition resulting from globalisation/internationalisation and changed technology. He highlights that these pressures have led to myriad responses, including individualisation and high road HRM strategies. Recent research (Barry and Wilkinson, 2011a; Gooberman et al., 2017) highlights that despite the decline in union power, collective employer associations have maintained, if not actually increased, their importance. In particular, Sheldon highlights that employer associations provide both collective and also selective goods for members.

A growing sub-set of employers who are particularly interesting and important actors in contemporary employment relations is multinational corporations (MNCs). MNCs as employers intersect with the state and political influence, institutional and regulatory agencies, and of course the relationship managers and employers develop with trade unions as counterpoised bargaining agents. Analysis about how MNCs diffuse practice highlights "forward diffusion", that is where MNCs bring practices from their home countries to foreign subsidiaries, but also that MNCs engage in "reverse diffusion", that is where lessons are drawn from new sites to inform corporate policy (Edwards et al., 2010; Edwards et al., 2013). Belizón (Chapter 14, this volume) highlights that MNCs often adopt a Janus-like role as an ER actor: on the one hand they act as a "rule-taker" with practices shaped by home and host countries to varying extents; on the other hand, they act as a "rule-maker" in both influencing public policy and in setting standards and practices for their subsidiaries to follow. MNCs are also active agents shaping regulations, laws and policy objectives of the national state around employment relations outcomes (see Cullinane et al., 2014; Dundon et al., 2014). These all make for fruitful insights about agency and the capacity of actors, as groups of individuals as well as collective associations, to shape the contours of work and employment rules and regulations.

Regulating employment relations

As outlined in the previous section, actors are a key focus of scholarship in employment relations. However, how these actors regulate the employment relationship often is what sets the ER approach apart from the disciplinary approaches outlined above. Allan Flanders (1970) famously defined ER as the institutions of job regulation. More recently Keith Sisson (2010, p. 4) defined ER as the study of 'the institutions involved in governing the employment relationship, the people and organisations that make and administer them, and the rule-making processes that are involved, together with their economic and social outcomes'.

Without doubt, the regulatory institution that has attracted the most attention from employment relations scholars has been that of collective bargaining. Beatrice and Sidney Webb (1894) highlighted that collective bargaining enabled the creation of "the common rule" where through collective representation, workers could lessen the power imbalance with employers. For Freeman and Medoff (1984), collective bargaining was the area where unions could exert their monopoly power the greatest. For much of the 1960s and 1970s trade unions and collective bargaining were the primary focus and the vehicle to achieve this, with more unions and collective bargaining seen as the answer to employment relations issues. As Pohler (Chapter 15, this volume) highlights, collective bargaining only carries out this function when embedded in a wider network of institutional support throughout society. With union decline, much has changed significantly; in ER we have seen a return to examining the employment relationship in broader terms and an expansion in the study of non-union forms of employment regulation (Gall and Dundon, 2013; Kaufman, 2014). The basis of the employment exchange is security and flexibility – employees receive rewards (tangible and intangible) in return for which employers acquire the right to direct them – and as noted earlier the nature of the exchange can be indeterminate, continuous, contradictory, co-operative but also exploitative at times. Regardless of whether trade unions are recognised, the process of exchange is political, involving ongoing negotiation in an unequal power relationship.

So collective bargaining is one process to deliver employment relations rule-making: other processes include consultation and non-union employee representative systems, informal social dialogue, mediation and conciliation, along with the law and contract status. Indeed, as Ackers and Wilkinson (2008) note, ER has long centred on the study of social institutions as well as the contract of employment. The Webbs began this process and the Oxford School carried forward this tradition of accumulating historical details about trade unions, collective bargaining and employers' associations as the core feature of industrial relations in regulating work rules and pay, for example (Kaufman, 2012). Employment relations has been criticised for its obsession with a highly limited range of social institutions, such as a narrow definition of contract, trade unions and collective bargaining, of which the latter are becoming less central to the sociology of contemporary society. But while the prominence of collective bargaining has declined markedly, it is still an integral part of the ER landscape across much of mainland Europe, the UK, the USA and Commonwealth countries like Australia, New Zealand and Canada.

Moreover, while the institutions of collective bargaining, the law or trade unionism have changed in various ways in many developed countries (Pohler, this volume), it is important to note that these are not the only mechanisms with which to regulate ER (Doellgast and Benassi, 2014; Wilkinson and Wood, 2012). Individual managers vary in their willingness to accept a curbing of managerial rights, depending on the subject matter under consideration. Most institutional ER work looks at regulatory and normative institutions, but cognitive institutions can also affect worker treatment due to their "taken-for-grantedness" (Scott, 2001) and negligible cost of implementation (Pohler, this volume).

After collective bargaining, employee voice has been a primary concern of employment relations, including informal and NER (non-union employee representation) channels for social dialogue (Wilkinson et al., 2014). In their classic formulation, the other face of trade unionism for Freeman and Medoff (1984) was that of voice. They regarded voice not just as a mechanism to raise grievances but also as something that could be associated with higher worker productivity and lower exit. "Voice" is a term which, as Barry et al. (Chapter 16, this volume) highlight, has been interpreted quite differently across disciplines such as ER, HRM, organisational behaviour and the sociology of work. Much early work on voice in ER focused on non-union workplaces and looked at systems designed to keep unions out (Gollan et al., 2014), but more recent work suggesting looking at non-union workplaces only through the lens of how they compare to union workplaces may not make sense, with the term "non-unionism' being limiting, in that firms are only analysed in relation to unionisation. Equally of interest are alternative mechanisms to regulate the workplace, including voice systems, although these are not always stable and rely on managers taking the system seriously and being prepared to devote time and effort to keep it going. Models of high commitment work practices include voice to challenge management decisions regarding discipline and some other matters because it enhances employees' perceptions of procedural justice, which may positively impact employee motivation and commitment (Mowbray et al., 2014). There is considerable literature on how employers should build a better dialogue with their workforce by considering alternative voice methods of engagement, including forms of dialogue to resolve possible disagreements (Barry et al., Chapter 16, this volume).

Colvin and Avgar (Chapter 17, this volume) highlight the trend towards the use of dispute resolution mechanism in workplaces. Growing attention to alternative dispute resolution (ADR) procedures illustrates how the field of ER is evolving by continuing to focus on institutions and regulatory processes in areas beyond its previous emphasis on unions and collective bargaining. ER research on ADR is investigating the use of traditional processes of mediation and arbitration in new domains, such as non-union workplaces, and the resolution of individual employment rights claims (Colvin and Avgar, this volume). Central to this endeavour is the traditional emphasis on understanding the conflicts and institutions of regulation of the employment relationship.

Interest in conflict has been a key part of employment relations, with conflict seen not as pathological but rather normal because managers and workers can have very divergent interests and competing priorities (Frangi et al., Chapter 18, this volume). As individual employees tend to be powerless in contrast to the resources available to an employer, conflicts are commonly pursued as collective forms of action (Dundon and Rollinson, 2011). While strike action has diminished in many countries, some argue that conflict has taken other forms, manifesting itself as 'flight' rather than 'fight'. In other words, workers may engage in unofficial, unorganised and even individualised forms of conflictual behaviours. Thus, Franghi et al. (2017) argue that a fundamental transformation of labour conflict is taking place due to the effects of globalisation on labour and work, which requires us to rethink our mental maps, where labour conflict was seen as collective employee mobilisation in the form of strikes (Kelly, 1998). But they suggest that labour conflict has not disappeared and employers have not transformed the *'recalcitrant worker' into the supine, docile and biddable worker* (Franghi et al., 2017) and indeed employees are resilient and determined to find new ways of resisting following the notion of labour conflict as a balloon, where constraints reduce pressure on one part but cause expansion in another and the balloon assumes a new configuration (Sapsford and Turnbull, 1994). Frangi et al. (Chapter 18, this volume) point to new actors (not just unions) and new loci (less likely to be at the plant gate): tribunals for individual claims; squares for social protest; and in the cybersphere too, so ER is played out on a much wider stage.

Broadening employment relations

The field of employment relations has evolved considerably since the likes of Dunlop put forward his systems theory. Similarly, while Clark Kerr and colleagues (1960) predicted that technology would lead to a convergence across the world as economic development unfolded, in fact, the trend could be argued to be in the opposite direction. This section of the volume seeks to track the broadening of the employment relationship in two ways: first, what are the identifiable trends in terms of the effects of globalisation on ER and secondly, what are the new areas of research being opened up by such changes?

An additional and broader area that has developed in ER has been a focus on precarious work. Guy Standing (2011) famously put forward the idea of the precariat as a particular social class who were subjected to the harshest end of the labour market as well as pernicious welfare state policy. As Benassi and Tekeste (Chapter 19, this volume) point out, risky and unstable working conditions have always affected part of the workforce, but the term "precarious work" refers to the growth of atypical, short-term, low-paid jobs in post-industrial economies since the seventies (Kalleberg, 2009). While in the post-war period western economies could provide relatively homogenous wages and working conditions to large segments of the workforce, especially based around manufacturing, the neoliberal economic model facilitated the precaritisation of the employment relationship. This growing sector of the economy and the way in which the work is regulated (or not) is a key feature of emerging research into work and employment. Issues surrounding ER also feature in domains other than the party political. A key development in recent times has been the emergence of what have been labelled "disruptive technologies", including robotisation and artificial intelligence, and management by algorithm. The effect of automation and robotisation has been held up by some as threatening vast numbers of middle-level jobs (Fabo et al., 2017). With the emergence of Uber, AirBnB, Deliveroo and other similar technological changes, debates about the employment relationship have been in focus. For reasons of insecurity, bogus self-employment and precarious work, many developments in this area of the economy have been viewed with concern by scholars in the area of ER. A mixture of new questions and reframed old issues has emerged in relation to developments such as these, including: how do we define an employee and hence an employment relationship; do developments such as these provide people with access to extra income with low barriers to entry or do they mark a further fragmentation in the direction of precarity; and how should governments respond to these developments in terms of taxation, social security and the likes?

Globalisation and changes in technology have increased the mobility of capital, work and workers, thereby weakening the influence of national laws, institutions and norms in shaping employment relationships and outcomes (Kochan and Bamber, 2009, p. 318), reflecting not so much the international mobility of labour, but rather a clearer international division of labour, including more offshoring of manufacturing (e.g. to China) and services (e.g. to India). With drivers of change such as globalisation and technological developments, the employment relationship has changed but continues to be a central feature of economic and social life (Frenkel, Chapter 20, this volume). Debates about work and its regulation in the context of globalisation played a central part in most major political debates in recent years. Take the 2016 Brexit referendum in the UK. A significant consequence arising from the decision to leave the European Union (EU) project is how ER will be regulated outside of the EU Directives and European Social Chapter (see also Doherty, Chapter 4, this volume). The Brexit issue further raises issues and debates around migration and the implications for labour market regulation (Hyman and Gumbrell-McCormick, 2017). Similarly, centre-left Italian Prime Minister Matteo Renzi faced major opposition to his 'Jobs Act', which sought to introduce greater flexibilities within the Italian labour market. This opposition set in train a series of opposition movements that ultimately led to his downfall. Thus, while industrial conflict is at an all-time low in many developed economies, the regulation of work and the political contestation of employment issues is still an important feature of economic and social life, though the parameters of the issues may shift.

An interesting recent change has been what appears to have been a political shift in terms of defenders and opponents of globalisation. Harvard political economist Dani Rodrik has highlighted that globalisation has seen a trilemma emerge where democratic governance loses out to corporate interests. Rodrik (2011) argues that pressures for a combination of open markets, democratic participation and regulation at the nation state level are incompatible, with at least one of these three principles being unsustainable in the presence of the other two. However, with phenomena such as the emergence of Trumpism and Brexit, an attack on globalisation has been launched by elements of the political right along nationalist lines. Some social democratic politicians and unions have defended moves towards cosmopolitanism from a cultural perspective but have argued that what is needed is greater capacity for transnational regulation. Consistent with this argument, Frenkel (Chapter 20, this volume) highlights that rather than seeking national responses to these pressures of globalisation, rethinking regulation to the international level is a better endeavour as globalisation has, in net terms, been beneficial, though it has had highly disruptive effects on workers in developed economies.

Globalisation has led to the emergence of new forms of work organisation and seen institutional responses in terms of its regulation. With the fall of technological and political barriers to trade, many large organisations have outsourced their production functions through the development of supply chains. These destinations are often chosen because of their low cost and low labour standards. Donaghey and Reinecke (Chapter 21, this volume) highlight that western MNCs have developed their own systems of "private labour governance" (Hassel, 2008) to regulate employment in these supply chains. However, to date much of the analysis has been based around exploring interfirm power relations, the activities of MNCs and/or "corporate social responsibility" (Donaghey and Reinecke, 2017) and the role of understanding the employment relationship can be seen as secondary. While the analysis of workplace issues has moved to the forefront in recent years (see Taylor et al., 2013), Donaghey and Reinecke highlight that more attention needs to be focused on the role of actors and how new and old actors are emerging across diverse supply chain networks within emerging developing economies.

One often overlooked factor has been that within this globalised economy, informal workers are important drivers within many economies in the developing world (Williams, Chapter 22, this volume). Without doubt, the field of ER has often had at its focus formal employment, whether it be secure, full-time and permanent or insecure and part-time. Williams highlights that in the context of internationalisation, ER scholars must expand their lenses and recognise that this dominant form of employment in much of the world requires much more attention from scholars and policy-makers in terms of the regulation of labour issues globally. This dominance of the informal model is seen as being the key feature within emerging economies. Picking up on these themes, Gunawardana (Chapter 23, this volume) highlights that within emerging economies the position of women workers is an issue of key concern. As outlined earlier in this chapter, labour markets do not operate as perfectly competitive: markets are highly segmented and create insiders and outsiders with winners and losers (Rubery, 1978). The effects of extreme segmentation is visible in emerging economies, where a combination of multiple factors including gender, ethnic origin, social class and migrant status can bring together multiple forms of disadvantage. In addition, as Gunawardana discusses, peak union leaders and corporate audits may further disempower female workers in attempts to overcome this disadvantage.

There remains widespread diversity in employment relations practices both within and between countries (Wilkinson et al., 2014b). But while the politics of the employment relationship has thrown up unexpected patterns in recent times, the embedded nature of national institutions also provides for significant political continuity. Hyman (2004) has highlighted the dominance of the "ethnocentric" nature of ER: actors embedded within national institutional frameworks. Supportive of this approach, Allen and Wood (Chapter 9, this volume) highlight that a key lesson from institutional accounts of ER is that convergence is not an inevitable consequence of institutional change. This resonates with the Varieties of Capitalism (VoC) approach, often criticised for its overly deterministic institutionalism, which makes an important point for scholars of employment relationships in highlighting the role of path dependency: national institutional configurations play key roles in differentiating the form, processes and outputs of the employment relationship (Barry and Wilkinson, 2011b; Gould et al., 2015).

The VoC approach has some strengths but also a number of weaknesses. A key strength has been its ability to help to explain the dynamics of policy choices within the arena of ER. Michel Lallement (2011) highlighted that political choices within Europe in response to the 2008 crisis were inherently linked to the national trajectory of institutions and political contingencies: France and Spain saw policies developed that protected insiders and increased labour market segmentation; Germany and Denmark saw adjustment through decreased working hours; while the UK and Ireland saw the growth of underemployment. The point here is that even in the context of globalisation, national political institutions still play a key role in shaping policy responses to issues of ER. However, a key critique of the VoC approach has been that it can overgeneralise similarities between economies by viewing them as falling within a narrow number of alternative models (Allen, 2004).

While much of the volume draws on research from developed economies, particularly North American and European, three chapters demonstrate the need to broaden our horizons as more economies emerge as industrialised. In response to the criticism of the VoC approach for overgeneralisation, Anner and Galhera (Chapter 24, this volume) highlight the "hierarchical market economy" nature of many Latin American economies: rather than disputing particular categories of economies, they utilise the general approach of VoC to argue for this new HME cluster, based in many Latin American economies. These economies differ significantly from the more commonly discussed "liberal" and "co-ordinated" market economies in terms of their shared colonial legacies, informality and segmentation, and political context.

Chan and Yunbing (Chapter 25, this volume) highlight the changes in the Chinese model as industrialisation has progressed. In particular, they note the complexities and contradictions that have emerged as China has sought to develop economically through a market-based strategy while maintaining its socialist governance system. The last decade has seen an increase in bottom-up pressure for the development of a less state-controlled model of collective bargaining. The theme of transition is also picked up by Dibben and Wood (Chapter 26, this volume), who provide an overview of the development of ER in African countries in the context of their relatively recent independence. This transition has seen the development of multinational sectors alongside indigenous industry with significantly different models of ER.

While global supply chains have seen the emergence of new institutional forms to regulate ER, the increased intensification of globalisation has seen a greater role for pre-existing supranational structures in the governance of employment relations. These institutional changes have generally been in addition to, rather than instead of, the pre-existing national frameworks (Marginson, 2015). Goyer and Valdivielso del Real (Chapter 27, this volume) use the examples of the EU and the International Labour Organization (ILO) to demonstrate their disruptive effects and the extent to which these supranational institutions can adapt to environmental changes in the regulation of ER. The development and effectiveness of supranational bodies in the governance of work is a particularly uneven terrain but one of increasing importance: Goyer and Valdivielso del Real highlight that the growth of such transnational institutions is far from being predictable and in generating solutions to some problems of globalisation, other unanticipated spillover effects may emerge.

A discourse that has developed in recent years has been that of business ethics. Business ethics in itself is based upon an assumption that business can provide a positive social function, and this runs contrary to the basic underpinnings of the radical approach to ER that the employment relationship is inherently exploitative in nature. Timming and Mansell (Chapter 28, this volume) argue that the imbalance of power between employers and employees is the source of all ethical problems in the field of ER and that employees are important stakeholders that could potentially have a moral right to participation in organisational decisions that affect them. They suggest taking up ideas of employee voice as a human right so we can then examine the intersection of ER, stakeholder theory and business ethics. This echoes earlier arguments advanced by neo-pluralists like Ackers and Payne (1998), who highlight that voice through partnership is a central part of an ethical approach to the employment relationship.

Contemporary reflections and future challenges

The final section reflects on both contemporary developments and future challenges concerning the spread of financial capitalism on employment relations issues. The literature on financialisation is based on the increased focus on shareholder value since the 1980s, reflecting structural changes in capitalism, a burgeoning of individualistic management ideology and practice, and characterised by the rise of financial intermediaries who increasingly make inroads in the value traditionally accruing to other stakeholders, most notably workers and long-term savers (see Batt, Chapter 27, this volume). A limitation of the literature on financialisation is that it has tended to assume strong homogenising pressures in global capitalism, when important differences remain between heavily financialised societies such as the UK and US, and many of the economies of northern Europe; in many continental European countries, the mainstay of the economy remains more orthodox sectors of industry, and, in key competitive areas, high labour standards with regulated rights (Wood and Wilkinson, 2014). Batt, in looking to the future, highlights that the emergence of new technologies alongside the emphasis of firms shifting from managerial structures of rule-making to financialised forms of capitalism has been a key factor in the regulatory dynamic of human agency, with workers being increasingly treated like any other resource within firms. The ramifications of these changes for ER are just beginning to emerge in research terms and this is certainly an issue that will be of increased importance in future years.

In a field where the study of institutions has always been central (Wilkinson and Wood, 2012), failures in market regulation and the global economic crisis have led both to pressures for a reduction of governmental capabilities for regulation and a renewed interest in the possibilities for meaningful institutional redesign. Many of the processes and institutions to regulate ER rules (eg among others, pay, working time, collective bargaining, voice, mediation, equality, supply chain networks or institutional forms) have become disconnected and at times fractured. Yet at other times and under other contexts, ER has displayed remarkable continuity and order. Institutions have a double social science value: as the place where social problems or issues are identified and analysed and providing the practical means whereby these can be solved (Ackers and Wilkinson, 2008).

In these times when so many of our problems appear intractable to the growing inequalities of contemporary economics, an understanding of employment relationships and the actors, institutions, contexts and processes reveals many of the outcomes and sources of consent and dissent shaping many present day social ills and the way organisations affect people's lives. We have seen how the big issues of our day – austerity, financialisation, workplace relationships, conflict, participation, feminisation of work, low pay and long hours – are all deeply connected to the study of work and employment with all its various forms and multiple perspectives. As a field of study ER is rich, dynamic and exciting. It can, as we have shown, make a call for the better management of people at work and help support a more informed individual (student) who can question the rhetorical claims of prescriptive best practice models. So while the employment relationship may be embedded in various constraints and ongoing tensions, there can be policy choices that can support a fairer, alternative equitable workplace while still meeting efficiency demands (Wilkinson et al., 2017). A study of ER helps us appreciate how organisations can meet the various competing demands of different actors and institutions to produce better outcomes for all, not just for one vested or corporate group. As Kochan (2015, xi) has suggested 'we are not just pawns controlled by globalisation, technological changes, or any other force totally out of our control. If we take the right actions and work together, we can shape the future of work in ways that work for all'. Indeed, the work of ER scholars has for decades positively engaged with and shaped government policy and organisational practice aimed at improving employee well-being, social justice and economic equality

References

Ackers, P. and Wilkinson, A. (2003). *Understanding Work and Employment: Industrial Relations in Transition.* Oxford: Oxford University Press.

Ackers P. and Wilkinson A. (2008). Industrial relations and the social sciences, in Blyton, P., Bacon, N., Firito, J. and Heery, E. (eds.) *The SAGE Handbook of Industrial Relations.* London: Sage, pp. 53–68.

Ackers, P. and Payne, J. (1998). 'British trade unions and social partnership: rhetoric, reality and strategy', *International Journal of Human Resource Management,* 9(3), pp. 529–550.

Allen, M. (2004). 'The Varieties of Capitalism paradigm: not enough variety?', *Socio-Economic Review*, 2(1), pp. 87–108.

Barry, M. and Wilkinson, A. (2011). 'Reconceptualising employer associations under evolving employment relations: countervailing power revisited', *Work, Employment & Society*, 25(1), pp. 149–162.

Barry M. and Wilkinson A. (2011b). *Handbook of Comparative Employment Relations*. London: Edward Elgar.

Barry, M. and Wilkinson, A. (2016). 'Pro-social or pro-management? A critique of the conception of employee voice as a pro-social behaviour within organizational behaviour', *British Journal of Industrial Relations*, 54(2), pp. 261–284.

Boxall, P. and Purcell, J. (2011). *Strategy and Human Resource Management*. 3rd edn. New York: Palgrave Macmillan.

Budd, J. (2004). *Employment With a Human Face: Balancing Efficiency, Equity, and Voice*. Ithaca: ILR Press.

BUIRA. (2008). *What's the Point of Industrial Relations?* Manchester (UK): British Universities Industrial Relations Association.

Burawoy, M. (2008). 'The public turn: from labor process to labor movement', *Work and Occupations*, 35(4), pp. 371–387.

Braverman, H. (1974). *Labor and Monopoly Capital: The Degradation of Work in the 20th Century*. New York: Monthly Review Press.

Clegg, H.A. (1975). 'Pluralism in industrial relations', *British Journal of Industrial Relations*, 13(3), pp. 309–316.

Commons, J. (1913). *Labor and Administration*. New York: Macmillan.

Commons, J.R. (1931). 'Institutional economics', *The American Economic Review*, 21(3), pp. 648–657.

Commons, J.R. (1911). 'Organized labor's attitude toward industrial efficiency', *The American Economic Review*, 1(3), pp. 463–472.

Crouch, C. (1993). *Industrial Relations and European State Traditions*. Oxford: Oxford University Press.

Crouch, C. (2000). 'The snakes and ladders of 21st-century trade unionism,' *Oxford Review of Economic Policy*, 16(1), pp. 70–83.

Cullinane, N., Donaghey, J., Dundon, T., Hickland, E. and Dobbins, T. (2014). 'Regulating for Mutual Gains: Non-Union Employee Representation and the Information & Consultation Directive', *International Journal of Human Resource Management*, 25(6), pp. 810–828.

Doellgast, V. and Benassi, C. (2014). Collective Bargaining, in Wilkinson, A., Donaghey, J., Dundon, T. and Freeman, R. (eds.) *Edward Elgar Handbook of Employee Voice*. Cheltenham: Edward Elgar.

Donaghey, J. and Reinecke, J. (2017). 'When Industrial Democracy Meets Corporate Social Responsibility – A Comparison of the Bangladesh Accord and Alliance as Responses to the Rana Plaza Disaster', *British Journal of Industrial Relations*. [online]. [Accessed: 7 December 2017]. Available at: 10.1111/bjir.12242

Donaghey, J., Reinecke, J., Niforou, C. and Lawson, B. (2014). 'From employment relations to consumption relations: balancing labor governance in global supply chains,' *Human Resource Management*, 53(2), pp. 229–252.

Dunlop J. (1958). *Industrial Relations Systems*. New York: Holt-Dryden.

Dundon, T. and Rollinson, D. (2011). *Understanding Employment Relations*. 2nd edn. London: McGraw-Hill.

Dundon, T., Dobbins, N., Cullinane, E., Hickland, J. and Donaghey, J. (2014). 'Employer occupation of regulatory space for the Employee Information and Consultation (I&C) Directive in Liberal Market Economies', *Work, Employment & Society*, 28(1), pp. 21–39.

Edwards, P.K. (1990). Understanding conflict in the labour process: the logic and autonomy of struggle, in *Labour Process Theory*. London: Palgrave Macmillan UK, pp. 125–152.

Edwards, P. K. (1986). *Conflict at Work*. Oxford: Blackwell.

Edwards, T. (1998). 'Multinationals, labour management and the process of reverse diffusion: A case study', *International Journal of Human Resource Management*, 9(4), pp. 696–709.

Edwards, T., Rees, C. and Coller, X. (1999). 'Structure, politics and the diffusion of employment practices in multinationals', *European Journal of Industrial Relations*, 5(3), pp. 286–306.

Edwards, T., Edwards, P., Ferner, A., Marginson, P. and Tregaskis, O. (2010). 'Multinational companies and the diffusion of employment practices from outside the country of origin,' *Management International Review*, 50(5), pp. 613–634.

Edwards, T., Marginson, P. and Ferner, A. (2013). 'Multinational Companies in Cross-National Context: Integration, Differentiation, and the Interactions between MNCS and Nation States: Introduction to a Special Issue of the ILR Review', *ILR Review*, 66(3), pp. 547–587.

Fabo, B., Karanovic, J. and Dukova, K. (2017). 'In search of an adequate European policy response to the platform economy', *Transfer: European Review of Labour and Research*, 23(2), pp. 163–175.

Flanders, A. (1970). *Management and Unions: the Theory and Reform of Industrial Relations*. London: Faber

Fox, A. (1966). 'Managerial ideology and labour relations', *British Journal of Industrial Relations*, 4(1–3), pp. 366–378.

Fox, A. (1974). *Beyond Contract: Work, Power and Trust Relations*. London: Faber & Faber.

Freeman, R.B. and Medoff, J.L. (1984). *What Do Unions Do?* New York: Basic Books.

Frege, C. and Kelly, J. (eds.) (2013). *Comparative Employment Relations in the Global Economy*. London: Routledge.

Gall, G. and Dundon, T. (2013). *Global Anti-Unionism*. London: Palgrave Macmillan.

Gollan, P., Kaufman, B., Taras, A. and Wilkinson, A. (2014). *Voice and Involvement at Work: Experience with Non-Union Representation Across Three Continents*. New York: Taylor & Francis.

Gooberman, L., Hauptmeier, M. and Heery, E. (2017). 'Contemporary employer interest representation in the United Kingdom', *Work, Employment and Society*. [online]. [Accessed: 7 December 2017]. Available at: doi.org/10.1177/0950017017701074.

Gould, A., Barry, M. and Wilkinson, A. (2015). 'Varieties of Capitalism Revisited: Current Debates and Possible Directions', *Industrial Relations*, 70(4), pp. 587–602.

Grimshaw, D. and Rubery, J. (2008). Economics and HRM, in Boxall, P., Purcell, J. and Wright, P.M. (eds.) *Oxford Handbook of Human Resource Management*. Oxford: Oxford University Press.

Guest, D.E. (1987). 'Human resource management and industrial relations [1]', *Journal of Management Studies*, 24(5), pp. 503–521.

Hall, P. and Soskice, D. (2001). An Introduction to the Varieties of Capitalism, in Hall, P. and Soskice, D. (eds.) *Varieties of Capitalism: The Institutional Basis of Competitive Advantage*. Oxford: Oxford University Press.

Hassel, A. (2008). 'The evolution of a global labor governance regime', *Governance*, 21, pp. 231–251.

Heery, E., Abbott, B. and Williams, S. (2012). 'The involvement of civil society organizations in British industrial relations: extent, origins and significance', *British Journal of Industrial Relations*, 50(1), pp. 47–72.

Heery, E, Abbott, B. and Williams, S. (2014). Civil society organizations and employee voice, in Wilkinson, A., Donaghey, J., Dundon, T. and Freeman, R. (eds.) *Edward Elgar Handbook of Employee Voice*. Cheltenham: Edward Elgar Press.

Holgate, J. (2009). Contested terrain: London's living wage campaign and the tensions between community and union organizing, in McBride, J. and Greenwood, I. (eds.) *Community Unionism: A Comparative Analysis of Concepts and Contexts*. Basingstoke: Palgrave Macmillan, pp. 49–74.

Howell, C. (2005). *Trade Unions and the State: The Construction of Industrial Relations Institutions in Britain, 1890–2000*. Princeton: Princeton University Press.

Hyman, R. (2004). Is industrial relations theory always ethnocentric?, in Kaufman, B.E. (ed.) *Theoretical Perspectives on Work and the Employment Relationship*. Champaign: Industrial Relations Research Association, pp. 265–292.

Hyman, R. and Gumbrell-McCormick, R. (2017). 'What about the workers? The implications of Brexit for British and European labour', *Competition & Change*, 21(3), pp. 169–184.

Inversi, C., Buckley, L.A. and Dundon, T. (2017). 'An analytical framework for employment regulation: investigating the regulatory space', *Employee Relations*, 39(3), pp. 291–307.

Jessop, B. (1995). 'Towards a Schumpeterian workfare regime in Britain? Reflections on regulation, governance, and welfare state', *Environment and Planning A*, 27(10), pp. 1613–1626.

Jessop, B. (2012). Rethinking the diversity and variability of capitalism: on variegated capitalism in the world market, in Lane, C. and Wood, G. (eds.) *Institutions, Internal Diversity and Change*. London: Routledge.

Kahn-Freund, O. (1967). 'A note on status and contract in British labour law', *Modern Law Review*, 30(6), pp. 635–644.

Kahn-Freund, O. (1977). *Labour and the Law*. London: Stevens.

Kalleberg A. (2009). 'Precarious Work, Insecure Workers: Employment Relations in Transition', *American Sociological Review*, 74(1), pp. 1–22.

Kaufman, B. (1993). *The Origins and Evolution of the Field of Industrial Relations in the United States*. Ithaca: ILR Press.

Kaufman, B.E. (2006). 'The institutional economics of John R. Commons: complement and substitute for neoclassical economic theory', *Socio-Economic Review*, 5(1), pp. 3–45.

Kaufman, B. (2004). *The Global Evolution of Industrial Relations: Events, Ideas and the IRRA*. Geneva: International Labour Office.

Kaufman, B.E. (2012). 'An institutional economic analysis of labor unions,' *Industrial Relations: A Journal of Economy and Society*, 51(s1), pp. 438–471.

Kaufman, B. (2014). 'History of the British Industrial Relations Field Reconsidered: Getting from the Webbs to the New Employment Relations Paradigm', *British Journal of Industrial Relations*, 52(1), pp. 1–3.

Kelly, J. (1998). *Mobilization, Collectivism and Long Waves*. London, Routledge.

Kerr, C., Dunlop, J.T., Harbison, F.H. and Myers, C.A. (1960). *Industrialism and Industrial Man*. Cambridge (MA): Harvard University Press.

Kochan, T. (2015). *Shaping the Future of Work*. New York: Business Express Press.

Kochan, T.A. and Bamber, G.J. (2009). Industrial relations and collective bargaining, in Wilkinson, A., Bacon, N., Redman, T. and Snell, S. (eds.) *The SAGE Handbook of Human Resource Management*. London: Sage.

Kochan, T.A., Katz, H.C. and McKersie, R.B. (1986). *The Transformation of American Industrial Relations*. Ithaca: Cornell University Press.

Lallement, M. (2011). 'Europe and the economic crisis: forms of labour market adjustment and varieties of Capitalism', *Work, Employment & Society*, 25(4), pp. 627–641.

Marginson, P. (2015). 'The changing nature of collective employment relations', *Employee Relations*, 37(6), pp. 645–657.

Meardi, G. (2014). 'The (claimed) growing irrelevance of employment relations', *Journal of Industrial Relations*, 56(4), pp. 594–605.

Meardi, G., Donaghey, J. and Dean, D. (2016). 'The strange non-retreat of the state: implications for the sociology of work', *Work, Employment & Society*, 30(4), pp. 559–572.

Morgan, G. (2007). 'National business systems research: Progress and prospects', *Scandinavian Journal of Management*, 23(2), pp. 127–145.

Mowbray, P.K., Wilkinson, A. and Tse, H.H.M. (2014). 'An Integrative Review of Employee Voice: Identifying a Common Conceptualization and Research Agenda', *International Journal of Management Reviews*, 17, pp. 382–400.

Offe, C. and Wiesenthal, H. (1980). 'Two logics of collective action: Theoretical notes on social class and organizational form', *Political Power and Social Theory*, 1(1), pp. 67–115.

Rodrik, D. (2011). *The Globalization Paradox: Why Global Markets, States, and Democracy Can't Coexist*. Oxford: Oxford University Press.

Rubery, J. (1978). 'Structured labour markets, worker organisation and low pay', *Cambridge Journal of Economics*, 2(1), pp. 17–36.

Sapsford, D. and Turnbull, P. (1994). 'Strikes and industrial conflict in Britain's docks: Balloons or icebergs?', *Oxford Bulletin of Economics and Statistics*, 59(3), pp. 249–265.

Scott, W. (2001). *Institutions and Organizations: Ideas and Interests*. New York: Sage.

Schmitter, P.C. (1974). 'Still the century of corporatism?', *The Review of Politics*, 36(1), pp. 85–131.

Sisson, K. (2010). *Employment Relations Matters*. [Online]. The University of Warwick. [Accessed: 7 December 2017]. Available at: www2.warwick.ac.uk/fac/soc/wbs/research/irru/erm

Smith, C. (2006). 'The double indeterminacy of labour power', *Work, Employment & Society*, 20(2), pp. 389–402.

Standing, G. (1997). 'Globalization, labour flexibility and insecurity: the era of market regulation', *European Journal of Industrial Relations*, 3(1), pp. 7–37.

Standing, G. (2011). *The Precariat: The Dangerous New Class*. London: Bloomsbury Academic.

Storey, J. and Sisson, K. (1993). *Managing Human Resources and Industrial Relations: Managing Work and Organizations*. Milton Keynes and Philadephia: Open University Press.

Streeck, W. and Thelen, K. (2005). *Beyond Continuity Institutional Change in Advanced Political Economies*. Oxford: Oxford University Press.

Streeck, W. (1992). *Social Institutions and Economic Performance: Studies of Industrial Relations in Advanced Capitalist Economies*. Sage: London.

Taylor, P., Newsome, K. and Rainnie, A. (2013). 'Putting labour in its place: global value chains and labour process analysis', *Competition and Change*, 17(1), pp. 1–5.

Thelen, K. (2012). 'Varieties of Capitalism: Trajectories of liberalization and the new politics of social solidarity', *Annual Review of Political Science*, 15, pp. 137–159.

Thompson, P. (2013). 'Financialization and the workplace: extending and applying the disconnected capitalism thesis', *Work, Employment & Society*, 27(3), pp. 472–488.

Webb, S. and Webb, B. (1894). *History of Trade Unionism*. London: Longmans, Green.

Wilkinson, A. and Fay, C. (2011). 'New Times for Employee Voice?', *Human Resource Management*, 50(1), pp. 65–74.

Wilkinson, A., Wood, G. and Deeg, R. (2014). *The Oxford Handbook of Employment Relations: Comparative Employment Systems*. Oxford: Oxford University Press.

Wilkinson, A., Donaghey, J., Dundon, T. and Freeman, R. (eds.) (2014). *The Handbook of Research on Employee Voice: Participation and Involvement in the Workplace*. Cheltenham: Edward Elgar Press.

Wilkinson, A., Barry, M., Gomez, R. and Kaufman, B. (2018). [Forthcoming]. 'Taking the pulse at work: an employment relations scorecard', *Journal of Industrial Relations*. (online) https://doi.org/10.1177/0022185617748990

Wilkinson, A. and Wood, G. (2012). 'Institutions and employment relations – the state of the art', *Industrial Relations: a Journal of Economy and Society*, 51(2), pp. 373–488.

Wilkinson, A. and Wood, G. (2017). 'Global Trends and Crises, Comparative Capitalism and HRM', *International Journal Of Human Resource Management*, 28(10), pp. 2503–2518.

Wood, G. and Wilkinson, A. (2014). Institutions and employment relations, in Wilkinson, A., Wood, G. and Deeg, R. (eds.) *The Oxford Handbook of Employment Relations: Comparative Employment Systems*. Oxford: Oxford University Press.

Wright-Mills, C. (1959). *The Sociological Information*. New York: Oxford University Press.

PART I

Perspectives on employment relations

2

THE FIELD OF EMPLOYMENT RELATIONS

A review

Niall Cullinane

Introduction

It is frequently observed that Employment Relations (ER) as a field of study is marked by a diversity of disciplinary and research traditions. Labour economics, sociology, political science, law, psychology and even geography all claim some authority over the study of work and employment. To do justice to such variety of interests in one chapter would be overly ambitious and confounded by the national-specific traditions of research characterising the field (Frege, 2007). Consequently, this chapter takes a more selective approach to its review. It begins by providing an account of dominant analytical traditions in the Anglophone literature, which have focused on the institutional regulation of the employment relationship, albeit with different degrees of emphasis. The chapter then turns to a particularly contemporary focus, reviewing the effects of the Great Recession on the institutional regulation of ER. The chapter concludes by returning to a concern that weighed heavily on earlier traditions in the field: the apparent 'problem' of labour and the associated 'problem of order'. With the withering away of the strike in developed economies and the modest levels of industrial contestation in the recent period of economic disruption, this chapter considers whether the resolution of ER injustices has been supplanted to the political sphere.

Analytical traditions within the field

Employment Relations as a field of study emerged as a response to the arrival of an organised working class and the industrial unrest accompanying such developments (Commons, 1959; Webb and Webb, 1902). The fruit of this analysis was the promotion of regulatory institutions, at a political and industrial level, to 'domesticate' worker behaviour and curb employer unilateralism. Broadly put, this project involved a combination of liberal democracy with welfare supports as well as the recognition of trade unionism and collective bargaining (Ackers and Wilkinson, 2008; Kaufman, 1993). In the immediate decades after the Second World War, the emergence of John Dunlop's (1958) "industrial relations system" in the United States and the British equivalent of "job regulation" (Bain and Clegg, 1974) heralded the cornerstones of the Anglophone field of study and gave it a distinctly pluralist character. Institutional economics, functionalist sociology and pluralist political theory were key influences, although these were quickly challenged by a more radicalised perspective offering Marxian interpretations of class conflict in capitalist society (Allen, 1971; Hyman, 1975).

Revisiting these traditions of pluralism and radicalism today reveals how both contained misplaced expectations for the trajectory of ER. The former tradition foresaw a future of pluralistic industrialism (Kerr et al., 1960), as if the Treaty of Detroit represented a microcosm of ER in mature capitalist societies. In contrast, the radical tradition assumed the long discontent of the 1970s would linger on as a symptom of class-divided societies (Goldthorpe, 1974). Both sets of expectations would need to be profoundly revised given the trajectory of later decades. Globalisation hollowed out the manufacturing zones that hosted unionised workers and progressively dismantled the post-war accord around which collective ER was constructed. Today, the source of 'disorder', to use a classic pluralist term (Maitland, 1983), is no longer found in the factories of striking workers, but is driven by the consequences of a heavily financialised capitalism (Glyn, 2006).

For contemporary pluralist and radical alike, this flavour of capitalism has not been welcomed. Although radicals tend to reject capitalism outright, there is also a mistrust of unfettered markets within the pluralist tradition (Heery, 2016). Such wariness stems from a conceptualisation of the employment relationship as marked by imbalances of power. Such imbalances are seen to be derived from employers' monopoly over capital stock and the need for individual workers to access such stock to sustain a livelihood. Capital has more readily available access to a stock of individual workers than individual workers have to stocks of capital. The decision of when, where and how to invest provides employers with the power to permit or deny individuals the opportunity to become or remain workers at all. Imbalance is more than an initial condition and infuses the ongoing relationship. Capital is possessed of a mobility power inaccessible to the more geographically rooted worker. Such imbalances, left untouched by social oversight, expose the worker to arbitrary employer power and risk the degradation of employment conditions.

A tenet of the pluralist tradition is that countervailing sources of power cushioning workers from employers' market superiority are not only desirable in shielding the weak from the strong, but necessary in protecting the strong from their own self-destructive tendencies (Commons, 1934, p. 143). Unregulated labour markets might offer quick returns to capital, but social costs may be inadequate pay, precarious work and a low-skill, low-productivity dynamic. These are said to rebound back on employers through 'under-consumption' problems or anti-establishment political trends seeking 'populist' solutions (Budd et al., 2004, p. 196). The desire for social regulation encouraged the defence of trade unionism. Trade unionism was said to not only protect workers' terms and conditions of employment, but act as a "sword of justice" in providing citizens with the opportunity for industrial voice (Flanders, 1970, p. 38–47). For the pluralist tradition, the right of workers to form unions and engage in bargaining was seen as a measure of the 'civilisation' of the capitalist system in accommodating different interests. For the radicals, this dynamic was a double-edged sword. In empowering labour to act independently, unionism strengthens the position of the worker. Yet by serving to control and limit the scale of worker demands, (see for example, Darlington, 1994), unionism checks encroachment upon a power structure that favours the reproduction of employers' dominance and labour's continued subordination.

The pluralist tradition remains unmoved by such claims. Joint regulation through collective bargaining was, at one point at least, pluralism's *cause célèbre* (Flanders, 1964). Yet experience has since led to some restraint in evaluating its achievements. Detached from wider institutional supports, autonomous islets of collective bargaining in deregulated seas of liberal capitalism are vulnerable to the fortunes of changing market tides. One of the lessons of the 1970s was that free collective bargaining at the point of production was ill-suited to ensuring stable macro-economic conditions (see Clegg, 1976a, p. 504–505). The insertion of the corporatist state as a coordinator between capital and labour was in some quarters deemed highly probable (Schmitter, 1974), though it was recognised that not all societies were endowed with a capacity to move in this direction (Goldthorpe, 1984). As the effects of product market competition, capital mobility and declining unionisation have taken hold, collective bargaining is no longer the defining regulatory mode in Anglophone ER. As detailed below, the retreat of this regulatory form has prompted a search for alternative modes of regulation to plug the gap in workers' representative capacities and restore a measure of power to labour.

If (re)investing workers with power is a prerequisite for the radical tradition in reconfiguring society in a non-capitalist direction (Atzeni, 2014), pluralist motivations remain different. For a start, the pluralist sympathy for ameliorating labour's position of weakness should not be taken to indicate a preference for workers' interests to override those of the employer. A mutually beneficial accommodation between conflicting interests is favoured, reflected in Budd's (2004) triptych of efficiency, equity and voice. Workers should have voice, but not so much that it disrupts 'economic performance'. 'Rights' in the pluralist tradition come with 'obligations'. As workers depend on the unit of capital that employs them for their livelihood, the pluralist tradition has sought to build co-operative employment relations that are not destructive of firm performance. Such sentiments prevail in the contemporary literature on state-led conflict resolution, for example (cf. Saundry and Dix, 2014). State employment tribunals provide workers with voice and a measure of equity in aiding remedial action against workplace wrongs. Yet 'too many' cases, in the face of scarce resources, is interpreted as a burden on 'efficiency', requiring the moderating effects of institutional reform.

Accommodating these different interests of capital, labour and society has been a long-running theme in the field. The classic literature pointed to high-trust informal reciprocity between management and sophisticated leader stewards as one route to moderating conflictual interests at workplace level (Batstone et al., 1978). Shop stewards were the 'lubricants' in managing workers' discontent and minimising disruptions to production (activities which, in radical quarters, could be portrayed as a union elite collaborating with employers at the expense of the membership). For pluralism, the management of discontent was the added value of trade unionism and collective bargaining in reinforcing 'order' and enabling management to secure control by sharing it. More contemporaneously, what might be termed the 'economic effects' literature is deployed by pluralists to argue positive spin offs from unionised workplaces in the form of higher productivity gains (the classic study in this regard being Freeman and Medoff, 1984; cf. Doucouliagos and Laroche, 2003). Applebaum et al. (2000) have argued that unions are compatible with new forms of flexible accumulation, helping to embed 'innovative' practices associated with 'high performance work systems'. In some accounts, the development of joint regulation with trade unions is said to promote sustained competitive advantage through generating inimitable firm-level characteristics like those articulated in resource-based views of the firm (Teague, 2005). Alternatively, work councils, ethical labour standards and/or state regulation are advanced as balancing competing interests. While such regulatory mechanisms may appear to employers as an encroachment on their prerogative, the pluralist tradition conceptualises these as 'beneficial constraints' (Streeck, 1997). Sources that circumscribe employer discretion push firms in the direction of 'high-road' employment practices that offer 'mutual gains' to capital and labour. Radical analysis, however, has countered that in a society with different class interests the optimal point of beneficial constraint varies for different classes, and that capitalist interests can be satisfactorily secured in ways that operate at the expense of other societal groups (Wright, 2004). The pluralist in response typically seeks to counter that such may be the case, but this is the best of all possible worlds in an otherwise imperfect world (Ackers, 2014).

Whatever differences remain between alternative traditions of pluralist and radical analysis, there is agreement regarding the desirability of constraint over the power of the employer. This consensus reflects a key demarcation between the field and alternative disciplinary traditions of work and employment found in neoclassical labour economics, human resource management (HRM) and organisational behaviour. These latter disciplines, in contrast, are comfortable with unilateral employer decision-making. Indeed, positive economic returns are seen to flow from such circumstances. The ER field is less sanguine. Take, for example, the HRM approach, which implicitly assumes that employer unilateralism is an unproblematic exercise in the strategic management of the firm's employees. Employment relations scholars have remained unconvinced by such claims, not only because it often fails to work on its own terms, but because it reduces labour to a subordinate or purely economic 'resource' (see critiques by Edwards, 2008; Kaufman, 2010; Thompson, 2011).

This aside, the ascendancy of employer choice has shaped much of the field's preoccupations in recent decades. While the power of employers waxes and that of labour wanes, existential questions have been presented to trade unionism. How unions may turn the tide and revitalise has been a pressing problem for many scholars in the field (cf. Frege and Kelly, 2004). In the radical tradition, scholarship has turned to long wave and global patterns in labour mobilisation to assess trends and prospects (Silver, 2003). The implications of such analysis suggest that treatments of union decline should avoid 'end of history' style, Western-centric assessments. If once Detroit and the UK's West Midlands lay at the heart of trade union mobilisation and growth, the new seedbeds, given capital flows, are likely to be Guangdong and Zhongzhan (Silver, 2014). The argument is not exclusively structural for much depends on whether unions can generate growth momentum by giving collective expression to workers' grievances and perceptions of injustice (Kelly, 1998; Lévesque and Murray, 2010). A closely affiliated offshoot of such analysis is an emphasis on 'organising' as a vehicle for revitalisation, which revolves around unions placing emphasis on the differences of interests between employers and workers to demonstrate the relevance of mobilising collectively (Milkman and Voss, 2004). Union-community alliances, new social movements and civil society organisations are part of these still largely experimental tools of workplace organising. In some cases, organising has taken on a transnational character through international union networks in recognition of the limits of national-specific action in a globalised economy (Brofenbrenner, 2007). In the pluralist tradition, concerns are shared with the radicals that new modes of production and harsher competitive environments challenge union security, but lines of enquiry often shy away from the adversarialism espoused by mobilisation advocates. With the spectre of marginalisation looming large, unions are counselled to offer positive collaboration with employers in the form of workplace partnership. Such productivity coalitions may ensure firm survival and job security in harsh economic conditions and stabilise the institutional presence of unions at the workplace level (Johnstone and Wilkinson, 2016). For the pluralist, adversarial mobilisation may provoke a militant backlash from employers, resulting in further union marginalisation.

New forms of regulation to plug the growing gap in workers' representative capacities increasingly feature in the field's analysis. One approach has been to examine statutory employment rights and case law, as mediated through formal systems of HRM (Lipsky and Avgar, 2004; Roche et al., 2014). In some circles, there is greater receptivity to employer-sponsored, non-union forms of representation (Kaufman, 2015), whilst legal initiatives, labour standards and new actors like non-governmental organisations all feature as part of the continued search for new regulatory forms (Locke et al., 2013). One obvious candidate for the institutional regulation of employment is of course the law. However, the law is not undifferentiated in its effects. Uneven mixtures of conformance and non-compliance are usually the norm and this is particularly so in common law systems. These are vulnerable to the discretionary behaviour of powerful actors because legal regulation is not closely allied to structures of social regulation, and there are often ample opportunities to challenge and overturn the law's provisions (Colling, 2010).

Rather than favouring one mode of regulation over others, a body of opinion increasingly leans towards a 'hybrid' approach: individual regulatory mechanisms work best when they are combined with others in an interlocking and complementary fashion (Freeman et al., 2007). An awareness that different forms of institutional regulation can combine and effectively reinforce each other has also directed attention to the macro-institutional form of capitalist economies. The Varieties of Capitalism literature, associated with Hall and Soskice (2001), has been influential in shaping analysis in the field over the last decade and a half (see Doellgast, 2009; Hamann and Kelly, 2008). The main contribution of this framework has been in the way it directs attention to how the structure, processes and outcomes of ER in any given economy, on matters like pay or skill formation, are influenced by the presence or absence of wider supportive institutional arrangements. If once ER tended to prioritise the structure of collective bargaining in thinking about national institutional variation (Clegg, 1976b), scholarship is now more accustomed to the influence of investment patterns and corporate governance structures (Gospel and Pendleton, 2006).

Allied to this trend is literature influenced by historical institutionalism. Although the field long recognised the importance of history and heritage, historical institutionalism has elevated the concept of path dependency as a corrective to notions that globalisation homogenises the experience of ER across countries (Thelen, 2004). Institutions are seen to mediate and refract globalisation in diverse ways, acclimatising with the history, politics and ideology of relevant nationally based actors (Hauptmeier, 2012). The German model is often the favoured stereotype of this explanatory dynamic in the Anglophone literature, with scholarship pointing to the collaborative tendencies of the country's institutional arrangement for sectoral bargaining and workplace councils. Studies have shown how the more coordinated German economy has been less prone to financialisation in comparison to liberalised economies, because international investors balk at the imposition of greater institutional constraints on managerial autonomy (Goyer, 2011). None of this is to say that institutions act in some unchanging or static way or that actors' behaviour in ER is exclusively path dependent. The case of Germany, for example, continues to find evidence of a drift from the traditional national model (Behrens, 2013). Studies of multinational corporations in national employment systems have indicated that while some actors have interests in isomorphic conformity for reasons of legitimacy (Ferner, 2010), others break from or marginalise institutional arrangements (Meardi et al., 2009). The debate on this matter remains unsettled, as scholarship has interpreted and reinterpreted developments in ER patterns at various levels, both across countries and within countries, to determine whether the evidence points towards convergence in the direction of market liberalisation or a divergent set of trajectories informed by national and sectoral specific traditions (Katz and Wailes, 2014). With the arrival of the Global Financial Crisis, subsequent Great Recession and ensuing low growth trajectory in developed capitalist economies, the response of capital, labour and the state to such events and the seeking out of new paths to economic growth are likely to further enhance the need for enquiry into the nature and fate of ER institutions going forward. To this end, a consideration of the global economic downturn's consequences for the field is appropriate.

Employment relations and the consequence of crisis

As perhaps the most significant episode of the early twenty-first century, the economic crisis emanating in 2007–2008 has had significant influence on the conduct of employment relations across countries. The crisis was itself a reflection and symptom of wider structural changes characterising ER in recent decades, in particular the weakening capacity of labour institutions to exercise influence over the definition of national and international public policy towards industry, work and regulation (Nolan, 2011). The working out of contradictions innate to the crisis and its aftermath are likely to be felt in ER for some time to come.

In liberal market economies, the pre-crisis model of growth, geared towards the finance, insurance and retail estate sectors, has been exposed as offering illusionary gains in income and wealth based on inflated asset prices, capital gains and rising household debt (Bellamy Foster and Magdoff, 2009). The subsequent bouts of post-crisis quantitative easing by central banks, ostensibly to stave off economic collapse, have deepened and magnified this trajectory further. The dysfunctional consequences of a financialised economy has been profound, evident by the bailout of rentiers, public austerity and the diversion of funds from productive sectors of the economy. In turn this has exacerbated social inequality and led to stagnant economic growth. Whereas previous economic fractures of this magnitude discredited pre-crisis orthodoxies, prevailing policy response has seen the "strange non-death of neoliberalism" (Crouch, 2011). Those who hoped the crisis might offer a Polanyian swing to the decommodification of the post-war Golden Age have found little comfort in existing policy responses. The power of global finance continues to impose severe constraints on national governments that might opt for macroeconomic policies favourable to labour. The dominance of financial interests also explains the anaemic return to growth in the post-crisis period (Wallerstein et al., 2014): money injected into the financial system in the form of quantitative easing has not found its way into the productive economy but circulated in the financial sphere of share buy-backs, dividend pay-outs and asset value growth. The persistence of relative stagnation in the productive sector may simply encourage the transfer of uninvested surpluses into the financial realm, leading to further asset bubbles (Roberts, 2016). In liberal market economies like the USA and UK, continued reliance on a low-productivity service sector and high trade deficits does not appear to offer hospitable terrain for sustained economic recovery. In the absence of any meaningful innovations, there may well be a long-term decline in advanced liberalised economies akin to the mediaeval Dark Ages (Streeck, 2016). Such outcomes would not necessarily concern the rent-seeking insiders of advanced economies in the same way it did not concern the expropriating elites of feudal times (Lane and Wood, 2014). For many sections of the workforce, however, continued stagnation is likely to mean the further erosion of living standards and impoverishment of employment relationships.

What the trajectory of ER institutions will be under these conditions is an important question. We might expect to see a degree of continuity with pre-crisis trends towards greater liberalisation, but with a further deepening of such pressures as policy-makers seek recovery through further labour market deregulation. There are social and political limits to such responses of course, increasingly evident in an emerging consensus around the problems of low-wage, insecure work as well as a growing debate on the merits and viability of universal basic incomes (Standing, 2017). To date the global crisis has had a heavy bearing on ER processes and outcomes, like pay and working time, across many countries, though national responses have been shaped by pre-existing institutional traditions (Glassner et al., 2011). In the USA and UK, the crisis has encouraged new legislative restrictions on unionisation in the public sector as part of an effort to weaken labour's opposition to austerity. In the USA newly adopted right to work laws in a number of Midwestern states now limit or eliminate public sector collective bargaining (Cantin, 2012). Legislation enacted by the British Conservative administration imposes further constraints on the balloting of union members for strike action, with an eye to weakening public sector unionism's opposition to austerity (Darlington and Dobson, 2015). Across a number of European states, government austerity programmes have reconfigured public sector ER in the form of pay freezes, deteriorating pensions and widespread redundancies (Bach and Bordogna, 2013), although with relative and patchy recovery in prospect clawbacks may now emerge. In some countries, radical reform has been forced through by governments without reference to existing systems of collective bargaining, a dynamic often provoked by explicit pressures from international, non-state institutions (Hyman, 2015). This is blatantly clear in the economies of southern Europe, where the crisis has been most severe. In these countries, the sovereign debt crisis led the European Commission, European Central Bank and International Monetary Fund to insist on radical reform of ER in exchange for financial support (Ioannou, 2013). The consequences are the dismantling of national and sectoral agreements and the introduction of local-level company derogation clauses.

In the northern European countries, a comparable but ultimately less austere trajectory is underway. A retreat from multi-employer bargaining and transference of pay determination to the company level is occurring, but the difference lies in how the process is managed (Marginson, 2015). The trend is for collective ER institutions at a national and industry level to shape a path-dependent form of organised decentralisation. Negotiated adjustments are seen to temper the worst features of the crisis relative to the often adversarial patterns evident in southern European states. Yet some counsel against overstating the nature and persistence of variance in institutional responses across countries. Rather, scholarship has pointed to convergence in the direction of market liberalisation and employer flexibility in the determination of pay and conditions (Howell and Kolins-Givan, 2011). In this argument, even where collective institutions designed to balance the interest of capital and labour formally persist, they are subject to 'plasticity' that reconfigures them in a fashion subservient to employer demands. Bolstering this position are findings that show how the inhibiting effect of collective bargaining institutions on income inequality in Europe has eroded in recent decades (Avdagic and Baccaro, 2014). Such institutions, while still present, are unable to secure outcomes different from those prevailing under market arrangements.

The endurance of collective institutions in many European countries, although in weakened forms with fewer redistributive powers, is partly a product of state strategy. In countries where organised labour has traditionally held a role in public policy or where unions' capacity to wield clout remains viable, the state is likely to leave existing institutions as they are to dodge political unrest; substantively, however, a creeping agenda of liberalisation is pursued (Baccaro and Howell, 2011). Unions face substantial tests in these circumstances (see Gumbrell-McCormick and Hyman, 2013 for a European-wide review). Where union strength weakens, the state may tighten the screw by further weakening unions politically and legally. Alternatively, the state may leave existing collective regulatory arrangements in place and allow their powers to be corroded by wider liberalisation. Where unions are not a potent force amongst the electorate, the state may opt for political and legal assaults, as in the USA and UK. In those countries where unions retain influence amongst the populace, the state may hold its fire. This second action seems to characterise state approaches in many parts of western Europe. Aside from weakening effects driven by economic liberalisation, this trajectory may be corrosive of unions' legitimacy, for under these circumstances they risk becoming detached from a burgeoning class of non-union 'outsiders'. The latter may come to perceive unions as protecting 'insiders' at their expense. In countries where union power is confined to the public sector, unions risk being branded as featherbedding a rent-seeking workforce from the discipline of 'market efficiency'. In countries where unions participate in the determination of terms and conditions for sectors and associated extension clauses, they end up negotiating conditions for large proportions of workers they do not formally represent. Force of circumstance may prod unions in the direction of privileging those groups they do represent at the expense of workers outside their control, or the outcomes they do negotiate may seem so limited to select groups as to weaken their wider credibility. The combination of economic weakness driven by exposure to the forces of liberalisation and political weakness driven by a lack of social legitimacy may produce a vicious cycle of decline and marginalisation.

The trajectory of conflict in employment relations

This weakening of labour in western economies is reflected in the declining incidence of industrial strikes (Kelly, 2015). While the absence of strike activity can in some contexts be interpreted as a measure of labour's strength, it is accepted that in the contemporary context it illustrates weakness. The withering away of the strike in advanced capitalism raises interesting questions for the field of ER, which originated in the midst of a 'labour problem' in the nineteenth and twentieth centuries. This is clearly less of a pressing matter for the field now. Only modest levels of industrial conflict were induced by the crisis and recession. What protests did occur left few indentations on the prevailing order, at least in comparison to previous crises (Howell, 2005; Silver, 2003). Elements of the radical tradition holding out for a wave of industrial mobilisation (Cohen, 2014) may prove to be like the characters in a latter day equivalent of *Waiting for Godot*. Of course, such pessimism may be too western centric. Strike decline is characteristic of the advanced capitalist countries but trends in the global south and east are more variable (Van Der Velden, 2007). Evidence from China points towards workers in the state-owned and private sectors protesting with great frequency, whilst formerly passive migrant workers have become more militant in the industrial cities on the southern and south-easterly coast (Chan, 2010; Friedman and Lee, 2010).

In the west, labour's quiescence has produced questions about the nature and trajectory of industrial conflict (Godard, 2011), particularly so when conditions generating workplace conflict still prevail. For example, British evidence from a national Work and Employment Relations Survey (WERS) (Van Wanrooy et al., 2013) documents real wage cuts, deteriorations in pension values, work intensification, increasing casualisation and the hollowing out of workplace consultation and collective bargaining. Yet paradoxically, employees report greater positivity about their working environments in this round of WERS than they did at the start of the century; a finding supported by the British Social Attitudes (BSA) Survey 2016 capturing job satisfaction (National Centre for Social Research, 2016). Although the meaning of job satisfaction is difficult to interpret in surveys of this sort, particularly when accompanied by reports of increased stress as in the BSA data, the findings have interesting implications – has labour increasingly modest expectations over what is achievable at work and has it adjusted to declining standards of employment quality as its power has declined?

It is conceivable that the collective manifestation of industrial conflict has been 'displaced' into alternative forms. Strike ballots in the UK, for example, might be seen as a form of leverage that has partially replaced, at a much lower scale, strike action. Industrial conflicts may have metamorphosed into individual actions at work, reflected by the rise in individual claims registered at dispute resolution bodies (Dix et al., 2009), even if these reflect specific complaints over legal entitlements rather than the kinds of non-legal injustices pervading wage-effort bargains. More subterranean forms of individual protest may also exist, although documenting the prevalence of these is difficult, even if a range of interesting case studies provide insight (Cushen and Thompson, 2012). More speculatively, potential deprivations in employment may be compensated by life outside work through consumerism and other forms of escapism or expressed in various social problems. Godard (2011) for example identifies alcohol and drug abuse, depression and low levels of civic and political participation as consequences of what he calls the "deinstitutionalisation of conflict". Yet such behaviours were readily evident in working class communities in periods when organised industrial conflict was high (Green, 1980) – although it is conceivable that 'anomic' behaviour has since deepened or become more widespread as levels of inequality surge (Wilkinson and Pickett, 2009). Alternatively, it could be that deprivations experienced at the point of production migrate in some repackaged form to the political sphere. Again this is not necessarily a new phenomenon for worker dissatisfactions have readily transferred to the political arena in the past. What may be novel is that such grievances are being articulated in new and different ways in different countries. For example, in European countries where collective bargaining remains relatively robust, the migration of conflict to the political sphere might be found in the increase in the number of general strikes against government reforms since the 1980s (Hamann et al., 2013). In Anglophone countries where collective bargaining coverage has declined, these options are less prevalent or prohibited by law. Nevertheless, governments can be influenced in other ways. With workers increasingly willing to switch party allegiances from one election to another or abstain altogether (Drummond, 2006), politicians pay more attention to voter preferences in order to appeal to a volatile and unpredictable population. Given that labour lacks leverage over mobile capital, western governments become a more useful target for they are after all geographically fixed and cannot escape the ire of the electorate.

The migration of workplace deprivations of, say, poor wage prospects, deteriorating pension values and labour market precariousness into the political arena may occur, as Standing (2011) has argued, in one of two ways: the 'politics of inferno' or the 'politics of paradise'. The latter revolves around a leftist programme of redistribution and income security. Its politics has risen in profile in the contemporary environment (Iglesias, 2015; Labour Party (UK), 2017; Sanders, 2016) but presently remains outside the corridors of power or, once inside, disciplined by international finance (Muddle, 2016). Rather, contemporary political trends increasingly replicate that of the 'inferno'. Dislocations in income inequality, deindustrialisation and changing demographics are sponsoring anti-establishment tendencies across the USA and the European continent, but these often take on nationalistic or even xenophobic characteristics. In many countries the prospects of stagnant growth, a downwardly mobile precariat, a reserve army of lumpen social elements and an increasingly visible migrant population offers a combustible mixture. If the forecasting of a new wave of automation and mass labour displacement comes to fruition (Brynjolfsson and McAfee, 2014), the combined effects, suggests the consolidation of a more harsh, vengeful and embittered society than we have known for a long time.

Conclusion

This review addressed three different facets of the field of ER. First it revisited analytical traditions in the field, focusing on the institutional regulation of the employment relationship. Historically trade unionism and collective bargaining have been the favoured means of institutional regulation, although experimentation with new modes is now *de rigueur* as the former weakens and declines. Second, the chapter considered the effects of the global economic crisis on the existing state of institutional regulation, with reference to international trends in the field. In the main, the outcomes for labour suggest, in the absence of any major policy shifts, a greater exposure to employer power and further weakening. Third, the chapter concluded with an assessment of labour opposition to this trajectory in the wider context of declining industrial action. It revisited ideas that labour acquiescence in the industrial sphere may have migrated to the political sphere, producing outcomes that increasingly reflect the 'politics of inferno'. Although the three areas are treated fairly distinctly they are of course related. As scholars maintain their preoccupation with the regulation of the employment relationship in a way that protects labour from the excesses of employer power, then the trends produced by the current crisis and how these are resolved will remain important areas of concern. Many of the conditions fostering contemporary social tensions originate from within the dynamic of employment relations, particularly in terms of how the rewards from production are distributed and the way in which work is organised. With such problems increasingly intruding on the political discourse of contemporary society, the relevance of ER as a field of study would seem well assured in the years ahead.

References

Ackers, P. (2014). 'Rethinking the employment relationship: a neo-pluralist critique of British industrial relations orthodoxy', *International Journal of Human Resource Management*, 25(18), pp. 2608–2625.

Ackers, P. and Wilkinson, A. (2008). Industrial relations and the social sciences, in Blyton, P., Bacon, N., Fiorito, J. and Heery, E. (eds.) *The SAGE Handbook of Industrial Relations*. London: Sage.

Allen, V.I. (1971). *The Sociology of Industrial Relations: Studies in Method*. London: Longman.

Applebaum, E., Bailey, T., Berg, P. and Kalleberg, A.L. (2000) *Manufacturing Advantage: Why High Performance Work Systems Pay Off*. Ithaca: Cornell University Press.

Atzeni, M. (2014). Introduction: neo-liberal globalisation and interdisciplinary perspectives on labour and collective action, in Atzeni, M. (ed.) *Workers and Labour in a Globalised Capitalism: Contemporary Themes and Theoretical Issues*. Houndsmill: Palgrave Macmillan.

Avdagic, S. and Baccaro, L. (2014). The future of employment relations in advanced capitalism: inexorable decline, in Wilkinson, A., Wood, G. and Deeg, R. (eds.) *The Oxford Handbook of Employment Relations*. Oxford: Oxford University Press.

Baccaro, L. and Howell, C. (2011). 'A common neoliberal trajectory: the transformation of industrial relations in advanced capitalism', *Politics and Society*, 39(4), pp. 521–563.

Bach, S. and Bordogna, L. (2013). 'Reframing public service employment relations: the impact of economic crisis and the new EU economic governance', *European Journal of Industrial Relations*, 19(4), pp. 279–294.

Bain, G.S. and Clegg, H.A. (1974). 'A strategy for industrial relations research in Great Britain', *British Journal of Industrial Relations*, 12(1), pp. 91–113.

Batstone, E., Boraston, I. and Frenkel, S. (1978). *The Social Organization of Strikes*. Oxford: Basil Blackwell.

Behrens, M. (2013). Germany, in Frege, C. and Kelly, J. (eds.) *Comparative Employment Relations in the Global Economy*. Abingdon: Routledge.

Bellamy Foster, J. and Magdoff, F. (2009). *The Great Financial Crisis: Causes and Consequences*. New York: Monthly Review Press.

Brofenbrenner, K. (ed.) (2007). *Global Unions: Challenging Transnational Capital through Cross Border Campaigns*. Ithaca: ILR Press.

Brynjolfsson, E. and McAfee, A. (2014). *The Second Machine Age: Work, Progress, and Prosperity in a Time of Brilliant Technologies*. New York: W.W. Norton & Co.

Budd, J.W. (2004). *Employment with a Human Face: Balancing Efficiency, Equity and Voice*. Ithaca: Cornell University Press.

Budd, J.W., Gomez, R. and Meltz, N.M. (2004). Why a balance is best: the pluralist industrial relations paradigm of balancing competing interests, in Kaufman, B. (ed.) *Theoretical Perspectives on Work and the Employment Relationship*. Champaign: Industrial Relations Research Association.

Cantin, E. (2012). 'The politics of austerity and the Conservative offensive against US public sector unions, 2008–2012', *Relations Industrielles/Industrial Relations*, 67(4), pp. 612–632.

Chan, C.K.C. (2010). *The Challenge of Labour in China: Strikes and the Changing Labour Regime in Global Factories*. London: Routledge.

Clegg, H.A. (1976a). *The System of Industrial Relations in Great Britain*. Oxford: Basil Blackwell.

Clegg, H.A. (1976b). *Trade Unionism under Collective Bargaining: A Theory Based on a Comparison of Six Countries*. Oxford: Blackwell.

Cohen, S. (2014). Workers organising workers: grass-roots struggle as the past and future of trade union renewal, in Atzeni, M. (ed.) *Workers and Labour in a Globalised Capitalism: Contemporary Themes and Theoretical Issues*. Houndsmill: Palgrave Macmillan.

Colling, T. (2010). Legal institutions and the regulation of workplaces, in Colling, T. and Terry, M. (eds.) *Industrial Relations: Theory and Practice*. Chichester: Wiley and Sons.

Commons, J. (1934). *Institutional Economics: Its Place in Political Economy*. New York: Macmillan.

Commons, J. (1959). *The Legal Foundations of Capitalism*. Madison: University of Wisconsin Press.

Crouch, C. (2011). *The Strange Non-Death of Neo-Liberalism*. Oxford: Polity Press.

Cushen, J. and Thompson, P. (2012). 'Doing the right thing? HRM and the angry knowledge worker', *New Technology, Work and Employment*, 30(2), pp. 352–365.

Darlington, R. (1994). *The Dynamics of Workplace Unionism: Shop Stewards' Organization in Three Merseyside Plants*. London: Mansell.

Darlington, R. and Dobson, J. (2015). *The Conservative Government's Proposed Strike Ballot Thresholds: The Challenge to Trade Unions*. Liverpool: Institute for Employment Rights.

Dix, G., Sisson, K. and Forth, J. (2009). Conflict at work: the changing pattern of disputes, in Brown, W., Bryson, A., Forth, J. and Whitfield, K. (eds.) *The Evolution of the Modern Workplace*. Cambridge (UK): Cambridge University Press.

Doellgast, V. (2009). 'Still a coordinated model? Market liberalization and the transformation of employment relations in the German telecommunications industry', *Industrial and Labor Relations Review*, 63(1), pp. 3–23.

Doucouliagos, C. and Laroche, P. (2003). 'What do unions do to productivity? A metaanalysis', *Industrial Relations*, 42(4), pp. 650–690.

Drummond, A.J. (2006). 'Electoral volatility and party decline in Western democracies: 1970–1995', *Political Studies*, 54(3), pp. 628–647.

Dunlop, J. (1958). *Industrial Relations Systems*. New York: Holt-Dryden.

Edwards, P. (2008). The employment relationship in strategic HRM, in Storey, J., Wright, P.M. and Ulrich, D. (eds.) *The Routledge Companion to Strategic Human Resource Management*. London: Routledge.

Ferner, A. (2010). HRM in multinational companies, in Wilkinson, A., Bacon, N., Redman, T. and Snell, S. (eds.) *The SAGE Handbook of Human Resource Management*. London: Sage.

Flanders, A. (1964). *The Fawley Productivity Agreements*. London: Faber and Faber.

Flanders, A. (1970). *Management and Unions: The Theory and Reform of Industrial Relations*. London: Faber and Faber.

Freeman, R.B. and Medoff, J.L. (1984). *What Do Unions Do?* New York: Basic Books.

Freeman, R.B., Boxall, P. and Haynes, P. (eds.) (2007). *What Workers Say: Employee Voice in the Anglo-American Workplace*. Ithaca: ILR Press.

Frege, C.M. (2007). *Employment Research and State Traditions: A Comparative History of the United States, Great Britain, and Germany*. Oxford: Oxford University Press.

Frege, C.M. and Kelly, J. (eds.) (2004). *Varieties of Unionism: Strategies for Union Revitalization in a Globalizing Economy*. Oxford: Oxford University Press.

Friedman, E. and Lee, C.K. (2010). 'Remaking the world of Chinese labour: a 30 year retrospective', *British Journal of Industrial Relations*, 48(3), pp. 507–533.

Glassner, V., Keune, M. and Marginson, P. (2011). 'Collective bargaining in a time of crisis: developments in the private sector in Europe', *Transfer: European Review of Labour and Research*, 17(3), pp. 303–322.

Glyn, A. (2006). *Capitalism Unleashed: Finance, Globalization and Welfare*. Oxford: Oxford University Press.

Godard, J. (2011). 'What has happened to strikes?', *British Journal of Industrial Relations*, 49(2), pp. 282–305.

Goldthorpe, J. (1974). 'Industrial relations in Britain: a critique of reformism', *Politics and Society*, 4(4).

Goldthorpe, J. (ed.) (1984). *Order and Conflict in Contemporary Capitalism: Studies in the Political Economy of Western European Nations*. Oxford: Clarendon Press.

Gospel, H. and Pendleton, A. (eds.) (2006). *Corporate Governance and Labour Management: A Comparative Study*. Oxford: Oxford University Press.

Goyer, M. (2011). *Contingent Capital: Short-Term Investors and the Evolution of Corporate Governance in France and Germany*. Oxford: Oxford University Press.

Green, J.R. (1980). *The World of the Worker: Labor in Twentieth-Century America*. New York: Hill and Wang.

Gumbrell-McCormick, R. and Hyman, R. (2013). *Trade Unions in Western Europe: Hard Times, Hard Choices*. Oxford: Oxford University Press.

Hall, P.A. and Soskice, D. (eds.) (2001). *Varieties of Capitalism: The Institutional Foundations of Comparative Advantage*. Oxford: Oxford University Press.

Hamann, K. and Kelly, J. (2008). Varieties of Capitalism and industrial relations, in Blyton, P., Bacon, N., Fiorito, J. and Heery, E. (eds.) *The SAGE Handbook of Industrial Relations*. London: Sage.

Hamann, K., Johnston, A. and Kelly, J. (2013). 'Unions against governments: explaining general strikes in Western Europe, 1980–2006', *Comparative Political Studies*, 46(9), pp. 1030–1057.

Hauptmeier, M. (2012). 'Institutions are what actors make of them: the changing construction of firm-level employment relations in Spain', *British Journal of Industrial Relations*, 50(4), pp. 737–759.

Heery, E. (2016). *Framing Work: Unitary, Pluralist and Critical Perspectives in the Twenty-First Century*. Oxford: Oxford University Press.

Howell, C. (2005). *Trade Unions and the State: The Construction of Industrial Relations Institutions in Britain, 1890–2000*. Princeton: Princeton University Press.

Howell, C. and Kolins-Givan, R. (2011). 'Rethinking institutions and institutional change in European industrial relations', *British Journal of Industrial Relations*, 49(2), pp. 231–255.

Hyman, R. (1975). *Industrial Relations: A Marxist Introduction*. Basingstoke: Macmillan.

Hyman, R. (2015). 'Three scenarios for industrial relations in Europe', *International Labour Review*, 154(1), pp. 5–14.

Iglesias, P. (2015). *Politics in a Time of Crisis: Podemos and the Future of Democracy in Europe*. London: Verso.

Ioannou, C.A. (2013). 'Greek public service employment relations: a Gordian knot in the era of sovereign default', *European Journal of Industrial Relations*, 19(4), pp. 295–308.

Johnstone, S. and Wilkinson, A. (2016). 'Developing positive employment relations: international experiences of labour-management partnership', in Johnstone, S. and Wilkinson, A. (eds.) *Developing Positive Employment Relations: International Experiences of Labour Management Partnership*. Basingstoke: Palgrave Macmillan.

Katz, H. and Wailes, N. (2014). Convergence and divergence in employment relations, in Wilkinson, A., Wood, G. and Deeg, R. (eds.) *The Oxford Handbook of Employment Relations*. Oxford: Oxford University Press.

Kaufman, B. (1993). *The Origins and Evolution of the Field of Industrial Relations in the United States*. Ithaca: ILR Press.

Kaufman, B. (2010). 'SHRM theory in the post-Huselid era: why it is fundamentally misspecified,' *Industrial Relations*, 49(2), pp. 286–313.

Kaufman, B. (2015). Employee involvement and voice at Delta Airlines: the leading edge of American practice, in Gollan, P.J., Kaufman, B.E., Taras, D. and Wilkinson, A. (eds.) *Voice and Involvement at Work: Experience with Non-Union Representation*. London: Routledge.

Kelly, J. (1998). *Rethinking Industrial Relations: Mobilization, Collectivism and Long Waves*. London: Routledge.

Kelly, J. (2015). 'Conflict: trends and forms of collective action', *Employee Relations*, 37(6), pp. 720–732.

Kerr, C., Dunlop, J.T., Harbison, F.H. and Myers, C.A. (1960). *Industrialism and Industrial Man*. Cambridge (MA): Harvard University Press.

Labour Party (2017). *For the Many, Not the Few*. London: Labour Party.

Lane, C. and Wood, G. (2014). Capitalist diversity, work and employment relations, in Wilkinson, A., Wood, G. and Deeg, R. (eds.) *The Oxford Handbook of Employment Relations*. Oxford: Oxford University Press.

Lévesque, C. and Murray, G. (2010). 'Understanding union power: resources and capabilities for renewing union capacity', *Transfer: European Review of Labour and Research*, 16(3), pp. 333–350.

Lipsky, D.B. and Avgar, A.C. (2004). 'Commentary: research on employment dispute resolution: toward a new paradigm,' *Conflict Resolution Quarterly*, 22(1), pp. 175–189.

Locke, R.M., Rissing, B.A. and Pal, T. (2013). 'Complements or substitutes? Private codes, state regulation and the enforcement of labour standards in global supply chain', *British Journal of Industrial Relations*, 51(3), pp. 519–552.

Maitland, I. (1983). *The Causes of Industrial Disorder: A Comparison of a British and a German Factory*. London: Routledge and Kegan Paul.

Marginson, P. (2015). 'Coordinated bargaining in Europe: from incremental corrosion to frontal assault?', *European Journal of Industrial Relations*, 21(2), pp. 97–114.

Meardi, G., Marginson, P., Fichter, M., Frybes, M., Stanojevic. M. and Toth, A. (2009). 'Varieties of multinationals: adapting employment practices in Central and Eastern Europe', *Industrial Relations*, 48(3), pp. 489–511.

Milkman, R. and Voss, K. (eds.) (2004). *Rebuilding Labor: Organizers and Organizing in the New Union Movement*. Ithaca: Cornell University Press.

Muddle, C. (2016). *Syriza: The Failure of the Populist Promise*. Basingstoke: Palgrave Macmillan.

National Centre For Social Research (2016). *British Social Attitudes Report 33*. NatCen Social Research: London.

Nolan, P. (2011). 'Money, markets, meltdown: the 21st century crisis of labour', *Industrial Relations Journal*, 42(1), pp. 2–17.

Roberts, M. (2016). *The Long Depression: Marxism and the Global Crisis of Capitalism*. Chicago: Haymarket Books.

Roche, W.K., Teague, P. and Colvin, A. (eds.) (2014). *The Oxford Handbook of Conflict Management in Organizations*. Oxford: Oxford University Press.

Sanders, B. (2016). *Our Revolution: A Future to Believe In*. New York: Thomas Dunne Books.

Saundry, R. and Dix, G. (2014). 'Conflict resolution in the United Kingdom', in Roche, W.K., Teague, P. and Colvin, A.J.S. (eds.) *The Oxford Handbook of Conflict Management in Organizations*. Oxford: Oxford University Press.

Schmitter, P.C. (1974). 'Still the century of corporatism?' *The Review of Politics*, 36(1), pp. 85–131.

Silver, B. (2003). *Forces of Labor: Workers' Movements and Globalization since 1870*. Cambridge (UK): Cambridge University Press.

Silver, B. (2014). Theorising the working class in twenty-first-century global capitalism, in Atzeni, M. (ed.) *Workers and Labour in a Globalised Capitalism: Contemporary Themes and Theoretical Issues*. Houndsmill: Palgrave Macmillan.

Standing, G. (2011). *The Precariat: The New Dangerous Class*. London: Bloomsbury Books.

Standing, G. (2017). *Basic Income: And How We Can Make It Happen*. London: Pelican.

Streeck, W. (1997). Beneficial constraints: on the economic limits of rational voluntarism, in Hollingsworth, J.R. and Boyer, R. (eds.) *Contemporary Capitalism: The Embeddedness of Institutions*. Cambridge (UK): Cambridge University Press.

Streeck, W. (2016). *How Will Capitalism End? Essays on a Failing System*. London: Verso.

Teague, P. (2005). 'What is enterprise partnership', *Organization*, 12(4), pp. 567–589.

Thelen, K.A. (2004). *How Institutions Evolve: The Political Economy of Skills in Germany, Britain, the United States and Japan*. Cambridge (UK): Cambridge University Press.

Thompson, P. (2011). 'The trouble with HRM', *Human Resource Management Journal*, 21(4), pp. 355–367.

van Der Velden, S. (2007). Introduction, in van Der Velden, S., Dribbusch, H., Lyddon, D. and Vandaele, K. (eds.) *Strikes Around the World, 1968–2005: Case-Studies of 15 Countries*. Amsterdam: Aksant.

Van Wanrooy, B., Bewley, H., Bryson, A., Forth, J., Freeth, S., Stokes, L. and Wood, S. (2013). *Employment Relations in the Shadow of the Recession: Findings from the 2011 Workplace Employment Relations Study*. Basingstoke: Palgrave Macmillan.

Wallerstein, I., Collins, R., Mann, M., Derluguian, G. and Calhoun, C. (eds.) (2014). *Does Capitalism Have a Future?* Oxford: Oxford University Press.

Webb, S. and Webb, B. (1902). *Industrial Democracy*. London: Longmans.

Wilkinson, R. and Pickett, K. (2009). *The Spirit Level: Why More Equal Societies Almost Always Do Better*. London: Allen Lane.

Wright, E.O. (2004). 'Beneficial constraints: beneficial for whom?', *Socio-Economic Review*, 2(3), pp. 407–414.

3

ECONOMICS AND EMPLOYMENT RELATIONS

Paul Willman

Abstract

As other chapters in this thematic unit illustrate, the field of employment relations touches on a number of different intellectual traditions, but arguably economics is the largest and most imperialistic discipline to influence the field; indeed, the founding father of personnel economics claims as much (Lazear, 2000). The interchange between discipline and field[1] has a long history, which must be summarised here in the broadest terms, and with a bias towards the most fruitful forms of interchange. This bias leads to a sampling of the discipline in favour of economists who are interested in institutions and specifically those who would accept the proposition that there is a difference between employment contracts and other forms of contract. The second bias is geographical: economics has tended to be more influential for US ER academics than for those elsewhere; one author has even suggested institutional economics is 'home turf' for the US ER tradition (Kaufman, 2010, p. 75).

The structure of this chapter is as follows. Section 2 uses a broad historical summary of the discipline's encounter with the field to try to explain the nature of the emerging relationship. The next three sections use arguably the three most influential concepts imported from economics to ER to illustrate the most fruitful elements of dialogue; these are, in order: incomplete contracts, collective action and voice. I will argue that all have been important to the ER field and have in turn been influential in developing economic ideas about what goes on within firms. The conclusion examines where the relationship might be going, and looks at the most proximate parts of the huge discipline of economics – personnel and organisational economics – to assess the possibility of further dialogue.

Introduction

As other chapters in this thematic unit illustrate, the field of employment relations (ER) touches on a number of different intellectual traditions, but arguably economics is the largest and most imperialistic discipline to influence the field; indeed, the founding father of personnel economics claims as much (Lazear, 2000). The interchange between discipline and field[2] has a long history, which must be summarised here in the broadest terms, and with a bias towards the most fruitful forms of interchange. This bias leads to a sampling of the discipline in favour of economists who are interested in institutions, and specifically those who would accept the proposition that there is a difference between employment contracts and other forms of contract. The second bias is geographical: economics has tended to be more influential for US ER academics than for those elsewhere; one author has even suggested institutional economics is 'home turf' for the US ER tradition (Kaufman, 2010, p. 75).

A history of dialogue?

Classical political economy was much concerned with employment relationships. Adam Smith famously discussed both the division of labour and the generation and distribution of economic surpluses; the *Wealth of Nations* also contains succinct descriptions of what later came to be called the 'principal–agent problem' in modern economics (Willman, 2014, pp. 37–48). For others, particularly Ricardo, the 'machinery question' was a central concern; this 'question' concerned the displacement or deskilling of employees by the introduction of new technology, particularly in the textile industries, and what ought to be done about it (Berg, 1980). For Marx, the centrality of the labour theory of value to his intellectual edifice places the employment contract and its dynamics centre stage (see, e.g. Giddens, 1971). All were profoundly influenced by the emergence of employment contracts within firms as a defining property of industrialisation.

It has become something of a cliché to remark on the disappearance of such concerns with the marginalist revolution in economics in the second half of the nineteenth century, so perhaps it is best here to focus on those components of the neoclassical approach that ensure its distancing from the ER field. Two stand out. First, beyond the production function, there is no theory of the firm in neoclassical economics within which to consider the dynamics of employment contracts. Second, employment contracts are not seen as distinctive; they have the same kinds of demand and supply curves as any other form of transaction; whereas the classical political economists saw the employment relationship in hierarchical terms, for the neoclassicist it does not matter much whether employers hire employees or vice versa (Alchian and Demsetz, 1972). It is axiomatic that, as Kaufman (2010, p. 76) puts it, labour is treated as a commodity in competitive markets.

The more general issue – which does not only affect the ER field – is that just at the time when the largest economies in the world were becoming dominated by vertically integrated large firms full of employees, economics goes missing; in Kay's (2004) terms, economists turned from concern about developments in the economy to an attempt to become physicists. Incidentally, this absence created an intellectual vacuum in which most of the current disciplines of the business school, such as accounting, operations management, marketing and strategy, developed to analyse (and prescribe best practice about) events within firms (Willman, 2014). For ER, with the exception of labour economists studying wage setting, differentials and trade union wage policy – all external to the firm – this absence lasts, as Piore (2011) has noted, from the late nineteenth through to the latter part of the twentieth century.

Although academic economics became estranged from the ER field, it would be an exaggeration to argue that the field of ER developed in isolation from a concern with economics, however. If we look at two Anglo-Saxon countries – the USA and UK – we can find in the work of the core founding figures of the academic field not only a concern with economic matters but the borrowing of economic ideas. For illustration, I examine here the work of John Commons in the USA and the Webbs in the UK. In both, there is clear evidence of the influence of three key economic ideas that have become central to the more modern analysis of ER. First, the conception of an employment contract as incomplete and distinctive, thus subject to conflict of interest; second, a concern with the ubiquity of collective action by employees; and third, the idea of voice as a mechanism for managing the dynamics of the employment relationship.[3]

In the neoclassical approach to labour contracts, wage and employment levels are set by the interaction of supply and demand; labour contracts are by implication complete. The dominant trend in ER is to see the employment contract as involving a hierarchical authority relationship, with an inequality of bargaining power between employer and employee, and as incomplete, that is with the opportunity, indeed necessity, for adaptation to changing circumstances. For the Webbs, this inequality was part of a more general pattern of social inequality that Fabian socialism sought to address, but for both the Webbs and Commons, the key deficiency of the neoclassical view of contracts is the omission of consideration of ownership and property rights. Consider the typical neoclassical production function, combining capital, land and labour. These are undifferentiated factors to combine, but typically (at the time) employers would own land and capital but rent labour, which thus became a more disposable factor of production (see also Kaufman, 2010, p. 88). For Commons in particular, the incompleteness of employment contracts was important because completion (i.e. agreement of precise terms in an ongoing relationship) entailed transaction costs; it followed that some forms of employment contract might be more efficient than others if they entailed lower transaction costs of completion. Although this insight was not fully followed up until the work of Williamson (see below) it pointed to the importance of the contractual governance mechanisms that might minimise transaction costs. For Commons, this pointed to the 'humanisation' of the workplace, ensuring the emergence of a win-win game in contract negotiations, as opposed to the then highly prevalent outcome of industrial conflict.

This divergence between field and discipline has proved enduring and it is worth exploring in some detail. To put it very simply, economics for many years had something to say about how wage rates might be struck but very little to say about how employees would subsequently be managed, and this followed from the absence of a theory of the firm. The most influential theory, that of Coase (1937), on which much subsequent work on the economics of the firm is based, has two characteristics relevant for the relationship between field and discipline. First, it generated very little interest within economics at the time; Coase spends much of his article justifying to a Marshallian audience why he is even asking why firms form, and his Nobel prize did not come until 1991. Second, it is a theory of market failure, not a theory of the firm. Specifically, firms arise when certain types of transaction in markets involve such costs of price discovery and enforcement that it becomes more efficient for an 'entrepreneur' to use 'authority' to direct resources to efficient ends. Strong boundaries emerge where the transaction costs of authority and market as allocative mechanisms are equal. Where 'entrepreneurs' come from, and what might be the basis of their 'authority', or the mechanisms through which it might be asserted, are not considered; they are assumptions.

This approach had little to say to academics trying to understand what was going on in firms like Ford, GM, DuPont and Sears that were dominating the US economy at the time; looking back, there must have been an *awful* lot of market failure around, if that were indeed the prime generator of firm formation and growth (Chandler, 1962). Assuming 'authority' involves zero or low transaction costs in turn assumes away most of the issues that Commons was trying to raise. As Bromiley (2005, p. 13) much later noted, the difference between a theory that explains why firms exist and one that explains what they do is similar to the difference between a theory of how fish evolved and one explaining how they swim. Coase had much more to say about the former than the latter.

This is an enduring rather than an historical point of interest. The intellectual heirs of the Coaseian approach are those who use the principal–agent theory to model how the 'entrepreneur' uses 'authority' to control intractable 'agents'. They regard the large public corporation as an 'aberration' and as inherently inferior to markets (Jensen and Meckling, 1976; Jensen, 1989). Those in the ER field who sought, like many other students of modern business, to understand how employment contracts were managed needed to develop their own theories and approaches, either to explain the nature of the contract itself or the system of contractual relationships that constituted the firm (e.g. Doeringer and Piore, 1971; Marsden, 1999; Osterman, 1987). For the modern economist, the Apple or Nike supply chains reveal the efficiencies of renting all of the factors of the production function, particularly for the advantage of shareholders. Many in the ER field retain a concern about what goes on in the factories within these supply chains that would have been familiar to Commons.

The second ER concern to feature in the work of both Commons and the Webbs is collective action by employees, primarily to address the structural power imbalances in the employment contract. Arguably, this was the central contribution of the Webbs to the UK ER field, covering the history of development of trade unions in Britain, their functions in workplace governance and their operation and administration. Commons similarly covered the union role in influencing the operation of the firm, and, most notably in his 1909 analysis of the Philadelphia shoemakers' union, the dynamics of union development as markets expanded and the division of labour progressed. As Kaufman (2010, pp. 76–78; see also Kaufman and Gall, 2015) has noted, in both cases there was a strong political dimension to this, since there was in the early twentieth century a widespread perception of a 'labour problem' in both the UK and USA, the outward sign of which was a high level of industrial conflict in both countries, the agents of which were trade unions. However, again the ER field entered an intellectual vacuum left by economics. High levels of collective action to raise wage rates should not occur for two, rather contradictory, reasons from a neoclassical perspective. First, it should not, given the benefits of free riding by individual employees, be possible, since employees can gain from union activity by enjoying the public goods it produces without paying the subscriptions it needs; this idea was much later formalised by Olson (see below). Second, it should be self-defeating, since raising the supply price of labour should reduce the overall level of labour demand, and thus employment levels would fall. Without collective action, under Say's law, the outcome will be full employment at equilibrium without government involvement. Needless to say, both the Webbs and Commons were in favour of government intervention in labour markets, as part of Fabian socialism on the one hand and the New Deal on the other.

One may tell another 'economics catch up story' here too. As ER writers stepped in to discuss the emergence of new institutions, economics arguably badly needed an efficiency argument. After all, something that is empirically very common in the economy needs an efficiency argument from an economics point of view – otherwise why would it exist? Firms should have a strong motivation to improve efficiency by getting rid of unions and employees should have a strong motivation to quit union membership and free ride. As we will see below, economists were to come up with influential work explaining why both need not happen (though they were better at explaining the first than the second) but there remains the curious fact that, for much of the period during which in advanced economies trade unions were powerful actors, economics struggled to explain why they were there. They did come up with influential theories about the objective functions of union organisations – i.e. the wage/employment trade-offs they pursued (e.g. Dunlop, 1944; Ross, 1948) – so we have in this instance the reverse position from that of the firm discussed above; in the case of trade unions, we have a theory about how fish swim but none about how they got there.

The final economic idea in the ER field we discuss that traces its lineage back this far is that of voice, although admittedly this more modern term is not used by either the Webbs or Commons. The central concern of both was the imbalance in authority and power in the employment relationship. The authority issue for the Webbs was that embedded in the law covering employment contracts in the UK, which was explicitly inherited from 'master and servant' acts going back several centuries. The core of the issue was the employer's generic right to give instructions and the employee's more limited right to disobey only if the instruction was unlawful or unreasonable (Wedderburn, 1971). The power issue was the imbalance of bargaining power in the employment relationship between the employer and the individual employee. In their treatise on industrial democracy, the Webbs were concerned to establish checks and balances on employer power and authority both by the introduction of counterweights to employer power (primarily the role of unions) and constraints on employer authority (primarily legislative proposals). Although the Webbs clearly thought such measures would be socially beneficial, they do not develop the efficiency arguments. By contrast, Commons did. 'Constitutional' government of contractual relations in industry would, he argued, lead to lower transaction costs in filling the 'silences' in employment contracts in firms and thus to greater efficiency. Where employees felt engagement in the terms of their contractual relationship, more co-operative relations were likely. In Commons, we find one of the earliest recognitions of the mantra that the management of people can generate competitive advantage.

Let us summarise the argument so far. Classical political economy was deeply concerned with ER because it saw the emergence of employment contracting and firms as a crucial part of the industrial revolution. Neoclassical economics shed this concern in an attempt to produce generalisable mathematical propositions which, *inter alia*, failed to recognise the idiosyncratic nature of employment contracts. Other academics and policy-makers – we have used the Webbs and Commons as exemplars – stepped into the vacuum economics left in order to analyse what was going on within the firms and institutions that neoclassical economics excised from its agenda as noise. They developed ways of analysing three key areas – employment contracts, collective action and contractual governance arrangements – which have remained influential within the ER field to date.

The final part of this argument concerns the return of the prodigal son. Although economics was not a source of core concepts for those concerned with employment contracts in the period we have discussed, it has become so. In the next three sections, we will argue that developments in institutional economics have become extremely influential in understanding how these three areas of activity central to the ER field operate. Simon and Williamson have developed the analysis of employment contracts, Hirschman and Olsen have developed the analysis of collective action, and Freeman and Medoff have contributed to the modern understanding of voice. We look at each in turn.

Authority and contract

Simon (1951) is one of the earliest and certainly the most influential to attempt to capture the distinctiveness of employment contracts from an economic perspective. Simon notes that most labour is (in 1951 in the USA) delivered under employment contracts and that these differ from sales contracts, which are the standard stuff of price theory. In the latter, the commodity to be exchanged and the price are completely specified, and the seller of the commodity does not care what happens to it after sale. By contrast, an employment contract exists when the employee 'agrees to accept the authority' of the employer (1951, p. 294) in return for a given wage. Simon addresses the two obvious questions: first, why would the employee accept the employer's authority and second, why would the employer want more than a sales contract?

The answer to the first question is simple: the employee is paid a premium for this concession; it is implicit in the argument that the more the employee cedes in terms of the range of this authority, the higher the wage premium will be. Simon specifies a range $(x_i \ldots \ldots x_n)$ of decision items across which the employee will in effect delegate decision-making to the employer in return for a premium in the employment contract over the sales contract price. The employer, by assumption, will in turn wish to have an employment contract as a way of purchasing discretion in decision-making. If they cannot predict which $(x_i \ldots \ldots x_n)$ will be needed at which time, then paying a premium for the right to choose may make sense.

This approach has influenced a range of subsequent developments in the analysis of employment contracts in economics, both for institutional economists such as Williamson and also for those who developed principal–agent theory into a formal model of the employment relationship (Jensen and Meckling, 1976), so it is worth making a number of general points. First, employment contracts are ubiquitous when Simon is writing, so they must have efficiency properties, otherwise all employment would be under sales contracts. These efficiency properties fundamentally lie in the absence of transaction costs and the management of uncertainty. Simon does not use the term transaction costs, but he is aware that the employment contract cannot be both continuously renegotiated and efficient. Uncertainty for the employer about the future demand for labour services carries a premium wage, and the greater the uncertainty, the greater the premium. So it is but a short step to the argument that authority is efficient. Its origins thus become unproblematic. Second, actors are presumed to be rational and would only enter employment contracts where it was in their own interests. Simon explicitly refers to the idea that an employment contract can be seen as a repeated game (1951, p. 294). They may be boundedly rational, being unable to predict how the future $(x_i \ldots \ldots x_n)$ will develop, but non-rational elements in employment contracts are not part of the model. The construction of an employment contract is thus from the employer's point of view similar to that of taking out an option on a trade; since they do not know when labour service x_j will be required, they purchase a call option. The employee takes the present value of this option as their wage.

This approach was developed by Simon's pupil, Williamson, who noted that some employment contracts look more like sales contracts than others. Before outlining his approach to employment contracts, it is important to be clear about the assumptions and core concept in his approach. Williamson is primarily concerned with two related issues: the Coaseian problem of the comparative efficiency of firms ('hierarchies' in his terms) on the one hand and markets on the other, and the efficiency properties of different types of hierarchy (Williamson, 1975, 1985). The step forward from Coase is precisely in his concern to theorise the dynamics of hierarchy; hierarchies may themselves differ in efficiency depending on the choice and mix of contractual forms with different levels of transaction costs. He assumes that firms will arise where assets are specific to a transaction – i.e. they have lower values outside the firm than inside (this follows from Coase).

Two further key assumptions about economic actors are important. He assumes individuals are boundedly rational and that complete contracts are difficult to write (this too follows from Simon). More controversially, he extends the conventional economic assumption that individuals pursue self-interest to the idea that they are 'opportunistic' in that they pursue 'self-interest seeking with guile' (1985, p. 47).

The scope of his work goes beyond employment contracts, but here we restrict our focus to employment. He distinguishes three broad contract types. *Sequential spot contracting* is a market-type transaction where employer and employee sustain no long-term commitments; they simply exchange cash for services as the need arises. A simple example might be that of a casually employed gardener or window cleaner paid by the householder as need arises.

A more modern example would be the use of such contracts in the 'gig economy', typified by app-driven employment in firms such as Uber (Habans, 2016). However, more complex institutional structures may emerge to govern sets of spot transactions. Longshore work in a variety of countries based on casual labour or, historically, the printing of newspapers appear to be institutionalised forms of spot contracting (Edwards, 1990; Sisson, 1975; Willman, 1986). Day hiring of labour in industries such as construction would be another example, as would the use of zero hours contracts.

Williamson identifies the strengths and weaknesses of this contractual type. From the employer perspective it has the advantage that labour does not become a fixed cost, but the disadvantage is that the employer cannot easily develop firm-specific skills. For the employee it allows choice of employment opportunities but has the disadvantage that all of the contractual risk falls on them. It is clear that the balance of advantage depends crucially on the supply/demand relationship. Spot contracts work well for employees where labour is, or can be made, scarce and a key strategy of unions (or other forms of collective action) in all of the industries above is to restrict the supply of labour and to maximise the number of bargaining opportunities.

Williamson's second type of employment contract is the *contingent claims* contract. In this arrangement the parties try to write a comprehensive contract itemising every employee task and setting a price for it. Again, there are historical examples. The making of shoes in the UK and USA was for many years based on extensive price lists for components such as soles and heels in which the cost of labour was included (Commons, 1909; Willman, 1986). The advantage for both employer and employee is reduction in uncertainty, and the problem for both is bounded rationality. Where events arise not covered in the comprehensive contract the haggling and thus transaction costs will emerge.

Williamson thus falls back on Simon's original idea (see also Simon 1991) of an authority relationship as having the most robust efficiency properties, and the example he relies heavily upon is Doeringer and Piore's (1971) 'enterprise market' – i.e. an internal labour market. Williamson (1975) describes it as an authority relationship with many contingencies spelt out. He emphasises several characteristics with efficiency properties: internal promotion ladders encourage the development of firm-specific skills; pay rates attached to jobs and a regularised promotion system lower the requirement to monitor employees intensively; job security encourages employee co-operation; and agreed procedures reduce haggling. In this contractual form, labour becomes a fixed cost and the employer bears much of the contractual risk (upside and downside) in return for a reduction in transaction costs.

One might find it ironic that such institutionalised forms of labour management arguably began to disappear in the USA just about the time Williamson wrote about their efficiency properties. However, there are two features of his analysis of ER that have enduring interest, not least because they embody major differences between economic approaches to employment relationships and those grounded in sociology or politics. They concern the outcome variables of efficient employment contracts, i.e. the avoidance of opportunism and the generation of consummate co-operation.

Opportunism – 'self-interest seeking with guile' – is an assumption about individual behaviour in contract negotiations, but in the analysis of employment contracts it emerges as a property exclusively of seller (i.e. employee) behaviour. The institutions of contractual governance are efficient to the extent that they control employee opportunistic behaviour such as deliberate underperformance or fraud. Employers (buyers) are assumed to be immune to opportunism (Willman, 1982). Consummate co-operation is defined as 'an affirmative job attitude – to include the use of judgement, filling gaps and taking initiative', contrasted with perfunctory co-operation, which is 'job co-operation of a minimally acceptable sort' (Williamson, 1975, p. 27). It is key to the generation of efficiency gains and firms that encourage it will out-compete those that do not. Again, it is a property of employees, not employers.

Williamson anticipates much of the later agenda about the relationship between human resource practices and competitiveness, in which a variety of terms have been used to describe desirable employee outcomes – most recently 'engagement'. However, his approach is also intellectually very similar to those embedded in more recent economic attempts to model employment contracts in economics, notably principal–agent theory (Jensen and Meckling, 1976), in three respects, all of which tend to make economic models of the employment contract unpalatable to many in the ER field. They are:

1. Authority of the employer is an assumption, not a variable. The Coaseian roots of the idea of authority in hierarchy as a source of efficiency means that its legitimacy is not questioned and its objectives are unexamined. Challenges to employer authority show up as transaction costs and thus efficiency losses. Most ER scholars regard power and authority as central to the analysis of employment contracts, and thus see economic approaches that sideline them as incomplete at best and biased towards the employer at worst (e.g. Edwards, 1990; Nolan 2012).
2. Efficiency is defined in terms of the appropriation of all economic rent by the employer. Appropriation of such rents by the employee is opportunism, and opportunism is seen as a property only of seller (employee) not buyer (employer) behaviour (Willman, 1982). The subsequent use of such rents is exogenous to the model of the employment contract.
3. The central problem of employment contracts is thus employee behaviour, specifically the avoidance of opportunism and perfunctory co-operation, and elimination of these undesirable outcomes, is a function of contract design.

It should be noted that developments in principal–agent theory share these features. Principals are risk-neutral and rational; agents are risk-averse and prone to generating information asymmetries. Those selecting agents must beware moral hazard and adverse selection. Management of agents involves a mix of monitoring and incentives and the design of this mix generates the desirable employee (agent) behaviours. As I have argued elsewhere, principal–agent theory is essentially a Taylorist approach to ER based on close monitoring and financial rewards (Willman, 2014, pp. 37–48).

The problem of collective action

Any theory in economics that stresses the difficulty of collective action is probably best regarded by those in employment relations as a constraint on theorising rather than a contribution to a field in which employee collective action is widespread. Olson's (1971) approach, mentioned above, must nonetheless feature here since it has provoked substantial debate within the ER field (Crouch, 1982; Kelly, 1998). However, much of this section will discuss another approach – that of Hirschman (1970) – which focuses in a more conventional economic way on the efficiency properties of a widely observed social phenomenon. Olson's approach does not have much to say about workplace representation, while Hirschman's explains much about the market for collective action; it also relates to the discussion of voice in Section 5 below.

Olson's approach relies on the one hand on the idea of calculative rationality and on the other hand on the distinction between public and private goods. By calculative rationality Olson primarily means that people will engage in collective action only where the benefits of doing so exceed the costs. The costs may be monetary (e.g. union subscriptions) and non-monetary (e.g. time involved). The central problem here is that for Olson, where collective action only produces public goods, free riding is more profitable than collective action. This is because a public good is one whose benefits are available to all, regardless of whether they have incurred the associated costs. Therefore, for Olson, private goods – restricted to those who have incurred costs – are essential if we are to avoid having a situation where everyone would benefit from the provision of public goods but there is no individual incentive for co-operation. He uses the term *selective incentive* to refer to private goods, and the term *special condition* to refer to forms of coercion or compulsion to compel individuals to engage in collective action.

Let us put all this into the language of ER. In this view, unions cannot only engage in collective bargaining, since typically the benefits of collective bargaining are a public good; non-members usually get the union-negotiated wage increase. They must provide private goods, typically individual benefits such as insurance or representation for individuals in disciplinary and grievance procedures. Where possible they will seek to make union membership compulsory by collective agreement, or encourage employers to advocate or facilitate union membership (for example by offering to deduct union subscriptions from salary). Much evidence indicates that unions, in the UK at least, do all of these things (e.g. Pencavel, 1971; Willman et al., 1993). Olson's analysis indicates how unions try to solve first- and second-order collective action problems; the first-order problem is how to overcome free riding to encourage membership growth, and the second is how to run collective action organisations so that the benefits to members are greater than the costs incurred (Willman, 2004; Willman et al., 2016).

There are two major problems with the Olson approach that have attracted the attention of ER researchers, however; the first is logical, the second empirical. As Elster (1989, p. 64) initially noted, the logical problem is that the union has to already exist in order to apply the selective incentives and special conditions that cause it to exist. The empirical objection (see Crouch, 1982; Kelly, 1998) is that there appears to be no good fit between historically observed bouts of union membership growth and the existence of special conditions. Partly as a result of these criticisms, the ER field has been influenced rather more by an approach to collective action that emphasises its efficiency consequences.

Hirschman (1970) was not initially setting out to solve an ER problem, and his approach is largely couched in terms of consumers rather than employees. Assume an organisation produces a good or service for consumers. Assume further that these customers experience a decline in quality of the good or service in question. The standard economic approach would say that consumers would then switch to the outputs of another organisation, until managers of the first organisation remedy the problem, when they might switch back. This is termed *exit* by Hirschman and he argues that it may be inefficient for all parties. For the organisation, exit is informationally inefficient; you know you are losing consumers, but it may take a long time to find out why and even longer to get them back. For the consumers, there may be substantial switching costs; in his words, consumers have *loyalty* – this is not irrational or affective, it simply refers to the costs of exit versus the alternative, which he terms *voice*. Voice involves consumers complaining directly to management about the quality decline, and doing so collectively. Managers get information and the consumer avoids the costs of switching. The reader may wish to think about what happens when an Apple product has a defect in order to assess how useful this approach is in understanding product market behaviour; switching away from your new iPhone means switching other products and services as well.

The approach has been applied successfully in the ER field, however, notably by Freeman and Medoff (1984) to explain aspects of unionisation and, particularly, voice. We discuss this in detail in the next section, but here we focus on the fact that Hirschman has, without particularly focusing on it, solved a number of the 'Olson' problems about collective action, and we close this section by summarising them.

Olson asserts that setting up collective action organisations is difficult and costly. Hirschman deals with this in three broad ways. First, he introduces the idea of switching costs. Where sunk costs of collective action are high, it may nonetheless be the case that switching costs are higher. To fall back on Williamson's language, the assets of both employer and employee may be so specific to the employment contract that both can bear the costs of employee collective action in order to sustain the contract. This leads to the second point, that the calculation of the costs and benefits of collective action is not put simply from the point of view of the individual considering union membership. The avoidance of costly employee exit may be worth invest-ment by employers, shareholders and even consumers in voice mechanisms that would prevent it. Third, he sidesteps the free rider problem central to Olson's analysis simply by allowing that individuals have different utility functions in considering collective action. Specifically, he assumes that there exists a subset of consumers (and by extension, employees) for whom the benefits of collective action are not the financial returns minus the costs but *the sum of the two*. These individuals are the activists who promote collective action for returns calculated in terms of both extrinsic and intrinsic rewards.

Hirschman's approach has been influential in the ER field but it is not without its critics. Several point to the difference between the consumer market roots of the approach and the hierarchical realities of employment contracts (e.g. Allen, 2014), suggesting that there are such fundamental differences that the model is inapplicable. Others have suggested that the exit, voice and loyalty categories are too simple, adding others, notably the idea of employee delib-erate 'neglect' as a response to any deteriorating employment situation (e.g. Farrell, 1983). But the main issues concern the scope of the term 'voice', which has a restrictive and remedial effi-ciency function for Hirschman, but a much broader set of interpretations in the ER field. We turn to it next.

Voice

One of the most influential books of the past 30 years in employment relations is by two labour economists, Freeman and Medoff (1984). It is remarkable in a number of ways. First, it is deriva-tive, in that it simply applies Hirschman's insights to the labour market. Second, it uses only a US data set but makes veridical claims about general relationships. Third, it assumes, without explicit justification, that unions are the most effective form of collective voice. However, it is highly cited and highly influential (Blanchflower and Bryson, 2004) and has defined the eco-nomic approach to voice within ER. In the book's title, the authors ask the question *What Do Unions Do?* However, they are not concerned with union activity itself but with its impact, on wages and the general performance of the economy. So the focus is not on unions per se, but on the impact of their presence in the firm on two key dependent variables, wages and productivity.

In their transaction costs approach, the net effect of unionisation is an empirical question that essentially consists of netting off the benefits of unionisation from the known costs. The known costs are monopoly wage gains and restrictive work rules. The key benefit is voice, which has simple Hirschman qualities of reduced exit and reduced information asymmetry. Let us look at each in turn. The conventional economic assumption underlying monopoly wage gains is that they should lead to reduced employment levels through the incentive to substitute capital for labour. The higher rates should also attract better quality labour (unless everyone else is doing the same). The approach does not deal directly with variation between firms in the extent to which capital might effectively displace labour nor the variable cost of capital. Unions naturally respond to this substitution effect either by opposing technical changes or by retaining prior employment levels in the face of technical change (Willman, 1986). The model contains no variables that might estimate the ability of unions to do so; supply/demand considerations do not really enter into it. The voice variable is in fact an interaction. It depends on the ability of employees to organise voice and the receptiveness of management to the information voice produces. For both of these reasons, it is probably not best conceptualised purely in terms of union activity. Since its effectiveness depends on management reception of its outputs, any form of voice that does not have to offset the imposition of restrictive work rules is likely to be more efficient in Hirschman terms.

However, from a field perspective, the approach has undoubted benefits. The list below is not intended to be exhaustive:

1. It stresses that the impact of unions on the dependent variable, productivity, is an empirical question – not an assumption. The unit of analysis for consideration of this question is the firm or the establishment.
2. The balance between pursuit of wage gains and restrictive work rules puts emphasis on the objective function of unions by focusing on the wage/employment trade off. Unions may seek to maximise the level of employment, or seek higher wages for a smaller number of employee members (Dunlop, 1944; Ross, 1948).
3. The balance between voice benefits and other costs depends on the extent of managerial responsiveness to voice. This is thus a more sophisticated version of the 'you get the union you deserve' argument, placing emphasis squarely on the effective management of the trade-offs in the model.
4. By extension, it defines the set of firms in which the net impact of unions on productivity can be positive. Where there are few opportunities for capital investment, where unions can impose restrictive work rules and where management 'quality' (as they define it) is poor, the impact of unions on the dependent variable will be negative (Willman, 2014, pp. 55–56).

What this approach does *not* do is examine the different mechanisms of voice in terms of their effects on productivity. This is more fully dealt with elsewhere in Chapter 16. The key point to make here is that because Freeman and Medoff assume that effective collective voice equates to union activity, two important issues are under-investigated. The first is the employer interest in voice promotion; there is substantial UK evidence that as union coverage declined employers invested substantially in other voice mechanisms (Budd et al., 2010; Gomez et al., 2010). The second is that there is evidence from the same data sets that employer-initiated voice mechanisms have efficiency advantages over unionised ones (Bryson et al., 2013).

The significance of employer investment in voice for an economist is that it emphasises the efficiency properties of voice for organisational performance. Many ER academics might look at employer-sponsored voice in terms of power and legitimacy. It might be seen as offering lower levels of representation and protection for employees than independent trade unionism. The Hirschman approach, as we have seen, sees its efficiency properties in terms of its ability to address an information asymmetry problem that adversely affects firm performance. The significance of any performance advantages of non-union voice is that it simply reflects the trade-offs in a make or buy decision. Firms may make voice mechanisms themselves in order to reap their benefits (non-union voice) or they may buy them (from a union).

A final point to make is that the idea of 'voice' within the ER field has developed beyond the economic view of it as an efficient alternative to exit as a reducer of information asymmetry. In the field, employee voice is studied for its effects *inter alia* on employee affective states such as job satisfaction and organisational commitment, and thus engages with debates within organisational psychology, and it is also related to issues concerning statutory rights within the workplace, and thus engages with the concerns of legal scholars. The impact of voice mechanisms on managerial behaviour represents only a fragment of these broader debates (see Wilkinson et al., 2014).

Conclusion

This chapter has tried to show the interplay between the field of employment relations and the discipline of economics. Neither is homogeneous; we have tried to proceed by showing how the two address problems that are seen as interesting from both perspectives, which has naturally led to a rather selective view of the concerns of both discipline and field. In ER, there are many who would see economics as secondary to sociology, politics and law, and in economics there are still those in denial about the existence of firms. So, in conclusion, we focus on differences between those in the field who think economics is relevant and those in economics who think the employment contract is distinctive.

The key distinction is, in fact, quite fundamental and conceptual. Even those in economics who acknowledge the distinctiveness of employment contracts feel that efficiency drives organisational outcomes and they do not focus on power. There is of course not space here to discuss how power might be conceptualised, but there are no mainstream economic models that deal with this, however defined. In Simon, Williamson, and agency theory the Coaseian assumption that the exercise of what they term *authority* rests with the employer is an unexamined assumption, not an empirically investigated variable, except in the very limited sense that it generates information asymmetry problems that need to be resolved.

This impacts on how economists deal with the silences in the employment contract, and again the base assumption is that the most efficient conflict resolution mechanism should prevail. Collective action and voice work to the extent that they improve firm performance. If they do not or, more realistically, more parsimonious collective action or voice mechanisms emerge, they will outcompete existing rivals. At the risk of labouring the point, it is worth emphasising the institutional agnosticism of economic approaches. Effective voice is whatever generates the best efficiency (productivity) outcome, normally measured as some return to the firm, rather than employees. This leads to a further point, which is that economic models make *employee* behaviour endemically problematic, but *employer* behaviour operates by assumption.

In closure, we focus on likely future relations between discipline and field. As readers will see from the dating of many economic references in this chapter, the high point of institutional economics appears to have passed and developments in personnel and organisational economics that focus on the same subject matter as ER operate with very different methods and assumptions. Their tendency to regard an organisation as an inferior substitute to a market, existing only where a market cannot work, tends to two inclinations. The first is to view the organisation as a nexus of constrained contracts that should operate as much like a market as possible. The second is to work out how the constraints on market operation can be removed to make the organisation dissolve into a market.

The growing field of personnel economics in particular is one that analyses some of the core activities of ER but uses economic and mathematical approaches to model outcomes. Lazear and Oyer (2013, pp. 479–481) for example, identify the scope of personnel economics as "focused on five aspects of employment relationships – incentives, matching firms to workers, compensation, skill development and the organisation of work". This set of issues is clearly part of the ER field, but they also identify its objective as "to describe how human resource practices

The Net Effect of Union Activity

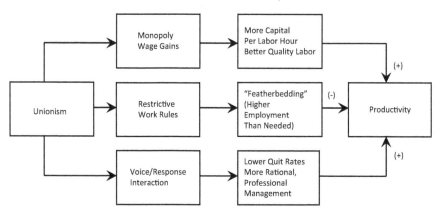

Figure 3.1 The net effect of union activity

can best address employers' goals". Collective action, power and authority relationships, conflict and bargaining take second stage where one seeks to optimise firm performance without a more pluralist analysis of the interests of other stakeholders. This pluralism has been a feature of the ER field since its origins, and it has only effectively engaged with economists who share it. An optimist might anticipate a return by economists to the classical concerns of political economy, in which employment contracts and their governance were central to an understanding of economic performance. A pessimist might point to the current contents of economic journals.

Notes

1 We use the two terms consistently throughout. 'Discipline' refers to economics; 'field' refers to employment relations. These terms are simply categorical, with no intended implications about the relative standings.
2 We use the two terms consistently throughout. 'Discipline' refers to economics; 'field' refers to employment relations. These terms are simply categorical, with no intended implications about the relative standings.
3 The references for the following paragraphs on the Webbs and Commons are listed in the reference list.

References

Alchian, A.A. and Demsetz, H. (1972). 'Production, Information Costs and Economic Organisation', *American Economic Review*, 62(5), pp. 777–795.

Allen, M.M.C. (2014). Hirschman and Voice, in Wilkinson, A., Dundon, A. and Freeman, R. (eds.) *The Handbook of Research on Employee Voice*. London: Edward Elgar, pp. 36–51.

Berg, M. (1980). *The Machinery Question and the Making of Political Economy*. Cambridge (UK): Cambridge University Press.

Blanchflower, D. and Bryson, A. (2004). 'What effect do unions have on wages now?' *Journal of Labor Research*, 25(3), pp. 383–414.

Bromiley, P. (2005). *The Behavioral Foundations of Strategic Management*. Oxford: Blackwell.

Bryson, A., Willman, P., Gomez, R., Kretschmer, T. (2013). 'The Comparative Advantage of Non-Union Voice in Britain, 1980–2004', *Industrial Relations*, 52(1), pp. 26–52.

Budd, J.W., Gollan, P.J. and Wilkinson, A. (2010). 'New approaches to employee voice and participation in organizations', *Human Relations*, 63(3), pp. 303–310.

Chandler, A. (1962). *Strategy and Structure: Chapters in the History of American Enterprise*. Cambridge (MA): MIT Press.

Coase, R.H. (1937). 'The Nature of the Firm', *Economica*, 4, pp. 386–405.

Commons, J.R. (1909). 'American Shoemakers, 1648–1895: A Sketch of Industrial Evolution', *The Quarterly Journal of Economics*, 24(1), pp. 39–84.

Commons, J.R. (1919). *Industrial Goodwill*. New York: McGraw-Hill.

Commons, J.R. (1934). *Institutional Economics: Its Place in Political Economy*. New York: Macmillan.

Commons, J.R. (1950). *The Economics of Collective Action*. Madison: University of Wisconsin Press.

Crouch, C. (1982). *Trade Unions; The Logic of Collective Action*. London: Fontana.

Davis, G. (2009). *Managed by Markets*. Oxford: Oxford University Press.

Doeringer, P. and Piore, M. (1971). *Internal Labour Markets and Manpower Analysis*. Lexington: D.C. Heath.

Dunlop, J. (1944). *Industrial Relations Systems*. New York: Holt.

Edwards, P.K. (1990). 'The Politics of Conflict and Consent: How the Labour Contract Really Works', *Journal of Economic Behavior and Organization*, 13, pp. 41–61.

Edwards, P.K. (2003). The Employment Relationship and the Field of Industrial Relations, in Edwards, P.K. (ed.) *Industrial Relations: Theory and Practice*. 2nd edn. London: Blackwell, pp. 1–36.

Elster, J. (1989). *The Cement of Society*. Cambridge (UK): Cambridge University Press.

Farrell, D. (1983). 'Exit, voice, loyalty and neglect as responses to job dissatisfaction; a multi-dimensional scaling study', *Academy of Management Journal*, 26(4), pp. 596–607.

Freeman, R. and Medoff, J. (1984). *What Do Unions Do?* New York: Basic Books.

Giddens, A. (1971). *Capitalism and Modern Social Theory*. Cambridge (UK): Cambridge University Press.

Gomez, R., Bryson, A. and Willman P. (2010). Voice Transformation: The Shift from Union to Non-Union Voice in Britain, in Wilkinson et al. (eds.) *Oxford Handbook of Participation in Organisations*. Oxford: Oxford University Press.

Habans, R. (2016). *Is California's Gig Economy Growing? Exploring Trends in Independent Contracting*. UCLA Institute for Research on Labor and Employment, 1099-MISC.

Hirschman, A. (1970). *Exit, Voice and Loyalty*. Cambridge (MA): Harvard University Press.

Jensen, M.C. (1989). 'Eclipse of the Public Corporation', *Harvard Business Review*, Sept-Oct, pp. 61–74.

Jensen, M.C. and Meckling, W.H. (1976). 'The Theory of the Firm: Managerial Behaviour, Agency Costs and Ownership Structure', *Journal of Financial Economics*, 3(4), pp. 305–360.

Kaufman, B.E. (2010). 'The Theoretical Foundation of Industrial Relations and its Implications for Labor Economics and Human Resource Management', *Industrial and Labor Relations Review*, 64(1), pp. 74–108.

Kaufman, B.E. and Gall, G. (2015). 'Advancing Industrial Relations Theory: An Analytical Synthesis of British-American and Pluralist-Radical Ideas', *Relations Industrielles/Industrial Relations*, 70(3), pp. 407–432.

Kay, J. (2004). *The Truth About Markets*. London: Penguin.

Kelly, J. (1998). *Rethinking Industrial Relations*. London: Routledge.

Lazear, E.P. (2000). 'Economic Imperialism', *Quarterly Journal of Economics*, 115(1), pp. 99–146.

Lazear, E.P. and Oyer, P. (2013). Personnel Economics, in Gibbons, R. and Roberts, J. (eds.) *Handbook of Organizational Economics*. Princeton: Princeton University Press, pp. 479–520.

Marsden, D. (1999). *The Theory of Employment Systems: Micro-foundations of Societal Diversity*. Oxford: Oxford University Press.

Nolan, P. (2012). 'Understanding the employment relationship: markets, hierarchies and power', *Industrial Relations Journal*, 43(4), pp. 359–369.

Olson, M. (1971). *The Logic of Collective Action*. Cambridge (MA): Harvard University Press.

Osterman, P. (1987). 'Choice of Employment Systems', *Industrial Relations*, 26(1), pp. 46–67.

Pencavel, J. (1971). 'The Demand for Union Services; An Exercise', *Industrial and Labor Relations Review*, 24(2), pp. 180–190.

Piore, M.J. (2011). 'Whither Industrial Relations: Does It Have a Future in Post-Industrial Society?' *British Journal of Industrial Relations*, 49(4), pp. 792–801.

Ross, M. (1948). *Trade Union Wage Policy*. Berkeley: University of California Press.

Simon, H.A. (1951). 'A formal theory of the employment relationship', *Econometrica*, 19(3), pp. 293–305.

Simon, H A. (1991). 'Organisations and Markets', *Journal of Economic Perspectives*, 5(2), pp. 25–44.

Sisson, K. (1975). *Industrial Relations on Fleet Street*. Oxford: Blackwell.

Webb, S. and Webb, B. (1897). *Industrial Democracy*. London: Longman, Greens.

Webb, S. and Webb, B. (1907). *The History of Trade Unionism*. London: Longman, Greens.

Wedderburn, K.W. (1971). *The Worker and the Law*. London: Penguin.

Wilkinson, A., Dundon, A. and Freeman, R. (eds.) (2014). *The Handbook of Research on Employee Voice*. London: Edward Elgar.

Williamson, O.E. (1975). *Markets and Hierarchies, Analysis and Anti-Trust Implications*. New York: Free Press.

Williamson, O.E. (1985). *The Economic Institutions of Capitalism*. New York: Free Press.

Willman, P. (1982). 'Opportunism and Labour Contracting: An Application of the Organisational Failures Framework', *Journal of Economic Behaviour and Organisation*, 2(1), pp. 83–98.

Willman, P. (1986). *Technological Change, Collective Bargaining and Industrial Efficiency*. Oxford: Oxford University Press.

Willman, P. (2004). Structuring Unions: the Administrative Rationality of Collective Action, in Kelly, J. and Willman, P. (eds.) *Union Organization and Activity*. London: Routledge, pp. 73–89.

Willman, P. (2014). *Understanding Management: The Social Science Foundations*. Oxford: Oxford University Press.

Willman, P., Morris, T.J. and Aston, B. (1993). *Union Business: Trade Union Organisation and Financial Reform in the Thatcher Years*. Cambridge (UK): Cambridge University Press.

Willman, P., Bryson, A. and Forth, J. (2016). *UK Trades Unions and the Problems of Collective Action*. IZA Discussion Paper No. 10043. Berlin.

4

EMPLOYMENT RELATIONS AND THE LAW

Michael Doherty[1]

Introduction

For many lawyers, the only perspective on employment relations (ER) that really matters is that gleaned through focusing on laws and legal mechanisms, the means by which rules and directives are made, by some authority, to direct behaviour and sanction deviance from established norms. Of course, as will be evident from other chapters in this section, and throughout the volume, it is clearly not only by looking at traditional legal instruments (such as constitutional provisions, presidential decrees, court decisions or acts of parliament) that we can understand the complexity of the employment relationship and how it is organised and controlled. Nonetheless, the law and the legal lens remain crucial to understanding employment regulation, and this chapter discusses how the law frames and interacts with other regulatory aspects of ER. There are, of course, significant variations in laws, and legal systems, throughout the world. The purpose of the chapter, therefore, is not to focus on specific laws themselves, but rather on the issues and challenges of the legal regulation of ER that appear, albeit to varying extents, in all jurisdictions.

First, the chapter looks at the role, and purpose, of the law in ER, tracing changing conceptions of these over time. Secondly, the chapter looks at the sources from which legal regulation of ER derives, considering the role of both 'hard' and 'soft' laws. The next section looks at one of the most controversial aspects of the legal regulation of ER: the scope and coverage of labour laws. At whom are such laws directed, who is excluded from their scope and what is the rationale for the legal regulation of particular actors, notably workers' representatives? The penultimate section considers the critical issue of compliance with, and enforcement of, labour laws. Here, the notion of the 'autonomous nature' of labour law is considered. The concluding section looks at some current and future challenges for the legal regulation of the employment relationship.

The role of law in employment relations

Kahn-Freund has described the law as "a technique for the regulation of social power" (Kahn-Freund, 1977, p.7). For him, key characteristics of society were the fact that firstly, such power is unequally distributed, and secondly, that the individual normally has little or no social power.

For Kahn-Freund, these characteristics were particularly true of the world of work, leading him to proclaim that:

> [t]he main object of labour law has always been, and we venture to say, will always be, to be a countervailing force to counteract the inequality of bargaining power which is inherent and must be inherent in the employment relationship.
>
> *(Kahn-Freund, 1977, p. 17)*

In a similar vein, Davis wrote that labour law's fundamental premise is "that it provides a framework within which workers can build a countervailing power to that of management" (Davis, 2002, p. 160). For much of the twentieth century, this perspective, that labour law should be defined by reference to its *protective* function, was the dominant one amongst labour law scholars (Creighton and Stewart, 2016; Wedderburn, 1965). Therefore, laws regulating ER should focus on protecting workers from unjust, unfair or exploitative treatment by employers. This could be by means of creating individual labour rights for workers, or permitting and/or encouraging collective representation of workers' interests, generally via trade unions, which would redress some or all of the power imbalances involved in negotiating terms and conditions of employment.

By the late twentieth century, however, the dominance of the protective perspective came to be questioned. Across most of the globe, trade union density and collective bargaining coverage has been dropping over the past 30 years, accompanied by a corresponding decline in industrial action, prompting some to identify a new 'individualism' amongst workers, which encompasses an ideological rejection of collective organisation and action (Beck, 2000; cf. Kelly, 1998). A range of social theorists have argued that work plays a much-diminished role in the contemporary life experience (Bauman, 1998; Beck, 2000, 1992; Sennett, 1998), with the emergence of a 'consumer society' in which work has lost its "privileged position as an axis around which all other efforts at self-constitution and identity-building rotate" (Bauman, 1998, p. 32). Moreover, it has been argued, the old 'top-down' logic of Taylorist management control has been turned on its head, with an increasingly well-educated workforce afforded a level of autonomy at work unthinkable in the era of the 'Fordist' model (Castells, 2004).

In terms of labour law, scholars have argued that the changed political landscape, and:

> in particular, the acceptance across party political divides of a market logic forcefully resistant to regulatory "interference" appeared to render futile any attempt to remain tied to old notions of labour law as state intervention to guarantee fair terms and conditions of employment.
>
> *(Dukes, 2014, p. 2)*

Attention has, therefore, focused increasingly on the interaction between *labour law* and *labour markets*, and the impact of legal regulation on competitiveness, flexibility and labour market access (Davies and Freedland, 2007; Deakin and Wilkinson, 2005). For Deakin and Wilkinson, the key question to be addressed is "what kind of normative or regulatory framework is needed in order for labour markets to function in the interests of a range of societal goals, of which efficiency is one?" (2005, p. 277). This approach requires labour law to extend beyond its traditional protective function, and become the "means for providing the institutional framework and mechanisms for redressing the deficiencies of markets for labour, and for promoting goals of flexibility and competitiveness in a socially sustainable way" (Frazer, 2008, p. 23; see also, Collins, 2001).

Of course, it is important to point out that for most scholars the protective function of labour law has never become irrelevant. For Dickens, worker protection was not to be promoted only as a good thing in itself, but could be "re-conceptualised as being about citizenship and individual rights in the workplace, and as a way of combating social exclusion" (2004, p. 607). Similarly, much literature focuses on the role of law in *protecting* workers from *systematic market failures*, such as asymmetric information and the problem of negative externalities (Deakin, 2001).

Guy Davidov (2016), in reviewing labour law literature and legislation in Israel, the UK and the USA, has outlined a number of the 'goals' of labour law. These include:

- Democracy, which can be understood as encompassing both 'voice' at work, and the fact that organisational decisions can be reached on the basis of compromise (via collective bargaining, for example); see Chapters 14 and 15 of this volume
- Redistribution of power, resources and risk, for example, via minimum wage laws or laws protecting against unjust dismissal
- Dignity, respect for which is crucial, given the economic, social and psychological importance of work; and social inclusion/citizenship, given that the workplace is a major forum of civil society
- Stability and security, which are not related only to job security, but also to all other arrangements that might render working life insecure or unstable (e.g. certain types of contractual arrangements or organisation of working time); this goal applies at the level of the individual, but also at the macro-economic level (the ability of economic systems to weather shocks and downturns)
- Efficiency: as noted above, labour law can contribute to the correction of market failures, and to improving both the competitiveness of organisations and national economies
- Social equality, which encompasses many of the ideas inherent in conceptions of workplace dignity and social inclusion, but also focuses on inequalities *outside* of the workplace and on the breaking of hierarchies between social classes; employment standards relating to free speech, privacy and whistleblowing operate to illustrate this argument.

Davidov is clear that these different goals have no claim to exclusivity: "in most cases different goals (or articulations) can live side by side with each other" (2016, p. 55).[2] Which goals are prioritised in a given place and time will depend, of course, on a range of normative, political, economic and social factors. It is also important to recognise the possibility of conflict between different areas of law in the pursuit of particular goals. A good illustration of this is the potential conflict between the efficiency goal of labour law and that of competition/antitrust law. Laws promoting collective bargaining, for example, might be justified by the need to remedy the structural imbalance and asymmetries of labour markets, as most workers do not have any alternative to earning their main income on the labour market; if wages fall below a certain level, they simply expand supply (e.g. by taking up another occupation or working overtime). A collective bargaining process is based on combining employees in order to alleviate the pressure to undercut the price of each other's labour (Novitz, 2015). However, competition/antitrust rules, at their core, prohibit cartels or agreements between undertakings that distort competition. These rules clearly conflict with the right to conclude binding collective agreements (often referred to as 'wage cartels'), the purpose of which is to set prices (wages). Therefore, courts and legislatures must grapple with ways of resolving such a conflict. Some solutions are to exclude collective agreements from the scope of competition/antitrust laws altogether; to exclude such agreements only if they fulfil certain objectives (e.g. directly contribute to the improvement of working conditions); or to restrict or prohibit binding collective agreements (see, for discussion, De Stefano, 2016). Other similar issues of conflict might arise, for example, between laws relating to corporate governance and laws promoting voice (e.g. board-level representation for employees).

Sources of legal regulation in employment relations

As with all areas of law, a starting point for any student or practitioner of labour law is to appreciate from where the relevant legal rules applicable to a particular scenario originate. It is also necessary to understand where the various legal rules fit into the overall system; is there a hierarchical framework if conflict arises and, if so, which legal rule will prevail over the others in the case of a conflict? Labour law is derived from a number of sources and the balance between these various sources is continuously changing. As a result, labour law tends to be an area that is quite dynamic and is persistently evolving, which reflects the reality that the employer-employee relationship itself is one that is constantly developing (Daly and Doherty, 2010). Adding to the complexity is the fact that in addition to the regular courts there is a variety of specific institutions and tribunals that deal with claims relating to employment disputes. We will examine these in greater detail below, but first we need to identify the principal sources of labour law.

At a global level, the International Labour Organization (ILO) is the tripartite United Nations (UN) agency that brings together governments and employer and worker representatives of its 187 Member States to set labour standards, develop policies and devise programmes promoting decent work (see Chapter 25). The ILO Constitution sets down core basic principles, most famously in the *Declaration of Philadelphia*, annexed to the Constitution, that "labour is not a commodity", and standards on particular areas of employment are outlined in the ILO's Conventions and Recommendations. States that ratify ILO Conventions are obliged to "take such action as may be necessary to make effective" their provisions (Article 19(5) of the Constitution), and the ILO Governing Body is supported by Committees of Experts, which hear complaints if a State is not securing the application of Conventions and issue Recommendations to the Member States. It is important to remember, however, that as an international law organisation, the ILO system ultimately relies on moral authority, the goodwill of its Member States and persuasion to achieve compliance with its goals. It does not have the capacity to issue the types of 'sanctions' that would be available for breaches of labour law in a typical nation state. The ILO, and its rules, remain symbolically very important though, as they are products of global, tripartite negotiation and compromise (Sengenberger, 2006).

Regional labour law standards can often have more obviously practical 'bite'. These may result from, for example, regional trade agreements, such as the North American Free Trade Agreement (NAFTA), which tend to have clauses, or chapters, on labour rights (Compa, 2006). The most powerful regional organisation, in terms of its impact on individual states' labour laws, is the European Union (EU). EU law (set out in the EU Treaties or in secondary legislation, such as EU Regulations and Directives) is binding in its entirety in all the Member States of the Union, and decisions of the EU Court of Justice (CJEU) similarly must be applied in all of the Member States' courts.

However, nation states still retain significant control over the legal regulation of ER within their borders.[3] National constitutions will generally sit at the apex of the domestic legal hierarchy, and set out basic principles applicable to the employment relationship, such as rights of equality, rights to property (including the right to own and operate a business) and rights to freedom of association and expression. Some constitutions will also include explicit provisions, for example, on the right to work and earn a livelihood, or the right to strike (Collins et al.,

2012, p. 658). However, below the level of constitutional principles, national legal systems vary significantly in how they regulate labour rights. Botero et al. (2004) point to the legal origins (common or civil law) of a given country's legal system as being a major factor in its approach to regulating the economy: "countries in different legal traditions utilise different institutional technologies for social control of business ... common law countries tend to rely more on markets and contracts, and civil law (and socialist) countries on regulation (and state ownership)" (2004, p. 1345).[4]

In the 'Anglo-Saxon' systems (e.g. the UK, USA, Australia), labour legislation generally provides a minimum 'floor of rights'; the adversarial common law system places a significant emphasis on judicial decision-making, and collective agreements tend not to be legally binding (but, rather, morally binding only on the parties to such agreements). By contrast, in the relatively highly regulated civil law systems of continental Europe (e.g. France, Germany) and some parts of Latin America (e.g. Argentina), and in 'mixed systems' such as the Chinese or Japanese legal systems, there tend to be more all-encompassing labour codes and statutory texts; comparatively less weight, in civil law systems, is accorded to court decisions as a source of law, and extensive mechanisms exist for the *erga omnes* extension of sectoral collective agreements to cover all employers and workers in that sector (including those not directly party to the agreements). The 'Nordic' civil law model of Sweden and Denmark tends to fall somewhere in-between; there is comprehensive regulation of the labour market, but much of this is based on voluntary co-operation and the conclusion of collective agreements between strong associations of employers and trade unions (Teague, 2001). Lastly, in mixed systems where religious law is prominent, labour rights will be heavily influenced by the tenets of the faith in question (e.g. Muslim law in countries like Pakistan and Sudan, or Jewish and Muslim Law in Israel).

Outside of the common/civil/mixed legal system classification, judicial decision-making is often analysed with a view to describing whether a given court can be described as 'activist'. There is no universally accepted definition of 'judicial activism' (Sherry, 2014), but aspects generally involve the extent to which courts are prepared to strike down laws passed by elected representatives, and/or the extent to which they are willing to develop, or expand, the bare text of legal instruments. The CJEU, for example, is often described as 'activist' for the expansive manner in which it has interpreted some key employment rights, such as the right to equal pay between men and women (Case 149/77 *Defrenne* [1978] ECR 136) and paid annual leave (Case C-350/06 *Schultz-Hoff* ECLI:EU:C:2009:18; for a contrary view, however, see Grimmel, 2014).

This account is necessarily somewhat stylised, and legal systems are constantly evolving (for a criticism of the 'legal origins' approach, see Deakin et al., 2007). Nonetheless, we can still conclude that significant national variations in the legal regulation of ER persist, and manifest most significantly in terms of the scope and nature of labour rights legislation, the role of the judiciary and the legal effects of collective agreements. However, it remains the case that in virtually all jurisdictions states regulate individual ER on the basis of an obligatory contract, the employment contract. We will return to this issue below.

'Soft law' and employment relations

It is important to restate that the regulation of employment relations does not only occur by means of 'hard' legal measures, such as legislation. We have already seen in previous sections that labour rights and obligations can flow from (legally non-binding) collective agreements and from international law. Similarly, rights and obligations can be derived from corporate codes of conduct, corporate social responsibility measures (see Chapter 27) or other forms of 'private law-making' (Snyder, 2003). In many jurisdictions, codes of practice or advisory codes issued by statutory bodies (for example, in the UK, the Advisory Conciliation and Advisory Service, ACAS) or by tax or social security authorities, which are not legally binding in themselves, can become quasi-legal sources if they are utilised in aiding courts and tribunals to come to decisions in cases before them.

Some labour scholars have focused in relatively recent times on the idea of 'reflexive' labour law (Rogowski, 2013; Rogowski and Wilthagen, 1994). Ashiogbor (2015, p. 125) refers to the 'reflexive turn' in labour law as the move from formal law (the exclusion of non-legal considerations from law-making and adjudication), to substantive law (the use of law as an instrument for purposive, goal-oriented intervention), to procedural law (where the focus is not on specifying concrete outcomes to be realised, but on laying down a procedural framework within which substantive outcomes can be determined, autonomously, via deliberative processes).

Reflexive labour law, therefore, marks a shift away from state-centred, top-down, rule-based, 'command and control' regulation of the workplace. Instead, national or international standard-setters (these could be national governments or organisations such as the ILO or EU) focus on the provision of expertise, incentives, bench-marking and learning and the co-ordination of best practices (ibid, pp. 125–126). It is for 'decentred' actors (the social partners, corporations, regional and local authorities, civil society actors, etc.) to negotiate the optimal substantive outcomes.

The advantages of reflexive law are said to be that it sidesteps the failings of traditional 'hard' regulation by focusing on self-regulation, participatory decision-making and local problem-solving, leading to regulatory solutions that are more likely to be internalised and observed by the subjects of the regulation (Rogowski, 2013). Furthermore, reflexive law is sometimes seen as a more viable solution to the problem of regulation in the context of the variety of legal systems outlined above. This can be easily illustrated by reference to the EU, where laws must bind 28 (at the time of writing) Member States, with their varying legal and ER traditions. However, equally, even *within* states with federal political structures (e.g. the US, Canada and India), a 'one size fits all' legal approach can be difficult to maintain.

Critics of the 'reflexive turn' in labour law have questioned whether reflexive regulation can readily be distinguished from non-regulation or deregulation (see McCrudden, 2007, writing in the context of the employment discrimination regime in the UK). Similarly, Streeck, commenting on the use of reflexive regulation in EU law, notes the danger that the outcomes of self-regulation could equate simply to market outcomes, or "results of a contingent distribution of power" (1994, p. 171). Arthurs (2012) raises the question as to whether reflexive theorists may unwittingly be furthering the interests of capital and the corporation, rather than those of the worker. Davidov notes that "even the strongest supporters of reflexive law approaches would not argue that 'soft' regulations should replace labour legislation setting *basic* standards" (2016, p. 2; emphasis in the original); he contends that the contexts in which self-regulation can be relied upon are bound to be relatively limited. Lastly, Ashiogbor (2015), in a sceptical account of the 'reflexive turn' she outlines, reminds us that collective bargaining, hardly a product of 'new governance' theories of reflexive law, itself can be understood as a form of reflexive regulation – albeit one with long-established rules of the game and clearly delineated actors.

The scope of the law in employment relations

The individual employment relationship

Although, as we have seen above, different legal systems (common law, civil law or, indeed, 'mixed' systems, such as China, South Africa, Japan or Israel) regulate employment relations in different ways, it can be broadly stated that the "starting point for the analysis of legal obligations arising in the context of working relations must always be the terms of any contractual arrangement" (Collins et al., 2005, p. 70). Kahn-Freund (1977) described the contract of employment as the cornerstone of the modern labour law system. Crucial are the questions, in law, of 'who is an employee?' and 'who is an employer?' This is because, as Davidov et al. (2015) point out, the approach to determining the coverage of labour law tends to be the same throughout the world, in being defined by reference to 'employee' and 'employer' (or similar terms); being categorised in these groups, therefore, carries important implications in terms of labour rights and obligations. Access to a range of statutory protections (e.g. minimum wage laws, unjust dismissal laws, working time laws) will generally depend on an individual's classification.

Moreover, 'employee' status has a range of other implications. In many legal systems, it will set the boundaries to an individual's access to social security systems (sick pay, unemployment insurance, etc.) and determine their taxation status. In the common law, particular terms, not set out explicitly in the contract, may be 'implied' by the courts into contracts of employment; for example, obligations of mutual trust and confidence (Brodie, 2008). In the law of tort, the contract of employment has been used to fix the scope of the vicarious liability of employers for the negligent acts of employees done in the course of employment. In terms of commercial/corporate law, employees are often granted particular rights (e.g. as 'preferential creditors') in the event that their employer becomes insolvent. Finally, we have already seen possible difficulties in the interface between collective bargaining and competition/antitrust laws. This is exacerbated in the case of non-employees, who, as independent undertakings, will generally be forbidden from coming to mutual arrangements over basic terms such as minimum payments as these will likely contravene competition/antitrust laws (Daly and Doherty, 2010, p. 41–42).

Given these factors, courts and tribunals must always be alive to the possibility that it may be in the interest of one, other or all of the parties to an employment relationship to seek to classify it as *not* involving a contract of employment. For example, the employer may try to evade taking on legislative responsibilities in relation to notice or redundancy requirements, while the worker might seek to maximise his/her tax or social security benefits. Employers may also seek to reduce their exposure to business risks by shifting these onto the worker through, for example, using a piece-work or performance-related remuneration system, or offering work on a casual basis. The more risks the worker agrees to bear the less likely it will be that he/she will be classed as an employee at all (Collins et al., 2005, p. 160).

The situation is complicated by the fact that labour legislation rarely includes guidance as to the precise meaning of the terms 'employee' or 'employer', leaving it to courts to interpret them and, thus, the scope of labour law. Courts around the world have essentially constructed a standard model of rules based on a 'binary divide' (Deakin and Morris, 2012, chapter 3) between employment and self-employment, between 'subordinated labour' (often to referred to as 'servants' in the older case law) and 'independent' or 'autonomous' work relations (which would include work done by what we might refer to nowadays as 'independent contractors' or 'service providers'; Deakin, 2007). Those who fall within the former category can claim to work under a *contract of employment*, while others, who work under a *contract for services*, fall outside of the 'employee' categorisation. The historical basis for such a distinction (reflecting the protective function of labour law) was that those in self-employment, those in business on their own, needed less protection against unemployment, sickness and old age than those in a 'master-servant' relationship.

It is important to note that this 'binary divide' has come in for criticism in recent years, given the increasingly differentiated organisation of contemporary working life (Deakin and Wilkinson, 2005; Davidov, 2005; Doherty, 2009). Freedland, for example, has heavily criticised the 'strict legal dichotomy' between the employed and self-employed (Freedland, 2003, p. 22). He has powerfully advocated a conceptual shift away from the contract of employment model to a model based on what he refers to as a "personal work nexus". This refers to the

> connection or connections, link or links, between a person providing a service personally and the persons, organisations or enterprises who or which are involved in the arrangements for, or incidental to, the personal work in question.
>
> *(Freedland, 2006, p. 16)*

Essentially, Freedland argues that the employment relationship should be re-conceptualised so that labour law recognises (and offers protection to) a wider set of relationships, categorised by *personal service* and *economic dependence* on the part of those working (even where these do not conform to the traditional model of contractual arrangement). This would necessitate the expansion of the idea of the traditional 'employer' to include trilateral or multilateral arrangements, whereby different 'employing entities' may have different and overlapping obligations to the same worker (as is the case in relation to agency work, for example; see Chapter 18). In some jurisdictions, tentative moves towards this model can be identified; in the US, the concept of the 'joint employer' (Carvell and Sherwyn, 2015), for example, and in German law the category of 'quasi-salaried workers', self-employed persons who are economically dependent on a single entity (Waas, 2010).

Prassl (2015) has built on Freedland's work by focusing on a reconceptualisation of 'the employer'. His 'functional concept of the employer' is one where the employing entity or entities are defined not via the absence or presence of a particular *factor* (such as 'control' over the employee), but via the exercise of specific *functions*. He identifies the key employer functions as the inception and termination of the employment relationship; receiving labour and its fruits (the duties owed by the employee to the employer, specifically to provide his or her labour and the results thereof, as well as rights incidental to it); providing work and pay; managing the internal market of the enterprise (that is the coordination, through control over all factors of production, up to and including the power to require both how and what is to be done); and managing the external market of the enterprise (that is undertaking economic activity in return for potential profit, whilst also being exposed to any losses that may result from the enterprise). Who owes the employer 'obligations', therefore, depends on who exercised the particular 'employer function', and, moreover, what is crucial is who actually had a *decisive* role in exercising that function.

As we will see in the concluding section, this debate has acquired new urgency in the context of the emergence of 'platform' work.

The growth of 'non-standard' or 'atypical' work (e.g. part-time, fixed-term, temporary and agency work) and precarious work (see Chapter 18) has been noted throughout this volume. In terms of legal regulation, it suffices to say here that in most countries the 'standard' employment relationship, based on an employment contract of an indefinite duration, is legally considered to be the norm. Under EU law, for example, Directive 1999/70 (on fixed-term work) states that "employment contracts of an indefinite duration are the general form of employment relationships and contribute to the quality of life of the workers concerned and improve performance". As Verhulp (2017) points out, this demonstrates that the status accorded standard ER is about more than just the protection of the employee: "[t]here is also a collective interest: the quality of life and the improvement of performance. The legal presumption is that an employment contract contributes to a healthy and happy workforce, resulting in high levels of productivity" (2017, p. 1).

Thus, in relation to atypical work, laws will usually try and strike a balance between protecting vulnerable atypical workers, and allowing – and, if necessary, promoting – flexible work relations where this is to the benefit of the parties; we see again the interaction between the 'protective' and 'labour market' functions of labour law. The approach the law takes, however, generally focuses on 'equal treatment': that those in atypical working relationships should not suffer less favourable terms and conditions of employment than comparable 'standard' workers. Two difficulties with this approach present. First, it hinges on finding a suitable 'comparator', and thus cannot address issues stemming from occupational segregation. If the entire workforce is part-time, and has poor terms and conditions of employment, against whom can an individual compare himself/herself? Secondly, of course, all that is required of the employer is equal treatment; the employer is free (subject to minimum legal standards, such as minimum wage laws, etc.) to treat all workers equally poorly, and the law will not intervene.

The collective employment relationship

Legal regulation of collective employment relations has traditionally focused on the law relating to trade unions, and, in particular, collective bargaining and collective action. Ewing (2005) has drawn the distinction between the 'representational' and 'regulatory' models of collective bargaining. In the representational model, typical of the Anglo-Saxon countries, collective bargaining is conceived of as a *private* market activity, conducted by unions at the level of the enterprise (or parts thereof) as agents of a tightly circumscribed bargaining unit. This requires the consent of workers to choose to be represented by a trade union (membership alone is not sufficient to raise such a presumption) and this consent is revocable (an individual worker can choose to deal directly with the employer, notwithstanding that the majority of his/her colleagues choose to be represented by a union).

By contrast, a regulatory model of collective bargaining is premised on the idea, prevalent, for example, in the 'Nordic' civil law countries, that trade unions are involved in a process of rule-making that has an impact beyond their members (or members' immediate colleagues). Here, collective bargaining takes on an explicit *public* role, as employment standards are set, and applied, not only for employers that recognise trade unions and union members, but for enterprises that do not engage in collective bargaining. This can happen through multi-employer collective bargaining, such as where joint industrial councils set standards for an industry or sector, or where legal mechanisms permit the extension of collective agreements to all employers in a sector; such standards may be mandatory even for employers not affiliated to sectoral or industry-level employer associations (Doherty, 2013).

Advocates for the representational model argue that it provides rights for workers to access union representation should they desire this. The declining membership of trade unions in most countries (see Chapter 11) can be pointed to as evidence that, in fact, union representation is not desired by most workers. As Brodtkorb (2012) argues, the law can impose a process or procedure for the establishment of collective bargaining arrangements, but for the law to seek to impose an outcome (mandated collective bargaining) would amount to undesirably excessive state intervention.

Critics, however, would point to the fact that the seeking of union representation is an extremely costly endeavour for workers in an organisation where the employer is hostile to trade unions. At one end of the scale this can manifest itself in unfair labour practices (ranging, for example, from the engagement of 'union busting' consultants, to the intimidation – or worse, actual or threatened violence – or impeding of union activists). Moreover, the employer's financial, communicative and organisational strength can be employed in more subtle ways to leave workers in little doubt as to potential adverse consequences of seeking representation. Again, this can take different forms, from actively seeking to shape (or re-shape) worker preferences through information (or mis-information!) campaigns to intimations of possible relocation, downsizing or even closure. For workers conscious of employer hostility, the seeming unlikelihood of successfully achieving collective representation rights, which is amplified where any campaign to do so is likely to take a not inconsiderable period of time, will also be a powerful deterrent (Doherty, 2013).

Bogg (2012, drawing on the work of Thaler and Sunstein, 2008) considers the issue in terms of 'choice architectures': the idea that regulatory structures can both frame the available options for choice and shape those preferences and choices. As a result, where the regulatory structures in place seem to indicate that a certain 'default' position (non-unionisation) will be unduly arduous to move from (due to the factors outlined in the preceding paragraph), workers are more likely to adapt their preferences to fit with the default position (the 'status quo bias'). The non-union default position then becomes 'sticky' and difficult to dislodge in the absence of 'asymmetry-correcting' regulatory intervention (Sachs, 2010, p. 662). In other words, where the existing position is that workers are well-disposed to union representation (or even neutral on the issue) but feel that the law (or state labour market policy) makes this difficult to achieve, their disposition is likely to change to accommodate the perceived 'reality' or 'practicality' of their situation.

In terms of collective action (which can take many forms, including strikes, work to rule, overtime bans, etc.; see Chapter 17), Kahn-Freund and Hepple (1972, p. 12) have noted that a strike (or a potential strike) is "an event which of necessity entails a waste of resources and damage to the economy" yet remains by general consent an indispensable element of a democratic society. This latter statement is confirmed by the recognition of a right to strike in many national constitutions and in international human rights treaties (Novitz, 2003), although, note Collins et al., "its recognition is matched only by the failure of many countries to meet the full extent of their obligations" (2012, p. 658).[5] Justifications for the legal protection of the right to strike include its character as a fundamental human right, linked with civil and political rights, such as the right not to be subjected to forced labour (Davies, 2009). Another conception of the right to strike is its status as an 'industrial relations right'. In this conception, legal protection for the right to strike is an integral aspect of the operation of an autonomous collective bargaining system; workers must have some 'muscle' to back up their bargaining positions (Ewing, 2004). Legal provisions regulating the right to strike, however, are almost universal; these generally focus on the need for trade unions to conduct ballots of members in advance of strike action, restrictions on the right to picket employers, and, in some jurisdictions, restrictions on the right to strike in 'essential services', like health, transport or security and policing (Adell et al., 2001).

Autonomy, enforcement and compliance

The 'autonomous' nature of labour law is often referred to in the literature, and indeed in pronouncements of the labour market actors. The concept (or, more accurately, concepts, as discussions on this topic often range widely) is somewhat ambiguous, and much contested (see Bogg et al., 2015). In this section, we will consider two key ways in which labour law might be said to be autonomous: the role of the key labour market actors (the social partners) and the nature of dispute resolution in labour law.

The social partners

We have already seen that the process of collective bargaining can create labour rights and obligations. Kahn-Freund described the UK system of labour law as "collective laissez-faire".

This description (which was broadly applicable to all Anglo-Saxon models) referred to a system of employment relations essentially regulated by free collective bargaining between worker and employer representative groups, with the role of the state confined primarily to providing a supportive framework for collective bargaining, and where the "principal purpose of labour law is to regulate, support and restrain the power of management and organised labour" (Kahn-Freund, 1977, p. 4). The implications of this were that employers and unions traditionally viewed with disfavour labour legislation, so that collective bargaining was the key element in the functioning of the ER system. The decline in both union density and collective bargaining coverage in the Anglo-Saxon world, and legislative intervention, have undermined the idea of 'collective laissez-faire', but collective bargaining continues (albeit generally at enterprise level), and unions and employer groups remain relatively 'privileged' actors, in the sense that they are generally consulted on the implementation, at least, of legislation affecting ER. For example, in the UK, the domestic legislation implementing the EU Temporary Agency Workers Directive (Directive 2008/104) came into force following a social partner agreement between the Confederation of British Industry (CBI) and the Trades Union Congress (TUC).

In other, civil law systems (see Section 3, above), of course, the social partners retain a strongly institutionalised role in terms of collective bargaining and/or socio-economic governance at a sectoral and/or national level, whilst in 'mixed' systems the role of the social partners tends to be heavily determined by the extent of state intervention in the labour market (extensive in countries like China and Japan, comparatively less so in countries like South Africa, and limited in countries like Malta or Cyprus).

At the level of the EU, the privileged status of the social partners is written into the EU treaties. Under Article 153 of the Treaty on the Functioning of the European Union (TFEU), Member States may entrust 'management and labour' at national level, with implementing EU directives. Furthermore, before submitting proposals in the social policy field, the European Commission (EC) must consult management and labour on the possible direction of EU action. Under Article 155 TFEU, management and labour (at EU level) may inform the EC of their wish to enter into dialogue, with a view to making agreements, on social policy issues. Such agreements may then be passed into law by the EU institutions. Successfully concluded agreements under this process, later translated into legally binding directives, have included important measures on fixed-term work, part-time work and parental leave.

The privileged role accorded to the social partners in many legal systems is not uncontroversial. In some systems, where the state is the central labour market actor, social partner organisations may be little more than extensions of the state itself (e.g. China). However, even wholly independent social partner organisations at national, or especially regional (e.g. EU), levels may be said to be too remote from their affiliates 'on the ground', and may be seen as unable to adequately represent the inevitable diversity of interests that exist within national, or even sectoral, organisations. Important questions of democratic legitimacy also arise when social partners are given law-making responsibilities that are normally the preserve of elected representatives. Key questions of *which* organisations and interests are to be deemed 'representative' (and by *whom*) arise; there is a danger of creating 'insiders' and 'outsiders', with only the former having input into labour law regulation (see Welz, 2008, chapter 2).

Dispute resolution and the law

Employment relations disputes differ from many other legal conflicts (and, in particular, from commercial actions, where the parties are generally dealing 'at arm's length'). The nature of the employment relationship means that disputes present complex and sensitive problems. While some issues (e.g. contractual interpretation, or the award of compensation for personal injury) can be approached according to general legal principles, other disputes will be more multifaceted. As Collins et al. put it:

> if the issue comes before a court for a legal determination of the rights and obligations of the parties, the court is likely to become involved in complex issues of fairness and the breakdown of informal and implicit understandings in working relations. Its intervention in the dispute can easily become portrayed as a political issue, where the court has the unappealing role of siding with either 'the bosses' or 'the workers'.
>
> *2012, p. 25*

The aim of dispute resolution systems in the employment sphere, therefore, is to solve disputes as close to the workplace, and as quickly, informally and cheaply, as possible (Doherty, 2009a). To achieve this, most legal systems tend to channel employment disputes away from the 'regular' courts, for example towards specialist tribunals, or tend to emphasise alternative dispute resolution (ADR) methods (such as mediation, conciliation and arbitration; see Chapter 16).

The focus on ADR, in the context of individual labour disputes, is controversial. Whilst one objective is to steer disputes away from the costs, delay and adversarial nature of a judicial, or quasi-judicial, hearing (ibid.), concerns may arise around access to justice and power imbalances. For example, in the USA, the Supreme Court has made clear that under the Federal Arbitration Act an employee can be required, *as a condition of employment*, "to submit virtually all federal and state statutory and common law claims to an arbitration system promulgated *unilaterally* by the employer" (Finkin, 2002, p. 76; my emphasis). Furthermore, ADR systems at the workplace may operate (or be designed) to exclude the actual, or potential, role of trade unions or other forms of collective representation of worker interests (Dau-Schmidt, 2011).

In terms of specialist labour dispute resolution fora, Corby and Burgess (2014) undertook a large-scale comparative study to look at how employment disputes are adjudicated across ten countries (France, Germany, Great Britain, Ireland, Italy, The Netherlands, New Zealand, South Africa, Sweden and the USA). The study considers the interaction between the 'regular' courts, specialised employment courts and tribunals and ADR practices, and touches on many of the controversies that surround this area.

First, there is the issue of the extent to which non-professional judges (typically employer and trade union nominees), which hear employment disputes in a number of jurisdictions, can adequately grapple with complex legal concepts. A counterpoint, of course, is that such judges can provide legitimacy ('knowledge of the shop floor') to employment dispute resolution processes. The related issue of the role of the social partners (see above) arises here; to what extent should employer groups and trade unions have a role in the formal adjudication of labour law disputes?

A second issue relates to access to justice; should, for example, access to employment tribunals be free (as in South Africa) or should a fee be imposed? Tribunal fees were introduced by the UK Government in 2013. There followed a dramatic decline in the number of claims taken, but whether this was due to the discouraging of 'unmeritorious actions' (the Government's claim), or simply to the fact that the cost to applicants was prohibitive, was a contested issue (Adams and Prassl, 2017). In any case, in 2017, the UK Supreme Court ruled (in *R (on the application of UNISON) v Lord Chancellor* [2017] UKSC 51) that the tribunal fees imposed were unlawful, as they obstructed the right of access to justice in the employment sphere. Thus, again, we see the interaction between various actors in the employment arena; the trade unions (who pursued the court action), the state (whose policy decision to impose fees was overturned), other 'third-party' actors (in this case, the UK Equality and Human Rights Commission made submissions to the Court) and the law courts (engaged here to protect fundamental rights of workers to access dispute resolution mechanisms).

Another key issue is the debate on to what extent procedures in labour courts or tribunals should reflect those of the 'regular' courts, or to what extent should employment dispute resolution fora be 'informal'? Here, the rights of the employer to natural justice/fair procedures (which might include taking evidence on oath, or cross-examination of witnesses) must be balanced against the need to encourage speedy and inexpensive resolution of disputes (Doherty, 2009a). This question is intimately bound up with the issue of access to legal representation, and whether this might be funded by the state, and the closely related issue of whether costs are awarded to litigants (as in Germany's appellate Labour Court) or not (as in Ireland).

In both areas, the role of the social partners and employment dispute resolution, the 'autonomous' nature of labour law is intimately bound up with the relative strength of labour and capital. Again, the decline in trade union density in most countries means a corresponding decline in the ability of trade unions to 'police' labour rights. Where trade union density has deteriorated most significantly, a decline in collective disputes (for example, in days lost to strike action) has been accompanied by a corresponding increase in the number of individual employment claims being taken to labour courts and tribunals (O'Sullivan et al., 2015; Pollert, 2005).

A decline in the social partner 'policing' role inevitably means more of a role for state enforcement of labour rights, usually by labour inspectorates. Public funding for such enforcement is heavily influenced by political and, especially, economic trends (Doherty, 2013, p. 381). A key concern, also, lies in the possibility of what Ford (2016) refers to as increasing 'collateral attacks' on workers' rights. By this, Ford refers to a practice of granting workers entitlements in law, but allowing "regulatory liberalism to triumph in fact" by placing so many financial and procedural burdens in front of individuals seeking redress as to render the possibility of obtaining a remedy in practice extremely unlikely (2016, p. 414).

Conclusions and future agendas

This chapter has given an overview of some of the key issues and challenges involved in the legal regulation of employment relations. Although legal systems across the world differ greatly, all of them need to confront these challenges to a greater or lesser extent. The nature of ER is dynamic and constantly evolving; the law must equally move and evolve in parallel. We will end with some very brief thoughts on some of the challenges that will present in the years ahead.

First, the transnational aspect of labour law will only gain in prominence in an increasingly interconnected, and globalised, world of work, in which capital, services and people can move more easily across national borders. This will create more complexity in terms of conflict of laws disputes, but also more opportunities, or at least demands, for greater cross-border co-operation between regulatory authorities and labour market actors (Erne, 2008). However, it will also raise concerns about 'social dumping' and the danger that the existence of high labour standards in some countries and their absence in others may give rise to unfair practices, whereby the latter base a comparative advantage on undercutting the former. This may give rise to a greater focus on 'universal' labour standards, and universal coverage of labour law. This may be welcomed as promoting global solidarity and reaching a larger segment of the global population in need of protection; however, there is a danger that such standards would promote a 'lowest common denominator' effect, and would be less efficient and effective than labour laws that selectively target groups in need (see Fudge et al., 2012).

Relatedly, we may well see an increasing appeal to fundamental human rights arguments in the context of labour law. This would move conceptions of labour law further away from their 'autonomous' roots (Bogg et al., 2015), and might involve Langille's (2011) formulation envisaging labour law as a tool to be used to help achieve, ultimately, the "maximising of human freedom" (2011, p. 114). At a very practical and local level, this might mean greater invocation in labour disputes of human rights law concepts, such as the right to a fair trial in the context of workplace disciplinary proceedings. This appeal to human rights has been questioned as, first, being framed too abstractly ('maximisation of human freedom') to be of practical significance to workers, and, secondly, as being a symptom of the labour movement's weakness, rather than a positive programme for the future (Doherty, 2013).

Finally, technological advances will continue to impact on the future of labour law. At least two dimensions can be mentioned. First, the so-called gig or platform economy, whereby service providers and end users are connected not by traditional 'employers' but app-based 'platforms', throw up significant challenges in terms of labour rights and obligations, particularly where services are performed remotely. Who is the employer? Are the service providers 'employees'? Does this model displace employment in the 'real' economy? Many of these issues are not wholly novel (see debate above on the scope of the employment relationship), but may require reconceptualising the employment relationship to ensure the protective and/or labour market functions of labour law can be maintained (Prassl, 2017).

Secondly, the 'digitalisation' of the workplace creates more challenges in the management of workers (Degryse, 2016). With the advent of smartphones, it is increasingly easy for employers to maintain surveillance of workers, with possible implications for the latter's private and family life, and, indeed, for the employer's potential vicarious liability. Equally, how valid is the regulation of working hours, when workers can be 'always on'? Again, the principles of regulation involved here may not be new, but the approaches to dealing with technological change will need to be carefully considered.

It is not time yet, to misquote Shakespeare, to kill all the (labour) lawyers.

Notes

1 I am very grateful to Sidar Yaylagül, University of Vienna, for her invaluable help in compiling this chapter.
2 Davidov is equally clear that the goals he identifies, and the proposals to achieve them he outlines, cannot be equally relevant to every legal jurisdiction. He gives examples from civil law, common law and mixed law jurisdictions, but devotes his attention to "relatively general questions – a level of generalisation at which the similarities between legal systems are great, and the differences small" (2016, p. 5). This is the approach also adopted in this chapter.
3 In an increasingly globalised world of work, transnational disputes arise more frequently, and are generally resolved by 'conflicts of law' rules, which establish which jurisdiction's laws should apply to the dispute.
4 For an excellent overview of the different legal systems in the world, see the work of the JuriGlobe research group, formed by professors from the Faculty of Law of the University of Ottawa: www.juriglobe.ca/eng/apropos/index.php.
5 Note, too, that in countries such as Ireland and the UK, there is no 'right' to strike. Rather, the law grants 'immunities' to those engaging in such action from being sued, or prosecuted, for the legal wrongs that will inevitably accompany strikes (e.g. conspiracy, interference with contractual relations, etc.). The granting of immunities is dependent upon compliance with legal formalities relating to the registration of worker organisations, the conduct of ballots, and so on.

References

Adams, A. and Prassl, J. (2017). 'Vexatious Claims: Challenging the Case for Employment Tribunal Fees', *The Modern Law Review*, 80(3), pp. 412–442.

Adell, B., Grant, M. and Ponak, A. (2001). *Strikes in Essential Services*. Kingston, Ont: IRC Press.

Arthurs, H.W. (2012). *Making Bricks Without Straw: The Creation of a Transnational Labour Regime*. Osgoode Hall Law School Research Paper Series 28/2012. [Online]. Available at: http://digitalcommons.osgoode.yorku.ca/cgi/viewcontent.cgi?article=1023&context=clpe.

Ashiogbor, D. (2015). Evaluating the Reflexive Turn in Labour Law, in Bogg, A., Costello, C., Davies, A.C.L. and Prassl, J. (eds.) *The Autonomy of Labour Law*. Oxford: Hart.

Bauman, Z. (1998). *Work, Consumerism and the New Poor*. Buckingham: Open University Press.

Beck, U. (2000). *The Brave New World of Work*. Cambridge (UK): Polity.

Beck, U. (1992). *Risk Society: Towards a New Modernity*. Cambridge (UK): Polity.

Bogg, A. (2012). 'The Death of Statutory Recognition in the United Kingdom', *Industrial Relations Journal*, 54(3), p. 409.

Bogg, A., Costello, C., Davies, A.C.L and Prassl, J. (eds.) (2015). *The Autonomy of Labour Law*. Oxford: Hart.

Botero, J.C., Djankov, S., La Porta, R., Lopez-de-Silanes, F. and Shleifer, A. (2004). 'The Regulation of Labour', *Quarterly Journal of Economics*, 119(4), pp. 1339–1382.

Brodie, D. (2008). 'Mutual Trust and Confidence: Catalysts, Constraints and Commonality', *Industrial Law Journal*, 37(3), pp. 329–346.

Brodtkorb, T. (2012). 'Statutory Union Recognition in the UK: A Work in Progress', *Industrial Law Journal*, 40(70).

Carvell, S.A. and Sherwyn, D. (2015). 'It is time for something new: a 21st century joint-employer doctrine for 21st century franchising', *American University Business Law Review*, 5(1), pp. 5–36.

Castells, M. (2004). Informationalism, Networks, and the Network Society: A Theoretical Blueprint, in Castells, M. (ed.) *The Network Society: A Cross-Cultural Perspective*. Cheltenham: Edward Elgar.

Collins, H. (2001). 'Regulating the Employment Relation for Competitiveness', *Industrial Law Journal*, 30(1), pp. 17–47.

Collins, H., Ewing, K.D. and McColgan, A. (2012). *Labour Law*. Cambridge (UK): Cambridge University Press.

Collins, H., Ewing, K.D. and McColgan, A. (2005). *Labour Law: Text and Materials*. 2nd edn. Oxford: Hart.

Compa, L. (2006). Labour Rights in the FTAA, in Craig, J. and Lynk, S. (eds.) *Globalisation and the Future of Labour Law*. Cambridge (UK): Cambridge University Press.

Corby, S. and Burgess, P. (2014). *Adjudicating Employment Rights: A Cross National Approach*. Basingstoke: Palgrave Macmillan.

Creighton, B. and Stewart, A. (2016). *Labour Law*. 6th edn. Sydney: Federation Books.

Daly, B. and Doherty, M. (2010). *Principles of Irish Employment Law*. Dublin: Clarus.

Dau-Schmidt, K.G. (2011). 'Promoting Employee Voice in the American Economy: A Call for Comprehensive Reform', *Marquette Law Review*, 94(3), pp. 766–836.

Davidov, G. (2016). *A Purposive Approach to Labour Law*. Oxford: Oxford University Press.

Davidov, G. (2005). 'Who is a Worker?', *Industrial Law Journal*, 34(1), p. 57.

Davidov, G., Freedland, M. and Kountouris, N. (2015). The Subjects of Labour Law: "Employees" and Other Workers, in Finkin, M. and Mundlak, G. (eds.) *Research Handbook in Comparative Labour Law*. Cheltenham: Edward Elgar.

Davies, A.C.L. (2009). *Perspectives on Labour Law*. 2nd edn. Cambridge (UK): Cambridge University Press.

Davies, P. and Freedland, M. (2007). *Towards a Flexible Labour Market*. Oxford: Oxford University Press.

Davis, D.D.M. (2002). Death of a Labour Lawyer, in Connaghan, J., Fischl, R.M. and Klare, K. (eds.) *Labour Law in an Era of Globalisation*. Oxford: Oxford University Press.

De Stefano, V. (2016). 'Non-Standard Work and Limits on Freedom of Association: A Human Rights-Based Approach', *Industrial Law Journal*, 44(2), pp. 1–23.

Deakin, S. (2007). 'Does the "Personal Employment Contract" Provide a Basis for the Reunification of Employment Law?', *Industrial Law Journal*, 36(1), p. 68.

Deakin, S. (2001). 'The Changing Concept of the "Employer" in Labour Law', *Industrial Law Journal*, 30(1), pp. 72–84.

Deakin, S. and Morris, G. (2012). *Labour Law*. 6th edn. Oxford: Hart.

Deakin, S., Pele, L. and Siems, M. (2007). 'The Evolution of Labour Law: Calibrating and Comparing Regulatory Regimes', *International Labour Review*, 146(3–4), pp. 133–162.

Deakin, S. and Wilkinson, F. (2005). *The Law of the Labour Market*. Oxford: Oxford University Press.

Degryse, C. (2016). *Digitalisation of the Economy and its Impact on Labour Markets*. ETUI Research Paper – Working Paper 2016.02. Available at: https://ssrn.com/abstract=2730550 (Accessed: 10 December 2017).

Dickens, L. (2004). 'Problems of Fit: Changing Employment and Labour Regulation', *British Journal of Industrial Relations*, 42(4), pp. 595–616.

Doherty, M. (2013). 'When You Ain't Got Nothin', You Got Nothin' to Lose… Union Recognition Laws, Voluntarism and the Anglo Model', *Industrial Law Journal*, 42(4), p. 369.

Doherty, M. (2009). 'When the Working Day is Through: the End of Work as Identity?', *Work, Employment & Society*, 23(1), p. 84.

Doherty, M. (2009a). 'Institutional Challenge: Tribunals, Industrial Relations and the Law', *Employment Law Review Ireland*, 2, p. 70.

Dukes, R. (2014). The Labour Constitution. Oxford: Oxford University Press.

Erne, R. (2008). *European Unions: Labour's Quest for a Transnational Democracy*. Ithaca: Cornell University Press.

Ewing, K.D. (2005). 'The Function of Trade Unions', *Industrial Law Journal*, 34(1), pp. 1–20.

Ewing, K.D. (2004). 'Laws Against Strikes Revisited' in Barnard, C., Deakin, S. and Morris, G. (eds.) *The Future of Labour Law*. Oxford: Hart.

Finkin, M. (2002). 'Employee Representation Outside the Labor Act: Thoughts on Arbitral Representation, Group Arbitration, and Workplace Committees', *University of Pennsylvania Journal of Labor & Employment Law*, 5(1), pp. 75–100.

Ford, M. (2016). 'The Effect of Brexit on Workers' Rights', *King's Law Journal*, 27(3), p. 404.

Frazer, A.D. (2008). 'Reconceiving Labour Law: The Labour Market Regulation Project', *Macquarie Law Journal*, 8(1), pp. 21–44.

Freedland, M. (2006). 'From the Contract of Employment to the Personal Work Nexus', *Industrial Law Journal*, 35(1), pp. 1–29.

Freedland, M. (2003). *The Personal Employment Contract*. Oxford: Oxford University Press.

Fudge, J., McCrystal, S. and Sankaran, K. (eds.) (2012). *Challenging the Legal Boundaries of Work Regulation*. Oxford: Hart.

Grimmel, A. (2014). 'The European Court of Justice and the Myth of Judicial Activism in the Foundational Period of Integration through Law', *European Journal of Legal Studies*, 7(2), pp. 61–83.

Kahn-Freund, O. and Hepple, B. (1972). *Laws Against Strikes*. London: Fabian Society.

Kahn-Freund, O. (1977). *Labour and the Law*. London: Stevens.

Kelly, J. (1998). *Rethinking Industrial Relations: Mobilisation, Collectivism and Long Waves*. London: Routledge.

Langille, B. (2011). Labour Law's Theory of Justice, in Davidov, G. and Langille, B. (eds.) *The Idea of Labour Law*. Oxford: Oxford University Press.

McCrudden, C. (2007). 'Equality Legislation and Reflexive Regulation: a Response to the Discrimination Law Review's Consultative Paper', *Industrial Law Journal*, 36(3), pp. 255–266.

Novitz, T. (2015). 'The Paradigm of Sustainability in a European Social Context: Collective Participation in Protection of Future Interests?', *International Journal of Comparative Labour Law and Industrial Relations*, 31(3), pp. 243–262.

Novitz, T. (2003). *International and European Protection of the Right to Strike*. Oxford: Oxford University Press.

O'Sullivan, M., Turner, T., Kennedy, M. and Wallace, J. (2015). 'Is Individual Employment Law Displacing the Role of Trade Unions?', *Industrial Law Journal*, 44(2), pp. 222–245.

Pollert, A. (2005). 'The Unorganised Worker: the Decline in Collectivism and New Hurdles to Individual Employment Rights', *Industrial Law Journal*, 34(3), pp. 217–238.

Prassl, J. (2017). *Humans as a Service*. Oxford: Oxford University Press.

Prassl, J. (2015). *The Concept of the Employer*. Oxford: Oxford University Press.

Rogowski, R. (2013). *Reflexive Labour Law in the World Society*. Cheltenham: Edward Elgar.

Rogowski, R. and Wilthagen, T. (eds.) (1994). *Reflexive Labour Law: Studies in Industrial Relations and Employment Regulation*. Deventer: Kluwer.

Sachs, B. (2010). 'Enabling Employee Choice: A Structural Approach to the Rules of Union Organising', *Harvard Law Review*, 123(3), pp. 655.

Sengenberger, W. (2006). International Labour Standards in the Globalised Economy: Obstacles and Opportunities for Achieving Progress, in Craig, J. and Lynk, S. (eds.) *Globalisation and the Future of Labour Law*. Cambridge (UK): Cambridge University Press.

Sennett, R. (1998). *The Corrosion of Character: The Personal Consequences of Work in the New Capitalism*. New York: W.W. Norton & Company Ltd.

Sherry, S. (2014). *Why We Need More Judicial Activism.* Vanderbilt Public Law Research Paper No. 13-3. Available at: https://ssrn.com/abstract=2213372 (Accessed: 10 December 2017)

Snyder, D.V. (2003). 'Private Law-making', *Ohio State Law Journal*, 64(2), pp. 375–450.

Streeck, W. (1994). 'European Social Policy after Maastricht: The Social Dialogue and Subsidiarity', *Economic and Industrial Democracy*, 15(2), pp. 151–177.

Teague, P. (2001). 'Deliberative Governance and EU Social Policy', *European Journal of Industrial Relations*, 7(1), p. 26.

Thaler, S. and Sunstein, C. (2008). *Nudge: Improving Decisions about Health, Wealth and Happiness.* New Haven: Yale University Press.

Verhulp, E. (2017). *The Notion of 'Employee' in EU-Law and National Laws.* Paper delivered at the Annual Conference of the European Centre of Expertise (ECE) in the field of labour law, employment and labour market policies, Frankfurt, April 27–28, 2017. [Online]. Available at: www.my.stibbe.com/mystibbe/attachment_dw.action?attkey=FRbANEucS95NMLRN47z%2BeeOgEFCt8EGQJsWJiCH2WAXlLxld8g770AoTWPQB5Bqg&fromContentView=1&nav=FRbANEucS95NMLRN47z%2BeeOgEFCt8EGQuf6KjHLHOBw%3D&attdocparam=pB7HEsg%2FZ312Bk8OIuOIH1c%2BY4beLEAe4lAh7Yab60s%3D.

Waas, B. (2010). 'The Legal Definition of the Employment Relationship', *European Labour Law Journal*, 1(1), p. 45.

Wedderburn, K.W. (1965). *The Worker and the Law.* London: Penguin.

Welz, C. (2008). *The European Social Dialogue Under Articles 138 and 139 of the EC Treaty.* Amsterdam: Kluwer.

5

EMPLOYMENT RELATIONS AND HISTORY

Greg Patmore

Introduction

There has been a long tradition of interest by industrial relations (IR), and later employment relations (ER), scholars in history. This chapter examines what we mean by 'history' and aims to indicate why historical methods are important for academics researching ER. It looks at the early links between history and ER and concludes with a review of the extent of historical research being undertaken by ER scholars.

What is history?

When dealing with issues in the world of work, we bring together perspectives based on the past, present and future. There are three temporal frames of reference based on the past, present and future: historicism, 'presentism' and futurism. At its worse historicism is antiquarianism, which focuses on history for its own sake and denies any link to the present or future concerns. Historians can also ignore the context in which events occur. At its best historicism allows theory generation and testing; history helps academics understand why things happen. For example, historians have tested and challenged Braverman's deskilling hypothesis (Patmore, 2006b, p. 32). History also provides researchers with a long-term perspective, allowing them to avoid the pitfalls of the snap shot. Gospel's historical study of British employers highlighted a long-term trend that may not necessarily have been picked up by a short-term study by establishing that firms gradually took direct control of labour management and grew less reliant on the internal labour market (Gospel, 1992, p. 10, 171).

History focuses on process and allows researchers to develop dynamic rather than static theoretical frameworks. Underlying the historical approach is a critique of the static approach taken to theorisation by the dominant social sciences such as economics and psychology. Jacoby (1990, pp. 319–320) in his discussion of the new institutional economics notes that orthodox economic theory is *synchronic*: an abstraction from reality that denies history or place. Most theories are based on fairly simple assumptions that X influences Y and ignore the temporal dimension. When did X occur and when did Y occur? What was the lag between the two? X and Y could also change over time during this lag. What is the rate of change? While X is impacting on Y, Y in the meantime could also impact on X. Mitchell and James

(2001, pp. 532–535) have suggested at least eight possible configurations of causality between X and Y when one introduces four time periods and two other different variables that X may have an impact on. Mitchell and James (2001, p. 537) also ask when does one measure X or Y? If relationships are cyclical then when one measures X or Y could be crucial. You can measure X at the peak of the season and measure Y at the trough. Theoretical perspectives that fail to take account of a changing economic, political and social climate have limited explanatory power.

'Presentism' denies the relevance of the past and claims that history, unlike the natural or social sciences, is idiographic in that it explores details of unique and irreproducible events. It ignores that historians can develop long-term theoretical perspectives (Mainzer, 2002, pp. 138–144). Futurism also has its limitations. Despite sophisticated econometric models and supercomputers it is difficult to predict the future. As physicists have noted in the world of quantum mechanics, systems can become chaotic. There is also a 'butterfly effect', where the smallest local change or event could have national and even international implications (Mainzer, 2002, p. 100). An isolated incident of bullying at a workplace could unexpectedly cascade into a strike and government intervention into the workplace. Despite these divisions, however, the three temporal frames of reference are linked.

The past and future are embedded in the present and the three fuse into a 'flux' in the human mind (Jacques, 1990, p. 25). The present is traditionally represented on the time axis in which the past and present come infinitely close. However, because time can vary due to differing psychological perceptions of the passage of time, the present may flow sluggishly or elapse instantaneously. The past pre-conditions the present through memory, while the future is based in the present in terms of expectations and hopes (Mainzer, 2002, pp. 127–128). Present concerns can also shape how we see the past and the questions we can ask concerning it. Futurism can become pure fantasy if it is not grounded in past or present experiences. As Bluedorn (2002, p. 138) notes the past "served as metaphor for the future: deep-past metaphors for deep-future concerns".

Historical methodology can be defined in two ways. First, it can be viewed temporally. Historical methodology is concerned with analysing the 'past' (Marshall and Rossman, 1989, p. 95). It is not clear when the 'past' ends or the 'present' begins. The 'past' may terminate yesterday, five years ago or at the beginning of the last decade. Evidence drawn from the 'past' can also help us understand the present.

Secondly, historical methodology has also been defined as a particular set of practices. The traditional image of the historian is someone who visits archives and interviews elderly people. There are claims that historical research is a craft, which involves the skills such as the ability to weigh up evidence, compress a range of events into a single trend, hold evidence up to "a dark Satanic light of evaluation", fill in gaps with "innovative detective work" and critically evaluate secondary sources (Markey, 1987, p. 7). However, these skills are not the exclusive domain of historians, but characterise all innovative research in the social sciences. Further, defining a distinctive historical methodology is a problem. For example, some researchers may view the survey as a contemporary research tool. However, one innovative English historian undertook a survey of Edwardian life by interviewing survivors of this period by the means of a quota sample based on the 1911 UK Census (Thompson, 1975).

Although it may be difficult to distinguish between the skills and methods of the contemporary researcher and the historian, there are differences. Both researchers of the present and the past use documents. However, the written word is not constant over time. Some words disappear, new words are invented and other words change meaning. These problems are greater for a historian studying the late nineteenth century than a researcher of current trade union amalgamations. The passage of time creates particular problems for the historical researcher, as crucial documents may be lost due to neglect or design or even faked, as in the case of the infamous 'Hitler diaries'. Further, while both contemporary and historical researchers use interviews, the problem of memory is greater for historians given the longer passage of time as well as the death of important participants (Patmore, 1998, p. 216). Consequently, the historical researcher has to weave together fragments of the 'past' to achieve understanding (Patmore, 1998, p. 215).

Sometimes contemporary research may not be possible on particular questions because of the implications for an individual's privacy and commercial considerations. Management may be reluctant to admit its role in provoking industrial disputes or reveal divisions over important issues. For historians passage of time may make these issues less sensitive. One particular issue of management sensitivity is the question of labour espionage against workers and unions. Jonathan Rees (2004), using previously confidential company records, found that Colorado Fuel and Iron (CF&I) in the US used spies to observe union meetings and union activities alongside its policies relating to encouraging worker voice through Employee Representation Plans (ERP).

Historical research is not restricted to qualitative methods but can also use quantitative methods such as regression analysis. Quantitative methods involve historians either using databases provided by the state, companies, unions, universities and other sources or developing new databases. Like social scientists, historians use quantitative methods in two ways. There is formalised description, which involves tables and graphs that measure and count. A more sophisticated approach is inferential statistics, where statistical methods such as multiple regressions are used to test hypotheses. Historians use quantitative methods to examine issues such as trade union growth, strikes, labour mobility and living standards. The advantage of quantification is that it allows greater precision in making statements (Patmore, 1998, pp. 224–225).

There are problems, however, with developing historical databases. If the data are poor then the outcomes of quantitative analysis will be useless. The definition of variables such as trade union membership and strikes changes over time. Data collection procedures may also change. Trade unions could submit their own returns concerning membership or a central statistical agency may undertake a general survey of union membership. Whether historical researchers rely on existing statistical data or construct their own, the problems of selectivity and bias still apply. A focus on quantitative data also narrows our understanding of the past to the measurable and may result in the rich detail of a particular period being ignored. There is also the problem of quantifying concepts such as class, power and nationalism (Jarausch and Hardy, 1991, pp. 1–2; Patmore, 1998, p. 225).

There can be different outcomes for those who rely on quantitative historical data, particularly where proxies are involved, and qualitative historical data (Strauss and Whitfield, 2008, p. 176). David Fairris (1995), in a reappraisal of US company unions using abstract industry data, notes that company unions or ERPs were beneficial for both shopfloor safety and productivity. Fairris (1995, p. 524) argues that these schemes "marked a definite improvement for the worker as well as the firm" in the 1920s by reducing labour turnover, fostering worker loyalty and allowing workers a voice in determining shopfloor conditions. Fairris's findings, however, clash with an unpublished internal management study of the CF&I ERP in 1924 which suggested that the economic benefits of the plan for management were disappointing. It certainly increased 'morale', but did not necessarily reduce costs and increase productivity (Patmore, 2016, p. 101). Ernest Burton (1926, p. 262) further argued in a major contemporary study of ERPs in the US that these schemes do not necessarily lead to greater output, increased efficiency or improved morale. Impediments that reduced the willingness of employee representatives to co-operate with management included the failure of management to provide satisfactory wages and conditions in comparison with competitors, managerial inefficiencies and how willing management was to share information about the company with employee representatives.

Historical methods are useful not only in the formulation of theories. They can be helpful in understanding the present and can thereby contribute to contemporary public policy debates such as the issue of employee voice. Ramsay (1977) in the UK and Wright (1995) in Australia have noted that employers have adopted a cyclical approach to worker participation driven by threats to management authority. The alternative "favourable conjunctures" thesis put forward by Michael Poole, Russell Lansbury and Nick Wailes (2001) rejects the inevitability of cycles and is more focused on factors that help explain the rise of industrial democracy. This approach acknowledges a "broad long-term trend towards greater experimentation and richness of forms" of industrial democracy. It also recognises "a discontinuous historical pattern, in which the main forms of industrial democracy have varied substantially in their incidence and impact at distinctive points in time." The favourable conjunctures model suggests four main sets of variables that influence industrial democracy within organisations: macro-conditions (external organisation); strategic choices of the actors; the power of actors; and organisational structures and processes at the level of the firm. The macro-conditions include favourable economic and technological variables, culture and the legal framework. Poole, Lansbury and Wailes also try to explain why particular forms of industrial democracy persist. They note that while there may be macro-conditions that favour industrial democracy, the adoption of employee participation at the level of the firm is subject to organisational choice. Both the cyclical and favourable conjunctures theses highlight that there is a long history of prior experimentation with schemes to promote worker voice in the workplace to draw upon in evaluating the success or failure of contemporary proposals. They also highlight the problem of 'amnesia' where a 'presentist' temporal frame of reference ignores or denies the value of previous experiments with employee voice (Patmore, 2006b, p. 34).

Why did such schemes for worker voice fail in earlier periods? Are the conditions for failure still present today? Historical research allows academics to explore these questions and provide another perspective for contemporary debates. When management attempts to introduce participatory practices, the past behaviour of management and employee expectations will influence whether the participatory practices will be successfully introduced. They are less likely to succeed if management in the past has acted autocratically rather than democratically with an interest in consulting employees. If employees anticipate that the new participatory practices are temporary and management will revert to autocratic behaviour they will be more hostile. They will be more favourable if they believe that there are increasing opportunities to participate in the future (George and Jones, 2000, pp. 669–670).

The recent decline in trade union membership in many western countries has rekindled interest in schemes of employee voice as a hope for the future. Scholars emphasise that workers without union representation no longer have a voice in the management of their workplaces. This 'representation gap' reduces the potential of workers to contribute to improving productivity and the quality of working life. The gap can be overcome through encouraging collectivist but non-union mechanisms such as works councils or joint consultative committees. The advocates of these forms of representation argue that they complement the call for 'high performance workplaces' or 'mutual gain enterprises' in an era of heightened global and domestic competition by encouraging decentralised decision-making, team forms of production and a climate of co-operation and trust (Dobbins and Dundon, 2014; Gollan and Hamberger, 2002, pp. 24–25; Kaufman and Taras, 2000, p. 4; Mizrahi, 2002).

In the US and Canada academics interested in overcoming the representation gap have explored their historical traditions, particularly in regard to ERPs prior to the outbreak of the Second World War (Kaufman, 2000a; MacDowell, 2000). The plan formed the foundation of a movement that spread throughout the US and covered 2,500,000 workers in various industries by 1935. Critics condemned these plans as 'sham organisations' that impeded labour organisation and they were outlawed in the 1935 National Labor Relations Act (Kaufman, 2000a, pp. 22–29). Despite this, Kaufman (2000b, p. 55) claimed that ERPs were "net, a constructive positive development for improved industrial relations". While the willingness of these scholars to undertake a historicist approach is welcome, one of the problems with these interpretations is a reluctance to explore the full historical context of the ERPs, particularly at the workplace level. At CF&I, for example, there was a long history of union avoidance activity at its Pueblo steel plant before the adoption of the ERP (Patmore, 2007, p. 847).

History and employment relations

In the United Kingdom and United States the relationship between history, particularly labour history, and industrial relations dates from the 1890s. Sydney and Beatrice Webb, the authors of a *History of Trade Unionism* (1894) and *Industrial Democracy* (1897), are cited as the founders of both areas of study in the UK. They were concerned with the 'problem', which encompassed both the rise of trade unionism and the extent of poverty among the British working class. The Webbs adopted a "scientific approach" to their work, believing that they could extract new laws from facts. Their empiricism excluded concepts such as working class ideology, which was "non-factual". They saw trade unions as a rational response by workers to the problems of industrialisation and charted in great detail the history of the organised labour movement to justify their views (Patmore, 1990, p. 8).

In the USA, John R. Commons and his colleagues at the University of Wisconsin pioneered both labour history and IR through the 11-volume *Documentary History of American Industrial Society* (1910–1911) and the first two volumes of the *History of Labour in the United States* (1918). They rejected the static assumptions of classical economics and saw historical research and statistics as a dynamic means of studying "industrial life". Commons and his colleagues wanted to demonstrate to orthodox economists that union rules and wages were compatible to the capitalist economy. They were concerned at the growing conflict between labour and capital at the end of the nineteenth century and looked for practical solutions for "labour problems". Like the Webbs, the 'Wisconsin school' emphasised highly detailed research findings and inductive theorising (Patmore, 1990, p. 8).

Since the Second World War labour history and industrial relations have drifted apart in the UK and USA for several reasons. Although post-war labour problems in both countries encouraged the growth of academic IR, and later employment relations, there was an increasing emphasis on labour economics and organisational behaviour. Researchers examining the world of work questioned the 'historical-institutionalist' approach and sought to establish a rigorous social science with quantitative and theoretically grounded analysis. Also, from the 1950s historians showed a greater interest in the history of workers and placing labour history in a broader context. The critiques of E.P. Thompson, Eric Hobsbawm and other British social historians broadened the horizons of labour historians in both countries. In the USA labour historians defined labour history as the history of the working class and explored issues such as working class culture and the shopfloor. Where IR academics did show an interest in labour history, they remained primarily concerned with trade unions and collective bargaining. Hugh Clegg, Alan Fox and A.F. Thompson's (1964, p. 1985) histories of British trade unions explicitly continued the work of the Webbs. There was an emphasis on empirical detail and a reluctance to incorporate unverifiable concepts – even the notion of a 'labour movement' (Campbell and McIlroy, 2010, pp. 100–101; Patmore, 1990, p. 9). According to Campbell and McIlroy, many union histories were commissioned, with some disclosing a "strong streak of antiquarianism" and others verging "on hagiography". One notable exception was Richard Hyman (1971), who drew important theoretical conclusions about how unions operated from his study of the developments of the Workers' Union from 1898 to 1929 (Campbell and McIlroy, 2010, pp. 100–101). According to Lyddon (2003, pp. 89–90, 113), who helped launch the journal *Historical Studies in Industrial Relations* at Keele University in 1996, by the beginning of the twenty-first century a continued tradition of problem solving among British IR academics, which was linked to a declining role in public policy and a decline in externally provided union education, led many industrial specialists to teach human resource management and adopt a broader ER approach, reinforcing an ahistorical approach among British ER academics.

There was a different pattern in Australia with labour history and IR. Participants in the Australian labour movement wrote celebratory histories of trade unions as early as 1888. Like the USA and UK there was little interest in the labour movement in university history departments until the 1950s. Labour historians formed the Australian Society for the Study of Labour History in 1961 and launched the journal *Labour History* in 1962. Labour problems arising from a full employment economy in the 1950s and the 1960s fuelled the growth of academic IR. Industrial relations courses commenced at the University of Sydney in 1953 and IR academics and practitioners founded the *Journal of Industrial Relations* in 1959. Australian and New Zealand IR academics formed an association in 1983, which has been holding regular conferences on IR teaching and research since then (Patmore, 1990, p. 9).

The links between industrial relations and labour history continued in Australia (Patmore, 2010, pp. 247–248, 251), with university departments of IR developing a growing influence on Australian labour historiography. Industrial relations in Australia was multidisciplinary, drawing upon economics, sociology, law and history. Labour history courses were part of IR programmes. As IR departments expanded during this period, they also employed labour historians who been trained in history departments, for example Bradon Ellem, John Shields, Ray Markey and Lucy Taksa. The main academic IR journals, *Labour and Industry* and *The Journal of Industrial Relations*, published labour history. While there had been an emphasis on prescriptive policy-making, IR scholars were increasingly interested in theoretical issues and even developing a radical political economy of industrial relations. Industrial relations academics were to further strengthen the interests of Australian labour history in areas such as history of the state, particularly compulsory arbitration, employers' associations, the labour process and comparative labour history. While IR departments, as in other countries, have been absorbed into larger departments of management, business and organisational studies and specific courses focusing on labour history have virtually disappeared, there are still strong links between labour history and IR, with both the major Australian journals in these fields being edited recently in the discipline of Work and Organisational Studies, the former Department of Industrial Relations, at the University of Sydney.

Despite the strong links between industrial relations and labour history in Australia, Lyddon and Smith (1996) argued that since 1979 historical articles had rarely been published in the UK IR journals or the two main US journals. A review of the *Journal of Industrial Relations* (Australia), *Industrial and Labor Relations Review* (US) and the *British Journal of Industrial Relations* (Patmore, 1998) published between 1990 and 1994 revealed that only 19 per cent used historical data – defined as pre-dating 1980. Industrial relations scholars engaged in historical research prefer quantitative methods. Of these 19 per cent the overwhelming majority of the historical articles in the *Review* and the *BJIR* employed quantitative data – 90 per cent and 62 per cent respectively. Examples include Boal's (1990) study of unionism and productivity in West Virginia coal mining during the 1920s and the study of British coal mining strikes by Church and his colleagues (1990). This highlighted the influence of labour economists within IR and reflected a general trend in IR towards quantitative methods, though this preference varied across countries: British and US industrial relations academics appeared reluctant to draw upon qualitative historical methods. Exceptions include Cobble's (1991) study of waitress unionism, which used both documentary and oral sources. By contrast approximately 75 per cent of the historical articles in the Australian journal employed qualitative techniques, a notable example being Sheridan's (1994) study of waterside workers.

What is the current situation? The three journals above are again reviewed for 2010–2014 with historical data redefined as pre-dating 2000 and a total of 543 articles. On the surface there has been surge in the proportion of articles using historical data: 34 per cent. Of these articles 69 per cent used quantitative methods, with 92 per cent of the historical articles in the US journal and 64 per cent in the UK journal using quantitative methods. The growth of quantitative methods is fuelled by the increasing availability of published longitudinal data obtained through various agencies, including the US Census, the US National Longitude Survey of Youth, which commenced in 1979, and the British Household Panel Survey, which began in 1991. Other important sources of these data include AWIRS, WES and Workplace Employment Relations in Australia, Canada and the UK respectively (Strauss and Whitfield, 2008, pp. 175–176). Examples of this sort of approach include use of data from the British Household Panel Survey from 1991 to 2010 to examine job satisfaction (Chongvilaivan and Powdthavee, 2014) and the use of the 1968, 1981 and 2000 Swedish Level of Living Surveys to examine the evolution of wage distribution in Sweden, comparing a period of centralised wage determination with a more flexible period of wage determination. There are exceptions to the reliance on this aggregate data, such as the study by Paul Deveraux and Robert Hart (2011), which examined strike activity in British engineering from 1920 to 1970 and concluded that strike outcomes for unions are more favourable when the strike rate is lower. They constructed a data set from the strike records of the member companies of the Engineering Employers' Federation in Great Britain, which covered 10,870 company-level strike incidents within the engineering, metal goods and automotive industries during the period examined.

By contrast the Australian journal, as in the previous period, favoured qualitative methods, with a notable increase in the percentage of qualitative historical articles – from 75 to 97 per cent of the total historical articles published. Examples of this approach include Cathy Brigden's (2012) innovative study of women leaders in the Female Confectioners' Union in Australia during the 1920s, which combines genealogical and archival sources and highlights women workers' collective strategies and the role of honorary union officials. This reflects the continued influence of Australian labour history on Australian industrial relations, with Australian labour historians preferring qualitative methods.

For ER scholars undertaking historical research, historical journals, particularly in the field of labour history, remain important outlets for this research. *Labor History*, edited by Craig Phelan at the University of Kingston (UK) and Gerald Friedman at the University of Massachusetts-Amherst, has sought to return the journal to its industrial relations roots and strengthen the links with ER scholars (Faue, 2010, p. 182). During 2013 and 2014 38 per cent of the articles contributed to *Labor History* originated from academics in ER and related disciplines with a primary focus on qualitative historical research methods. Ray Markey (2013) uses a diachronic comparative methodology, which compares two separate historical sets of events, to examine the Australian federal elections of 1929 and 2007, which resulted in both the defeat of the government and the respective Prime Ministers losing their seats. Following radical labour reforms by the respective governments, industrial relations were a major issue in both elections. Despite the different historical contexts, he notes similarities in the drive for change in terms of productivity and international competitiveness, and highlights a union pressure group style campaign based on grassroots organising. Ralph Darlington (2014) examines the interplay between strike waves, union growth and rank and file versus bureaucracy in Britain for the periods 1889–1890, 1910–1913 and 1919–1920. He uses a qualitative approach to reassess Gerald Friedman's (2008) *Reigniting the Labour Movement* argument for the restoration of past militant action to reignite the contemporary labour movement, and concludes "the containment of workers and trade unionism to capitalism is anything but a simple and automatic process, even in quiet times".

There has been willingness by some labour history journals to broaden their focus and examine management strategies in regard to labour that echo influences ranging from labour process theory to human resource management (Wright, 2011). The recent decline of the trade unions in a number of western countries has also highlighted the importance of examining the historical experience of unorganised workplaces and forms of non-union employee representation. As noted previously Bruce Kaufman has reignited the debate in regard to non-union forms of employee representation, particularly focusing on ERPs with several of his articles (2000b, 2015) appearing in *Labor History*, and similar articles (Markey and Patmore, 2009; Patmore, 2006a) on this question appearing in *Labor* (US) and *Labour History* (Australia).

The willingness of labour history journals to publish articles that focus on examining management labour strategies highlights the potential for ER academics to publish in business and management history journals. Generally business historians in the United States have shown little interest in labour management issues, focusing on issues such as technological change and ownership structures (Boyce and Ville, 2002, p. 119). Alfred Chandler in *The Visible Hand* (1977, p. 497) argued that "neither the labor unions or the government has taken part in carrying out the basic functions of modern business enterprise". While Sanford Jacoby (1985, p. 8) has argued that Chandler's claim is correct for essential functions of top management such as marketing or production, he argues that this is not true for the employment sphere and that Chandler too readily accepts the American manager's bias that employment is a secondary corporate function.

Richard John (1997, pp. 190–191) further reinforced these concerns about *The Visible Hand*. Workers made possible the economies of speed that assisted Chandler's managerial revolution, but also delayed productive reorganisation in order to retain control over the labour process. They helped establish internal labour markets in large bureaucratic organisations, to increase job security and restrict the power of foremen and subcontractors, and aided the extensive development of corporate paternalism. In the USA the state played a role in limiting the ability of workers to mobilise through the activities of anti-labour lawyers, judges and legislators.

Chandler (1990, p.13) later acknowledged the importance of labour management for the industrial enterprise in *Scale and Scope*, his study of big business in the USA, Britain and Germany, but excluded the discussion of it on the grounds of insufficient space in the book. Jürgen Kokcha (1990, p. 711) also justified Chandler's exclusion of "changing labor relations" with the need to make the comparative study more manageable. For Germany particularly this a significant omission given the role of works councils during the Weimar Republic in allowing worker representatives a role in management decision-making and open access to company information (Patmore, 2013, p. 533). Whatever the reasons for Chandler excluding labour management, there is a current recognition within business history for the need for greater co-operation with researchers who focus on the history of work. Lars Magnusson (2014, p. 72) argues "it is necessary to treat both work and its processes in connection with the historical organisation of business. To a large degree they are part of the same process of change and transformation".

Two examples of studies published by ER scholars in business history journals are Westcott (2008) and Jhatial, Cornelius and Wallace (2014). Westcott provided a detailed qualitative historical case study of Tooth's & Co., a major Australian brewer, to examine how the product market conditions faced by managers influence their labour management policies. Increasing competition in the 1970s and poorer company performance led to a greater focus on returns, a tightening up of labour management and removal of inconsistent practices by supervisors in their relationships with workers. Jhatial, Cornelius and Wallace, using qualitative methods, examine how colonial laws and administrative practices shaped the evolution of employment management in Pakistan. They highlight how the legacies of important mechanisms established in the period of the British Raj and the influence of clan and ethnicity in recruitment and selection, for example, still shape ER in the country today.

Beyond journals books make an important contribution to understanding the history of employment. Books have the advantage of providing historians, particularly qualitative historians, with the length to explore issues over long periods and across a number of countries and to meet the elaborate archival referencing required by archives for documentary sources. Sanford Jacoby (1985, 1997, 2005) has written several major books that allow ER scholars to understand long-term trends such as the bureaucratisation of work and challenge myths. Jacoby in *Modern Manors* reminds us of the persistence of welfare capitalism after the Great Depression of the 1930s and that most workplaces in the USA were unorganised in the immediate post-war period, when unions were at their peak, and that to some degree non-union voice has always been an issue for most US workers. Howard Gospel (1992) and Chris Wright (1995) provide important historical analyses of employer strategies for ER over extensive periods for the UK and USA. Bruce Kaufman (2008, 2010) has re-examined the early years of human resource management in the USA. Chris Howell (2005) challenges the concept of voluntarism in British ER in the twentieth century by arguing that the state played a prime role in developing the forms of ER, using "a narrative of crisis" to justify new forms of ER.

Books on ER history do not only cover extensive periods of time but can also focus on particular events that are 'turning points' in the development of ER. A good example of this is Joseph McCartin's study (2011) of the Professional Air Traffic Controllers Organization strike in 1981, which he argues not only led to a long period of labour decline in the US but also was a foretaste of the current campaigns against public sector workers in the US.

Conclusion

There are different temporal frames of reference based on the past, present and future. These are historicism, presentism and futurism. Historical analysis enables one to subject 'dominant paradigms' to closer scrutiny, develop dynamic as opposed to static theory and question claims of 'transformation'. Presentism can also be associated with historical 'amnesia', where ideas such as employee participation are seen as new but have in fact been experimented with in the past. Historicism allows us to ask the simple question of whether the conditions that led to failure in the past are still present. As ideas such as the 'butterfly effect' highlight, it is extremely difficult to predict the future. The past, present and future are linked and to deny the relevance of any temporal dimension is problematic.

The link between historical research and employment relations established by the Webbs and the Wisconsin School persists in ER through the growth of quantitative historical research, particularly in the USA, where the influence of labour economists and growing availability of historical databases encourage this form of research. Quantitative historical research has limitations in that it restricts researchers to the measurable and does not illuminate the processes by which change occurs. There can also be problems with the use of proxies to cover factors that may not be readily measurable. However, qualitative historical research persists in ER in Australia, particularly with the continued influence of labour history there, and can be found in historical journals such as *Labor History*. Business history and management history also provide another potential area of further publication for qualitative historical study in industrial relations, with the recognition of the need to link business history to the world of work.

References

Albrecht, J., Björklund, A. and Vroman, S. (2011). 'Unionization and the Evolution of the Wage Distribution in Sweden: 1968 to 2000', *Industrial and Labor Relations Review*, 64(5), pp. 1039–1057.

Boal, W. (1990). 'Unionism and Productivity in West Virginia Coal Mining', *Industrial and Labor Relations Review*, 43(4), pp. 390–405.

Boyce, G. and Ville, S. (2002). *The Development of Modern Business*. Houndmills: Palgrave.

Brigden, C. (2012). 'Tracing and Placing Women Trade Union Leaders: A Study of the Female Confectioners Union', *Journal of Industrial Relations*, 54(2), pp. 238–255.

Bluedorn, A. (2002). *The Human Organization of Time: Temporal Realities and Experience*. Stanford: Stanford University Press.

Burton, E. (1926). *Employee Representation*. Baltimore: Williams & Wilkins.

Campbell, A. and McIlroy, J. (2010). Britain: The Twentieth Century, in Allen, J., Campbell, A. and McIlroy, J. (eds.) *Histories of Labour: National and International Perspectives* London: Merlin Press, pp. 99–136.

Chandler, A. (1977). *The Visible Hand: The Managerial Revolution in American Business*. Cambridge (MA): Harvard University Press.

Chandler, A. (1990). *Scale and Scope: The Dynamics of Industrial Capitalism*. Cambridge (MA): Harvard University Press.

Chongvilaivan, A. and Powdthavee, N. (2014). 'Do Different Work Characteristics Have Different Distributional Impacts on Job Satisfaction? A Study of Slope Heterogeneity in Workers' Well-Being', *British Journal of Industrial Relations*, 52(3), pp. 426–444.

Church, R., Outram, Q. and Smith, D. (1990). 'British Coal Mining Strikes 1893–1940: Dimensions, Distribution and Persistence', *British Journal of Industrial Relations*, 28(3), pp. 329–349.

Clegg, H. (1985). *A History of British Trade Unions since 1889. Volume II 1911–1933*. Oxford: Clarendon Press.

Clegg, H., Fox, A. and Thompson, A.F. (1964). *History of British Trade Unions Since 1989. Volume I 1889–1910*. Oxford: Clarendon Press.

Cobble, D. (1991). 'Organising the Postindustrial Work Force: Lessons from the History of Waitress Unionism', *Industrial and Labor Relations Review*, 44(3), pp. 419–436.

Commons, J.R., Phillips, U.B., Gilmore, E.A., Sumner, H.L. and Andrews, J.B. (1910–1911). *Documentary History of American Industrial Society*. Cleveland: The A.H. Clark Company.

Commons, J.R., Saposs, D.J., Sumner, H.L., Mittleman, E.B., Hoagland, H.G., Andrews, J.B. and Perlman, S. (1918). *History of Labour in the United States*. New York: Macmillan.

Darlington, R. (2014). 'Strike waves, union growth and the rank-and-file/bureaucracy interplay: Britain 1889–1890, 1910–1930 and 1919–1920', *Labor History*, 55(1), pp. 1–20.

Devereux, P. and Hart, R. (2011). 'A Good Time to Stay Out? Strikes and the Business Cycle', *British Journal of Industrial Relations*, 49(Suppl.1), pp. 70–92.

Dobbins, T. and Dundon, T. (2014). Non-union Employee Representation, in Wilkinson, A., Donaghey, J., Dundon, T. and Freeman, R. (eds.) *Handbook of Research on Employee Voice*. Cheltenham: Edward Elgar, pp. 342–362.

Fairris, D. (1995). 'From Exit to Voice in Shopfloor Governance: The Case of Company Unions', *Business History Review*, 69(4), pp. 493–529.

Friedman, G. (2008). *Reigniting the Labor Movement: Restoring Means to Ends in a Democratic Labor Movement*. London: Routledge.

Faue, E. (2010). The United States of America, in Allen, J., Campbell, A. and McIlroy, J. (eds.) *Histories of Labour: National and International Perspectives*. London: Merlin Press, pp.164–197.

George, J. and Jones, G. (2000). 'The Role of Time in Theory and Theory Building', *Journal of Management*, 26(4), pp. 657–684.

Gollan, P. and Hamberger, J. (2002). Enterprise-based employee representation in Australia – employer strategies and future options, in Gollan, P., Markey, R. and Ross, I. (eds.) *Works Councils in Australia: Future Prospects and Possibilities*. Sydney: Federation Press, pp. 24–36.

Gospel, H. (1992). *Markets, Firms and the Management of Labour in Modern Britain*. Cambridge (UK): Cambridge University Press.

Howell, C. (2005). *Trade Unions and the State: The Construction of Industrial Relations Institutions in Britain, 1890–2000*. Princeton: Princeton University Press.

Hyman, R. (1971). *The Workers' Union*. Oxford: Clarendon Press.

Jacoby, S. (1985). *Employing Bureaucracy: Managers, Unions, and the Transformation of Work in American Industry, 1900–1945*. New York: Columbia University Press.

Jacoby, S. (1990). 'The New Institutionalism: What Can It Learn from the Old?', *Industrial Relations*, 29(2), pp. 316–359.

Jacoby, S. (1997). *Modern Manors: Welfare Capitalism since the New Deal*. Princeton: Princeton University Press.

Jacoby, S. (2005). *The Embedded Corporation: Corporate Governance and Employment Relations in Japan and the United States*. Princeton: Princeton University Press.

Jacques, E. (1990). The Enigma of Time, in Hassard, J. (ed.) *The Sociology of Time*. London: Macmillan, pp. 21–34.

Jarausch, K. and Hardy, K. (1991). *Quantitative Methods for Historians: A Guide to Research, Data, and Statistics*. Chapel Hill: University of North Carolina Press.

Jhatial, A.A., Cornelius, N. and Wallace, J. (2014). 'Rhetorics and realities of management practices in Pakistan: colonial, post-colonial and post-9/11 influences', *Business History*, 53(6), pp. 456–484.

John, R. (1997). 'Elaborations, Revisions, Dissents: Alfred D. Chandler, Jr.'s The Visible Hand after Twenty Years', *Business History Review*, 71(2), pp. 151–200.

Kaufman, B. (2000a). Accomplishments and Shortcomings of Nonunion Employee Representation in the Pre-Wagner Act Years: A Reassessment, in Kaufman, B. and Taras, D. (eds.) *Non-Union Employee Representation: History, Contemporary Practice and Policy*. Armonk: M.E. Sharpe, pp. 21–60.

Kaufman, B. (2000b). 'The Case for the Company Union', *Labor History*, 41(3), pp. 321–351.

Kaufman, B. (2008). *Managing the Human Factor: The Early Years of Human Resource Management in American Industry*. Ithaca: Cornell University Press.

Kaufman, B. (2010). *Hired Hands or Human Resources? Case Studies of HRM Programs and Practices in Early American Industry*. Ithaca: Cornell University Press.

Kaufman, B. (2015). 'Divergent fates: company unions and employee involvement committees under the railway labor and national labor relations acts', *Labor History*, 56(4), pp. 423–458.

Kaufman, B. and Taras, D. (2000). Introduction, in Kaufman, B. and Taras, D. (eds.) *Non-Union Employee Representation: History, Contemporary Practice and Policy*. Armonk: M.E. Sharpe, pp. 3–18.

Kokcha, J. (1990). 'Germany: Co-operation and Competition', *Business History Review*, 64(4), pp. 711–716.

Lyddon, D. (2003). History and Industrial Relations, in Akers, P. and Wilkinson, A. (eds.) *Understanding Work and Employment: Industrial Relations in Transition*. Oxford: Oxford University Press, pp. 89–118.

Lyddon, D. and Smith, P. (1996). 'Editorial: Industrial Relations and History', *Historical Studies in Industrial Relations*, 1, pp. 1–10.

MacDowell, L. (2000). Company Unionism in Canada, 1915–1948, in Kaufman, B. and Taras, D. (eds.) *Non-Union Employee Representation: History, Contemporary Practice and Policy*. Armonk: M.E. Sharpe, pp. 196-220.

McCartin, J. (2011). *Collision Course: Ronald Reagan, The Air Traffic Controllers, and the Strike that Changed America*. Oxford: Oxford University Press.

Magnusson, L. (2014). 'Business history and the history of work – a contested relationship', *Business History*, 56(1), pp. 71–83.

Mainzer, K. (2002). *The Little Book of Time*. New York: Copernicus Books.

Markey, R. (1987). Labour History and Industrial Relations in Australia, in Hince, K. and Williams, A. (eds.) *Contemporary Industrial Relations in Australia and New Zealand: Literature Surveys*. Wellington: The Association of Industrial Relations Academics of Australia and New Zealand, pp. 169–198.

Markey, R. (2013). 'Tragedy or farce? The repetition of Australian industrial relations history, 1929 and 2007', *Labor History*, 54(4), pp. 355–376.

Markey, R. and Patmore, G. (2009). 'Employee Participation and Labour Representation: ICI Works Councils in Australia, 1942–75', *Labour History*, 97(2), pp. 53–73.

Marshall, C. and Rossman, G. (1989). *Designing Qualitative Research*. Newbury Park: Sage.

Mitchell, T. and James, L. (2001). 'Building Better Theory: Time and the Specification of When Things Happen', *Academy of Management Review*, 26(4), pp. 530–547.

Mizrahi, S. (2002). 'Workers' Participation in Decision-Making Process and Firm Stability', *British Journal of Industrial Relations*, 40(4), pp. 689–708.

Patmore, G. (1990). History and Industrial Relations, in Patmore, G. (ed.) *History and Industrial Relations*. Sydney: Australian Centre for Industrial Relations Research and Teaching, pp. 1–15.

Patmore, G. (1998). Digging Up the Past: Historical Methods in Industrial Relations Research, in Whitfield, K. and Strauss, G. (eds.) *Researching the World of Work: Strategies and Methods in Studying Industrial Relations*. Ithaca: Cornell University Press, pp. 213–226.

Patmore, G. (2006a). 'Employee Representation Plans in the United States, Canada, and Australia: An Employer Response to Workplace Democracy', *Labor*, 3(2), pp. 41–65.

Patmore, G. (2006b). Time and Work, in Hearn, M. and Michelson, G. (eds.) *Rethinking Work: Time, Space and Discourse*. Melbourne: Cambridge University Press, pp. 21–38.

Patmore, G. (2007). 'Employee representation plans at the Minnequa Steelworks, Pueblo, Colorado, 1915–1942', *Business History*, 49(6), pp. 788–811.

Patmore, G. (2010). Australia, in Allen, J., Campbell, A. and McIlroy, J. (eds.) *Histories of Labour: National and International Perspectives*. London: Merlin Press, pp. 231–261.

Patmore, G. (2013). 'Unionism and non-union employee representation: The interwar experience in Canada, Germany, the US and the UK,' *Journal of Industrial Relations*, 55(4), pp. 527–545.

Patmore, G. (2016). *Worker Voice: Employee Representation in the Workplace in Australia, Canada, Germany, the UK and the US 1914–1939*. Liverpool: Liverpool University Press.

Poole, M., Lansbury, R. and Wailes, N. (2001). Participation and Industrial Democracy Revisited: a Theoretical Perspective, in Markey, R., Gollan, P., Hodgkinson, A., Chouraqui, A. and Veersma, U. (eds.) *Models of Employee Participation in a Changing Global Environment: Diversity and Interaction*. Aldershot: Ashgate, pp. 23–34.

Ramsay, H. (1977). 'Cycles of Control: Worker Participation in Sociological and Historical Perspective', *Sociology*, 11(3), pp. 481–506.

Rees, J. (2004). 'X, XX and X-3: Labor Spy Reports from the Colorado Fuel and Iron Company Archives,' *Colorado Heritage*, pp. 28–41.

Sheridan, T. (1994). 'Australian Wharfies 1943–1967: Casual Attitudes, Militant Leadership and Workplace Change', *The Journal of Industrial Relations*, 36(2), pp. 258–284.

Strauss, G. and Whitfield, K. (2008). Changing Traditions in Industrial Relations Research, in Blyton, P., Bacon, N., Fiorito, J. and Heery, E. (eds.) *The SAGE Handbook of Industrial Relations*. Los Angeles: Sage, pp. 170–186.

Thompson, P. (1975). *The Edwardians: The Remaking of British Society*. London: Weidenfeld and Nicholson.

Webb, S. and Webb, B. (1894). *The History of Trade Unionism*. London: Longmans, Green & Co.

Webb, S. and Webb, B. (1897). *Industrial Democracy*. London: Longmans, Green & Co.

Westcott, M. (2008). 'Markets and managerial discretion: Tooth and Co. 1970–1981', *Business History*, 50(5), pp. 602–618.

Wright, C. (1995). *The Management of Labour: A History of Australian Employers*. South Melbourne: Oxford University Press.

Wright, C. (2011). 'Historical Interpretations of the Labour Process: Retrospect and Future Research Directions', *Labour History*, 100, pp. 19–32.

6

SOCIOLOGY, THE LABOUR PROCESS AND EMPLOYMENT RELATIONS

Bill Harley

Introduction

Employment relations (ER) is a field that has been informed by a number of core disciplines, each of which brings its own theoretical lens to bear on the employment relationship and highlights particular aspects of it. The strength of sociological research on the employment relationship is primarily that it locates its analysis of workplace issues within broader social and economic frameworks, thereby providing a holistic model of the factors shaping, and being shaped by, ER.

The discipline of sociology has been particularly important in informing critical analyses of the employment relationship, which focus on power and control in capitalist production systems. Within sociology, arguably the most significant body of work on ER is that done within the labour process theory (LPT) tradition. This approach, based on the work of Marx (1954) and initially developed by Braverman (1974), has come to occupy a central role, particularly in the Anglophone world, in critical understandings of work and employment. For this reason, this chapter will focus primarily on the LPT tradition.

The first part of the chapter discusses what is distinctive about "the sociological imagination" (Mills, 1959) and why this makes the sociological lens a particularly appropriate one through which to examine ER. Section 2 provides an overview of the LPT tradition, starting with Braverman's (1974) work and then considering subsequent developments. The discussion is structured around key contributions of the tradition that are particularly significant for understanding ER. In the third section, a brief discussion is provided on insights about gender and ER that have emerged from sociological research. The final substantive section of the chapter takes stock of the legacy that sociology has left to the field of ER.

The sociological imagination and employment relations

While there are different views about precisely when and where sociology emerged as a discipline, we can understand it primarily as a product of the Enlightenment and its growth as inextricably linked to industrialisation (see Sica, 2011). Reflecting this trajectory of development, a concern with work and employment has been central to sociology, and the 'parents' of sociology – Durkheim, Marx and Weber – were all motivated to a significant extent by this concern (Crompton, 2008; Grint, 1998; Thompson and Smith, 2009; Vallas, 2011). This in turn makes it unsurprising that the field of ER has been shaped in important ways by insights from sociology.

Traces of the influence of Durkheim, Marx and Weber can be found in numerous places in the broader literature on work and employment. For example, Durkheim's argument that when social ties are replaced by economic ones dysfunctions arise can be seen echoed in the work of the Human Relations School in the mid-twentieth century and among the post-Fordists in the 1980s and 90s (Vallas, 2011, p. 420). Marx's emphasis on conflict has underpinned LPT and radical industrial relations scholarship more generally (e.g. Braverman, 1974; Hyman, 1975), as well as institutional analysis associated with the French Regulation School (see Boyer, 1990). Weber's work has also informed some variants of LPT as well as neo-institutionalism in ER theory (Thompson and McHugh, 2003, pp. 370–374).

Employment relations as a field is multidisciplinary. It draws on a diverse range of disciplines, including sociology, economics, management, social psychology and law (Mueller-Jentsch, 2004). Different disciplines draw attention to different aspects of the employment relationship, and it would be foolish to argue that sociology alone provides all the resources required to understand ER, but nonetheless the sociological lens provides a way of understanding the employment relationship that is particularly useful (see Watson and Korczynski, 2011 for a systematic discussion of the ways in which sociology has been applied to understanding work and organisations).

In *The Sociological Imagination*, C. Wright Mills argued that sociology was distinctive in its ability to bring together understandings of social structures, history and the experiences of individuals within societies:

> Whatever the specific problems of the classic social analysts, however limited or however broad the features of social reality they have examined, those who have been imaginatively aware of the promise of their work have consistently asked three sorts of questions:
>
> (1) What is the structure of this particular society as a whole? What are its essential components, and how are they related to one another? How does it differ from other varieties of social order? Within it, what is the meaning of any particular feature for its continuance and for its change?
>
> (2) Where does this society stand in human history? What are the mechanics by which it is changing? What is its place within and its meaning for the development of humanity as a whole? How does any particular feature we are examining affect, and how is it affected by, the historical period in which it moves? And this period – what are its essential features? How does it differ from other periods? What are its characteristic ways of history-making?
>
> (3) What varieties of men and women now prevail in this society and in this period? And what varieties are coming to prevail? In what ways are they selected and formed, liberated and repressed, made sensitive and blunted? What kinds of 'human nature' are revealed in the conduct and character we observe in this society in this period? And what is the meaning for 'human nature' of each and every feature of the society we are examining?
>
> *(Mills, 1959, pp. 6–7)*

Watson neatly sums up the implications of this Millsian view for what sociologists do:

> To be a sociologist, then, is to be able to take the smallest everyday action, routine or even artefact and see how it relates, first, to the type of society in which it is happening or exists, and, second, to the important changes and trends which are occurring at the societal or 'structural' level.
>
> *(Watson 2009, p. 863)*

This feature of sociological inquiry is what makes it so valuable for understanding ER. It allows scholars to link levels of analysis and to explore how the daily experiences of workers are shaped by social structures and processes that exist beyond any individual and which are more than the aggregation of individual phenomena. At the same time, sociology apprehends the way that individual actions can in turn shape these larger social structures and processes. It apprehends social phenomena as being embedded in particular contexts, which shape and are shaped by them.

Thus, a sociological view of ER emphasises the interactions between human actors – notably employers, managers and workers – and how these interactions are shaped by, and shape, complex systems of institutions and social and economic forces. It recognises that the employment relationship is not just an economic one, although that is an important facet of it, but also a social and political one (Vallas, 2011, p. 419). Moreover, it recognises that ER structures and processes reflect the specific features of the social and economic frameworks in which they are embedded, notably capitalism and its attendant structures, and that they change as capitalism changes. Furthermore, changes in the structures of capitalism are influenced by workplace-level struggles and their outcomes. This perspective allows sociologists to develop holistic accounts of workplace relations, which include consideration of the mechanisms through which practices emerge and operate in specific contexts.

A second important reason that sociology appears to have been influential in the field of ER is that there is an 'activist' impulse in much of sociology (see Burawoy, 2004, 2008). That is, many sociological scholars have followed the lead of Durkheim, Marx and Weber and seen their role as being not just the analysis of society, but the attempt to intervene and improve it. This kind of activist orientation appears to have been appealing to scholars and practitioners in ER.

This chapter does not pretend to consider all of the ways that sociology has influenced ER (for a useful discussion of the role of different sociological schools in the field of ER during the twentieth century, see Kaufman, 2004). Rather, the focus is on overtly critical approaches informed by sociological theory and research. There is a particular focus on LPT, because this is the approach that has had the most profound impact on the field, although attention is also given to the contribution of feminist sociologists.

Historically, much of the activity of industrial relations scholars has focused on institutions, particularly the institutions that regulate bargaining between employers and employees (Cullinane, 2014), but also trade unions. A sociological analysis of institutions has been central to a number of strands of research in ER. It should be noted, however, that a persistent criticism of the labour process tradition has been that its focus on workplace phenomena, shaped by capitalist relations, has led scholars working within it to downplay the role of specific institutions (Vidal and Hauptmeier, 2014). It is certainly the case that Braverman (1974) downplayed the role of national institutional configurations and unions and assumed a certain uniformity of outcomes of developments in the labour process. More recently, however, some scholars within this tradition have given more attention to institutions (see Smith, 2015). Because of the relative lack of focus on institutions in LPT and because institutions are dealt with elsewhere in this volume (Chapters 9 and 11), they will not be a focus of the remainder of this chapter.

Labour process theory and employment relations

As already noted, work has been central to sociological inquiry more or less since the birth of the discipline. The more significant contributions of sociology to ER are rather more recent and are associated with the LPT tradition. In the discussion that follows, the emergence and development of this tradition are discussed.

Marx, Braverman and the emergence of labour process theory

The most obvious influence of sociology on understandings of ER has been via LPT. The influence of this body of theory and research has waxed and waned, and it has undergone a series of shifts in concerns and emphases over time. Nonetheless, the LPT approach to understanding the employment relationship has endured for 150 years, with its roots in Karl Marx's *Capital Volume One*, published in 1867 (Marx, 1954). Marx's approach to understanding the dynamics of the employment relationship was rooted in his political economy and apprehended the fact that this relationship was necessarily a function of capitalism, which determined key facets of it. His insights into the nature of relations between managers and employees within capitalist production provided the foundations for contemporary LPT.

The significance of Marx's analysis for our understanding of ER lay in his argument that the employment relationship was necessarily shaped by the profit motive and that this made it one characterised by conflict. Put simply, Marx argued that the owners of the means of production (in practice, commonly their agents in the form of managers) had to extract surplus value from workers. That is, they must seek to 'squeeze' from workers labour of a higher value than they paid them for. This meant that the employment relationship was fundamentally exploitative. Moreover, it meant that the structurally determined role of managers was to find ways to wrest control of production from workers so that the latter expended the necessary effort to generate surplus value. Part Three of *Capital Volume One* sets out Marx's argument in full (Marx, 1954).

While Marx can be seen as the 'parent' of LPT, it is important to note that some scholars in this tradition have also been influenced by Max Weber's work. Like Marx, Weber recognised the control imperative in organisations and highlighted the role of bureaucratic structures as control mechanisms (Thompson and McHugh 2003, pp. 370–374). Nonetheless, it was Marx's work that most obviously laid the foundation for LPT.

Marxian LPT only really came to prominence a century after *Capital Volume One*, when Harry Braverman published *Labor and Monopoly Capital* (1974). Braverman's central thesis is well known, so it will be discussed fairly briefly here. It can be summarised as follows. In the advanced economies, the organisation of the labour process is shaped by capitalist social structures. The antagonistic relations between labour and capital, which arise because capital exploits labour to generate surplus value, mean that capital must find ways to control workers and maximise their labour output. Control is enacted primarily through the application of mechanised production and the application of the principles of Taylorism or Scientific Management (see Taylor, 1911).

The combination of technology and Taylorist management exerts control on workers by a process of deskilling. Workers are stripped of their discretion and skill, which are built into management and production systems, and the division of labour is increased. The result is that work is degraded, while managerial control is enhanced. Braverman had much more than this to say about occupational change and class structure, but for the purposes of this chapter the points above set out the key contributions.

Braverman's work is significant for a number of reasons. First, and most importantly, it brought Marx's labour process analysis to centre stage in sociological analyses of work and employment and presented a radical alternative to the utopianism of the work of contemporary scholars such as Daniel Bell (1973). Second, it is an exemplar of sociological analysis of work and employment. This is because Braverman located changes in the experience of work within a broader understanding of capitalism at a particular historical point, thus exemplifying the Millsian view of the role of sociological analysis. Third, prior to Braverman, the study of work and ER was fragmented and spread across different disciplines. *Labor and Monopoly Capital* sought to put forward an integrated and holistic account of the nature of work under capitalism (see Littler and Salaman, 1982). Finally, Braverman identified two themes that continue to be central to LPT: control and deskilling. While Braverman laid the foundations for the field by identifying some enduring features of the capitalist labour process, his work was subject to extensive critique and the field has shifted and become more complex and diverse over time.

Writing nearly 25 years ago, Brown observed that:

> Whilst Braverman's formulations remain important, and are likely to be referred to for some time to come, a very much more complex and less deterministic picture of the relations between capital and labour, and of industrial and employing organisations, emerges from the many and diverse contributions to this debate.
>
> *(Brown, 1992, p. 188)*

This statement remains true to this day, in the sense that while LPT has further developed since the time Brown was writing, nonetheless it continues to build on the work of Braverman. While Braverman's work has been subjected to numerous critiques – some of which will be considered below – there can be no doubt that his work was foundational. By arguing that the structures of capitalism shaped the experience of work and by suggesting that control was a necessary corollary of capitalist production, Braverman produced an insight that has profoundly shaped LPT. Moreover, his approach had clear implications for the study of ER. From a Bravermanian perspective, to understand the nature of the employment relationship and the institutions and practices around it, it was necessary to understand the relationship as being inherently a conflictual one, in which managers sought to control and exploit labour. Further, it was necessary to understand the employment relationship as embedded in social relations, which shaped both its character and the need for its regulation.

Subsequent developments in labour process theory

Labour process theory has continued to develop since Braverman's germinal work. The more important developments in this tradition can all be understood as originating in critiques of Braverman's work, which emerged in the late 1970s and 1980s. At the heart of the majority of these critiques is the argument that his analysis was too deterministic and presented too simple and uniform an account of the nature and dynamics of the employment relationship (see Brown, 1992, pp. 188–222). More specifically, there are three, partially overlapping, issues around which criticisms of Braverman's thesis can be organised. Each of these led to developments of this body of theory that strengthened it and made it better able to inform analysis of ER. Each is discussed in turn below.

The nature of the employment relationship

For Braverman, the employment relationship was inherently an antagonistic one, because it was exploitative and necessarily involved conflicting interests. Littler and Salaman (1982) argued that this was a fundamental flaw in Braverman's work. They suggested that, on the basis of his reading of Marx, Braverman simply assumed that this conflictual character was a necessary and enduring feature of the employment relationship (1982, p. 253). Others also challenged Braverman's view and argued that the employment relationship had a dualistic character. For example, Cressey and McInnes (1980) argued that employers required the co-operation of workers and needed to harness their creativity, while at the same time workers had an interest in the viability of enterprises that paid their wages. Thus, it increasingly became accepted that the relationship between capital and labour was not a purely conflictual one, but rather a contradictory relationship.

Perhaps the most useful and influential intervention in the debates around the nature of conflict was Paul Edwards' (1990) chapter 'Understanding Conflict in the Labour Process'. Edwards argued that it was not enough to knock down the 'straw man' of Braverman's overdeterministic account and simply to observe that the reality was a mixture of conflict and co-operation in which manager and workers reached accommodations with each other. Rather, it was necessary to specify in theoretical terms the precise nature of the relationship and to explain how it was played out in practice in the workplace. This led Edwards to characterise the employment relationship as one of 'structured antagonism'. He summarised his argument as follows:

> There is a basic conflict of interest (or, to use a more precise term…a structured antagonism) between capital and labour. This antagonism does not determine what happens at the level of day-to-day behaviour, but it exerts definite pressures. Workers and employers respond to these pressures and in doing so develop traditions and understandings that are used to interpret their relations.
>
> *(Edwards 1990, p. 126)*

The significance of Edwards' argument is that it recognised the fact that there was indeed a necessary conflict at the heart of the employment relationship, which co-existed with the potential for co-operation. This antagonism could not be removed, but it did not shape ER in a deterministic way. The specific character of ER was, to this extent, autonomous, which explained differences in ER that emerged in different times and places, in spite of the fact that all employment relationships are at heart antagonistic.

This understanding of the employment relationship has profound implications for understanding ER. It provides us with a way to make sense of the fact that while clearly the kind of 'win-win' outcomes espoused by unitarism are nonsensical, nonetheless there are occasions when mutual gains are possible. At the same time, this theorisation apprehends the fact that even at the most harmonious moments in the employment relationship, there remains an inherent conflict present. Further, this theorisation provides an understanding of the outcomes of the employment relationship as shaped by capitalist social relations, but not determined by them.

Structured antagonism in the employment relationship is now so widely accepted among labour process scholars that it constitutes one of the core assumptions underlying LPT (Thompson and Harley, 2007, p. 150). It has informed numerous studies, including recent ones that have investigated the ways in which managerial practices might simultaneously deliver benefits to managers and employees (e.g. Belanger and Edwards, 2007; Edwards, Belanger and Wright, 2006; Harley, Sargent and Allen, 2010).

Managerial control strategies

A second set of critiques concerned Braverman's focus on control. An early and influential example of this criticism can be found in Littler and Salaman's 'Bravermania and Beyond'

(1982). Echoing themes from their critique of the Bravermanian conception of the employment relationship, these authors accuse him, *inter alia*, of assuming that control of the labour process to extract surplus value is the *only* way for capitalists to generate profit, and ignoring other factors – taxation regimes or pricing, for example – which are likely to influence the performance of organisations. They argue that Braverman assumed, based on his "Marxist functionalism" (Littler and Salaman, 1982, p. 256), that the focus on control which characterised Taylorist production systems at a particular point in time was a necessary feature of all capitalist production.

This points to a second criticism of Braverman, which opened up very fruitful avenues for research and theorising by subsequent labour process scholars. This was the assumption that Taylorism was the dominant control mechanism. One line of criticism relates to deskilling. Braverman's deskilling thesis is a good corrective to the excessive optimism of 'post-industrial' and 'post-Fordist' scholars who predicted a generalised upskilling arising from technological change (see Wood, 1989). Nonetheless, it suffers from shortcomings that have limited its utility as an analytical tool. The most commonly identified limitation of the deskilling thesis is that it is based on a simple binary distinction between pre-industrial craft production – characterised by high levels of skill and autonomy and a unity of conception and execution – and deskilled industrial production. Numerous critics have argued that this is simplistic and overlooks the extent of variation in both pre-industrial and industrial eras, where patterns of work organisation and skill utilisation have varied a great deal (see Brown, 1992, p. 221).

Moreover, patterns of change in skills since Braverman's time suggest a much more varied set of changes than a simple trajectory towards deskilling (or upskilling, for that matter). For example, Thompson and Harley (2007) argue that recent research has highlighted a number of trends that confound Braverman's predictions, with employers often requiring a wider range of skills from employees, particularly 'soft' social skills, and work being intensified qualitatively rather than quantitatively by mobilising employees' problem-solving skills (Thompson and McHugh, 2003, pp. 362–364).

The second line of critique relates to control mechanisms being more broadly defined. Friedman's (1977) work was particularly significant here. He argued that there were at least two control strategies available to managers. The first was "direct control" of the kind discussed by Braverman, while the second was what he called "responsible autonomy". Put simply, he argued that in some settings, where workers had relatively high levels of power, they would resist direct control strategies, so a better way to harness their effort was to allow them a degree of discretion and responsibility as a means to gain loyalty. Further, he argued that both strategies might be used within the same organisation, for different groups of workers.

Others developed additional categorisations of control, notable among them being Richard Edwards' (1979) framework based on a historical study of control in US organisations. Edwards proposed three forms of control. Simple control was characteristic of small, often entrepreneurial, firms and involved managers interacting directly and personally with staff, supervising their work. In larger and more complex organisations, he argued, two systems could be identified: technical control involved the use of mechanised or computerised systems, with the Fordist assembly line being a good example; bureaucratic control arose in response to the limits of technical systems and the need for reward and disciplinary systems to control employees, and involved the use of policies and procedures to regulate behaviour.

This is not by any means a full account of the critiques of, and alternatives to, Braverman's account of control. These two examples, however, are illustrative of an important point. Post-Braverman LPT recognised that control was not the only preoccupation of managers and that Taylorism was but one of the many possible ways in which control of labour was enacted.

More recently, with the emergence of a strand of LPT informed by post-structuralism, scholars have described forms of control that focus on employee subjectivity (Willmott, 1993; Willmott and O'Doherty, 2009). Others, also influenced by poststructuralism, but simultaneously drawing on resources from Weber's work, highlight the role of norms and peer pressure in team-based work as control mechanisms (Barker, 1993; Sewell, 1998). It has also been recognised that control mechanisms can be combined into hybrid systems involving both 'soft' normative mechanism and 'hard' technical surveillance (Frenkel et al., 1995; Sewell, 1998).

Clearly control remains absolutely central to LPT. A defining feature of LPT is a recognition of the indeterminacy of labour, which leads to a need for control systems (Thompson and Harley, 2007). The research and theorising that has come after Braverman, however, has demonstrated very clearly that there are many possible control mechanisms, both 'hard' and 'soft', which are deployed by contemporary organisations. Moreover, we have witnessed new forms of control alongside old ones, as well as the extension of control into new spheres of work.

Employee responses

A persistent theme in LPT has been employee responses to control strategies, most notably employee resistance. Strangely, in spite of the amount of attention paid to employee resistance subsequently, Braverman's germinal work paid it scant attention. Brown observes:

> …Braverman largely discounted the question of the varying willingness and ability of workers to resist managerial control. Other writers, however, have given considerable attention to such considerations, and it is clear that in this respect Braverman's account is seriously deficient.
>
> *(Brown 1992, p. 206)*

This would seem to be a strange omission on Braverman's part, given his assumptions about the innately conflictual and exploitative nature of the employment relationship.

Later labour process scholars made resistance central to their accounts. Early contributors include Edwards (1979) and Friedman (1977). The possibility of resistance introduces a dynamic element into the employment relationship, in the sense that if employees resist control strategies, then it is likely that alternative control strategies will be introduced to counter this resistance. For example, Friedman proposed that responsible autonomy might be used in situations where direct control led to resistance. This would suggest that specific patterns of control and resistance are likely to develop within particular workplaces and industries through a dynamic interaction between control and resistance.

Post-Braverman LPT, however, has pointed to the fact that resistance is not the only worker response to control strategies. Burawoy's (1979) germinal work on consent is particularly noteworthy in this regard. Edwards (1986) and Edwards and Scullion (1982) pointed to the way in which patterns of control and employee responses varied widely, with all manner of accommodations being made on both sides, albeit within a relationship that inevitably had at least a partial conflictual character. The work done since Braverman has led to a widespread recognition that in fact "there is a continuum of possible, situationally driven, and overlapping worker responses to relations of ownership and control in the workplace – from resistance to accommodation, compliance and consent" (Thompson and Harley, 2007, p. 150).

Post-Braverman developments in theorisations of control and resistance have clear implications for our understanding of ER. They suggest firstly that while control mechanisms are likely to be pervasive features of workplace relations, there is likely to be variation in how control is enacted. Second, these developments suggest that many practices aimed at eliciting employee effort will not be simple or direct ones. Third, employee responses are likely to vary considerably, depending on the nature of control mechanisms as well as other workplace features. Overall, this suggests that in many settings a simple dynamic in which managers seek to exert control and workers resist, with attendant patterns of industrial conflict, is unlikely.

Sociology, gender and employment relations

Another chapter of this volume is devoted to gender and ER (see Hebson and Rubery, Chapter 7), so gender issues will not be discussed at length here. Nonetheless, a discussion of sociology and ER would be incomplete without some mention of gender. As noted earlier in this chapter, a significant strength of sociological approaches to work and employment is that they seek to explain the experiences of individuals and groups in workplaces with reference to the larger social structures in which they are embedded.

Feminist sociologists have contributed to our understanding of work and employment in important ways, notably concerning the way that gendered work and employment practices within workplaces both reflect and shape gendered social structures beyond the workplace (see Adkins, 1995; Game and Pringle, 1983; Walby, 1986; West 1990). The early 1980s appear to have been a very rich period for research by those informed explicitly by LPT, with numerous studies being produced that explored the different experiences of women and men at work as well as the mechanisms through which work was gendered (Ackroyd, 2014, p. 576). Sociological research informed by feminist theory has pointed to the fact that numerous factors, including wider social perceptions about what constitutes 'men's' and 'women's' jobs, informal interactions at work and the domestic division of labour, shape what happens at work.

The extent to which insights from the work of feminist sociologists has flowed through to the field of ER remains contested, however. Writing nearly 20 years ago, Jucy Wajcman observed that "[w]hile feminist scholarship has reshaped the social sciences, it has made surprisingly few inroads into the field of industrial relations – this despite the feminization of the paid labour force, one of the most important social changes in the twentieth century" (2000, p. 183). Her argument was that the focus of research in ER has remained on institutions, which are assumed to be gender neutral. When gender is considered, it is commonly in terms of 'women's issues' – for example pay equity – rather than reflecting a recognition that the entire world of work is gendered.

Since that time, numerous other scholars have made similar arguments about the limited extent to which feminist scholarship has reshaped ER. In the introductory editorial to a special issue of *Industrial Relations Journal* (2006), Healy and colleagues set out an overview of the promise, and the challenges, for feminism in reshaping ER. More recently, Ledwith (2012) argues that in spite of the influence of feminism in social science, ER remains gendered, both in terms of theory and practice, and in part this reflects the fact that female ER scholars and their work are still to an extent marginalised within the academy. It seems clear that sociology, particularly that which is informed by feminist theory, has much to offer the field of ER (Holgate et al., 2006). It seems equally clear, however, that the field has not yet fully accepted the offer.

The legacy of sociology in employment relations

Having discussed some of the key contributions of sociology to studies of work and employment, the final issue to be discussed in this chapter is what legacy sociology has left to the field of employment relations. Sociological analysis in the LPT tradition has made distinctive contributions, both methodological and theoretical (Thompson and Newsome, 2004).

First, critical sociologists in the labour process tradition have made a methodological contribution, in the form of a focus on the workplace level of analysis and the use of qualitative methods to explore processes and outcomes (Thompson and Newsome, 2004, p. 133). This is not to say that there have not been quantitative studies informed by sociological theorising (see for example: Harley, 1999; Harley, Sargent and Allen, 2010; Ramsay, Scholarios and Harley, 2000), but rather that sociologists demonstrated the value of qualitative studies as appropriate to understand important phenomena at a workplace level. In particular, they demonstrated the value of qualitative, often ethnographic, studies as a means to understand what goes on 'beneath the surface' of institutional ER. Of course, this focus was not invented by labour process scholars and indeed industrial sociology had a rather longer tradition of workplace studies, but nonetheless labour process scholars brought this approach to the centre of ER research (Thompson and Smith, 2009, p. 916).

Second, and turning to theoretical issues, the focus of data collection at the workplace level reflected the recognition that to understand the employment relationship and attendant phenomena, it was necessary to go beyond institutions and look at what was going on in individual workplaces. Moreover, labour process scholars brought issues of work organisation and technology into their accounts, again going beyond institutional rules and processes (Deery, Plowman and Walsh, 1997, p. 1.13).

Third, while focusing on workplace phenomena, labour process scholars recognised that these phenomena could only be understood by locating them in wider social structures, most obviously capitalism, but also patriarchal societies. In this sense, sociologists sought to develop a holistic theory of what happens in workplaces, embedded in social structures. This has particularly profound implications for the field of ER. Edwards' (1990) concept of structured antagonism provides a powerful tool for understanding patterns of conflict and accommodation within ER, without sliding into either the unitarist assumption that conflict can be removed from the employment relationship or the view that there can never be any shared interests between capital and labour.

Fourth, in seeing workplace phenomena as embedded in this way, post-Braverman LPT appreciates that social structures shape the nature and outcome of the employment relationship, but do not determine it. This characteristic of this body of theory allows it to apprehend different patterns of relations in different contexts, without abandoning the insight that capitalist social relations fundamentally shape them.

Conclusion

In taking stock of the influence of labour process theory, it would be fair to say that insights from this tradition are now widely accepted in employment relations scholarship. In spite of its profound and distinctive contributions, however, LPT has not displaced other disciplinary influences in the field of ER. Much ER scholarship still focuses on institutions and formal processes and much is informed by economics and law. Further, critical approaches in ER are seen by some as under attack due to the growing influence of mainstream organisational behaviour research, which is typically informed by social psychological theory and adopts a more managerialist orientation (Barry and Wilkinson, 2016; Godard, 2014; Harley, 2015).

Looking to the future, it seems unlikely that the imprint of sociology will disappear from the field of ER. It provides a lens that allows insights which simply are not accessible through other disciplines. Ultimately, however, the continued influence of labour process theory will depend on its ability to continue to evolve and to develop new insights that apprehend new developments, while simultaneously retaining its distinctive core.

References

Ackroyd, S. (2014). British Industrial Sociology and Organization Studies: a Distinctive Contribution, in Adler, P., du Gay, P., Morgan, G. and Reed, M. (eds.) *The Oxford Handbook of Sociology, Social Theory and Organization Studies*. Oxford: Oxford University Press.

Adkins, L. (1995). *Gendered Work*. Buckingham: Open University Press.

Barker, J. (1993). 'Tightening the Iron Cage: Concertive Control in Self-Managing Teams', *Administrative Science Quarterly*, 38(3), pp. 408–437.

Barry, M. and Wilkinson, A. (2016). 'Pro-Social or Pro-Management? A Critique of the Conception of Employee Voice as a Pro-Social Behaviour within Organizational Behaviour', *British Journal of Industrial Relations*, 54(2), pp. 261–284.

Belanger, J. and Edwards, P. (2007). 'The Conditions Promoting Compromise in the Workplace', *British Journal of Industrial Relations*, 45(4), pp. 713–734.

Bell, D. (1973). *The Coming of Post-Industrial Society: a Venture in Social Forecasting*, New York: Little, Brown.

Boyer, R. (1990). *The Regulation School: A Critical Introduction*. New York: Columbia University Press.

Braverman, H. (1974). *Labor and Monopoly Capital: The Degradation of Work in the Twentieth Century*. New York: Monthly Review Press.

Brown, R. (1992). *Understanding Industrial Organisations: Theoretical Perspectives in Industrial Sociology*. London: Routledge.

Burawoy, M. (1979). *Manufacturing Consent: Changes in the Labor Process Under Monopoly Capitalism*. Chicago: University of Chicago Press.

Burawoy, M. (2004). 'Public Sociologies: Contradictions, Dilemmas and Possibilities', *Social Forces*, 82(4), pp. 1603–1618.

Burawoy, M. (2008). 'The Public Turn: From Labor Process to Labor Movement', *Work and Occupations*, 35(4), pp. 371–387.

Cressey, P. and McInnes, J. (1980). 'Voting for Ford: Industrial Democracy and Control of Labour', *Capital and Class*, 11(2), pp. 5–33.

Crompton, R. (2009). *Class and Inequality*. 3rd edn. Cambridge (UK): Polity.

Cullinane, N. (2014). Institutions and the Industrial Relations Tradition, in Wilkinson, A., Wood, G. and Deeg, R. (eds.) *The Oxford Handbook of Employment Relations: Comparative Employment Systems*. Oxford: Oxford University Press, pp. 222–240.

Deery, S., Plowman, D. and Walsh, J. (1997). *Industrial Relations: A Contemporary Analysis*. Sydney: McGraw-Hill.

Edwards, R. (1979). *Contested Terrain*. New York: Basic Books.

Edwards, P. (1986). *Conflict at Work: A Materialist Analysis of Workplace Relations*. Oxford: Blackwell.

Edwards, P. (1990). Understanding Conflict in the Labour Process: The Logic and Autonomy of Struggle, in Knights, D. and Willmott, H. (eds.) *Labour Process Theory*. London: Macmillan.

Edwards, P. and Scullion, H. (1982). *The Social Organization of Industrial Conflict: Control and Resistance in the Workplace*. Oxford: Blackwell.

Edwards, P., Belanger, J. and Wright. M. (2006). 'The Bases of Compromise in the Workplace: a Theoretical Framework', *British Journal of Industrial Relations*, 44(1), pp. 125–145.

Frenkel, S., Korczynski, M., Donoghue, L. and Shire, K. (1995). 'Re-Constituting Work: Trends Towards Knowledge Work and Info-Normative Control', *Work, Employment & Society*, 9(4), pp. 773–796.

Friedman, A. (1977). 'Responsible autonomy versus direct control over the labour process', *Capital and Class*, 1(1), pp. 43–57.

Game, A. and Pringle, R. (1983). *Gender at Work*. Sydney: Allen and Unwin.

Godard, J. (2014). 'The Psychologisation of Employment Relations?', *Human Resource Management Journal*, 24(1), pp. 1–18.

Grint, K. (1998). *The Sociology of Work*. 2nd edn. Cambridge (UK): Polity.

Harley, B. (1999). 'The Myth of Empowerment: Work Organisation, Hierarchy and Employee Autonomy in Contemporary Australian Workplaces', *Work Employment & Society*, 13(1), pp. 41–66.

Harley, B. (2015). 'The One Best Way? 'Scientific' Research on HRM and the Threat to Critical Scholarship', *Human Resource Management Journal*, 25(4), pp. 399–407.

Harley, B., Sargent, L. and Allen, B. (2010). 'Employee Responses to 'High Performance Work Systems' Practices: an Empirical Test of the 'Disciplined Worker Thesis'', *Work, Employment & Society*, 24(4), pp. 740–760.

Healy, G., Hansen, L. and Ledwith, S. (2006). 'Editorial: Still Uncovering Gender in Industrial Relations', *Industrial Relations Journal*, 37(4), pp. 290–298.

Holgate, J., Hebson, G. and McBride, A. (2006). 'Why gender and 'difference' matters: a critical appraisal of industrial relations research', *Industrial Relations Journal*, 37(4), pp. 310–328.

Hyman, R. (1975). *Industrial Relations: A Marxist Introduction*. London: Palgrave.

Kaufman, B. (2004). *The Origins and Evolution of the Field of Industrial Relations in the United States*. Ithaca: ILR Press.

Ledwith, S. (2012). 'Outside, Inside: Gender Work in Industrial Relations', *Equality, Diversity and Inclusion: An International Journal*, 31(4), pp. 340–358.

Littler, C. and Salaman, G. (1982). 'Bravermania and Beyond: Recent Theories of the Labour Process', *Sociology*, 16(2), pp. 251–269.

Marx, K. (1954). *Capital: Volume One*. Moscow: Progress Publishers.

Mills, C. (1959). *The Sociological Imagination*. New York: Oxford University Press.

Müller-Jentsch, W. (2004). Theoretical Approaches to Industrial Relations, in Kaufman, B. (ed.) *Theoretical Perspectives on Work and the Employment Relationship*. Ithaca: ILR Press, pp. 1–40.

Ramsay, H., Scholarios, D. and Harley, B. (2000). 'Employees and High Performance Work Systems: Testing Inside the Black Box', *British Journal of Industrial Relations*, 38(4), pp. 501–531.

Sewell, G. (1998). 'The Discipline of Teams: the Control of Team-Based Industrial Work Through Electronic and Peer Surveillance', *Administrative Science Quarterly*, 43(2), pp. 397–428.

Sica, A. (2011). A Selective History of Sociology, in Ritzer, G. (ed.) *The Wiley-Blackwell Companion to Sociology*. Hoboken: Wiley, pp. 25–54.

Smith, C. (2015). Rediscovery of the Labour Process, in Edgell, S., Gottfried, H. and Granter, E. (eds.) *The SAGE Handbook of the Sociology of Work and Employment*. London: Sage.

Taylor, F. (1911). *The Principles of Scientific Management*. New York: Harper and Brothers.

Thompson, P. and McHugh, D. (2003). *Work Organisations: A Critical Introduction*. 3rd edn. London: Palgrave.

Thompson, P. and Newsome, K. (2004). Labour process theory, work and the employment relationship, in Kaufman, B. (ed.) *Theoretical Perspectives on Work and the Employment Relationship*. Ithaca: Cornell University Press.

Thompson, P. and Harley, B. (2007). HRM and the Worker: Labour Process Perspectives, in Boxall, P., Purcell, J. and Wright, P. (eds). *The Oxford Handbook of HRM*. Oxford: Oxford University Press.

Thompson, P. and Smith, C. (2009). 'Labour Power and the Labour Process: Contesting the Marginality of the Sociology of Work', *Sociology*, 43(5), pp. 913–930.

Vallas, S. (2011). Work and Employment, in Ritzer, G. (ed.) *The Wiley-Blackwell Companion to Sociology*. Hoboken: Wiley, pp. 418–443.

Vidal, M. and Hauptmeier, M. (2014). Comparative Political Economy and Labour Process Theory: Towards a Synthesis, in Hauptmeier, M. and Vidal, M. (eds.) *Comparative Political Economy of Work*. London: Palgrave.

Wajcman, J. (2000). 'Feminism Facing Industrial Relations in Britain', *British Journal of Industrial Relations*, 38(2), pp. 183–201.

Walby, S. (1986). *Patriarchy at Work*. Cambridge (UK): Polity.

Watson, T. (2009). 'Work and the Sociological Imagination: The Need for Continuity and Change in the Study of Continuity and Change', *Sociology*, 43(5), pp. 861–877.

Watson, T. and Korczynski, M. (2011). *Sociology, Work and Organisation*. 6th edn. London: Routledge.

West, J. (1990). Gender and the Labour Process: A Reassessment, in Knights, D. and Willmott, H. (eds.) *Labour Process Theory*. London: Macmillan.

Willmott, H. (1993). 'Strength is ignorance; slavery is freedom: managing culture in modern organisations', *Journal of Management Studies*, 30(4), pp. 515–552.

Willmott, H. and O'Doherty, D. (2009). 'The decline of labour process analysis and the future sociology of work', *Sociology*, 43(5), pp. 931–951.

Wood, S. (1989). The Transformation of Work?, in Wood, S. (ed.) *The Transformation of Work?* London: Unwin Hyman.

7

EMPLOYMENT RELATIONS AND GENDER EQUALITY

Gail Hebson and Jill Rubery

Introduction

Gender equality has increasingly become a central theme of employment relations (ER) research. This is in itself an achievement. In 1995 one of the current authors pointed to the complete absence of any reference to women or female in the indexes of core industrial relations textbooks (Rubery and Fagan, 1995). The now commonplace inclusion of gender equality within ER research and teaching reflects a number of developments, including, of course, the rising number of women both in employment and as a share of trade union members. Growing female trade union membership has partially compensated for declining male membership and women now account for around 44 per cent of Europe's trade union members (ETUC, 2014). Gender equality has also emerged as a core theme and objective of trade union activity, particularly in the public sector, although this varies across countries. In France equality bargaining is now mandatory (Gregory and Milner, 2009) and UK trade unions have used European Union (EU) law to establish or defend employment rights, with many of the key legal cases related to women's equality rights. Finally, but by no means least, important scholarship has contributed to the understanding of gender within ER and the wider issue of work and employment. This scholarship includes contributions that have primarily critiqued the lack of a gender lens, both in industrial relations (Rubery and Fagan, 1995; Wajcman, 2000) and human resource management (Dickens, 1998), alongside contributions that focus on how women and their interests are being represented within trade unions and collective bargaining, through direct organisation and representation of women (Briskin, 1999; Colgan and Ledwith, 2002; Kirton, 2015) or more indirectly through organising on the margins or among non-standard employees (Heery and Conley, 2007).

Notwithstanding the importance of these specific contributions, our purpose here is somewhat different again and that is to map the impact of the development of a gender lens on ER on the fundamentals of the discipline or subject itself. Our contention is that a gender lens has led to major changes in ER as a subject area or discipline. Four key impacts are identified. First, a gender lens has expanded the scope of ER as a subject area; the tradition of embedding workplace ER within product market, political and education and training institutions has been extended to the family, welfare and gender institutional arrangements. Second, the integration of a gender dimension has extended the traditional class-based focus on inequality and thereby promoted, we argue, a multilayered and intersectional perspective on inequalities that can be extended beyond gender to include other dimensions such as ethnicity or age. Third, a gender lens has challenged customary pay hierarchies and working time arrangements but has also revealed the problems of developing new, more inclusive arrangements without ceding new areas of control to employers. Fourth, research with a gender focus has revealed not only gender differences in experience of work but also how work itself involves 'doing gender'.

Beyond employment: embedding employment in the family and welfare system

The core contribution of a feminist approach to employment relations is to put the social reproduction system centre stage alongside the production system and to make unpaid work visible alongside paid work. Nancy Fraser in her 1994 article calling for a universal caregiver approach to social organisation identified three different scenarios for the organisation of both production and care work that could promote greater gender equality beyond the male breadwinner model. The first is the universal breadwinner model in which both men and women engage full-time in wage work and care is provided through paid labour services. This, she argues, would either result in a care deficit, as not all care can be provided by services, or in only a partial assimilation of women into the breadwinner role. Women would still take more responsibility for care (or employers would assume they still had ultimate responsibility) and would therefore remain in subordinate positions in wage work. The second scenario, the caregiver parity model, explicitly assumes women would continue with their specialisation in care but their work would be higher valued and directly rewarded (for example through a basic income). However, the outcome would be a highly gender segmented labour market. The third scenario, the universal caregiver model, would dissolve boundaries between care work and wage work and ultimately between genders, as both men and women participate equally in both work forms. This last model requires a completely new approach to the management and organisation of wage labour, with care needs driving the capitalist economy as, following Polanyi's vision, the economy is re-embedded within society and its needs rather than vice versa. These scenarios emerge from a feminist perspective that rejects the normal taken-for-granted assumptions of the dominance of the capitalist production and wage work model. This is also a core flaw in the exposition (Rubery, 2015) as there is no theorisation as to how or why the capitalist system of work organisation would give way to a change in the gender regime. Social progress towards gender equality may thus require simultaneous policy developments on both the organisation of wage and care work. Nevertheless, the imagining of a new world order driven by care needs puts in question the notion that there is only one way to organise production relations and that production relations should dominate societal needs.

Feminist perspectives on the importance of the social reproduction systems in shaping the employment regime have also served to complement and refocus the debates on the impact of welfare systems on shaping both labour supply and employment, sparked by Esping-Andersen's (1990) analysis of the three worlds of welfare capitalism. At an early stage in the comparative welfare state debates, feminists such as Orloff (1993), Lewis (1992) and Sainsbury (1996), pointed out decommodification by the state, at the core of Esping-Andersen's analysis, only applied if labour was first commodified, that is participated in the wage economy, while many women remained in practice excluded from wage employment. Orloff argued for extending state-market relations to state-market-family relations, Sainsbury pointed to differences among states in treating women primarily as wives, mothers or workers and Lewis proposed a classification of welfare states according to support for a male breadwinner model. In the Nordic weak male breadwinner model women were more fully integrated into the wage labour market on a continuing basis, supported by leave entitlements and high benefits that reduced dependency on male partners. The outcome was not only an adult worker model where everyone was a breadwinner but also a labour market with a high share of public sector jobs as public services replaced some domestic unpaid labour. Wages in the Nordic systems could also be compressed around a high minimum level, in part because state support, in the form of generous paid leave and subsidised childcare, reduced reliance on male wages to cover wives and children's reproduction costs. In contrast the German strong male breadwinner model reinforced the notion of male breadwinner wages as women were treated primarily as dependants and disincentivised from working as the tax system supported wives who stayed at home or worked in marginal part-time jobs, called mini jobs, exempt from taxation. Just these two country examples illustrate how wage systems, employment contracts and sectoral divisions between public and private sectors, all topics at the heart of ER, cannot be understood without this expanded social reproduction lens. These interrelationships underline why bargaining over gender equality and issues such as childcare or parental leave are not matters for 'special interest groups' (even if in this case the group is half the population), but also address the major issues of labour market organisation.

Furthermore, while debates on varieties of welfare states and employment systems focused on political origins and development paths, feminist contributions related historical patterns of women's inclusion or exclusion from wage employment to current diversities in employment arrangements. Pfau-Effinger's (1998) comparative work on Finland, the Netherlands and Germany thus sought to explain, *inter alia*, the tendency for women to work full-time in Finland by the continuity of women's involvement in wage activities in Finland, from agriculture to industrial and service employment. In contrast women's involvement in part-time work in the other two countries reflected its use as a mechanism to draw women back into wage employment from housewife status. Likewise the high full-time employment rate of women in Portugal is not accounted for by its welfare and family systems but by the mobilisation of women to replace men – in employment and in family budgets – who left Portugal either on military activities or as guest workers (Távora, 2012). These different historical contexts illuminate the very marked differences in shares of part-time work among women across European countries and suggest that women's demand for part-time versus full-time work is linked to their history of integration into or exclusion from the wage labour market. Although this work remains largely focused on OECD (Organisation for Economic Co-operation and Development) countries, it has been applied to developing countries. For example, Abu Sharkh and Gough (2009) have extended the advanced country welfare regime typologies by adding two types of family regimes in developing countries, distinguishing between informal security regimes reliant on community and family systems and insecurity regimes where even stable informal systems are lacking. Where there are informal family and community-based security systems women's integration into market work will be more conditioned by that family and community system, but in insecurity systems women's relationship to market work may be more individualised.

The interactions between labour demand and women's labour supply have also been considered through the application of Marx's notion of women as a reserve army of labour. This approach assumes both that women's labour can be mobilised in times of high demand and expelled at times of low demand, and that its availability as an alternative cheap labour supply poses a potential threat to labour standards (Karamessini and Rubery, 2013; Rubery, 1988). This was the fear of trade unions after the two world wars and in part explains women's subsequent exclusion from the jobs into which they were mobilised. The extent and form of women's role as a reserve army of labour, however, is context- and time-specific and shaped by patterns of gender segregation. Thus, although women may provide a flexible buffer of employment in some contexts and sectors, gender segregation reduces the likelihood that women would provide a flexible buffer across all segments and they may even be found in protected segments, less affected by the downturn in demand. The balance between these two effects varies as is illustrated by changes in the effects of the recessions of the 1970s and 1980s and the 2008 economic crisis and subsequent austerity. Women in many European countries had become more integrated permanently into employment and in the latter recession the buffer role was taken on primarily by migrants and the young. Contrary to a simple reserve army hypothesis, integration eventually becomes effectively non-reversible as the experience of integration changes not only women's aspirations but also consumption patterns, reducing the scope for domestic labour to be an alternative to wages in family budgets, such that integration eventually becomes effectively non-reversible (Humphries and Rubery, 1984). Furthermore, while public sector work, which is dominated by women, protected women's employment in the earlier downturns and in the immediate period after the 2008 crisis, under austerity it was public sector employment that became vulnerable to displacement or downgrading of pay and conditions.

A third role that women may play is as a cheap labour substitute for male labour. Reskin and Roos (1990) identified a range of sectors or occupations that in the United States moved rapidly from being male- to female-dominated under the influence of both changes in technology, service or product delivery systems and the upgrading of women's qualifications. In the process occupations became downgraded or subdivided, with women concentrated in the bottom rungs. Substitution is easier in the upturn when jobs are expanding even though downturns may incentivise substitution to reduce costs. Beyond these employment effects there is also the impact of women's concentration in particular forms of work – such as part-time work – which can have an impact on overall conditions in the labour market. A particular example is the provision of additional payments for working evenings or weekends. In the UK these premiums in trades such as retail were first of all eroded through the deployment of part-time workers who were excluded from such premiums. Eventually this led to premiums for many full-time staff being reduced or cancelled on the grounds that they were no longer 'competitive' with part-time staff (Rubery, 1998). The formation of part-time and effectively women-dominated service sectors – for example in cleaning and catering – has also been used as a means of reducing total labour costs.

These examples suggest that it is through the concentration of female labour in specific employment forms that women's employment can be used as a vehicle to exercise downward competitive pressure on employment standards (ibid.). This is, therefore, less likely to occur where women are fully integrated into wage work, have rights to retain their employment positions over periods of childbirth through extended paid leave, and where comprehensive collective bargaining and/or employment rights reduce the scope for undercutting employment standards. Thus the development of more inclusive and regulated labour markets may be beneficial for both men and women and from both an ER and gender equality perspective. These commonalities of interests need to be recognised by both feminists and ER actors. Nancy Fraser has posited that feminists may have inadvertently fuelled the new spirit of neoliberalism, by arguing against 'restrictive practices' in reproducing the male breadwinner model. However, it is the case that trade unions have often been slow to pursue more inclusive and progressive policies that promote the interests of women alongside those of men, such that, for example, recent research on wages has revealed the continuing favouring of male wages in countries such as Germany through collective agreements (Schäfer and Gottschall, 2015). It is to these problems of how to address more than one dimension of inequality – that is both class and gender – through the institutions and practices of ER that we now turn.

Beyond class inequalities: addressing multiple inequalities and intersectionality

Introducing a gender lens challenges the traditional employment relations focus on class-based identities and interests. However, far from undermining ER we argue that a feminist perspective has been pivotal to the renewal and revitalisation agenda of the trade union movement and the discipline as a whole. By applying a gendered lens to analyse the changing institutions and practices of ER it is possible to see the interaction between the need to attract and represent women members to the trade union movement and a deeper engagement with feminist theorising relating to democracy, representation and intersectionality.

The conflict between the increasing female membership in trade unions and the under-representation of women's interests has led to a plethora of studies on gender democracy in the union movement. A burgeoning literature on different conceptualisations of democracy and which forms are more inclusive draws on the political theory of Iris Marion Young (2000) and her distinction between aggregate and deliberative democracy and between democratic outcomes and democratic processes. For Young aggregate democracy, under which democrat-ically elected representatives are assumed to deliver fair outcomes for all, will fail to include the interests of marginalised groups if they remain absent in decision-making processes. The aggregate approach, akin to the traditional representative democracy approach, provides few ways for a minority to influence decision-making beyond being able to cast a vote (Kirton, 2015, p. 487). In contrast a deliberative model of democracy involves marginalised groups in decision-making processes and structures and offers the most potential to include marginalised groups' perspectives and interests (Young, 2000, p. 35). This has informed the many feminist scholars' critiques of the union focus on gender proportionality, which assumed an increase in women's membership and representation would increase the representation of their interests (see McBride's analysis of UNISON, 2001). Kirton (2015) argues that participatory democracy is consequently now widely accepted as the 'ideal' in the UK union movement, as is reflected in gender equality strategies such as women's committees, networks and conferences that widen opportunities for women's participation in decision-making. Briskin's (1999) work has shown the need for a balance between autonomy and integration if these types of structures are to be effective; that is, the strong voice that separate structures can give needs to be integrated into the decision-making structures of unions to guarantee marginalised voices gain access to organisational decision-making. Healy and Kirton's (2000) research on the UK Manufacturing, Science and Finance Union (now part of Unite) highlights the possibilities and tensions that separate structures generate as actors seek to achieve the fine balance between integration and maintaining autonomy. Significantly these debates have provided a framework for how to the-orise and assess the integration of other marginalised groups in the trade union movement (see Marino, 2015 on the inclusion of migrant workers).

However, the pursuit of gender democracy in unions via separate structures appears to be changing. Using SERTUC data over a 25-year period, Kirton argues that the union democracy project is changing, with increased activity on other equality strands and resources being focused on integrated equality structures and strategies, noting "action on women seemed to be standing still" (Kirton, 2015, p. 502). While this is itself problematic as despite a narrowing pro-portionality gap women are still under-represented in union structures, she recognises that the integrated equalities approach extends capacity to respond to multiple and intersecting iden-tities (op cit, p. 502). Indeed, the inability of separate structures to capture intersecting identities constitutes a major flaw that can serve to perpetuate existing inequalities, as research revealed white middle-class women tended to dominate women's groups and black men tended to dominate black groups (Healy et al., 2004). This shift may be both a response to resource issues and a reflection of a growing feminist preoccupation with intersectionality that is now shaping both the subject discipline and the practices of trade unions. It remains to be seen whether such a shift to generic equalities approaches will be able to reflect and integrate the interests of those with multiple identities.

While debates around intersectionality have had less influence on ER research compared with other disciplines (McBride et al., 2015), its influence is strongly evident in the debates on gender and trade unions. Originating in the black feminist critique of white feminism, intersectionality was a term originally used by Crenshaw (1991) to capture the distinct oppression of black women who experienced the inequalities of both gender and 'race'. This led the way to an 'intersectionally sensitive' approach in feminist theorising that cautioned against treating women as a homogenous group, recognised women's heterogeneous and different interests and considered key strands of inequality relating to gender, ethnicity, nationality, age, disability, sexuality, religion, class and migration all to be legitimate areas of study. That said, there remains much debate over what is intersecting, and how they intersect.

Indeed the additive approach, which is inherent in some descriptions of "double disadvantage" and "multiple burdens"(Bradley, 2007), has been critiqued on the grounds that multiple inequalities do not simply mean 'more' or 'worse' inequality but may actually change the nature of how each inequality is experienced (Walby, Armstrong and Strid, 2012). A key problem of 'doing intersectionality' (Healy et al., 2011) is deciding which aspect of inequality to prioritise (Durbin and Conley, 2010) and which to leave out. Durbin and Conley highlight how prioritising one strand over others is hard to avoid and show how some theorists openly prioritise one form of inequality over another (for example they highlight Acker's (2006) prioritisation of class in her inequality regimes approach while Collins (2000) prioritises race). This issue of prioritisation is particularly pertinent in the ER context, where class has been openly pursued as the most important strand of inequality to address in both research and practice. Feminist scholars and women trade unionists are introducing competing priorities but research shows these need not always be contentious. Healy and Kirton (2000), in their comparison of US and UK women union leaders, found that while their class union identity was prioritised, gender and class identities could coexist. Durbin and Conley's (2010) realistic appraisal that "perhaps intersectionality is not the panacea some thought it might be but it does represent a key departure from analyses solely based on gender or class" (p. 198) is particularly relevant for ER. A gender lens influenced by 'intersectional sensitivity' has paved the way for research on multiple dimensions of inequality and included groups previously marginalised in ER research and institutions. This can be seen clearly in research focused on ethnicity and ethnic women's union participation, which shows how community activism can shape union activism and how family life and religious obligations are central to the working lives of both ethnic minority men and women (Kirton, 2010). Intersectionality has also provided a way to explore social divisions across the life course as age inequalities intersect with other inequalities to shape employment opportunities (Moore, 2009). The recognition of these intersections has come from a gendered lens and goes beyond Wacjman's (2000) call for an analysis of the gendered character of work and institutions for both men and women. Now, it is often the intersections with other forms of inequalities that shape how ER scholars use a gender lens to analyse gendered work and institutions. Yet in other regards ER as a discipline has failed to make progress, particularly in relation to how a gendered analysis is useful for its study of men. Wacjman noted that "it is women who are marked as 'gendered', the ones who are different" (p. 184) and Briskin (2006) also notes men remain "ungendered" in ER. We will discuss this in more detail in the last section, which looks at the informal and cultural ways women and men 'do' gender.

Beyond structures and practice: gender and the organisation and valuation of work

Employment relations actors, particularly trade unions, tend to have an ambiguous attitude towards traditional systems of valuing and organising work. On the one hand the very existence of trade unions and collective bargaining suggests that these issues cannot be simply left to the market or to managerial discretion. Yet at the same time much collective activity is aimed at preserving and defending existing pay differentials and forms of work organisation and hierarchy, in part because defending institutionalised arrangements provides some protection against arbitrary managerial decisions, often cloaked in the legitimacy of the market. The development of a gender lens through which to scrutinise customary arrangements has, we will argue, revitalised critiques of the existing order and reinforced awareness of the social construction of customary arrangements. Yet at the same time, as we explore, by adopting a gender lens to challenge and open up ways of organising and valuing work, there is the danger that employers may use the opportunity to legitimise change that is to the overall detriment of workers.

As we have argued above, pursuing both gender and class interests may raise challenges but may also extend and renew collective organisation. Examples of such renewal can be found in the organisation of domestic workers in countries as diverse as the United States and Uruguay, which is among an almost exclusively female group that has often been excluded from employment rights altogether (UN, 2015). We explore these issues with respect to both the valuation of women's work and working time organisation and the challenges posed by the apparent adoption of work-life balance policies.

One of the main causes of the gender pay gap is the tendency to undervalue women's work (Grimshaw and Rubery, 2007). This may occur within a workplace, and provided there is a male comparator working in a similar job or in work that can be considered to be of equal value, it can in principle be remedied through equal pay legislation. However, there are many other ways in which women's work may be undervalued that are not susceptible to remedy through the core equal pay legislation. Even within a workplace there is nothing in European law to say that pay should be proportional to its value, so provided men's work is shown to be at least slightly higher in value it can be paid much more than work done by women. Much of the undervaluation of women's work is associated with gender segregation, such that women may be employed in female-dominated areas where the few men employed may either be paid the same low rates as women or have managerial posts. These types of female-dominated work include employment forms such as part-time work, occupations such as care assistants or teachers, firms such as specialist cleaning or catering companies used for outsourcing or whole sectors such as retail or social care.

Five factors – the five Vs – can be identified as being used to legitimise or drive undervaluation (Grimshaw and Rubery, 2007). The first V is visibility; many of women's skills are not made visible in either pay structures or occupational and skill classifications. Men's occupations are classified and rewarded according to much more fine-grained divisions between type and degree of skill compared with much of women's work, which tends to be aggregated together, for example in clerical, retail or care work. The next V is valuation, such that even where women's skills are made visible, the reward for those skills may be low. The lack of career ladders in social care has, for example, recently been highlighted by a UK parliamentary committee. In our own research senior care workers were usually paid less than £1 an hour more than standard care workers on close to the minimum wage. The third V is vocation; this notion is used to legitimise low pay on the grounds that women derive so much satisfaction from their work that there is no need to pay them more than a minimum rate (Hebson et al., 2015). This approach takes an essentialist position on gender differences in orientations and regards women as inherently more altruistic than men. A fourth V is value-added; this term refers to the tendency for women to be under-represented in sectors with high value added, where the cost of labour is a relatively low proportion of all costs and where employers have more discretion to pay higher wages without this damaging competitiveness. In other words, women lose out in the distribution of economic rents. Finally the fifth V is variance; this highlights the tendency for women to be paid less simply because they are not able to fit in with the male breadwinner norms such as long working hours. Part-time workers are paid less not because they are less productive per hour but because they are expected to pay a penalty for working in a different way from the standard. Moreover, many part-timers have to negotiate specific arrangements with their employers and as a consequence have limited bargaining power.

These tendencies towards undervaluation are not just historical legacies but can reappear in many formats. For example, the apparent high job satisfaction among social care assistants in the UK is used to suggest that the outsourcing of social care work and subsequent decline in pay for these staff is not a problem, even though shortages of social care staff persist (Hebson et al., 2015). Likewise where women have entered previously male-dominated occupations, there is evidence from the United States that these jobs tend to move down the pay hierarchy (Mandel, 2013; Reskin and Roos, 1990) or develop more pronounced subdivisions with women largely confined to the lower rungs of a profession – for example in banking as retail, not corporate, bankers (Crompton and Sanderson, 1990) or as salaried lawyers, not partners in the firm (Bolton and Muzio, 2007).

This recognition of undervaluation has led to various policy responses from both governments and trade unions and employers. Much hope was originally placed in both Europe and the USA on the effectiveness of analytical job evaluation for addressing problems of undervaluation. These expectations of progress have not been fully realised for a large number of reasons (Rubery and Grimshaw, 2015), including the limited adoption of analytical job evaluation, its limited effects due to the need to apply it company by company, particularly when some companies have only a narrow range of jobs, the trends away from job-based to performance-related pay and the problems that the implementation of new pay systems can pose for ER. This is exemplified in Acker's (1989) study of the implementation of comparable worth in Oregon, where management went along with the plan but with motivations other than gender equality in mind.

> …comparable worth presented the possibility to management to strengthen its power over the labor unions in wage setting … If management controls the job evaluation process, unions have even less influence. … The feminist proposal to eliminate gender inequity exacerbated class conflict threatening to place feminists on the side of management, even though the most broad-based support for comparable worth outside the women's movement came from organised labor.
>
> *(Acker, 1989, p. 202)*

Despite these disappointments and the increasing recognition that wage setting is a political process that prevents job evaluation offering a simple technical solution (Figart et al., 2002), there are some positive outcomes, particularly in the public sector where because of the scale of the employer the impacts can be greater on women's pay. In the UK the opportunity to use European Union gender equality law to promote new pay systems in the public sector provided public sector trade unions with a new rationale that helped sustain public sector unionism. However, the longer-term impacts have been less favourable, in part because of disputes over how far trade unions prioritised protecting men's pay against downgrading versus maximising women's access to pay arrears for underpayment (Deakin et al., 2015). It is also the case that some improvements to women's pay have been circumvented, first by outsourcing and more recently by centralised wage freezes and caps on pay below inflation. Recently the focus of campaigns for gender equality at the workplace has moved from comparable worth or equal pay for work of equal value towards more general gender pay audits. These are found to be more likely to have positive effects when trade unions have a role in scrutinising the audits and in developing action plans, as for example in Quebec (Chicha, 2006).

A gender lens is also challenging traditional systems of working time organisation. Without the integration of women en masse into employment the current concern and debate about work-life balance and flexible working times is unlikely to have developed, or not to the same extent. The assumption that work should be undertaken on a full-time continuous basis has clearly acted to exclude women from the labour market, and the current greater diversity of working time arrangements may be reducing exclusion but not without dangers and downsides, both for women and for employment standards more generally. These include first the fact that regular hours may be more helpful than part-time hours for organising work and family commitments, and in some countries women tend to favour regular full-time work over part-time work (Távoro, 2012), which they associate with irregular hours and poor working conditions. Where full-time hours are also irregular and long and childcare services inadequate or expensive, part-time hours may be the only viable option. The best arrangements tend to be found where there are opportunities to work flexibly – including on reduced hours – in a job previously held as a full-time job or in jobs where all workers are enabled to work flexibly, for example through compressed work weeks or combining working at home with office-based work to reduce commuting time. In contrast jobs designed as part-time jobs may often be low paid and lacking in career paths (Fagan et al., 2012). Another problem is that the move towards diversity may allow employers to use working time to increase productivity through the cutting out of less productive hours (Supiot, 2001), when for example customer demand is low, thereby raising work intensity and creating more uncertainty and irregularity in shift patterns, including split shifts or fragmented work arrangements. However, all these forms of work tend to be labelled flexible working and presented as if beneficial for employees even when some are driven by employer interest only (Rubery et al., 2015). Fleetwood (2007) has in fact argued that the current concern with work-life balance provides a smokescreen for the trend towards less family- or life-friendly working hours. Limited accommodation of employee preferences is occurring alongside a general trend towards more employer-driven and family-unfriendly working times.

What both these examples suggest is that there is a need to interrogate the impact of new practices, even those apparently adopted under gender equality objectives, and to make new policies as inclusive and comprehensive as possible to reduce opportunities for evasion. For example, it may be desirable to extend equal pay comparisons along the supply chain to guard against equal pay policies incentivising employers to seek new forms of low-cost outsourcing both at home and abroad. Likewise work-life balance policies need to address the overall pattern of working times in the workplace, for only if all employees have rights to working arrangements compatible with family life and care responsibilities is it likely that gender equality can be achieved. Otherwise work-life balance policies may simply reinforce traditional gender divisions of labour over care responsibilities.

Beyond the gender neutral work experience: new understandings of work and work behaviours

In this final section we show how a gender lens has opened up new research agendas that recognise the more informal ways women and men 'do gender' in the workplace, that is "how gender is created in the situation rather than existing *a priori*" (Nentwich and Kelan, 2014, p.122). In particular, concepts of femininities, masculinities, sexualities and embodiment have become pivotal areas of gender research, where gender is theorised as a 'social practice' that conceptualises "gender identity as an ongoing activity or a 'doing' within everyday life" (op cit, p. 123). Early examples of studies of male-dominated sectors such as printing by Cockburn (1985) showed this in practice; by performing technical jobs in printing male workers were also 'doing gender' and therefore they felt emasculated when their technical skills were no longer needed due to technological change. Pringle's (1989) research on secretaries showed how traditional notions of femininity were central to how the job was structured and how women enjoyed and performed this part of the job again showing how, as Nentwich and Kelan (2014) describe, "individuals doing a job are doing gender at the same time" (op cit, p. 126). These issues do not only apply to women, and studies of how men 'do gender' (Norman et al., 2014) have revealed how men are also constrained by constructions of masculinity: for example, fathers, while valued as employees, felt "invisible at work in their paternal role" (Burnett et al., 2013, p. 632). Furthermore men working in female-dominated non-traditional occupations have been found to "both do and undo masculinity and femininity – supporting and subverting the status quo – as they seek security and legitimacy within their non-traditional role" (Pullen and Simpson, 2009, p. 581). Regardless of whether women and men were attached to these concepts, what became clear in these workplace studies was that these cultural ideas of what constitutes femininity and masculinity, linked with the sexualisation of women, were key ways power relations were being perpetuated in the workplace.

This was particularly the case for women working in male-dominated workplaces, where narrow definitions of femininity kept women in their place as the 'other'. McDowell's (1997) study of women in corporate banking showed how women had to be careful not to be too feminine or too sexual in their dress, while also being careful not to be too masculine. McDowell argued men and women "'do' gender in the workplace" (1997, p. 133) by dressing and behaving in ways that either confirm or transgress acceptable forms of femininity and masculinity. While such studies showed a focus on women's appearance and dress at the informal level of the workplace, the more recent studies of aesthetic labour, which have been informed by an ER and labour process tradition (Warhurst and Nickson, 2007), show how 'doing' gender in this way has become part of the requirement of many service sector jobs in a more overt way. For example, Williams and Connell (2010) found that management in retail legitimised discriminatory hiring practices that entrenched gender, race and class stereotypes of how women should dress and look by appealing to customer expectations. They found that in retail "the right aesthetic is middle class, conventionally gendered and typically white" (Williams and Connell, 2010, p. 350) and thus aesthetic labour criteria often built on gendered stereotypes that intersect with other dimensions of inequality to reinforce job segregation, race and gender discrimination.

Such research puts the customer as an important part of the analysis of ER when adopting a gender lens. This is particularly the case when charting how sexuality and sexual harassment have been theorised in gender research. Collinson and Collinson's (1989) classic study of shopfloor culture showed how sexual banter was part of the way men bonded at work, and even when men were uncomfortable with this it was difficult to challenge. Many studies have shown how such sexualised 'banter' can promote high levels of sexual harassment (Hearn and

Parkin, 2001). Studies continue to show that women managers and women in male-dominated sectors are particularly vulnerable to this from male colleagues (McLaughlin et al., 2012). Studies of the hospitality sector also show the ways women are at risk from male customers, as they are expected to put up with abusive and sexual behaviour in the name of customer service (Guerrier and Adib, 2000), and research has shown how customers' sexualised stereotypes of particular ethnicities (Kang, 2013) are central to ethnic minority women's experiences of work.

A sexualised workplace is based on a norm of heterosexuality, which also has implications for lesbian, gay and bisexual (LGB) people at work. In research carried out with LGB workers, Colgan et al. (2007) found that one in five LGB respondents experienced discrimination on the grounds of sexuality in the past five years. This 'heteronormativity' creates particular tensions for women who work in male-dominated workplaces. A study by Wright (2011) of the transport and construction industries shows how women's embodiment and sexuality are particularly significant in strongly masculine workplaces. Wright shows that the discourse of 'the lesbian' is present regardless of whether the women employed identify with this label. While this means some women can avoid the unwanted advances from male colleagues, even those women who don't conform to 'heteronormativity' continue to be defined by their sexuality in these male dominated industries.

This focus on identities and sexuality reflects the 'cultural turn' in gender research, which is not only reflective of post-modern and post-structural thinking (Bradley, 2007) but also reflects wider feminist theorising that tries to balance material and cultural dimensions of gendered experiences and inequalities. For example, Acker's (2006) inequalities regimes recognises the gendered organisational processes that are more structural in nature, such as wage setting and recruitment practices, rely on cultural assumptions about male and female bodies and how these are mutually reinforced at the informal level of interactions in the workplace, and the gender, race and class based assumptions that shape the ways people interact at work (op cit, p. 451). Fraser's (1997) distinction between a politics of redistribution and a politics of recognition has also been highly influential, as it balances a material focus on the redistribution of socio-economic resources (such as equal pay and equal access to paid work) with a focus on the need to validate the cultural and symbolic values of marginal groups if equality is to be achieved.

Interestingly, a final way to explore this gender lens of balancing material and cultural dimensions of inequalities can be seen in newer conceptualisations of body work (Wolkowitz et al., 2013). Body work has been defined as the work involving a direct focus on the body of a service recipient, which involves "assessing, diagnosing, handling, treating, manipulating, and monitoring bodies, that thus become the object of the worker's labour" (Twigg et al., 2011, p. 177). Wolkowitz et al. (2013) argue the concept is a complement to emotional labour (Hochschild, 1983) and that it extends the focus on bodies and sexuality from the informal workplace relations we have discussed to the formal level; "it recognises the incorporation of body work (and sex work) within market relationships, and emphasises the role of paid workers in social reproduction" (op cit, p. 3). This area of study puts under the radar new occupations for ER to look at, not just in terms of health and social care jobs, but also sex work, aesthetic services such as beauty work and protective and security services (op cit, p. 3). To fully develop our understanding of body work within ER and how and why it remains both low paid and invisible requires a number of cultural processes to be theorised: these include how the clients and producers negotiate the sexualisation and desexualisation of the work; how the client shapes the employment relationship as well as the employer; and how racialised dynamics shape the experience of this work (Wolkowitz et al., 2013).

What becomes clear is that this goes beyond exposing the gender-neutral depictions of work experience; gendered experiences and ways of 'doing gender' that intersect with other forms of inequalities have created new research agendas around identities, sexualities and embodiment and provide exciting opportunities for ER, informed by a gender lens, to illuminate wider social inequalities in the contemporary workplace.

Conclusions

The opening contention of this chapter was that the application of a gender lens to employment relations has expanded and enriched the disciplinary field across a wide array of dimensions, reflecting the innovative and challenging nature of feminist scholarship. We have argued that the key outcomes have been embedding the disciplinary field within family and welfare state systems; expanding theoretical and practical understandings of the complex problems of representing diverse and potentially conflicting interests among the workforce; challenging the social construction of key characteristics of work organisation and work values, notably the construction of skill, working time and pay systems; and recognising that not only are experiences of work gendered but also that work itself involves the constant 'doing of gender'. The interactions between gender and other dimensions of inequality call for the development of an intersectional sensitivity to understand the complex world of work. New concepts such as emotional labour, body work and aesthetic labour have been developed with a gendered perspective from the outset and have been used to understand the ways in which social inequalities along several dimensions are being reproduced in new forms of work and organisation. This success story needs tempering by reference to two continuing issues. The first is the failure to develop an equally gendered analysis for men at work. The second is a concern that there is often still no systematic gender analysis in ER, except when either the subjects studied are women or the topic has a specific gender label. The situation has undoubtedly improved from the mid 1990s, when key critiques of ER were launched based on the identification of the absence of gender from textbooks and journal contributions. The extent of change is an empirical issue and adopting a gendered lens is a continuing challenge for ER scholars and the discipline as a whole; indeed the analysis of content within all the chapters in this handbook could itself be one way to investigate whether the discipline is stepping up to the challenge.

References

Abu Sharkh, M. and Gough, I. (2009). *Global Welfare Regimes: A Cluster Analysis*, CDDRL Working Paper No. 91. [Online]. Available at: https://cddrl.fsi.stanford.edu/sites/default/files/No_91_SharkhGough_Global_Regime.pdf.

Acker, J. (1989). *Doing Comparable Worth*. Philadelphia: Temple University Press.

Acker, J. (2006). 'Inequality Regimes: Gender, Class and Race in Organisations', *Gender and Society*, 20(4), pp. 441–464.

Bolton, S. and Muzio, D. (2007). 'Can't Live with 'Em; Can't Live without 'Em: Gendered Segmentation in the Legal Profession', *Sociology*, 41(1), pp. 47–64.

Bradley, H. (2007). *Gender*. Cambridge (UK): Polity Press.

Briskin L. (1999). 'Autonomy, diversity and integration: union women's separate organizing in North America and Western Europe in the context of restructuring and globalization', *Women's Studies International Forum*, 22(5), pp. 543–554.

Briskin, L. (2006). 'Victimisation and agency: the social construction of union women's leadership', *Industrial Relations Journal*, 37(4), pp. 359–378.

Burnett, S., Gatrell, C., Cooper, C. and Sparrow, P. (2013). 'Fathers at work: a ghost in the organizational machine', *Gender, Work & Organization*, 20(6), pp. 632–646.

Chicha, M.T. (2006). *A Comparative Analysis of Promoting Pay Equity: Models and Impacts.* Declaration Working Paper No. 49. Geneva: International Labour Organization.

Cockburn, C. (1985). *Machinery of Dominance.* London: Macmillan.

Colgan, F. and Ledwith, S. (eds.) (2002). *Gender, Diversity and Trade Unions: International Perspectives.* London: Routledge, pp. 319.

Colgan, F., Creegan, C., McKearney, A. and Wright T. (2007). 'Equality and diversity policies and practices at work: lesbian, gay and bisexual workers', *Equal Opportunities International,* 26(6), pp. 590–609.

Collins, P.H. (2000). 'Gender, Black Feminism and Black Political Economy', *The Annals of the American Academy of Political and Social Sciences,* 568(1), pp. 41–53.

Collinson, M. and Collinson, D.L. (1989). Sexuality in the workplace: the domination of men's sexuality, in Hearn, J., Tancred-Sherrif, P., Sheppard, D. and Burrell, G. (eds.) *The Sexuality of Organization.* London: Sage, pp. 91–109.

Crenshaw, K. (1991). 'Mapping the margins: intersectionality, identity politics, and violence against women of color', *Stanford Law Review,* 43(6), pp. 1241–1299.

Crompton, R. and Sanderson, K. (1990). *Gendered Jobs and Social Change.* London: Unwin Hyman.

Deakin, S., Butlin, S., McLaughlin, C. and Polanska, A. (2015). 'Are Litigation and Collective Bargaining Complements or Substitutes for Achieving Gender Equality? A Study of the British Equal Pay Act', *Cambridge Journal of Economics,* 39(2), pp. 381–403.

Dickens, L. (1998). 'What HRM means for gender equality', *Human Resource Management Journal,* 8(1), pp. 23–40.

Durbin, S. and Conley, H. (2010). Gender, labour process theory and intersectionality: une liaison dangereuse?, in Thompson, P. and Smith, C. (eds.) *Working Life: Renewing Labour Process Analysis.* Basingstoke: Palgrave Macmillan.

Esping-Andersen, G. (1990). *The Three Worlds of Welfare Capitalism.* Princeton: Princeton University Press.

ETUC (European Trade Union Confederation) (2014). *Bargaining Equality.* Brussels: ETUC.

Fagan, C., Lyonette, C., Smith, M., and Saldaña-Tejeda, A. (2012). *The Influence of Working Time Arrangements on Work-Life Integration or 'Balance': A Review of the International Evidence.* (Conditions of Work and Employment Series). Geneva: International Labour Office.

Figart, D., Mutari, E. and Power, M. (2002). *Living Wages, Equal Wages: Gender and Labour Market Policies in the United States.* London: Routledge.

Fleetwood, S. (2007). 'Why work-life balance now?' *International Journal of Human Resource Management,* 18(3), pp. 387–340.

Fraser, N. (1994). 'After the Family Wage: Gender Equity and the Welfare State', *Political Theory,* 22(4), pp. 591–618.

Fraser, N. (1997). *Justice Interruptus: Critical Reflections on the 'Post-Socialist' Condition.* New York: Routledge.

Gregory, A. and Milner, S. (2009). 'Trade Unions and Work-life Balance: Changing Times in France and the UK?' *British Journal of Industrial Relations,* 47(1), pp. 122–146.

Grimshaw, D. and Rubery, J. (2007). *Undervaluing Women's Work.* Equal Opportunities Commission Manchester, Working Paper Series No 53. [Online]. Available at: www.researchgate.net/profile/Jill_Rubery/publication/267854289_Undervaluing_Women's_Work/links/55277d360cf2520617a71230.pdf.

Guerrier, Y. and Adib, A. (2000). 'No we don't provide that service: harassment of hotel employees by customers', *Work, Employment & Society,* 14(4), pp. 689–705.

Healy, G., Bradley, H. and Mukherjee, N. (2004). 'Individualism and Collectivism Revisited – A Study of Black Minority Ethnic Women', *Industrial Relations Journal,* 35(5), pp. 451–466.

Healy, G., Bradley, H. and Forson, C. (2011). 'Intersectional Sensibilities in Analysing Inequality Regimes in Public Sector Organizations', *Gender, Work & Organization,* 18(5), pp. 467–487.

Healy, G. and Kirton, G. (2000). 'Women, power and trade union government', *British Journal of Industrial Relations,* 38(3), pp. 343–360.

Hearn, J. and Parkin, W. (2001). *Gender, Sexuality and Violence at Work in Organisations.* London: Sage.

Hebson, G., Rubery, J. and Grimshaw, D. (2015). 'Rethinking job satisfaction in care work: looking beyond the care debates', *Work, Employment & Society,* 29(2), pp. 314–330.

Heery, E. and Conley, H. (2007). 'Frame Extension in a Mature Social Movement: British Trade Unions and Part-Time Work, 1967–2002', *Journal of Industrial Relations,* 49(1), pp. 5–29.

Hochschild, A. (1983). *The Managed Heart: the Commercialization of Human Feeling.* Berkeley: University of California Press.

Humphries, J. and Rubery, J. (1984). 'The reconstruction of the supply side of the labour market: the relative autonomy of social reproduction', *Cambridge Journal of Economics*, 8(4), pp. 331–346.

Kang, M. (2013). What does a manicure have to do with sex: racialised sexualisation of body labour in routine beauty services, in Wolkowitz, C., Cohen, R., Sanders, T. and Hardy, K. (eds.) *Body/Sex/Work*. London: Palgrave Macmillan.

Karamessini, M. and Rubery, J. (2013). Economic crisis and austerity: challenges to gender equality, in Karamessini, M. and Rubery, J. (eds.) *Women and Austerity: The Economic Crisis and the Future for Gender Equality*. London: Routledge.

Kirton, G. (2010). Work-life balance: attitudes and expectations of young black and minority ethnic graduates, in Healy, G., Kirton, G. and Noon, M. (eds.) *Equalities, Inequalities and Diversity*. Basingstoke: Palgrave Macmillan.

Kirton, G. (2015). 'Progress towards gender democracy in UK unions 1987–2012', *British Journal of Industrial Relations*, 53(3), pp. 484–507.

Kirton, G. and Healy, G. (2013). 'Commitment and collective identity of long-term union participation: the case of women union leaders in the UK and USA', *Work Employment & Society*, 27(2), pp. 195–212.

Lewis, J. (1992). 'Gender and the Development of Welfare Regimes', *Journal of European Social Policy*, 2(3), pp. 159–173.

Mandel, H. (2013). 'Up the Down Staircase: Women's Upward Mobility and the Wage Penalty for Occupational Feminization, 1970–2007', *Social Forces*, 91(4), pp. 1183–1207.

Marino, S. (2015). 'Trade unions, special structures and the inclusion of migrant workers: on the role of union democracy', *Work, Employment & Society*, 29(5), pp. 826–842.

McBride, A. (2001). *Gender Democracy in Trade Unions*. Farnham: Ashgate Publishing.

McBride, A., Hebson, G. and Holgate, J. (2015). 'Intersectionality: are we taking enough notice in the field of work and employment relations?', *Work, Employment & Society*, 29(2), pp. 331–341.

McDowell, L. (1997). *Capital Culture: Gender at Work in the City*. Oxford: Blackwell.

McLaughlin, H., Uggen, C. and Blackstone, A. (2012). 'Sexual Harassment, Workplace Authority, and the Paradox of Power', *American Sociological Review*, 77(4), pp. 625–647.

Moore, S. (2009). '"No matter what I did I would still end up in the same position": age as a factor defining older women's experience of labour market participation', *Work, Employment & Society*, 23(4), pp. 655–671.

Nentwich, J.C. and Kelan, E. (2014). 'Towards a topology of 'doing gender': an analysis of empirical research and its challenges'. *Gender, Work and Organization*, 21(2), pp. 121–134.

Norman, H., Elliot, M. and Fagan, C. (2014). 'Which fathers are the most involved in taking care of their toddlers in the UK? An investigation of the predictors of paternal involvement', *Community, Work and Family*, 17(2), pp. 163–180.

Orloff, A. (1993). 'Gender and the Social Rights of Citizenship: The Comparative Analysis of Gender Relations and Welfare States', *American Sociological Review*, 58(3), pp. 303–328.

Pfau-Effinger, B. (1998). Culture or structure as explanations for differences in part-time work in Germany, Finland and the Netherlands?, in O'Reilly, J. and Fagan, C. (eds.) *Part-time Prospects: Part-Time Employment in Europe, North America and the Pacific Rim*. London: Routledge.

Pringle, R. (1989). *Secretaries Talk: Sexuality, Power and Work*. London: Sage.

Pullen, A. and Simpson, R. (2009). 'Managing Difference in Feminized Work: Mens Otherness and Social Practice', *Human Relations*, 62(4), pp. 561–587.

Reskin, B.F. and Roos, P. (eds.) (1990). *Job Queues, Gender Queues: Explaining Women's Inroads into Male Occupations*. Philadelphia: Temple University Press.

Rubery, J. (ed.) (1988). *Women and Recession*. London: Routledge and Kegan Paul, p. 294.

Rubery, J. (1998). Part-Time Work: A Threat to Labour Standards, in O'Reilly, J. and Fagan, C. (eds.) *Part-time Prospects: Part-Time Employment in Europe, North America and the Pacific Rim*. London: Routledge.

Rubery, J. (2015). 'Regulating for Gender Equality: A Policy Framework to Support the Universal Caregiver Vision', *Social Politics*, 22(4), pp. 513–538.

Rubery, J. and Fagan, C. (1995). 'Comparative Industrial Relations Research: Towards Reversing the Gender Bias', *British Journal of Industrial Relations*, 33(2), pp. 209–236.

Rubery, J. and Grimshaw, D. (2015). 'The Forty Year Pursuit of Equal Pay: A Case of Constantly Moving Goal Posts', *Cambridge Journal of Economics*, 39(2), pp. 319–344.

Rubery, J., Grimshaw, D., Hebson, G. and Ugarte, S. (2015). '"It's all about time": time as contested terrain in the management and experience of domiciliary care work in England', *Human Resource Management*, 54(5), pp. 753–772.

Sainsbury, D. (1996). *Gender Equality and Welfare States*. Cambridge (UK): Cambridge University Press.

Schäfer, A. and Gottschall, K. (2015). 'From wage regulation to wage gap: how wage-setting institutions and structures shape the gender wage gap across three industries in 24 European countries and Germany', *Cambridge Journal of Economics*, 39(2), pp. 467–496.

Supiot, A. (ed.) (2001). *Beyond Employment: Changes in Work and the Future of Labour Law in Europe*. Oxford: Oxford University Press.

Távora, I. (2012). 'The southern European social model: familialism and the high rates of female employment in Portugal', in *Journal of European Social Policy*, 22(1), pp. 63–76.

Twigg, J., Wolkowitz, C., Cohen, R. and Nettleton, S. (2011). 'Conceptualising Body Work in Health and Social Care', *Sociology of Health and Illness*, 33(2), pp. 171–188.

UN Women (2015). *Progress of the World's Women 2015–16: Transforming Economies, Realizing Rights*. New York: United Nations.

Wajcman, J. (2000). 'Feminism facing industrial relations in Britain', *British Journal of Industrial Relations*, 38(2), pp. 183–201.

Walby, S., Armstrong, J. and Strid, S. (2012). 'Intersectionality: multiple inequalities in social theory', *Sociology*, 46(2), pp. 224–240.

Warhurst, C. and Nickson, D. (2007). 'Employee experience of aesthetic labor in retail and hospitality', *Work, Employment & Society*, 21(1), pp. 103–120.

Williams, C. and Connell, C. (2010). 'Looking good and sounding right: aesthetic labor and social inequality in the retail industry', *Work and Occupations*, 37(3), pp. 349–377.

Wolkowitz, C., Cohen, R., Sanders, T. and Hardy, K. (eds.) (2013). *Body/Sex/Work*. London: Palgrave Macmillan.

Wright, T. (2011). Exploring the intersections of gender, sexuality and class in the transport and construction industries, in Healey, G., Kirton, G. and Noon, M. (eds.) *Equality, Inequalities and Diversity*. Basingstoke: Palgrave.

Young, I.M. (2000). *Inclusion and Democracy*. Oxford: Oxford University Press.

8

EMPLOYMENT RELATIONS AND HUMAN RESOURCE MANAGEMENT

Brian Harney, Tony Dundon and Adrian Wilkinson

Introduction

Employment relations (ER) has both informed and been influenced by key shifts in our understanding about how people at work are managed. One significant development in the field of ER concerns the prominence of human resource management (HRM). Since the mid 1980s HRM has been 'contested' yet also recognised as the 'conventional' academic perspective for analysing the management of employment and all its associated relationship tensions and ambiguities (Keenoy, 2007). HRM has equally been diffused widely into practice and many see HR as a legitimate and professional career choice (Tamkin, Reilly and Hirsh, 2006). The traction of HRM has been underpinned by a colonisation of business school content, with dedicated undergraduate specialisms and postgraduate level qualifications in HRM replacing more traditional ER provisions. Professional bodies, including the Chartered Institute of Personnel Development (CIPD) and the Society for Human Resource Management (SHRM), have created HRM norms and gold standards while promoting the beneficial impact of HRM for individuals, organisations and society (Kochan, 2007). The current CIPD tag line of "championing better work and working lives" is indicative of this broad ambition, even though scholars point out that these claims may be indicative of rhetoric rather than reality (e.g. Legge, 2005; Thompson, 2011).

Proponents of HRM link its ascendancy to the performance benefits it can yield for firms in enhancing competitiveness and realising strategic advantage. From this view HRM is very much a relative of strategic management (Jackson, Schuler and Jiang, 2014), typically seeing matters through the eyes of managers and shareholders (rather than workers and other stakeholders). In some measure HRM filled the lacuna left by former industrial relations research, which afforded limited attention to the role, impact and dynamics of management (Dundon and Rollinson, 2011). Others have focused more vehemently on HRM as being distinct from personnel management (Storey, 1995), or as a natural extension of it (Torrington et al., 2014). These fault lines of debate have been reflected in significant research efforts. Early HRM researchers sought empirical evidence to explore the nature and diffusion of HR practices, before seeking to demonstrate its viability and assessing its contribution to key organisational and employee outcomes. This latter HRM performance agenda has dictated much of the recent terms of reference for HRM researchers.

The extent to which HRM can be differentiated from or subsumes ER will very much depend on the definition of HRM. Explorations of HRM as an exclusive and distinct approach to managing people are evidenced in literature focusing on high-commitment management, high-involvement management, best practice HRM and High Performance Work Systems (HPWS) (see Wall and Wood, 2005). A more inclusive understanding can be found from one leading outlet for HRM, the *Human Resource Management Journal*, which highlights an all-encompassing scope in seeking "to publish scholarly articles on any aspect of *employment studies* but especially those focused on issues related to the management of *people at work*. Articles should make a substantive contribution to *contemporary issues... .*" (our italics).[1] There are however varying levels of emphasis in research and approach. A ten-year content analysis of the leading US-based journal, *Human Resource Management*, finds a dominance of keywords such as strategic HRM, selection, careers, leadership, turnover and firm performance. It is only beyond the 40 most frequently used keywords where one finds evidence more aligned with ER, e.g. the employment relationship, trade unions, conflict, bargaining power, politics and labour shortages (Townsend and Wilkinson, 2014).

This chapter seeks to locate the emergence and significance of key intersections of HRM and ER. In so doing the first section of the chapter traces the origins of HRM, highlighting the importance of long-standing domain assumptions that formed the conceptual heritage of the term. The second section of the chapter explores three waves of research that have characterised the field since the mid 1980s, including an emphasis on strategy, HRM-performance linkages and employee outcomes. The final section of the chapter draws on a 5C framework to provide a critical evaluation of HRM. Overall, this serves to illuminate the value of more ER-grounded understanding and ongoing conversation between related modes of thinking about the management of people at work in contemporary society.

Origins and domain assumptions of human resource management

It is difficult to find a consensus on the precise origins of HRM (Kaufman, 1999). Gospel (2009) makes a useful distinction between the historically occurring activity of human resource management (lower case), as distinct from the specific conceptualisation of Human Resource Management (upper case) that emerged in the mid 1980s. Focusing on the former understanding, the industrial revolution served as a key catalyst for the development of specific techniques for people management as a factory model of employment mandated new modes of working and organising labour. This heralded the beginning of the mass-producing capitalist enterprise moving from direct control to more technical systems, founded on a clear separation between the owners of capital and waged employee labourers. The period saw the rise of a more professional 'managerial' class, essentially acting as agents for and on behalf of owners in controlling and managing people under the emergent factory system. The era was also characterised by low wages and very poor working conditions, which were confounded by weak labour power and the absence of a vehicle for collective mobilisation or resistance (Niven, 1967).

There were some shades of light in this early industrial context, however, as more enlightened employers, frequently guided by entrenched moral values or religious beliefs, looked to better the conditions of employment for their workers. A frequently highlighted forerunner to contemporary emphasis in HRM comes from the Quaker tradition that emerged in the late nineteenth century, as exemplified by the likes of Cadbury, Fry's and Rowntree's. These were welfare-orientated organisations that employed dedicated welfare officers and encouraged worker participation in committees examining issues such as health and leisure time. In a similar vein, as early as 1817 social reformers such as Robert Owen looked to place minimal age thresholds on child labour in factories, while also calling for a more balanced work day via the slogan "*Eight hours labour, eight hours recreation, eight hours rest*". At this time these social and industrial welfare programmes became a place of pilgrimage for statesmen and social reformers, whilst also illustrating to the governing classes that philanthropy could be reconciled with profit-making (Cole, 1930). These more progressive employers still provide a context for academic pilgrimage today, representing an opportune basis for HRM researchers to highlight an employee well-being orientated legacy.

If the industrial revolution provided the initial impetus for the specific consideration of employment and management issues, this tendency was solidified via the scientific management movement popularised by Frederick Winslow Taylor (1856–1917) and subsequently manifest as Fordist production. Taylor is frequently termed the father of modern management theory for his role in introducing practicable, replicable, standard and efficiency driven means to manage production processes and employees therein. The imprinting logic of many HRM practices – from sophisticated recruitment and selection to a division of labour job design system, pay for performance and talent planning – can be found in the control rationality of scientific management. Scientific management had the goal of eliminating uncertainty and reducing any variability in the system. Employees were conceptualised as mere cogs in an industrial system. This not only reflected the engineering mindset of Taylor, but also a derogatory attitude to the immigrant labour that compromised much of the workforce at the time (Grey, 2009). Whilst scientific management brought forward practices founded on transparency and formality, it also provided a clear divide and ongoing justification for the separation of those tasked with policy formation (management) and those responsible for implementation (employees). Overall, in many ways scientific management serves as the ultimate prescriptive template for aligning desired organisational goals and objectives with the means of organising the workforce to realise these. It is perhaps unsurprising therefore that in the 1920s the need to take a strategic approach to managing people in the workplace was already articulated by many organisations (Kaufman, 2007).

With its foundation on rational efficiency and a means-end logic, it is perhaps inevitable that scientific management would be subject to staunch critique. In a practical sense, employees working under such conditions were subject to boredom, frustration, minimal autonomy and alienation, which ultimately became manifest as forms of resistance and employee turnover (Mowday, Porter and Steers, 1982). A solid stream of workplace research gradually emerged, unpacking these dynamics and re-introducing human agency into the equation, including the Human Relations movement. Building on its origins in Elton Mayo's Hawthorne experiments, human relations stressed the imperative of paying due attention, not simply to the physical conditions of work, but equally to employee needs and motivation in the form of group dynamics, informal recognition and individual expectations. HRM has a close allegiance to the behavioural insights and modes of understanding associated with the human relations movement. Indeed, HRM's emergence and significance as a contrast to traditional personnel management can be seen as echoing this earlier historical surge from scientific management towards a more normative form of control (Barley and Kunda, 1992).

Domain assumptions

While often depicted as vastly contrasting modes of people management, in reality both scientific management and human relations were founded on common domain assumptions that would be readily assimilated into HRM. Both scientific management (with its rationality on 'economic logic') and human relations (with a focus on 'social legitimacy') were underpinned by a fundamental desire to control the labour process in order to enhance productivity and maximise private profit. As a basis for understanding how this may be achieved, both had a penchant for a hard and positivistic science paradigm, with a belief that the tasks of employees could be accurately defined, measured and assessed with specific predictability. Finally, an underlying ideological imperative of both approaches was that organisations should operate without any countervailing force or alternative voices, so that all employees were aligned to the objectives of the organisation, i.e. a nascent form of unitarism. Thus although human relations is frequently touted as being more humane in its treatment of employees owing to its social and psychological antecedents, compared with the harder economic basis of scientific management, at its core was a desire to "discover how psychology could be used to raise productivity, resist unionisation and increase workers' co-operation with management" (Kiechel, 2012, p. 66). Indeed, a deeper historical inspection provides further insights into the managerial biased undertone, revealing that both Taylor and Mayo had commercial vested interests that were intertwined with a nascent business school agenda underpinning the ideology of leading industrialists Joseph Wharton and John D. Rockefeller respectively (Bruce and Nyland, 2011). In his wonderful excavation of the social and historical context framing the Hawthorne studies, Hassard (2012, p. 1434) suggests that "the narrative developed by Mayo's research group emerged as much from internal politics at Harvard as scientific evidence from Hawthorne". In surfacing domain assumptions related to performance maximisation, faith in the scientific paradigms and a managerialist heritage, these early schools of thought bare a forceful imprint in how mainstream (prescribed best practice) HRM conceptualises work and work relations as something for the good of a pro-market ideology (Godard, 2014; Harley, 2015; Thompson, 2011).

Contemporary emergence of HRM

Personnel management emerged as a welfare-orientated role addressing the needs of employees, but equally as a dedicated function necessitated by more large-scale, diversified organisations (Chandler, 1962). By the 1970s this was accompanied by a requirement for specialist expertise to deal with a growing stream of legislation governing the employment relationship (e.g. in areas such as pay, hours, holidays, equality, redundancy and employment protection). Yet this growth in demand for personnel specialists did not automatically equate to an elevated status for the function. Early commentary found personnel management to be a dumping ground for many unwanted tasks, heavily criticised for being a combination of the functions of file clerk, social worker and firefighting (Drucker, 1954). Personnel management was also perceived in a gendered fashion. In particular, it had a feminised welfare role that was contrasted with the more masculine technical professions of finance and accounting, or indeed with the bargaining and negotiation associated with ER (Legge, 1995). Even less complimentary impressions come from Harry Callaghan, the no-nonsense San Francisco police detective played by Clint Eastwood in the movie series *Dirty Harry*, when he responds to his internal transfer to personnel: "What? To personnel! That's for arseholes".[2]

Debates and tensions concerning HRM meanings were evidenced in models that highlighted the diversity of personnel practice and the variety of roles carried out by managers. Taking Tyson and Fell's (1986) building analogy as an example, key personnel management roles ranged from an administrative 'clerk of works' through to a more sophisticated, employee-focused 'contracts manager' and finally the 'architect' with significant influence operating at the level of strategy and top management. In practice, personnel management was still largely seen as an administrative function dealing with the 'labour problem' rather than contributing to strategic goals. During the 1970s in particular, much of the personnel manager's time was consumed with ER firefighting. In many ways with this descriptive, administrative and reactive stereotype, personnel management served as the perfect foil to set out the virtues of the new HRM orthodoxy as it emerged with force in the early 1980s (Wilkinson et al., 2009).

HRM was founded on a mantra that it represented *a*, if not *the*, means to generate competitive sustainable advantage for firms. This strategic discourse emanated in the context of intensive global competition, most notably from Japan, and the emergence of more people-intensive service and knowledge-based industries. Academic models originating from the likes of Harvard Business School (Beer et al., 1984) and Michigan (Fombrun, Tichy and Devanna, 1984) lent credence and practitioner impetus to HRM. Overall, there was a consensus that organisations were best served when employees "were given broader responsibilities, encouraged to contribute, and helped to take satisfaction in their work" (Walton, 1985, p. 77). The focus shifted from controlling workers to eliciting commitment and creating an infrastructure and environment whereby employees could flourish, ultimately yielding "tangible dividends for the individuals and the company" (ibid.). This commitment emphasis also served to fill some of the analytical space left void by ER scholarship, which tended to privilege the conflict dimension of the employment relationship to the neglect of more mutual or collaborative aspects (Ackers and Wilkinson, 2003; Delbridge, 2007). HRM flipped the terms of reference forcefully to the other extreme, privileging unitarism as the presumed basis and outcome of HRM prescriptions (Geare et al., 2014).

It is perhaps unsurprising that early contributions examining the rise of the new HRM were concerned to define it and specifically contrast it with a more traditional approach to personnel management (e.g. Guest, 1987). Beyond the US, HRM was (initially at least) received with more scepticism. HRM was at once seen as a commitment-orientated approach to people management (Storey, 1995), "a wolf in sheep's clothing" (Keenoy, 1990) or as "old wine in a new bottle" (Legge, 1995). Others highlighted an undercurrent of individualisation of the employment relationship and purposeful marginalisation of trade unions (Nolan and Wood, 2003). Indeed HRM's emphasis on management, strategy and enterprise coalesced neatly with the prevailing economic and ideological consensus of the 1980s, born of Reagan in the US and Thatcher in the UK. The theoretical significance of HRM was that it could serve as a substitute for traditional employment regulatory approaches. Where an exclusive definition of HRM was offered it was somewhat easier to differentiate HRM from its predecessors. Picking up the emphasis on commitment and competitive advantage, Storey proffered a definition of HRM as "a distinctive approach to employment management which seeks to achieve competitive advantage through the strategic deployment of a highly committed and capable workforce, using an integrated array of cultural, structural and personal techniques" (1995, p. 5).

While definitional debate continued and empirical evidence of HRM remained patchy at best, there was some consensus on what normative HRM should look like. In addition to its focus on employee commitment, a core argument was the necessity that the way people were managed should support and align with organisational strategy. In terms of understanding the connections with the management of employment relationships, HRM was inherently unitarist, with policies and practices driven by business needs above all other interests (Wilkinson, Redman and Dundon, 2017). Former ER traditions such as the rise in specialist bargaining expertise were considered reactionary to issues arising from mass union growth, while the new HRM targeted operational responsibilities at individual line managers who were often intolerant of distant personnel experts removed from the immediate demands of getting products out the door. In business terms, HR was to be a strategic business partner advising on strategy, including via board representation, while local managers who know best how to do a job become empowered to implement change. However, clear lines of differentiation between old personnel and new

HRM were premised more on normative ideals rather than an empirical reality (Legge, 2005). In strategic terms HRM has always been a lower order factor compared with corporate or business objectives (Boxall and Purcell, 2008). In moving beyond the impasse, efforts to develop and legitimise HRM can be characterised by three waves of understanding and emphasis, all of which formed part of an ongoing journey to formulate and refine the meanings of HRM and how it connects with firm decisions as well as employee well-being concerns.

Matching models

Matching models of HRM represent a form of contingency theory, guided by the implicit assumption that the most successful organisations are those that display a 'Chinese box' type consistency between the external environment and internal organisation (Miles and Snow, 1984). Deciphering HRM's linkage to strategy has been at the core of the HRM agenda since the mid 1980s. An early and influential development was the Michigan model of 'Hard HRM' developed by Fombrun et al. (1984). This model detailed a tight and calculative (hard) fit between the business needs of organisations and the way people were managed to ensure optimal alignment and maximum employee effort and performance. In this model the focus was on Human *Resource* Management, with HRM operating via strict rules related to selection, training and reward, and employees ultimately judged as factors of production to be assessed on purely efficiency grounds. By contrast, a matching model developed at Harvard Business School emphasised more 'soft' variants of HRM, whereby employees were treated as assets to be nurtured and developed. This *Human* Resource Management approach pioneered by Beer et al. (1984) included multiple stakeholder interests (including government and trade unions), multifaceted employee outcomes and also long-term implications for individuals and well-being. While considered to be more analytically grounded, it was more difficult to specify this range of descriptive elements and also evaluate softer dimensions and human attributes (Wilkinson, Redman and Dundon, 2017). This is a problem that continuously haunts HRM, meaning that much of this richer heritage has been neglected. A narrower conceptualisation of HRM, illuminating the direct linkages and desired role behaviours mandated of various organisational strategies (frequently referred to as 'best fit'), became the core focus of HRM by the late 1980s (e.g. Schuler and Jackson, 1987)

Matching models were intuitively appealing to practitioners and enabled HRM researchers to leverage the legitimacy of related fields such as strategic management. Critiques of matching models claim that they overestimate the clarity and rationality of the process. Strategy may often emerge retrospectively, while rigid 'fit' may actually hinder the innovativeness and flexibility mandated for success. Assuming consensus on end objectives may be a flawed starting point as this process is likely to be messy, contested and shaped by power relations. As long-standing critiques of contingency theory note "politics cannot be simply left to the end as part of the problem of application" (Wood, 1979, p. 342). Underpinning matching models is an implicit determinism, leaving little room for the agency of HR managers (or workers and their representative bodies), who are expected to choose and operate from a predetermined and narrow palette of HR options. Rich qualitative case studies, even of leading-edge organisations, found little of what matching models would predict, with commentators indicating that firms actually express a preference for more 'flexible' approaches (Tyson, 1997). While extensive research claims to have demonstrated the mediating role of strategy in enhancing the HRM performance linkage (Youndt et al., 1996), results have been subject to ambiguous definitions and varying interpretations. Arthur's (1992) study of steel minimills claims a significant association between HRM systems and business strategy choices, yet 40 per cent of the mills in Arthur's study with a strategy of differentiation did not have a matching commitment-based HRM system (1992, p. 502). In the meantime, authors have put forward accounts depicting fit as more multifaceted and complex than a narrow strategy-HRM relationship would allow for (e.g. environmental fit and legitimacy). Matching models clearly enhanced the business case for HRM, although rather than being addressed, key conceptual and empirical concerns were ignored or overshadowed by the HRM-performance wave of scholarship.

HRM and performance

If matching models privilege exclusivity for a managerial class, the last two decades have been characterised by attempts to validate precisely how important HRM is for organisational profit. HRM-performance research has been consumed by attempts to demonstrate the positive relationship between HRM practices and organisational performance. The HRM labels used in this type of research – High-Performance Work Systems (HPWS), Best Practice HRM, High-Commitment Management – signal above all else some demonstrable boost to a firm's bottom line via people management policies. This line of research found a theoretical bedfellow in the resource-based view (RBV) of the firm, which argues that the essence of advantage resides in the internal capabilities and processes of organisations, including the way people are managed (Harney and Trehy, 2016). While building on the logic of matching models, HRM-performance research is much more universalistic in its argument, holding that certain human resource practices have a direct and positive impact on organisational performance irrespective of the context in question. Initially, the universalistic focus was on single HR practices such as pay and staffing. Over time, research evolved to examine how mutually reinforcing bundles of HRM practices could have a synergistic impact on financial performance. Typical HR practices advocated as part of such bundles include sophisticated recruitment tests, internal promotions, job security, extensive training and performance-related pay schemes. A key watershed in the HRM performance movement was research by Mark Huselid (1995), which demonstrated that the use of a high-performance work system (an index of 13 HRM practices) was significantly and positively related to lower turnover and higher profits, sales and market value for the firms studied. Over time researchers have tried to hone in more precisely on the size effect and impact of HRM (Jiang et al., 2012). The HRM-performance debate has clearly shaped the terms of reference in HRM, with efforts at extension and replication remaining common yet also contestable (Pauwee, Guest and Wright, 2013).

The HRM-performance wave of research has played a huge role in facilitating HR managers to demonstrate impact (Wall and Wood, 2005). This discourse has been eagerly embraced by consultants in justifying their interventions. However, many still grapple with what precisely constitutes performance practice bundles, especially if they are to be held up as a best practice or a distinct variant to earlier paradigms of ER. While there is agreement at a broad level on the principles of enhancing employee motivation, skill and ability from better people management processes, these same principles have informed industrial relations analysis since the Donovan Commission in the 1960s in Britain (Seifert, 2015). In contemporary HRM studies, however, there appears to be contradictory prescriptions as to the precise mix of practices actually involved, and little consensus on how they should be measured (e.g. indexes, scales, clusters) (Posthuma et al., 2013).

Definitional issues aside, if such HRM practices are so beneficial, what explains their limited diffusion across organisations? Clearly, the magnitude of the economic benefits from adopting new HRM systems will be qualified by the vagaries of market forces, contextual influences and institutional factors (Wilkinson, Redman and Dundon, 2017). It may also be the case that financial performance is simply too distal to capture the impact of HRM interventions. Attempts also tend to ignore the sector-specific nature of turnover and performance, while also relegating discussion of intensified competition to something controllable; a rationale supportive of the adoption of best practices rather than something that may actually militate against them. HRM-performance arguments are largely founded on certain types of firms (large, private sector) from certain regions (Anglo-Saxon) and so the significance of institutional context is not given due acknowledgement. As Boselie et al. (2001) point out, high-commitment practices that are discretionary under neoliberal regimes such as the USA and UK are often part of the legislative framework elsewhere, such as in the Netherlands. In their review of low-wage work across a number of high-income countries in Northern Europe, the UK and the USA, Appelbaum and Schmitt (2009) argue that institutions including the legal framework and the power of organised labour have a strong influence over the take-up of HRM. Thus high-commitment HRM depends not just on employers but also corporate governance and actors at the national as well as the organisation level (see Marchington et al., 2016, p. 70–71).

A long-standing debate is whether HRM leads to performance or whether the impetus flows in the opposite direction, i.e. a firm's success results in more sophisticated HRM. Equally concerning is that recent re-examination of key contributions has found their original findings severely wanting. Gerhart's (2007) review of Ichniowski et al. (1997) finds nothing to support a performance impact from HR bundles, while Porter and Siggelkow's (2008) reassessment of MacDuffie (1995) dismisses the notion of a universal impact of HR practices (with the one exception of formal teams), suggesting that HR practices exhibit significant 'contextuality'. This is important as it has long been recognised that employers may purposefully deploy unique employment practices as a distinctive means of product market competition (Brown, 2008). A core criticism of HRM performance studies is that they represent the unitarist assumptions of HRM scholarship, writ large. Until recently HRM-performance scholarship was exclusively about management (HR practices) for management (various performance outcomes), with limited appreciation of the dynamics of the employee side of relationship.

Employee-centric HRM

Early content analysis revealed HRM-performance studies paid scant attention to workers (Wilkinson, Redman and Dundon, 2017). Employee perspectives have been gradually incorporated into analyses, largely as part of efforts to provide more rigorous and robust explanations of the HRM-performance relationship or "unlocking the black-box" (Jiang et al., 2012). This wave of more employee-centric research has been buffered by a (renewed) emphasis on a socio-psychological dynamic of the employment exchange relationship (Dundon and Rollinson, 2011), with recognition of various collective and individual workforce orientations at play that affect the 'strength' of the HR system (Bowen and Ostroff, 2004). Research has pointed to the importance of line managers as key intermediaries in the delivery of HRM (Harney and Jordan, 2008; Townsend and Dundon, 2015). In this regard the employee-centric agenda may be seen as seeking to put workers back into the equation as active agents capable of shaping their work experiences and the arrangements under which they are expected to generate value and performance (Grant and Shields, 2002; Heffernan and Dundon, 2016).

In contrast to the unitarist penchant in most HRM literatures, contemporary employee-centric assessments tend to paint a more pluralist perspective of the divergent co-operative and antagonistic basis of work relations (Boxall and Purcell, 2008). Research in this area has countered the assumed mutual 'win-win' argument in much extant HRM and shown that HPWS impacts could have been achieved through work intensification (Ramsay, Scholarios and Harley, 2000). Analysis now supports the idea of competing hypotheses and a recognition of key tensions and contradictions likely to characterise the HRM-performance relationship (Ehrnrooth and Björkman, 2012). Moreover, beyond many surface-level prescriptions there is evidence of empirical tensions. Research has shown that even where HR has achieved the status of a fully integrated 'strategic partner', this may not necessarily be beneficial for employees; indeed, it can lead to feelings of estrangement and frustration (Hope-Hailey, Farndale and Truss, 2005). Kochan (2007) bemoans the alignment of HR and business interests, arguing that this is the root cause of the lost credibility and lack of trust in HR professionals. Marchington (2015) adds that the problem lies in the HRM function losing sight of its principle welfare tradition and instead becoming obsessed with 'looking up' to the boardroom to stress short-term performance validity for the existence of HR. Further, it is posited that financialised neoliberal modes of accumulation have meant that many managers fail to deliver on their side of the bargain, owing to global economic pressures and demands out of their control (Thompson, 2013). Lepak and Snell's reasoning is equally instructive: "managers do not have the necessary resources to invest in developing knowledge-based employees. In particularly dynamic environments, firms may not believe they will be able to fully recoup human capital investments in even their core workers" (Lepak and Snell, 2002, p. 537). Critical accounts have long stressed that HRM operates as a pseudo-gemeinschaft, with arguments that perceived best practice HRM as actually leading to work intensification and negative employee outcomes.

ER and HRM: 5Cs for conversation

This chapter has presented the evolution of HRM from its early origins through to contemporary waves of research and the desire for performance-enhancing employment paradigms. Despite this development many commentators provide damning indictments of progress, pointing to the poor status and strategic influence of the HR function (Kaufman, 2012; Kochan, 2007). The performance agenda that has dictated recent focus exemplifies a field struggling to demonstrate its role and impact (Guest, 2011). In order to expand on some of the deficiencies of extant HRM and explore insights from ER, this section draws on the 5Cs of 'complexity, context, contingency, causality and critique' as an organising framework. The 5Cs have been identified as "central to the concerns" of researchers studying the management of people at work (Delbridge and Whitfield, 2007).

C1 Complexity

A common critique directed at HRM is that it provides a sterile account of HRM interventions. Research into HR in some of the top performing firms has found an undercurrent of emergence, highlighting an entangled nature of formal policy and informal dynamics on the shopfloor (Gratton et al., 1999). Recognition of a disparity between intended and realised HRM practice has fostered a dedicated line of research founded on the unitarist assumption that this gap can be easily bridged or minimised, largely through more or better management, or via ready-made solutions to 'fix' some managerial or organisational deficiency.

An alternative ER approach would suggest that such disparity leaves analysis open to the concept of emergence, informality and complexity, not a defined problem to be fixed but reflective of the diverging interests and structured antagonism at the heart of the employment relationship (Dundon and Dobbins, 2015; Edwards, 1986). HRM decisions may not always be introduced or enacted as a result of strategic foresight, as traditionally understood, but rather reflect tactical optimums strived for by management, who often fumble or just "muddle-through" on a day-to-day basis (Lindblom, 1959). A concern with complexity also allows for the informality of practice that substitutes for, or fills, the silences of formal policy (Edwards, 1995). In reality, managers in all organisations navigate between rationality, formality, personal preference and idiosyncrasy as the occasion demands. A long heritage of workplace studies provides a wealth of concepts related to the "leeway function of rules" (Gouldner, 1954) or the role of custom and practice (Brown, 1972). Overall, the dimensions of complexity (emergence, informality and conflicted collaboration) point to a nuanced world of HRM that cannot be collapsed neatly into fixed practices, categories or outcomes (Marchington and Suter, 2013).

C2 Context

With its universalistic emphasis HRM offers scientific insights; however, these can also be independent of both its mode of operation and place of application. There is a tendency to reify and abstract features of organisations, imbuing them with formal characteristics in the pursuit of rational, predetermined goals. Edwards (2005) argues for 'context sensitive research' meaning that HRM cannot be dislocated from the totality of political and economic relations. These form the enabling conditions for the dynamic fluidity of the employment relationship and a means to conceptually enrich C1, the complexity issue, previously discussed. A focus on macro-context enables an understanding of HRM as an ongoing process constantly being enacted and re-enacted, as opposed to a one-off structural intervention. The imperative of this approach is evidenced in an era of 'financialisation', previously noted, where financial transactions and relationships external to the organisation (and independent of physical products or services), are deemed to be defining the employment relationship (Applebaum, Batt and Clark, 2013; Cushen and Harney, 2014). This context exposes the deficiency of imposing a biased preconceived ideal of HRM.

The context in which HRM is enacted clearly matters. Normative prescriptions in HRM (e.g. 'business partner' aspirations or 'championing better working lives') risk becoming de-contextualised from the power relations required for them to be realised or constrained. Likewise, employees are not passive recipients of HRM. Needs, demands and previous experiences of employees, including gender and feminisation, are all important factors that will inform the nature of HRM and the way it is applied under segmented labour contexts (Grimshaw and Rubery, 2008). For instance, when examining employee voice in SMEs, Wilkinson, Dundon and Grugulis (2007, p.1291) refer to the "paradox of organisational action", whereby "social actors inject their own interpretations, meanings and interests which results in a more complex set of social interactions associated with managing human resources". Contextual issues such as the extent of pay dispersion, the size of a firm or the nature of 'give and take' on a shopfloor may hold greater import in understanding employee experiences of work than (pre)judging them on a narrow or predefined number of formal HR practices in place. This discussion of context suggests that in order to give meaning to debates, HRM researchers might pay greater attention to work rooted in the traditions of understanding the institutions and systems of work and employment inequalities, while appreciating contextually grounded definitions that are more sensitive to local interpretation and variance.

C3 Contingency

Except in the form of moderators or limited 'control variables' (e.g. age, sector, unionisation), HRM has been slow to engage with the impact of key contingency variables. More traditional research has long pointed to product market competition and labour market conditions as fundamental to appreciating employment relations. In introducing an emphasis on management actions, HRM has served to overplay managerial rationality and decision-making capability and underplayed constraints or structural realities. This is most obvious in the limited attention HR scholars have paid to the impact from the likes of legal regulation, trade union modernisation or informal modes of labour resistance and misbehaviour on ER (van den Broek and Dundon, 2012). An emphasis on contingencies in this situation is not analogous to the over-simplified contingency or best fit matching models of the 1980s, but is rather an appreciation of the necessity for research to allow for, and accommodate, uneven dynamic interventions between a firm, its environment and among its stakeholders. Kaufman (2010) has made a strong case for a demand-driven conception of HR, noting that researchers should be less consumed by whether a certain type of HRM is inevitable or the degree of investment in a practice, and instead focus on the more "fruitful problem" of developing theoretically informed accounts that consider patterns of diffusion and the actual practices utilised. The desired performance outcome of firms is also likely to be a relative concept, wherein financial performance or profit maximisation may not always be objective criteria owing to differences in context (e.g. sector or ownership types) and complexity (e.g. informality).

C4 Causality

HRM has been dominated by a "big science" approach to empirical research (Wall and Wood, 2005). This is frequently based on counts of practices, a quest for event regularities and theoretical exploration via mediation, moderation or structural equation modelling. This line of inquiry offers a limited basis for understanding the various contexts and complexities under which HRM is actually enacted. Moreover, correlation between variables is often falsely equated with explanation and confirmation (Harney, 2009). By contrast, historical workplace studies exhibit a richer form of analysis, involving in-depth case analysis founded on uncovering the processes of "complex causality" (George and Bennett, 2004) and its project of explaining the observed features of the "real world" by reference to the underlying mechanisms that are responsible for them. Indeed, it has long been noted that a complete understanding of the employment relationship requires that we analyse the social relations that underpin them. Alternative modes of understanding in HRM including more intensive and longitudinal research would ensure that explanatory accounts are privileged, that processes of HRM in firms are adequately contextualised and that complexity is accommodated. Ultimately HR practices and rules have to be interpreted in action (Edwards, 2003). Greater analytical purchase may also help with the incorporation of dimensions of well-being, employee voice, organisational democracy, justice and other outcomes that do not sit well with the dominant HPWS quantitative paradigm.

C5 Critique

In addition to the 4Cs suggested by Delbridge and Whitfield (2007), the role of immanent critique is a fifth 'C' that ought to be of concern for HRM researchers. In one respect this may seem obvious; however, much of the normative HRM model, coupled with a prescriptive and managerial bias in a lot (although not all) of its teaching in mainstream business schools, mean a conversation about critical reflection is warranted (Dundon, Cullinane and Wilkinson, 2017). Immanent critique and the problematisation of extant HRM acts not only as a basis to position research but also serves as a reflexive process to ensure HRM researchers do not automatically perpetuate the status quo (e.g. Godard, 1994). Recognition of 'complex' structural layers, 'contextual' diversity and 'causal' ambiguity mean there is scope for ongoing critical dialogue, encouraging sensitivity to *contingent* processes and events rather than proffering immediate, universal solutions (Edwards, 2005). Current debates in HRM are largely consumed by technical issues, which may result in an ideological 'immiseration' of the field of study, including its teaching and practical application across some (although not all) business school programmes (Dundon, Cullinane and Wilkinson, 2017). With respect to performance there is little recognition of the multiple outcomes initially proffered by Beer et al. (1984) and others. Likewise, there is little cross fertilisation from related fields, such as the application of Budd's (2004) analytical prism for understanding the balance of "efficiency, equity and voice", or the intersectionality of Organisational Behaviour and Employment Relations disciplines to inform "pro-social silence and voice" within the workplace (Barry and Wilkinson, 2016). In many ways conceptual advancement in HRM is hindered by a "consensus orientation" (Keegan and Boselie, 2006). As a consequence, HRM proponents neglect critical trends found in related fields of ER and Organisational Analysis (e.g. outsourcing, trade unions, conflict management, whistle-blowing, identity, top management fraud) that run counter to untiarist models and frames of reference (Batt and Banerjee, 2012). Concepts such as engagement and well-being also risk being interpreted in a narrow, managerialist fashion, at odds with their more holistic, employee-centric origins. As Guest (2017) notes, while the dominant models within HRM theory and research have focused largely on ways to improve performance, with employee concerns regarded as a secondary consideration, pressures at work are creating an increasing threat to employee well-being, and if these concerns are to be taken seriously a different analytic framework for HRM is required.

Overall, many research efforts in HRM typically suffer from a failure to appreciate the key attributes of the 5Cs; 'complexity' is downplayed or (deliberately) eroded by managerialism; 'context' is lacking or deemed homogenous; 'contingencies' are notably absent or superficially controlled; prescriptions are derived from large-scale positivist research founded on a simplistic Humean notion of 'causality'; and a consensus orientation overshadows immanent 'critique', all of which can engender the ideological immiseration of the field. Employment Relations, on the other hand, affords greater contextual sensitivity with its understanding of reciprocity surrounding an economic, social and psychological exchange relationship.

Grounded by these type of insights HRM may be better placed to appreciate the interaction between the structural forces both inside and outside the immediate work milieu that shape the management of those in employment. Of particular utility in this vein is the more inclusive definition of 'analytical HRM' (Boxall and Purcell, 2008), treating the subject as "those activities associated with the management of work and people in firms" (2008, p. 1). This is accompanied by a commitment to explaining what happens in reality: "taking account for the way that management actually behaves and therefore privileging <u>understanding</u> and <u>explanation</u> over prediction" (Boxall, Purcell and Wright, 2007, p. 4, emphasis added). Important to stress here is the necessity of the process and not to predetermine or dictate the form that any bundle of HR practices will take. This avoids the common problem in much HRM analysis whereby its meaning is exhausted by those who prescribe. Very much connected to this is the important point that analytical HRM moves towards embracing the inevitability of tension and contradiction, and so steps away from a unitarist and exclusively normative managerialist agenda. The power and politics inherent in the operation of the employment relationship are acknowledged through the notion of 'plurality' of goals, interest and strategic tensions (Boxall and Purcell, 2008). While analytical HRM is seen to hold much promise, it should also be appreciated that it is hardly novel, and some of its key principle lessons have an established pedigree in the antecedents of earlier related literatures (Gospel, 2009; Gouldner, 1954; Jain and Murray, 1984; Prandy, Stewart and Blackburn, 1983).

Conclusion

While HRM is often assumed to be ahistorical, this chapter has suggested that HRM is very much informed by its conceptual and ideological heritage, including its connections to the deeper social science anchor points of ER. Likewise, the challenges facing the HR practitioner reflect long-standing dynamics and tensions inherent to all efforts of managing the employment relationship, however defined. Paradoxically, as much as HR might be criticised for its managerialist focus, it has elevated and sustained the employment relationship as a key means of understanding organisations, where other perspectives have fallen somewhat short. Moreover, "tactical engagement with HRM" (Jacques, 1999, p. 216) as the conventional means for analysing the employment relationship provides the basis for informed insights and a balanced assessment about the management of people at work. On the matter of more inclusive definitions, there is scope for mutual influence and an analysis that is sensitive not just to the needs and interests of shareholders (employers), but considers the interactions and obligations of a range of stakeholders (workers and others) connected in a complex web of institutional structures and process-driven informalities. This is one means to help avoid the trap of partial understanding born of disciplinary myopia.

Notes

1 http://onlinelibrary.wiley.com/journal/10.1111/(ISSN)1748–8583/homepage/ForAuthors.html
2 See Torrington et al., 2014 or YouTube clip of the scene: www.youtube.com/watch?v=qvG3R-xOMzE

References

Ackers, P. and Wilkinson, A. (2003). *Understanding Work and Employment: Industrial Relations in Transition.* Oxford: Oxford University Press.

Applebaum, E. and Schmitt, J. (2009). 'Low wage work in high income countries: labour market institutions and business strategy in the US and Europe', *Human Relations*, 62(2), p. 34.

Applebaum, E., Batt, R. and Clark, I. (2013). 'Implications of Financial Capitalism for Employment Relations Research: Evidence from Breach of Trust and Implicit Contracts in Private Equity Buyouts', *British Journal of Industrial Relations*, 51(3), pp. 498–518.

Arthur, J. (1992). 'The link between business strategy and industrial relations systems in American steel minimills', *Industrial and Labor Relations Review*, 45(3), pp. 488–505.

Barley, S. and Kunda, G. (1992). 'Design and devotion: surges of rational and normative ideologies of control in managerial discourse', *Administrative Science Quarterly*, 37(3), pp. 363–399.

Barry, M. and Wilkinson, A. (2016). 'Pro-social or pro-management? A critique of employee voice as pro-social behaviour within organisational behaviour', *British Journal of Industrial Relations*, 54(2), pp. 261–284.

Batt, R. and Banerjee, M. (2012). 'The scope and trajectory of strategic HR research: evidence from American and British journals', *International Journal of Human Resource Management*, 23(9), pp. 1739–1762.

Beer, M., Spector, B., Lawrence, P., Mills, Q. and Walton, R. (1984). *Managing Human Assets.* New York: The Free Press.

Boselie, P., Paauwe, J. and Jansen, P. (2001). 'Human resource management and performance: lessons from the Netherlands', *International Journal of Human Resource Management*, 12(7), pp. 1107–1125.

Bowen, D. and Ostroff, C. (2004). 'Understanding HRM-Performance Linkages: The Role of the 'Strength' of the HRM System', *Academy of Management Review*, 29(2), pp. 202–222.

Boxall, P. and Purcell, J. (2008). *Strategy and Human Resource Management.* 2nd edn. London: Palgrave Macmillan.

Boxall, P., Purcell, J. and Wright, P. (2007). Human Resource Management: scope, analysis and significance, in Boxall, P., Purcell, J. and Wright, P. (eds.) *Oxford Handbook of Human Resource Management.* Oxford: Oxford University Press, pp. 1–16.

Brown, W. (1972). 'A consideration of custom and practice', *British Journal of Industrial Relations*, 10(1), pp. 42–61.

Brown, W. (2008). The influence of product markets on Industrial Relations, in Blyton, P., Bacon, N., Fiorio, J. and Heery, E. (eds.) *Handbook of Industrial Relations*. London: Sage, pp. 113–127.

Bruce, K. and Nyland, C. (2011). 'Elton Mayo and the deification of Human Relations', *Organization Studies*, 32(3), pp. 383–405.

Budd, J.W. (2004). *Employment with a Human Face: Balancing Efficiency, Equity and Voice*. Ithaca: Cornell University Press.

Chandler, A.D. (1962). *Strategy and Structure*. Cambridge (MA): MIT Press.

Cole, A.D.H. (1930). *The Life of Robert Owen*. London: Macmillan.

Cushen, J. and Harney, B. (2014). Broken promises: why SHRM does not always work, in Harney, B. and Monks, K. (eds.) *Strategic HRM: Research and Practice in Ireland*. Dublin: Orpen.

Delbridge, R. (2007). 'Explaining conflicted collaboration: a critical realist approach to hegemony', *Organization Studies*, 28(9), pp. 1347–1357.

Delbridge, R. and Whitfield, K. (2007). 'More than mere fragments? The use of the Workplace Employment Relations Survey data in HRM research', *International Journal of Human Resource Management*, 18(12), pp. 2166–2181.

Drucker, P.F. (1954). *The Practice of Management*. New York: Harper and Row.

Dundon, T. and Dobbins, T. (2015), 'Militant partnership: a radical pluralist analysis of workforce dialectics', *Work, Employment & Society*, 29(6), pp. 912–931.

Dundon, T. and Rollinson, D. (2011). *Understanding Employment Relations*. London: McGraw-Hill.

Dundon, T., Cullinane, N. and Wilkinson, A. (2017). *A Very Short, Fairly Interesting and Reasonably Cheap Book About Studying Employment Relations*. London: Sage.

Edwards, P. (1986). *Conflict At Work: A Materialist Analysis of Workplace Relations*. Oxford: Blackwell.

Edwards, P. (1995). 'From Industrial Relations to the Employment Relationship', *Relations Industrielle*, 50(1), pp. 39–65.

Edwards, P. (2003). The employment relationship and the field of industrial relations, in Edwards, P. (ed.) *Industrial Relations: Theory and Practice*. Oxford: Blackwell, pp. 1–36.

Edwards, P. (2005). 'The challenging but promising future of industrial relations: developing theory and method in context sensitive research', *Industrial Relations Journal*, 36(4), pp. 264–282.

Ehrnrooth, M. and Björkman, I. (2012). 'An Integrative HRM Process Theorization: Beyond Signalling Effects and Mutual Gains', *Journal of Management Studies*, 49(6), pp. 1109–1135.

Fombrun, C., Tichy, N. and Devanna, M. (1984). *Strategic Human Resource Management*. New York: Wiley.

Geare, A., Edgar, F., McAndrew, I., Harney, B., Cafferkey, K. and Dundon, T. (2014). 'Exploring the ideological undercurrents of HRM: workplace values and beliefs in Ireland & New Zealand', *International Journal of Human Resource Management*, 25(16), pp. 2275–2294.

George, A. and Bennett, A. (2004). *Case Studies and Theory Development*. Cambridge (MA): MIT Press.

Gerhart, B. (2007). Modelling HRM and Performance Linkages, in Boxall, P., Purcell, J. and Wright, P. (eds.) *Oxford Handbook of Human Resource Management*. Oxford: Oxford University Press.

Godard, J. (1994). 'Beyond Empiricism: Towards a Reconstruction of IR Theory and Research', *Advances in Industrial and Labor Relations*, 6, pp. 1–35.

Godard, J. (2014). 'The psychologisation of employment relations?' *Human Resource Management Journal*, 24(1), pp. 1–18.

Gospel, H. (2009). HRM: a historical perspective, in Wilkinson, A., Bacon, N., Redman, T. and Snell, S. (eds.) *The SAGE Handbook of Human Resource Management*. London: Sage, pp. 12–30.

Gouldner, A.W. (1954). *Patterns of Industrial Bureaucracy*. New York: Free Press.

Grant, D. and Shields, J. (2002). 'Researching employee reactions to human resources management', *Journal of Industrial Relations*, 44(3), pp. 313–334.

Gratton, L., Hope-Hailey, V., Stiles, P. and Truss, C. (1999). *Strategic Human Resource Management: Corporate Rhetoric and Human Reality*. Oxford: Oxford University Press.

Grey, C. (2009). *A Very Short, Fairly Interesting and Reasonably Cheap Book About Studying Organisations*. 2nd edn. London: Sage.

Grimshaw, D. and Rubery, J. (2008). Economics and HRM, in Boxall, P., Purcell, J. and Wright, P.M. (eds.) *Oxford Handbook of Human Resource Management*. Oxford: Oxford University Press.

Guest, D. (1987). 'Human resource management and industrial relations', *Journal of Management Studies*, 24(5), pp. 503–521.

Guest, D. (2011). 'Human resource management and performance: still searching for some answers', *Human Resource Management Journal*, 21(1), pp. 3–13.

Guest, D. (2017). 'Human Resource Management and Employee Well-Being: Towards a New Analytic Framework', *Human Resource Management Journal*, 21(3), pp. 3–13.

Harley, B. (2015). "The one best way?" 'Scientific' Research on HRM and the threat to critical scholarship', *Human Resource Management*, 25(4), pp. 399–407.

Harney, B. (2009). *Exploring the road less travelled in HRM-Performance research: a critical realist alternative to big science*. Proceedings of the Labor and Employment Relations Association 61st Annual Meeting LERA. [Online]. Available at: www.researchgate.net/publication/261697573_Exploring_the_road_less_travelled_in_HRM-Performance_research_A_critical_realist_alternative_to_big_science.

Harney, B. and Jordan, C. (2008). 'Unlocking the black box: line managers and HRM performance in a call centre context', *International Journal of Productivity and Performance Management*, 57(4), pp. 275–296.

Harney, B. and Trehy, J. (2016). Resource-based view, in Wilkinson, A. and Johnstone, S. (eds.) *Encyclopedia of Human Resource Management*. Cheltenham: Edward Elgar, pp. 377–378:

Hassard, J. (2012). 'Rethinking the Hawthorne Studies: The Western Electric research in its social, political and historical context', *Human Relations*, 65(11), pp. 1431–1461.

Heffernan, M. and Dundon, T. (2016). 'Cross-level effects of high-performance work systems (HPWS) and employee well-being: the mediating effect of organisational justice', *Human Resource Management Journal*, 26(2), pp. 211–231.

Hope-Hailey, V., Farndale, E. and Truss, C. (2005). 'The HR department's role in organisational performance', *Human Resource Management Journal*, 15(3), pp. 49–66.

Huselid, M.A. (1995). 'The impact of human resource practices on turnover, productivity, and corporate financial performance', *Academy of Management Journal*, 38(3), pp. 635–672.

Ichniowski, C., Shaw, C. and Prennushi, G. (1997). 'The effects of human resource management on productivity: a study of steel finishing lines', *American Economic Review*, 87(3), pp. 291–313.

Jackson, S.E., Schuler, R.S. and Jiang, K. (2014). 'An aspirational framework for strategic HRM', *Academy of Management Annals*, 8(1), pp. 1–56.

Jacques, R. (1999). 'Developing a tactical approach to engaging with 'Strategic' HRM', *Organization*, 6(2), pp. 199–222.

Jain, H. and Murray, V. (1984). 'Why the human resource management function fails', *California Management Review*, XXVI(4), pp. 95–110.

Jiang, K., Lepak, D., Hu, J. and Baer, J. (2012). 'How does human resource management influence organizaional outcomes? A meta-analytic investigation of mediating mechanisms', *Academy of Management Journal*, 55(6), pp. 1264–1294.

Kaufman, B. (1999). 'Evolution and Current Status of University HR Programs', *Human Resource Management Review*, 38(2), pp. 103–110.

Kaufman, B. (2007). The development of HRM in historical and international perspective, in Boxall, P., Purcell, J. and Wright, P. (eds.) *Handbook of Human Resource Management*. Oxford: Oxford University Press, pp. 19–47.

Kaufman, B. (2010). 'A theory of the firm's demand for HRM practices', *International Journal of Human Resource Management*, 21(5), pp. 615–636.

Kaufman, B. (2012). 'Strategic Human Resource Management Research in the United States: A Failing Grade After 30 Years?' *Academy of Management Perspectives*, 26(2), pp. 12–36.

Keegan, A. and Boselie, P. (2006). 'The lack of impact of dissensus inspired analysis on developments in the field of human resource management', *Journal of Management Studies*, 43(7), pp. 1491–1511.

Keenoy, T. (1990). 'HRM: rhetoric, reality and contradiction', *International Journal of Human Resource Management*, 1(3), pp. 363–384.

Keenoy, T. (2007). *Chasing the shadows of HRM*. Paper presented at the Critical Management Studies Conference, University of Manchester, July 11–13.

Kiechel, W.I. (2012). 'The management century', *Harvard Business Review*, 90(11), pp. 63–75.

Kochan, T. (2007). Social legitimacy of the HRM profession: a US perspective, in Boxall, P., Purcell, J. and Wright, P. (eds.) *Oxford Handbook of Human Resource Management*. Oxford: Oxford University Press.

Legge, K. (1995). *Human Resource Management: Rhetoric and Realities*. Basingstoke: Macmillan.

Legge, K. (2005). Preview/PostScript for the anniversary edition – Times they are a-changing: HRM Rhetoric and Realities Ten Years on, in *Human Resource Management*. Basingstoke: Macmillan.

Lepak, D.P. and Snell, S. (2002). 'Examining the human resources architecture: the relationships among human capital, employment and resource configurations', *Journal of Management*, 28(4), pp. 517–543.

Lindblom, C.E. (1959), 'The science of 'muddling through', *Public Administration Review*, 19 (Spring), pp. 79–88.

Marchington, M. (2015). 'Human resource management (HRM): too busy looking up to see where it is going longer term?' *Human Resource Management Review*, 25(2), pp. 176–187.

Marchington, M. and Suter, J. (2013). 'Where Informality Really Matters: Patterns of Employee Involvement and Participation (EIP) in a Non-Union Firm', *Industrial Relations*, 52(1), pp. 284–313.

Marchington, M., Wilkinson, A., Donnelly, R. and Kynighou, A. (2016). *Human Resource Management at Work*. 6th edn. London: Chartered Institute of Personnel and Development.

MacDuffie, J.P. (1995). 'Human resource bundles and manufacturing performance: organizational logic and flexible production systems in the world auto industry', *Industrial and Labor Relations Review*, 48(2), pp. 197–221.

Miles, R. and Snow, C. (1984). 'Designing strategic human resource systems', *Organizational Dynamics*, 13(1), pp. 36–52.

Mowday, R., Porter, L.W. and Steers, R. (1982). *Employee–Organization Linkages: The Psychology of Commitment, Absenteeism, and Turnover*. New York: Academic Press.

Niven, M. (1967). *Personnel Management, 1913–63: The Growth of Personnel Management and the Development of the Institute*. London: Institute of Personnel Management.

Nolan, P. and Wood, S. (2003). 'Mapping the future of work', *British Journal of Industrial Relations*, 41(2), pp. 165–174.

Paauwe, J., Guest, D. and Wright, P. (2013). *HRM and Performance: Achievements and Challenges*. Chichester: Wiley.

Porter, M. and Siggelkow, N. (2008). 'Contextuality within activity systems and sustainability of competitive advantage', *Academy of Management Perspectives*, 22(2), pp. 34–56.

Posthuma, R., Campion, M., Masimova, M. and Campion, M. (2013). 'A High Performance Work Practices Taxonomy: Integrating the Literature and Directing Future Research', *Journal of Management*, 39(5), pp. 1184–1220.

Prandy, K., Stewart, A. and Blackburn, R.M. (1983). *White Collar Unionism*. London: Macmillan.

Ramsay, H., Scholarios, D. and Harley, B. (2000). 'Employees and high performance work systems: testing inside the blackbox', *British Journal of Industrial Relations*, 38(4), pp. 501–531.

Schuler, R.S. and Jackson, S.E. (1987). 'Linking competitive strategies with human resource management practices', *Academy of Management Executive*, 1(3), pp. 207–219.

Seifert, R. (2015). 'Big bangs and cold wars: the British industrial relations tradition after Donovan (1965–2015)', *Employee Relations*, 37(6), pp. 746–760.

Storey, J. (ed.) (1995). *Human Resource Management: A Critical Text*. London: Routledge.

Tamkin, P., Reilly, P. and Hirsh, W. (2006). *Managing and Developing HR Careers: Emerging Trends and Issues*. London: CIPD.

Thompson, P. (2011). 'The trouble with HRM', *Human Resource Management Journal*, 21(4), pp. 355–367.

Thompson, P. (2013). 'Financialization and the workplace: extending and applying the disconnected capitalism thesis', *Work, Employment & Society*, 27(3), pp. 472–488.

Torrington, D., Hall, L., Taylor, S. and Atkinson, C. (2014). *Human Resource Management*. London: Pearson.

Townsend, K. and Wilkinson, A. (2014). 'Guest Editors' Note: Time to Reconnect the Silos? Similarities and Differences in Employment Relations and Human Resources', *Human Resource Management*, 53(2), pp. 203–210.

Townsend, K. and Dundon, T. (2015). 'Guest editorial: Line Managers and Employee Relations', *Employee Relations*, 27(4), pp. 1–7.

Tyson, S. (1997). 'Human resource strategy: a process for managing the contribution of HRM to organisational performance', *International Journal of Human Resource Management*, 8(3), pp. 277–290.

Tyson, S. and Fell, A. (1986). *Evaluating the Personnel Function*. London: Hutchinson.

van den Broek, D. and Dundon, T. (2012). '(Still) Up to No Good: Reconfiguring Worker Resistance and Misbehaviour in an Increasingly Unorganized World', *Relations Industrielles/Industrial Relations*, 67(1), pp. 97–121.

Wall, T. and Wood, S. (2005). 'The romance of human resource management and business performance, and the case for big science', *Human Relations*, 58(4), pp. 429–462.

Walton, R.E. (1985). 'From control to commitment on the workplace.' *Harvard Business Review*, 63(2), pp. 77–84.

Wilkinson, A., Bacon, N., Redman, T. and Snell, S. (2009). *The SAGE Handbook of Human Resource Management*. London: Sage.

Wilkinson, A., Dundon, T. and Grugulis, I. (2007). 'Information but not consultation: exploring employee involvement in SMEs', *International Journal of Human Resource Management*, 18(7), pp. 1279–1297.

Wilkinson, A., Redman, T. and Dundon, T. (2017). *Contemporary Human Resource Management: Text and Cases*. 5th edn. London: Pearson.

Wood, S. (1979). 'A reappraisal of the contingency approach to organisation', *Journal of Management Studies*, 16(3), pp. 334–354.

Youndt, M.A., Dean, J.W. and Lepak, D.P. (1996). 'Human Resource Management, Manufacturing Strategy and Firm Performance', *Academy of Management Journal*, 39(4), pp. 836–866.

9
INSTITUTIONAL THEORY AND EMPLOYMENT RELATIONS

Matthew M.C. Allen and Geoffrey Wood

Introduction

Institutions matter. They help to shape the decisions that individual and collective actors, such as managers, workers, unions and politicians, make (Hall and Soskice, 2001; Hollingsworth and Boyer, 1997; Jessop, 1997; North, 1990; Steinmo and Thelen, 1992; Streeck, 2011a). As institutions vary between different countries and regions within countries, the typical patterns of interactions between managers, on the one hand, and workers and their representatives, on the other, will also differ. This encompasses not just the formal mechanisms by which employees and employee representatives engage with management in seeking to negotiate wages and working conditions, and the social and technical organisation of work, but also the informal, daily social interactions within and between firms that involve potential compromises and ad hoc solutions. Fundamental institutional effects include the relative rights and responsibilities accorded to employers, the degree of countervailing power enjoyed by employees and other stakeholders, and the room available for compromise and mutually beneficial accommodations (Hall and Soskice, 2001; La Porta, Lopez de Silanes and Shleifer, 1999). However, there is much debate within the institutional camp as to the relative opportunities accorded for the latter, how they may have diminished over time, and, indeed, whether they are desirable at all (Streeck, 2013; Whitley, 2010; Wright, 2004).

Institutional theory has a long and rich history, covering different aspects of how institutions influence employment relations (Hall and Taylor, 1996; Katzenstein, 1985; Morgan and Hauptmeier, 2014; Shonfeld, 1965; Steinmo and Thelen, 1992; Zysman, 1984). This chapter focuses on three particularly influential approaches within the institutional literature; much comparative work on ER draws on them (Wilkinson and Wood, 2012, 2014). They are: 1) Varieties of Capitalism (VoC) and the broadly related business systems approaches (Hall and Soskice, 2001; Whitley, 1994, 1999, 2007); 2) historical institutionalism (Streeck, 1997, 2011a; Thelen, 2014); and 3) the *régulation* approach, which has led to the 'social systems of innovation and production' sub-school of analysis (Amable, 2003; Hollingsworth and Boyer, 1997) and the literature on 'variegated capitalism' (Jessop, 2012a).

The differences between these three approaches are not always as clear in practice, as we set out here. Indeed, work by individual researchers does not necessarily fit coherently or consistently into one of these three categories. Our classification does, though, enable us to highlight key differences between the approaches and to demonstrate how those differences result in contrasting analytical foci and explanations of variation in ER. The two factors that we focus on to distinguish the different approaches are 1) explanations of institutional change, and 2) the emphasis on, and conceptualisation of, internationalisation (Allen, 2013; Boyer and Juillard, 2002; Hall and Soskice, 2001; Jessop, 1997; Morgan, 2007b; Streeck, 1997; Whitley, 2007, 2010).

The three institutionalist approaches that we examine here contrast with rational, hierarchical accounts within the mainstream economics and finance literatures (Djankov et al., 2003; North, 1990). These perspectives and the three institutional theories that this chapter focuses on share an emphasis on the role of formal and embedded 'rules' in governing long-term national developmental trajectories; there are, however, clear differences. First, the former tend to highlight the importance of formal rules rather than formal *and* informal ones. Second, the rational, hierarchical approaches often adopt a 'narrow' view of institutions and their influences, meaning that institutions either have a positive or negative link to important outcomes, such as economic growth or firm innovation (Allen and Aldred, 2013; Boyer, 2011; Campbell, 2007; Jackson and Deeg, 2008; Whitley, 2003). Indeed, some of the former approaches assume that a single institutional feature, private property rights, overrides all other institutional features and that the strength of this alone determines the prosperity of nations (Djankov et al., 2003; Glaeser, et al., 2004).

Third, the rational, hierarchical approaches assume that institutions and actors can be conceived as discrete, analytically distinct entities that are separate from one another. As North (1990, p. 4) noted: "Conceptually, what must be clearly differentiated are the rules [of the game] from the players [of it]". Within rational, hierarchical frameworks, then, institutions primarily serve as providers of incentives or disincentives to rational actors, encouraging them to make optimal or sub-optimal choices. In contrast, the latter approaches that we focus on in this chapter conceive institutions and actors to be a duality, meaning that actors and institutions are mutually constitutive, inter-related entities (Allen, 2013). Fourth, as a corollary of the preceding point, the rational, hierarchical approaches to institutions tend to downplay 1) the varying nature of firms in different locations and 2) the possibility that institutions can enable particular outcomes, but do not always lead to that outcome (Jackson and Deeg, 2008; Steinmo, 2008). What is rational for actors will, therefore, depend upon their socio-economic context.

Finally, perhaps the most salient difference between rational hierarchical approaches and socio-economic alternatives is that whilst the former continues to develop along a very distinct trajectory, encompassing deeply embedded – and at times fact-resistant – assumptions as to the inherent and consistent superiority of liberal markets (Buccirossi et al., 2013), the latter sub-schools of thought have increasingly found common ground between each other, even if these commonalities are often not explicitly recognised by the proponents of each approach (Kristensen and Morgan, 2012a; Streeck, 2010, 2011a; Thelen, 2014; Whitley, 2010).

The Varieties of Capitalism framework and business systems theory

These frameworks seek to explain how institutions help or hinder companies to solve co-ordination problems, such as recruiting and retaining particular kinds of employees, facilitating investments in certain skills or re-configuring organisational capabilities (Hall and Soskice, 2001; Harcourt and Wood, 2007; Whitley, 1999, 2007). The business systems approach differs from the VoC framework and predates it (Allen, 2014); however, the two share an analytical focus on the varying type of co-ordination challenges that firms face and the role that institutions play in influencing companies' abilities to overcome those problems (Hall and Soskice, 2001; Whitley, 1999).

The main difference is that the VoC approach draws quite extensively on rational choice economics, with its assumptions that actors' decision-making will be guided by their efforts to maximise their distributional benefits (Wood, 2011). However, they depart from orthodox economics in the assumption that in interacting with each other, actors are inevitably forced into compromises that will contribute to institutional building and maintenance, and that such compromises may leave the parties better off than if they had been able to pursue their interests independently. In contrast, business system theory's foundations lie in industrial sociology; it draws on Weberian traditions to develop ideal types that are logically consistent and that do not necessarily reflect empirical reality (Morgan, 2007a). In practical terms, whilst both claim to be firm-centred accounts, the VoC approach places a stronger emphasis on the form and scale of macro-societal accommodations between broadly based actors, and the business systems approach highlights the distinct nature of both different state traditions and social relationships, whether involving individuals or collectives, within the workplace (Allen, 2014).

Both accounts agree, however, that the influence of institutions on firm behaviour results in companies that are located in some institutional settings being better able to compete in particular industries than their rivals in other locations, and that the foundations for variations in competitive abilities stem from the nature of regional and national institutional influences. For instance, firms in Germany benefit from institutions that, *inter alia*, support intra-employer co-operation, industry-level vocational training, patient investor behaviour and workplace co-determination, making them competitive in incrementally innovative areas of activity, such as mechanical engineering and automobiles. By contrast, the institutional framework in the USA promotes the competitiveness of both breakthrough innovative industries, such as bio-technology and IT, as well as low-end service sector work (Hall and Soskice, 2001; Whitley, 1999, 2010). Such firms appear to cope relatively well with adversarial competition, highly mobile and speculative investors, and flexible labour markets. This enables innovative startups to more easily secure funding. Weak security of job tenure and high levels of inter-job mobility enable firms to cope with sudden fluctuations in demand. In particularly innovative sectors, such mobility helps to transfer skills and knowledge between firms.

Hence, both approaches argue that institutions influence the ability of firms to pursue par-ticular competition strategies successfully, as different strategies have implications for how firms manage their employees and organise work (Casper, 2009; Goyer, 2011; Hotho, 2014; Whitley, 2000, 2010). As a result, institutions help to explain international patterns of comparative advan-tage (Allen, Funk and Tüselmann, 2006; Hotho, 2014; Schneider and Paunescu, 2012; Witt and Jackson, 2016). However, unlike the regulation approach, which not only critiques the inherent contradictions and inequalities associated with contemporary capitalism, but also suggests that the contexts with the weakest institutional mediation are the least desirable, these approaches make no explicit assumptions as to the operational or moral superiority of a particular national institutional regime (Dore, 2008; Hall and Soskice, 2001; Howell, Culpepper and Rueda, 2015; Howell, 2003; Whitley, 1999, 2007).

Institutional change

As a result of the emphasis on the benefits that companies gain from their institutional settings, both approaches have tended, at least until recently, to assume that institutions and patterns of economic organisation are relatively stable (Campbell, 2010; Crouch and Farrell, 2004; Hall and Thelen, 2009; Hancké, Rhodes and Thatcher, 2007; Howell et al., 2015; Jackson and Deeg, 2006; Jessop, 2012a; Morgan, 2007a). The VoC approach, in particular, assumes that companies will adapt their competition strategies to take advantage of the institutional resources that are available to them in their national economies (Allen, 2004; Crouch, 2005). Dominant firms, in other words, derive competitive advantages from their institutional setting (Hall and Soskice, 2001; Whitley, 1999). This, in turn, implies that leading firms will not seek to fundamentally alter the existing institutional frameworks (Howell et al., 2015; Wood and Frynas, 2006; Wood, 2001), as the benefits that these groups derive from existing institutions outweigh their costs and the risks posed by embarking on unfamiliar trajectories. The VoC approach and the business systems framework have not, until relatively recently, analysed in detail how and why institutional change occurs.

This does not mean, however, that these approaches have ignored institutional change. When they focus on institutional dynamics, they highlight factors 'outside' the institutional system. For instance, the approaches have highlighted how exogenous shocks, such as the globalisation of capital markets, the demise of state socialism in Central and Eastern Europe in the 1990s and the increasing speed and functionality of information and communication technology, have, in general, weakened 'non-market' forms of economic co-ordination (Hall and Soskice, 2001; Lane, 2005; Morgan and Kubo, 2005; Whitley, 2010). Consistent, then, with the emphasis on the benefits of institutions within these two approaches, institutional change does not result from developments within institutional domains themselves.

However, the VoC literature has increasingly recognised that even more mature capitalist archetypes may be subject to change, and that the predominant pressures will be for greater liberalisation. Hall and Gingerich (2009) note that as actors forge accommodations to reconcile competing demands whilst maximising their personal distributional benefits, they will naturally seek to enhance the latter, and continuously push back on any constraints. In practice, this means that given strong global pressures towards liberalisation, key players have an opportunity to maximise their benefits, which they will seek to capitalise on; this has meant strong pressures towards the greater marketisation of ER (see Hall and Gingerich, 2009; Whitley, 2010).

Such pressures entice companies, irrespective of their institutional setting, to focus to an even greater extent on financial outcomes and increasing the requirement for more 'flexibility' in the employment relationship between employers and wider groups of employees (Morgan, 2016). The increasing international spread of activist short-termist investors capitalise on systemic reforms to promote short-term shareholder returns at the expense of longer-term financial and organisational objectives and co-ordinating capabilities (Whitley, 2010), potentially leading to a use of agency workers or employees on short-term contracts (Allen et al., 2017).

As the VoC and business systems approaches tend to downplay institutional change, they are both, in some respects, ahistorical (Jessop, 2012b). In focusing on linear developmental trajectories (regardless of whether such trajectories are converging) the VoC and business systems literature neglects the extent to which the mature capitalist archetypes as described represent relatively recent phenomena (cf. Morgan, 2007a). Liberal markets were considerably less liberal, and liberal market-based firms typically did not focus on financial returns to the same extent that they do today up until the 1980s (Lazonick, 2010).

A further issue is, even if co-ordinated markets are quite durable, whether other types of capitalism are converging to the liberal market model. As noted above, the early VoC literature saw all other economies as being in a transitional phase prior to becoming more like one of the mature models. However, it has been increasingly recognised that other types of capitalism may be quite viable, and result in sufficient benefits for key players so as to persist (Hancké et al., 2007; Wood and Frynas, 2006). This has led to much debate on what these other types of capitalism might be, with new archetypes including hierarchical market economies (Latin America), segmented business systems (Africa), mixed market economies (the European Mediterranean economies), dependent market economies (Eastern Europe), and the transitional periphery

(Central Asia, Caucasus and Ukraine) (Hancké et al., 2007; Nölke and Vliegenthart, 2009; Witt and Jackson, 2016; Wood and Frynas, 2006).

As the business systems framework never accepted the two mature models thesis, this line of thinking was always more open to such approaches (Whitley, 1999, 2007; Witt and Jackson, 2016). The growing emphasis on multi-archetype models reflects empirical reality, but raises questions as to what really sets different types of capitalism apart, especially as the proliferation of models leads to a loss of parsimony, which is the *raison d'être* of the theorising process.

Internationalisation

As noted above, recent work on institutional change within the VoC and business systems frameworks often focus on how internationalisation can decrease the institutional restrictions on collective actors to be opportunistic, increase the heterogeneity of actors and hamstring actors' attempts to engage in long-term, high-trust dealings with one another (Hall and Soskice, 2001; Morgan, 2005; Whitley, 2010, 2012). As an example, the decreasing barriers to trade increase the competitive pressures on domestic firms by foreign firms, especially in markets for commoditised goods. This can reduce domestic firms' abilities to restrict aggressive price competition and maintain working conditions, even in situations where a highly motivated workforce would benefit companies in the long term (Hall and Soskice, 2001, pp. 56–60; Whitley, 2010).

Recently, the business systems framework, in particular, has highlighted the position of multinational corporations (MNCs) as collective actors who are rooted in different and potentially contrasting institutional settings and who are often significantly less committed to particular production facilities and modes of operation than their purely domestic counterparts. As a result, they are more likely to question taken-for-granted assumptions and ways of organising work in both home and host countries (Kristensen and Morgan, 2012b; Morgan and Kristensen, 2006; Morgan, 2012). This represents a significant shift from early VoC and business system work that downplayed the importance of MNCs and assumed that social ties bound firms to a specific institutional setting and that firms could not easily ignore these ties (Allen, 2004).

Historical institutionalism

Historical institutionalism focuses on 1) the circumstances under which institutional arrangements are established or bedded down, and 2) the long-term processes that involve internal and external forces and that lead to institutional change (Hall and Taylor, 1996; Hassel, 2014; Steinmo and Thelen, 1992; Steinmo, 2008; Streeck, 2009; Thelen, 2012). As is the case with regulationist theory, historical institutionalism is strongly influenced by Polanyian notions of double movements and pressures that impel nations towards greater statism or marketisation (Streeck, 2009).

However, historical institutionalists emphasise that the forms that states and markets assume will vary according to long-term historical processes; this is, of course, a point that is integral to Polanyi's writing (Polanyi, 2001 [1944]), but is somehow lost in optimistic strands of the industrial relations literature, which assume that state mediation will be in the labour-friendly form of the 1950s' welfare state. However, statism is often not benign; for example, the role of ostensibly neoliberal states in supporting an ecosystem of firms that, whilst unable to compete on market terms, occupy oligopolistic positions in tendering for outsourced state functions and that reap increased profits as a result (Wood and Wright, 2015).

Unlike early regulationist thinking, historical institutionalism has always accorded particular attention to issues of scale; in other words, it highlights national political traditions and associated party politics, and the relative fortunes of different sections of workers in different settings (Busemeyer, 2009; Steinmo, 2008; Streeck, 2013).

Institutional change

Historical institutionalism assumes that institutions change as a result of the different and sometimes competing interests of collective actors (Crouch and Farrell, 2004; Regini, 2003; Streeck, 2011a). This does not, however, mean that historical institutionalists predict when any specific institutional framework will change (Streeck, 2012). It does, though, presuppose that specific historical circumstances help to create particular institutional frameworks, leading to institutions that are legitimate – whilst also being contested – within temporally specific limits (Steinmo and Thelen, 1992; Streeck, 2012). For instance, institutional arrangements that reflect social democratic values in Europe came into being in the late 1940s and 1950s when certain collective actors, including the occupying powers in West Germany, were able to impose institutions, such as the extension of workers' rights, in the coal and steel industries, influencing later national legislation (Jackson, 2005).

A corollary of this approach is that economic and financial elites are not able to determine which institutions will change in which ways. Instead, these collective actors must compromise and seek to change existing institutional arrangements where they can. Institutions will, of course, shape the interests of these elites and mediate how any institutional change will proceed. In general, however, economic and financial elites are likely to encourage the greater use of market relations within, as well as between, individual firms (Goyer, 2011; Regini, 2003; Thelen, 2012). For example, the 2008 financial crisis has led some historical institutionalists to argue that national institutions which impede deregulated labour markets are gradually being eroded in different countries, resulting in labour markets in all countries being characterised by greater 'flexibility' and the commodification of more types of employment and non-economic activities (Crouch, 2013; Howell et al., 2015; Regini, 2003; Streeck and Thelen, 2005; Streeck, 2012, 2013, 2014).

Indeed, Streeck's recent research argues that countries are in the early stages of a liberalisation process rather than at the end of such a process (Streeck, 2011a, 2012, 2013, 2014). This suggests that companies in various countries are likely to focus more on short-term financial objectives and trying to make labour markets more flexible. Evidence from German employer associations buttresses these claims: many of these associations lobbied aggressively for liberalisation in the 2000s (Kinderman, 2014 cf. Goerres and Höpner, 2014). Improvements in Germany's economic performance have lessened these claims to some extent (Kinderman, 2014); however, many policy-makers still adhere to neoliberalism, despite the financial crisis (Crouch, 2013).

Indeed, crises in the global economy create opportunities for, as well as pressures on, different collective actors, especially property owners, to seek to change existing institutional structures (Crouch, 2013; Palier and Thelen, 2010; Streeck, 2013; Thelen, 2012). In contrast to both the VoC framework and the business systems approach, therefore, historical institutionalism emphasises the importance of endogenous institutional change (Streeck, 2012). Property owners often create these changes as they seek to expand in scope and depth the areas dominated by market relations (Crouch, 2016; Kinderman, 2014; Streeck, 2012). Consequently, historical institutionalists often view institutional change as a contested, political process that is instigated and led by those seeking to improve their position within the institutional framework. Those with liquid assets, such as shareholders and financiers, are frequently within this group (Goyer, 2011; Schnyder, 2012; Wood and Wright, 2015; cf. Streeck, 2012). A further implication of the assumptions that underpin institutional change within historical institutionalism is that the government is the key actor in ensuring work relations (Rogers and Streeck, 1995; Streeck,

2012) and that governments of various hues in different countries will come under pressure to liberalise existing economic activities and marketise other, non-economic areas of social life (Crouch, 2011, 2016; Regini, 2014; Streeck, 2012, 2013).

However, some historical institutionalists argue that some companies in co-ordinated market economies will attempt to protect existing institutions and their associated modes of operation. For example, some German employers continue to support vocational training schemes, as they help to create collaborative workplace environments (Thelen, 2014). In addition, the focus on national-level regulations within much of the historical institutionalism literature can obscure areas of continuity in firm-level policies and practices as well as in sectoral or local institutional arrangements (Busemeyer, 2009; Hassel, 2014; Streeck, 2014; Thelen, 2009, 2014, cf. Sako and Jackson, 2006).

Internationalisation

The focus on politics and social outcomes within historical institutionalism results in internationalisation being conceptualised primarily as a process that is driven by international capital markets and that puts pressures on national governments to cut deficits, increase taxes, decrease welfare spending, de-regulate labour markets and curtail the role of collective bargaining (Crouch, 2016; Streeck, 2011b, 2012).

In part as a result of these pressures on all democratic, capitalist countries, historical institutionalists argue that research should focus to a greater extent on the commonalities across different forms of capitalism rather than their differences (Streeck, 2010). As Streeck has written:

> It is hard to see how a view as sanguine as this [that emphasises the persistence of distinct and autonomous national variants of capitalism] could survive the experience of the global crisis and its proliferation along the transnational linkages created by dynamically expanding international markets, in particular for finance.
>
> *(Streeck, 2010, p.38)*

As the above quotation illustrates, historical institutionalism highlights the internationalisation of *markets* rather than *firms*. This has important implications as it suggests that the market logic will expand in breadth and depth across countries but that it will be difficult to establish a common governance structure across those different nations (Crouch, 2016; Streeck, 2010), leading to the deregulation of labour markets, for instance. By focusing on markets rather than firms, historical institutionalism implicitly invokes a view of markets as non-agentic, homogeneous entities that pursue an autogenic logic of ever greater expansion. This leads to pessimistic assessments about the possibilities that exist for polities and international organisations, such as the European Union, to resist pressures to deregulate markets, including labour markets.

By contrast, a focus on firms would reveal the diversity of actors within markets as well as their sometimes coherent and sometimes competing interests (Goyer, 2011). This has implications for the extent to which common regulations that govern certain practices, such as collective redundancies, will be adopted in different institutional contexts. Even if financial markets and the accompanying logic that firms which are owned by a dispersed group of shareholders should be run primarily to create 'shareholder value' have become more international, that does not mean that other types of firm owner no longer exist in countries where such priorities were not traditionally the norm. This continued diversity of actors within different financial markets can mean that some employment practices, such as large-scale lay-offs, are more prevalent in the UK than they are in France (Goyer, Clark and Bhankaraully, 2016).

A further corollary of the emphasis on markets rather than firms is that historical institutionalism tends to assume that increasing breadth and depth of markets will lead to less diversity (Crouch, 2016; Streeck, 2010). By contrast, a focus on firms would reveal the importance of institutional variation to firms, as it enables them to conduct different types of activities in different locations that have diverse institutional settings (Allen, 2013; Kristensen and Morgan, 2012a; Lane, 2008). As a result, firms cannot be assumed to be homogeneous or to have the same interests and preferences for deregulation at all times and in all locations.

Regulation theory

The interrelated elements of regulation theory (RT) are the industrial paradigm (how the technical and social division of labour is governed), the mode of regulation (that examines the influences on individuals' behaviour), the accumulation or growth regime (how a national economy grows as a result of the usual patterns of consumption and production) and the modes of development (how the previous factors combine to ensure a relatively lengthy period of economic growth) (Boyer, 2005, 2011; Jessop, 1990, 2001, xxvii; Lipietz, 1997). More specifically, a mode of regulation is the "ensemble of norms, institutions, social networks and patterns of conduct that can stabilise an accumulation regime", and the latter in turn, "a complementary pattern of production and consumption" (Jessop, 2001, p. 93). Both are spatially and temporarily confined, and the former is of very much shorter duration and scale than the traditional Marxist concept of a mode of production.

Institutional change

Regulation theory presupposes that all forms of capitalism are inherently dynamic; as a result all forms of capitalism are likely to experience crises from time to time. In other words, crises are a quintessential part of capitalism. Even if institutional frameworks appear to be stable, they are only temporary, contingent, and spatially and temporally specific solutions to particular challenges (Jessop, 2012b). For instance, Boyer (2011, p.67) has contended that "a capitalist economy is never stuck in a stationary state since it is affected by the process of accumulation, the recurrence of social conflicts, major crises and the impact of radical innovations."

A corollary of such thinking is that institutional change is often the result of endogenous processes (Boyer, 2005, 2011; Jessop, 2001, 2012a): the inherent dynamism of capitalist modes of production largely explains institutional change rather than any outside or exogenous factors (Boyer and Juillard, 2002; Coriat, 2002). Of course, this does not mean that exogenous and endogenous change cannot occur at the same time or that the two can be easily identified in practice (Bohle and Greskovits, 2007; Bruff and Horn, 2012; Vidal, 2013b). For example, domestic firms that pursue 'shareholder value' may seek to extend the use of contingent, low-paid workers as well as make use of such workers as a result of regulatory changes wrought by international companies and the internationalisation of product markets.

Regulation theory is distinct from the VoC approach in another way: RT does not view the firm as a simple venue in which formal and informal rules are 'automatically' enacted or reproduced as the VoC tends to assume (Allen, 2004; Crouch, 2005), but emphasises how different and sometimes competing interests around the production process make the influence of institutions on actors' behaviour contingent and contested (Jessop, 2012a; Lipietz, 1993).

An initial focus in RT was, therefore, to explain how Fordist modes of production and consumption provided stable growth over a relatively long period of time, but eventually declined

(Boyer, 2005; Jessop, 2001). Although RT demonstrated how the Fordist model was practised differently in various countries, the approach also highlighted the similarities across those countries as well as the common challenges posed in finding viable alternative modes of production and consumption when Fordism declined (Boyer, 2005; Jessop, 2001).

Initially, the RT approach did not preclude the possibility that new institutional arrangements that would solve these challenges within capitalist systems would be based on collaboration within workplaces (Bliek and Parguez, 2008; Jessop, 2001). This, in part, was a corollary of the policy preferences of regulationists in France in the early 1980s as well as the optimistic outlook of analysts in the UK who had been influenced by regulationist thinking and who examined 'post-Fordist' models of capitalism (Bliek and Parguez, 2008; Jessop, 2001, xvii).

However, writing within the regulationist tradition always stressed that modern capitalism is inherently dysfunctional, albeit that the Althusserian radicalism of early RT has been tempered over the years. Indeed, in many respects historical institutionalists and regulation theorists are as pessimistic as one another about the ability of *capitalism* to deliver simultaneously rising profits and increasing wages; both, moreover, focus on the declining quality of many jobs that have limited autonomy, few opportunities for promotion or training, and have become increasingly precarious (Beynon, 2016; Vidal, 2013a, 2013b).

Internationalisation

Regulation theory examines internationalisation in two broad ways. The first focuses on the implications of internationalisation for workers and their employment conditions. The second assesses internationalisation at a conceptual rather than an empirical level, and highlights key distinctions between RT and VoC, in particular.

Regulation theory acknowledged that many jobs within Fordist production and consumption models did not offer high levels of discretion to employees; these jobs did, however, provide relatively high wages. Internationalisation has changed this (Vidal, 2013a). The heightened competitive pressures on companies that stem from the increasing internationalisation of product and capital markets as well as the growing importance of the service sector have led many firms to externalise as many jobs and activities as possible, resulting in reduced wages, lower-quality jobs, fewer training opportunities for many workers and an increase in the precariousness of some forms of employment (Vidal, 2013a). These trends have affected all countries, albeit to varying degrees (Hauptmeier, 2010; Vidal, 2013b).

At a more abstract level, scholars who draw on RT have emphasised how internationalisation raises important theoretical questions about how different varieties of capitalism interact with one another. In particular, RT focuses on the 'compossibility' of different forms of capitalism (Jessop, 2012b); in other words, whether one type of capitalism is able to co-exist with another. In general, RT argues that as a result of increasing competitive pressures and political decisions, market relations have gained in both breadth and depth, undermining the ability of politicians and other collective actors to maintain institutional regimes that support higher-quality jobs (Jessop, 2012b). This perspective contrasts with the VoC and business systems approaches, which assume that different varieties of capitalism can co-exist with one another as they can provide distinct benefits to companies within their borders, enabling them to compete globally in particular markets, such as cars or pharmaceuticals. Within RT, the USA occupies a dominant position, being able to shape the institutional settings in other countries to a greater extent than any other country. This influence stems, in part, from the USA having a currency that is used as a global reserve, enabling it to have a large and growing trade deficit (Jessop, 2012b).

Empirical evidence

A growing body of research has sought to test the veracity of the predictions of the theories against real-world evidence. This body of research can be divided into two broad categories. The first seeks to compare national institutional archetypes against broad societal trends (Allen et al., 2006; Boyer, 2004; Hotho, 2014; Schneider and Paunescu, 2012; Witt and Jackson, 2016). In general terms, this work confirms the predictions of the literature on comparative capitalism, but recognises that relatively slow systemic change may be taking place. Amable's (2003) capitalist archetypes are themselves derived from a cluster analysis of societal and macro-economic features.

The second body of research looks at firm-level practices, paying particular attention to work and employment relations. This includes a series of articles based on the Cranet comparative surveys that examine HR practices at different points of time in a large number of countries (Brewster et al., 2014, 2007; Brewster, Wood and Brookes, 2008; Farndale, Brewster and Poutsma, 2008). Research that has drawn on these data has explored the relative veracity of Whitley's (1999) original categorisations, Hall and Soskice's (2001) dichotomous classification, Hancké et al.'s (2007) taxonomy (which introduced the emerging market economy (Eastern Europe) and mixed market economy (Mediterranean) types) and Amable's (2003) framework that draws on cluster analysis. The methodology adopted in the latter study means that it provides the most accurate predictor of firm-level practices (Goergen et al., 2012).

The second strand of empirical evidence broadly confirms that 1) liberal market economies, such as the USA and the UK, are very different to other types of capitalism, 2) many workers are worse off in such contexts than in mature co-ordinated markets and 3) these differences have endured over time, despite claims that a process of convergence is underway (Brewster et al., 2014, 2007; Croucher et al., 2012; Harcourt and Wood, 2007). Challenges for future research include a closer analysis of the bounded nature of diversity amongst firms and inter-firm networks within national settings (existing work suggests that there is as much diversity within national systems as there is between them) and a closer examination of whether some liberal markets are more extreme than others (Brewster et al., 2014). Similarly, co-ordinated markets have always encompassed considerable diversity, and many smaller firms follow practices quite removed from the co-ordinated market ideal type (Allen, 2004; Brewster et al., 2014; Crouch, 2005).

By the same measure, no particular broad set of institutional conditions is ever immutable, no matter how much a limited range of key players may benefit from it; indeed, if, as is presently the case with both the US and the UK, a system systematically worsens, a large component of society and the existing social order will come under pressure. This does not necessarily signify a progressive moment, as it may result in a drive to narrow identity-based politics; however, by the same measure, such moves may challenge existing institutional arrangements (Skocpol and Williamson, 2012). Again, the strain unification placed on the German model, and wilful misunderstandings of the Japanese so-called lost decade, led to chronic misinterpretations of the viability of the largest co-ordinated markets; since 2008, the inherent strengths of both countries have become much more visible, and, by the same measure, forces for change may have been easily over-estimated.

Assessment

There is a tendency within all three of the institutional approaches reviewed here to assume that national institutional frameworks are relatively closely coupled (Crouch, 2005; Crouch,

Schröder and Voelzkow, 2009; Hall and Soskice, 2001; Streeck, 2010; Whitley, 1999, 2007 cf. Allen, 2013). Recent evidence has highlighted the importance of institutional diversity within national economies, even if that diversity is bounded by institutions (Lane and Wood, 2009; Walker, Brewster and Wood, 2014; Wood, 2013). This internal institutional diversity stems from 1) the persistence of regional or sectoral production networks, 2) the variable extent of institutional change and 3) local responses to reform pressures (Lane and Wood, 2009).

Regional institutional systems that involve industrial policies by regional authorities and the provision and maintenance of a highly skilled local workforce can facilitate the formation of strong inter-firm ties that, in turn, support firms' competition strategies (Crouch et al., 2009; Kristensen and Morgan, 2012a). In addition, variation exists between sectors within countries. For instance, within the US, certain sectors, such as defence, ICT and health, receive a large amount of state funding that other sectors do not (Allen, 2013; Keller and Block, 2013), helping to support the competition strategies of firms within those sectors and providing the basis for some well-remunerated and rewarding jobs.

Institutional change does not affect all collective actors in the same way. As the development of co-determination in Germany after the Second World War shows, institutional reform can be piecemeal, and will affect firms in certain sectors, such as coal and steel, before it has an impact on firms in other sectors (Jackson, 2005). Indeed, the number of employee representatives who sit on supervisory boards depends upon the size of the firm.

The effects of institutional change at the national level will have uneven consequences and result in new local variations while reinforcing old ones. For instance, financial market reforms at the national level have benefited, in general, those in London and the south east of England, increasing income inequality with the rest of the UK and helping to create stronger national cleavages, in particular between England and Scotland. As a result, Scotland has developed institutions that are distinct from those in England, with the aim of developing along more a social-democratic trajectory (Scott and Wright, 2012). This has created variation in the extent of privatisation of public-sector services between Scotland, where the role of the market is relatively marginal, and England, where it is greater (ibid.). The employment terms of those in private companies that provide some of the services to hospitals are likely to become more precarious and less well paid than those of public-sector employees who performed the same tasks.

Conclusion

A core tenet of the socio-economic literature on comparative capitalism is that there are many viable national economic models – even if the emphasis on the distinctiveness of those models varies within the three institutional perspectives examined here. A second key premise is that it is possible for firms to prosper when workers' legal rights are relatively strong. However, the literature has increasingly found common ground around the view that all institutional mediation is temporary and contingent, never closely coupled and that all institutional systems have disadvantages, shortfalls and internal contradictions. In turn, this makes national institutional orders inherently vulnerable to disruptions from both inside and outside the system.

As noted above, the three institutional approaches reviewed here tend, on the whole, to highlight the negative consequences of institutional change for workers' employment conditions. However, the literature also highlights the possibility of new institutional fixes, indicating that national employment regimes do not necessarily inevitably face deregulation with a commensurate degradation in employment relations and working life. At the same time, major institution building or redesign is a risky and complex process that in broad historic terms is relatively unusual. This would explain why a very broad body of literature, from Marx (1992 [1885]) to the reactionary writings of Calhoun (2012 [1837]), emphasises that almost all societies are characterised by large-scale labour coercion. The challenge for employment relations scholars is to avoid the trap of pessimism, through focusing on those alternatives that have proved most resilient to crisis and exploring the conditions under which these proven forms of institutional mediation may be replicated or extended (Wood and Lane, 2012; Wood and Wright, 2015).

References

Allen, M.M.C. (2004). 'The varieties of capitalism paradigm: not enough variety?' *Socio-Economic Review*, 2(1), pp. 87–108.

Allen, M.M.C. (2013). 'Comparative capitalisms and the institutional embeddedness of innovative capabilities', *Socio-Economic Review*, 11(4), pp. 771–794.

Allen, M.M.C. (2014). Business systems theory and employment relations, in Wilkinson, A., Wood, G. and Deeg, R. (eds.) *The Oxford Handbook of Employment Relations.* Oxford: Oxford University Press, pp. 86–113.

Allen, M.M.C. and Aldred, M.L. (2013). 'Business regulation, inward foreign direct investment, and economic growth in the new European Union Member States', *Critical Perspectives on International Business*, 9(3), pp. 301–321.

Allen, M.M.C., Funk, L. and Tüselmann, H. (2006). 'Can variation in public policies account for differences in comparative advantage?' *Journal of Public Policy*, 26(1), pp. 1–19.

Allen, M.M.C., Liu, J., Allen, M.L. and Imran Saqib, S. (2017). 'Establishments' use of temporary agency workers: the influence of institutions and establishments' employment strategies', *The International Journal of Human Resource Management*, 28(18), pp. 2570–2593.

Amable, B. (2003). *The Diversity of Modern Capitalism.* Oxford: Oxford University Press.

Beynon, H. (2016). Beyond Fordism, in Edgell, S., Gottfried, H. and Granter, E. (eds.) *The SAGE Handbook of the Sociology of Work and Employment.* London: Sage, pp. 306–328.

Bliek, J.-G. and Parguez, A. (2008). 'Mitterrand's turn to conservative economics: a revisionist history', *Challenge*, 51(2), pp. 97–109.

Bohle, D. and Greskovits, B. (2007). 'Neoliberalism, embedded neoliberalism and neocorporatism: Towards transnational capitalism in Central-Eastern Europe', *West European Politics*, 30(3), pp. 443–466.

Boyer, R. (2004). 'New growth regimes, but still institutional diversity', *Socio-Economic Review*, 2(1), pp. 1–32.

Boyer, R. (2005). 'How and why capitalisms differ', *Economy and Society*, 34(4), pp. 509–557.

Boyer, R. (2011). 'Are there laws of motion of capitalism?' *Socio-Economic Review*, 9(1), pp. 59–81.

Boyer, R. and Juillard, M. (2002). The United States: Goodbye, Fordism!, in Boyer, R. and Saillard, Y. (eds.) *Régulation Theory: The State of the Art.* London: Routledge, pp. 238–246.

Brewster, C., Brookes, M., Johnson, P. and Wood, G. (2014). 'Direct involvement, partnership and setting: a study in bounded diversity', *The International Journal of Human Resource Management*, 25(6), pp. 795–809.

Brewster, C., Croucher, R., Wood, G. and Brookes, M. (2007). 'Collective and individual voice: convergence in Europe?' *The International Journal of Human Resource Management*, 18(7), pp. 1246–1262.

Brewster, C., Wood, G. and Brookes, M. (2008). 'Similarity, isomorphism or duality? Recent survey evidence on the human resource management policies of multinational corporations', *British Journal of Management*, 19(4), pp. 320–342.

Bruff, I. and Horn, L. (2012). 'Varieties of capitalism in crisis?' *Competition and Change*, 16(3), pp. 161–168.

Buccirossi, P., Ciari, L., Duso, T., Spagnolo, G. and Vitale, C. (2013). 'Competition policy and productivity growth: an empirical assessment', *The Review of Economics and Statistics*, 95(4), pp. 1324–1336.

Busemeyer, M.R. (2009). 'Asset specificity, institutional complementarities and the variety of skill regimes in coordinated market economies', *Socio-Economic Review*, 7(3), pp. 375–406.

Calhoun, J.C. (2012). Speech on the reception of abolition petitions, in McKitrick, E.L. (ed.) *Slavery Defended: The Views of the Old South.* Whitefish (MT): Literary Licensing.

Campbell, J.L. (2007). 'Why would corporations behave in socially responsible ways? An institutional theory of corporate social responsibility', *Academy of Management Review*, 32(3), pp. 946–967.

Campbell, J.L. (2010). Institutional reproduction and change, in Morgan, G., Campbell, J.L., Crouch, C., Pedersen, O.K. and Whitley, R. (eds.) *The Oxford Handbook of Comparative Institutional Analysis*. Oxford: Oxford University Press, pp. 87–116.

Casper, S. (2009). 'Can new technology firms succeed in coordinated market economies? A response to Herrmann and Lange', *Socio-Economic Review*, 7(2), pp. 209–215.

Coriat, B. (2002). France: the end of Fordism…and no successor in sight, in Boyer, R. and Saillard, Y. (eds.) *Régulation Theory: The State of the Art*. London: Routledge, pp. 247–253.

Crouch, C. (2005). *Capitalist Diversity and Change: Recombinant Governance and Institutional Entrepreneurs*. Oxford: Oxford University Press.

Crouch, C. (2011). *The Strange Non-death of Neo-liberalism*. Cambridge (UK): Polity Press.

Crouch, C. (2013). *Making Capitalism Fit For Society*. Cambridge (UK): Polity Press.

Crouch, C. (2016). *The Knowledge Corrupters: Hidden Consequences of the Financial Takeover of Public Life*. Cambridge (UK): Polity Press.

Crouch, C. and Farrell, H. (2004). 'Breaking the path of institutional development? Alternatives to the new determinism', *Rationality and Society*, 16(1), pp. 5–43.

Crouch, C., Schröder, M. and Voelzkow, H. (2009). 'Regional and sectoral varieties of capitalism', *Economy and Society*, 38(4), pp. 654–678.

Croucher, R., Wood, G., Brewster, C. and Brookes, M. (2012). 'Employee turnover, HRM and institutional contexts', *Economic and Industrial Democracy*, 33(4), pp. 605–620.

Djankov, S., Glaeser, E., La Porta, R., Lopez de Silanes, F. and Shleifer, A. (2003). 'The new comparative economics', *Journal of Comparative Economics*, 31(4), pp. 595–619.

Dore, R. (2008). 'Best practice winning out?' *Socio-Economic Review*, 6(4), pp. 779–784.

Farndale, E., Brewster, C. and Poutsma, E. (2008). 'Co-ordinated vs liberal market HRM: The impact of institutionalisation on multinational firms', *The International Journal of Human Resource Management*, 19(11), pp. 2004–2023.

Glaeser, E.L., La Porta, R., Lopez de Silanes, F. and Shleifer, A. (2004). 'Do institutions cause growth?' *Journal of Economic Growth*, 9(3), pp. 271–303.

Goergen, M., Brewster, C., Wood, G. and Wilkinson, A. (2012). 'Varieties of capitalism and investments in human capital', *Industrial Relations*, 51(S1), pp. 501–527.

Goerres, A. and Höpner, M. (2014). 'Polarizers or landscape groomers? An empirical analysis of party donations by the 100 largest German companies in 1984–2005', *Socio-Economic Review*, 12(3), pp. 517–544.

Goyer, M. (2011). *Contingent Capital: Short-term Investors and the Evolution of Corporate Governance in France and Germany*. Oxford: Oxford University Press.

Goyer, M., Clark, I. and Bhankaraully, S. (2016). 'Necessary and sufficient factors in employee downsizing? A qualitative comparative analysis of lay-offs in France and the UK, 2008–2013', *Human Resource Management Journal*, 26(3), pp. 252–268.

Hall, P.A. and Gingerich, D.W. (2009). 'Varieties of Capitalism and institutional complementarities in the political economy: an empirical analysis', *British Journal of Political Science*, 39(3), pp. 449–482.

Hall, P.A. and Soskice, D. (2001). An introduction to varieties of capitalism, in Hall, P.A. and Soskice, D. (eds.) *Varieties of Capitalism: The Institutional Foundations of Comparative Advantage*. Oxford: Oxford University Press, pp. 1–56.

Hall, P.A. and Taylor, R.C.R. (1996). 'Political science and the three new institutionalisms', *Political Studies*, 44(5), pp. 936–957.

Hall, P.A. and Thelen, K. (2009). 'Institutional change in varieties of capitalism', *Socio-Economic Review*, 7(1), pp. 7–34.

Hancké, B., Rhodes, M. and Thatcher, M. (2007). Introduction: beyond varieties of capitalism, in Hancké, B., Rhodes, M. and Thatcher, M. (eds.) *Beyond Varieties of Capitalism: Conflict, Contradictions, and Complementarities in the European Economy*. Oxford: Oxford University Press, pp. 3–38.

Harcourt, M. and Wood, G. (2007). 'The importance of employment protection for skill development in coordinated market economies', *European Journal of Industrial Relations*, 13(2), pp. 141–159.

Hassel, A. (2014). 'The paradox of liberalization – understanding dualism and the recovery of the German political economy', *British Journal of Industrial Relations*, 52(1), pp. 57–81.

Hauptmeier, M. (2010). Reassessing markets and employment relations, in Blyton, P., Heery, E. and Turnbull, P. (eds.) *Reassessing the Employment Relationship: Management, Work and Organisations*. Basingstoke: Palgrave Macmillan, pp. 171–194.

Hollingsworth, J. and Boyer, R. (1997). Coordination of economic actors and social systems of production, in *Contemporary Capitalism: The Embeddedness of Institutions*. Cambridge (UK): Cambridge University Press, pp. 1–47.

Hotho, J.J. (2014). 'From typology to taxonomy: a configurational analysis of national business systems and their explanatory power', *Organization Studies*, 35(5), pp. 671–702.

Howell, C. (2003). 'Varieties of Capitalism: and then there was one?' *Comparative Politics*, 36(1), pp. 103–124.

Howell, C., Culpepper, P.D. and Rueda, D. (2015). 'On Kathleen Thelen, varieties of liberalization and the new politics of social solidarity', *Socio-Economic Review*, 13(2), pp. 399–409.

Jackson, G. (2005). Contested boundaries: ambiguity and creativity in the evolution of German codetermination, in Streeck, W. and Thelen, K. (eds.) *Beyond Continuity: Institutional Change in Advanced Political Economies*. Oxford: Oxford University Press, pp. 229–254.

Jackson, G. and Deeg, R. (2006). *How many varieties of capitalism? Comparing the comparative institutional analyses of capitalist diversity*. Max Planck Institute for the Study of Societies MfiG Discussion Paper (Vol. 06/2). [Online]. Available at: doi.org/10.2139/ssrn.896384.

Jackson, G. and Deeg, R. (2008). 'Comparing capitalisms: understanding institutional diversity and its implications for international business', *Journal of International Business Studies*, 39(4), pp. 540–561.

Jessop, B. (1990). 'Regulation theories in retrospect and prospect', *Economy and Society*, 19(2), pp. 153–216.

Jessop, B. (1997). 'Capitalism and its future: remarks on regulation, government and governance', *Review of International Political Economy*, 4(3), pp. 561–581.

Jessop, B. (2001). Capitalism, the regulation approach, and critical realism, in Brown, A., Fleetwood, S. and Roberts, J. (eds.) *Critical Realism and Marxism*. Abingdon: Routledge, pp. 88–115.

Jessop, B. (2012a). Rethinking the diversity and varieties of capitalism: on variegated capitalism in the world market, in Lane, C. and Wood, G.T. (eds.) *Capitalist Diversity and Diversity Within Capitalism*. Abingdon: Routledge, pp. 209–237.

Jessop, B. (2012b). The world market, variegated capitalism, and the crisis of European integration, in Nousios, P., Overbeek, H. and Tsolakis, A. (eds.) *Globalisation and European Integration: Critical Approaches to Regional Order and International Relations*. New York: Routledge, pp. 91–111.

Katzenstein, P.J. (1985). *Small States in World Markets: Industrial Policy in Europe*. Ithaca: Cornell University Press.

Keller, M.R. and Block, F. (2013). 'Explaining the transformation in the US innovation system: the impact of a small government program', *Socio-Economic Review*, 11(4), pp. 629–656.

Kinderman, D. (2014). *Challenging Varieties of Capitalism's account of business interests: The new social market initiative and German employers' quest for liberalization, 2000–2014*. Max Planck Institute for the Study of Societies MfiG Discussion Paper No. 14/16. Cologne.

Kristensen, P.H. and Morgan, G. (2012a). 'From institutional change to experimentalist institutions', *Industrial Relations*, 51(S1), pp. 413–437.

Kristensen, P.H. and Morgan, G. (2012b). Theoretical contexts and conceptual frames for the study of twenty-first century capitalisms, in Whitley, R. and Morgan, G. (eds.) *Capitalisms and Capitalism in the Twenty-first Century*. Oxford: Oxford University Press, pp. 11–43.

La Porta, R., Lopez de Silanes, F. and Shleifer, A. (1999). 'Corporate Ownership Around the World', *The Journal of Finance*, 54(2), pp. 471–517.

Lane, C. (2005). Institutional transformation and system change: changes in the corporate governance of German corporations, in Morgan, G., Whitley, R. and Moen, E. (eds.) *Changing Capitalisms? Internationalization, Institutional Change, and Systems of Economic Organization*. Oxford: Oxford University Press, pp. 78–109.

Lane, C. (2008). 'National capitalisms and global production networks an analysis of their interaction in two global industries', *Socio-Economic Review*, 6(3), pp. 227–260.

Lane, C. and Wood, G. (2009). 'Capitalist diversity and diversity within capitalism', *Economy and Society*, 38(4), pp. 531–551.

Lazonick, W. (2010). 'Innovative business models and Varieties of Capitalism: financialization of the U.S. corporation', *Business History Review*, 84(2), pp. 675–702.

Lipietz, A. (1993). From Althusserianism to "regulation theory," in Kaplan, E.A. and Sprinker, M. (eds.) *The Althusserian Legacy*. London: Verso, pp. 99–138.

Lipietz, A. (1997). 'The post-Fordist world: labour relations, international hierarchy and global ecology', *Review of International Political Economy*, 4(1), pp. 1–41.

Marx, K. (1992). *Capital: A Critique of Political Economy*, Vol. II. London: Penguin Books.

Morgan, G. (2005). Introduction: Changing capitalisms? Internationalization, institutional change, and systems of economic organization, in Morgan, G., Whitley, R. and Moen, E. (eds.) *Changing Capitalisms? Internationalization, Institutional Change, and Systems of Economic Organization*. Oxford: Oxford University Press, pp. 1–18.

Morgan, G. (2007a). 'National business systems research: Progress and prospects', *Scandinavian Journal of Management*, 23(2), pp. 127–145.

Morgan, G. (2007b). 'The theory of comparative capitalisms and the possibilities for local variation', *European Review*, 15(3), pp. 353–371.

Morgan, G. (2012). International business, multinationals and national business systems, in Wood, G. and Demirbag, M. (eds.) *Handbook of Institutional Approaches to International Business*. Cheltenham: Edward Elgar, pp. 18–40.

Morgan, G. (2016). 'New actors and old solidarities: institutional change and inequality under a neo-liberal international order', *Socio-Economic Review*, 14(1), pp. 201–225.

Morgan, G. and Hauptmeier, M. (2014). Varieties of Institutional Theory in Comparative Employment Relations, in Wilkinson, A., Wood, G. and Deeg, R. (eds.) *The Oxford Handbook of Employment Relations: Comparative Employment Systems*. Oxford: Oxford University Press, pp. 190–221.

Morgan, G. and Kristensen, P.H. (2006). 'The contested space of multinationals: varieties of institutionalism, varieties of capitalism', *Human Relations*, 59(11), pp. 1467–1490.

Morgan, G. and Kubo, I. (2005). 'Beyond path dependency? Constructing new models for institutional change: the case of capital markets in Japan', *Socio-Economic Review*, 3(1), pp. 55–82.

Nölke, A. and Vliegenthart, A. (2009). 'Enlarging the varieties of capitalism: The emergence of dependent market economies in east central Europe', *World Politics*, 61(4), pp. 670–702.

North, D.C. (1990). *Institutions, Institutional Change, and Economic Performance*. Cambridge (UK): Cambridge University Press.

Palier, B. and Thelen, K. (2010). 'Institutionalizing dualism: complementarities and change in France and Germany', *Politics & Society*, 38(1), pp. 119–148.

Polanyi, K. (2001). *The Great Transformation: The Political and Economic Origins of Our Time*. Boston (MA): Beacon Press.

Regini, M. (2003). 'Work and labour in global economies: the case of western Europe', *Socio-Economic Review*, 1(2), pp. 165–184.

Regini, M. (2014). 'Models of capitalism and the crisis', *Stato E Mercato*, 1, pp. 21–44.

Rogers, J. and Streeck, W. (1995). The study of works councils: concepts and problems, in Rogers, J. and Streeck, W. (eds.) *Works Councils: Consultation, Representation, and Cooperation in Industrial Relations*. Chicago: The University of Chicago Press, pp. 3–26.

Sako, M. and Jackson, G. (2006). 'Strategy meets institutions: the transformation of management-labor relations at Deutsche Telekom and NTT', *Industrial and Labor Relations Review*, 59(3), pp. 347–366.

Schneider, M.R. and Paunescu, M. (2012). 'Changing varieties of capitalism and revealed comparative advantages from 1990 to 2005: a test of the Hall and Soskice claims', *Socio-Economic Review*, 10(4), pp. 731–753.

Schnyder, G. (2012). 'Varieties of insider corporate governance: the determinants of business preferences and corporate governance reform in the Netherlands, Sweden and Switzerland', *Journal of European Public Policy*, 19(9), pp. 1434–1451.

Scott, G. and Wright, S. (2012). 'Devolution, social democratic visions and policy reality in Scotland', *Critical Social Policy*, 32(3), pp. 440–453.

Shonfeld, A. (1965). *Modern Capitalism: The Changing Balance of Public and Private Power*. Oxford: Oxford University Press.

Skocpol, T. and Williamson, V. (2012). *The Tea Party and the Remaking of Republican Conservatism*. Oxford: Oxford University Press.

Steinmo, S. (2008). Historical institutionalism, in della Porta, D. and Keating, M. (eds.) *Approaches and Methodologies in the Social Sciences: A Pluralist Perspective*. Cambridge (UK): Cambridge University Press, pp. 118–138.

Steinmo, S. and Thelen, K. (1992). Historical institutionalism in comparative politics, in Steinmo, S., Thelen, K. and Longstreth, F. (eds.) *Structuring Politics: Historical Institutionalism in Comparative Analysis*. Cambridge (UK): Cambridge University Press, pp. 1–32.

Streeck, W. (1997). 'German capitalism: does it exist? Can it survive?' *New Political Economy*, 2(2), pp. 237–256.

Streeck, W. (2009). *Re-forming Capitalism: Institutional Change in the German Political Economy*. Oxford: Oxford University Press.

Streeck, W. (2010). *E pluribus unum? Varieties and commonalities of capitalism.* Max Planck Institute for the Study of Societies MfiG Discussion Paper. [Online]. Available at: https://papers.ssrn.com/sol3/papers.cfm?abstract_id=1805522.

Streeck, W. (2011a). 'Taking capitalism seriously: towards an institutionalist approach to contemporary political economy', *Socio-Economic Review*, 9(1), pp. 137–167.

Streeck, W. (2011b). 'The crises of democratic capitalism', *New Left Review*, 71, pp. 5–29.

Streeck, W. (2012). 'How to study contemporary capitalism?' *European Journal of Sociology*, 53(1), pp. 1–28.

Streeck, W. (2013). *Gekaufte Zeit: Die Vertagte Krise des Demokratischen Kapitalismus.* Berlin: Suhrkamp Verlag.

Streeck, W. (2014). 'How will capitalism end?' *New Left Review*, 87(May/June), pp. 35–64.

Streeck, W. and Thelen, K.A. (2005). Introduction: Institutional change in advanced political economies, in Streeck, W. and Thelen, K. (eds.) *Beyond Continuity: Institutional Change in Advanced Political Economies.* Oxford: Oxford University Press, pp. 1–39.

Thelen, K. (2009). 'Institutional change in advanced political economies: first annual lecture of the BJIR', *British Journal of Industrial Relations*, 47(3), pp. 471–498.

Thelen, K. (2012). 'Varieties of Capitalism: trajectories of liberalization and the new politics of social solidarity', *Annual Review of Political Science*, 15(1), pp. 137–159.

Thelen, K. (2014). *Varieties of Liberalization and the New Politics of Social Solidarity.* Cambridge (UK): Cambridge University Press.

Vidal, M. (2013a). 'Low-autonomy work and bad jobs in post-Fordist capitalism', *Human Relations*, 66(4), pp. 587–612.

Vidal, M. (2013b). 'Postfordism as a dysfunctional accumulation regime: a comparative analysis of the USA, the UK and Germany', *Work, Employment & Society*, 27(3), pp. 451–471.

Walker, J.T., Brewster, C. and Wood, G. (2014). 'Diversity between and within varieties of capitalism: transnational survey evidence', *Industrial and Corporate Change*, 23(2), pp. 493–533.

Whitley, R. (1994). 'Dominant forms of economic organization in market economies', *Organization Studies*, 15(2), pp. 153–182.

Whitley, R. (1999). *Divergent Capitalisms: The Social Structuring and Change of Business Systems.* Oxford: Oxford University Press.

Whitley, R. (2000). 'The institutional structuring of innovation strategies: business systems, firm types and patterns of technical change in different market economies', *Organization Studies*, 21(5), pp. 855–886.

Whitley, R. (2003). 'From the Search for Universal Correlations to the Institutional Structuring of Economic Organization and Change: The Development and Future of Organization Studies', *Organization*, 10(3), pp. 481–501.

Whitley, R. (2007). *Business Systems and Organizational Capabilities: The Institutional Structuring of Competitive Competences.* Oxford: Oxford University Press.

Whitley, R. (2010). Changing competition models in market economies: the effects of internationalization, technological innovations, and academic expansion on the conditions supporting dominant economic logics, in Morgan, G., Campbell, J.L., Crouch, C., Pedersen, O.K. and Whitley, R. (eds.) *The Oxford Handbook of Comparative Institutional Analysis.* Oxford: Oxford University Press, pp. 363–397.

Whitley, R. (2012). Internationalization and the institutional structuring of economic organization: changing authority relations in the twenty-first century, in Morgan, G. and Whitley, R. (eds.) *Capitalisms and Capitalism in the Twenty-first Century.* Oxford: Oxford University Press, pp. 211–236.

Wilkinson, A. and Wood, G. (2012). 'Institutions and Employment Relations: The State of the Art', *Industrial Relations*, 51(Suppl.1), pp. 373–388.

Wilkinson, A. and Wood, G. (2014). 'Special Issue of International Journal of Human Resource Management – Global trends and crises, comparative capitalism and HRM', *The International Journal of Human Resource Management*, 25(19), pp. 2748–2750.

Witt, M.A. and Jackson, G. (2016). 'Varieties of Capitalism and institutional comparative advantage : a test and reinterpretation', *Journal of International Business Studies*, 47(7), pp. 778–806.

Wood, G. (2011). Governance, finance and industrial relations, in Townsend, K. and Wilkinson, A. (eds.) *Research Handbook on the Future of Work and Employment Relations.* Cheltenham: Edward Elgar, pp. 279–295.

Wood, G. (2013). 'Institutional diversity: current contestations and emerging issues', *The Journal of Comparative Economic Studies*, 8(1), pp. 7–20.

Wood, G. and Frynas, J.G. (2006). 'The institutional basis of economic failure: anatomy of the segmented business system', *Socio-Economic Review*, 4(2), pp. 239–277.

Wood, G. and Lane, C. (2012). Institutions, change, and diversity, in Lane, C. and Wood, G. (eds.) *Capitalist Diversity and Diversity Within Capitalism.* Abingdon: Routledge, pp. 1–31.

Wood, G. and Wright, M. (2015). 'Corporations and new statism: trends and research priorities', *Academy Management Perspectives*, 29(2), pp. 271–286.

Wood, S. (2001). Business, government, and patterns of labor market policy in Britain and the Federal Republic of Germany, in Hall, P.A. and Soskice, D. (eds.) *Varieties of Capitalism: The Institutional Foundations of Comparative Advantage.* Oxford: Oxford University Press, pp. 247–274.

Wright, E.O. (2004). 'Beneficial constraints: beneficial for whom?' *Socio-Economic Review*, 2(3), pp. 407–414.

Zysman, J. (1984). *Governments, Markets, and Growth: Financial Systems and the Politics of Industrial Change.* Ithaca: Cornell University Press.

10

RESEARCH METHODS IN EMPLOYMENT RELATIONS

Keith Whitfield and Suhaer Yunus

Abstract

Building on previous work that has examined the use of research methods in industrial relations/ employment relations (IR/ER), particularly Whitfield and Strauss (2000), this chapter updates its empirical work and re-examines its key postulates. IR/ER research continues to show a wide range of research methods and approaches. It is highly empirical, with a large proportion of papers published in its leading journals involving data collected by the author(s), and there is still a significant level of research that has a policy orientation. A significant number of case studies are undertaken by IR/ER researchers, but perhaps not as many as is generally thought. There is little evidence of the development of multi-method research, despite a recognition that such an approach could be beneficial for the development of the field. Instead, authors tend to stick to their own preferred approach. This might change as researchers in the field take a greater interest in epistemological/ontological issues, especially as this is leading to a greater interest in critical realism.

Introduction

Industrial relations/employment relations (IR/ER) research displays a wide range of research methods. It is one of its hallmarks as a field of study. This is possibly to be expected in a subject area that is multidisciplinary, with a very strong policy orientation and situated at the meeting point of a range of very disparate disciplines and fields as diverse as economics, sociology, psychology, politics, history and business/management studies, among others. It has also evolved its own distinctive approaches to research, most notably detailed case study analysis (Brown and Wright, 1994), as well as pioneering the undertaking of large workplace surveys in a number of countries (Bryson and Frege, 2010).

Such heterogeneity in the range of methods used by IR/ER researchers can, on the one hand, be seen as a major strength, yielding powerful empirical analysis and rich insights into how the world of work works, and allowing the customisation of research to the specific needs of the topic at hand. It could also potentially allow the field to free itself of the criticisms directed towards allied fields and disciplines, for example labour economics and organisational psychology, that they are too narrow in their research approach, too reliant on a narrow range of methods and therefore potentially missing key insights (Godard, 2014; Spencer, 2013). Yet the field has not prospered in recent years, and has been in decline in many areas of academia. It may even be the case that the heterogeneity of research methods deployed in IR/ER is a curse for the field, something that has hastened its decline as an area of academic enquiry. The wide range of approaches could have given IR/ER the air of a field of study that has no central core to its approach, perhaps one where there is profound disagreement as to ways of seeing and doing, and thereby an area to be avoided at all costs.

For such heterogeneity to be a strength rather than a weakness, it is pivotal that it reflects a carefully thought-through approach to research design that results from matching research methods to the tasks at hand and involves the deployment of a mix of approaches that allows the weaknesses of specific methods to be mitigated by the simultaneous use of methods that are less prone to such weaknesses (even though they may have problems of their own that are less prevalent in other methods used). In its most developed form, such a research programme could be expected to evolve and yield ever-increasing insights into the core phenomena being investigated, developing a body of knowledge that would not only suggest academic progress, but also offer increasingly prescient advice to policy-makers and practitioners. Whether such a world is evolving in IR/ER is therefore a key issue.

The aim of this chapter is to review the current state of research methods in the IR/ER area, to consider the current state of its methodological mix and to suggest how its approach to undertaking research might be developed to strengthen the standing of the field in academia and beyond. It builds on similar conjectures developed by George Strauss and Keith Whitfield at the end of the twentieth century (Whitfield and Strauss, 1998, 2000) and further considered in a follow-up piece early in the new millennium (Whitfield and Strauss, 2008). It also builds on the ideas of other authors who have considered methods and IR/ER, most notably Carola Frege's paper on how internationalisation has affected the nature of IR/ER research (Frege, 2005).

The chapter is focused around three key questions:

1) What is the current state of play in the use of research methods in IR/ER research?
2) What are the trends in the use of research in IR/ER?
3) Is the heterogeneity of methods used in IR/ER research a good or a bad thing for the development of the field?

What's in a name?

There has undoubtedly been a major set of changes taking place in the field of study traditionally known as industrial relations (IR), and now more commonly known as employment relations (ER). No longer is the focus principally on union-management relations; it has broadened to include a number of key issues relating to the way in which the world of work operates. As the core subject area of the field of IR, collective bargaining, has declined, so the subject matter of the renamed field has expanded to take on board emerging interests in, *inter alia*, "high performance" human resource practices, equality and diversity, employee well-being and comparative international employment systems. The consequence has been an inevitable broadening in the range of methods used across the field.

This change has undoubtedly expanded the scope of the subject, but has simultaneously reduced its distinctiveness as a field of study. Whereas traditional IR had a very clear core, albeit one that its scholars built on in all manner of directions, the new ER is much more diffuse, its core subjects typically going well beyond the IR/ER mainstream *per se*, into areas such as the impact of human resource management (HRM) on organisational performance and the business case for employer initiatives in areas of benefit to employees, such as well-being and work-life balance. Increasingly, scholars who feel that their principal discipline or field is not IR/ER are crossing swords with those who do so identify, but often with very different approaches and methods. Most notably, there has been increasing cross-over between the subject area and labour economics (Spencer, 2013) and organisational psychology (Godard, 2014). Neither of these cross-overs has been unproblematic and both have raised issues for IR/ER in general, and in particular with regard to the deployment of research methods therein. The distinctiveness of the IR/ER approach to research has consequently eroded.

For many, the 'golden age' of IR research is seen to have exhibited a highly distinctive approach to research methods – detailed case study research based on workplace-based fieldwork, heavily focused on observation and semi-structured interviews with key participants (Brown and Wright, 1994). The essence of this approach was that the researchers "talked to their data", and attempted to explain key aspects of the employment relationship by relating these, "… to a broader structure of societal power" (ibid, p.154). The approach was highly inductive and, at most (but not that often), attempted to develop some form of middle-level theory. A contrast was often made with the more deductively-inclined approach of mainstream labour economists, involving the use of increasingly powerful quantitative techniques and the secondary analysis of survey data, most notably the workplace IR surveys that developed, particularly in the United Kingdom, in the last quarter of the twentieth century. This latter approach has been seen to crowd out the more traditional case study approach, and thereby change the nature of IR/ER research as its subject focus has shifted, as the more often quoted letter changed from 'I' to 'E', and, possibly more crucially, the nature of the researchers undertaking research in this subject area, and most notably their training, has changed.

Some have bemoaned many of the changes taking place in the field (Brown and Wright, 1994; Whitfield and Strauss, 1998); others have welcomed it, but the dominant mood has possibly been a desire for the various approaches to work in harmony to produce an understanding of the complexities of the employment relationship that transcends simple methodological approaches (Delbridge and Whitfield, 2007). That such a multifaceted programme of work has not emerged is possibly a reason why IR/ER has experienced such a period of introspection and concern about its academic status. Part of the problem is perhaps that while the range of methods used in IR/ER has expanded, there has not been the development of a core of researchers or research teams who are proficient across this range and who have become adept at combining different methods into a coherent and far-reaching approach to research. In particular, there does not seem to have been an increase in the development of multi-method research approaches, despite much rhetoric as to their importance.

Epistemological and ontological issues

To a considerable extent, the research methods and designs deployed by researchers reflect their ontological (assumptions about the nature of reality) and epistemological (beliefs about how such a reality can best be studied) stances. In short, those taking a more positivistic stance are inclined towards large-scale surveys (and increasingly 'big data') and quantitative analysis. While there might be some differences in the quantitative methods used, for example in terms of using parametric and non-parametric methods and techniques such as factor and cluster analysis, the focus has been on the testing of hypotheses using statistical inference. A major contrast can be seen with those adopting a more post-structural stance, who are much more likely to adopt qualitative methods, especially observation and unstructured or semi-structured interviewing. The whole notion of hypothesis testing is deemed a chimaera and avoided totally. In between

Table 10.1 Nature of papers published in main IR/ER journals, 2015

	2015					
	BJIR	*IRJ*	*ILRR*	*IR*	*RI*	*JIR*
Articles coded	32	21	40	28	28	31
Basic approach						
Deductive	15	2	36	22	14	9
Inductive	16	19	3	6	14	22
Primary orientation						
Discipline orientation	25	11	33	18	25	24
Policy orientation	7	10	7	10	3	7
Data						
Yes	31	21	40	28	28	31
Subject area						
Union-management relations	6	6	8	2	6	6
Level of analysis						
Individual/household	8	5	17	12	14	4

Source: Whitfield and Yunus (2017)

these two polar opposites are the critical realists, who typically adopt a mixed position and considerable differences to one another in their attitudes towards different forms of analysis and the degree to which hypothesis testing can be deemed in any way meaningful (see, for example, the variety of approaches outlined in Edwards, O'Mahoney and Vincent, 2014).

Industrial/employment relations researchers take a wide range of ontological/epistemological stances, but typically they do not express an explicit position on such matters, though sometimes echoes of a particular stance (or more than one) can be detected. This has led to the frequent accusation that the 'facts' are allowed to speak for themselves or more critically that the field "heaps facts on the plains of human ignorance". Edwards (2006) has suggested that a critical realist approach can be discerned in much IR/ER research, even though this is rarely stated explicitly. However, it is also noted that such studies lack certain key factors that would be required of a fully articulated critical realist analysis. In particular, IR/ER is seen to be overly inductive in its approach, "… and it has not lent itself to more formal and rigorous approaches that might speak to more conventional modes of analysis." (ibid., p. 11).

An examination of the current IR/ER literature (see Table 10.1 above) suggests that the inductive and deductive approaches to the subject are equally prevalent, with US research favouring the latter and research elsewhere being more balanced between the two.

Changing times

The nature of IR/ER research has changed in a number of ways in the last half-century. Two analyses of the contents of leading journals in the field (Frege, 2005; Whitfield and Strauss, 2000) charted these changes up to the advent of the new millennium, taking slightly different stances in relation to their key dimensions. Whitfield and Strauss's analysis focused on changes in the papers published in six of the leading journals in the field in an attempt to see how much change there had been in how research was undertaken between 1952 and 1997. Frege's analysis focused on how the internationalisation of the global economy had affected IR research.

Whitfield and Strauss (2000) concluded that between the early 1950s and late 1990s:

1) There had been a shift away from research that is primarily inductive, qualitative and concerned with policy, towards research that is quantitative, deductive and concerned with theory-building and testing.
2) There were substantial and continuing differences in research style among the journals and the countries in which they were published.
3) There was an increase in the proportion of papers using empirical data, especially quantitative data, and a large increase in the proportion of papers using such data that involved a multivariate analysis.
4) In 1997, in all but the two US journals analysed, the majority of papers were based on the primary analysis of data collected by the researcher.
5) Only about one-fifth of papers involved case studies.
6) Few articles were based on multi-method research strategies.
7) The proportion of papers on union-management relations was fairly constant at just below 50 per cent.
8) The period witnessed an increased focus on the attitudes and behaviours of individuals and households.

In short, there had been a definite shift in the way in which research had been undertaken during this period, away from what was regarded as the traditional IR approach towards an approach that was already well established in sub-disciplines and fields with which IR/ER overlapped, such as labour economics and organisational psychology. The shift seemed most pronounced for the two leading US journals, reflecting a distinct difference in how research was undertaken in the USA as opposed to Europe, especially continental Europe and, to some extent, Canada. However, there was still evidence of some of the hallmarks of the traditional approach in place – most notably the primary analysis of data collected by the researcher him/herself, and a continued emphasis on union-management relations. By contrast, the analysis of case studies was not, and had never been, the dominant approach to research in the subject area.

Frege's findings were perhaps more chastening. Her analysis suggested that "… the ongoing globalisation of the economy and of the research community has not yet translated itself into a strong international research environment in the Anglo-Saxon countries, although it has to a certain extent in Germany… . The prominent absence of international topics in the USA seems to confirm the stereotype of US research as being parochial and ethnocentric." (Frege, 2005, p. 203). Her analysis also suggested that there were distinct patterns of IR research in the USA, UK and Germany. Such differences were seen to be shaped by differences in the countries' national IR systems.

Together, these two analyses suggest that the pressures promoting how research is undertaken in IR/ER are by no means universal, and are strongly shaped by national imperatives. Moreover, there is a definite tendency towards a form of research that departs from what might be called the traditional IR way of detailed case study at the workplace level – though there might be doubts about whether it was ever thus. This is much more marked in the US than elsewhere.

The move towards a more deductive orientation, with greater emphasis on multivariate analysis, is not necessarily a bad thing for the field. It could add a dimension to the more detailed case-based analysis that allows the key insights of such research to be examined in a much more general setting, and thereby to see how universal the insights of key cases are. There could

Table 10.2 Type of data and methods of analysis used, 2015

Articles with data	2015					
	BJIR	*IRJ*	*ILRR*	*IR*	*RI*	*JIR*
	31	*21*	*40*	*28*	*28*	*31*
Type of data						
Quantitative	15	3	36	21	13	9
Multivariate analysis	15	2	35	21	13	7
Data collected by						
Author	13	14	13	12	20	24
Case study	14	14	6	4	9	16
Multi-method	9	11	3	1	3	8

Source: Whitfield and Yunus (2017)

develop an articulation between the two approaches that allows a more holistic perspective to develop. On the other hand, it is possible that the advent of the workplace survey and its analysis by ever more complex multivariate analysis could well be crowding out aspects of the more detailed approach to research that has contributed so much to our understanding of the key processes underlying behaviour in the subject area. The absence of meaningful interaction between the two approaches in the research literature seems to suggest that maybe the latter has been the dominant outcome.

An updating of the Whitfield and Strauss (2000) analysis for the new millennium (Whitfield and Yunus, 2017) suggests that many of the trends highlighted in the earlier study have continued in recent years. The results for 2015 for all six journals are shown in Tables 10.1 and 10.2, and the changes in the four journals for which there is a continuous record over the period 1967 to 2015 (*British Journal of Industrial Relations, Industrial and Labor Relations Review, Industrial Relations, Journal of Industrial Relations*) are shown in Table 10.3.

The deductive approach has become even more dominant, with nearly two-thirds of papers taking this stance in these four journals. This contrasts with just over one-half in 1982 and 1997, and just one-fifth in 1967. Even more striking is the move towards a discipline focus as opposed to a policy focus, which now accounts for three-quarters of papers, in contrast to just over two-fifths in 1967.

The key finding in the new analysis is the decline in research on union-management relations, from nearly 50 per cent of all papers to just over one-quarter. This no doubt reflects the decline in unionism around the world, but also a shift of focus among ER researchers both towards studying non-union workplaces and issues that typically, or perhaps increasingly, do not involve unions, even in unionised settings. The scale of the change is substantial and reflects a major change in the nature of the field.

The decline in interest in union-management relations might have been expected to have been associated with an increase in the number of papers on individuals and households, but that does not seem to have occurred, with a significant decline in the proportion of papers focused at this level. The key area of growth has undoubtedly been the study of workplace HRM practices, particularly in relation to issues such as HRM and performance and the development of high performance/commitment systems.

Table 10.3 Change in the nature of papers published, 1967–2015

	1967	*1982*	*1997*	*2015*
Articles coded (number)	**76**	**93**	**90**	**131**
Basic approach				
Deductive (percentage)	21	55	57	64
Primary orientation				
Discipline orientation (percentage)	42	67	68	76
Data used (percentage)	75	92	96	99
Subject area				
Union-management relations (percentage)	42	42	46	26
Level of analysis				
Individual/household (percentage)	13	31	41	31
Articles with data (number)	**57**	**86**	**87**	**130**
Type of data				
Quantitative (percentage)	46	76	71	62
Multivariate analysis (percentage)	7	48	57	60
Data collected by author (percentage)	30	39	38	48
Case study (percentage)	14	19	15	31
Multi-method (percentage)	9	17	16	16

Source: Whitfield and Strauss (2000); Whitfield and Yunus (2017)

All but one paper published in the four journals in 2015 contained data of some form. The field is heavily empirical. Multivariate analysis has also become even more dominant as the analytical method of choice, and was used in three-fifths of 2015 papers, in contrast to just seven per cent in 1967. It is, however, notable that there was a decline in the proportion of papers that were based primarily on quantitative data, from 71 per cent in 1997 to 62 per cent in 2015. There was also an increase in papers using data collected by the author/authors, increasing from 38 per cent in 1997 to 48 per cent in 2015. An even larger increase was in the undertaking of a case study, which increased from 15 per cent of papers in 1997 to 31 per cent in 2015.

There was no increase in the proportion of papers that used a multi-method strategy. This remained at just 16 per cent of papers. It therefore seems that single-method research is still dominant in the field, despite a wide heterogeneity of methods in use, and much rhetoric about the importance of using a range of methods either to triangulate research findings or broaden the breadth and depth of research undertaken.

Workplace surveys: curse, blessing or foundation?

The advent of a series of national workplace surveys in a range of countries has had a major impact on how research is undertaken in IR/ER. Pioneered in the UK in the 1980s, there have been nationally representative workplace surveys in Australia, Britain (six in total with a number of linked surveys), Canada, France, Germany and Norway (Bryson and Frege, 2010). These have been the basis of a large number of research studies, mostly on a country-specific basis, but sometimes cross-nationally (e.g. Caroli and van Reenen, 2001; Mumford and Smith, 2003; Whitfield et al., 1994).

The workplace surveys have allowed researchers to uncover the magnitudes of key workplace structures, map the distribution of structures between differing types of workplace and contextualise case studies and more limited surveys. They have also been the basis of a wide range of investigations of key behavioural relationships in the ER domain.

The development of the workplace surveys has been widely supported in the IR/ER research community, though there have been some dissenting voices (e.g. McCarthy, 1994), which have suggested that the existence of readily available survey data has crowded out more appropriate data for the task at hand. Less widely accepted is the use of survey data to examine behavioural relationships. Not only has the acceptability of the key proxy variables used in such studies been questioned, but so has the ability of researchers to make causal inferences on the back of cross-sectional data.

What has been notably absent is a programme of research that has workplace data at its heart, but which complements it with data that is more detail-rich and focused on a particular issue (Delbridge and Whitfield, 2007). There has been something of a tendency to see workplace survey data and more qualitative forms of information as 'either/ors' rather than as different aspects of understanding a complex phenomenon. This is partly a resource issue, but also one involving the respecting of anonymity and confidentiality.

Two interesting developments in relation to national workplace survey data that have both emphasised the power and at the same time the limitations of the approach have been the analysis of successive surveys in the same country and the analysis of surveys between countries. A prime example of the former is Brown et al. (2009), which analysed the first five of the WIRS/WERS surveys (1980 to 2004). This allowed changes in key aspects of the British ER system to be mapped over a quarter of a century. A strong advantage of the WIRS/WERS series is that many variables were deliberately kept as they were in successive surveys and so a full time-series could be built. However, many of the variables inevitably changed their structure in successive surveys as the underlying world of work changed, meaning that time-series were sometimes incomplete or not fully consistent across their range. Moreover, the nature of the institutions themselves has evolved through time, and thus the same question may be tapping different phenomena in one survey relative to another. A prime example concerns employee participation in decision-making, which has evolved from a more pluralistic set of structures to one that is much more managerial in its focus in recent years. Nonetheless, an interesting story can be told of change in a system of industrial/employment relations that has undergone fundamental change in some areas but exhibited high levels of continuity in others.

The second example of innovative use of workplace surveys is in relation to comparative international analysis. This area has been particularly powerful in relation to the British workplace surveys and both the Australian and French surveys. Potentially these allow the undertaking of nationally representative comparisons of key IR/ER structures and institutions, involving lots of controls for key differences between the countries concerned. However, in practice, the comparisons tend to be, at most, proximate, requiring the invocation of a plethora of conditions that weaken the strength of the conclusions reached. The surveys tend to differ in many respects – nature of sample (especially the lower size-band for workplaces), the precise structures that are investigated, the dimensions of the structures that are examined, whether employees are investigated too, and if so, which ones, and to whom the questions are asked. In short, there are always grounds for the more sceptical reviewer to doubt the exactitude of the match between seemingly similar national surveys, even those that are deliberately kept as closely similar as possible.

A key issue for research in the IR/ER area is that institutional detail varies markedly across both time and space, and that such detail is of crucial importance in understanding why phenomena take the forms that they do and why they change in particular ways. This will always result in a degree of disjuncture between theoretical concepts and empirical constructs and thereby an imprecision in the testing of key hypotheses. There will always be grounds for scepticism about the precision of analyses using workplace data, especially when the analyses involve comparisons across time and across space.

Whither employment relations research methods?

There is very little doubt that employment relations has a much greater variety in terms of the research methods its researchers use than most disciplines, sub-disciplines and fields of study. This yields major advantages, but also significant threats. The result is diversity in terms of research undertaken and the potential to develop an all-round understanding of the topics under investigation. The cost is potentially the failure to develop a clear identity for the field and a widely accepted set of research approaches to guide those entering its domain.

The IR/ER approach to undertaking is undoubtedly distinctive. It is overwhelmingly an empirical field, with most papers involving the analysis of data of some type. There is a high emphasis on authors collecting their own data, often 'talking to the data'. A considerable amount of research involves case study analysis, and significant work based primarily on qualitative data. Although the issues analysed are predominantly discipline/field-focused, there is still a considerable volume of work that takes a policy orientation.

There are clearly varying ways of doing research in the IR/ER field, and researchers tend to stick to the approach that suits them best. This reflects to some extent the fact that there are differing ways of seeing/ontological stances among the researchers themselves. The difference is essentially between those taking a 'scientific method' epistemological orientation to their analysis and those following a more critical realist approach. A prime example is the variety of approaches taken to the debate about whether performance-oriented HRM improves an organisation's performance. The results of analyses in this area have been far from definitive, and fail to give a clear steer to those involved in the practice of HRM. One response has been to develop a case for 'big science', that is "…large-scale, long-term research at a level of magnitude that probably can only be achieved through partnerships between research, practitioner and government communities." (Wall and Wood, 2005, p. 429). In contrast, Fleetwood and Hesketh (2006), from a critical realist perspective, suggest that the problem lies not so much in method as in philosophy and the need for more theorising. They advocate that the science actually becomes "smaller" rather than larger, and builds from the local to the general rather than the reverse. Similarly, Edwards (2006) has called for a programme of qualitative comparative analysis (QCA) as a way of turning the implicit critical realist approach within much IR/ER research into a more formal programme of analysis. Such an approach is seen to encourage the researcher to "…identify logical possibilities and then go through the evidence systematically to see what combination of factors is necessary and sufficient for a given outcome" (Edwards, 2006, p. 16).

What is notable, largely by its absence, is research that applies a multi-method approach. It might have been expected that a field such as IR/ER would be a pioneer in this area, but it has failed to take hold. Instead, authors tend towards a primarily single-method, and increasingly quantitative, approach to their research. There is possibly much scope for the development of a multi-method approach, particularly as doctoral programmes in the social sciences in general typically involve instruction in both quantitative and qualitative methods, though possibly not how they can best be used in tandem, as research complements. Perhaps this is an area in which the subject, through its professional bodies, such as the International Labour and Employment Relations Association (ILERA), Labor and Employment Relations Association (LERA) and British Universities Industrial Relations Association (BUIRA), and the various subject groups and departments in differing universities, can take a lead. Maybe multi-method instruction can be introduced strongly into the doctoral streams at national and international conferences, and the various bespoke doctoral conferences and related events that regularly take place.

In conclusion, it can probably be said that the heterogeneity of research methods used in IR/ER research is neither a curse nor a blessing, but a reflection of a field of study that is itself heterogeneous in its objectives and in the perspectives that its researchers bring to it. Few signs exist of the development of a distinctive and comprehensive programme of IR/ER research that uses a range of methods in conjunction to build a body of knowledge that underpins strong academic progress and increasingly insightful policy and practitioner advice. There is, though, scope for considerable development in terms of how research methods are deployed within the field of study and, in particular, a need for researchers to use a mix of methods in a complementary way to allow for greater depth in the nature of the research they undertake.

Acknowledgements: Thanks are due to Ed Heery, Jimmy Donaghey and members of Cardiff University's Employment Research Unit for perceptive comments on an earlier draft of this paper, and to George Strauss for the intellectual stimulation he has generated for the issues covered in this paper. We are grateful to Wiley for allowing us to publish material from Whitfield and Strauss (2000).

Appendix: Classification used in Tables 10.1, 10.2 and 10.3

Basic approach

This was 'deductive' if the primary objective was to test a hypothesis or to establish the magnitude of a conceptual relationship, and 'inductive' if the aim was to uncover empirical regularities to assist in conceptual development. Articles that are primarily descriptive are 'unclassified'.

Primary orientation

This was 'policy' if the prime objective was to examine an organisational or governmental policy-related question, and 'discipline-oriented' if the prime objective was to examine a conceptual issue or present findings without immediate policy implications.

Subject area

'Yes' indicates that the focus was on the relationship between unions and employers and not just one of these parties.

Level of analysis

This relates to the level of the entity that was the primary focus of the analysis. The analysis focuses on the number of papers based on the individual or household.

Type of data

This was 'quantitative' if the paper included statistical material, and 'qualitative' if it focused on data not presented in quantitative form (although quantitative data could be presented as background or in providing examples).

Multivariate analysis

It was 'multivariate' if based at least in part on the simultaneous analysis of at least three variables.

Data collection

'Author' indicates that the information was collected by the author; this includes the collation of published information from a variety of sources as well as surveys and interviews (if the collation was conducted or designed by the author). 'Other' indicates that the data were taken from a single source or small number of sources, such as one of the Workplace Industrial Relations Surveys or a small set of manuscripts.

Case study

'Case study' means that the approach involved the conduct of case studies, which are explicitly designed to suggest, develop or test generalisations with broader application.

Multi-method

'Multi-method' means that more than one method is used, with the explicit aim of triangulation or transcending the insights gleaned from a single method. The use of two or more methods in conjunction, without either aim (such as the statistical analysis of survey data), was not deemed multimethod.

N.B. Literature reviews were not classified.

References

Brown, W., Bryson, A., Forth, J. and Whitfield, K. (2009). *The Evolution of the Modern Workplace*. Cambridge (UK): Cambridge University Press.

Brown, W. and Wright, M. (1994). 'The Empirical Tradition in Workplace Bargaining Research', *British Journal of Industrial Relations*, 32(2), pp. 154–164.

Bryson, A. and Frege, C. (2010). 'The Importance of Comparative Workplace Relations Studies', *British Journal of Industrial Relations*, 48(2), pp. 231–234.

Caroli, E. and van Reenan, J. (2001). 'Skill-based Organizational Change? Evidence from a Panel of British and French Establishments', *The Quarterly Journal of Economics*, 116(4), pp. 1449–1492.

Delbridge, R. and Whitfield, K. (2007). 'More than Mere Fragments: The Use of Workplace Employment Relations Survey Data in HRM Research', *International Journal of Human Resource Management*, 18(12), pp. 2166–2182.

Edwards, P. (2006). *Industrial Relations and Critical Realism: IR's Tacit Contribution*. Warwick Papers in Industrial Relations, Number 80, May.

Edwards, P., O'Mahoney, J. and Vincent, S. (2014). *Studying Organizations Using Critical Realism: A Practical Guide*. Oxford: Oxford University Press.

Fleetwood, S. and Hesketh, A. (2006). 'HRM-Performance Research: Under-Theorised and Lacking Explanatory Power', *International Journal of Human Resource Management*, 17(11), pp. 1977–93.

Frege, C. (2005). 'Varieties of Industrial Relations Research: Take-over, Convergence or Divergence?' *British Journal of Industrial Relations*, 43(2), pp. 179–207.

Godard, J. (2014). 'The Psychologisation of Employment Relations?' *Human Resource Management Journal*, 24(1), pp. 1–18.

McCarthy, W. (1994). 'Of Hats and Cattle: Or the Limits of Macro-Survey Research in Industrial Relations', *Industrial Relations Journal*, 25(4), pp. 315–322.

Mumford, K. and Smith, P. (2003). 'Determinants of Current Job Tenure: A Cross-Sectional Comparison', *The Australian Journal of Labour Economics*, 6, pp. 597–608.

Spencer, D. (2013). 'Barbarians at the Gate: A Critical Appraisal of the influence of Economics on the Field and Practice of HRM', *Human Resource Management Journal*, 23(4), pp. 346–359.

Wall, T. and Wood, S. (2005). 'The Romance of Human Resource Management and Business Performance, and the Case for Big Science', *Human Relations*, 58(4), pp. 429–462.

Whitfield, K., Marginson, P. and Brown, W. (1994). 'Workplace Industrial Relations under Different Regulatory Systems: A Survey-Based Comparison of Australia and Britain', *British Journal of Industrial Relations*, 32(3), pp. 319–338.

Whitfield, K. and Strauss, G. (1998). *Researching the World of Work: Strategies and Methods in Studying Industrial Relations*. Ithaca: ILR Press.

Whitfield, K. and Strauss, G. (2000). 'Methods Matter: Changes in Industrial Relations Research and their Implications', *British Journal of Industrial Relations*, 38(1), pp. 141–152.

Whitfield, K. and Strauss, G. (2008). Changing Traditions in Industrial Relations Research, in Blyton, P., Bacon, N., Fiorito, J. and Heery, E. (eds.) *The SAGE Handbook of Industrial Relations*. Sage: Los Angeles, pp. 170–186.

Whitfield, K. and Yunus, S. (2017). *Changing Research Methods in Industrial Relations: The New Millennium*. Discussion Papers in Management, Cardiff Business School.

PART II

Actors in employment relations

11

THE STATE AND EMPLOYMENT RELATIONS

Continuity and change in the politics of regulation

Miguel Martínez Lucio and Robert MacKenzie

Introduction

The question of the state is fundamental to employment relations[1] or work and employment issues more broadly. The state is in many ways the guarantor and coercive force ensuring the establishment of the explicit rules and regulations that govern ER. The state is key to the public regulation and control of the contractual basis of such relations. The importance of having a clear understanding of what is commonly called the state is vital if we are to study the rules of engagement and the spheres of influence that govern our work. The state is also, as we will discuss below, not a monolithic actor even when it appears to be so, but rather the conglomeration of various institutions and agencies. At one level the state can be seen as a set of institutions comprising, *inter alia*, mechanisms of public governance, social and economic management, coercive forces, public enterprises and non-departmental public bodies; a varied and varying set of institutions – some directly democratically accountable, in liberal democratic contexts, some not. Yet the state is more than a set of institutions: it reflects the social relations of the capitalist mode of production and in turn serves to reproduce these social relations, providing a logic to the role of the state that abstracts from the potentially contradictory activities of state bodies at the concrete level. At the concrete level, it cannot be assumed that all bodies of the state act in concert. Sub-units of the state may have competing interests and divergent agendas causing them to act in contrast to the interests of other sub-units, or even in contrast to the policy agenda of elected governments. Even in the United Kingdom at the height of the Thatcher government's reassertion of a unitarist model of management's right to manage, the non-departmental public body ACAS (Advisory, Conciliation and Arbitration Service) continued to propagate a more pluralistic approach. However, the state may not function in the manner in which it is intended or even in the manner it espouses. In reality, in terms of its reach and efficacy, the state may not be as omnipotent as sometimes assumed. What is more, the state may govern or regulate for a specific set of interests and enshrine or support the role and activities of certain actors and organisations over the interests of others. Therefore understanding, conceptually, the meaning of the state and 'what it does' has to coincide with an attempt to grasp its problems and its limitations in the face of other interests. As Kelly (1998) highlighted, until recently there has been a failure of the industrial relations (IR) tradition in terms of its theoretical endeavours to engage with the state: a failure of analysis, and even lack of interest. In IR, and in the study of human resource management (HRM), there has been a general abdication of debate on the state to the arena of law. The study of politics – i.e. the study of the distribution of power and related institutions – has been marginalised to a great extent as well. Business schools especially have a variable record in terms of the way in which questions of regulation and political context are studied.

This chapter aims to assist in the task of reviving the analysis of the state in various ways. Firstly, it explores the way we formally understand the state in relation to ER, and how the state plays a range of roles and executes various functions. We start with an outline of the tensions between schools of thought in discussing these issues. Secondly, we locate this binary within a discussion of what are often labelled as the three 'perspectives' within ER: the unitarist, pluralist and radical or Marxist approaches to ER. We add a new dimension to these perspectives by dividing them into what could be labelled direct, state-oriented approaches and more indirect approaches to the role of the state. This emphasis on direct and indirect approaches, broadly speaking, allows us to appreciate that the state can vary in form and that its political objectives, viewed across such perspectives, can be achieved in different ways. The third section will focus on the emergence of an approach that is focused on a broader understanding of the state's role – building on the insights from previous sections – and which attempts to synthesise to some extent the different perspectives around a more nuanced interest in regulation and coordination issues. In this respect, the impact of regulation theory and regulatory space are important for the reshaping of a more nuanced approach, which addresses how the state intervenes in a range of ways. This approach builds on the analysis of changes the state and the economy faced in the 1970s and 1980s, in relation to the transformation of the Fordist economy in developing countries, the emergence of privatisation and political questions about the role of the modern state: it is concerned with the "the transformation of social relations, which creates new forms – both economic and non-economic – organised in structures and reproducing a determinate structure, the mode of reproduction" (Aglietta, 1982p. 14; as quoted in Boyer, 1990, p. 17). The fourth section focuses explicitly on the rethinking of state roles in an age of greater globalisation, neoliberalism and economic crisis. The aim here is to focus the vital question of the current transformations of the role of the state as its capacity and resources – and roles – are challenged by economic and political developments. We also note the way in which new debates address the changing parameters of the state in a globalised and market-oriented context. This section will also look at the tensions these changes create for – and within – the state, as it grapples with questions of social responsibility and the support of long-term economic development and stability.

Throughout the chapter we will focus on the way debates have emerged with new schools of thought, allowing us to comprehend the role of the state in novel and more nuanced ways. It will highlight key developments in our handling and understanding of the state in relation to work and employment. In many ways the fundamental transformations of the economy and of society call upon us not to abandon any traditional view or understanding of the state but to underpin analysis with a more dynamic approach that allows us to appreciate its ongoing transformation and its ongoing roles.

Competing roles and approaches to the state: from consensus and representation to politics and conflict

In terms of explicit debates on the state there has been, overall, a paucity of systematic discussion within the ER tradition. Much was due to the way dominant views of the state emerged within the discipline historically, with different positions on the state being discernable within the various traditions within literature. The historically dominant pluralist view of ER presents the state as one actor amongst others in the interplay that constitutes the regulation of employment: yet it was an actor that could assist in the redressing of the balance of power between capital and labour, or workers and managers. The pluralist view (Clegg, 1976) sees the state as an actor that in effect stands outside the employment process. The realm of pluralism within ER is, of course, quite broad and with a range of internal tensions (see Poole, 1981, pp. 72–91). Increasingly, however, the pluralist tradition within the field of ER became detached from the pluralist view of the state within political science, which posits the state as a disaggregated plurality of potentially competing power centres. Employment relations pluralists were concerned with processes of regulation between the state and, more importantly, unions and employers' bodies, in particular focusing on the role of collective bargaining as a vehicle for containing conflict (Clegg, 1976). Here the state played various roles as 'honest broker', 'negotiator', as a guardian and developer of rules, and perhaps ultimately as an arbiter. The assumption in this pluralist approach was that the imbalances of the economic system could be rebalanced through the role of the political sphere, which could develop public policies and state institutions to redress or tilt the balance of power in one direction or another. Yet within the UK's pluralist tradition there has also been a strain of ethical concerns and a focus on the social role of regulation through a strong social-democratic, progressive bias in the work of Clegg and others. More recently, this tradition has been manifest in relation to how a relatively more radical sociology of work was fused with IR (Ackers, 2011). It would be fair to say, however, that the state has not been systematically analysed as an entity and actor but rather it has been approached in a more empirical manner.

Within developed economies, particularly in western Europe, interest in the macro-level, political management role of the state led to the debate on the corporatist state. The development of the corporatist debate in the 1970s – which can be seen to be linked to the pluralist tradition within politics and sociology – saw the state as a quasi-autonomous, macro-level actor, intermediating between the peak organisations of capital and labour. The state was a player alongside these other actors in the regulation of the economy and labour market. The state was an actor that sought consensus and concertation between capital and labour, and access to their regulatory capacities, in order to provide a centralised and co-ordinated approach to economic and social policy. This school of thought represented a second stream of debate on the state within a broader pluralist paradigm, focusing on macro-level questions of regulation and representation. For Schmitter (1974), *societal* corporatism was seen to be a "post-liberal form of interest intermediation". The post-Second World War era saw a process of intermediation where the state attempted to include capital and labour organisations within decision-making processes regarding public and economic matters: this agenda was driven as much by political imperatives – the need to include, and so contain, subordinate classes – as economic ones (ibid).

This representation of corporatism reproduced pluralist assumptions in the way each actor was autonomous, entering into tripartite relations due to economic necessity and political imperatives; however, the theory of corporatism did recognise a counter point in cases where the state forces social dialogue and relies upon a more authoritarian approach to controlling the social actors (see the discussion on authoritarian unitarism below and critical views of the repressive role of the state). Furthermore, as Hyman (1989) pointed out, the liberal or societal corporatist view shared the pluralist perspective of the state being just another actor, a negotiator amongst others. In effect, the theory of corporatist concertation was based on a vision of 'bargained' IR.

However, there has been a distinctly Marxist, and broadly critical, view of this type of corporatist state, which saw it as conducting more than just a form of political bargaining. From this perspective, corporatism represented the state's encroachment into the details of joint regulation and economic activity due to the failure of socio-economic actors to deliver stable, effective and consistent economic results. Panitch (1981) and Jessop (1982) argued that the state was attempting to create the basis for social cohesion through macro-level negotiated or managed 'inclusion' of trade unions and other social actors. However, Panitch (1981) argued that in the long term all this did was further politicise labour conflict by bringing the state directly into matters of IR, and matters of IR directly into the state. Marxist-corporatist theories of the state were dominated therefore by concerns over its role as a vehicle for economic and coercive action, or for undermining labour autonomy and action in the long term through the incorporation of its leadership.

Building on these antecedents, Kelly (1998) attempts to reintroduce a political sensitivity to the debate. Here the state is viewed as an actor in the process of mobilisation within civil society, as a form of repressive intervention, which can be seen to politicise questions and struggles regarding perceived injustices. Beyond the politicising of labour mobilisations in specific instances, Kelly sees the state as primarily providing a repressive dimension to the process of IR. This position reflects a tradition in which the state is seen as a player with coherent interests, directed from some pivotal elite within and around the state. The question of its autonomy, be it total, relative or potential (see Jessop (1990) for a discussion on this topic, as well as Poulantzas (1974) and Skocpol (1979)), was not really discussed within IR until the emergence of new debates around regulation: the spaces and activities within which the state intervenes were not seen as integral to any discussion of the state and its roles. The links between the different elements of the state, the links between these elements of the state and other actors, and the context of state action need to be considered more carefully. Even if we take the extreme example highlighted by Kelly concerning the repressive role of the state, this has historically not been conducted in a unitary and unilateral manner. As Darlington and Lyddon (2003) point out, in the British strike wave of 1973 an array of intelligence and coercive state apparatus was mobilised in alliance with reactionary aspects of the media, private agencies dedicated to blacklisting and particular employers. Thus, even this coercive feature of the state is part of a process of co-ordination with actors within civil society. Kelly himself, in a discussion of the 1984–1985 Miners' Strike in the UK, points to such developments:

> The 1984–85 Miners' Strike, however, witnessed radical changes in both the nature and scale of police tactics as the forces of the state engaged with an unusually large number of determined strikers. *Regional police forces* achieved an unprecedented degree of co-ordination and centralisation in decision-making. *Riot police*, first pioneered in 1970s as a response to the strike wave of that period, were frequently deployed and anti-strike tactics became markedly aggressive... In the midst of the strike, *the courts* began to attach novel conditions to bail awards which prevented striking miners travelling within a specified radius... A few years earlier (1980) the *welfare benefit system* had been altered so that social security benefits were reduced by sixteen pounds per week (the amount of union strike pay miners were deemed to receive whether they did or not). And urgent needs payments to strikers and their families were abolished. Finally, *the intelligence services* were allegedly involved in a variety of ways: surveillance, telephone tapping, deployment of agent provocateurs and maintenance of at least one secret agent in the upper reaches of the miner's union.... Files were kept in the 1960s and 1970s and probably since on senior trade union leaders and regularly passed to *government ministers* who met them. ... Until its demise, in the 1990s, and organisation called the *Economic League* (founded 1919) have maintained files on thousands of trade union activists...
>
> *(Kelly, 1998, p. 57) (Italics added.)*

Whilst certain governments have used various agencies and organisations (public and private) to pursue anti-union practices at specific times, this detailed direct quote reveals that the role of the state, even when focusing on the repressive dimension, is complex. It involves an array of policies and actors across a period of time. Whilst Kelly (1998) is advocating mobilisation theory to show how the state's responses politicise IR, the quote also alludes to the complex nature of the state's repressive character. The links between these policies and practices were also the product of a set of alliances based on shared ideological predispositions (and, ultimately, class interests) amongst a number of dominant elites and institutions. Therefore, we need to observe the pattern of state intervention in terms of a wider time frame than is often the case, and with sensitivity to the array of actors involved, within and beyond the state. This critical perspective is important for stretching our understanding of the state and countering the more passive institutional views of it.

Within the various approaches reviewed above, the emphasis may be seen as less focused on representation and more on a juridical role and formal type of intervention. However, we need an approach to critical analysis that allows us to go beyond an obsession with the degree of maturity or development in a country's system of joint regulation and to focus on the way various state agencies intervene – effectively or not – in the context of ER. Much depends on the context in question and the extent of trade union and worker rights. However, we can begin to map more broadly the way the state operates across representative and regulatory mechanisms, as well as repressive and more coercive mechanisms, in terms of its relation to key actors in ER. Such an approach also allows us to appreciate the impact of the level of national resourcing of the state, within particular cases, and the extent of the legitimacy and capacity the various actors called upon to bolster these resources may or may not have.

The state and traditional perspectives on employment relations: thinking in terms of macro- and micro-level state roles

The previous section outlined the basic tensions and approaches to viewing the state: critical approaches have vied with more institutionalised, generically pluralist approaches over understanding the purpose and roles of the state. This section will develop this analysis by locating it within a broader set of views and at different levels of state intervention, in terms of the macro (national policy level) and the micro level (pertaining to the workplace). Within the study of ER, the treatment of public policy and the role of the state has an uneven history; one way of trying to characterise this unevenness is by recognising that there are different ideologically and theoretically informed approaches to the issue. Budd and Zagelmeyer (2010) (building on Budd and Bhave, 2008), in a review of debates on public policy in relation to employee participation and involvement, provide a summary of various ways in which we can approach these questions. They build on the well-established discussions of the aforementioned three perspectives that are the mainstay of textbooks on ER (see Blyton and Turnbull, 2004 for example): unitarism; pluralism; and conflict/critical approaches (or what we have termed above, radical/Marxist). Budd and Zagelmeyer (ibid.) actually add a fourth approach, subdividing what is usually presented as unitarism with the addition of a perspective they call egoism. The egoist perspective is based on a more transactional, market-based approach to ER, one that corresponds to orthodox, neoclassical economic analysis of the employment relationship in which self-seeking economic agents freely interact towards the ends of economic efficiency. In this idealised model, the role of public policy is reduced to being mainly focused on fixing market failures and ensuring a limited role for regulation on employment issues. The second perspective is the unitarist approach, into which the egoist perspective is normally conflated due to, in our view, the tendency within

ER to view employer-oriented approaches as fundamentally unified and non-problematic. However, Budd and Zagelmeyer (ibid.) differentiate these more employer-oriented positions. They argue that, unlike the market reductionism of egoism, unitarism sees equity and voice, along with psychological satisfaction, as being important within the employment relationship, albeit framed by employers and management. The role of public policy is to prevent the destructive dimensions of competition. In such a context the state must facilitate the dialogue between worker and management, albeit in the interests of the employer; voice has to be constructed in some way within unitarism rather than being left to being a natural by-product of free interaction within the labour market, as within egoism. The next category is the pluralist approach – which in many ways is more diverse than Budd and Zagelmeyer acknowledge – and which argues that questions of efficiency, equity and voice are all important and it is the role of the state and public policy to balance these interests and equalise the bargaining between the actors. The final perspective is labelled the critical approach in Budd and Zagelmeyer – as noted, terms vary, with radical/Marxist often being the preferred label. In their account, the critical approach views equity and voice issues as paramount. In the capitalist context, whilst the state can offset some of the imbalances in power between workers and employers, its main interest is to sustain these imbalances, presumably due to the view that the capitalist form of ER is the most efficient system. It should be noted that more radical positions within this critical approach would eschew issues of equity and voice as sometimes disguising the true nature of the capitalist employment relationship.

Hence, we can see the general perspectives approach allows us to understand the state in different ways and the rationales underpinning different views of the state. The problem with the perspectives approach is that it can introduce an element of relativism to the debate on ER, i.e. that it is all a case of what position suits your political approach, and thus it is not a robust framework for comparing positions and narratives. Yet the approach allows us to ground different perspectives in terms of narratives of power and policy developments; also, it has some uses in understanding the language of policy and state activity as well as the academic traditions analysing it. However, our view is that we need to differentiate the *form* of state and the nature of proactive and reactive state roles that emerge. The state and public policy have many dimensions, as outlined earlier, and so these perspectives can be further subdivided, broadly speaking, by two dimensions: these additional dimensions allow us to broaden the analysis of the different roles of the state. Our argument is that questions of coercion and consensus, as well as direct and more indirect roles, run throughout these perspectives, and in highlighting these additional dimensions we can arrive at a more nuanced approach to how we understand the state within a critical account of its the capitalist context.

When we consider unitarism, which fundamentally highlights the common character and interests of employers and workers, we need to break these into two sets.[2] The first is one where the state and public policy are concerned with underpinning 'dialogue' through regulations that highlight the prerogative of management. Policy focuses on the micro level of dialogue at the firm or workplace in a way that highlights equity issues first but allows for individual social issues to be dealt with, in a passive manner. Japanese ER in the post-war period up until the 1980s would be an example of this, in terms of enterprise unionism and micro-level, firm-based (and oriented) labour relations (Jeong and Aguilera, 2008: see Urano and Stewart, 2009 for a critique). The aim of public policy is to underpin this formally independent system and support it through firm-based social and welfare systems. However, there are many other ways the state can do this job, and some of these approaches are relevant for 'non-democratic' and/or developing economy contexts. The state can coerce such dialogue through direct and authoritarian means; not just by isolating workers and their organisations and even repressing them – as in Italy in the 1930s, Spain in the 1940s–1970s, or even Argentina in the 1980s – but by then actively creating a system of 'dialogue' through systems of worker representation dominated by the state. This approach links to the debate about the difference between state and societal corporatism (Schmitter, 1974). The point is that there are different ways the state, employers and workers engage around debates on social and economic issues. In the form that was prevalent in authoritarian contexts such as the fascist dictatorships in Italy and Spain in the early-to-mid twentieth century, we saw the state subverting organised labour and creating joint structures of representation between workers and employers at various levels, which were in effect dominated by the state and its key party. It could be argued this is similar in the case of China under the ideologically contrasting communist context: labour representation was – and is to a great extent – dominated by the one-party state, albeit with different social ends compared to the previous two examples, which were located in capitalist contexts. In effect the unitary character of ER is enforced and pushed in a specific political direction. By contrast, the societal approach Schmitter refers to is built on that fact that dialogue at the national level is voluntary and based on acceptance of difference. We return to the nature of the societal when discussing the pluralist approach, where it is less focused on unitary concerns. The point is, we need to understand that the state supports ER in quite different ways even when the perspective appears essentially unitarist.

The pluralist approach can also be seen to contain very different standpoints in terms of the nature of the state. On the one hand, and following on from the emphasis on the micro-level approach outlined above, the state can play a key role in ensuring that dialogue between actors such as worker organisations and employers can be based on relatively more balanced power relations. The emergence of a liberal democratic system of ER in various developed economy contexts, and in a selection of developing economies in parts of West Africa, for example, has been based on an acceptance of independent unions and systems of open collective bargaining that are legally underpinned by the state, to a greater or lesser extent. In such a system, the role of the state is to ensure the rules of engagement, systems of representation and generalisation of agreements between actors such as trade unions and management, on the basis of the autonomous nature of each. In turn, the state can provide assurances, resources and obligations, such as the requirement for trade unionists to have time to work on questions of ER issues in their workplace (in the UK this is known as facility time). However, the state can also be proactive on such matters and actually develop macro-level strategies that frame the indirect wage of the workforce, in terms of social welfare and health benefits as well as educational and developmental services. This corresponds to some features of a societal approach to corporatism as outlined above, in terms of elements of macro-level tripartite dialogue, but also links to broader models of the welfare state (Esping-Andersen, 1990). It could be argued that this is the difference between US approaches, historically, which largely correspond to the former, less interventionist approach, and the more social dialogue based model of the Nordic countries that correspond to the latter, more proactive approach. So the state engages with ER in a pluralist context again in a variety of ways, sometimes combining these approaches and sometimes separating them. Clearly these are generalisations but it is vital to acknowledge that these different approaches have macro- and micro-level features. The problem is that the study of these social and macro issues are usually the preserve of political scientists and social policy academics, and have not been systematically incorporated into ER analysis until recently. Yet, as Meardi, Donaghey and Dean (2016) point out, the role of welfare state studies and the focus on different welfare regimes is an important reference point for comprehending the broader roles of the state, thus allowing appreciation of the social wage, and the support and intervention of workers as a whole and not just the prototypical male, stably employed individual.

This leads us to the third approach, variously called the critical approach (a term that undermines its more positive identity and history) or the radical/Marxist perspective. The argument here is that the state is normally viewed as working on behalf of employers – capitalists in most cases – and in the interests of the incumbent socio-economic system: capitalism. Yet how it does this and through what forms are highly complex. The problem with the general perspectives approach is that it fails to see how the state can be ambivalent in relation to individual capitalists, and how it is not so much a case of supporting their every whim but of ensuring the long-term interests of capital, more broadly conceived, and the reproduction of the capitalist system. The state's actions may indeed contradict the interests of individual or groups of capitalists in pursuit of these ends, especially given the propensity for capitalists to pursue short-term gain over long-term stability (Poulantzas, 1974), and this is why some talk of the relative autonomy of the state. In effect it reflects a tension in Marxist traditions between those who see the state as simply an arm of the dominant class and those who see the state as a relatively autonomous set of institutions that clasp back onto those classes to ensure they, and not just the workforce, behave and deliver specific outcomes that ensure systemic sustainability. On the one hand, the state has to ensure the illusion of there being a balance of interests between workers and their employers, through specific types of rights to representation, for example, and legal redress (Hyman, 1975). The language of fairness is deployed to ensure that aggressive or assertive behaviours are contained (ibid). In effect, through specific legislation and an ideology that stigmatises certain 'militant' behaviour, the state can intervene to ensure 'peace' (MacKenzie and Martínez Lucio, 2014). Additionally, the state can deploy more concerted roles, through the use of the types of welfare and social strategies mentioned earlier (in relation to the macro-level policy approach highlighted by pluralists), but which in this case can be seen as mechanisms to deter workers from an antagonistic approach to their employers and to pacify class conflict. On the other hand, there is the potential use of authoritarian means, which the state can deploy through repressive forces (both overtly coercive and in the form of covert intelligence) to limit the role of any one group: usually organised labour. This approach is very common, unfortunately, in both authoritarian contexts and also liberal democratic ones, as seen through the use of blacklists and laws that curtail worker rights. Hence the state can be more or less autonomous of dominant class interests and can also deploy both micro- and macro-level strategies to condition the development of ER.

Using the perspectives approach as an analytical tool and less as a set of normative views allows us to provide a more nuanced insight into the diverse activities and forms of the state in relation to ER: one which is valid beyond the common focus of developed economies. For example, the developmental state can be better understood when we see that in terms of unitarist approaches the state can actually contribute to employer colonisation of worker representation at either the macro or micro level – or both (MacKenzie and Martínez Lucio, 2005). The state can play a role in ensuring an employer-dominated system of company-based ER, or through the state manufacturing or dominating the political space of labour representation, as seen in China (although this is changing). Curiously, whilst a unitarist approach may actually celebrate this outcome (showing that unitarism is not to be seen simply as a liberal market approach, ironically), the 'conflict-based' approaches would acknowledge such initiatives as being a reality of some developmental contexts. The state pursues systemic interests through subverting organised labour – for example – at the national and workplace level via coercive means or by mimicking it through state network-controlled labour organisations. In this respect, the interest in revealing the coercive side is important as is the way state-led proxies are developed. However, more recently in Malaysia and Indonesia the role of the developmental state has been more significant in the way it has actually attempted to ensure some semblance of pluralist-like dialogue at the micro level. Such dialogue is sustained by a system of quasi-liberal labour law, but one that does not develop a broader plurality and balance between capital and labour at the macro political and welfare level, although it is increasingly under pressure to do so (see Kumar and Martínez Lucio, 2014). Therefore, there is a need to look at different levels of dialogue and mutual engagement across the actors, as this may reveal the emergence of pluralistic democratic dynamics, albeit limited.

The outline of the perspectives approach – and our variation on it above – are generalisations. There are also overlaps, as in the case of a micro-level, unitarist approach overlapping with a micro-level, pluralist-oriented context in the UK in the 1980s and 1990s, as the former was being propagated under the Conservative governments of the time. However, what we are able to see is how different narratives of class conflict and co-operation are structured across these perspectives and in terms of different approaches within them. Broadly speaking, the macro and micro levels and the consensual and coercive aspects of state policy and behaviour become visible, which takes us beyond the blanket term of public policy. We can see how the state plays a variety of roles and how it negotiates and attempts to frame the basic interactions within the employment relationship. In this respect we can broaden the framework of the analysis of the state and stretch across various aspects of institutional and organisational behaviour. It is to this that we now turn, as we outline the ways in which regulation itself as a central feature of ER is being conceptualised and reimagined in a set of contemporary debates regarding the diverse roles of the state.

Mapping the state over time and across roles and institutions: an emergent synthesis in understanding regulation, coordination and ideology

There have been attempts to try and balance the institutionalist approach of pluralism with a more systematic attempt to look at the diverse roles of the state, and the workings of different levels of the state in relation to ER and the political economic context in general. The work of Clark (1995) sought to re-envision the state in terms of its transformation, and increasing complexity, in the age of deregulated and flexible labour markets. Clark was far from alone in depicting the state as having withdrawn – at one level – from the regulation of the employment relationship and the economy through policies to free up market forces. The neoliberal rhetoric of the state and its ideological 'mobilisation' against regulation and collectivism was a salient feature of the latter decades of the twentieth century. In this approach, the state facilitates the interests of capital through its rhetoric and the strategic nature of its withdrawal across various fronts of engagement

The activities of the state and its role across a range of dimensions of the economy and society are confronted in another set of debates, which have located the state within varieties of capitalism (Hall and Soskice, 2001). The case of the UK, for example, is seen as being linked to a liberal market economy where shareholder interests and a more short-term, less regulated approach to ER has prevailed (ibid). This is in part due to the uneven nature of industrial and Fordist developments in terms of work organisation, and a history of a libertarian, laissez faire approach to regulation (Clark, 2000).

However, whilst the state is viewed in terms of its different roles within the Varieties of Capitalism approach, these are discussed primarily in relation to questions of economic context and the way the state links into different political agendas or traditions. The conclusion, applied with varying degrees of sophistication by exponents of this approach, is that coordinated market economies have more proactive states in terms of regulation, welfare and economic activity than their liberal market counterparts. This is a debate that has allowed regulation and the state to enter more directly into questions of economic and social context but which does not then problematise the state per se. Mechanisms of coordination occur in liberal market economies but the assumption is repeated that such marketised arrangements reflect some sort of idealised laissez faire antithesis of state involvement. The focus of such academic approaches is on the various functions of the state and their role in different national contexts (see Hyman 2008, p. 263). In this respect, such regulation-based understandings of the state are concerned with an overarching purpose and narrative. This is reflected in Crouch's interest in locating state action across various dimensions of contestation, pluralism and corporatism (Crouch, 1993: see Hyman, ibid) and with the way weak market-facing approaches undermine more concerted and coordinated alternatives, or more regulated, worker-oriented approaches, within the state (Crouch, 1993). For Crouch, the issue of coordination within IR systems is a key feature of the extent to which they are more robust and more socially oriented, along with supportive political alliances and underpinning ideologies such as social democracy.

This leads to a need to engage with the role of regulation theory and its contribution to the debate on the state in ER. The IR discipline has addressed some of the issues, as we have outlined above, but the informality and complexity of regulation has faded from the debate in the UK. Given the Anglo-Saxon context, this has been in part due to the nature of regulatory development during the twentieth century, where the state has not been as overt a player as in other cases (Clark, 1995, 2000). Clark has argued for the need to embed any analysis in an approach that is sensitive to the economic and industrial structures of a national context: the way Fordist structures have or have not evolved generally, in terms of the structure of economic governance and the dynamics of labour market policies. Clark was one of the first IR scholars to embed regulation theory from a political economy perspective into IR analysis. Some contributions have been implicitly or tangentially concerned with the internal dynamics and politics of regulation: attention has been drawn to the questions of informal regulatory processes, actors and relations more broadly and the way regulation is discretely constructed in different cases (see the development of Hancher and Moran's (1989) notion of regulatory space by MacKenzie and Martínez Lucio, 2005, which in part builds on work done by Crouch, 1986). We, therefore, focus on the lessons learnt from developments within the UK context because of the peculiar – though not necessarily superior – characterisation of the state as the curious 'other', due to its uneven and distinctive development as a regulatory actor. Within the UK, the apparatus of regulation has been developed in quite formally 'de-centred' ways during the twentieth century: the extent of 'deregulation' and withdrawal are formally extensive, but there are examples of new forms of 'arm-length' regulation that are suggestive of novel forms of intervention and political relations between actors. Ironically, the UK context is held up as a paradigm of change and economic, regulatory withdrawal within Europe, yet there are quite novel forms of re-regulation that raise pertinent questions about how we view both regulation and the state (Howell, 2005).

The state must be understood in terms of a much broader comprehension of regulation, one that recognises the processes by which the state *manages*, *shares* and in effect *shifts* the locus of regulation between different sites. This is done through modes of representation, intervention or even coercion. Jessop has sought to ensure that we understand that the capitalist state is an ensemble of institutions of representation, intervention and administration (Jessop, 1982). The structuralist tradition has also demonstrated the importance of mechanisms that support and underpin the role of the state in the economy, such as IR institutions like collective bargaining or social relations as reflected in the family. This recognition has been transformed within the regulation school generally into a less reductionist approach, which highlights the need to understand the co-ordination of regulation within the state and between the state and social actors as issues in their own right (Jessop, 1990, 1995; Théret, 1994). This conforms to Baldwin, Scott and Hood's (1998) third typology of theories of regulation, which views it as "all mechanisms of social control – including unintentional and non-state processes..." (ibid, p. 4)[3]: "... the state can be described as a relatively unified ensemble of socially embedded, socially regularised, and strategically selective institutions, organisations, social forces, and activities organised around (or at least involved in) making collectively binding decisions for an imagined political community..." (Jessop, 2002, p. 40).

The state can therefore be viewed, as far as Jessop is concerned, at six levels of activity: modes of political representation; internal articulation of the state apparatus; modes of intervention and their articulation; political projects articulated by different social forces; prevailing state projects and discourses; and broad hegemonic projects that link and legitimise the state. Any discussion of regulation in relation to current changes in employment must also be sensitive to the meaning and function of regulation (Howell, 2005; MacKenzie and Martínez Lucio, 2005). Regulation theory facilitates an awareness of the contradictory and crisis-ridden nature of state development, linked to different historical approaches to accumulation and the uneven autonomy between the state and the economic context (Howell, 2005, pp. 31–33). For example, Howell attempts to fuse regulation theory with IR approaches in his seminal UK-based study. Such an approach allows the role of the state to be appreciated in its fuller and yet, ironically, more limited sense. Within IR debates, Hyman (2008) has developed a parallel agenda, which looks at the state across various dimensions: its role as an employer; establishing procedural regulation; substantive employment rights; economic (including demand and supply side) roles; and indirect wage/welfare intervention. Thus the state can be mapped across such competing roles. On the basis of such mapping, the form and the spaces of regulatory intervention by the state, internally and externally, can be understood.

On the other hand, it is also important to recognise the role of different sites, spheres and actors that populate the regulatory landscape, and the relationship between them (MacKenzie and Martínez Lucio, 2005). Interplay and tensions exist within a context in which the state is one amongst many actors. Such an approach should be sensitive to a multidisciplinary, socio-political understanding of regulation and regulatory change. It is important to chart the role of the state in terms of both its relationships with other actors at the macro and micro levels, and relationships within the state itself. To these ends, the notion of regulatory space, a term used by Hancher and Moran (1989) and on which we have built is significant.

We would view the panoply of regulation through an analytical framework made up of a variety of levels, spaces and sites that are adjacent and at times inter-locking, both mutually supportive and potentially competing (MacKenzie and Martínez Lucio, 2014). This terrain is populated by a range of regulatory actors, such as state bodies, trade unions or management networks, to name some key examples. The site represents the point of interaction between regulatory actors, where regulatory outcomes are arrived at through the interaction of actors, and often reflected in institutional constructs. The site of regulation is circumscribed by a regulatory space, a recognised boundary of jurisdiction for the regulatory processes in question. Various actors may intervene in the process within this space, and there may be an overlap between the boundaries of regulatory spaces, but within these spaces each actor will also operate within their own sphere of influence, or jurisdiction, within which they are the sole actor. For example, trade unions and management interact within a given regulatory space, within which each traditionally operates their own sphere of jurisdiction (the fact that the boundaries are fluid and contested by extant and potential new entrant actors, who may even pose a threat to the continued existence of these spheres of jurisdiction, is key to the processes of regulatory transfer with which we are concerned). Regulatory actors may operate across a number of levels, sites and spaces, and furthermore the actors that occupy given spaces of regulation may vary by location. The regulation of certain social and economic relationships may in one location be served by the local state, whilst in another this role may be played by capital, for example through the dominance of local communities by monopolistic employers in so-called company towns or corporate-centred welfare as seen in Japan. In other circumstances, key regulatory roles may be played by social institutions such as religious bodies, local community groups or a combination of these actors.

The regulation of workplace health and safety in the UK provides a further example, which depending on context may vary between the involvement of employers, the state and trade unions. Union involvement in the regulation of workplace health and safety depends on a union presence in the workplace. Therefore actor entry or exclusion can turn on a recognition agreement, or alternatively de-recognition, which would in effect represent the colonisation of the regulatory space by management. In either case, these actors would continue to share the regulatory space with the state, in the form of the Health and Safety Executive. With antecedents in the nineteenth century Factory Acts, which saw the government enter the regulatory space as a new actor, the Health and Safety Executive is itself a product of shifting boundaries and the colonisation of regulatory space through its absorbing of historic regulatory bodies such as the Factories Inspectorate and the Railways Inspectorate. Hence, the space is the broad arena around which different actors coalesce, within which economic and social actors can act with relative confidence regarding the actions of others. The advantage of this approach is that it allows for observance of the political interplay and contestation between actors. In some cases, actors may compete with each other over the right to represent a specific constituency, as in the development of the living wage in the UK, especially in London, in the past 20 years: the space may become increasingly contested with a greater amount of political competition than co-operation. It is therefore important to distinguish between this conceptualisation of regulatory space and its use within a pluralist discourse of negotiation and accommodation: conflict and mobilisation, as well as problems of representation and voice, are just as significant.

These spaces exist at various levels, from micro to macro, dealing with operational, strategic or policy issues. These levels are conceptually discrete but interlocking and mutually informing. Relationships between actors within a regulatory space, for example management and unions at the level of the workplace, may be informed by regulatory processes in the form of regional and national bargaining structures, the policy processes of the nation state and, increasingly, supranational mechanisms of regulation. In terms of supranational developments, recent decades have seen unions and employers, alongside non-government organisations, establish a series of agreements on employment practices within specific contexts, albeit essentially 'soft regulation' (MacKenzie and Martínez Lucio, 2014). European Union social and labour market regulation perhaps serves as a more significant example of supranational influence. In turn, the implications of Brexit promise future examples of shifting boundaries of regulatory space, new actor entry and the colonisation of regulatory roles.

The organisational, institutional and economic dimensions of the state are also supported by discursive and ideological dimensions (Jessop, 1982), or what can be called narrative dimensions (Howell, 2005, pp. 39–41). As previously noted, Hyman (1975) pointed to the importance of such prevailing ideologies in framing and contextualising the nature of state intervention, such as in the use of 'fairness' to curtail class conflict and politics. This discursive side to the role of the state is rarely a point of discussion in the study of the state in IR analysis. The way the state can propagate ideas and visions of future or preferable forms of management-union/worker relations through its various agencies and political mechanisms can play an important part in establishing a narrative that underpins the long-term perspective of work and employment change. For example, there may be very explicit political discourses stigmatising the role and behaviour of certain actors, as in the case of the UK in the 1980s and the impact of 'New Right' political discourse on the legitimacy of trade unions (MacKenzie and Martínez Lucio, 2014). Furthermore, very specific policies and support mechanisms on questions of good practice or preferred practice, such as the use of consultancy and learning facilities through the state's conciliation strategy, may also assist transformations in the conduct of managers and worker representatives (Martínez Lucio and Stuart, 2011). So such narratives may operate at a macro level or a micro level through a range of political and ideological interventions.

Meardi, Donaghey and Dean (2016) try to underpin such growing sensitivities in terms of an approach to the state by citing various academic sources and disciplinary based inputs. They make a point of academics tending to ignore the role of gender studies in explanations of the mechanisms of regulatory inclusion and exclusion, labour market structure, welfare support and politics, and the general language of rights and regulation – as noted previously. To this extent the growing interest in a more open and inclusive academic conceptualisation of regulation allows for a socially more sensitive approach to the subject, not least when the nature of work and workers is being fundamentally transformed.

In a curious way these debates on regulation have allowed academics to generate instruments to study the role of the state – and ER more generally – across different national contexts, which are more open to broader questions of regulation across time and space. We can see how to understand the way certain issues are highlighted in different contexts in different ways (Locke and Thelen, 1995), but also how different agencies and strategies of the state mobilise in relation to them. These new approaches focus on, for example, institutional regimes, the societal context and the pattern of rule-making. They point to the importance of context in historical terms and how these can frame developments as logics of action; these are created in specific moments of time but referenced in subsequent developments as actors jostle for position and thus resurrect previous practices that may have been inactive. Therefore, specific naratives, institutional practices and relations may find that they are used in different contexts as part of this interplay. Increasingly, this dynamic and cross-referencing analysis of the spaces and temporal contexts of ER has become important in how the state is studied and understood.

The death and rebirth of the state in the context of neoliberalism, fragmentation and austerity

The question of the state is, as has been outlined above, a curious and important feature of how we understand ER. There are various approaches and debates that attempt to explain its diverse and varied roles. Observers from pluralist, unitarist and more critical perspectives have argued that with the affirmation of a liberal market perspective and market-oriented approach in politics and economics in recent decades, the role of the state has diminished. Yet, there is a growing tranche of literature arguing that things are not so simple – even if change is perceptible. This argument has been an emergent and significant current in ER debates.

Firstly, during the 1990s there was an emergent interest in new forms of social dialogue with a more strategic nature, given the growing impact of the neoliberal environment: for example, the way training and supply-side issues became a salient feature of the state's role in its attempts to facilitate a more competitive economy and productive workforce, along with new forms of management-worker collaboration. This has been a key feature of the state's growing role: the way it has facilitated the greater flexibility and deployment of workers across and within workplaces in an attempt to move away from a traditional and crisis-ridden Fordist model of production (Jessop, 2002). The state begins to play a more coercive role in part, notably in the way welfare is organised, so as to compel workers into the labour market. Other means include the use of training for new forms of qualifications and work-related skills development, although in some cases this may involve a degree of social dialogue with trade unions and employers (Heyes, 2007). Within the EU this shift has formed a key part of policy-making and funding for sector- and firm-level flexibility and learning initiatives (Stuart, 2007). What is more, the state continues to intervene in establishing minimum thresholds in relation to pay and operational features of the employment relationship, although in some cases whether it is developing this to achieve a model employer or fair employment relations is another point of debate (Heyes and Clark, 2011). However, the state's role is embedded in the very DNA of the employment relationship. In fact, even during processes of deregulation and change, as in the adoption of policies to decentralise collective bargaining and enhance managerial prerogative, we see the state having to deal with a range of repercussions and new forms of conflict. Koukiadaki, Tavora and Martínez Lucio (2016) studied deregulation and change within collective bargaining systems during the period 2008–2015 in those parts of the EU most affected by economic austerity measures and neoliberal policies. Their conclusions highlight the way the state, through the courts and mediation services, has had to deal with the greater fragmentation of regulation and the inconsistent outcomes that it brings in terms of wages and employment (Koukiadaki et al., 2016).

Secondly, in some respects the state has had to underpin its role through the development of new forms of 'soft regulation' through the establishment of labour standards and new forms of labour rights (Martínez Lucio and MacKenzie, 2011). This has become an important feature of the role of the state at the national and transnational levels. These interventions are called soft regulation because they do not have clear forms of implementation and sanctions that are deployed when non-compliance occurs (Kuruvilla and Verma, 2006). They are, for example, indicative frameworks and templates for companies to base their internal systems and standards on, establishing a set of general expectations. However, it is not mandatory for actors to comply with them, and hence can be categorised primarily at the first level of Baldwin et al.'s (1998) schema, operating as a weak form of coercion. The state therefore 'returns' to the establishment of standards through a range of practices. In some cases the state actually uses its learning and mediation spheres to provide consultancy and training to social actors as a way of endearing or orienting them towards specific types of organisational practices, such as partnership practices in the UK and the EU more generally (Martínez Lucio and Stuart, 2011). In the UK, we have seen the state increasingly fascinated by a new language of fairness and justice at work – noting the way the state uses campaigns and marketing increasingly – although this may in part be a response to the limitations of its own direct role. At the international level we see such an investment in the notion of new forms of soft regulation as forming the backdrop for a more co-ordinated attempt at creating labour standards. Through initiatives from the ILO and other international bodies such as the ISO 26000, there have been attempts to establish a basis of corporate social responsibility, albeit in a voluntary form (Mueckenberger and Jastram, 2010). The effectiveness and consistent implementation of these standards are, however, arguably problematic.

Thirdly, *the state continues to play a policing and coercive role* – the extent of which is dependent on the political situation and extent of freedoms in any given context. Even in developed economy contexts, such as the UK, there has been an ongoing concern with the use of intelligence services, informal blacklists and the way trade unions and trade unionists have been subject to surveillance (Kelly, 1998). This is a much darker feature of the reality of ER. In the case of Spain, the right wing government of 2011–2015 used laws that had precedence in the previous dictatorship to undermine the role of trade unionists during picketing and other forms of collective action (Fernández Rodríguez, Ibáñez Rojo and Martínez Lucio, 2016). The manner in which the state intervenes in overt and covert ways within ER has become a more pressing subject of study, not least given the growing concern with labour rights in a context of globalisation. As Gamble (1994) asserted when discussing the UK, the move to a greater market orientation leads to more direct and coercive state roles in the way it responds to the negative social and economic outcomes of the marketisation process. Hence the state remains an important albeit ethically ambivalent actor in what is a more brutal period of capitalism (Coates, 2014; Streeck, 2011).

Fourth, we see *the boundaries between the state and the market* becoming slightly more porous, which leads to new forms of alliances between the state and corporate capital around specific public goods. We also see the exposure of internal regulatory actors to external 'market' pressures, through processes of privatisation, subcontracting and shifts in organisational boundaries (MacKenzie, 2002). The representation of the 'market' within the state, and the imperatives it is perceived to unleash, has been a vital ingredient of change in the past few decades. During privatisation processes, references are made to what the new market requires, and what new forms of organisational behaviour are now relevant to the state and its structures (Crouch, 2011).

The context of individualisation, capital internationalisation, greater labour mobility and migration geographically (often involuntary), plus the impact of fiscal crisis and instability, means that the state does not so much withdraw as rethink its roles: a process that also calls on academics to draw on a wider set of approaches in relation to its study (MacKenzie and Martínez Lucio, 2005; Meardi, Donaghey and Dean, 2016). The ambivalence of regulation and its likely capturing by various other actors – and potential re-capturing by the state – is an important issue we need to account for (Majone, 1994; Martínez Lucio and MacKenzie, 2004). There are curious new roles for the supposedly 'diminished' state, in being brought back into ever wider and more complex scenarios of engagement, which require a new language and set of policies (Crouch, 2011, 2013; Rubery, 2011).

Conclusion

After a period of muted interest, the role of the state has returned as a point of discussion within the areas of ER and HRM, albeit only in the past decade or so. Much of this interest has been prompted by the fact that a period of crisis in capitalism has been changing the character and roles of the state within different contexts. The increasing privatisation of state services and their reduction in some areas has been reconfigured into new roles and new types of intervention. This chapter has therefore tried to outline the different ways in which the state intervenes within ER and the new roles it is attempting to achieve in a more globalised and competitive context: a context that is also bringing forth major social challenges and questions of fairness and dignity within the language of ER. Just as unitarism has be newly problematised (Budd and Zagelmayer, 2010), so pluralism and more critical approaches need to be set against two sets of developments, irrespective of where the commitments and loyalties of the authors may lie.

The first is the need to widen our approach to engaging with these traditional perspectives, in terms of drawing on other academic disciplines. This approach can bring us to a point where we look at the different perspectives in terms of how they relate to the role of the state at both the micro and macro levels. The fact is that there are different spaces and levels within the way ER are regulated and 'managed' by the state (MacKenzie and Martínez Lucio, 2005). We cannot simply refer to one level without an awareness of the other – something that until recently has been the negative contribution and handicap of Anglo-Saxon studies of the subject. The need to emphasise the role of the macro within each perspective helps us to widen the lens by which we study the state and the way it tries to steer the nature of ER.

This leads to a second development, which is outlined above: the focus on regulation theory and regulatory space, and the synthesis of these developments. Whilst some observers come from an avowedly Marxist tradition and others from a pluralist one, there seems to be an engagement with this approach towards regulation: one that is much more attuned to a historical, materialist and political engagement in terms of conceptualising the state. In some respects, the irony will not be lost on many observers that it is a theoretical framework linked to the notion of regulation that has helped salvage and rejuvenate the ER tradition on the state – although the concept of regulation is utilised in a very different way to what the term stood for in the past.

Finally, the paper ends with a discussion on the way the state plays a new set of roles, and remains entangled in the question of work and employment, partly in a deliberate manner and partly in an unintentional one. The state is having to return to the 'field of play' in a variety of ways, in order to respond to the new challenges thrown up by a more globalised and marketised system of work, employment and economy. In effect the state is having to resolve new tensions and new problems, as employers continue to challenge the established patterns of work and employment while simultaneously failing to provide a sustainable and innovative system of social and economic regeneration. In conclusion, the chapter brings to the fore a range of new debates on how we need to understand the more fractured and continuous role of the state, within and beyond the limits of the current economic context, and the implications that this holds.

Notes

1 We use the term employment relations in preference to industrial relations not simply as a more contemporary nomenclature but to signal a broadening of analysis beyond formal types of regulation and organisational actors towards a more sociological and labour market-orientated approach. However the terms employed will vary according to how they were used by authors we cite.
2 Although the egoist position as discussed by Budd and Zagelmeyer (2010) is relevant it does not quite acknowledge the role of the state in having to construct and support mechanisms of employment relations as such: as noted, the egoist approach is based on an orthodox economic view of labour market interaction, where the role of public policy is mainly focused on fixing market failures, with a limited role for regulation. We are therefore liable to accusations of re-conflating egoism with unitarism.
3 Baldwin et al. (1998, p. 4) suggest that contributions to the debate on regulation tend to fall into one of three categories. The first views regulation in terms of 'targeted rules' "accompanied by some mechanism, typically a public agency, for monitoring and promoting compliance". The second view is to be found in the area of political economy, which conceptualises regulation as being the state and its attempt to manage the economy. However, there is a third view that considers regulation to be "all mechanisms of social control – including unintentional and non-state processes…" (Baldwin et al., 1998, p. 4).

References

Ackers, P. (2011). 'The changing systems of British industrial relations, 1954–1979: Hugh Clegg and the Warwick sociological turn', *British Journal of Industrial Relations*, 49(2), pp. 306–330.
Aglietta, M. (1982). *Régulation et crises du capitalisme*. Paris: Calmann-Levy.

Baldwin, R., Scott, C. and Hood, C. (1998). Introduction, in Baldwin, R., Scott, C. and Hood, C. (eds.) *A Reader on Regulation*. Oxford: Oxford University Press.

Blyton, P. and Turnbull, P. (2004). *The Dynamics of Employee Relations*. 3rd edn. Basingstoke: Palgrave.

Boyer, R. (1990). *The Regulation School*. New York: Columbia University Press.

Budd, J.W. and Bhave, D. (2008). Values, Ideologies and Frames of Reference in Industrial Relations, in Blyton, P., Bacon, N., Fiorito, J. and Heery, E. (eds.) *The SAGE Handbook of Industrial Relations*. London: Sage, pp. 92–112.

Budd, J. W. and Zagelmeyer, S. (2010). Public Policy and Employee Participation, in Wilkinson, A., Gollan, P.J., Marchington, M. and Lewin D. (eds.) *The Oxford Handbook of Participation in Organisations*. Oxford: Oxford University Press.

Clark, I. (1995). The State and the New Industrial Relations, in Beardwell, I.J. (ed.) *Contemporary Industrial Relations*. Oxford: Oxford University Press.

Clark, I. (2000). *Governance, the State, Regulation and Industrial Relations*. London: Routledge.

Clegg, H. (1976). *Trade Unions Under Collective Bargaining*. Oxford: Blackwell.

Coates, D. (2014). 'Studying comparative capitalisms by going left and by going deeper', *Capital & Class*, 38(1), pp. 18–30.

Crouch, C. (1986). Sharing Public Space: States and Organised Interests in Western Europe, in Hall, J. (ed.) *States in History*. Oxford: Basil Blackwell.

Crouch, C. (1993). *Industrial Relations and European State Traditions*. Oxford: Oxford University Press.

Crouch, C. (2011). *The Strange Death of Neoliberalism*. Cambridge (UK): Polity Press.

Crouch, C. (2013). *Making Capitalism Fit for Society*. Cambridge (UK): Polity Press.

Darlington, R. and Lyddon, D. (2003). *Glorious Summer: Class Struggle in Britain in 1972*. London: Bookmarks.

Esping-Andersen, G. (1990). 'The three political economies of the welfare state', *International Journal of Sociology*, 20(3), pp. 92–123.

Fernández Rodríguez, C.J., Ibáñez Rojo, R. and Martínez Lucio, M. (2016). 'Austerity and collective bargaining in Spain: the political and dysfunctional nature of neoliberal deregulation,' *European Journal of Industrial Relations*, 22(3), pp. 267–280.

Gamble, A. (1994). *The Free Economic and the Strong State*. 2nd edn. London: Palgrave.

Hall, P.A. and Soskice, D. (eds.) (2001). *Varieties of Capitalism. The Institutional Foundations of Comparative Advantage*. Oxford: Oxford University Press.

Hancher, L. and Moran, M. (1989). Organising Regulatory Space, in Hancher, L. and Moran, M. (eds.) *Capitalism, Culture and Economic Regulation*. Oxford: Oxford University Press.

Heyes, J. and Clark, I. (2011). *The State and Employment Relations*, in Townsend, K. and Wilkinson, A. (eds.) *Research Handbook on the Future of Work and Employment Relations*. Cheltenham: Edward Elgar.

Heyes, J. (2007). 'Training, social dialogue and collective bargaining in Western Europe', *Economic and Industrial Democracy*, 28(2), pp. 239–258.

Howell, C. (2005). *Trade Unions and the State*. Princeton: Princeton University Press.

Hyman, R. (1975). *Industrial Relations: A Marxist Introduction*. London: Macmillan.

Hyman, R. (1989). *The Political Economy of Industrial Relations*. London: Macmillan.

Hyman, R. (2008). The state in industrial relations, in Blyton, P., Bacon, N., Fiorito, J. and Heery, E. (eds.) *The SAGE Handbook of Industrial Relations*. London: Sage Publications.

Jeong, D.Y. and Aguilera, R.V. (2008). 'The Evolution of Enterprise Unionism in Japan: A Socio-Political Perspective', *British Journal of Industrial Relations*, 46(1), pp. 98–132.

Jessop, B. (1982). *The Capitalist State*. Oxford: Martin Robertson.

Jessop, B. (1990). *State Theory*. Oxford: Polity Press.

Jessop, B. (1995). 'The regulation approach, governance and post-Fordism: alternative perspectives on economic and political change?' *Economy and Society*, 24(3), pp. 307–333.

Jessop, B. (2002). *The Future of the Capitalist State*. Cambridge (UK): Polity Press.

Kelly, J. (1998). *Rethinking Industrial Relations*. London: Routledge.

Koukiadaki, A., Tavora, I. and Martínez Lucio, M. (2016). Joint regulation and labour market policy in Europe during the crisis: a seven-country comparison, in Koukiadaki, A., Tavora, I. and Martínez Lucio, M. (eds.) *Joint Regulation and Labour Market Policy in Europe During the Crisis*. Brussels: ETUI.

Kumar, N. and Martínez Lucio, M. (2014). Developing contexts of human resource management and industrial relations: globalization and employment relations strategies and narratives, in Martínez Lucio, M. (ed.) *International Human Resource Management: An Employment Relations Perspective*. London: Sage.

Kuruvilla, S. and Verma, A. (2006). 'International labor standards, soft regulation, and national government roles', *Journal of Industrial Relations*, 48(1), pp. 41–58.

Locke, R.M. and Thelen, K. (1995). 'Apples and Oranges Revisited: Contextualized Comparisons and the Study of Comparative Labor Politics', *Politics & Society*, 23(3), pp. 337–367.

MacKenzie, R. (2002). 'The migration of bureaucracy: contracting and the regulation of labour in the telecommunications industry', *Work, Employment & Society*, 16(4), pp. 599–616.

MacKenzie, R. and Martínez Lucio, M. (2005). 'The Realities of Regulatory Change: Beyond the Fetish of Deregulation', *Sociology*, (39)3, pp. 499–517.

MacKenzie, R. and Martínez Lucio, M. (2014). 'The colonisation of employment regulation and industrial relations? Dynamics and developmnents over five decades of change', *Labor History*, 55(2), pp. 189–207.

Majone, G. (1994). 'The rise of the regulatory state in Europe', *West European Politics*, 17(3), pp. 77–101.

Martínez Lucio, M. and MacKenzie, R. (2004). 'Unstable Boundaries? Evaluating the 'New Regulation' within Employment Relations', *Economy and Society*, 33(1), pp. 77–97.

Martínez Lucio, M. and MacKenzie, R. (2011). Regulation and Change in Global Employment Relations, in Harzing A.W. and Pinnington, A. (eds.) *International Human Resource Management*. 3rd edn. London: Sage.

Martínez Lucio, M. and Stuart, M. (2011). 'The state, public policy and the renewal of HRM', *The International Journal of Human Resource Management*, 22(18), pp. 3661–3671.

Meardi, G., Donaghey, J. and Dean, D. (2016). 'The strange non-retreat of the state: implications for the sociology of work', *Work, Employment & Society*, 30(4), pp. 559–572.

Mueckenberger, U. and Jastram, S. (2010). 'Transnational norm-building networks and the legitimacy of corporate social responsibility standards', *Journal of Business Ethics*, 97(2), pp. 223–239.

Panitch, L. (1981). 'Trade unions and the Capitalist State', *New Left Review*, 125, pp. 21–45.

Poole, M. (1981). *Theories of Trade Unionism*. London: RKP.

Poulantzas, N. (1974). *Classes in Contemporary Capitalism*. London: NLB.

Rubery, J. (2011). 'Reconstruction amid deconstruction: or why we need more of the social in European social models', *Work, Employment & Society*, 25(4), pp. 658–674.

Schmitter, P. (1974). 'Still the Century of Corporatism', *Review of Politics*, 36(1), pp. 85–131.

Skocpol, T. (1979). *States and Social Revolutions: A Comparative Analysis of France, Russia and China*. New York: Cambridge University Press.

Streeck, W. (2011). 'Taking capitalism seriously: towards an institutionalist approach to contemporary political economy', *Socio-Economic Review*, 9(1), pp. 137–167.

Stuart, M. (2007). 'The industrial relations of learning and training: a new consensus or a new politics?', *European Journal of Industrial Relations*, 13(3), pp. 269–280.

Théret, B. (1994). 'To have or to be: on the problem of the interaction between state and economy and its 'solidarist' modes of regulation', *Economy and Society*, 23, pp. 1–46.

Urano, E.I. and Stewart, P. (2009). Beyond Organised Labour in Japan – The Case of the Japanese Community Union Federation, in McBride, J. and Greenwood, I. (eds.) *Community Unionism*. Basingstoke: Palgrave Macmillan, pp. 121–138.

12

UNIONS

Paul F. Clark

Introduction

Unions, also commonly referred to as labour unions or trade unions, are an important part of the workplaces of most nations. The objectives and structures of these organisations vary widely in response to the economic and political environment in which they function. However, the definition of a union first proposed in 1920 by the scholars Sidney and Beatrice Webb is still widely accepted as accurate. The Webbs defined unions as "continuous associations of wage earners for the purpose of maintaining or improving the conditions of their working lives" (1920).

The union movements of each country have their own distinct history, forms and structures, but there are also common issues and challenges that labour movements around the world have faced. The focus of this chapter will be the experience and role of labour unions in the United States (US), but many of the issues discussed will also resonate with labour unions in other countries, while at the same time reflecting the often unique nature of American exceptionalism.

In addressing the role that unions play in the social and economic system of the US, the chapter will identify and discuss the main developments in the evolution of these organisations over the last 250 years, as well as the challenges they face today. These developments will be analysed through a review of the scholarly literature, which has grown substantially over time.

The history of American unions

Origins

Modern American unions had their origins in the European craft guilds of the Middle Ages, although historians differ on the degree to which unions directly descend from these medieval organisations. Guilds were basically mutual aid organisations that sought to protect groups of skilled workers by controlling access to the occupation through apprenticeship training. By limiting access, guilds protected the incomes of their members. Guilds also functioned as benevolent societies, assisting members and their families in times of illness, injury or death (Epstein, 1995).

Guilds, however, differed from today's unions in that membership consisted of both merchants/masters and journeymen. As Western society transitioned from feudalism to capitalism and the industrial revolution spread, merchants/masters became employers. It was the inherent conflict between the interests of employers and the interests of their employees that is built into the capitalist system that led to the rise of unions (Curl, 2012; Epstein, 1995).

This conflict plays out in the labour market, where employers, whose goal is to maximise profit, attempt to do so by keeping their labour costs as low as possible. At the same time, employees, who want to maximise what they receive for their labour, attempt to push labour costs higher. Employers have almost always had the upper hand in this process, given the power advantage they have over a single employee. The most effective way workers have found to counter the power of employers is to band together and use their collective strength to balance that of employers. In doing so, the organisations they formed came to be called unions.

These early unions were formed first in Great Britain and other parts of Europe, and then in the US, by workers in skilled trades, such as printers, shoemakers and carpenters. They carried over some of the functions of guilds, particularly apprenticeship training and benevolent services. And like guilds, their power came from control over the supply of skilled labour, which they exercised by limiting access to each of the occupations. These craft unions then used this power to improve wages and working conditions (Curl, 2012).

The nineteenth century

During the first half of the nineteenth century, the union movement consisted largely of craft unions representing skilled workers. However, as the industrial revolution gained momentum, mechanisation was introduced in industry after industry. One of the very earliest industries to be mechanised was the textile industry. Technological advances led to the establishment of larger and larger workshops and eventually factories. Increasingly productive spinning and weaving machines made it possible to turn out textiles made of wool, silk and cotton in enormous quantities. Such workplaces required more and more labour to keep the machines operating (DeFranceso and Segal, 2014).

The low pay and poor working conditions of these early factories soon led to labour unrest. In some cases, strikes sprung up spontaneously, without the organisation of a union, as occurred in Pawtucket, RI in 1824. In other cases, textile workers formed some of the earliest factory or industrial unions prior to engaging in job actions. In 1934, the girls and young women working in the textile mills of Lowell, MA organised a union and walked out over wage cuts (Bloy, 2016; DeFranceso and Segal, 2014).

Other groups of semi-skilled and unskilled workers, such as iron workers, molders, railroad workers and miners, also began to form unions in the first half of the nineteenth century as a result of new technologies that accompanied the industrial revolution (Dubofsky and Dulles, 2010).

The first effort to form a national labour organisation in the US occurred in 1866 when the National Labor Union (NLU) was founded. The NLU was actually a federation of unions that came together to fight for the eight-hour day and other labour law reforms. While craft unions made up a significant part of its membership, the NLU also worked to help industrial workers form unions. It ceased to function by 1873 (Dubofsky and Dulles, 2010).

The Knights of Labor (KOL) was, technically, the first national union in the US (as opposed to a federation of unions like the NLU), as well as the first national organisation to endure for a significant period of time. The KOL brought together skilled and unskilled workers from almost all industries and occupations into one union that would grow to 700,000 members by 1886.[1] Both the NLU and KOL were notable for their opposition to the emerging wage system and their commitment to social and economic transformation. The KOL, in particular, advocated replacing the capitalist system with workplace co-operatives where workers would share the profits generated by the enterprise. However, a lack of effective leadership, combined with the rise of another national labour organisation, the American Federation of Labor (AFL), during the later 1880s, led the KOL to suffer a precipitous membership decline. By 1890, KOL membership had fallen to 100,000 members, and by 1900 it had basically withered away (Dubofsky and Dulles, 2010; Hild, 2010).

The AFL was founded in 1886 by craft unions disenchanted with the lack of substantive progress made by the KOL. Having witnessed the KOL accomplish little, the AFL took a fundamentally different approach to representing workers. Whereas the KOL offered membership directly to workers, the AFL was a federation of unions. Workers became members of a union and their union joined the AFL. And while the KOL was open to all workers, including women and African-Americans, the AFL affiliates were craft unions that largely restricted membership to workers in the skilled trades. As most of the skilled trades limited membership to white males at this point in time (and for years to come), so did the AFL (Dubofsky and Dulles, 2010).

The AFL, and its member unions, was also significantly more conservative and pragmatic than the KOL in terms of its goals and objectives. It largely accepted capitalism and the role of employers, and opposed workers' co-operatives. Its focus was primarily on making the lives of its members better in tangible ways by winning higher wages, better working conditions and fewer hours. Founding members of the AFL included the cigar makers, typographers, hat makers and carpenters' unions (ibid.).

The twentieth century

By the turn of the century, the craft unions of the AFL were well established and their memberships were growing. However, with the demise of the KOL, the growing number of unskilled and semi-skilled workers labouring in the mills, mines and factories of the burgeoning textile, metals and manufacturing industries did not have unions to turn to. This void was, in part, filled in 1905 by the creation of a new labour organisation called the Industrial Workers of the World (IWW) (Dubofsky and Dulles, 2010).

The IWW was national in scope, organising mill and factory workers in the eastern part of the country and ore miners, loggers and farm workers in the western US. Many of its early leaders and much of its philosophy would come from another union – the Western Federation of Miners (WFM). The IWW was, in many ways, the antithesis of the AFL as it welcomed any and all workers, regardless of gender, race, national origin, industry, occupation or skill level. It viewed the world through a class lens, referring to itself as the "first continental congress of the working class" and had as its goal the creation of "one big union" that would overthrow the capitalist wage system. Its aggressive style was built around class struggle and direct action such as strikes, boycotts and slowdowns. While the IWW has been portrayed as engaging in violence, the evidence suggests that it was, in fact, more often the victim of violence by police, vigilantes and company agents than it was a perpetrator (Dubofsky, 1969; Taft and Ross, 1969).

The IWW grew rapidly in the first two decades of the twentieth century, reportedly reaching a high of 150,000 members by 1917. However, just as rapidly, the union disintegrated in the face of government repression, including arrests and deportation, and internal divisions. By 1925, the IWW no longer functioned as a significant labour organisation (Dubofsky, 1969).

Four years after the demise of the IWW, the US saw the beginning of one of the most traumatic periods in its history, the Great Depression. Precipitated by the crash of the stock market and widespread bank failures, unemployment during this period reached 25 per cent overall and 37 per cent for all non-farm workers. When Franklin D. Roosevelt was elected in 1932, he embarked on a plan to address the crisis and get the nation's economy back on track. This plan, known as the New Deal, created a much bigger role for the government in the American economy. One of the parts of the New Deal that was a radical change from the past was the National Labor Relations Act (NLRA), also known as the Wagner Act (Dubofsky and Dulles, 2010).

Since the earliest unions had arisen in the late 1700s, government at all levels had taken, with just a few exceptions, one of two positions in the ongoing struggles between labour and management. Most often government assumed a laissez faire position, standing by and letting the conflict between the parties play out without intervening. Such a position almost always favoured employers since they consistently had more power, more resources and more organisation than the nascent unions. When the government did take a position regarding labour-management disputes, it most often intervened on behalf of employers. This intervention ranged from deputising private police forces hired and operated by companies (as in the case of the iron and coal police), calling out state and national troops to break strikes, convincing courts to issue injunctions banning actions by unions and persuading legislative bodies to pass anti-union legislation (ibid.).

In light of this long history, the passage of the NLRA was radical by any definition as it positioned the federal government to play a very different role in labour-management relations than it had previously. This legislation granted most American private sector workers the legal rights to organise unions, bargain collectively and engage in concerted activity (i.e. strikes, boycotts, picketing, etc.) and gave the responsibility to protect those rights to the federal government.[2] This meant that the government would now intervene on behalf of employees when it believed employers were violating their rights. Not surprisingly, employers rejected the law and vowed to ignore it, expecting that it would soon be ruled unconstitutional. Even when the US Supreme Court affirmed the constitutionality of the law in the 1937 Jones and Laughlin case, many employers still refused to abide by the provisions of the Act (Cooke, 1985).

Nonetheless, the passage of the NLRA signalled a new era for American labour. Workers immediately began exercising their rights by flocking to join unions. In 1937, when the AFL's craft unions declined to organise the millions of American workers in the rapidly expanding auto, steel, rubber and electrical manufacturing industries, a small number of unions, led by the United Mine Workers (UMW) and its President John L. Lewis, broke with the Federation. They then created a new labour federation – the Congress of Industrial Organizations (CIO) (ibid.).

The CIO quickly began to form new unions to organise the major American industries. By 1938, the CIO had spawned the United Steelworkers (USW), the United Auto Workers (UAW), the United Rubber Workers (URW) and 35 other new unions, whose total membership was approximately three million. At the same time, the AFL had grown to four million members. Together, the two federations, along with some unions that did not belong to either the AFL or the CIO, now represented a labour movement of eight to nine million members (Olson, 2001).

Despite the success that both the AFL and CIO had in organising new members, the two federations, and their unions, saw each other as rivals. This adversarial relationship continued into the 1950s, when changing circumstances removed many of the reasons for the rivalry. Merger talks took place over a number of years and in 1955 the two federations merged to form the AFL-CIO (Dubofsky and Dulles, 2010).

The next significant event for the American union movement occurred during the 1960s and 1970s. When the NLRA was passed, one of the groups of employees who were excluded from the Act's protections was public sector employees (i.e. anyone working for federal, state or local government). Since the Act's passage in 1935, the pay of private sector workers had been increasing, while that of public sector employees had not. Over time, public employees began to clamour for the same workplace rights their counterparts in the private sector enjoyed (ibid.).

The first step toward gaining those rights came in 1963 when President John F. Kennedy issued Executive Order 10988. This Order granted all federal employees the right to organise unions and engage in collective bargaining over a limited number of issues. They were not, however, permitted to bargain over economic issues such as pay and benefits, nor were they permitted to strike (limitations that continue to the present) (ibid.).

Kennedy's Executive Order did not cover the millions of state and local government workers whose legal status regarding unionisation is governed by state law. The fact that each state has the authority to grant these employees the rights to unionise, bargain collectively and strike, or to deny them those rights, has led to a "patchwork quilt" of different state laws.

Wisconsin was the first state to grant state and local employees union rights when it extended the rights to form unions and bargain collectively (but not to strike) to teachers and local government employees in 1959 (IFEBP, 2011). Over the next several years, New York, New Jersey and California passed similar laws. In 1970, Pennsylvania passed the first law giving public employees the right to strike (police, firefighters and prison guards were excluded). Today, 41 states allow at least some of their public employees to organise and bargain. Eleven of these allow some of their employees to strike. Nine states either have no law or prohibit their public employees from engaging in collective bargaining (Budd, 2012).

A majority of state public sector bargaining laws were passed during the 1970s and 1980s. The result was that membership in public sector unions grew rapidly, from 3.1 million in 1973 to a high of 7.9 million in 2009. This infusion of members helped pushed total union membership in the US from 18.1 million in 1973 to 21.0 million in 1979 (Hirsch and Macpherson, 2003).

Period of decline for American unions

When, in 1979, overall union membership began a steady 35-year decline that resulted from a precipitous drop in the number of private sector union members, the growing public sector membership provided a lifeline for the American labour movement. By 2009, as shown in Figure 12.1 below, public sector union membership exceeded private sector membership for the first time ever (although the private sector caught up again in 2013). For that same year (2009), union density (the percentage of the workforce belonging to a union) in the public sector (37.4 per cent) was more than five times higher than in the private sector (6.7 per cent) (ibid.).

The boost in membership that public sector unions brought to the American labour movement in the 1960s and 1970s was followed by a long period of decline that fundamentally changed the position of unions in American society. The decline began in the early 1980s. Two major factors – one political and the other economic in nature – are considered to have precipitated this crisis.

The first factor was the Professional Air Traffic Controllers Organization (PATCO) strike of 1981. PATCO was a union of federal government employees who had the stressful job of guiding planes through the nation's air space. After years of unsuccessful negotiations with the Federal Aviation Agency to upgrade working conditions, reduce stress, improve safety and win better wages, the PATCO leadership led 12,000 of their 17,000 members out on strike on August 3, 1981 (McCartin, 2011).

As federal employees, PATCO members were prohibited by law from striking. For that reason, their action evoked a strong response from President Ronald Reagan, a stalwart conservative

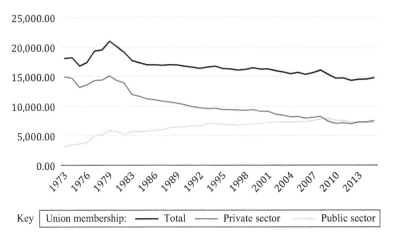

Figure 12.1 Union membership: private sector, public sector and total, 1973–2014
Source: Hirsch and Macpherson, 2003

and nemesis of unions, who had been elected in 1980. In a press conference Reagan made his position on the PATCO strike clear: "They [the members of PATCO] are in violation of the law and if they do not report within 48 hours, they have forfeited their jobs, and will be terminated" (ibid.). When they did not return to work, Reagan followed through on his threat. The PATCO members were fired and strike replacements took their jobs. As a result, the strike collapsed and the union was decertified (ibid.).

The PATCO strike took on great significance as it portrayed Reagan as a strong leader. His decisive actions are credited with signalling to private sector employers that an aggressive response to unions was the right, and the effective, course of action. In fact, the 1980s saw employers taking a much harder line in bargaining with existing unions and in organising drives by potential unions. This would be the hallmark of labour-management relations for decades to come (ibid.).

The second major factor that contributed to the long-term diminution of the US labour movement was the growing globalisation of the economy. The reasonably strong and stable economy of the 1950s through the 1970s, and the growth of union membership during this time frame, were both products of a halcyon period in industrial production. Basic industries like steel, coal, rubber, copper and aluminium, and manufacturing industries like aircraft, paper and textiles, boomed during this period. The unions that represented workers in these indus-tries, and in the industries that supported them – rail, airlines, trucking, utilities, etc. – also grew steadily (Baldwin, 2003).

However, as the world moved to an increasingly globalised economy in the 1980s, more and more employers closed their mills, plants and factories in the US and moved them abroad. This process of deindustrialisation fundamentally restructured the American economy and the unions that represented workers in these industries were hit hard. While the heavily unionised industrial and manufacturing sectors of the economy declined, the service sector grew. This sector included banking and finance, wholesale and retail trade, and professional services, including healthcare, communications and software. The result was that high-paying union jobs in the industrial sector were replaced by low paying non-union jobs in the service sector (ibid.).

The events of the 1980s precipitated a crisis in the American labour movement that threatened its continued relevance. Deepening the crisis was the fact that most unions were slow to adapt and respond to the 'new' economy they faced. Eventually, unions began to focus on organising and representing workers who were a part of the low-wage service industry. In many cases, these workers were recent immigrants to the US from Latin America, Asia and other parts of the world. Many did not speak English and were in the US illegally. Unions began adjusting their organising strategies to better connect with these workers, including hiring organisers who spoke Spanish and Russian, as well as Mandarin, Cantonese, Korean, Vietnamese, Ethiopian and other languages (Kim, 2015).

Some unions made organising their top priority, while others took a more cautious, wait and see, attitude. In 2005, several unions demanded that the AFL-CIO push its affiliates to make organising a higher priority. The AFL-CIO's reluctance to do so, as well as conflicts between the AFL-CIO's leadership and that of several unions, resulted in those unions breaking away from the AFL-CIO to form a new labour federation called Change to Win (CTW). The affiliates of CTW were the Service Employees International Union (SEIU), the Teamsters, the Union of Needletrades, Industrial, and Textile Employees (UNITE), the United Food and Commercial Workers (UFCW), the Laborers, the United Farm Workers (UFW), and, briefly, the Carpenters Union. Within a few years, several of the founding unions left CTW and reaffiliated with the AFL-CIO. As of 2015, only three unions – SEIU, the Teamsters and the UFW – remained affiliates of CTW. Formed to lead the revitalisation of organising among American unions, the evidence indicates that the breakaway federation was unsuccessful in this regard. During its short time in existence, CTW failed to gain significant momentum and it ultimately had little lasting impact (Aleks, 2015; Meyerson, 2013).

Globalisation and the increasingly aggressive approach of employers to labour-management relations, combined with the inability of unions to effectively adjust to these and other challenges, had a devastating impact on the US labour movement. Between 1980 and 2015, overall union membership fell from 20,095,300 to 14,786,300 and union density declined from 23 per cent to 11 per cent. Private sector unions, particularly manufacturing/industrial unions, were severely impacted. Between 1980 and 2015, union membership in the private sector fell in 27 out of 36 years (Hirsch and Macpherson, 2016). And from 1973, the membership of the four leading industrial unions in the country fell dramatically, as illustrated in Table 12.1.

One of the consequences of the decline in membership was a decrease in the number of national unions making up the American labour movement. In 1985 there were 178 national unions with more than 1,000 members; by 2015 only 87 national unions remained. While in some cases the membership of national unions dwindled to the point that they just quietly expired, in most cases the reduction occurred as a result of mergers and consolidations.

The USW has been among the most active unions in absorbing smaller unions. Since the 1980s, the USW has absorbed numerous unions, including the Paper, Allied-Industrial, Chemical and Energy Workers International Union (250,000 members); the United Rubber Workers (98,000 members); the Aluminum, Brick, and Glass Workers International Union (40,000 members); the

Table 12.1 Membership of leading industrial unions, 1973 and 2015

	1973	*2015*
United Auto Workers	1,500,000	409,000
United Steelworkers	1,200,000	591,000
International Association of Machinists	760,000	569,000
United Mine Workers	213,000	71,000

Source: Roper Center, 1994 and Center for Union Facts, 2016

American Flint Glass Workers Union (12,000 members); the Upholsterers International Union (55,000 members); and the Industrial, Wood and Allied Workers (50,000 members). In 2005, it officially changed its name to the United Steel, Paper and Forestry, Rubber, Manufacturing, Energy, Allied Industrial, and Service Workers International Union (although it still refers to itself as the United Steelworkers) (USW, 2016).

The Teamsters have also been active in mergers. Since 2004, the union has absorbed the Graphic Communications International Union (60,000 members), the Brotherhood of Maintenance of Way Employees (40,000 members) and the Brotherhood of Locomotive Engineers (36,000 members), along with a number of smaller unions. The UAW, CWA, UFCW and the Machinists unions have also engaged in significant mergers in recent years (Teamsters, 2016).

These mergers were largely driven by the declining memberships of many mid-sized to small unions. Dwindling memberships resulted in a lack of resources that made it difficult for smaller unions to function effectively, or even to remain financially solvent, as independent organisations. As a result, many of them were 'absorbed' by larger unions (Chaison, 1996; Proper, 2013).

In 2015, union density in the private sector dropped to 6.7 per cent, the lowest rate since records started being kept in 1973. This level of density indicated that private sector unions, as a force in American society, were now a shadow of what they once were. However, the relatively strong position of public sector unions (35.2 per cent density) meant that the labour movement still had influence in the political arena, where public sector unions were particularly effective (Hirsch and Macpherson, 2016).

There is a significant amount of evidence that in the 2000s, anti-union interest groups like the American Legislative Exchange Council, the State Policy Network, Americans for Prosperity, the National Right to Work Committee and the US Chamber of Commerce, having seen unions in the private sector decimated, turned their attention to public sector unions. Because public sector unions provide significant manpower and support for liberal causes in general, and the Democratic Party's election efforts in particular, weakening them, or putting them out of business entirely, would give Republicans a big advantage in electoral politics at all levels of government. And if public sector unions could be debilitated to the extent that private sector unions had, the American labour movement would cease to have any meaningful influence in either the political or economic arenas (Hertel-Fernandez, 2015; Kroll, 2011).

These interest groups used a number of mechanisms to weaken public sector unions. These assaults occurred on a state-by-state basis and tended to begin with narrow strategic attacks such as the introduction of 'paycheck protection' legislation. This legislation would weaken unions financially by limiting their ability to collect 'fair share' dues to cover the representation services public sector unions are mandated by law to provide. The attacks would then escalate to include more significant measures such as restricting, or completely eliminating, bargaining rights for public employees (Hertel-Fernandez, 2015; Kroll, 2011).

The most successful of these efforts took place in Wisconsin. Using a budget crisis for justification, Governor Scott Walker pushed legislation through the Republican state legislature that effectively stripped most state and local government employees in Wisconsin of their collective bargaining rights. One estimate indicated that as a result, the National Education Association affiliate in Wisconsin saw its membership drop by 33 per cent, the American Federation of Teachers affiliate lost half of its membership and AFSCME's membership fell by 70 per cent (Samuels, 2015).

Following the passage of the public sector legislation in Wisconsin, laws restricting government employees' bargaining rights or unions' ability to collect 'fair share' dues through payroll deductions were passed in 15 states, including Tennessee, Oklahoma, Michigan, Maine, Pennsylvania, New Jersey, Minnesota and Ohio (Lafer, 2013). Other efforts are underway in additional states.

In sum, as the American labour movement moves toward the third decade of the 2000s, it finds itself trying to fend off multiple threats to its continued existence.

Theories explaining the American labour movement

Having looked at the manner in which unions were conceived and how they evolved over time in the US, it is useful to turn to the literature on unions to learn how scholars have viewed the development of labour organisations and the labour movement.

As far back as the early 1900s, scholars have formulated theories in an effort to better understand unions and their evolution as organisations. Theory is a very useful tool because it connects facts and information and helps pull them together into a coherent whole. It endeavours to explain "the 'how' and the 'why' of whatever is being examined" (Larson and Nissen, 1987). One of the early scholars of unions, Robert Hoxie, wrote in 1917 that:

> …there is no normal type to which all union variants approximate, no single labor movement which has progressively adapted itself to progressive change of circumstances, no one set of postulates which can be spoken of as the philosophy of unionism. Rather there are competing, relatively stable union types, functional and structural, the outcome of permanent differences in the temperament and situation of different groups of wageworkers.
>
> *(Hoxie, 1917)*

Hoxie then went on to construct a typology, or method for categorising, unions by both structure and function. In terms of structure, Hoxie identified four types of unions and did so in terms of the sequence in which they emerged. The first type was the simple craft union, which he defined as an organisation of 'wage-workers engaged in a single occupation' (Hoxie, 1917). Examples of these, according to Hoxie, were the unions formed by glass bottle blowers, horseshoers and locomotive engineers.

The second type of union identified by Hoxie was a federation formed by these early craft unions. The craft unions in a geographic area joined these federations to promote their mutual self-interest. In doing so, they also retained their own individual sovereignty. Hoxie pointed to the Chicago Federation of Labor, the Illinois Federation of Labor and the American Federation of Labor, all formed in the 1800s, as examples.

Industrial unions were the third type of union identified by Hoxie. These unions differed from craft unions in that they organised all workers – skilled, semi-skilled and unskilled – in a single industry or enterprise involved in putting out a product. Hoxie used as an example a coal-mining company. The union in this workplace would include the skilled workers – the shotfirers and engineers – as well as the semi-skilled – the miners, drivers and trackmen – and the unskilled miners' helpers and dumpmen (ibid.).

The fourth type of union identified by Hoxie was the general union. This type of union transcended the first three by organising all workers in a geographic area, regardless of craft or industry. These organisations might be based in local communities or in larger geographic areas such as districts, states or even nationally. Hoxie cited the Knights of Labor as the best example of this kind of union in the US around the beginning of the 1900s, when he was writing.

As the labour movement continued to grow and evolve, Hoxie's typology remained useful. Craft unionism became the heart and soul of the American labour movement through the 1930s and continues to play a big role today. The AFL flourished, eventually merged with the CIO and lives on as part of the AFL-CIO. The rise of the CIO and the formation of unions on an industrial basis in the auto, steel, rubber, electrical and manufacturing industries validated Hoxie's industrial union category. And the IWW appeared soon after Hoxie published his typology and fell clearly in the general union category given its "one big union" philosophy.

Hoxie also classified unions by function. Of the five types he cited, three most accurately described the unions that developed in the US. The first functional type of union identified was business unions. Business unions were narrowly focused on winning economic improvement for their members – higher wages, shorter hours and better working conditions. This type of union accepted capitalism and the wage system and strove to have their members prosper within that system. Hoxie identified craft unions, as well as the early railroad unions, as examples of this type of union.

Uplift unions, the second functional type, were characterised by Hoxie as idealistic in nature. These unions worked to elevate:

> the moral, intellectual, and social life of the worker, to improve the conditions under which he works, to raise his material standards of living, give him a sense of personal worth and dignity, secure for him the leisure for culture, and insure him and his family against the loss of a decent livelihood by reason of unemployment, accident, disease, or old age.
>
> *(Hoxie, 1917, p. 213)*

One of the main mechanisms they employed in pursuit of these goals was mutual insurance. The KOL is cited as the prime example of uplift unionism (Hoxie, 1917).

Hoxie identified the third type of union as revolutionary unions. Unions in this category promoted class consciousness and worked to weaken and eventually eliminate capitalism and the wage system. Ultimately, their goal was to have workers take over the means of production and engage in class-based political action. Hoxie pointed to the WFM and the IWW as examples of revolutionary unions (ibid.).

Other labour theorists focused on the goals of the unions that developed in the US over the last 200 years. Two well-known American theorists, John R. Commons and Selig Perlman, saw unions primarily as a mechanism for integrating American workers into the capitalist system. The primary goal of these groups was to build bargaining power as a way of improving the lives of their members in pragmatic ways – increasing wages, reducing hours and making workplaces safer. This, of course, is consistent with the business unionism approach identified by Hoxie.

Two of the earliest theorists in the UK, Sidney and Beatrice Webb, believed that the ultimate goal of unions was to promote industrial democracy. The democratisation of the workplace would result, the Webbs believed, in increasing standards of living for workers, greater opportunities for education and skill development, and fairer treatment. The labour organisation that most closely aligned with this goal was the KOL. Their approach to unionism, however, never caught on with American workers (Webb and Webb, 1920).

Theorists who looked at unions through a Marxist lens argued that the goal of unions was the revolutionary transformation of the capitalist system. Rather than focusing on incremental gains in the workplace, their objective was to bring about fundamental change to society in a way that would benefit workers. Certainly there were a small number of unions that advocated this view and that captured the interest and imagination of hundreds of thousands of American workers. The WFM and the IWW fell into this category and, in many ways, so did the KOL. However, the societal change that these organisations promised their members, and American workers in general, never materialised. And when they could not deliver, members left the organisations as quickly as they had joined (Larson and Nissen, 1987).

Ultimately, revolutionary unionism never had a real foothold in the US. Why the US is one of the few industrialised nations in the world never to have a significant socialist movement is a question that has been much examined. Alexis de Tocqueville, one of the earliest observers of American democracy, noted a number of significant characteristics of American society and polity that he believed were unique to the US. Other writers have cited these traits as responsible, in part, for the lack of a sustained American socialist movement. These characteristics included:

> its relatively high levels of social egalitarianism, economic productivity, and social mobility (particularly into elite strata), alongside the strength of religion, the weakness of the central state, the earlier timing of electoral democracy, ethnic and racial diversity, and the absence of feudal remnants, especially fixed social classes.
>
> *(Lipset and Marks, 2000)*

De Tocqueville saw these characteristics as exceptional. In fact, many scholars attribute the term and the concept "American exceptionalism" to him. American exceptionalism is the belief that the US' origin and history, and the system of government that developed as a result, is unique among countries. The belief also includes the ideas that the US is special, even superior, compared with other countries. The lack of a socialist movement is one of a number of factors explained by American exceptionalism, according to those who subscribe to this belief (Lipset, 1996).

Whether a function of American exceptionalism or other factors, it is the case that a socialist/revolutionary movement, and socialist/revolutionary unions, never gained traction in the US. This has been a significant factor in shaping the American labour movement and in differentiating it from most other labour movements around the world (ibid.).

While two of the functional types of unions that Hoxie identified – uplift and revolutionary – did not gain a footing in the US, the third type, business unionism, has survived and endured. Most modern building trade unions continue to exemplify this approach to unionism. However, in the middle of the twentieth century another approach to unionism, not included in Hoxie's typology, appeared. Social unionism is generally understood to involve "both engagement with social justice struggles beyond the workplace and methods of union activity beyond collective bargaining" (York, 2007, p.16). Walter Reuther, and the union he led, the UAW, was a leader in bringing social unionism to the fore.

Reuther's view of the role of unions in society differed substantially from the business unionism view. Reuther believed in "a labor movement whose philosophy demands that it fight for the welfare of the public at large" (Featherstone, 2016). Consistent with this view, Reuther and the UAW were active supporters of the civil rights and social justice movements of the 1960s. At a time when many building trade unions either ignored, or actively opposed, the civil rights movement, Reuther befriended Dr Martin Luther King Jr, marched with civil rights activists in Mississippi and was one of the few non-African American speakers at the 1963 Freedom March on Washington. The UAW helped finance that march, as well as others in Detroit and in the south. At the behest of Reuther, the UAW was one of the strongest backers, financially and otherwise, of Cesar Chavez and the United Farm Workers' struggle to organise agricultural workers in the southwestern US. Reuther was also one of the earliest American labour leaders to recognise the need for labour to organise on an international basis if it was to successfully confront multinational corporations. Toward that end, Reuther was a founding member of the International Confederation of Free Trade Unions (ibid.).

A small number of American unions shared Reuther's commitment to social unionism as far back as the 1940s. These included the United Electrical, Radio and Machine Workers of America (UE); the Retail, Wholesale, Department Store Union (RWDSU); and a handful of other unions. However, in the 1970s and 1980s, a number of larger, more mainstream, unions began to adopt many of the tenets of social unionism. The USW, under the leadership of Lynn Williams, the Machinists under William Wimpisinger, and SEIU, under John Sweeney, broadened the scope of their unions' work beyond simply serving their members. And as globalisation and more aggressive attacks on unions began to decimate American labour in the 1980s, 1990s and 2000s, other unions recognised the need to expand the narrow focus they had held for decades.

The last 25 years has seen another discussion in the American labour movement about a fundamental principle related to unions. Partly as a result of the success of unions in the 1950s, 1960s and 1970s, many had adopted a way of operating referred to as the servicing model. In the 1980s and 1990s, labour activists and academics decried this approach to union representation as a dated strategy that needed to change given the new circumstances unions faced at the turn of the century (Hurd, 2004).

A union employing the servicing model is often compared to an insurance company. Instead of paying premiums, union members purchase services from the union by paying dues. When a member has a problem – they face discipline or are turned down for a promotion they believe they deserve, for example – they go to their full-time union representative and the union representative solves the problem. When it comes time to negotiate a new contract, a representative negotiates on behalf of the members and then presents them with a new contract. To most members, 'the union' is the representatives who are paid to provide the services of the union. The involvement with or contribution to the work of the union for most members begins and ends with the payment of dues. The critique of this approach suggests that this 'insurance agency' or 'trade association' form of unionism might have been well suited for an era in which unions were growing and union density and power were relatively high, but it does not work in the circumstances the labour movement finds itself in today (ibid.).

An alternative to the servicing model, the organising model is based on the premise that the members are 'the union' and that every member has a responsibility to not only pay dues, but to actively participate in and contribute to the work of the union. The central focus of this model is member mobilisation and the goal is to have members accept greater responsibility for the work of the union (ibid.).

When a local union faces negotiations, for example, the responsibility for negotiating a new contract is not ceded to a full-time representative, rather members are involved as much as possible in the process. Input from the members is sought to set the union's bargaining priorities, they participate in regular actions to communicate to the employer the degree to which the members support their negotiating team, and they are kept informed at every step of the negotiation process. A greater emphasis is also placed on members participating in the governance and operation of the local union. This might mean creating an expanded committee and steward structure, where a high percentage of members hold some formal position such as committee members or chairs, stewards and assistant stewards. The benefits of such a system are a much greater sense of engagement and a higher level of commitment to the union on the part of the membership, which ultimately makes the union a stronger organisation that is better positioned to deal with the challenges it faces (Fletcher and Hurd, 1988).

Supporters of the organising model also advocate expanding its focus from internal 'organising', i.e. the running of the local union, to external organising. They contend that labour's future can only be assured by organising new members and that the most effective way to organise is through a grassroots, member to member strategy. And one additional benefit of the organising model is that as members take more responsibility for representing themselves, resources, money and staff, formerly devoted to representation, can be reallocated to external organising (Booth, 2015).

Many in and out of the labour movement believe that the optimal type of union for the twenty-first century are those that combine the 'organising union' model with the broad outlook of social unionism. Such unions would be member-driven and democratic, with a high level of member involvement and commitment. And they would focus on both the problems and issues its own members face in their workplace and the larger problems and issues of both unorganised and organised workers in other industries.

Ultimately, the theories of the labour movement shed significant light on the origins of American unions, the variety of structures and functions they adopted, the goals they had and the degree to which they accomplished these goals. Looking at labour history through the framework of these theories provides significant insight into the current state of the labour movement.

American unions in the twenty-first century

There is little doubt that American unions and union leaders were slow to recognise the significance of the structural changes in the economy and the more aggressive approach of employers toward unions that occurred from the early 1980s. However, in the last decade the evidence suggests that much of the traditional labour movement now recognises the seriousness of the existential crisis it faces.

Coalition building

One reaction of unions in the US to this crisis has been to reach out and form coalitions with partners that share their values. The labour movement has recognised that it can be more effective working in common cause with like-minded partners than going it alone. In recent years individual unions and the AFL-CIO have formed alliances with religious, civil rights, immigrant rights, human rights, community, environmental and womens' groups, both at the domestic and international levels (Kazin, 2013).

These alliances even extend to groups with whom the labour movement is not always in agreement. For example, Leo Gerard, President of the United Steelworkers, co-chairs the Blue-Green Alliance, an environmental coalition, with the Executive Director of the Sierra Club (Blue-Green Alliance, 2016). This is significant because historically many unions have disagreed with the Sierra Club's agenda, contending that it costs their members jobs. Gerard and his union support the coalition even though they disagree with the Sierra Club on the controversial Keystone pipeline project (Efstathiou, 2013). Another example of the labour movement working in coalition with other kinds of organisation is its involvement with the National Paid Sick Days Coalition. This coalition brings together a dozen unions and hundreds of other national, state and local women's, civil rights, health, children and faith-based organisations committed to the passage of national paid sick days legislation (National Paid Sick Days Coalition, 2016).

Constituency groups

One of the best examples of labour's efforts to broaden its constituency by reaching out and embracing new groups is in the area of immigrant rights. Prior to the 1980s, the AFL-CIO and most unions' views and policies in this area could be characterised as anti-immigrant. During this period, many in the labour movement held the view that immigrants were a threat to Americans' jobs and that they were flooding the labour market and pushing down wages. For this reason, most unions consistently supported legislation that restricted immigration and promoted stronger enforcement of immigration laws. However, in the 1980s and 1990s, unions and union leaders' position on immigration gradually changed. In 2000, the AFL-CIO Executive Board officially reversed its position and adopted a pro-immigration agenda for the labour movement, which included support for increased immigration, a call for a 'blanket amnesty' for undocumented immigrants and more lenient enforcement of immigration laws in general (AFL-CIO, 2001; Briggs, 2001; Kazin, 2013).

The change in the labour movement's attitudes towards immigrants and immigration was critically important. In subsequent years, as Latinos became the fastest-growing segment of the American workforce, unions strengthened their pro-immigrant position and built increasingly strong ties with the Latino community. The Labor Council for Latin American Advancement (LCLAA) is the official constituency group for Latino union leaders and members. Within the AFL-CIO, constituency groups like LCLAA serve as labour's 'bridge to diverse communities, creating and strengthening partnerships' with unions and the community. While LCLAA had been around since 1972, it took on a bigger role after the AFL-CIO changed its immigration stance in 1980. It is now involved in a wide range of activities, including immigration policy, registering and mobilising Latino workers to vote, networking with other Latino advocacy groups and working with interest groups within the Latino labour community such as young workers, women, domestic workers and farm workers (LCLAA, 2016).

In recent years, the AFL-CIO and individual unions have extended their connection with Latino workers by working with, and supporting, organisations independent of the AFL-CIO, including the National Day Laborer Organizing Network, the National Guestworker Alliance and the National Domestic Workers Alliance (AFL-CIO, 2016).

Similar efforts are being made to develop stronger relationships with other immigrant communities. The AFL-CIO also has an allied group that focuses on the Asian labour community. The Asian Pacific American Labor Alliance (APALA) was formed in 1982. Like LCLAA, it serves to connect the labour movement with Asian union members and the larger Asian community and is involved in voter registration, political action on behalf of candidates it believes are supportive of its issues, and organising low-wage Asian workers. Towards these ends it has created its own organising programme, the Asian Pacific American Organizing Institute, as well as a similar programme just for Asian women and its own Leadership School for developing potential Asian-American leaders for the labour movement (APALA, 2016).

The efforts of the AFL-CIO and other unions to embrace immigrant workers and get them more involved in the labour movement have taken a number of different forms. The most direct way to bring immigrants into the labour movement is to make them union members. Some American unions had already begun to focus their organising efforts on low-wage Latino workers even prior to the AFL-CIO's policy change on immigration. SEIU had actually begun a large-scale organising campaign called Justice for Janitors in the mid-1980s that focused on janitors in Denver and Los Angeles; it eventually expanded to Houston and Miami. By the early 2010s, the campaign had organised 225,000 janitors in 29 cities in the US and several cities in Canada. A high percentage of these workers were Latino. This campaign gained a great deal of attention nationally and began to change the perception among many in the immigrant community that unions were hostile to immigrant workers (Milkman, 2006; UCLA, 2016).

Another example of successful organising efforts that targeted low-wage sectors with a predominately immigrant workforce was the United Steelworkers effort to organise car wash workers in California. These were mostly Central American immigrants who faced significant problems, including below minimum wage pay; exposure to toxic chemicals; and the denial of water, shade and rest breaks. After several years of effort, the first contract was signed with a carwash in Santa Monica in 2011. Since then 23 car washes have agreed to union contracts (Roosevelt, 2014).

These types of organising drives helped increase the number of Latino union members in the American labour movement by 21 per cent between 2002 and 2012. Given that Latinos are the fastest-growing, and most widely exploited, group in the US workforce, many in the labour movement believe that when 'the labor movement and the immigrant rights struggle unite, both complement each other...' (Lozano, 2011). And the organising of immigrant workers clearly has the potential to slow, or even turn around, the steady decline in union membership of the last 35 years (Elmer, 2013).

Alt-labour organisations

As unions have struggled to survive and adapt to the changing circumstances of the early twenty-first century, they have begun to support alternative approaches to organising non-traditional workers and the organisations they form. Many of these workers are not covered by the NLRA or other labour laws and therefore the organisations that organise them have to use innovative and creative approaches outside the traditional processes and protections of labour law. These groups have come to be known as alt-labour, or alternative labour, organisations.

Traditional unions were slow to recognise these organisations since they fell outside the legal definition of a union (although interestingly, they appear to fit under the definition of a union as first suggested by the Webbs in 1920, see page 1). Over the years, the AFL-CIO and its affiliate unions have come to recognise that while alt-labour groups may not be, strictly speaking, 'unions', they clearly are a part of the labour movement. These alt-labour organisations have the advantage of being able to reach workers who have not been given the legal right to organise under the NLRA or some other law, or, for some other reason, have not been included in past organising efforts. They also lack some of the things that traditional unions have, such as steady sources of revenue, as their members are usually low-wage workers who do not pay dues on a regular basis (Edelson, 2013).

The alt-labour phenomenon is significant as it has the potential to expand what is thought of as the labour movement in the US. In the past, the labour movement has largely been made up of the different types of unions recognised by law. This would include craft unions in the building trades; industrial unions; public sector unions; sectoral unions, such as those in the air-line, rail, entertainment and professional sports sectors; and general unions, as well as the labour federations to which they affiliate (the AFL-CIO and CTW). This widely accepted, and relatively longstanding, definition of what constitutes the labour movement is one of the reasons it has taken time for traditional unions to accept alt-labour groups.

Towards this end, the labour movement has invested in helping workers form non-traditional organisations to bring immigrant workers together to address employment and work-related problems. Many of these groups take the shape of 'worker centres'. These are 'community-based and community-led organisations that engage in a combination of service, advocacy, and organising to provide support to low-wage workers' (Fine, 2005); they often serve immigrant workers.

While worker centres advocate for higher wages and better working conditions, help workers integrate into the communities in which they work, assist with immigration matters, and provide advice on housing, healthcare and schools, they are not subject to the provisions of the NLRA (ibid.).

One way of looking at alt-labour groups is as minority unions. Worker centres and other alt-labour groups normally have less than a majority of workers of any given workplace involved in their organisation (if they had a majority, they could probably file for an NLRB election and become a traditional union).

In a 2016 statement, the AFL–CIO articulated its position on alt-labour organisations:

> The union movement works to improve the lives of *all* people who work – not just those who have the benefits of union membership. In fact, the AFL–CIO has formed partnerships with worker centers and other groups of working people who do not have the legal right to collective bargaining… . All workers deserve fair treatment, respect and a voice at work, regardless of how they are classified by employers or regarded by labor law.
>
> *(AFL-CIO, 2016)*

One count puts the overall number of these groups at 214. Many of these organisations, including the National Day Laborer Organizing Network (NDLON), the National Domestics Workers Alliance (NDWA), Making Change at Wal-Mart and the Restaurant Opportunities Center United (ROC United), have relationships or affiliations with the AFL–CIO or national unions (Furchgott-Roth, 2013).

In 2012, SEIU, for example, gave $2.5 million to New York Communities for Change, a worker centre that helps fast-food employees advocate for better wages and working conditions. Among other unions that actively support worker centres are the UFCW, UNITE-HERE and the USW (Maher, 2013; Marculewicz and Thomas, 2012).

Another type of alt-labour group involves workers who are considered independent contractors, and are thus excluded from labour law protection. Among these workers are taxi drivers. Despite their legal status, the National Taxi Workers Alliance (NTWA) has organised chapters in New York City, Philadelphia and San Francisco. These chapters have been successful in advocating for the needs of taxi drivers with the companies they work for and the taxi commissions in their cities. In 2011, the NTWA became the first alternative worker organisation to be invited to be an affiliate of the AFL–CIO (Struckman, 2012).

One of the most successful alt-labour campaigns is the 'Fight for $15' movement. Fight for $15 was started when a few hundred restaurant workers in New York City struck for a pay raise to $15 an hour and the right to have a union. With significant financial and logistical support from SEIU, the campaign has grown into a full-blown international movement, operating in more than 300 cities on six continents, which has expanded to include not only fast-food workers, but other low-wage workers such as home health aides, retail employees, airport workers and child care workers (Fight for $15, 2016). The campaign has won increases in the minimum wage to $15 in cities such as Seattle, New York City and San Francisco, and more recently in the states of California and New York (Scheiber and Lovett, 2016).

While traditional unions and union leaders increasingly accept alt-labour groups as a part of the labour movement, differences remain as to the role they should, and will, play in labour's future. Some observers believe that they are the future of the labour movement, and that traditional unions have outlived their usefulness. Others believe that traditional unions remain the core of the American labour movement, but that alt-labour organisations play an important function in broadening the ways that workers can be a part of this movement.

This debate extends to the manner in which unions advocate for, and represent, workers. In this regard there are those who believe that the system of collective bargaining established by the NLRA is irreparably broken, or that it is unsuitable for many of the new employer-employee relationships that have developed in recent decades. They argue that given the structural changes in the economy, there is simply "no way to rebuild exactly the models of unionism that won such brilliant gains in the mid-twentieth century" (Dean, 2016). The logical conclusion of this view is that the types of union that were formed to operate in this system are not the types of union needed in a post-NLRA era and that worker centres and alt-labour organisations are the way of the future.

People in and out of the labour movement who believe this to be the case often also suggest that the labour movement should abandon, or at least de-emphasise, the NLRA's approach to organising unions (get 30 per cent of workers to sign cards, conduct a campaign, have an election, win a majority and represent all members of the bargaining unit). Instead, some believe that direct action and corporate and community campaigns designed to pressure employers to recognise a union could be a more effective strategy (Voss and Sherman, 2003).

However, many others are not convinced that these alt-labour groups have the potential to serve as the structural framework for the American labour movement, as unions have done since its founding. One of things sceptics point to is the issue of sustainability. In most cases, these organisations do not have the ability to generate revenue or funding on an ongoing basis, as they do not receive dues. And few could operate without the significant funding that unions provide. As Lance Compa, a labour scholar and former union official, points out "despite many accomplishments, Alt-labor has not solved the test of creating stable, mass, dues-paying organizations" (2015).

Compa argues that the labour movement should not be too quick "to ditch the NLRA, forsake traditional unions, and start the labor movement afresh". While acknowledging that labour currently faces significant challenges, he argues that this point in time is not unique. He points out that throughout history unions have been organised "in the face of capital's superior power". And as evidence that traditional unions are still serving the purpose they were created to serve, he notes that today they win a high percentage of the organising drives they undertake. He also calls attention to the fact that in recent years the labour movement has successfully organised large groups of workers, including 12,000 dealers and other casino workers, 25,000 private bus system workers and more than 10,000 adjunct faculty members, in addition to winning elections with many smaller groups of employees in a range of industries (Compa, 2015).

Paul Booth, another veteran union organiser and leader, makes the case that unions still have the capacity to organise and bring large numbers of workers into the labour movement. He argues that the transition many unions have made over the last 25 years from a servicing to an organising approach has made a significant difference. He points out that the labour movement has organised millions of workers over the last 40 years; however, the offshoring of union jobs, deindustrialisation and a number of other factors have resulted in unions losing more members than they have organised. And while he does not believe that alt-labour groups are the answer to labour's dilemma, he does believe they have made significant contributions. Ultimately, he argues that if these organisations can combine with traditional unions in a way that will allow them to sustain, and even grow, the work they have been doing, the labour movement would benefit (Booth, 2015).

Unions and politics

There is also discussion within the labour movement on how, and to what extent, unions should be involved in the political process. Unions long ago recognised that if they were to improve the lives of their members they needed to be effective on two fronts – in the workplace and in the political and legislative process. Labour needs to be involved in politics because Congress and state legislatures can pass laws that can have beneficial or detrimental impacts on workers.

Over the years the labour movement has been the driving force behind the passage of many laws that have significantly benefited workers, including the NLRA, workers and unemployment compensation laws, the Occupational Safety and Health Act, various workplace discrimination laws and state laws extending union rights to public employees. However, numerous laws have also been passed that weaken unions, such as state right-to-work laws and laws that limit or eliminate the collective bargaining rights of public employees.

In an effort to promote and defend their interests, unions engage in political action to help elect candidates that share their values and priorities, and lobby legislatures at the state and national levels. And they devote a great deal of time, effort and money to doing so. For example, SEIU alone reportedly spent $60.7 million to help elect President Obama in 2008. They also "knocked on 1.87 million doors, made 4.4 million phone calls and sent more than 2.5 million pieces of mail" to support him (Codevilla, 2009). Altogether American unions spent $600 million on politics in 2012 (compared with $9.5 billion by the American business community) (Blumenthal and Jamieson, 2014). In that same election cycle unions reportedly mobilised three to four million members to work on behalf of their endorsed candidates (Cooke, 2012).

Given the support they provided, many union leaders and activists were disappointed with Obama's efforts on labour issues during his two terms in office. In particular, there was considerable anger that he failed to make the passage of the Employee Free Choice Act, a bill that would have made it easier for unions to organise, a priority in his first two years, when Democrats controlled both the US House and Senate. His stand on the Trans-Pacific Partnership, a major trade agreement, further alienated many in the labour movement. And while he was given credit for naming a union-friendly majority to the National Labor Relations Board (NLRB) that resulted in consistently pro-labour decisions over the latter years of his presidency, many in the labour movement wondered if their investment in Obama had been worth the price (Scheiber, 2015).

The disappointment in President Obama left many in the labour movement with a feeling of déjà vu. Union supporters had similarly mixed emotions about his two Democratic predecessors (Bill Clinton and Jimmy Carter) and Democratic congressional leaders they had supported in the past. This disappointment has caused some to wonder whether the resources spent on supporting politicians could be better spent on organising. Others argued for a 'Labor Party', which would be more responsive to union priorities. A failed effort to form such a party in the 1980s, however, convinced all but the most ardent advocates of the idea that it was a pipedream (Archer, 2010). Ultimately, there appears to be a consensus in the labour movement that in the face of conservative forces bent on dismantling unions, labour has little choice but to defend itself by supporting 'pro-labour' (i.e. Democratic) candidates for political office.

The future

What is the future of unions in the US? One opinion commonly espoused is that while unions played an important and necessary role in the past, they have outlived their usefulness. In fact, unions are sometimes referred to as dinosaurs, the implication being that their time has come and gone. But is this true?

As discussed in this chapter, unions were formed in the US at the beginning of the nineteenth century. They were created in response to the inherent conflict between employers and employees built into the capitalist system. That basic conflict still exists today and, as was the case 200 years ago, employers still have the upper hand in that relationship. And, just as workers then saw uniting together to use their collective strength as the most effective way to balance the power of the employer in their workplace, so do many workers today.

Despite the presence of this conflict between employers and employees, predictions of the demise of unions have been commonplace for decades. For example, "in 1932, the president of the American Economic Association said the labor movement was dying and would disappear in a decade" (Compa, 2015). This was before the rise of industrial unionism in the 1930s, before the labour movement's heyday in the 1950s and 1960s when it tripled its size relative to 1932, and before millions of public sector workers flooded into unions in the 1960s and 1970s.

It can be argued that these predictions are off base because the need for unions actually remains unchanged. Over the last several decades, as union membership has declined, middle class incomes have steadily fallen and income inequality has increased dramatically (see Figures 12.1 and 12.2 below). The lives of the people who could benefit by having a collective voice in their workplaces have steadily worsened. It seems clear that there is still a role for unions in the modern American workplace.

As union membership rates decrease, middle-class incomes shrink

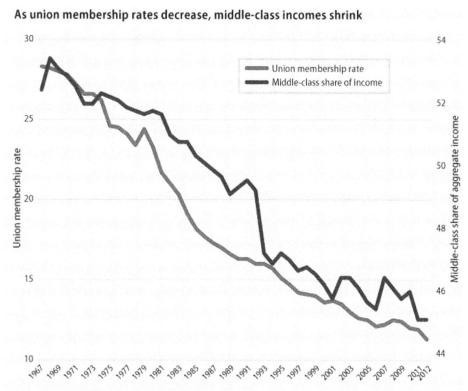

Source: Union membership rate is from Barry T. Hirsch, David A. MacPherson, and Wayne G. Vroman, "Estimates of Union Density by State," Monthly Labor Review 124 (7) (2001). Middle-class share of aggregate income is from the U.S. Census Bureau, Current Population Survey (Department of Commerce).

Figure 12.2   As union membership rates decrease, middle class incomes shrink
Source: Union membership rate is from Hirsch, MacPherson and Vroman (2001), 'Estimates of Union Density by State', *Monthly Labor Review*, 124(7), pp. 51–55; middle-class share of aggregate income is from the Bureau of the Census (2015), Current Population Survey (Department of Commerce)

Percent Change In Real Income: 1980–2012

—Top 0.01% — Bottom 90%

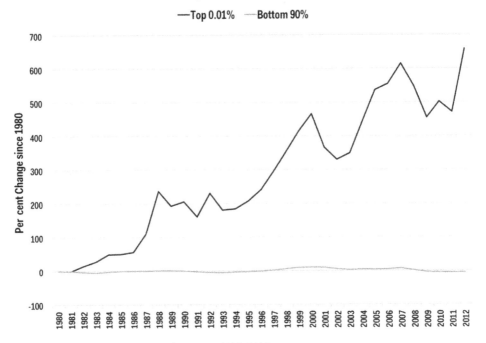

Figure 12.3   Per cent change in real income: 1980–2012
Source: Mishel, Gould, and Bivens, 2015

Unions exist because they serve a purpose that no other organisation serves – as a check and balance on the power of employers by giving workers a collective voice in the workplace. But as the circumstances that workers face change, the unions that represent them need to change as well. This chapter has identified a number of ways in which the labour movement is, indeed, changing. The most critical of these is the effort to involve the growing immigrant workforce in the labour movement. And if it takes multiple types of organisations to do this – traditional unions, constituency groups and worker centres – then involving these groups is what the movement needs to do.

Another change the labour movement needs to be open to involves the strategies it employs to gain a voice in the workplace. The view that, despite its imperfections, the traditional approach of organising under the NLRA still works for many workers needs to be considered. At the same time, it seems clear that the innovative strategies that have been developed to organise outside of the framework of the NLRA present new opportunities for workers.

In earlier periods in American history, workers were presented with different forms of unions, e.g. craft, uplift and revolutionary unionism. Workers tried each of these approaches, but ultimately only craft unionism endured, because it delivered on its promise of making life better for workers and their families. Later, factory workers in the mass production industries of auto, steel, rubber and electrical manufacturing sought to organise and industrial unionism joined craft unionism as forms of unionism that worked effectively for American workers. Over time, some unions broadened the kinds of workers they sought to organise. Today, these unions are best described as general unions.

Today's labour movement is made up of craft, industrial and general unions, with alt-labour groups bringing in a new generation of workers. All of these groups have the potential to contribute to building a stronger labour movement.

Ultimately, given the fast-changing world in which workers and unions exist, having multiple approaches that fit the very different circumstances that workers face is most likely a strength and not a weakness. It may, in fact, be this ability to adapt that provides the strongest reason to expect that unions will endure in American society.

Notes

1 The KOL accepted almost all workers, but barred groups of people it considered "non-producers", including liquor dealers, professional gamblers, lawyers, bankers and stockbrokers (Hild, 2010).
2 The following types of workers were excluded from coverage by the NLRA: government workers, supervisors, railway and airlines workers (who were covered by the Railway Labor Act of 1926), domestic workers, agricultural workers and independent contractors (NLRA, 2016).

References

AFL-CIO. (2001). Resolution 5: A Nation of Immigrants. Available at: https://aflcio.org/resolution/nation-immigrants.

AFL-CIO. *Worker Centers.* Available at: www.aflcio.org/About/Worker-Center-Partnerships (Accessed: 18 December 2017).

Aleks, R. (2015). 'Estimating the Effect of "Change to Win" on Union Organizing', *ILR Review*, 68(3), pp. 584–605.

Archer, R. (2010). *Why Is There No Labor Party in the United States?* Princeton: Princeton University Press.

Asian Pacific American Labor Association (APALA). Home page. Available at: www.apalanet.org/ (Accessed: 17 December 2017).

Baldwin, R. (2003). *The Decline of U.S. Labor Unions and the Role of Trade.* Washington, DC: Peterson Institute.

Bloy, M. (2016). *A Web of English History.* Available at: www.historyhome.co.uk/peel/trade-us/tu1830%2B.htm (Accessed: 18 December 2017).

Blue-Green Alliance. Board of Directors. Available at: www.bluegreenalliance.org/about/board-of-directors (Accessed: 18 December 2017).

Blumenthal, P. and Jamieson, D. (2014). 'Koch Brothers Are Outspent By A Labor Force Millions Of Times Their Size, But…' *The Huffington Post.* [Online]. 15 March. [Accessed: 18 December 2017]. Available at: www.huffingtonpost.com/2014/03/15/kochs-brothers-labor_n_4966883.html.

Booth, P. (2015). 'Labor at a Crossroads: The Case for Union Organizing'. *American Prospect.* (Online). 23 January. Available at: http://prospect.org/article/labor-crossroads-case-union-organizing. (Accessed: 18 December 2017).

Briggs, V. (2001). *Immigration and American Unionism.* Ithaca: Cornell University Press.

Budd, J. (2012). *Labor Relations: Striking a Balance.* New York: McGraw-Hill Irwin.

Bureau of the Census. (2015). *Historical Income Tables: Households.* Available at: www.census.gov/data/tables/time-series/demo/income-poverty/historical-income-households.html (Accessed: 18 December 2017).

Center for Union Facts. (2016). Home page. Available at: www.unionfacts.com (Accessed: 18 December 2017).

Chaison, G. (1996). *Union Mergers in Hard Times: The View from Five Countries.* Ithaca: Cornell ILR Press.

Codevilla, A. (2009). 'From Citizens to "Stakeholders": The New American Constitution'. *The American Spectator.* (Online). 8 September. Available at: http://spectator.org/articles/40981/citizens-stakeholders-new-american-constitution. (Accessed: 18 December 2017).

Compa, L. (2015). 'Careful What You Wish For: A Critical Appraisal of Proposals to Rebuild the Labor Movement', *New Labor Forum*, 24(3), pp. 11–16.

Cooke, S. (2012). 'Elections 2012: Why Labor's Rank and File Won't Campaign for Obama'. *Global Research.* (Online). 16 March. Available at: www.globalresearch.ca/elections-2012-why-labor-s-rank-and-file-won-t-campaign-for-obama/29802. (Accessed: 18 December 2017).

Cooke, W.N. (1985). *Evolution of the National Labor Relations Act, in Union Organizing and Public Policy: Failure to Secure First Contracts*. Kalamazoo: W.E. Upjohn Institute for Employment Research, pp. 1–21.

Curl, J. (2012). *For All the People: Uncovering the Hidden History of Cooperation, Cooperative Movements, and Communalism in America*. 2nd edn. Oakland: PM Press.

Dean, A.B. (2016). 'Experiment with change', *New Labor Forum*, 25(1), pp. 13–14.

DeFranceso, J. and Segal, D. (2014). 'Labor History: The First Factory Strike'. *In These Times*. (Online). 1 September. Available at: http://inthesetimes.com/article/17050/the_mother_of_all_strikes. (Accessed: 18 December 2017).

Dubofsky, M. (1969). *We Shall Be All: A History Of The Industrial Workers Of The World*. Chicago: Quadrangle Books.

Dubofsky, M. and Dulles, F.R. (2010). *Labor in America: A History*. 8th edn. Hoboken: Wiley-Blackwell.

Edelson, J. (2013). 'Alt-Labor'. *The Prospect*. [Online]. 29 January. [Accessed: 18 December 2017]. Available at: http://prospect.org/article/alt-labor.

Efstathiou, J. (2013). 'AFL-CIO Courts Sierra Club Despite Keystone Disagreement'. *Bloomberg News*. (Online). 9 September. Available at: www.bloomberg.com/news/articles/2013-09-09/afl-cio-courts-sierra-club-despite-keystone-disagreement. (Accessed: 18 December 2017).

Elmer, V. (2013). 'The State of the Union is Weak: Young Americans Are Not Joining Unions Anymore'. *Quartz*. (Online). 1 September. Available at: http://qz.com/120260/the-state-of-the-american-union-young-workers-out-latinos-in/.(Accessed: 18 December 2017).

Epstein, S. (1995). *Wage Labor and Guilds in Medieval Europe*. Chapel Hill: The University of North Carolina Press.

Featherstone, T. 'No Greater Calling: The Life of Walter P. Reuther'. Walter P. Reuther Library, Wayne State University Library. (Online). Available at: http://reuther100.wayne.edu/bio.php?pg=1. (Accessed: 18 December 2017).

Fight for $15. About Us. Available at: http://fightfor15.org/about-us/ (Accessed: 18 December 2017).

Fine, J. (2005). 'Worker Centers: Organizing communities at the edge of the dream'. *Economic Policy Institute*. (Online). 13 December. Available at: www.epi.org/publication/bp159/. (Accessed: 18 December 2017).

Fletcher, B. and Hurd, R. (1988). Beyond the Organizing Model: The Transformation Process in Local Unions, in Bronfenbrenner, K., Friedman, S., Hurd, R., Oswald, R. and Seeber, R. (eds.) *Organizing to Win*. Ithaca: Cornell ILR Press, pp. 37–53.

Furchgott-Roth, D. (2013). 'What You Should Know About Job Killing 'Worker Centers''. *Real Clear Markets*. (Online). 30 July. Available at: www.realclearmarkets.com/articles /2013/07/30/what_you_should_know_about_job_killing_worker_centers_100510.html. (Accessed: 18 December 2017).

Hertzel-Fernandez, A. (2015). *New Conservative Strategies to Weaken America's Public Sector Unions*. Scholar Strategy Network. Available at: www.scholarsstrategynetwork.org/brief/new-conservative-strategies-weaken-americas-public-sector-unions (Accessed: 18 December 2017).

Hild, M. (2010). *Greenbackers, Knights of Labor, and Populists: Farmer-Labor Insurgency in the Late-Nineteenth-Century South*. Athens (GA): University of Georgia Press.

Hirsch, B.T. and Macpherson, D.A. (2016). *2016 Union Membership and Earnings Data Book*. Arlington: Bloomberg BNA.

Hirsch, B.T., Macpherson, D.A. and Vroman, W.G. (2001). 'Estimates of Union Density by State', *Monthly Labor Review*, 124(7).

Hoxie, R.F. (1917). *Trade Unionism in the United States*. New York: Appleton and Company.

Hurd, R. (2004). The Rise and Fall of the Organizing Model in the U.S., in Wood, G. and Harcourt, M. (eds) *Trade Unions and Democracy: Strategies and Perspectives*. Manchester (UK): Manchester University Press.

Kazin, M. (2013). 'How Labor Learned to Love Immigration'. *New Republic*. (Online). 13 May. Available at: https://newrepublic.com/article/113203/labor-and-immigration-how-unions-got-board-immigration-reform. (Accessed 18 December 2017).

Kim, E.T. (2015). 'Organizing the Unorganizable'. *Dissent*. (Online). Spring. Available at: www.dissentmagazine.org/article/worker-centers-immigrant-organizing. (Accessed: 18 December 2017).

Kroll, A. (2011). 'Wisconsin Gov. Scott Walker: Funded by the Koch Bros'. *Mother Jones*. (Online). 18 February. Available at: www.motherjones.com/mojo/2011/02/wisconsin-scott-walker-koch-brothers. (Accessed: 18 December 2017).

Labor Council for Latin American Advancement (LCLAA). (2017). Home page. Available at: www.lclaa.org/.

Lafer, G. (2013). 'The Legislative Attack on American Wages and Labor Standards, 2011–2012'. Economic Policy Institute. (Online). 31 October. Available at: www.epi.org/publication/attack-on-american-labor-standards/. (Accessed: 18 December 2017).

Larson, S. and Nissen, B. (1987). *Theories of the Labor Movement*. Detroit: Wayne State University Press.

Lipset, S.M. (1996). *American Exceptionalism: A Double-Edged Sword*. New York: W.W. Norton & Co., Inc.

Lipset, S.M. and Marks, G. (2000). *It Didn't Happen Here: Why Socialism Failed in the United States*. New York: W.W. Norton and Company.

Lozano, P. (2011). 'Latinos, immigrants and labor form strategic alliance'. *People's World*. (Online). 20 AprilAvailable at: www.peoplesworld.org/latinos-immigrants-and-labor-form-strategic-alliance/. (Accessed: 18 December 2017).

Maher, K. (2013). 'Worker Centers Offer a Backdoor Approach to Union Organizing: Community Groups Aren't Restricted by National Labor Laws Governing Unions'. *Wall Street Journal*. (Online). 23 July. Available at: www.wsj.com/video/a-backdoor-approach-to-union-organizing/4FB0ECA8-9589-4564-970A-ED28224235DF.html. (Accessed: 18 December 2017).

Marculewicz, S. and Thomas, J. (2012). 'Labor Organizations by Another Name: The Worker Center Movement and its Evolution into Coverage under the NLRA and LMRDA', *Engage: The Federalist Society*, 13(3), pp. 79–98.

McCartin, J. (2011). *Ronald Reagan, the Air Traffic Controllers, and the Strike that Changed America*. Oxford: Oxford University Press.

Meyerson, H. (2013). 'Back in the Big Labor Fold'. *The American Prospect*. (Online). 12 August. Available at: http://prospect.org/article/back-big-labor-fold. (Accessed: 18 December 2017).

Milkman, R. (2006). 'Organizing the Unorganizable: The unlikely spark for a rebirth of labor'. *Boston Review*. (Online). 11 September. Available at: https://bostonreview.net/ruth-milkman-the-rebirth-of-organized-labor. (Accessed: 18 December 2017).

Mishel, L., Gould, E. and Bivens, J. (2015). 'Wage Stagnation in Nine Charts'. Economic Policy Institute. Available at: www.epi.org/publication/charting-wage-stagnation/ (Accessed: 18 December 2017).

National Paid Sick Days Coalition. 'About Us'. Available at: www.paidsickdays.org/about-us/about-coalition.html#.Vxq2eD_1YqI (Accessed: 18 December 2017).

Olson, J. (2001). *Historical Dictionary of the Great Depression, 1929–1940*. Westport: Greenwood Press.

Proper, C. (2013). 'Unions, Money, and Mergers'. (Online). 18 July. Available at: https://carlproper.com/2013/07/18/unions-money-and-mergers-2/.

Roper Center. (1994). 'Transformation: Declining and Shifting Union Membership'. *The Public Perspective*. (Online). July-August. Available at: http://ropercenter.cornell.edu/public-perspective/ppscan/55/55009.pdf. (Accessed: 18 December 2017).

Roosevelt, M. (2014). 'Union-Backed Car Wash Workers Fight for More Pay, Shade'. *Orange County Register*. (Online). 31 August. Available at: www.ocregister.com/articles/car-633355-workers-wash.html. (Accessed: 18 December 2017).

Samuels, R. (2015). 'Walker's Anti-Union Law Has Labor Reeling in Wisconsin'. *Washington Post*. (Online). 22 February. Available at: www.washingtonpost.com/politics/in-wisconsin-walkers-anti-union-law-has-crippled-labor-movement/2015/02/22/1eb3ef82-b6f1-11e4-aa05-1ce812b3fdd2_story.html. (Accessed: 18 December 2017).

Scheiber, N. (2015). 'As His Term Wanes, Obama Champions Workers' Rights'. *New York Times*. (Online). 31 August. Available at: www.nytimes.com/2015/09/01/business/economy/as-his-term-wanes-obama-restores-workers-rights.html. (Accessed: 18 December 2017).

Scheiber, N. and Lovett, I. (2016). '$15-an-Hour Minimum Wage in California? Plan Has Some Worried'. *New York Times*. (Online). 28 March. Available at: www.nytimes.com/2016/03/29/business/economy/15-hour-minimum-wage-in-california-plan-has-some-worried.html

Struckman, Robert. (2012). 'Taxi! Taxi! Cabbies Form Unlikely Union'. *People's World*. (Online). 14 May. Available at: www.peoplesworld.org/article/taxi-taxi-cabbies-form-unlikely-union/

Taft, P. and Ross, P. (1969). American LaborViolence: Its Causes, Character, and Outcome, in Graham, H.D. and Gurr,T.R. (eds.) *The History of Violence in America: A Report to the National Commission on the Causes and Prevention of Violence*. New York: Frederick A. Praeger.

Teamsters. Teamster History Visual Timeline. Available at: https://teamster.org/content/teamster-history-visual-timeline (Accessed: 18 December 2017).

Justice for Janitors History Project. About. Available at: http://socialjusticehistory.org/projects/justiceforjanitors/about (Accessed: 18 December 2017).

United Steelworkers (USW). Our History. Available at: www.usw.org/union/history (Accessed: 18 December 2017).

International Foundation of Employee Benefit Plans. (2011). *Collective Bargaining: What It Is and Its Place in Wisconsin's History*. (Press release). Available at: www.ifebp.org/AboutUs/PressRoom/Releases/pages/pr_022411.aspx. (Accessed: 18 December 2017).

Voss, K. and Sherman, R. (2003). You Just Can't Do It Automatically: The Transition to Social Movement Unionism in the United States, in Fairbrother, P. and Yates, C.B. (eds.) *Unions in Renewal: A Comparative Study*. London: Continuum, pp. 51–73.

Webb, S. and Webb, B. (1920). *The History of Trade Unionism*. London: Longmans, Green, and Co.

York, S. (2007). 'Varieties of Social Unionism: Towards a Framework for Comparison', *Just Labor: A Canadian Journal of Work and Society*, 1(Autumn), pp. 16–34.

13

EMPLOYERS, MANAGERS AND EMPLOYMENT RELATIONS

Peter Sheldon

Introduction

For an employer, the practice of employment relations (ER) starts with a *contract of employment* that establishes an individual *employment relationship* with an employee. At its simplest, that employment relationship (and ER) then proceeds as the employer specifies the work the employee is to do and those conditions, beyond the initial contract of employment, under which the employee will perform it. Under time-based hiring, the employer offers the certainty of a pay rate and particular employment conditions in exchange for an expected level of employee performance during the time paid for. The employer therefore buys that employee's *potential* performance during that time, not any specific level of output, service or even behaviour. This represents the core ambiguity within the employment relationship. Under output-based payment systems, the performance-time-pay calculus works differently but employees can still seek to manipulate production processes and measurement to their benefit.

Thus, the full terms of these wage-effort bargains are often unclear and they change over time, particularly as an employer's own production requirements may alter. As Fox (1974, p. 183) puts it:

> Since no employment contract could anticipate all relevant contingencies arising in work relations, many issues had to be settled during the everyday conduct of business. How hard was the employee to work? Under what material, social, and psychological conditions? With what tools, machines, and materials? With what rights to demur against specific instructions, managerial policies, and proposals for change?
>
> *(Fox, 1974)*

Overall too, the greater the number of employment relationships an employer has to manage, the greater the organisational complexities they face with regard to ER.

Organising employment and work is a central task of 'management', an organisational function and process directing the organisation for the employer. Management is variously understood as, for example, a series of tasks – like Fayol's planning, organising, command, coordination and control – or managerial roles – such as Mintzberg's ten roles grouped under three categories: interpersonal; informational; and decisional (Mintzberg, 1973; Paucelle and Guthrie,

2013). More tangibly, management is the people carrying out those tasks or in those roles on the employer's behalf, with organisationally legitimated power through their formally delegated positions. This provides them with substantial influence for achieving the managerial purpose of getting work done through other people on behalf of the employer.

Larger and more complex organisations usually produce more managers and managerial levels as well as more managerial ER specialists. Furthermore, with every new employee the employer hires – perhaps through a manager – they encounter an existing ER context for that employment relationship, including its own particular market forces, other actors and institutions. All this occurs within a broader environment of labour, product and financial markets and institutions, including those of the state.

As employees are both a cost and a source of potential earnings (or other contribution), employers, in pursuing profits (or other performance markers), seek to manage ER to minimise those costs and maximise those earnings/contributions. Nonetheless, a goal of cost minimisation may provoke very different managerial strategies and policies when directed, for example, to short-run as against longer-run horizons. In one situation, high employee turnover may be an acceptable consequence of a cost minimisation strategy if, overall, it costs less to lose those employees than seek to retain them. However, the opposite may be the case where those leaving take with them valuable organisational and/or technical knowledge; labour markets are tight for those categories; the costs of recruiting and training replacements are high; and/or where that turnover has other disruptive effects on the organisation's internal operations – including on workforce morale. In these cases, it may cost more to lose those employees than to seek to retain them (see e.g. Sheldon and Li, 2013).

This chapter examines how employers seek to address this ambiguity inherent in the employment relationship, how organisational and ER contexts influence their choices, and how those employers contribute, in turn, to shaping those contexts. Its focus ranges from employer management of the individual employment relationship to employer involvement in the functioning of national labour markets.

In discussing 'employment relations', this chapter includes the overlapping fields of industrial relations (IR) and human resource management (HRM). This helps bring together the interacting individual and collective dimensions of ER and the formal and informal forces shaping them. It allows practitioners and researchers to shift focus, as needed, to roles and relationships within single organisations, among organisations and to their interactions with other elements within their wider environments. Nevertheless, the world of ER is greater than the sum of its IR and HRM parts (see also Gardner and Palmer, 1997). This is because interactions among distinctively IR and HRM elements dynamically re-shape lived experiences within organisations, particularly where there is a patchwork of regulation by statute, public policy, collective bargaining and union activity, and employers' own rules (for a recent Chinese example, see Kim and Chung, 2016).

The breadth of this topic and its voluminous relevant literature necessitated severe authorial choices. First, there is a vast literature on management, including HRM, but much less on employer associations. Given this volume includes an entire chapter on HRM, this author provides no separate section on HRM, despite its importance, but does include a section on employer associations. As there are also entire chapters on multinationals and global supply chains, this chapter largely ignores them despite their increasing importance to this topic. Furthermore, to understand employer behaviour requires historical understanding. Yet, because this volume also includes a historical chapter, this suggested severely limiting historical explanation.

Other decisions included balancing presentation of theory and concrete examples. The approach chosen is to present a few key themes, theories, models and illustrative examples in sufficient depth to help explain the chapter's main arguments. Another important choice made was to showcase contributions from different disciplines. In making these choices, the author also sought to balance 'classic' (older) theories with more recent elaborations and to widen the range of countries used as examples, including East Asian economies.

The next section briefly explores ways in which the ER literature examines employer engagement in ER. It then proposes a well-known schema for making sense of this behaviour.

Ways of exploring and explaining employers and employment relations

Given the vastness of this topic, its often highly contested nature and its central importance to individuals, organisations and societies, two questions immediately arise. The first concerns explanatory focus. Simply, how can we most usefully organise our examination and understanding of employers, managers and ER? Scholars provide a variety of approaches. For example, Gardner and Palmer (1997) prioritise the role of strategy. However, they prefer to see strategy as implicit and often unplanned; it can be read back over what may initially appear as a number of ad hoc, pragmatic and even apparently inconsistent choices and conducts of action. This stands in contrast to idealised notions of strategy as formalised, explicit, long-term planning that brings policies together in a coherent and consistent whole (see e.g. Bacon, 2008). For Bray et al. (2014), the focus is on regulation within the world of work through rules and rule-making. They thus define the field (p. 18) as "the study of the formal and informal rules which regulate the employment relationship and the social processes which create and enforce these rules". Others have privileged the study of power and conflict (Hyman, 1975), control or even culture. This chapter particularly looks to (implicit) strategy and rule-making.

Like Gospel (1992), this author has delineated employer strategy into levels of action and analysis. However, two of Gospel's levels – 'industrial relations' and 'human resources' – separate employers' IR from their HRM activity (the third, 'work organisation', embraces both). Instead, this chapter presents its three levels – the individual employee, the organisation and the wider labour market – so that there is at least some role for both IR and HRM in each. This is important given this author's contention that ER is more than the sum of its IR and HRM parts.

Broader systems of beliefs and values regarding ER influence employer strategies and the rules they produce. This suggests a second question concerning the underlying meanings attributed to ER. Put simply, how do employers and other ER parties – and researchers – interpret the phenomena this chapter discusses? One influential interpretative schema is Fox's (1974) distinction between unitarist, pluralist and radical 'frames of reference'.

A unitarist assumes there is no fundamental conflict of interests between employer and employees. Employees don't have group interests, only individual ones, and these they share (or should share) with the employer – as indicated by organisational success. The expectation is that these values, enmeshed in a rhetoric of organisations as families or teams, should produce common purpose and workplace harmony. Conflict over ER is thus aberrant and counterproductive; for some even deviant (ibid.). Confucian paternalism, long influential in East Asia, is a unitarist variant, but one that more strongly embraces mutual obligations (e.g. Chen, Su and Zeng, 2016; Thomas and Peterson, 2014).

Pluralists expect there to be a variety of interests within and among the ER parties. Alongside shared interests on some issues, they expect – and see as legitimate – the emergence of conflicting responses over others. The resulting individual and social conflicts are then open to being managed, for example through negotiation. Ideally, agreement produces new rules (Fox, 1974; Bray et al., 2014).

Radical approaches assume that in capitalist societies, employment is a central site for broader class conflicts. A core conception is that the ownership of, control over and profits from employing organisations remain in the hands of the few while the many, with little other source of subsistence, are constrained to offer their labour – and therefore themselves – for wages. This fundamental class divide is a perpetual source of potential conflicts, even if these only appear sporadically (see Fox, 1974; Hyman, 1975).

As mentioned above, choices – including unconscious choices – of frames of reference also condition how ER practitioners understand their situations and actions. Some authors have used these frameworks to help construct typologies of employer IR 'styles' that focus largely on whether, and if so on what terms, employers accept unionism and collective bargaining. This question was at the core of Fox's (1974) own six-category typology. With non-unionism increasingly pervasive in many industries and countries, Fox's emphasis on attitudes to unions has become less relevant, in many cases, than other factors. Thus, attention has also shifted to another dimension, owing more to HRM. It concerns the degree to which employers seek to invest in the development of their employees (Bacon, 2008). We discuss this further below.

The next section expands discussion on how the management of employment relationships represents a core ER challenge facing employers, particularly in contexts that constrain managerial autonomy and power. Subsequent sections consecutively analyse employers' managerial strategies inside the organisation and then outside. Inside the organisation, there is first discussion of management focused on the individual employee, and then on the wider organisational processes and dynamics. In looking outside the workplace, it explains employer activity in the wider labour market and public policy arena, particularly through employer associations.

Employment relations contexts, employer autonomy and managerial strategies

For most of human history, employment relations have been confined to employment relationships: individualised, informal and based on verbal understandings. These situations give employers almost complete discretion (or 'managerial prerogative') over the main elements of employment relationships: hiring; firing; remuneration; work scheduling and duration; work intensity; work breaks; discipline; and workplace health and safety. In the absence of labour market protections for workers – through unions, collective bargaining, works councils and state labour market regulation – employers have faced very few, mostly weak, constraints on their choices to abuse that power. Such constraints have derived from societal norms, religious law, labour market exigencies – such as skill shortages – and forms of early collective regulation of skilled work through and within organisations like craft guilds (Deakin, 2001).

Formal, explicit recognition that employers would inevitably abuse their unfettered workplace power already appeared as employment law in the Jewish Bible (or Christian Old Testament), compiled some 2,500 to 3,000 years ago. One example is:

> You shall not abuse a needy and destitute labourer, whether a fellow countryman or a stranger in one of the communities of your land. You must pay a worker's wages on the same day, before the sun sets, for he is needy and urgently depends on it. Deuteronomy 24:14–15
>
> *(Plaut, 1981, pp. 1499–1500)*

With industrialisation and modernity, employment relations have also gained a collective dimension across developed and developing countries. The spread of unionism and collective bargaining confronts employers with particular challenges. As Flanders (1975) pointed out, this collective dimension, a 'political' process involving joint rule-making with unions, provides individual employees with a protective, rights-based platform. The terms specified in their individual contracts of employment, and the treatment they receive through the employment relationship, cannot fall below this platform.

Laws that support the rights of individual employees or their unionism have a similar effect, reshaping the making, terms and administration of individual employment contracts and hence relationships. In some countries, like the United States, Italy, Germany and Australia, collective agreements have long had some form of legislative or judicial force (Bean, 1994). In an important change facing employers in China, the Employment Contracts Law 2008 requires them to provide employees with *written* employment contracts that specify reciprocal rights and obligations (Wang et al., 2016). This reduces the sorts of unilateral discretion employers enjoy when employment rests solely on verbal agreements. All these factors that reduce employers' areas of unilateral discretion and (potential) coercive power produce further challenges to be managed.

For employers then, management of the employment relationship, based as it is upon an apparently simple contractual arrangement, can be very complex. This reflects the subjectivity inherent in employing labour in a world of very unevenly distributed material resources and power. The most apparent sign of this, as the radical frame of reference explains, is the employment relationship itself. An employee, in selling their time (and capabilities) to an employer as a commodity (or 'human capital'), cares about how that employer treats what they are selling – essentially a lease of themselves. As most employment relationships (and jobs) in the modern era are longstanding – often over years – employees continue to care. These factors combine to intensify, for individual employees, the psychological elements of their employment relationships.

Employees can influence, through action and inaction, the quality and quantity of their own performance. At an individual level, an employee can co-operate with management directions enthusiastically or begrudgingly, mix co-operation with apathy or denial depending on the issue, resist or sabotage aspects of their expected workload, protest or leave that employment relationship. Collectively, employees may engage in all the above responses while also adding collective 'voice' options like going on strike. As individuals or as collectives, employees may also seek external regulatory intervention, particularly from state agencies.

Moreover, employment relationships develop within patterns of workgroup identity, custom, practice and organisational cultures that condition how people perceive the employer's treatment of them. The work sociology literature provides examples of work groups, at times supported by local cultural values from outside the workplace, creating and enforcing their own norms that restrict employee effort, whether under time- or output-based pay systems (Burawoy, 1979; Mulholland, 2004; van den Broek, 2002).

Thus, employers require strategies that force, persuade or inspire employees to produce and sustain expected performance levels. During periods of early industrialisation, and particularly under authoritarian regimes, employers have often been free to impose feudal styles of coercive control. For example, in Britain in the first half of the nineteenth century, the operation of master and servant laws provided employers with a range of coercive powers over their 'servants', including having them imprisoned for absconding during the term of their employment contracts or for other disobedience (Deakin, 2001). During the 1970s and early 1980s, with (South) Korea under military dictatorships, high-level managers of Korea's family-controlled business groups (*chaebols*) enforced their authority over unskilled factory and construction workers through militaristic cultures of labour management backed by the threat of instant dismissal. Managers – some of them former army officers – demanded short haircuts, strict time control and intrusive supervision of company-provided dormitory accommodation. Employees had to follow orders, even if they brought substantial safety risks (Jun and Sheldon, 2018).

Within modern democracies, these extremely coercive employer behaviours still exist episodically and at the margins. However, they mostly run foul of regulatory oversight, union involvement and public opinion. More generally and overly simplifying, it can be helpful to categorise employer approaches, within the organisation and without, as either 'hard' or 'soft', or as pursuing a 'low road' or a 'high road'. Another, similar categorisation speaks of 'control-oriented' as against 'commitment-oriented'. The first in each case focuses on employers actively subordinating labour, as a production factor, solely to their own interests. The second takes greater cognisance of and attempts to meet some employee interests and needs, including for skill development, work autonomy and participation (Guest, 1999). Research from Germany and Australia suggests that in practice, employers also use hybrid models, targeting different workforce segments with different approaches (Hauff, Alewell and Hansen, 2014; Sarina and Wright, 2015).

With the development of work roles that are more skilled, customer-oriented and knowledge-intensive, or that involve vulnerable, highly expensive plant and equipment, employers have come to require more subtle and sophisticated management strategies that ensure employee commitment, not just compliance. Many employers have also restructured their organisations to have flatter hierarchies by removing levels of management. This increases the 'span of control' for remaining managerial roles, reducing their capacities for direct control over subordinates. How then to ensure employees sustain expected levels of performance to justify the costs of hiring and employing them?

The field of organisational behaviour (OB) is a response to these challenges. The scope of this challenge is evident in tertiary OB curricula projecting high-road perspectives towards productivity improvement, with core topics like motivation, leadership, managing groups and teams, organisational change and organisational culture (Kaufman, 2014). It is also evident in OB research on employee 'voice' that focuses only on individual employee initiatives functional to employer interests, rather than as individual or collective expressions of employee interests (Barry and Wilkinson, 2016). As OB provides the HRM field's conceptual underpinnings, they each seek to inform managers – or aspiring managers – about how to persuade subordinates to align their attitudes and performance with employers' expectations.

The effectiveness of such persuasion depends on a complex mixture of economic and non-economic factors, and can be highly variable among employees over time, space and even culture (Thomas and Peterson, 2015, chapter 7). These factors complicate management's choices. The next section introduces a perspective from micro OB (or organisational psychology) that confronts the challenge of motivation at the level of the individual employee.

Management of the individual employee: psychological contracts

The idea of a 'psychological contract' in employment has become very influential for high-road approaches to employee management at the individual level. It refers to beliefs that individual employees hold regarding mutual obligations between them and their employer, these felt obligations having both transactional and relational dimensions (Rousseau, 1990). Stronger psychological contracts can motivate employees to contribute greater discretionary effort. This operates through the employee's increasing commitment to the employing organisation, and by them accepting greater employer discretion over decisions. Therefore, developing and maintaining strong psychological contracts is an important way for employers to reduce, to their advantage, the employment relationship's ambiguity and consequent potentially contrasting views over the wage-effort bargain. Employers can develop general policies that boost or maintain psychological contracts across an organisation or work unit, but managers can also target individuals by negotiating to deliver particular benefits to them (so-called I-Deals) – with the aim of generating more focused reciprocity (Rousseau, Ho and Greenberg, 2006).

Employee beliefs change over time, however – causing psychological contracts to shrink or expand – and are open to influence from an employee's experience within an organisation, including perceived treatment from the employer. Indeed, with time, employees can come to expect more from their employer and to feel that they owe the employer less (Robinson, Kraatz and Rousseau, 1994). Thus, when an employer breaches employee expectations, a common occurrence, employees redress the balance by, for example, lowering their commitment (Coyle-Shapiro and Kessler, 2000). This can produce patterns of employee decisions to leave, reduce their effort or to respond collectively, including through unions. These represent challenges to employers at the organisational level.

Management initiatives at the organisational level

Researchers have produced a very varied picture of employer intentions, motivations and strategic processes regarding how they manage employment at the organisational level. This variation has its roots in local conditions. Important are history, politics and culture, and stages of economic and industrial development. So too are the nature of the industry, employing organisation, workplace and work unit, and the approaches – including ideologies – of employers and their managers.

For example, is the employing organisation large or small, new or old, a first-mover or a follower? What is the ownership structure of the organisation: domestic or foreign, private or state owned, family based or publicly owned? How competitive is its product market, and how fully has it engaged in product differentiation, in vertical and horizontal integration? Can it access investment finance easily, and at what cost – including by compromising ownership and control? How capital or labour intensive are its main productive processes? What sorts of labour does it require and to what extent can the external labour market adequately respond? Does it face unions and, if so, under what circumstances? What role does or could the state play in relation to the various markets it is involved in? (See e.g. Adams, 1995; Bacon 2008; Gospel, 1988, 1992; Gospel and Littler, 1983; Lazonick, 1991; Littler, 1982; Rowlinson, 1998; Sisson, 1987; Tolliday and Zeitlin, 1991). The following five sub-sections address variants – both empirical and theoretical – of organisation-level employer strategies.

Labour process theory and the question of control

The exercise of managerial control – including highly coercive control – over individual employees has long been an important low-road strategy. It can also serve to break down collective employee coordination that constrains managerial prerogative, whether via informal workgroup norms or workplace union activism. Since the mid 1970s, the (sociological) labour process literature has stressed management's use of workplace control structures and processes, including cognitive ones, to reap maximum value from an employee's time or effort at work.

Historically, these strategies have included: simple versions involving close personal supervision of employee effort; deliberative choices of employee-controlling technology – such as assembly line systems and machine monitoring; the force of bureaucratic organisational rules; and payment systems linked to output. Most recently, digital surveillance systems, for example in call centres, have brought together simple and technological control mechanisms (Mulholland, 2004; van den Broek, 2002). Some labour process theorists have also developed a focus on employer strategies to gain employee consent and commitment, not just compliance. Such strategies include using more targeted recruitment/selection, training, and performance management and rewards to have employees internalise official company norms and values. These can work with policies that deliver greater employee autonomy – a high-road option – alongside those of direct control (Burawoy, 1979; Thompson and McHugh, 2002).

Among criticisms of labour process theory is that it greatly overstates, for employers, the importance of controlling labour relative to other employer concerns that need managing, like financial controls, firm borrowings, marketing, product development, brand image and sales. Increasingly, researchers are recognising the need to understand how these various other challenges/roles interact with the management of employment (Bray et al., 2014).

Internal labour markets: employee commitment through security and advancement

In developing an internal labour market (ILM), an employer chooses a high-road response to the organisational challenges of coordination and control, employee commitment and the diffusing of knowledge that produces more functionally flexible workforces (Gospel, 1988, 1992; Lazonick, 1991). Institutional economists and IR scholars have particularly pointed to three main ILM characteristics. Each can contribute to psychological contract strength as each involves employers explicitly taking responsibility for employees' welfare. The first is extensive job security. The second is the availability of extensive promotion opportunities via organisational 'job ladders'. Supporting this are extensive in-house training plus opportunities for internal secondments or transfers to gain more experience across the organisation. Thus, in organisations with strong ILMs, internal appointees typically hold the top jobs after having climbed those job ladders. Entry from the external labour market is mostly through 'ports of entry' at the organisation's lower levels. Finally, clear systems of rules, rewards and sanctions governing the first two characteristics ensure clarity in expectations of mutual rights and obligations between employer and employees (Doeringer and Piore, 1971).

These three characteristics normally generate others: pay structures that reflect internal logics rather than external labour market conditions; seniority as a high-priority criterion for pay and promotion; and, where it exists, more stable patterns of collective bargaining. Employers developed ILMs particularly in large firms, in firms facing less competitive product markets where stability and predictability are important, and where it has been important for employers to retain employees' organisational knowledge and firm loyalty. Throughout the world, ILMs have been pervasive in public sector employment, in banking and finance, in large-scale manufacturing, railways and large-scale retailing. Large firms in Japan have provided famous examples marked by life-time employment and enterprise-based unionism (Jackson, 2005; Taira, 1970). Authoritarian ILM versions have dominated ER under central planning in state socialist societies, most notably the Soviet Union and China (Chen, Su and Zeng, 2016).

In many instances, employers have also added substantial employee welfare schemes to their ILM systems. Particularly in the USA, these represented paternalistic employer attempts to win employee loyalty in order to keep unions out. At other times, company welfarism has co-existed with unionism and collective bargaining. Nonetheless, many employers have reserved ILMs and the benefits they provide employees for certain sections of their workforce, particularly those where skills and knowledge are firm-based and employee loyalty is more valuable (Jacoby, 1998; Rowlinson, 1998).

Flexibilities for employers plus commitment from employees

Since the late 1970s, there has been a growing decline in employer commitment to employee security and welfare more generally. This phenomenon has emerged and developed unevenly across nations and industries but it has weakened support for and investment in ILMs. Central have been employer drives to gain new forms and greater levels of flexibility over how they use labour and capital. The forms of flexibility to which employees must increasingly submit concern expansion of managerial prerogatives over their employment security, their working hours (and days), the tasks they do and how they do them, where they work and with whom, and the pay they receive. It can also include employer discretion in using labour hire workers.

Important contextual influences for these shifts include intensified international price competition with the rise of East Asian economies, more fluid product markets, the rising importance of financial markets with their focus on the short term, and rapid and 'disruptive' technological change. Often overlooked though are the ascendancy of governmental and managerial ideologies founded in neoclassical economics and the powerful influence of executive remuneration schemes.

The practical results, alongside massive 'offshoring' by employers, particularly to China, have notably included widespread organisational 'disaggregation', 'downsizing' and 'delayering'. These have, respectively, hived off large organisational units, retrenched substantial numbers of employees and stripped out whole layers of management. Through each, employers have gutted ILM opportunities once available in organisations with more units, larger workforces and taller hierarchies. Furthermore, there has been a growing trend for employers to seek cost reductions by outsourcing whole functions or units or using labour hire/dispatched labour arrangements to avoid direct employment. Many of these phenomena may have first come to prominence in the USA but they have spread widely, even to newly developed, post-transition economies like China (Cappelli, 1999; Cooke and Brown, 2015; Knox, 2010; Peck, Theodore and Ward, 2005).

Having retreated from previous commitments to job security, employers have advanced ideas of 'portfolio careers', in which employees themselves become solely responsible for their career advancement and income security through enhancing their 'employability'. This contradicts notions of building strong psychological contracts. Yet, where knowledge work, flexible production and reduced-inventory systems increase firms' product and labour market vulnerabilities, employers still need to motivate employees to supply discretionary effort. This has encouraged some to choose a higher-road flexibility approach. They have also adopted HRM strategies that seek to build employee 'alignment' – in the unitarist sense – with employer perspectives and goals. These may also involve top-down attempts to develop an approved organisational culture and styles of leadership and teamwork, including through managing employee socialising outside work (Cappelli, 1999; Grugulis, Dundon and Wilkinson, 2000; Thompson and McHugh, 2002).

High-performance work systems

Initiatives to achieve high-performing workplaces/systems (HPWS) – or high-involvement management – represent a recent high-road response that can also preserve some ILM characteristics – like job security – that support psychological contracts. Here, improved organisational performance, for instance higher productivity and innovation, is to come through at least one of these three avenues: raising the quantity of employee effort; increasing the quality of that effort; and improving work processes. The first two go to the heart of the management challenge founded in the employment relationship. For Bryson, Forth and Kirby (2005, p. 460) such results flow from high-performing workplaces that offer some combination of:

task-related practices, which aim to maximise employees' sense of involvement in their work, and human resource management (or personnel) practices that aim to maximise employees' commitment to the wider organisation.

Given this, core areas for management HPWS initiatives include autonomous teams (however defined), training for multi-skilling and communication skills. These require support via employee participation and from employment practices like job security, internal promotion, equal employment opportunities and performance-related pay. For Kalmi and Kauhanen (2008, p. 431), this can be summarised as "participation, incentives and skills". While the literature has suggested that the best results come through combining all three elements, recent UK research found that they operate separately (Wood et al., 2015). Despite the sustained popularity of these ideas in recent decades, few employers have adopted them and most have implemented only very few practices, and haphazardly (Boxall, 2012). Employers have typically neglected participation initiatives, particularly where this includes representation.

Employers and strategic choices about representative employee participation

Employers often view proposals for employee participation in workplace employment relations management as challenges to their managerial prerogative. Nonetheless, sometimes employers must, or choose to, have participation schemes (Fox, 1974). This raises strategic questions: with whom should employers share power; how; over which areas; and to what extent? Finally, should these mechanisms be formal or informal?

Institutional options include works councils and/or unions and collective bargaining. Widely used in Europe, works councils may exist under supportive statutory provisions – as in Germany, Austria and the Netherlands – but the degree of their autonomy from and influence over management varies: in Germany, works councils have traditionally had more autonomy and authority; in other countries, management may dominate works councils more, and provide information but little consultation and no co-determination. In some instances, employers use them for union avoidance; in others, like Germany, while being formally separate, unions have, in fact, taken councils over. European Union legislation has mandated that multinational companies establish Europe-wide councils. Overall, from an employer perspective, even at their most powerful, works councils are more attuned to the commercial success of the employing organisation than unions. However, they allow employee representatives much greater crucial information about, and sometimes authority over, how the organisation runs (Jenkins and Blyton, 2008).

Employers confront similar choices regarding union representation. In some countries, legislation has supported unionisation and/or collective bargaining. Thus, Australian employers widely accommodated strong state support for unionisation and bargaining for nearly a century until the early 1990s. In contrast, in the USA, apart from a few decades after the Second World War, private sector employers have often fought long and bitterly – and with almost every means – to keep their employees from unionising and bargaining, even for a time, in defiance of federal law. During 2016, on behalf of the *chaebols*, South Korea's (elected) government returned to strident union harassment strategies not seen since before the country's dramatic democratisation in 1987.

Where unionisation and collective bargaining appear inevitable, employers can sometimes choose the terms of their acceptance: which union is to be involved and how is it connected to the workplace? One aspect is bargaining level. Strong preferences by larger employers for enterprise-based unions – as in Japan and South Korea – or enterprise- or workplace-level bargaining with 'locals' or branches of industry or occupational unions – as in the USA, Canada and, more recently, the UK – most directly and potentially intrusively enmesh rule-making with an employer's workplace operations. Nonetheless, enterprise unions are open to employer influence and capture, and enterprise bargaining avoids having to compromise with other – potentially competitor – employers in managing union claims. Similarly, they offer the best opportunities for employers to use 'concession bargaining' by threatening local employment, as has been common in the USA since the 1990s. Finally, decentralised bargaining systems mostly mean that smaller employers completely escape union attention and collective bargaining (Bean, 1994).

On the other hand, it is much easier for an employer to restrict the scope of bargaining – and thereby insulate the firm from union pressures – by combining in multi-employer bargaining. Both processes encourage formalisation and standardisation of ER routines as the employer hires specialist staff (or brings in consultants), develops policies and procedures, produces manuals and provides relevant training. The next section discusses employers' initiatives beyond their organisations in response to wider ER challenges.

Beyond the workplace: employers, management and collective employment relations

Broader external labour market, legislative and policy considerations also constrain or encourage employers' range of options. Here, like unions, they have choices between political and industrial strategies. Similarly, they can also strategically involve themselves in policy debates over labour market regulation and social welfare provision, vocational education and training, and immigration policy. This may include choices to act alone or in loose co-ordination with other firms, via their employer association, or to collaborate with public sector bodies (Li and Sheldon, 2014; Sheldon and Thornthwaite, 2005; Wright, 2017).

Very large employers have the resources to confront those challenges alone – for example by lobbying governments – but mostly, they operate via employer associations, particularly where this involves engagement in institutionalised collective ER. The most complete version of this is tripartite (or corporatist) arrangements headed by government and including separate employer association and union representation. Such arrangements have been very important, at times, in Europe, Australia and South Korea, and central to Singapore's IR and economic success (Sheldon, Gan and Morgan, 2015; Siaroff, 1999).

Employer associations

Employer associations are voluntary, membership-based business associations for whom labour market matters are an important part of their vocation. Akin to 'bosses' unions' they are highly influential in much of Europe, southern and eastern Asia, Latin America and Australia. They have also formed a series of international confederations for bargaining, lobbying and representation in supranational forums. Historically, the 'Western' literature on employer associations suggests that employers have formed them to confront labour market challenges from unions and state intervention, or from other employers who either pay wages too high or too low for competitors to match. Lacking the necessary resources to confront, individually, these communal challenges, employers associate to increase their power via resource-sharing, co-ordination, solidarity and a more substantial political profile. These motivations subsequently became associations' principal sources of organisational purpose (Sheldon and Thornthwaite, 1999; Windmuller and Gladstone, 1984).

Organisational purposes generate strategic choices among activities that associations embrace on behalf of employers. Thus in 'Western' employer association traditions, early association activity focuses first on providing 'collective goods' (Olson, 1971). These are non-exclusive, non-market solutions to employers' needs: in particular leading or coordinating employers in multi-employer collective bargaining; lobbying governments; and mounting public policy campaigns. Such activities allow employers to express their collective ER preferences in the wider labour market and policy arenas, for example over minimum wages, restrictions to working hours, employment security, workplace health and safety regulation, or training policy. Over time, original purposes and strategic choices of activity generate associations' core roles and contribute to their organisational identities (Schmitter and Streeck, 1999).

Particularly where unions are strong, collective bargaining more centralised, and governments more willing to regulate employer behaviour, an association's collective goods serve as important resources for employers' own ER needs. As firms, both members and potential members, are a major part of that association's 'product market', it thus also depends, indirectly, on those labour market conditions that make membership of it attractive (Sheldon et al., 2016). For much of the second half of the twentieth century, in countries like Australia, Denmark, Sweden, (West) Germany, the UK, the Netherlands and Italy, those conditions provided associations with very high profile roles and, in many cases, substantial power over their memberships (Sheldon and Thornthwaite, 1999; Windmuller and Gladstone, 1984).

Nonetheless, reliance on collective goods leaves associations vulnerable to free-riding. As association revenues traditionally depend heavily on membership subscriptions, widespread free-riding undermines those resources as well as its representativeness. Many associations therefore provide 'selective goods' (Olson, 1971): free and mostly standardised services directly to and solely for members. These include information on industry trends, published advice on labour regulations, guidelines for collective bargaining and call centre advisory services on individual ER matters (Sheldon et al., 2016).

Selective goods are a crucial association response to challenges to its 'associability' and 'governability' (Traxler, 1999). That is, associations must first attract and retain member firms; they must then find a way to effectively represent member firms' often differing interests in situations where firms can often choose to act against association policy. How associations 'structure' themselves can assist with these challenges arising from membership heterogeneity by having recruitment domains reflecting product (and/or labour) market characteristics of member firms. Territorial associations recruit all firms within a geographical area, irrespective of industry. Sectoral (or industry) associations recruit within one or a few related industries. National federations of associations bring together sectoral and/or territorial bodies. Because one of the major cleavages within associations is between the interests of small versus large firms, another way for associations to reduce governability challenges is through adopting structures closely mirroring firm size.

As multi-employer collective bargaining has long provided associations with central institutional roles, its recent decline in some countries brings associations severe associability, and hence financial, challenges, like those that undercut US associations after the 1970s (Kochan, Katz and McKersie, 1986; Sheldon and Thornthwaite, 1999). Some associations are responding by marketing 'elective goods' – customised, commercially-priced products and services – to members and non-members. This assists associations in developing new revenue streams but can also act as a membership recruitment tool (Sheldon et al., 2016).

In some East Asian countries, the motivations for association formation and development have differed greatly. In South Korea, when *chaebols* formed their Korea Employers' Federation in 1970, its original purpose was to develop selective, not collective, goods. With South Korea under a pro-business military dictatorship, those employers faced no collective threats from unions or government regulation (Jun and Sheldon, 2006). In 1980, Singapore's employers acceded to activist pressure from Lee Kwan Yew's government to merge two existing associations in founding the Singapore National Employers' Federation. Once again, the traditional collective IR challenges were absent; the government's motivation was to streamline its tripartite planning and decision-making structures (Sheldon, Gan and Morgan, 2015). Finally, the recent history of association development in China is very complex but includes instances of local associations of foreign-invested enterprises (FIEs) responding collectively to predatory employee poaching and rising wage levels from more recently arrived FIEs (Lee, Sheldon and Li, 2011).

Employers and the shaping of employment relations systems

It is useful to explore how and why there has been substantial variation across countries in the interactions between employer behaviours and IR systems. Clegg's (1976) influential study argues that it has been the structures of management and employer associations that have been most responsible for shaping cross-national differences in the configuration, content and impact of collective bargaining. The collective bargaining dimensions he works with include its level, scope, extent and union security. More recent work tends to support this argument (Bacon, 2008)

Apart from Adams (1995) and Sisson (1987), there has been little research into how the role of employers in collective bargaining varies across countries. Adams points out how Western European employers have typically behaved quite differently towards unions from those in North America. In the former, employers are organised into strong associations that collectively bargain with unions (and the state). By contrast, in North America, employers have generally not formed strong associations. While Adams was writing before the growing trend among employers, in some European countries, to decentralise collective bargaining and leave associations, his general point still stands.

The emergence of China as the world's dominant manufacturer has probably been the largest single external factor to have shaken ER systems around the world. Its rise has debilitated manufacturing industries – traditional heartlands of collective IR – in most advanced industrial societies. The rise of knowledge work and service industries has also been important for changes to ER in those countries. Ideologically, there has been a growing international trend to public anti-union stances and strongly unitarist positions from employers, one that Kochan, Katz and McKersie (1986) earlier identified among US employers. All these factors have encouraged a greater employer emphasis on shrinking their ER focus to managing the *individual* employment relationship. Reinforcing this, and concomitant with the intensification of global competition and changing sectoral composition, has been the growth of OB and HRM as fields of practice, theorising and empirical research (Kaufman, 2014).

Employers can either work from the bottom-up or top-down, and their efforts can seek to destroy employees' collective rights and power or establish or improve frameworks that embrace a collective employee voice. Associations have been employers' main vehicle for seeking top-down changes. Bottom-up attempts to destroy employee combination were a hallmark of individual US corporations prior to the Second World War, and since the late 1970s. Bottom-up collaborative approaches are more apparent at regional or industry level, for example in Australia's engineering industry in the 1980s. Top-down approaches have been important in Sweden where, in 1938, employers agreed to collaboratively build a centralised collective bargaining framework with unions. Sixty-odd years later, they were seeking to dismantle as much of it as they could.

Conclusion

This chapter has examined employers, management and employment relations across three levels: the individual employee; the organisation; and the wider labour market. It has used theories from a number of disciplines and examples from different countries to help explain how employers choose to manage ER and why they may choose some approaches over others. As well, it has also very briefly explained how employers have been seeking to reshape ER in recent years, both inside and outside their workplaces. In this they have strategically chosen, and sometimes meshed, high-road and/or low-road approaches depending on their product and labour market contexts, their technological profiles, the nature of institutional regulation they face and their own frames of reference. The overall direction would seem to be in combining some elements of high-commitment HRM – like training and teamwork – with a preference for increasing managerial autonomy and flexibilities over the use of labour.

Nonetheless, it is difficult to predict broad trends. Despite claims for cross-national convergence, there remains abundant diversity across countries and industries. Given this, it is not clear what the limits are for employers' low-road strategies beyond more vulnerable labour market segments. Similarly, it is unclear whether individual employers will invest more or less in ILMs, HPWS or other high-road organisational innovations aimed at employees' psychological contracts, which employees will receive more favoured treatment, and what this might entail.

Global competition, domestic politics and technological change will continue to strongly influence employer decisions. However, there are reasons to believe that these will not all play out in the same direction as previously. China appears to be approaching its low-wage production frontier at a time when its party-state has legitimated unionism and collective bargaining (albeit within constraints). With prices, costs and wages rising, many Chinese employers are already having to engage in the sorts of strategic choices over ER that their western, Japanese and South Korean competitors have been dealing with for decades. They too are having to think more about psychological contracts and employee commitment, and/or labour flexibilities and cost-minimising, atypical employment. Cost pressures on China's employers may well give employers in developed economies new opportunities. Linked to this are domestic political factors. Over recent decades, employer strategies have increasingly developed under neoliberal regimes that legitimate and reinforce managerial prerogatives; economic globalisation; and weakened employee protections. Populist backlashes sweeping many countries during 2016 and 2017 suggest that employers may have to factor in this sentiment in managing employment relations.

References

Adams, R.J. (1995). *Industrial Relations under Liberal Democracy: North America in Comparative Perspective.* Columbia: University of South Carolina Press.

Bacon, N. (2008). Management Strategy and Industrial Relations, in Blyton, P., Bacon, N., Fiorito, J. and Heery, E. (eds.) *The SAGE Handbook of Industrial Relations.* Los Angeles: Sage, pp. 241–257.

Barry, M. and Wilkinson, A. (2016). 'Pro-social or pro-management? A critique of the conception of employee voice as a pro-social behaviour within organizational behaviour', *British Journal of Industrial Relations*, 54(2), pp. 261–284.

Bean, R. (1994). *Comparative Industrial Relations: An Introduction to Cross-national Perspectives.* 2nd edn. London: Routledge.

Boxall, P. (2012). 'High performance work systems: what, why, how and for whom?' *Asia Pacific Journal of Human Resources*, 50(2), pp. 169–186.

Bray, M., Waring, P., Cooper, R. and MacNeil, J. (2014). *Employment Relations: Theory and Practice.* 3rd edn. North Ryde, NSW: McGraw-Hill Education.

Bryson, A., Forth, J. and Kirby, S. (2005). 'High-involvement management practices, trade union representation and workplace performance in Britain', *Scottish Journal of Political Economy*, 52(3), pp. 451–491.

Burawoy. M. (1979). *Manufacturing Consent: Changes in the Labor Process Under Monopoly Capitalism.* Chicago: University of Chicago Press.

Cappelli, P. (1999). *The New Deal at Work: Managing the Market-driven Workforce.* Boston (MA): Harvard Business School Press.

Chen, L., Su, Z-X. and Zeng, X. (2016). 'Path dependence and the evolution of HRM in China', *International Journal of Human Resource Management*, 27(18), pp. 2034–2057.

Clegg, H.A. (1976). *Trade Unionism under Collective Bargaining: A Theory Based on Comparisons of Six Countries.* Oxford: Blackwell.

Cooke. F.L. and Brown, R. (2015). *The Regulation of Non-standard Forms of Employment in China, Japan and the Republic of Korea*, Conditions of Work and Employment Series No. 64. Geneva: International Labour Office.

Coyle-Shapiro, J. and Kessler, I. (2000). 'Consequences of the psychological contract for the Employment Relationship: A large-scale survey', *Journal of Management Studies*, 37(7), pp. 903–930.

Deakin, S. (2001). 'The contract of employment: a study of legal evolution', *Historical Studies in Industrial Relations*, 11, pp. 1–36.

Doeringer, P.B. and Piore, M.J. (1971). *Internal Labor Markets and Manpower Analysis.* Lexington: D.C. Heath and Co.

Flanders, A. (1975). Collective Bargaining: A Theoretical Analysis, in Flanders, A. (ed.) *Management and Unions: The Theory and Reform of Industrial Relations.* London: Faber and Faber.

Fox, A. (1974). *Beyond Contract: Work, Power and Trust Relations.* London: Faber and Faber.

Gardner, M. and Palmer G. (1997). *Employment Relations: Industrial Relations and Human Resource Management in Australia.* 2nd edn. South Melbourne: Macmillan.

Gospel, H.F. (1988). 'The management of labour: Great Britain, the US and Japan', *Business History*, 30(1), pp. 104–115.

Gospel, H. (1992). *Markets, Firms and the Management of Labour in Modern Britain.* Cambridge (UK): Cambridge University Press.

Gospel, H.F. and Littler, C.R. (1983). *Managerial Strategies and Industrial Relations: An Historical and Comparative Study.* London: Ashgate.

Grugulis, I., Dundon, T. and Wilkinson, A. (2000). 'Cultural control and the 'culture manager': employment practices in a consultancy', *Work, Employment & Society*, 14(1), pp. 97–116.

Guest, D. (1999). 'Human Resource Management – the workers' verdict', *Human Resource Management Journal*, 9(3), pp. 5–25.

Hauff, S., Alewell, D. and Hansen, N.K. (2014). 'HRM systems between control and commitment: occurrences, characteristics and effects on HRM outcomes and firm performance', *Human Resource Management Journal*, 24(4), pp. 424–441.

Hyman, R. (1975). *Industrial Relations: A Marxist Introduction.* London: Macmillan.

Jackson, G. (2005). 'Stakeholders under pressure: corporate governance and labour management in Germany and Japan', *Corporate Governance: An International Review*, 13(3), pp. 419–428.

Jacoby, S.M. (1998). *Modern Manors: Welfare Capitalism Since the New Deal.* Princeton: Princeton University Press.

Jenkins, J. and Blyton, P. (2008). Works Councils, in Blyton, P., Bacon, N., Fiorito, J. and Heery, E. (eds.) *The SAGE Handbook of Industrial Relations.* Los Angeles: Sage, pp. 346–357.

Jun, I. and Sheldon, P. (2006). 'Looking beyond the West? The Korea Employers' Federation and the challenges of membership adhesion and cohesion', *Economic and Labour Relations Review*, 17(1), pp. 203–226.

Jun, I. and Sheldon, P. (2018). [Forthcoming]. *Korea's Business Groups, Their Association and Industrial Relations.* London: Routledge.

Kalmi, P. and Kauhanen, A. (2008). 'Workplace innovations and employee outcomes: evidence from Finland', *Industrial Relations*, 47(3), pp. 430–459.

Kaufman, B.E. (2014). 'The historical development of American HRM broadly viewed', *Human Resource Management Review*, 24(3), pp. 196–218.

Kim, S. and Chung, S. (2016). 'Explaining organizational responsiveness to emerging regulatory pressure: the case of illegal overtime in China', *International Journal of Human Resource Management*, 27(18), pp. 2097–2118.

Kochan, T., Katz, T. and McKersie, R. (1986). *The Transformation of American Industrial Relations.* New York: Basic Books.

Knox, A. (2010). '"Lost in translation": an analysis of temporary work agency employment in hotels', *Work, Employment & Society,* 24(3), pp. 449–467.

Lazonick, W. (1991). *Business Organization and the Myth of the Market Economy.* Cambridge (UK): Cambridge University Press.

Lee, C.-H., Sheldon, P. and Li, Y. (2011). Employer Associations, in Sheldon, P., Kim, S., Li, Y. and Warner, M. (eds.) *China's Changing Workplace: Dynamism, Diversity and Disparity.* London: Routledge, pp. 301–319.

Li, Y. and Sheldon, P. (2014). 'Collaborations between foreign invested enterprises and China's VET schools: making the system work amid localized skill shortages', *Journal of Vocational Education and Training,* 66(3), pp. 311–329.

Littler, C.R. (1982). *The Development of the Labour Process in Capitalist Societies.* London: Heinemann.

Mintzberg, H. (1973). *The Nature of Managerial Work.* New York: Harper & Row.

Mulholland, K. (2004). 'Workplace resistance in an Irish call centre: slammin', scammin', smokin', an' leavin'', *Work, Employment & Society,* 18(4), pp. 709–724.

Olson, M. (1971). *The Logic of Collective Action: Public Goods and the Theory of Group.* Cambridge (MA): Harvard University Press.

Paucelle, J-L. and Guthrie, C. (2013). Henri Fayol, in Witzel, M. and Warner, M. (eds.) *The Oxford Handbook of Management Theorists.* Oxford: Oxford University Press, pp. 49–73.

Peck, J., Theodore, N. and Ward, K. (2005). 'Constructing markets for temporary labour: employment liberalization and the internationalization of the staffing industry', *Global Networks,* 5(1), pp. 3–26.

Plaut, W.G. (ed.) (1981). *The Torah: A Modern Commentary.* New York: Union of American Hebrew Congregations.

Robinson, S.L., Kraatz, M.S. and Rousseau, D.M. (1994). 'Changing obligations and the psychological contract: a longitudinal study', *Academy of Management Journal,* 37(1), pp. 137–152.

Rousseau, D.M. (1990). 'New hire perceptions of their own and their employer's obligations: a study of psychological contracts', *Journal of Organizational Behavior,* 11(5), pp. 389–400.

Rousseau, D.M., Ho, V.T. and Greenberg, J. (2006). 'I-deals: idiosyncratic terms in employment relationships', *Academy of Management Review,* 31(4), pp. 977–994.

Rowlinson, M. (1998). 'Quaker Employers', *Historical Studies in Industrial Relations,* 6, pp. 163–198.

Sarina, T. and Wright, C.F. (2015). 'Mutual gains or mutual losses: organisational fragmentation and employment relations outcomes at Qantas Group', *Journal of Industrial Relations,* 57(5), pp. 686–706.

Schmitter, P. and Streeck, W. (1999). *The Organization of Business Interests: Studying the Associative Action of Business in Advanced Industrial Societies.* Cologne: MPIfG Discussion Paper 99/1. Available at: http://www.mpi-fg-koeln.mpg.de/pu/mpifg_dp/dp99-1.pdf.

Sheldon, P. and Li, Y. (2013). 'Localized poaching and skills shortages of manufacturing employees among MNEs in China', *Journal of World Business,* 48(2), pp. 186–195.

Sheldon, P. and Thornthwaite, L. (1999). *Employer Associations and Industrial Relations Change: Catalysts or Captives?* Sydney: Allen & Unwin.

Sheldon, P. and Thornthwaite, L. (2005). 'Employability skills and vocational education and training policy in australia: an analysis of employer association agendas', *Asia Pacific Journal of Human Resources,* 43(3), pp. 404–425.

Sheldon, P., Gan, B. and Morgan, D.E. (2015). 'Making Singapore's tripartism work (faster): the formation of the Singapore National Employers' Federation in 1980', *Business History,* 57(3), pp. 438–460.

Sheldon, P., Paoletti, F., Nacamulli, R. and Morgan, D.E. (2016). 'Employer association responses to the effects of bargaining decentralization in Australia and Italy: seeking explanations from organizational theory', *British Journal of Industrial Relations,* 54(1), pp. 160–191.

Siaroff, A. (1999). 'Corporatism in 24 industrial democracies: meaning and measurement', *European Journal of Political Research,* 36(2), pp. 175–205.

Sisson, K. (1987). *The Management of Collective Bargaining: An International Comparison.* Oxford: Blackwell.

Taira, K. (1970). *Economic Development and the Labor Market in Japan.* New York: Columbia University Press.

Thomas, D.C. and Peterson, M.F. (2015). *Cross-cultural Management: Essential Concepts.* 3rd edn. Los Angeles: Sage Publishing.

Thomson, P. and McHugh, D. (2002). *Work Organisations.* 3rd edn. Basingstoke: Palgrave.

Tolliday, S. and Zeitlin, J. (1991). National models and international variations in labour management and employer organization, in Tolliday, S. and Zeitlin, J. (eds.) *The Power to Manage? Employers and Industrial Relations in Comparative Historical Perspective.* London: Routledge.

Traxler, F. (1999). 'Employers and employer organisations: the case of governability', *Industrial Relations Journal*, 30(4), pp. 345–354.

van den Broek, D. (2002). 'Monitoring and surveillance in call centres: some responses from Australian workers', *Labour & Industry*, 12(3), pp. 43–58.

Wang, F., Song, H., Cheng, Y., Luo, N., Gan, B., Feng, J. and Xie, P. (2016). 'Converging divergence: The effect of China's Employment Contract Law on signing written employment contracts', *International Journal of Human Resource Management*, 27(18), pp. 2075–2096.

Windmuller, J.P. and Gladstone, A. (eds.) (1984). *Employers Associations and Industrial Relations: A Comparative Study*. New York: Clarendon Press.

Wood, S., Burridge, M., Rudloff, D., Green, W. and Nolte, S. (2015). 'Dimensions and locations of high-involvement management: fresh evidence from the UK Commissions' 2011 Employer Skills Survey', *Human Resource Management Journal*, 25(2), pp. 166–183.

Wright, C.F. (2017). 'Employer organizations and labour immigration policy in Australia and the United Kingdom: the power of political salience and social institutional legacies', *British Journal of Industrial Relations*, 55(2), pp. 347–371.

14

MULTINATIONALS AS EMPLOYMENT RELATIONS ACTORS

María Jesús Belizón

Introduction

Much has been written about employment relations (ER) actors since John T. Dunlop's seminal work, *Industrial Relations Systems* (1958). His simple, concise and neat categorisation – employers, trade unions and state – constituted the starting point and bedrock for the systematisation of the study of ER across the globe. The differing and unique interlocking relationships among these actors in different nations have been the focus of numerous international comparative studies, providing scholars, practitioners and policy-makers with a universal 'convention' with which to describe, analyse, criticise, modify and shape the employment relationship (Bellemare, 2000, p. 383). Elaborating on this foundational convention, scholars have reached out for new actors in their attempt to reconceptualise the industrial relations (IR) system (Kochan, 2004), either by delving into the variety of these tripartite networks or into new actors that were somewhat excluded. End users, governmental and private agencies, educational entities, non-governmental organisations (NGOs) and even religious organisations are somewhat active agents within the ER system of a given country and internationally. However, current ER is not just defined as a simple system of economic actors but involves a human face aimed at the protection of efficiency, equity and voice as they embody the objectives of the employment relationship (Budd, 2004; Edwards, 2003). This chapter is concerned with one of the three primary actors, namely, a significant employer, the multinational corporation (MNC), and with how MNCs' behaviours and interactions play out in relation to other actors and their ER objectives more broadly.

MNCs are viewed as global employers due to their prominent and active role in the worldwide economy (Lévesque et al., 2015). They are the movers and shakers of global economic activity, but are by no means operating under free will. In this context, MNCs have been studied through the lenses of institutional theory in an attempt to decipher to what extent they conform to local legal, social or cultural requirements that ultimately grant them legitimacy within the host country. The institutional leeway MNCs enjoy in certain locations confers them with the possibility of exercising their strategic freedom and embrace best practices, which often entails a replication of home country practices that headquarters deems essential to the successful running of the business (Geary and Aguzzoli, 2016; Pudelko and Harzing, 2007). Concomitantly, MNCs are seen as both ER actors and a contested or co-operative socio-political space where ER take place at the different levels at which the social actors interact with their respective counterparts. Particular consideration has recently been given to the analysis of MNCs as drivers of change in ER and as diffusers of new ER practices across borders. Thus, this chapter will situate the MNC as an ER actor by considering its role in the global economy as well as the role of MNCs as *rule-takers* and *rule-makers*. The myriad of political interplays and dynamics that occur within the so-called regulatory space (Berg et al., 2005; Dundon et al., 2014) will be considered at the macro and micro levels, where the different ER actors engage in their power struggles in an attempt to occupy this regulatory space as much as they possibly can by gaining power resources or optimising those already possessed. The overarching conceptualisation of power upon which each of these forms of macro- and micro-politicking and their impact on ER is generally built is the 'Lukesian' triple typology of power dimensions (Dundon et al., 2014; Ferner, Edwards and Tempel, 2012; Geary and Aguzzoli, 2016; Lukes, 2005). Table 14.1 outlines how power can be sourced from different reservoirs, namely, resources, processes and meaning along with some examples of managerial implications within MNCs.

MNCs: the global employer

MNCs are the largest employers worldwide in terms of proportions and geographical extension (Lévesque et al., 2015). Every year the United Nations Conference in Trade and Development (UNCTAD) publishes the World Investment Report (WIR), aimed at informing all economic actors of the trajectory of foreign direct investment (FDI) at a global scale in order to serve, *inter alia*, as a means to drive international policy-making on cross-border investments, with a particular emphasis on developing and transition economies. Although global FDI inflows have fallen since the commencement of the economic recession, investment made by MNCs originating in developing countries has reached record levels (UNCTAD, 2015). The last WIR estimated that nine out of the twenty largest investor nations were developing and transition economies, pointing to developing Asia as the largest investor region. According to past years' estimations, MNCs' corporate taxes provide developing countries with an average of ten per cent of their budgeted revenue. By 2010, the UNCTAD reported the existence of more than 82,000 MNCs operating worldwide, employing some 77 million people across the globe (UNCTAD, 2010). By 2015, despite the bumpy recovery after the global financial crisis, which slowed down FDI flows at a global scale and led to multiple divestment decisions, MNCs' workforces still accounted for over 75 million employees. It is precisely this vast, far-reaching breadth of the MNC that makes it the most influential of all employers. Hence, to what extent are MNCs framing the broader agenda for economic development? Are MNCs the most powerful actors in the so-called social dialogue? As Batt, Holman and Holtgrewe (2009, p. 474) note, MNCs "disproportionately influence the direction of change" in the workplace.

From an international business perspective, besides their role in collective bargaining at national, sectoral and company levels, MNCs have the capacity to affect IR praxis and employment conditions directly by disseminating existing or novel employment practices across borders; indirectly by either threatening national economies with their exit or the closure of different sites – what has been termed 'regime-shopping' (Streeck, 1997) – or alternatively, by engaging in FDI incentive schemes within the host economies. Additionally, MNCs may shape and steer certain changes in ER politically by getting involved in lobbying activities aimed at influencing the industrial order and social peace in a given country (Meardi, 2012). But are MNCs pursuing their own agendas without careful and deep consideration of their impact on the welfare of employees and their families, other stakeholders, the economy at large and the common good of all citizens?

Table 14.1 Lukesian conceptualisation of power and some implications for ER practices

Power dimension	Roots of power	Managerial implications in MNCs
Power of resources	Concerns the very essence and nature of the decisions that are made, and the resources needed to carry them out	Is the MNC's presence in the host location and its impact on the local economy and employment levels a source of power within the social dialogue instigated by trade unions? Is the local subsidiary in an advantageous position to negotiate with headquarters due to the possession of critical resources that are key to the financial sustainability of the entire MNC? To what extent does the workers involvement become key to these negotiations between subsidiary and headquarters?
Power of processes	Refers to the latitude that actors enjoy to influence and recast the agenda, by ignoring or incorporating issues, and more specifically by formulating the rules of decision-making	What is the role of the workforce in managerial decision-making and what are the voice mechanisms available (i.e. to influence, facilitate or block the transfer of parent ER practices to a specific subsidiary)? Is there any form of co-determination as part of the decision-making in the dispersed units? Does the subsidiary partake of the development and formulation of ER practices globally, and to what degree do local managers rely on the workforce's views?
Power of meaning	Captures the ability by which some actors exercise domination over others 'by influencing, shaping or determining their very wants', oftentimes through 'the control of information', 'the mass media' and 'the process of socialisation' (p. 27)	Is the MNC involved in lobbying activities within the local economy? Is the MNC able to mobilise other ER actors such as community groups, NGOs, etc. to its own advantage directly or indirectly? Do non-union practices such as double-breasting undermine the power of trade unions within MNCs? Do these practices have an impact on the trade union agendas? Do trade unions take an opportunistic approach along with mass media resources to obtain public support and gain power in their negotiations with MNCs?

Source: Dundon et al. (2014); Geary and Aguzzoli (2016); Luke (2005)

MNCs as ER actors in the global arena

Originally, the well-established globalisation debate focused on the impact that MNCs may potentially have on the employment relationship. Two broad perspectives on how MNCs' behaviour will influence employment rights and obligations were advanced. Some scholars suggested that globalisation will undoubtedly impoverish labour standards as MNCs are continually seeking out cost minimisation, particularly in the least developed and regulated economies (Bartram et al., 2015 ; Morley and Collings, 2004; Royle, 2000). This has been termed the 'bleak house' or 'race to bottom' approach. In contrast, a more positive take on globalisation and labour benchmarks is adopted by some other scholars, who argue that globalisation has brought about constructive changes and new practices in the area of equality and diversity that have benefited society at large and some minority groups in particular. Further societal improvements were highlighted in the area of talent management, whereby talented staff with high potential from disavantanged countries have often taken advantage of alternative and prosperous career opportunies abroad (Bartram et al., 2015; Morley and Collings, 2004).

As research has moved forward, a good deal of different concerns around MNCs and their ER gained significance, namely: the global-local tension in the transfer of employment practices from the home country to the foreign operations; the home and the host country effects shaping ER practices; the strategic approaches towards ethnocentric, polycentric or global MNCs' international structure and its impact on ER practices; the 'Americanisation' of certain ER practices, such as a preference for non-unionism in voluntarist industrial relations systems and individual employment regulation; the incidence of European-style work councils in MNCs; and the extent of local subsidiary autonomy over IR practices (Almond et al., 2005; Belizón et al., 2014; Collings, 2008; Fenton-O'Creevy, Gooderham and Nordhaug, 2008; Geary and Aguzzoli, 2016; Gooderham, Nordhaug and Ringdal, 2006; Gunnigle, Lavelle and McDonnell, 2009; Marginson et al., 2010; Vo and Rowley, 2010). Recently, a relatively incipient line of enquiry has centred on the political interplays around the MNC, either between MNCs, the states and trade unions, or between the different units within MNCs, namely, between headquarters and subsidiary dispersed units (Ferner, Edwards and Tempel, 2012; Geary and Aguzzoli, 2016; Morgan, 2001; Williams and Geppert, 2011). This relatively novel angle to the study of the MNC and its ER practices enhances the understanding of the political dynamics and conflict of interests between different actors by portraying the MNC concomitantly as a *rule-taker* and *rule-maker* in constant interaction with other ER actors (Dörrenbacher and Geppert, 2014). In this vein, previous relevant debates are seen in the light of that somewhat contested space in which the MNC operates so that it becomes clearer what role MNCs have taken as actors in the IR systems in every nation, and to what extent their input and *modus operandi* have, *de facto*, challenged the position of the state and trade unions, by, in some cases, forcing new rules for the game (Lévesque et al., 2015).

MNCs as rule-takers

An extensive effort has been made on unearthing and comparing similarities and differences around unique and distinctive IR systems worldwide and on patterning how smooth or problematic it might become for MNCs to transfer their home employment practices to the different host locations (Almond et al., 2005; Almond and Ferner, 2006; Belizón et al., 2014; Fenton-O'Creevy, Gooderham and Nordhaug, 2008; Ferner et al., 2011; Pudelko and Harzing, 2007). This work constitutes a longstanding thread of contributions on several fronts. Ostensibly, not only has research consistently demonstrated that institutional pressures mould management practices but also that this is particularly prominent in IR. Studies of the MNC as *rule-taker* in the home country and the country of operations have been commonplace. The so-called home country effect refers to the impact of the country of origin's institutional settings on the employment practices pursued by the MNC overseas (Almond et al., 2005). National legislation on IR and employee voice, minimum wages, vocational training systems and diversity and equality matters have proven to have a particular impact on the international integration of employment practices as some MNCs attempt to transfer their home practices on the basis of fostering best practices in their foreign operations (Almond et al., 2005; Belizón, Gunnigle and Morley, 2013; Ferner et al., 2011; Geary and Aguzzoli, 2016). This is indeed the case of US MNCs operating in analogous liberal markets economies such as Ireland and the UK, where union avoidance becomes a feasible alternative (Ferner et al. 2011; Gunnigle, Lavelle and McDonnell, 2009; Lamare et al., 2013). In some cases, MNCs have opted for what has been termed 'double-breasting', which entails the cohabitation of unionised and non-unionised sites in the same host country (Lamare et al., 2013). This practice has been extensively adopted by US MNCs operating in Ireland and particularly so in the case of geographical expansion through green field investment.

These are examples of country-of-origin effects manifested in certain employment practices MNCs are able to pursue overseas by engaging in what has been termed 'institutional layering' (Geary and Aguzzoli, 2016; Streeck and Thelen, 2005, pp. 14–19), whereby MNCs bypass existing institutions in the host country, taking advantage of legal vacuums or 'spaces of uncertainty' (Ferner, Edwards and Tempel, 2012; Geary and Aguzzoli, 2016). Consider, for example, the union-free approaches to ER widely adopted by US MNCs (Dundon, 2002; Gunnigle, Collings and Morley, 2005; Gunnigle, Lavelle and McDonnell, 2009; Logan, 2006; Marginson et al., 2010). Union avoidance is possible in voluntarist IR systems where employers have considerable latitude to recognise union representation (or not) through a statutory provision of union recognition (Roche, 2001). In theory, at least, voluntarist IR systems allow employers to have differing preferences over the union representation structures established in their workplaces due to the management prerogative they enjoy. Examples of voluntarist IR systems are the American, British, Irish and Canadian. Oftentimes in these contexts, when employees have come together to engage in indirect representation union avoidance approaches on the part of MNCs can be also manifested in many ways, such as intimidation of workers willing to pursue union representation, substitution of unions with collective consultation channels, development of sophisticated human relations practices or disincentives to unionisation among others (Dundon, 2002). Country-of-origin effects of this sort can easily end up recasting the institutional arrangements of the host country, propelling MNCs into the host country as ruletakers and rule-makers concomitantly (Geary and Aguzzoli, 2016). Notorious has been the role of US MNCs' behaviour in reshaping public policy regulating union recognition in Ireland (Geary and Roche, 2001; Gunnigle, Collings and Morley, 2005). Nonetheless, the influence that MNCs can exert over institutional settings will most likely rely on the malleability of the national business system or the host country's institutional vulnerability to other economic actors' endeavours (Quintanilla, Susaeta and Sanchez-Mangas, 2008).

Non-unionism in MNC: bypassing the rules

Examining non-unionism in MNCs has been commonplace for researchers and practitioners since the beginning of the new millennium (Dundon et al., 2015; Gall and Dundon, 2013). Employer motives for non-union voice mechanisms are not only circumscribed by a preference for union avoidance but can be triggered by other logics, such as a strong focus on business objectives for growth or a deliberate strategy to create union-free spaces whereby an unitarist ideology favouring individual human resources practices and working conditions prevails (Dundon et al., 2015; Gunnigle, Lavelle and McDonnell, 2009; Roche, 2001). Non-unionist approaches are 'materialised' in many ways, such as a persistent resistance to union recognition (Gall, 2004; Marginson et al., 2010); the emergence of union avoidance practices through 'double-breasting' (Dundon et al., 2015; Gunnigle, Lavelle and McDonnell, 2009; Lamare et al., 2013) or the implementation of direct voice mechanisms aimed at the individual negotiation of working conditions and a smoother micro-management of the psychological contract between employer and employee (Dundon and Gollan, 2007).

Non-unionism in MNCs and home country effects

Country of origin matters when referring to union status and union avoidance approaches (Marginson et al., 2010). There are two apparent examples illustrating that the country wherein MNCs are headquartered will influence the management style used by local managers in their dealings with employee representation. British MNCs are generally known by the different approaches they have pursued in dispersed host locations such as the USA, Germany or Japan by adopting a chameleonic behaviour (Ferner et al., 2005; Tüselmann, McDonald and Heise, 2003; Wilkinson, Morris and Munday, 1993). On the other hand, US MNCs have left a strong legacy of non-unionism, particularly in countries where legislation allowed scope to take these approaches (Dundon, 2002; Gall and Dundon, 2013; Gunnigle, Collings and Morley, 2005; Gunnigle, Lavelle and McDonnell, 2009; LeRoy, 2006; Logan, 2006; Marginson et al., 2010). The latter case is indeed well documented. As Marginson et al. (2010, p. 155) note "there is a potential asymmetry between MNCs headquartered in countries such as the USA, with a tradition of anti-unionism, and those based in the countries of continental western Europe, which provide institutional and legal support to collective employee representation and consultation, in choice of voice practice in an institutionally permissive host environment such as the UK." Previous research on our topic has limited its scope to a small number of countries such as Germany, the UK, Japan or the USA. Although some existing research has treated Europe as a cluster of countries, little is known about how MNCs approach their employee representation policies in other parts of Europe besides the UK or Germany, and in other parts of the world (Marginson et al., 2010). Quantitative studies in the USA, UK, Ireland and Canada have also focused on employee voice and representation; less so on its absence. Previous research has called attention to the need for investigating the absence of employee representation – union and non-union – in less permissive host countries such as Spain, Italy or France (Ferner et al., 2005; Marginson et al., 2010). Taking stock of the evident intra-model variation that US-owned MNCs present, that is, variation in their employee representation approaches by sector of operations or size of the subsidiaries (Almond and Ferner, 2006; Ferner and Varul, 2000; Katz and Darbishire, 2000; Marginson et al., 2010), recent studies show evidence to argue that US MNCs still prefer non-union approaches while pursuing direct voice mechanisms in their operations located in Ireland and the UK, where non-unionism is permissible (Colling et al., 2006; Ferner et al., 2005; Marginson et al., 2010). Thus, variations in the approaches to employee representation are also shaped by the country of operations and its national labour market legislation, IR system and union legacy (Almond and Ferner, 2006; Fenton-O'Creevy, Gooderham and Nordhaug, 2008; Gall and Dundon, 2013). Referring to IR practices, scholars often talk about permissive host countries such as the USA, the UK or Ireland and about regulated host countries such as those in Southern Europe. There is increasing literature supporting the idea that MNCs pursuing union-free strategies in their country of origin are more likely to do so in their foreign operations located in permissive regimes than in more rigid host countries (Belizón et al., 2014; Dundon, 2002; Gall and Dundon, 2013; Gunnigle, Lavelle and McDonnell, 2009).

Non-unionism in MNCs and host country effects

Additionally, host country effects have been defined as "the degree to which MNC subsidiaries are embedded in national regulation in the host location. It does not only capture, as is sometimes implicitly assumed, the constraining (and enabling) influences of legislation or of national collective bargaining and representation structures, but also incorporates the societally informed rationality of host country managers" (Almond et al., 2005, p. 281). MNCs operating within the same environment tend to assume similar characteristics in conforming to local requirements (Kostova and Roth, 2002). Referred to as "isomorphism" by DiMaggio and Powell (1983), it has been employed as a lens in several studies examining policy and practice transfer issues in MNCs (e.g. Kostova, 1999; Kostova and Roth, 2002). Three types of isomorphism have been categorised: coercive, mimetic and normative. The first refers to practices that the host environment effectively forces firms to adopt, meaning that practices are imposed by a higher authority. The second type comprises specific practices employed because managers consider them useful in helping the MNC avoid some uncertainty facing the local scenario. The third type refers to the "conditions and methods" of a specific profession in the host environment, i.e. the way professionals develop their managerial tasks in a particular industry, shaped mainly by the local education system (DiMaggio and Powell, 1983). In light of these contributions, some scholars argue that foreign-owned MNCs adopt approaches aligned with the formal and informal rules and behaviours that characterise the host environment. In so doing, these foreign operations aim to achieve efficiency and legitimacy within the local institutional context (Kostova and Roth, 2002).

From an international business (IB) perspective, Kostova and collaborators developed a conceptual framework of the "institutional dualism" that subsidiaries experience (Kostova, 1999; Kostova and Roth, 2002; Kostova, Nell and Hoenen, 2016; Hauptmeier and Morgan, 2014). Institutional arrangements are viewed here in a broad sense as the elements of the external institutional environment in which the MNC operates, and include regulations, formal and informal norms, cultural schemas and language barriers, and social and political aspects (Kostova, Roth and Dacin, 2008). Their assumption implies that the greater the institutional distance (ID) between the home and the host country, the more intricate the integration of practices from headquarters to the subsidiary becomes. Building on this, some scholars have argued that MNCs originating in certain countries are more likely to transfer and implement corporate employment practices (e.g. US or Japanese MNCs). On the other hand, where foreign subsidiaries encounter highly regulated labour market regimes, the adaptation of local practices becomes necessary as an alternative to the transfer of employment practices from headquarters (Almond et al., 2005; Bélanger et al., 2013; Belizón et al., 2014; Ferner et al., 2011; Hauptmeier and Morgan, 2014). Thus the longstanding body of research exploring and analysing MNCs' behaviour in their home and host countries points toward the MNC as a rule-taker, abiding by the rules of the game in every external environment wherein they operate in order to seek survival.

There is a myriad of examples of MNCs adapting to the local IR systems worldwide, particularly in the areas of Europe and Eastern Europe where economies and labour markets are highly regulated (Hauptmeier and Morgan, 2014). Turning to our example of union avoidance approaches, it makes little sense to speak of union avoidance in non-voluntarist IR systems such as in Germany, France, Italy or Spain. There is very limited scope for union avoidance approaches, as understood by the Anglo-Saxon literature, in right-based IR contexts.

As Gumbrell-McCormick and Hyman (2006, p. 473) note "the notion of non-union employee representation, as the term is usually understood in the English-speaking world, has little resonance in most countries of continental western Europe". In right-based IR systems, social actors encounter a wide range of rights and responsibilities to which they have to respond (ibid.) and in particular, employers do not benefit from management prerogative. In the majority of western Europe, companies employing at least 50 workers are obliged to deal with employee representation – union or non-union – by statutory provision. This is the case in Germany, France, Italy, Spain and Portugal (Belizón et al., 2014; Gumbrell-McCormick and Hyman, 2006; Molina, 2014). Offering better conditions than those created by collective agreements at the sectoral, regional or national level that have been negotiated through the so-called social dialogue might potentially become the only means to bypass unions at the company level. Even in this scenario, 'absence of employee representation at company level' in western Europe would be a more suitable term than that of 'union avoidance', which is technically not possible due to legal constraints.

Non-unionism in MNCs and firm-specific factors

Criticism has arisen in response to an excessive focus on institutional effects in the study of employment practices in MNCs and on employee voice more specifically (Bechter, Brandl and Meardi, 2012; Lamare et al., 2013; Marginson et al., 2010). This criticism, along with a need to descend to the organisational levels where the transfer of employment practices occur, has led some scholars to explore firm-specific factors such as the sector of operations, the degree of diversification of product, the extent of subsidiary autonomy over employment practices and other aspects of the HR function. Understanding the importance of micro-level factors in MNC approaches to employee representation has become vital in recent research (Lamare et al., 2013).

At the subsidiary level, an increasing interest has been shown in the potential impact of the sector of operations on IR practices (Bechter et al., 2012; Lamare et al., 2013; Marginson et al., 2010; Meardi et al., 2009). First, legislation on employee representation is operationalised by sector of operations via sectoral collective agreements, which have a long pedigree in the history of IR in European countries such as Italy, Germany, France, Portugal and Spain. Second, much has been written about the high levels of unionisation in the manufacturing sector compared with those in the services (Lamare et al., 2013). These contributions show that MNCs in the services sector are more likely to report a greater use of non-union approaches than MNCs operating in the manufacturing sector. Diversification of product has been found to influence MNCs' approach to employee representation (Lamare et al., 2013; Marginson et al., 2010). In this sense, Marginson et al. (2010, p. 172) argue that MNCs focused on a single business are more likely to take non-union approaches while emphasising direct channels of employee representation. They also found evidence to state that MNCs diversified into related businesses are not so inclined to union avoidance approaches, and hence are more likely to have a wider variety of employee representation channels.

At departmental level, local management autonomy over union engagement has been identified as one of the aspects influencing union avoidance in MNCs operating in the UK, Ireland, Canada and Spain (Lamare et al., 2013). Subsidiaries and headquarters are often seen as the two sides of a political interplay in which each part seeks and defends their own interests (Bélanger et al., 2013; Morgan and Kristensen, 2006). Within this interplay, a centralisation approach habitually places subsidiaries in an inferior position caused by them having to implement policies that crystallise headquarters' expectations or being compelled to embrace policies transferred from the central office (Bélanger et al., 2013; Ferner, Edwards and Tempel, 2012). Lamare et al. (2013) posit that higher levels of subsidiary autonomy will facilitate the presence of unionised forms of employee representation, particularly in countries where employee representation practices prevail locally. Furthermore, individual-related HR practices have been linked to union avoidance due to their potential capacity to provide benefits beyond those offered by conventional employee representation (Roche, 2001). A handful of scholars have given recognition to the role of 'soft' individual-related HR practices in substituting or preventing unionised representation. However, some others have emphasised that this might only be the case in a minority of companies. As Roche (2001, p. 39) notes "the findings on the impact of 'soft' HRM practices on [union] recognition are inconclusive". These 'soft' practices are categorised into three areas where the practices are able to be individualised: pay, training and direct communication. Individualised practices foster a direct relationship between the employer and the employee, meaning the employee might not need the intervention of employee representation (ibid.).

Beyond institutional effects: MNCs as *rule-makers*

Scholars have perhaps overly focused on the effects of the home and host institutional settings on the employment practices used in MNCs (Almond et al., 2005; Batt et al., 2009; Collings, 2008; Ferner, Edwards and Tempel, 2012). Additionally, these accounts are "often founded on macro-data, and with only limited attention being accorded to internal diversity and details of actual practice" (Wilkinson, Wood and Deeg, 2014, p. 1). Research on MNCs and their ER has centred on elucidating to what extent the different institutional settings are conducive to re-shaping or blocking employment practices, but considerably less attention has been given to the power and political dynamics of the MNC as an ER actor. There is certainly a growing body of literature pointing towards a "relational, dynamic and multilevel explanation of institutional effects" (Geary and Aguzzoli, 2016, p. 3; Geppert and Dörrenbächer, 2014). Katz and Wailes (2014) have emphasised that explicating phenomena such as the global integration and localisation of employment practices in MNCs demands some detachment from rigid and static conceptualisations of institutions, allowing for the inclusion of change and the conflicting preferences and interests of the key actors and their power struggles. As a result of the dynamic complexity and scope of globalisation, MNCs are viewed not solely as mere ER actors but as socio-political spaces where decision-making takes place at different levels by a wider suite of ER actors, such as local managers and trade unions, local entities, community groups and agencies, and end users (Dörrenbächer and Geppert, 2014) – each of them pursuing different and often conflicting interests and making use of different power resources and capabilities to achieve their preferred ends.

First, MNCs viewed as ER actors are part of the work of Geppert, Ferner and other MNCs scholars who show evidence to argue that the external institutional arrangements are re-framed by the power and behaviour of MNCs and their pressurising lobbying activities in the home and host countries at macro and sub-national levels (Almond, 2011; Almond and Ferner, 2006; Dörrenbächer and Geppert, 2011; Ferner, Edwards and Tempel, 2012; Geary and Aguzzoli, 2016; Gunnigle et al., 2015; Kristensen and Zeitlin, 2005; Lévesque et al., 2015; Hauptmeier and Morgan, 2014; Morgan and Kristensen, 2006; Tregaskis et al., 2010). Second, academics and practitioners have witnessed the work, primarily of Dörrenbächer and Geppert, on the MNCs as a contested and co-operative space where ER practices are developed and transferred under different power dynamics, which is worth examining. They bring to our attention the fact that politicking, defined as the political manoeuvering of

ER actors, has largely been neglected in "international business and management literature, which sees power and politics in organisations as an exception, being nothing more than 'dirty business' preventing organisations from doing their normal work". This work has been complemented and subsequently reinforced by even more recent studies on the distribution of power resources and capabilities and how different actors are able to mobilise themselves to exert this power over others (Lévesque et al., 2015; Aguzzoli and Geary, 2014). This work has focused more specifically on the micro-level explanatory factors determining MNC engagement with trade unions at the company level. Some of the predictors of trade union engagement in MNCs identified by this literature are the distribution of the subsidiary's power and capability of its local managers, and the structural power of workers or the workers' associational power, among other factors.

Rapid changes in the external national settings in which the world of work takes place are the source of straining pressures on MNCs, trade unions and states across the globe, and they all need to evolve with the times, modifying their practices and policies (Kochan, 2004). Seemingly, the roots of these changes are obvious: the globalisation of best practices; advances in new technological equipment and processes; the demographic evolution of the population in different countries; and the decreasing role of workers in the manufacturing sector as they are overtaken by increasingly effective technology and digital devices. However, as Kochan (2004, p. 1) notes "these changes pose several additional questions: can these actors regain control over their destiny and over the destiny or performance of their industrial relations systems in light of changes in these external contexts?" Research prior to the global financial crises in 2008–2009 suggested that there are crucial moments in the history of economies, generally triggered by substantial economic downturns that propel economic actors to exercise their strategic freedom in order to seek survival in the complex and challenging aftermath of a financial recession. This is often translated into changes of institutions and their subsequent influence over the IR systems (ibid). This is also termed 'institutional plasticity' (Katz and Wailes, 2014), which relies on the assumption that institutional arrangements are not static but malleable to a certain extent. The emergence of new patterns of ER and their impact on social dialogue have been explained by several factors (Lane and Wood, 2009). First, the increasing implementation of neoliberalist and deregulation policies. Second, the escalating growth of FDI inflows in national economies are a clear source of diversity, both in terms of nationality and culture but also in management styles and different approaches to ER; new ideas and novel *modus operandi* transferred by MNCs are often able to bypass national regulations. Finally, the lack of political union among countries and their uneven pace of institutional changes results in a higher degree of diversity in national capitalisms, to which MNCs need to react in differing ways.

Against this backdrop, MNCs are also viewed as *rule-makers*. Some prominent scholars have posed that MNCs have the potential capacity to transform the context wherein they operate. Are MNCs able to inform macro-institutional settings? Do MNCs have the power to shape their environment by changing institutional arrangements or neglecting trade unions, and ultimately ignoring employee representation altogether? And if so, where do they source this power from? Not so long ago Kochan (2004) rhetorically reflected on the MNCs and other ER actors' capacity and volition to respond to changes in the environment. However, other authors are devoting their efforts to elucidating to what extent the environment is able to change as a response to MNCs' behaviour (Batt et al., 2009; Ferner, Edwards and Tempel, 2012; Geary and Aguzzoli, 2016). Ferner et al. reveal some relevant aspects around this topic in their attempt to complement the Kostovian, institutional approach. MNCs, key and active players in the globalisation process, have a relevant role and voice in the world economic system (Ferner,

Edwards and Tempel, 2012, p. 168) – but what are the macro implications of this role? What type of changes are MNCs able to instigate? Some scholars point to the capacity of MNCs to modify the rules of the economic game and, as Ferner et al. (2012) observe, to exercise power "at a systemic level through their ability to shape the decision-making rules governing international economic activity" (p. 168). For instance, Ireland is identified as a particular national case where the scale and influence of US MNCs has helped reshape the industrial promotion strategies to favour inward investment and to resist moves to strengthen regulations regarding collective employee representation and, especially, trade union recognition (Gunnigle, Collings and Morley, 2005). As Lévesque et al. (2015, p. 188) point out, "this shift in the balance of power has reinforced the capacity of MNCs to shape labour relations according to their interests and preferences, seemingly irrespective of institutional setting".

Prior to the economic recession, ER at the national level seemed to vanish among the political agendas and priorities of MNCs across the globe (Meardi, 2012). This is not precisely due to a growing general belief in a decline of the relevance of ER, as if economic actors operated on the assumption that ER are no longer needed as labour markets become flawless systems where workers are always respected (Meardi, 2014). Indeed, this fallacy has been rooted in the tenet that "work could be professionally managed, rather than socially negotiated" (Meardi, 2014, p. 2). Employment relations understood as the framework of social dialogue to solve social problems in the workplace was jeopardised by an attempt to reduce IR to direct negotiations between employers and employees by seeking common ground through the so-called best practices, and ultimately through collective bargaining at company level (Lavelle, Gunnigle and McDonnell, 2010). Many countries beheld low trade union memberships, while collective bargaining at the national level has been at stake not only in countries with longstanding liberal market economies but also in developing economies that were embracing neoliberal labour approaches, such as Mexico, Argentina and the nascent market economies from the east of Europe (Lévesque et al., 2015).

As Meardi (2012, p. 3) argues, "overall, multinational companies tend to comply with national collective bargaining structures: their collective bargaining coverage is the same, or even higher (in the case of the UK), than for the national average. However, MNCs do shift the balance of collective bargaining by being more active in company-level bargaining, which appears more pertinent to their product markets and organisation structures. In France and Spain, where sectoral collective agreements mostly limit themselves to setting relatively low minimum pay levels, MNCs can often easily afford higher pay levels and therefore find sectoral agreements, however binding, of little relevance – a point which undermines the political argument that the collective bargaining structure of these countries would hamper foreign direct investment."

The most disturbing and illustrative case of an MNC forcing its influence on a national IR system is that of Fiat in Italy in 2011, when the company closed two of its operations through legal channels and re-opened the two sites 'anew' so that the negotiations about their employment conditions were subsequently changed to suit its own interests. Trade unions, employer associations and the government in Italy responded to this with an agreement reforming the Italian IR systems to promote some forms of 'flexicurity', which overall benefited MNCs more than other social partners. Over recent years developing and developed economies have experienced a shift in trade union attitudes and approaches to collective bargaining at all levels, as unions have made substantial concessions on the conditions of employment, union rights inclusive, with a view to avoiding alternative detrimental consequences such as relocations or total site or division closures (Meardi, Strohmer and Traxler, 2013).

MNCs as contested spaces and the implications for employment relations practices

Turning to the micro level of analysis of employment relations practices in MNCs, two different forms of micro-political spaces have been identified (Dörrenbächer and Geppert, 2011; Geary and Aguzzoli, 2016). The first form refers to the relationship between head-quarters and subsidiary management, while the second encapsulates the political interplays between local managers and subsidiary employees. The variety of actors involved in this micro contested space, namely, headquarter and host country managers, subsidiary employees, and other economic actors from the local communities, engage in tussles over a diverse range of often conflicting interests and agendas, which rather implies a concious and strategic use of power. Simplistic considerations as to whether headquarters might hold a stronger position than their subsidiaries over time have been overcome. The locus of power (resources, processes and meaning) can be placed in the subsidiary in different fashions. For instance, the subsidiary might possess critical resources or occupy a relevant role within the global value chain, which will grant local managers a stronger voice in their negotiations and dealings with head-quarters (Bouquet and Birkinshaw, 2008). In other instances, it is up to the subsidiary to have the ability to gain power over processes through initiative taking and the reverse diffusion of employment practices, profile building, issue selling and lobbying activities (Bouquet and Birkinshaw, 2008; Dörrenbächer and Gammelgard, 2016; Dutton et al., 2001; Edwards et al., 2010; Gammelgard, 2009). Regarding how subsidiary managers can exercise a greater power of meaning, Kostova, Nell and Hoenen (2016) note that reducing local managers' bounded rationality would provide them with a more comprehensive understanding of headquarters' interests and intentions, which will ultimately have a positive impact on the outcomes of any policy transfer between corporate and local managers. In this vein, a low-bounded rationality of headquarters' wants and extensive knowledge and experience of navigating the local arena might provide local managers with the power to pursue their own interests and those of their workforce. Subsidiary power originating from resource, process and meaning forms has been positively associated with higher levels of subsidiary autonomy over employment practices (Dörrenbächer and Geppert, 2014; Gunnigle et al., 2015).

At the micro level, there is another power dynamic that remains crucial to contouring ER practices, namely the relationship between local managers and the subsidiary workforce (Geary and Aguzzoli, 2016). The nature of this relationship is particularly shaped by the nationality of the local managers (whether they are nationals, expatriates from the home country or come from third countries). This interplay will also have considerable influence on the degree of subsidiary power and autonomy in relation to headquarters (Dörrenbächer and Geppert, 2014). The transfer of employment practices from headquarters to local operations can be hindered by the oppo-sition and resistance of the host country workforce. This is very much so in the case of vested interests shared by local managers and the subsidiary's workforce. One of the direct sources of power in relation to local workers' involvement is their initiative in any of the subsidiary capabil-ities already discussed, particularly production processes or new employment practices. However, there is a call for workers and their representatives "to get involved in political processes and power struggles between corporate management and their subsidiary, as there is too much at stake for them: quality of work, levels of employee involvement and voice, and last but not least jobs" (ibid., p. 300). Workers and workers' representatives' involvement in the political and power interplays depends heavily on their knowledge of the local IR systems and their ability to build a robust toolkit based on the legal protection offered by the state (Dörrenbächer and Geppert, 2014; Williams and Geppert, 2011). Properly qualified workers with a legal education will be able to make better use of this toolkit to offer resistance to corporate intentions, as has been the case of MNCs operating in France and Finland. Additionally, workers' involvement in local initiatives might help leverage higher degrees of systemic power. Finally, one last determining factor enhancing workers' involvement in the power and political interplays in MNCs has been the presence of regional employee representation bodies such as an European work councils, which generally serve as a vehicle of support for transnational workers.

Conclusion

MNCs are active and powerful ER actors; they drive new patterns of employment relations practices and the diffusion of new practices into the lives of workers as well as into the institutional environments in which they operate in different locations (Geary and Aguzzoli, 2016). Hence, MNCs have proven to be active ER actors, changing the course of history of other ER across the globe, especially in the last few decades.

Changes driven and disseminated by MNCs are sometimes tempered by different national regulatory frameworks. However, research has shown substantial evidence of the endogenous power that MNCs are in fact exerting over national regulations in different business systems, some of which have been reformed and redesigned in response to MNCs' attempts (often successful) to avoid employee representation and their pressurising and lobbying activities. As discussed in this chapter, this is illustrated by the cases of US MNCs following non-union approaches, adopting 'double-breasting' practices and developing new individual HRM practices aimed at bypassing trade union engagement (Roche, 2001).

Future research should delve more deeply into the relational nested nature of the different levels of analysis of the MNC (Snape and Redman, 2010; Wilkinson, Wood and Deeg, 2014). An over-emphasis on single-level conceptualisations has directed research towards a biased view of the MNC as an ER actor, normally seen at the macro level. Research to date has been unable to identify the relative explanatory power of subsidiary capabilities or of workers' involvement in relation to the 'omnipotent' power of MNC headquarters, which pursue their preferred practices by bypassing and modifying legislation in different host locations. Revealing how different combinations of power interplay at the different levels of analysis might shed some more light on the actual role of MNCs in IR systems.

A potential line of enquiry also entails the study and theorisation of the interaction of MNCs and new ER actors, such as end users, governmental and private agencies, educational entities, NGOs, and community and religious organisations. As Cooke and Wood (2014, p. 11) argue, "not all new actors' involvement will lead to enhanced workers' conditions. Instead, they may weaken the regulatory capacity of host governments, and indeed lead to the dispossession of peasants and the erosion of the bargaining power of workers." The emergence of new interplays between some of these new actors and MNCs might redirect the current role of MNCs as ER actors. Future studies might concentrate on patterning how new ER actors are able to reshape MNCs' behaviour and employment practices.

References

Aguzzoli, R. and Geary, J. (2014). 'An "emerging challenge": the employment practices of a Brazilian multinational company in Canada', *Human Relations*, 67(5), pp. 587–609.

Almond, P. (2011). 'The sub-national embeddedness of international HRM', *Human Relations*, 64(4), pp. 531–551.

Almond, P., Edwards, T., Colling T., Ferner, A., Gunnigle, P., Müller-Camen, M., Quintanilla, J. and Wächter, H. (2005). 'Unravelling home and host country effects: an investigation of the HR policies of an American multinational in four European countries', *Industrial Relations: A Journal of Economy and Society*, 44(2), pp. 276–306.

Almond, P. and Ferner, A. (2006). *American Multinationals in Europe: Managing Employment Relations Across National Borders*. Oxford: Oxford University Press.

Bartram, T., Boyle, B., Stanton, P., Burgess, J. and McDonnell, A. (2015). 'Multinational enterprises and industrial relations: a research agenda for the 21st century', *Journal of Industrial Relations*, 57(2), pp. 127–145.

Batt, R., Holman, D. and Holtgrewe, U. (2009). 'The Globalization of Service Work: Comparative Institutional Perspectives on Call Centers', *Industrial and Labor Relations Review*, 62(4), pp. 453–488.

Bechter, B., Brandl, B. and Meardi, G. (2012). 'Sectors or countries? Typologies and levels of analysis in comparative industrial relations', *European Journal of Industrial Relations*, 18(3), pp. 185–202.

Bélanger, J., Lévesque, C., Jalette, P. and Murray, G. (2013). 'Discretion in employment relations policy among foreign-controlled multinationals in Canada', *Human Relations*, 66(3), pp. 307–332.

Belizón, M.J., Gunnigle, P. and Morley, M.J. (2013). 'Determinants of central control and subsidiary autonomy in HRM: the case of foreign-owned multinational corporations in Spain', *Human Resource Management Journal*, 23(3), pp. 262–278.

Belizón, M.J., Gunnigle, P., Morley, M.J. and Lavelle, J. (2014). 'Subsidiary autonomy over industrial relations in Ireland and Spain', *European Journal of Industrial Relations*, 20(3), pp. 237–254.

Bellemare, G. (2000). 'End Users: Actors in the Industrial Relations System?', *British Journal of Industrial Relations*, 38(3), pp. 383–405.

Berg, S., Gasmi, F. and Tavara, J.I. (2005). *Glossary for the body of knowledge on the regulation of utility infrastructure and services*. World Bank. Available at: http://regulationbodyofknowledge.org/glossary/.

Bouquet, C. and Birkinshaw, J. (2008). 'Weight versus voice: how foreign subsidiaries gain attention from corporate headquarters', *Academy of Management Journal*, 51(3), pp. 577–601.

Budd, John W. (2004). *Employment with a Human Face: Balancing Efficiency, Equity, and Voice*. Ithaca: ILR Press.

Colling T., Gunnigle, P., Quintanilla, J. and Tempel, A. (2006). Collective representation and participation, in Almond, P. and Ferner, A. (eds.) *American Multinationals in Europe*. Oxford: Oxford University Press.

Collings, D. (2008). 'Multinational corporations and industrial relations research: a road less travelled', *International Journal of Management Reviews*, 10(2), pp. 173–193.

Cooke, F.L. and Wood, G. (2014). New Actors in Employment Relations, in Wilkinson, A., Wood, G. and Deeg, R. (eds.) *The Oxford Handbook of Employment Relations: Comparative Employment Systems*. Oxford: Oxford Handbooks Online, pp. 1–13.

DiMaggio, P.J. and Powell, W.W. (1983). 'The iron cage revisited: institutional isomorphism and collective rationality in organizational fields', *American Sociological Review*, 48(2), pp. 147–160.

Dörrenbächer, C. and Gammelgard, J. (2016). 'Subsidiary initiative taking in multinational corporations: the relationship between power and issue selling', *Organisation Studies*, 37(9), pp. 1249–1270.

Dörrenbächer, C. and Geppert, M. (2011). *Politics and Power in the Multinational Corporation: The Role of Institutions, Interests and Identities*. Cambridge (UK): Cambridge University Press.

Dörrenbächer, C. and Geppert, M. (2014). 'Power and politics in multinational corporations: towards more effective workers' involvement', *Transfer*, 20(2), pp. 295–303.

Dundon, T. (2002). 'Employer hostility to union organising in the UK', *Industrial Relations Journal*, 33(3), pp. 234–245.

Dundon, T. and Gollan, P. (2007). 'Re-conceptualising non-union voice', *International Journal of Human Resource Management*, 18(7), pp 1182–1198.

Dundon, T., Dobbins, T., Cullinane, N., Hickland, E. and Donaghey, J. (2014). 'Employer occupation of regulatory space of the Employee Information and Consultation (I&C) Directive in liberal market economies', *Work, Employment & Society*, 28(1), pp. 21–39.

Dundon, T., Cullinane, N., Donaghey, J., Dobbins, T., Wilkinson, A. and Hickland, E. (2015). 'Double-breasting employee voice: an assessment of motives, arrangements and durability', *Human Relations*, 68(3), pp. 489–513.

Dunlop, J.T. (1958). *Industrial Relations Systems*. New York: Holt Rinehart and Winston.

Dutton, J.E., Ashford, S.J., O'Neil, R.M. and Lawrence, K.L. (2001). Moves that matter: issue selling and organizational change', *Academy of Management Journal*, 4, pp. 716–736.

Edwards, P.K. (2003). *Industrial Relations: Theory and Practice*. 2nd edn. Oxford: Blackwell.

Edwards, T., Edwards, P., Ferner, A., Marginson, P. and Tregaskis, O. (2010). 'Multinational companies and the diffusion of employment practices from outside the country of origin', *Management International Review*, 50(5), pp. 613–634.

Fenton-O'Creevy, M., Gooderham, P. and Nordhaug, O. (2008). 'HRM in US subsidiaries in Europe and Australia', *Journal of International Business Studies*, 39(1), pp. 151–166.

Ferner, A. and Varul, M. (2000). 'Internationalisation and the personnel function in German multinationals', *Human Resource Management Journal*, 10(3), pp. 79–96.

Ferner, A., Almond, P., Colling, T. and Edwards, T. (2005). 'Policies on union representation in US multinationals in the UK: between micro-politics and macro-institutions', *British Journal of Industrial Relations*, 43(4), pp. 703–728.

Ferner, A., Tregaskis, O., Edwards, P., Edwards, T., Marginson, P., Adam, D. and Meyer, M. (2011). 'HRM structures and subsidiary discretion in foreign multinationals in the UK', *International Journal of Human Resource Management*, 22(3), pp. 483–509.

Ferner, A., Edwards, T. and Tempel, A. (2012). 'Power, institutions and the cross-national transfer of employment practices in multinationals', *Human Relations*, 65(2), pp. 163–187.

Gall, G. (2004). 'British employer resistance to trade union recognition', *Human Resource Management Journal*, 14(2), pp 36–53.

Gall, G. and Dundon, T. (2013). (eds.) *Global Anti-unionism: Nature, Dynamics, Trajectories and Outcomes.* London: Palgrave Macmillan.

Gammelgaard, J. (2009). 'Issue Selling and Bargaining Power in Intrafirm Competition: The Differentiating Impact of the Subsidiary Management Composition', *Competition and Change*, 13(3), pp. 214–228.

Geary, J.F. and Roche, W.K. (2001). 'Multinationals and Human Resource Practices in Ireland: A Rejection of the 'New Conformance Thesis'', *International Journal of Human Resource Management*, 12(1), pp. 109–127.

Geary, J. and Aguzzoli, R. (2016). 'Miners, politics and institutional caryatids: accounting for the transfer of HRM practices in the Brazilian multinational enterprise', *Journal of International Business Studies*, 47(8), pp. 1–29.

Geppert, M. and Dörrenbächer, C. (2014). 'Politics and Power within Multinational Corporations: Mainstream Studies, Emerging Critical Approaches and Suggestions for Future Research', *International Journal of Management Reviews*, 16(2), pp. 226–244.

Gooderham, P.N., Nordhaug, O. and Ringdal, K. (2006). 'National Embeddedness and HRM in US Subsidiaries in Europe and Australia', *Human Relations*, 59(1), pp. 1491–1513.

Gumbrell-McCormick, R. and Hyman, R. (2006). 'Embedded collectivism? Workplace representation in France and Germany', *Industrial Relations Journal*, 37(5), pp. 473–491.

Gunnigle, P., Collings, D.G. and Morley, M.J. (2005). 'Exploring the Dynamics of Industrial Relations in US Multinationals: Evidence from the Republic of Ireland', *Industrial Relations Journal*, 36(3), pp. 241–256.

Gunnigle, P., Lavelle, J. and McDonnell, A. (2009). 'Subtle but deadly? Union avoidance through 'double breasting' among multinational companies', *Advances in Industrial and Labor Relations*, 16(1), pp. 51–73.

Gunnigle, P., Pulignano, V., Edwards, T., Belizón, M.J., Navrbjerg, S., Olsen, K. and Susaeta, L. (2015). 'Advancing Understanding on Industrial Relations in Multinational Companies: Key Research Challenges and the INTREPID contribution', *Journal of Industrial Relations*, 57(2), pp. 146–165.

Hauptmeier, M. and Morgan, G. (2014). Ideas and Institutions: The Evolution of Employment Relations in the Spanish and German Auto Industry, in Hauptmeier, M. and Vidal, M. (eds.) *Comparative Political Economy of Work*. Basingstoke: Palgrave Macmillan, pp. 162–185.

Katz, H.C. and Darbishire, O. (2000). *Converging Divergences: Worldwide Changes in Employment Systems.* Ithaca: ILR Press/Cornell University Press.

Katz, W. and Wailes, N. (2014). Convergence and Divergence in Employment Relations, in Wilkinson, A., Wood, G. and Deeg, R. (eds.) *The Oxford Handbook of Employment Relations: Comparative Employment Systems*. Oxford: Oxford University Press.

Kochan, T.A. (2004). 'Collective actors in industrial relations: what future? *Industrielle Beziehungen: Zeitschrift für Arbeit/ Organisation and Management*, 11(1), pp. 6–14.

Kostova, T. (1999). 'Transnational transfer of strategic organizational practices: a contextual perspective', *Academy of Management Review*, 24(2), pp. 308–324.

Kostova, T. and Roth, K. (2002). 'Adoption of organizational practices by subsidiaries of multinational corporations: institutional and relational effects', *Academy of Management Journal*, 45(1), pp. 215–233.

Kostova, T., Roth, K. and Dacin, M.T. (2008). 'Institutional Theory in the Study of MNCs: A Critique and New Directions', *Academy of Management Review*, 33(4), pp. 994–1007.

Kostova, T., Nell, P.C. and Hoenen, A.K. (2016). 'Understanding agency problems in headquarters-subsidiary relationships in multinational corporations: a contextualized model', *Journal of Management*. Available at: http://journals.sagepub.com/doi/10.1177/0149206316648383.

Kristensen, P.H. and Zeitlin, J. (2005). *Local Players in Global Games: The Strategic Constitution of a Multinational Corporation*. Oxford: Oxford University Press.

Lamare, J.R., Gunnigle, P., Marginson, P. and Murray, G. (2013). 'Union Status and Double-Breasting at Multinational Companies in Three Liberal Market Economies', *Industrial and Labor Relations Review*, 66(3), pp. 696–722.

Lane, C. and Wood, G. (2009). 'Diversity in Capitalism and Capitalist Diversity', *Economy and Society*, 38(4), pp. 531–551.

Lavelle, J., Gunnigle, P. and McDonnell, A. (2010). 'Patterning employee voice in multinational companies', *Human Relations*, 63(3), pp. 395–418.

LeRoy, M. (2006). 'The power to create or obstruct employee voice', *Socio-Economic Review*, 4(2), pp. 311–319.

Lévesque, C., Bensusán, G., Murray, G., Novick, M., Carrillo, J. and Gurrera, M.S. (2015). 'Labour relations policies in multinational companies: a three country study of power dynamics', *Journal of Industrial Relations*, 57(2), pp. 187–209.

Logan, J. (2006). 'The Union Avoidance Industry in the United States', *British Journal of Industrial Relations*, 44(4), pp. 651–675.

Lukes, S. (2005). *Power: A Radical View*. Basingstoke: Palgrave Macmillan.

Marginson, P., Edwards, P., Edwards, T., Ferner, A. and Tregaskis, O. (2010). 'Employee representation and consultative voice in multinational companies operating in Britain', *British Journal of Industrial Relations*, 48(1), pp. 151–180.

Morley, M. and Collings, D. (2004). 'Contemporary Debates and New Directions in HRM in MNCs: Introduction', *International Journal of Manpower*, 25(6), pp. 487–499.

Meardi, G., Marginson, P., Fichter, M., Frybes, M., Stanojevic, M. and Toth, A. (2009). 'Varieties of multinationals: adapting employment practices in central eastern Europe', *Industrial Relations*, 48(1), pp. 489–511.

Meardi, G. (2012). *European Industrial Relations Under International Pressure: A Six-Country Comparison*. Technical Report. Management & Business Studies. Economic and Social Research Council.

Meardi, G. (2014). 'The (claimed) growing irrelevance of employment relations', *Journal of Industrial Relations*, 56(4), pp. 594–605.

Meardi, G., Strohmer, S. and Traxler, F. (2013). 'Race to the East, race to the bottom? Multinationals and industrial relations in two sectors in the Czech Republic', *Work, Employment & Society*, 27(1), pp. 39–55.

Molina, O. (2014). 'Self-regulation and the state in industrial relations in Southern Europe: back to the future?' *European Journal of Industrial Relations*, 20(1), pp. 21–36.

Morgan, G. (2001). The multinational firm: Organizing across institutional and national divides, in Morgan, G., Kristensen, P.H. and Whitley, R. (eds.) *The Multinational Firm: Organizing Across Institutional and National Divides*. Oxford: Oxford University Press, pp. 1–24.

Morgan, G. and Kristensen, P.H. (2006). 'The contested space of multinationals: varieties of institutionalism, varieties of capitalism', *Human Relations*, 59(1), pp. 1467–1490.

Pudelko, M. and Harzing, A.-W. (2007). 'Country-of-origin, localization, or dominance effect? An empirical investigation of HRM practices in foreign subsidiaries', *Human Resource Management*, 46(4), pp. 535–559.

Quintanilla, J., Susaeta, L. and Sanchez-Mangas, R. (2008). 'The diffusion of employment practices in multinationals: 'Americanness' within US MNCs in Spain?' *Journal of Industrial Relations*, 50(5), pp. 680–696.

Roche, W.K. (2001). 'Accounting for the Trend in Trade Union Recognition in Ireland', *Industrial Relations*, 21(1), pp. 37–54.

Royle, T. (2000). *Working for McDonald's in Europe: The Unequal Struggle?* London: Routledge.

Snape, E. and Redman, T. (2010). 'HRM Practices, Organizational Citizenship Behaviour, and Performance: A Multi-Level Analysis', *Journal of Management Studies*, 47(7), pp. 1219–1247.

Streeck, W. (1997). 'Industrial citizenship under regime competition: the case of European work councils', *Journal of European Public Policy*, 4(4), pp. 643–664.

Streeck, W. and Thelen, K. (2005). Introduction: institutional change in advanced political economies, in Streeck, W. and Thelen, K. (eds.) *Beyond Continuity: Institutional Change in Advanced Political Economies*. Oxford: Oxford University Press, pp. 1–39.

Tregaskis, O., Edwards, T., Edwards, P., Ferner, A. and Marginson, P. (2010). 'Transnational learning structures in multinational firms: organisational context and national embeddedness', *Human Relations*, 63(4), pp. 471–499.

Tüselmann, H., McDonald, F. and Heise, A. (2003). 'Employee relations in German multinationals in an Anglo-Saxon setting: toward a Germanic version of the Anglo-Saxon approach?', *European Journal of Industrial Relations*, 9(3), pp. 327–349.

UNCTAD (2010). *World Investment Report: Investing in a Low Carbon Economy*. New York and Geneva: United Nations.

UNCTAD (2015). *World Investment Report: Reforming International Investment Governance*. New York and Geneva: United Nations.

Vo, A.N. and Rowley, C. (2010). 'The internationalization of industrial relations? Japanese and US multinational companies in Vietnam', *Asia Pacific Business Review*, 16(1), pp. 221–238.

Wilkinson, B., Morris, J. and Munday, M. (1993). 'Japan in Wales: a new industrial relations', *Industrial Relations Journal*, 24(4), pp. 273–283.

Wilkinson, A., Wood, G. and Deeg, R. (2014). Comparative Employment Systems, in Wilkinson, A., Wood, G. and Deeg, R. (eds.) *The Oxford Handbook of Employment Relations: Comparative Employment Systems*. Oxford: Oxford University Press.

Williams, K. and Geppert, M. (2011). Bargained globalization: employment relations providing robust "tool kits" for socio-political strategizing in MNCs in Germany, in Dörrenbächer, C. and Geppert, M. (eds.) *Politics and Power in the Multinational Corporation: The Role of Interests, Identities, and Institution*. Cambridge (UK): Cambridge University Press, pp. 72–100.

PART III

Core employment relations processes and issues

15

COLLECTIVE BARGAINING

Dionne Pohler

Introduction

Employment relations (ER) scholars have long recognised that fundamental conflicts of interest exist between employers and employees (Barbash, 1984; Commons, 1935; Webb and Webb, 1902). Industrial relations (IR) scholars in particular assume there is a structural imbalance of power in the employment relationship that favours the employer when individual employees attempt to negotiate over wages and working conditions (Kaufman, 2008). Collective bargaining can reduce this structural imbalance of power, but usually only when other institutional actors (i.e. governments) create rules to legitimise, rather than obstruct, it.

Collective bargaining in the context of ER can be succinctly defined as a process through which workers come together to negotiate with their employer(s) over terms and conditions of employment and/or the rules that will govern the processes that decide these same terms and conditions. Collective bargaining is a form of collective action among workers, though it is generally more structured than other forms of worker collective action. It involves negotiations, joint decision-making or joint regulation that results in formal and binding contracts, as opposed to looser and more flexible forms of consultation or joint problem-solving between employers and employees that are often employer-led (Doellgast and Benassi, 2014).

Collective bargaining takes place within a set of established rules and institutions; many countries have legislation that shapes its form and function, such as the Wagner Act in the USA or the legislative provisions in Germany supporting industry-level collective bargaining and extension of collective agreements. Direct participation by employees and employers in collective bargaining may occur, but the process is often undertaken by individuals or groups chosen to represent the interests of the respective parties (e.g. union leaders, management, employers' associations, etc.). In some circumstances collective bargaining may also include other parties to the employment relationship, such as tripartite arrangements involving government agencies. Elected officials may intervene in the collective bargaining process when public safety becomes a concern, though direct government intervention is often highly controversial. Government plays a unique part in public sector collective bargaining due to its multiple and sometimes conflicting roles as legislator and employer.

Collective bargaining has been recognised by the International Labour Organization (ILO) as a fundamental human right; however, constitutional and/or human rights protections for freedom of association among workers are notably absent, even in many developed countries. Advocates of the position that 'bargaining rights are human rights' have argued that all ILO member countries are required to ensure collective bargaining is not only recognised as a human right, but also legislated as a minimum employment standard; however, there is a long way to go to reach this goal (Adams, 2011). In practice, the standards, processes, structures and outcomes of collective bargaining vary greatly across countries due to a variety of different historical, legal, social, political and economic factors.

In this essay, I will develop a multi-level framework that identifies the critical variables required to understand the collective bargaining processes, structures and outcomes across different contexts, and discuss some of the research that has been done on the various aspects of this framework. The intention of this essay is not to be comprehensive, but rather to highlight the main developments and more recent research findings in an annotated and highly interdisciplinary review of the literature. I will then discuss issues that have received relatively short shrift, and in doing so have limited our understanding of collective bargaining across contexts.

Collective bargaining: elements of a framework

Figure 15.1 outlines a conceptual framework for understanding the IR institutions, structures and processes of collective bargaining, and its outcomes. This model has notable similarities and differences from previous IR frameworks. Two in particular deserve mention here: Dunlop's (1958) Industrial Relations Systems Model and Kochan, Katz and McKersie's (1986) Three-Levels of Industrial Relations Activities.

Dunlop's classic framework identified key factors affecting outcomes of the employment relationship: environmental forces, interactions between IR actors (labour, management and government) and the rules that are produced from these interactions to govern the employment relationship. Kochan, Katz and McKersie's strategic choice framework provided another major contribution to the field by highlighting the IR activities undertaken at different levels of analysis. They also brought agency to the forefront, emphasising the effect of actors' strategic choices on employment relationship outcomes.

The collective bargaining framework developed here elaborates upon many of the factors identified in these two seminal IR frameworks. However, both of these contributions were developed in the context of the American IR system, making them difficult to apply to understand collective bargaining systems across different countries, especially those with completely different sets of institutions.

While collective bargaining processes and outcomes are affected by rules, which are central to Dunlop, and the strategic choices and activities of actors at different levels, which are central to Kochan, Katz and McKersie, the following framework emphasises how the allocation of power shapes, and is shaped by, collective bargaining institutions, rules and processes, and also how allocations of power may change through the processes and outcomes of collective bargaining. My framework puts emphasis on the various sources of power in the employment relationship. Each of the framework's elements and processes are explored in turn.

Institutions

Many countries lack rule of law and thus basic IR institutions, or they have minimal legislative protections for workers. In these countries, collective bargaining at best is either absent or ad hoc, and at worst, results in deadly confrontations, often between workers and the state.

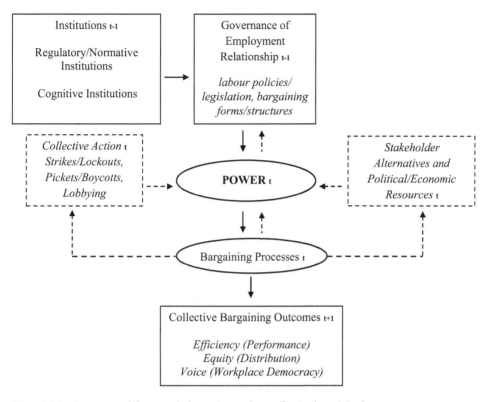

Figure 15.1   A conceptual framework for understanding collective bargaining[1]

In early 2014, police fired assault rifles at a crowd of striking garment workers in Phnom Penh, Cambodia, killing at least four people and injuring more than 20 others. These types of incidents are still quite common in countries at earlier stages of industrial development, and the patterns closely mirror what happened in the past as workers fought to improve their wages and working conditions in what are now fully industrialised countries. For instance, in 1919 in Canada, a general workers' strike in Winnipeg, Manitoba led to police brutality, ultimately resulting in the deaths of two people and over 40 injuries.

Regulatory and normative institutions

Some examples of institutions that impact collective bargaining structures and processes include the assignment of property rights that determine who owns the factors of production in society, the existence (or not) of human rights laws protecting freedom of worker association, labour/employment legislation that enables (or constrains) collective bargaining and industrial action, and normative expectations about worker treatment and what constitutes unfair labour practices. How these types of regulatory and normative institutions determine the governance of the employment relationship, and in particular, the existence, forms and structures of collective bargaining, has been extensively explored by comparative IR scholars and institutional economists.

Comparative IR scholars have proposed that there are broad archetypes of country-level institutions, and that variation across these archetypes has a substantive impact on collective bargaining outcomes. The following patterns and differences across many country-level institutions can be broadly summarised by this excerpt:

> According to the Varieties of Capitalism framework (Hall and Soskice, 2001), relative to liberal market economies, coordinated market economies have been characterised by greater legislative requirements for the employment relationship and government policies generally supportive of monitoring and sanctions for non-compliance, greater non-market arrangements, more strategic interaction between employers and different institutional actors, including Works Councils, industry-level bargaining over employment, and high unionisation rates (Marginson et al., 2013; Hall and Soskice, 2001). CMEs [coordinated market economies] have also been associated with greater normative expectations surrounding what is considered fair and responsible worker treatment (Doellgast, 2012). LMEs [liberal market economies] are generally characterised by highly decentralised labour markets and terms of employment agreed upon between employers and employees at the workplace level with relatively little government interference, subject to some minimum level of regulation (Colvin and Darbishire, 2013; Hall and Soskice, 2001)... .[employers] from liberal market economies may be more accustomed to unilaterally determining employment practices than [employers] from coordinated market economies.
>
> *Pohler and Riddell (2018)*

Notwithstanding the similarities across countries categorised into broader archetypes, scholars have cautioned against ignoring the variation that exists within these archetypes. For instance, Colvin and Darbishire (2013) have documented varying patterns of convergence and divergence across liberal market countries.

The Varieties of Capitalism framework is also limited for helping understand IR institutions from emerging economies. Countries in earlier stages of industrial development such as India, China and Taiwan are proposed to lack many basic employment laws and protections for workers. A recent OECD report cites many Asian countries as having lower employment regulations overall compared with developed countries (OECD, 2013). Notwithstanding these similarities, comparative research has also documented variation in IR institutions in the political economies of different Asian countries (Frenkel and Kuruvilla, 2002).

Cognitive institutions

Cognitive institutions are not as immediately visible as regulatory or normative institutions, and as such they have received less attention in the collective bargaining literature to date. However, cognitive institutions are no less important to understanding collective bargaining. Cognitive views of institutions highlight that institutions are socially constructed, and emphasise that individuals do not seek only to maximise benefits or to conform to society's normative expectations. In many circumstances, compliance occurs "because other types of behaviour are inconceivable; rules and routines are followed because they are taken for granted as 'the way we do these things'" (Scott, 2001, p. 57).

In practice, regulatory, normative and cognitive institutions are mutually reinforcing. Regulatory institutions formalise a particular set of societal norms and/or ways of viewing the world when they provide legal or other recourse for a particular set of rights (e.g. protection of private property), and thus legitimise the corresponding efficiency and distributional consequences of a particular power allocation. The efficiency and distributional consequences of this power allocation in turn influence future norms and ways of seeing the world, which may (or may not) lead to changes in future regulatory institutions. These institutions ultimately shape stakeholder power, incentives, identities and capacity for collective action.

Cognitive institutions also have an independent effect on governance of the employment relationship. For example, Canada and the USA share a very similar legislative framework for collective bargaining, yet the interpretation and practical application of the laws and regulatory framework are perceived through the lenses of vastly different world views that have been shaped by different histories, geographies, political ideologies, cultures and values of the actors in both countries (Colvin and Darbishire, 2013). Many Asian countries in earlier stages of development exhibit weak employment protection norms compared with more developed countries (Frenkel and Kuruvilla, 2002). Social norms greatly matter for how work is organised and how workers are treated at the workplace level (Doellgast, 2012).

Governance of the employment relationship: collective bargaining forms and structures

Governance of the employment relationship is the framework that determines which actors (e.g. employees, employers, governments, regulatory bodies) have the authority to participate in decision-making over employment factors (e.g. wages and working conditions, bargaining decision rules, conflict resolution processes), at what level (e.g. firm, industry, state, etc.), and through what forms and structures (e.g. unions, works councils, associations, etc.) If workers have no legitimate authority, and/or they cannot draw on informal sources of power to affect any of these decisions (to be discussed), collective bargaining is non-existent.

Collective bargaining forms and structures have a direct impact on the relative power of the parties, and thus the outcome of bargaining (Livernash, 1963). Given this, the design of bargaining structures is often a source of intense political debate and ongoing controversy between stakeholders in the employment relationship. The vast majority of research on collective bargaining forms and structures has focused on regions/countries that have more developed IR institutions, such as those in North America, Australia/New Zealand and Europe. While some research has been conducted on IR institutions and employment regulations in developing countries in Asia (Frenkel and Kuruvilla, 2002; Kim, Han and Zhao, 2014) and Central and South America (Amengual, 2014; Gindling, Mossaad and Trejos, 2015), English language research on many developing countries is still relatively scarce, particularly in mainstream IR journals. However, comparative IR work increasingly includes an examination of institutions and regulations across developing countries (Vadlamannati, 2015).

Collective bargaining forms and structures in countries that have been more widely researched can be categorised along a number of key dimensions. The dimensions that have received the most attention include the extent of collective bargaining coverage, the extent of union coverage, single-employer versus multi-employer bargaining, degree of bargaining centralisation, extent of coordination across stakeholder groups, and extent and type of government involvement in bargaining. Each of these dimensions is covered briefly.

Doellgast and Benassi (2014) document variation in legal provisions across OECD countries that provide for mandatory extension of collective agreements to firms and/or sectors that are more poorly organised. These provisions have had a major impact on both bargaining coverage and union density, though the two outcomes are not completely correlated. While they showed that union density has declined over the 20-year period from 1990–2010 in most OECD countries, there have been different trends in collective bargaining coverage. Countries that underwent changes to labour laws undermining union recognition and mandatory extension procedures, such as Australia, New Zealand, the UK and Portugal, have seen the greatest decrease in bargaining coverage, while others countries such as Belgium, Austria, Spain and the Netherlands have had bargaining coverage remain quite stable, or even increase (ibid.).

Single- versus multi-employer bargaining can be differentiated by whether individual employers negotiate agreements with workers or their representatives at the company/workplace level, or employers form associations to bargain with one or more unions and/or their associations (Jackson, 2005, cf. Doellgast and Benassi, 2014). Multi-employer bargaining also differs in the degree of centralisation (where national-, sectoral- or industry-level agreements regulate employment) and the extent of coordination across stakeholder groups, each of which is highlighted in turn.

At one time, IR scholars argued that a variety of economic, political and organisational factors were leading to a long-term historical trend toward greater bargaining centralisation and expansion of negotiating units (Kochan, 1980; Weber, 1967). While this trend has continued in countries like Italy (Baccaro, 2002), for most countries, the trend toward centralisation appears to have reversed (Doellgast and Benassi, 2014; Katz, 1993). Only a few OECD countries (e.g. Belgium, France, Germany and Ireland) are characterised by widespread national-, sectoral- and/or industry-level bargaining. Moreover, the tripartite social partnerships in Ireland collapsed in 2010 (Doellgast and Benassi, 2014) and German collective bargaining is only at the industry and sectoral levels. France does have both national-level collective bargaining, as well as industry-level agreements. In other continental European countries, as well as Australia and Israel, sectoral bargaining has been dominant, though Australia has shifted to predominantly enterprise-level bargaining in recent decades (Colvin and Darbishire, 2013). Local or company bargaining is the dominant structure in almost all Anglo-American countries, Slovakia, Poland, Estonia, Mexico, Chile, Japan and South Korea (Visser, 2011, cf. Doellgast and Benassi, 2014).

The degree of bargaining coordination generally refers to the extent to which company-level actors adhere to agreements reached by peak employer and labour associations. This depends on the levels of formal and/or informal control these associations are able to exert over other players. However, even in countries with few or no peak associations, little state intervention and greater decentralisation through company- or establishment-level bargaining, coordination can still occur. Often this takes the form of pattern bargaining, whereby agreements set by major bargaining agents from large firms or industries set the standard that other employers and unions follow.

Government plays a variety of roles in collective bargaining – and sometimes these roles can be in conflict. Government sets the labour policy, legislation and regulatory framework within which collective bargaining occurs (or does not), and its agencies enforce (or do not) these rules. Government may intervene in the collective bargaining process, such as when it legislates wage freezes in certain sectors or industries (often the public sector) or forces striking workers to return to work. Government agencies often oversee or play arbitration, mediation and/or conciliation roles in resolving conflicts between employers and employees. Government is also an employer, and negotiates over the terms and conditions of employment with public sector workers. It is in this role that government most often faces a direct conflict of interest.

The extent and type of government involvement in bargaining takes different forms across countries that exist on a continuum from voluntarism (very little state intervention in IR) to a tripartite model of social partnership (Katz, Lee and Lee, 2004). In countries like Italy, and in Ireland prior to 2010, government agencies were actively involved in the negotiation processes with employers and employees through centralised and tripartite arrangements (i.e. social pacts) to generate trade-offs between wage restraint, inflation and job creation. However, even in

Italy a substantial amount of variation still exists across industries and workplaces (Regalia and Regini, 2004).

When taken together, the permutations and combinations of the dimensions previously outlined result in almost as many different collective bargaining forms and structures as there are countries to examine, and the variation in forms and structures that exists within countries is likely as substantive as that which exists between countries.

There are also differences in the extent to which the different dimensions of collective bargaining forms and structures are legislated in any given country, and the extent to which various forms of collective bargaining and industrial action are encouraged or constrained by legislation. For instance, in Canada and Australia, there are many non-union associations that bargain collectively with employers over wages and working conditions (e.g. Kaufman and Taras, 2010), yet in the USA, non-union employee representation groups are not allowed under the Wagner Act, though they are under the Railway Labor Act (Kaufman, 2015). Some countries, such as Germany, have greater legislative requirements for worker co-determination – that is, workers play a greater role in company management.

Whether and the extent to which different dimensions of collective bargaining and/or particular forms and structures are enforced or protected through legislation raises an interesting question about whether legislative protections for collective bargaining are required for workers to be able to engage in 'meaningful' collective bargaining. Directly relevant to this question is the assumption about where the balance of power lies in the employment relationship – and specifically, whether it favours the employer. If it does, for employees to engage in 'meaningful' collective bargaining, whether unionised or not, they must have recourse to some credible threat mechanism (e.g. threat of unionisation, strike, substantial financial penalties imposed by a state regulator, mandatory interest or final-offer arbitration) to force the employer to bargain in good faith.

A recent Supreme Court judgement in Canada upheld this idea in principle, ruling that government legislation restricting public sector workers' right to strike in one Canadian province was in violation of public sector workers' constitutional right to freedom of association. The judgement stated that:

> Where good faith negotiations break down, the ability to engage in the collective withdrawal of services is a necessary component of the process through which workers can continue to participate meaningfully in the pursuit of their collective workplace goals.
>
> *(Supreme Court of Canada, 2015)*

Another chapter in this Companion covers important elements of regulation of ER in more depth. See also Gollan, Patmore and Xu (2014), who review and compare regulation of collective bargaining across the USA and Australia, including enforcement of "good-faith" bargaining and sanctions for unfair labour practices.

The type and extent of legislative protections matter greatly for rectifying any structural imbalance of power that exists between employers and employees, and ultimately for determining the form and structure of collective bargaining. For instance, empirical research has shown that specific legislative and regulatory provisions about union certification processes, recognition and security matter a lot for union certification success. Union certification success rates in one Canadian province declined by an average of 19 percentage points under a secret ballot voting regime versus a card-check procedure (Riddell, 2004), most likely due to management opposition and union suppression tactics (Riddell, 2001, 2004). Enforcing legislation that reduces election delays can mitigate some of this and increase certification success (Campolieti,

Riddell and Slinn, 2007; Riddell, 2010). In the USA, state-level right-to-work laws have arguably had a negative effect on union density in those states (Ellwood and Fine, 1987). Taken together, this research suggests that even relatively minor differences between legislative and regulatory provisions (and their enforcement) across jurisdictions can have a substantial impact on collective bargaining forms and structures, and thus the distribution of power between stakeholders.

Power

Central to this framework of collective bargaining is the distribution of power amongst key stakeholders. Power manifests itself formally through the set of institutions at the state and industry level that determine the authority and limits of different stakeholders to make decisions about the existence, forms and structures of collective bargaining, as well as the terms and conditions of the employment relationship. Power also manifests informally through: 1) leverage arising from the current distribution of economic/political resources to different stakeholders; 2) the broader economic context that determines the parties' reservation points and their best alternatives to a negotiated agreement; 3) the leverage that arises from the ability of different stakeholders to effectively solve their collective action problem; and 4) the way the bargaining process itself influences any of these sources of power. Formal sources of authority and informal sources of power ultimately determine who has a say in the decisions about the distribution of benefits, and through what processes – in other words, *who gets to decide what and how*.

The bargaining process

The negotiation process and its associated conflict resolution procedures is one of the central topics of interest for both scholars and practitioners interested in collective bargaining. There has been a plethora of theoretical and empirical work on negotiations, not to mention a substantial body of work that is focused on providing prescriptive advice to negotiators. This is not surprising, given that it is often the most visible part of the collective bargaining process.

Economists have provided substantial insights into general bargaining processes through the application of game theory. Game theory predicts whether negotiators will reach an agreement and what the particulars of that agreement will be by outlining the conditions that define how decisions will be made and attaching utility to all combinations of negotiator options (Bazerman and Moore, 2012). However, game theoretical models assume actor rationality, and thus predictions do not often hold up in real-world applications. Alternatively, decision-analytic approaches have focused on how rational negotiators *should* approach the bargaining process to both create shared value and to capture value. By understanding the structure of the situation, identifying each party's alternatives, interests and the relative importance of those interests, and working to avoid systematic decision-making errors and biases, it is argued that the parties can create value (i.e. maximise efficiency) while at the same time maximising their own distributive outcomes based on their relative bargaining power (Bazerman and Moore, 2012; Raiffa, 1982). This has been a major focus of scholars and practitioners engaged in the study and application of interest-based or mutual gains bargaining (Avgar and Owens, 2014; Kochan and Osterman, 1994).

However, three major problems plague the application of both game theoretic and decision-analytic approaches to understanding negotiations in collective bargaining. First, the complexity of the negotiations (e.g. multiple issues that include multiple parties) and uncertainty over future events make it virtually impossible to describe all options and accurately predict all associated outcomes. Second, individuals and groups do not consistently act in a rational manner, and are subject to a variety of decision-making biases that are extremely difficult to overcome. Finally, both the preferences and the bargaining power of each side are not necessarily fixed, as they ultimately depend on the strategies and bargaining power available to the other side, and how these are employed.

Scholars have responded to these limitations in predicting or explaining the outcomes of collective bargaining by examining how real people make decisions in real situations. Empirical research has explored the outcomes and effectiveness of different bargaining strategies and tactics, and pays detailed attention to the role played by communication and the characteristics of the negotiators (for a review, see Bazerman et al., 2000). This research further modifies assumptions about rationality by incorporating a wider range of theories from social psychology that better explain the observed outcomes of negotiation processes (Thompson, 2012). Researchers have also incorporated the role that emotion and affect play in negotiations (Kopelman, Rosette and Thompson, 2006; Kumar, 1997), given the role emotions have been found to play in overall judgement and decision-making (Bazerman and Moore, 2012).

Scholars have argued that collective bargaining works in reaching agreements through the facilitation of trade-offs through negotiations and the *threat* of resorting to industrial action, which predominantly comes from the parties' relative economic power (Cox, 1958). Notwithstanding this, institutional scholars have placed a great deal of importance on describing the role that historical, political, economic and institutional factors play in influencing the negotiation process and its associated outcomes. These factors directly influence the relative bargaining power of each stakeholder, level of trust between the parties and the social norms that impact the extent to which the parties perceive the need to engage in 'good-faith bargaining'.

Finally, there is a substantive literature on the role of dispute resolution in the bargaining process, such as the use of mediation, conciliation and arbitration, in attempting to come to an agreement between the parties (see another chapter of this handbook). Requirements to engage in these processes during negotiations and/or prior to, or in lieu of, industrial action (e.g. strikes or lockouts) by either party vary substantially both across and within countries.

Collective bargaining outcomes

A useful framework for categorising the outcomes of collective bargaining is Budd's (2004) presentation of the three primary objectives of the employment relationship: efficiency, equity and voice. Budd proposes that efficiency, equity and voice are mutually reinforcing and inextricably linked; however, it is in the inevitable situations where these objectives may conflict with each other that questions will arise about what the appropriate trade-offs should be. Collective bargaining institutions, forms and structures have an impact on all three of these employment relationship objectives, but the majority of empirical research on outcomes of collective bargaining has focused on the impact of unions.

Efficiency

Efficiency is a standard of economic performance that seeks to minimise waste through the most productive or effective allocation of scarce resources. Neoclassical economic theory suggests that collective bargaining, especially through unions, will lead to inefficiencies at both the firm and societal levels. Only firms in a monopoly position will be able to compete over the long term as unions generate wages for workers above market rates, unless all employers in an industry are unionised or employers respond by creating industry-level employer associations to take wages out of competition. Union wage increases may also lead to inflation and reduced employment at the societal level (Hayek, 1984; Lindbeck and Snower, 1986).

Institutional economists who founded the IR discipline (Commons, 1935; Webb and Webb, 1902), as well as many subsequent IR scholars, have been highly critical of the neoclassical model. These scholars argue that labour markets are imperfect and different from other factor markets on a variety of grounds, not least of which is the ethical consideration that labour is embodied in human beings and thus should be treated differently than other factor markets (Budd, 2004).

At the macroeconomic level, research has examined the extent to which tripartite or centralised bargaining has led to improved economic competitiveness and control of inflation across a variety of countries (Avdagic, Rodes and Visser, 2011; Molina and Rhodes, 2002; Regini, 2000). Many social pacts were once thought to have been beneficial in helping countries better respond to economic downturns; however, many of these pacts have not survived in more recent years (Katz, Lee and Lee, 2004). Country-level studies face a variety of endogeneity problems associated with linking collective bargaining institutions to outcomes, which can also lead to conflicting findings. For instance, some evidence suggests that more centralised systems and/or countries with a higher degree of bargaining coordination may be better able to control inflation and weather economic shocks, but countries with highly decentralised systems have also been linked to strong macroeconomic performance (see Doellgast and Benassi, 2014 for a more in-depth review of this research).

There has been a substantial amount of empirical research examining the role of collective bargaining in organisational performance, most of which has focused on the impact of unions on workplace- and firm-level outcomes. Indeed, unions have been linked to lower employment growth at the firm level (Long, 1993; Pohler and Luchak, 2015), and they have been found to have negative, slightly positive or non-existent effects on productivity depending on a variety of factors (Doucouliagos and Laroche, 2003, 2009).

However, collective bargaining may also have positive outcomes by providing an effective conflict resolution mechanism that promotes industrial peace and minimises the potential for more destructive and/or insidious conflict. Indeed, the vast majority of collective agreements are settled without parties resorting to any form of industrial action; however, these peaceful settlements do not receive as much media attention as striking workers.

Collective bargaining through unions can correct inefficiencies that arise from information asymmetries by getting worker input into production processes (e.g. Addison et al., 2000; Hübler and Jirjahn, 2003). By encouraging the development of internal labour markets, unions may also increase firm-level productivity and reduce costs by providing an efficiency wage, reducing shirking and turnover, and encouraging greater firm-specific investments by employees (e.g. Doeringer and Piore, 1971; Freeman and Medoff, 1984). Unions may also 'shock' management into finding cost-savings elsewhere (Slichter, Healy and Livernash, 1960). There is also recognition of the fact that unions by themselves are neither good nor bad for productivity or efficiency; rather their effect is contingent on the union-management-employee relationship and the type of work system in place (Hirsch, 2004; Pohler and Luchak, 2014, 2015).

Equity

Equity in employment relations encompasses fairness in the distribution of material outcomes as well as how workers are treated (Budd, 2004). With regard to the former, unions have been linked to higher wage and benefit premiums in Anglo-American countries (Budd and Na,

2000; Hildreth, 2000) and reduced wage inequality (Jacobs and Myers, 2014; Koeniger, Leonardi and Nunziata, 2007). Unions have also been linked to greater employee satisfaction and working less unpaid overtime, particularly when employees have access to voice through multiple channels (Pohler and Luchak, 2014).

In many cases, minimum employment and labour standards have only been adhered to because of the presence of a union. Indeed, there is research in economics and IR on compliance with employment laws in the US that documents unionised workplaces exhibiting higher compliance with regulatory provisions, including workers' compensation (Hirsch, Macpherson and DuMond, 1997), occupational health and safety (Weil, 1991) and employment/labour standards (Pohler and Riddell, 2018; Trejo, 1993). Unions also reduce employees' fear of speaking up due to the potential for retribution (Freeman and Medoff, 1984; Kaufman, 2004).

However, collective bargaining also has its disadvantages. Striking workers and other disruptions can pose health and safety concerns or major economic risks for the broader public (Raskin, 1967), though governments will often intervene in these cases. As previously mentioned unions have also been shown to increase inequality between unionised workers and other workers by lowering overall employment and creating unequal wage distributions and lower job security for non-unionised workers (Hayek, 1984; Lindbeck and Snower, 1986). However, this can be reduced by the presence of other collective bargaining laws and institutions, such as mandatory extension of collective agreements to non-unionised workers, more centralised bargaining institutions, higher minimum wages, and/or norms around worker solidarity and coordinated and inclusive bargaining (see Doellgast and Benassi, 2014 for a review).

Voice

Voice has been defined as the ability for employees to have meaningful input into decisions that affect their working lives (Budd, 2004). If we value workplace democracy, collective bargaining may be intrinsically valuable as a form of worker voice, whether or not it ultimately alters the distribution of material rewards. However, for collective bargaining to be a legitimate form of voice, it must also be accompanied by a mechanism that gives employees a credible threat, or a legitimate source of power that could, theoretically, alter the distribution of rewards by forcing the employer to make trade-offs to reach an agreement.

Collective bargaining matters as a form of 'meaningful voice' because it can actually change how workers are being treated or the distribution of their outcomes by giving voice to their concerns. In Nordic countries, where there are generally stronger participation rights and more encompassing bargaining institutions than in Anglo-American countries (Doellgast and Benassi, 2014), worker participation is greater, and workers have more autonomy and influence over their day-to-day work tasks (Esser and Olsen, 2012; Gallie, 2009). While collective bargaining institutions and processes are not the only access workers have to voice mechanisms (see Wilkinson et al., 2014 for a comprehensive review of voice mechanisms), it is the only approach that relies on both worker collective action and self-determination.

Research on grievance filing, however, suggests that employees may face retribution for using voice (Lewin, 1990). Moreover, even if employees make proactive suggestions, they will only speak up if they think it will make any difference, and they feel it is psychologically safe to do so (Morrison, 2011). While unions do not always eradicate management retribution for using voice (Lewin 1999; Lewin and Peterson, 1999), the ability for employees to voice concerns through a collective bargaining process may solve classic free rider and collective action problems. Recent research shows that encouraging employee voice may be more effective for both organisations and employees in the presence of a union (Pohler and Luchak, 2014).

Conclusion

There is an often implicit assumption in industrial relations research about the distribution of power in the employment relationship – that is, a structural imbalance of power exists favouring the employer when employees bargain individually over the terms and conditions of employment. Collective bargaining institutions may alter this structural imbalance of power, but only if they are paired with institutions and mechanisms that force the employer, and/or other parties to the employment relationship, to bargain in good faith. Thus, institutional actors (i.e. governments) must be careful to create rules to level the playing field between employees and employers by legitimising and encouraging collective bargaining and its associated mechanisms.

If society cares about the productive use of resources and macroeconomic performance (efficiency considerations), fair and equitable distribution of the fruits of labour to workers (equity considerations), and workers having some kind of meaningful input into decisions that affect their working lives because labour is ultimately embodied in a human being (voice considerations), then it is difficult to envision this society not ensuring a minimum level of protection for collective bargaining.

There is a paucity of research on IR institutions in developing countries, arguably because collective bargaining institutions are notably absent in many of these countries. However, collective bargaining institutions are also breaking down in many developed countries: union density is declining, tripartite arrangements are failing and bargaining is becoming increasingly decentralised. IR scholars need to conduct explorations into the novel approaches that workers are using in both developing and developed countries (if any) to address imbalances of power, and the effectiveness and outcomes of these approaches.

Research on cultural differences in understandings about collective bargaining processes would also be helpful in determining whether certain types of collective bargaining institutions are more or less effective, and/or are understood differently across cultures. Related, the role of cognitive institutions has not been explicitly incorporated into research on collective bargaining – most institutional IR research to date has focused on regulatory and normative institutions. However, cognitive institutions can be just as powerful in affecting worker treatment (good or bad), and maybe even more so than regulatory institutions in certain contexts, due to their "taken-for-grantedness" (Scott, 2001) and negligible cost of implementation.

Given the substantial variation that exists even within countries (i.e. within industries, sectors and even organisations), more research needs to be conducted on how collective bargaining plays out at the workplace level, and what types of variables complement and/or hinder effective collective bargaining.

While I attempted to do so in this review chapter, adopting a more comprehensive systems approach to understanding collective bargaining requires more detailed cross-level theorising of the individual, workplace, organisational, industry, sector, national and societal level factors that impact various components and processes of collective bargaining. This would be useful to disentangle what can most effectively be done, and at what level, to improve specific outcomes.

Finally, almost all collective bargaining frameworks discuss power, but explicit incorporation of power is generally lacking. Employment relations scholars should do more to theorise the antecedents and consequences of power in the employment relationship, including the various sources of power and the implications of different sources of power for the distribution of both material and social outcomes to stakeholders of the employment relationship. The framework developed here explicitly incorporates power into a dynamic process model of collective bargaining. Given the potential for IR institutions and rules and collective bargaining forms and structures to have a major impact on the distribution of power amongst stakeholders of the employment relationship, it is no surprise that these institutions, rules, forms and structures are sources of ongoing contestation and political struggles between stakeholders.

Scholars have recently proposed that the employment relationship is a major source of societal inequality, as this is where workers are allocated jobs and determinations are made about the distribution of rewards (Bidwell et al., 2013; Cobb, 2016). If the employment relationship is indeed where broader societal power struggles are played out, continuing to develop a better understanding of collective bargaining in this context will also yield greater insights into outcomes beyond the employment relationship.

Note

1 Note that the *t-1* variables are used in this model as initial conditions. Regulatory, normative, and cognitive institutions and governance structures are relatively stable – or the process through which they change takes a much longer period of time – and changes to these variables are directly tied both to the processes and outcomes of collective bargaining, as well as other political and societal processes such as changes in government or broader social movements. While the model is portrayed as fairly linear, in reality many of these processes operate simultaneously and are endogenous. As a result, feedback loops are employed in various places to capture some of the most important dynamics.

References

Adams, R. (2011). 'Collective bargaining as a minimum employment standard', *Economic and Labour Relations Review*, 22(2), pp. 153–164.

Addison, J., Siebert, S., Wagner, J. and Wei, X. (2000). 'Worker participation and firm performance: evidence from Germany and Britain', *British Journal of Industrial Relations*, 38(1), pp. 7–48.

Amengual, M. (2014). 'Pathways to enforcement: labor inspectors leveraging linkages with society in Argentina', *Industrial & Labor Relations Review*, 67(1), pp. 3–33.

Avdagic, S., Rodes, M. and Visser, J. (2011). *Social Pacts in Europe: Emergence, Evolution, and Institutionalization*. Oxford: Oxford University Press.

Avgar, A. and Owens, S. (2014). Voice in the mutual gains organization, in Wilkinson, A., Donaghey, J., Dundon, T. and Freeman, R. (eds). *The Handbook of Research on Employee Voice*. Cheltenham and Northampton (MA): Edward Elgar, pp. 327–341.

Baccaro, L. (2002). 'The construction of "democratic" corporatism in Italy', *Politics and Society*, 30(2), pp. 327–357.

Barbash, J. (1984). *The Elements of Industrial Relations*. Madison: University of Wisconsin Press.

Bazerman, M.H., Curhan, J.R., Moore, D.A. and Valley, K.L. (2000). 'Negotiation', *Annual Review of Psychology*, 51(1), pp. 280–314.

Bazerman, M.H. and Moore, D.A. (2012). *Judgment in Managerial Decision Making*. 8th edn. Hoboken: John Wiley & Sons.

Bidwell, M., Briscoe, F., Fernandez-Mateo, I. and Sterling, A. (2013). 'The employment relationship and inequality: how and why changes in employment practices are reshaping rewards in organizations', *The Academy of Management Annals*, 7(1), pp. 61–121.

Budd, J.W. (2004). *Employment With a Human Face: Balancing Efficiency, Equity, and Voice*. Ithaca: Cornell University Press.

Budd, J.W. and Na, I.G. (2000). 'The union membership wage premium for employees covered by collective bargaining agreements', *Journal of Labor Economics*, 18(4), pp. 783–807.

Campolieti, M., Riddell, C. and Slinn, S. (2007). 'Labor law reform and the role of delay in union organizing: empirical evidence from Canada', *Industrial & Labor Relations Review*, 61(1), pp. 32–58.

Cobb, J.A. (2016). 'How firms shape income inequality: stakeholder power, executive decision making, and the structuring of employment relationships', *Academy of Management Review*, 41(2), pp. 324–348.

Colvin, A. and Darbishire, O. (2013). 'Convergence in industrial relations institutions: the emerging Anglo-American model?' *Industrial and Labor Relations Review*, 66(5), pp. 1047-1212.

Commons, J. (1935). *History of Labor in the United States*. Vols. 3–4. New York: Macmillan.

Cox, A. (1958). 'The duty to bargain in good faith', *Harvard Law Review*, 71(8), p. 1409.

Doellgast, V. (2012). *Disintegrating Democracy at Work: The Future of Good Jobs in the Service Economy*. Ithaca: Cornell ILR Press.

Doellgast, V. and Benassi, C. (2014). Collective bargaining, in Wilkinson, A., Donaghey, J., Dundon, T. and Freeman, R. (eds.) *The Handbook of Research on Employee Voice*. Cheltenham and Northampton (MA): Edward Elgar, pp. 227–246.

Doeringer, P. and Piore, M. (1971). *Internal Labor Markets and Manpower Analysis*. Lexington: Heath Lexington Books.

Doucouliagos, C. and Laroche, P. (2003). 'What Do Unions Do to Productivity? A Meta-Analysis', *Industrial Relations: A Journal of Economy and Society*, 42(4), pp. 650–691.

Doucouliagos, C. and Laroche, P. (2009). 'Unions and profits: a meta-regression analysis', *Industrial Relations: A Journal of Economy and Society*, 48(1), pp. 146–184.

Dunlop, J. (1958). *Industrial Relations Systems*. New York: Holt, Rinehart, and Winston.

Esser, I. and Olsen, K.M. (2012). 'Perceived job quality: autonomy and job security within a multi-level framework', *European Sociological Review*, 28(4), pp. 443–454.

Ellwood, D.T. and Fine, G. (1987). 'The impact of right-to-work laws on union organizing', *Journal of Political Economy*, 95(2), pp. 250–273.

Freeman, R. and Medoff, J. (1984). *What Do Unions Do?* New York: Basic Books.

Frenkel, S. and Kuruvilla, S. (2002). 'Logics of action, globalization, and changing employment relations in China, India, Malaysia, and the Philippines', *Industrial and Labor Relations Review*, 55(3), pp. 387–412.

Gallie, D. (2009). 'Institutional regimes and employee influence at work: a European comparison', *Cambridge Journal of Regions, Economy and Society*, 2(3), pp. 379–393.

Gindling, T.H., Mossaad, N. and Trejos, J.D. (2015). 'The consequences of increased enforcement of legal minimum wages in a developing country: an evaluation of the impact of the Campaña Nacional de Salarios Mínimos in Costa Rica', *Industrial and Labor Relations Review*, 68(3), pp. 666–707.

Gollan, P., Patmore, G. and Xu, Y. (2014). Regulation of employee voice, in Wilkinson, A., Donaghey, J., Dundon, T. and Freeman, R. (eds.) *The Handbook of Research on Employee Voice*. Cheltenham and Northampton (MA): Edward Elgar, pp. 363–380.

Hall, P. and Soskice, D. (2001). *Varieties of Capitalism: The Institutional Foundations of Comparative Advantage*. New York: Oxford University Press.

Hayek, F.A. (1984). *1980s Unemployment and the Unions: Essays on the Impotent Price Structure of Britain and Monopoly in the Labour Market*. London: Institute of Economic Affairs.

Hildreth, A.K. (2000). 'Union wage differentials for covered members and nonmembers in Great Britain', *Journal of Labor Research*, 21(1), pp. 133–147.

Hirsch, B.T. (2004). 'What do unions do for economic performance?' *Journal of Labor Research*, 25(3), pp. 415–455.

Hirsch, B.T., Macpherson, D.A. and DuMond, J.M. (1997). 'Workers# x0027; Compensation Recipiency in Union and Nonunion Workplaces', *Industrial and Labor Relations Review*, 50(2), pp. 213–236.

Hübler, O. and Jirjahn, U. (2003). 'Works councils and collective bargaining in Germany: the impact on productivity and wages', *Scottish Journal of Political Economy*, 50(4), pp. 471–491.

Jackson, G. (2005). Contested boundaries, ambiguity and creativity in the evolution of German coordination, in Streeck, W. and Thelen, K. (eds.) *Beyond Continuity: Institutional Change in Advanced Political Economies*. New York: Oxford University Press, pp. 229–254.

Jacobs, D. and Myers, L. (2014). 'Union strength, neoliberalism, and inequality contingent political analyses of us income differences since 1950', *American Sociological Review*, 79(4), pp. 752–774.

Katz, H. (1993). 'The decentralization of collective bargaining: a literature review and comparative analysis', *Industrial and Labor Relations Review*, 47(1), pp. 3–22.

Katz, H.C., Lee, W. and Lee, J. (2004). *The New Structure of Labor Relations: Tripartism and Decentralization*. Ithaca: Cornell University Press.

Kaufman, B.E. (2004). 'What unions do: insights from economic theory', *Journal of Labor Research*, 25(3), pp. 351–382.

Kaufman, B. (2008). 'Paradigms in industrial relations: original, modern and versions in-between', *British Journal of Industrial Relations*, 46(2), pp. 314–339.

Kaufman, B. (2015). 'Divergent fates: company unions and employee involvement committees under the railway labor and national labor relations acts', *Labor History*, 56(4), pp. 423–458.

Kaufman, B.E. and Taras, D.G. (2010). *Employee Participation Through Non-Union Forms of Employee Representation*. Oxford: Oxford University Press.

Kim, S., Han, J. and Zhao, L. (2014). 'Union recognition by multinational companies in China: a dual institutional pressure perspective', *Industrial and Labor Relations Review*, 67(1), pp. 34–59.

Kochan, T. (1980). *Collective Bargaining and Industrial Relations.* Homewood (IL): Richard D. Irwin.

Kochan, T.A., Katz, H.C. and McKersie, R.B. (1986). *The Transformation of American Industrial Relations.* Ithaca: Cornell University Press.

Kochan, T. and Osterman, P. (1994). *Mutual Gains Bargaining.* Boston (MA): Harvard Business.

Koeniger, W., Leonardi, M. and Nunziata, L. (2007). 'Labor market institutions and wage inequality', *Industrial and Labor Relations Review*, 60(3), pp. 340–356.

Kopelman, S., Rosette, A.S. and Thompson, L. (2006). 'The three faces of Eve: strategic displays of positive, negative, and neutral emotions in negotiations', *Organizational Behavior and Human Decision Processes*, 99(1), pp. 81–101.

Kumar, R. (1997). 'The role of affect in negotiations an integrative overview', *The Journal of Applied Behavioral Science*, 33(1), pp. 84–100.

Lewin, D. (1990). 'Grievance procedures in nonunion workplaces: an empirical analysis of usage, dynamics, and outcomes', *Chicago-Kent Law Review*, 66(3), pp. 823–844.

Lewin, D. (1999). Theoretical and empirical research on the grievance procedure and arbitration: a critical review, in Eaton, A. and Keefe, J. (eds.) *Employment Dispute Resolution and Worker Rights in the Changing Workplace.* Madison: Industrial Relations Research Association, pp. 137–186.

Lewin, D. and Peterson, R.B. (1999). 'Behavioral outcomes of grievance activity', *Industrial Relations: A Journal of Economy and Society*, 38(4), pp. 554–576.

Lindbeck, A. and Snower, D. (1986). 'Wage setting, unemployment, and insider-outsider relations', *American Economic Review*, 76(2), pp. 235–239.

Livernash, E. (1963). 'The relation of power to the structure and process of collective bargaining', *Journal of Law and Economics*, 6(October), pp. 10–40.

Long, R.J. (1993). 'The effect of unionization on employment growth of Canadian companies', *Industrial and Labor Relations Review*, 46(4), pp. 691–703.

Marginson, P., Lavelle, J., Quintanilla, J., Adam, D. and Sanchez-Mangas, R. (2013). 'Variation in approaches to European Works Councils in multinational companies', *Industrial and Labor Relations Review*, 66(3), pp. 618–644.

Molina, O. and Rhodes, M. (2002). 'Corporatism: the past, present, and future of a concept', *Annual Review of Political Science*, 5(1), pp. 305–331.

Morrison, E. (2011). 'Employee voice behavior: integration and directions for future research', *Academy of Management Annals*, 5(1), pp. 373–412.

OECD (2013). *OECD Employment Outlook 2013.* (Online). Available at: http://dx.doi.org/10.1787/empl_outlook-2013-en.

Pohler, D. and Luchak, A. (2015). 'Are unions good or bad for organizations? The moderating role of management's response', *British Journal of Industrial Relations*, 53(3), pp. 423–459.

Pohler, D. and Luchak, A. (2014). 'Balancing efficiency, equity and voice: the impact of unions and high involvement work practices on work outcomes', *Industrial and Labor Relations Review*, 67(4), pp. 1063–1094.

Pohler, D. and Riddell, C. (2018). 'Multinationals' compliance with employment law: an empirical assessment using administrative data from Ontario, 2004–2015'. Forthcoming *at Industrial and Labor Relations Review*.

Raiffa, H. (1982). *The Art and Science of Negotiation.* Cambridge (MA): Harvard University Press.

Raskin, A. (1967). Collective bargaining and the public interest, in Ulman, L. (ed.) *Challenges to Collective Bargaining.* Englewood Cliffs: Prentice-Hall.

Regalia, I. and Regini, M. (2004). Collective bargaining and social pacts in Italy, in Katz, H., Lee, W. and Lee, J. (eds.) *The New Structure of Labor Relations.* Ithaca: Cornell University Press, pp. 59–83.

Regini, M. (2000). 'Between deregulation and social pacts: the responses of European economies to globalization', *Politics and Society*, 28(1), pp. 5–34.

Riddell, C. (2001). 'Union suppression and certification success', *Canadian Journal of Economics/Revue canadienne d'économique*, 34(2), pp. 396–410.

Riddell, C. (2004). 'Union certification success under voting versus card-check procedures: evidence from British Columbia, 1978–1998', *Industrial and Labor Relations Review*, 57(4), pp. 493–517.

Riddell, C. (2010). 'The causal effect of election delay on union win rates: instrumental variable estimates from two natural experiments', *Industrial Relations: A Journal of Economy and Society*, 49(3), pp. 371–386.

Supreme Court of Canada (2015). Saskatchewan Federation of Labor v. Saskatchewan, 2015 SCC 4, [2015]. 1 S.C.R. 245. (Online). Available at: www.canlii.org/en/ca/scc/doc/2015/2015scc4/2015scc4. html?autocompleteStr=saskatchewan%20fe&autocompletePos=1.

Scott, R. (2001). *Institutions and Organizations*. 2nd edn. Thousand Oaks: Sage Publications.

Slichter, S., Healy, J. and Livernash, E.R. (1960). *The Impact of Collective Bargaining on Management*. Washington, DC: Brookings Institution.

Thompson, L. (2012). *The Heart and Mind of the Negotiator*. 5th edn. Upper Saddle River (NJ): Pearson Education, Inc.

Trejo, S.J. (1993). 'Overtime pay, overtime hours, and labor unions', *Journal of Labor Economics*, 11(2), pp. 253–278.

Vadlamannati, K.C. (2015). 'Rewards of (dis) integration economic, social, and political globalization and freedom of association and collective bargaining rights of workers in developing countries', *Industrial and Labor Relations Review*, 68(1), pp. 3–27.

Visser, J. (2011). *ICTWSS: Database on Institutional Characteristics of Trade Unions, Wage Setting, State Intervention and Social Pacts in 34 countries between 1960 and 2007*. Amsterdam: Advanced Institute for Advanced Labour Studies.

Webb, S. and Webb, B. (1902). *Industrial Democracy*. New York: Augustus M. Kelley.

Weber, A. (1967). Stability and change in the structure of collective bargaining, in Ulman, L. (ed.) *Challenges to Collective Bargaining*. Englewood Cliffs: Prentice-Hall, p. 26.

Weil, D. (1991). 'Enforcing OSHA: the role of labor unions', *Industrial Relations*, 30(1), pp. 20–36.

Wilkinson, A., Donaghey, J., Dundon, T. and Freeman, R. (2014). *The Handbook of Research on Employee Voice*. Cheltenham and Northampton (MA): Edward Elgar.

16

EMPLOYEE VOICE

Conceptualisations, meanings, limitations and possible integration

Michael Barry, Tony Dundon and Adrian Wilkinson

Introduction

In the concluding chapter of a volume on employee voice, John Budd (2014) noted that interest in the subject matter has never been stronger. There are two points to make about this comment. First it is apparent that there is a burgeoning literature on voice, and second, that interest in voice is spread across a number of academic disciplinary areas. Voice research cuts across the academic discipline areas of industrial/employment relations (ER), labour process theory (LPT), human resource management (HRM) and organisational behaviour (OB), and even beyond these areas there is broader interest in voice in terms of workplace and political democracy (Budd, 2004; Budd and Zagelmeyer, 2010; Foley, 2014). However, while it seems that everyone has an interest in voice, research agendas and indeed core meanings and conceptualisations are very different. Across disciplinary boundaries, views about what voice is and how it should be examined diverge strongly. While there have been explicit efforts to draw research together in what are said to be integrative reviews of the field (Klaas, Olson-Buchanan and Ward, 2012; Morrison, 2011, 2014; Mowbray, Wilkinson and Tse, 2015), the research on voice remains stuck in self-contained and self-referential silos (Kaufman, 2015; Pohler and Luchak, 2014). Thus, a feature of voice studies is how little interest in or awareness there has been of developments in other fields (Wilkinson and Barry, 2016).

A key aim of this chapter is to explain how voice is conceptualised across disciplinary divides, and to highlight what can be gained from integrating different perspectives. In doing so the chapter notes that much work remains to be done. Recent OB reviews on voice have had a tendency to reinforce narrow disciplinary approaches to the study of the topic, based on looking at individual pro-social motivations for voice (see Klaas, Olson-Buchanan and Ward, 2012; Morrison, 2011, and critiques by Barry and Wilkinson, 2016; Mowbray et al., 2015). Equally, ER studies on voice maintain a preoccupation with indirect forms of collective voice, and have tended to exhibit a preference for voice through institutions such as union representation. The latter focus runs counter to the decline in unionisation, which has created a representation gap (Freeman and Rogers, 1999) and a need to explore alternative meanings of voice, through both indirect and direct mechanisms as well as informal avenues in which workers articulate a voice (Dundon et al., 2004; Marchington, 2015a; Wilkinson et al., 2004). This chapter will attempt to point to some possible ways that the disparate views on voice can be integrated. It concludes that the concept of stupidity management (Alvesson and Spicer, 2012) discourages employees from expressing a dissenting voice, which in turn can lead to inferior managerial communications and poor decision-making processes.

Untangling the meanings and conceptualisations of voice

If there is a common starting point for the analysis of voice it would appear to be Hirschman's (1970) work on exit/voice/loyalty. Hirschman defined voice as "any attempt to change rather than escape from an objectionable state of affairs". If Hirschman represents a common conceptual grounding for voice, even if his work was actually about consumers, contemporary studies are very much moulded by the distinct disciplinary boundaries and different actor interpretations of what voice means to them. At times other terms are used such as 'employee involvement', while others – often unitarist OB or HRM accounts – prefer to use terms like 'communication strategy', 'engagement' or 'empowerment', while more ER or LPT ideas draw on ideas of 'worker participation' or 'industrial democracy'. Additional ambiguities and alternative interpretations can exist when realising that voice across cultures and countries can differ considerably. In European Union member states, for example, a wide range of regulatory provisions exist that affect the dimensions of voice in both individual and collective ways (Dundon et al., 2014a). In contrast, in countries such as America, New Zealand or Australia there exists less regulatory prescription such as works councils or worker directors on company boards (Marchington, 2015b; Marchington and Dundon, 2017). Yet across and within these varying contextual backgrounds, there can and do exist further differences even within a single company, and dissonance of terms and practices can be compounded depending on the presence or absence of a trade union or what might be termed 'double-breasting' voice, where employers seek to restructure a workforce site or location along union and non-union voice arrangements (see Dundon et al., 2014b).

Thus the meanings for voice can differ widely across organisational-level practices and international boundaries, as well as between academic disciplinary perspectives. Indeed, there is no reason to assume that more voice necessarily leads to better voice outcomes, and there are valid arguments to assume a high degree of silence might prevail in an organisation, even where voice structures and systems may exist (at least on paper). For example, Donaghey et al. (2011) argue that by controlling internal voice mechanisms and setting the voice agenda on certain issues, management can engineer worker silence by manipulating voice mechanisms to minimise or exclude worker contributions to decision-making. The wide-ranging ambiguity concerning the various meanings of voice warrants a further unpacking of disciplinary perspectives of the fields of ER, HRM, LPT and OB.

OB Voice

In OB research there is a unitarist assumption of an alignment between the interests of workers and managers in voicing. It is assumed that workers want to speak up, to provide ideas and suggestions to management, and that management would want to capture voice because of its value to the firm. OB researchers focus on the micro-level 'antecedents' of voice by asking what factors prompt an employee to voice for the benefit of the organisation. In mainstream OB research voice is therefore portrayed as a 'prosocial behaviour', initiated by employees for the benefit of the organisation as a whole or their work unit. The highly cited and generally accepted OB definition of voice by Van Dyne and LePine (1998) sees voice as an extra role, discretionary, individual, communicative behaviour. Morrison (2011) has gone further in defining voice by saying that it is not about complaining. To do so would presumably not be of benefit to the organisation. That complaining is not voice is an interesting departure, given that OB scholars (as well as other discipline researchers) cite Hirschman as the foundational study of voice. For Hirschman, dissatisfaction was *the* trigger for voice. In Hirschman's study it was repeated consumer dissatisfaction that lowered customer loyalty, leading perhaps to exit (or to suffer in silence until more favourable conditions emerge or are introduced).

In the OB world, voicing is presented as a choice on the part of employees (it is discretionary behaviour), which occurs as an individual rather than collective action, and that generally takes place through verbal communication by an employee speaking up to a supervisor or higher-level leader. So voice is generally seen as informal rather than institutional. Of critical interest to OB are the antecedents of voice, which might be understood as key factors that would make employees favourably disposed to voicing, such as their own personal traits, as well as leadership style and employee perceptions of managerial openness. Receptiveness to voice can be seen as critical to the willingness of employees to speak up, by giving workers a sense that management is really interested in acting on voice, and that employees will feel safe that voicing will not lead to retribution (Pohler and Luchak, 2014).

While OB emphasises the antecedents of direct voice, there is little consideration of formal voice structures – and this is a critical difference between OB and ER. Indeed, in her review of the voice literature Morrison (2011) suggests that ER studies of voice should not be considered voice studies at all, because ER looked at voice structures rather than discretionary individualistic voicing behaviours. Accordingly, she excluded these studies because they did not match "current [OB] conceptualisations" (Morrison, 2011, p. 381). It is arguable, therefore, that OB interpretations about how to conceptualise voice create distinctive barriers with other academic boundaries and further constrain knowledge generation and dissemination given the narrow exclusivity of the OB academic space.

Within OB research there is also a small stream of work, labelled justice-oriented voice, which examines employee efforts to voice as a response to organisational failure or wrongdoing (Klaas, Olson-Buchanan and Ward, 2012). However, as Mowbray, Wilkinson and Tse (2015) point out, this is not the central tendency of OB research, which is very much dominated by the pro-social strand of voice. Moreover, it is important to note that the justice stream of voice in OB is not seen as a vehicle for the expression of employee views and interests, but more to do with exposing wrongdoing via actions such as whistleblowing. There is also a pejorative inference about employee behaviour that is not pro-social within this strand of OB. Thus in their review of the voice literature Klaas et al. (2012) referred to the "dark side" of employee voice, where employees attempt to exact revenge when they feel that management has violated the psychological contract. To some extent such approaches reflect a positivistic ontology predicated on seeking employee inputs 'for' management (or company) improvement, in which it is assumed that employee attitudes and behavioural traits can be easily managed or even manipulated through policy design (Dundon, Cullinane and Wilkinson, 2017).

HRM Voice

In HRM voice has a long history, with the notion that informing and allowing employees an input into work and business decisions can help create better decisions and more understanding, and hence commitment (Boxall and Purcell, 2003). This has been recently linked with efforts by employers to introduce high-performance work practices and HR systems to garner employee commitment (Wilkinson, Dundon and Marchington, 2013).

Since the mid 1990s high-performance work systems (HPWS) have come to prominence in HRM research, and this has given voice greater recognition in HRM, although there is earlier evidence of interest in voice with the employee involvement schemes of the 1980s and 1990s (Marchington et al., 1992). The logic is clear in that if HPWS provide jobs that are enriching for workers, then there is more likelihood that employees will want to participate in all aspects of their work, including by voicing in ways that enhance performance. Harley (2014) argues that the HPWS is now the dominant conceptual model for explaining the link between HRM and organisational performance, and voice occupies a central place in HPWS research. HPWS also have the potential to be seen as a means to benefit workers and even unions, and proponents have used terms such as mutual gains and partnership to describe how workers and their representatives can benefit from and play an active role in the adoption and implementation of these systems (Kochan and Osterman, 1994). Critics of HPWS might however argue that the performance effects are not as marked as proponents suggest. For example, the costs of adopting such systems can be much greater than is generally acknowledged (Godard, 2004), and outcomes such as improved employee satisfaction and affective commitment have been found wanting under HPWS regimes (Heffernan and Dundon, 2016).

HRM voice research shares a number of unitarist similarities with OB voice research. HRM is interested in management-led voice, and how efforts by management promote voice to enhance the bottom line. Employee input into decision-making is supported on the grounds that it is good for organisational performance. This is not to say that HR voice offers nothing for workers. The HPWS model incorporates a bundle of ER practices, such as employment security, performance-based wages, some level of employee autonomy, involvement in decision-making and skill development.

Consistent with OB, HRM research focuses primarily on direct rather than representative voice. Harley (2014) identifies three main components of direct voice from a HR perspective. These are firstly high-autonomy jobs, secondly the structuring of work into autonomous or semi-autonomous teams and thirdly that employees have access to communication channels that allow them to input into higher-level decision-making. Marchington (2008) provides a similar but somewhat broader categorisation of direct voice, comprising task-based mechanisms and upward-problem solving schemes (that support higher-level decisions), to which he adds complaints about fair treatment.

If these are the main mechanisms for HR voice, what is less clear is the extent of input employees are granted and over which issues employee input is allowed. Does voice mean that employees are simply informed about decisions that are taken by management, or is there genuine consultation prior to decision-making? These questions raise issues related to the depth of voice, which is defined as voice that occurs over a wide number of substantive employment issues and on a regular basis. Importantly, depth also means that employee input is influential in decision-making on matters that affect workers individually and collectively, for otherwise there can be voice without muscle (Kaufman and Taras, 2010) or trickle up voice (Wilkinson, 2015). The test of deep voice might be that there are a range of HR (and other) channels through which issues can be raised by workers and that matters raised are dealt with by line managers in a timely manner (Marchington, 2008).

ER Voice

The ER view of voice is very different from that found in OB, and similar to what has been defined as the employee-centric strand of HRM (Wilkinson, Redman and Dundon, 2017; see Harney et al., this volume). In part this reflects traditional differences of perspective between those fields, with ER adopting a critical view about the efficacy of pro-social voice and some HR studies questioning the validity of HR bundles as inherently or always performance-enhancing (Boxall and Macky, 2014). The ER perspective would see workers as having views and interests of their own, which can be expressed as a voice independent of the interests of the firm. Formal structures, such as unions, works councils and grievance procedures, would be seen by ER researchers as strong preconditions for promoting employee voice on employees' terms. Therefore employee-centric HR voice would be more likely to flourish in contexts where structures are underwritten by laws, labour market institutions and societal cultures that give employees formal rights to exercise voice, or indeed to co-determine work processes (Barry et al., 2014; Malos, Haynes and Bowal, 2003). It follows that pro-social voice, or management-led voice, would be more likely to be promoted in contexts where formal structures of employee voice are less socially embedded, weak or absent, and where employment relationships function on a predominantly individualistic basis.

ER studies of voice have been strongly guided by the approach taken by Freeman and Medoff (1984), which saw unions as the key institution of voice. Adapting the pioneering work of Hirschman on exit, voice and loyalty, Freeman and Medoff saw unions as providing workers with a formal voice that would act as a strong alternative to employee exit. Publication of Freeman and Medoff's book was the point at which voice started to be popularised in ER.

A key difference between ER and OB perspectives is the importance given, in the former, to the context surrounding the act of voicing. Context might include organisational and institutional considerations. Whether a firm has a deskilled assembly line process, or semi-autonomous teams of employees working together and problem solving, or whether there is high labour or capital intensity, high or low skilled employees, etc. are key organisational factors that might increase or decrease the likelihood of voice being promoted. For ER, whether there are unions present or absent at the workplace or industry level, or whether laws provide extensive or limited rights for workers to be consulted about organisational change, play as much, or more, of a role in promoting voice than the individual traits such as whether an employee is extroverted or a manager is receptive to employee voice (Kaufman, 2015). Marchington and Dundon (2017) usefully set out a range of contextual variables relevant across different liberal market economies (e.g. UK, Australia, Ireland and New Zealand), from macro-regulatory frameworks, labour and product markets, technology, intermediary forces such as employer groups and voluntary state agencies, down to the level of supervisory skills and management style and worker interests, to show how voice systems can be promoted or impeded by the alignment of these variables. The more highly coordinated regulatory frameworks, with higher skilled workers and greater employer commitment to involvement schemes, tend to produce conditions most likely to be strongly supportive of voice. This reasoning is consistent with literature which shows that employers and employees are incentivised to invest in high-involvement practices such as autonomy and skill development where workers are tied to long-term employment through employment security (e.g. Mares, 2003). Again, ER approaches tend to incorporate broader macro factors and institutional arrangements that play an important role in firm-level outcomes. In coordinated economies, collective bargaining produces greater standardisation of wages and conditions than in neoliberal free market economies and this allows for investment in training, skill development and decision-making inclusion because it acts as a disincentive to competitive poaching (Hall and Soskice, 2001).

LPT and voice

Labour process theorists would have some alignment to ER, especially the sociological disciplinary perspectives examining industrial democracy, workplace conflict and changing patterns of financialised capitalism and employment regulation (Ramsay, 1977; Thompson, 2013; and see Harley, this volume).

A key distinguishing feature of the LPT perspective is its critical stance concerning the extent to which employee voice can coalesce competing (even opposing) employer and employee interests. Marks and Chillas (2014) suggest that it is because of such a critical starting point that the LPT perspective offers a 'robust counter' to the OB and managerial HRM accounts of how voice is conceptualised and interpreted. The contribution of LPT to voice is the connection between workplace issues and the broader political economy in which corporations operate and function. Notwithstanding debate as to whether LPT is a theory at all, or an approach to study phenomena and issues (Jaros, 2000; Thompson and Vincent, 2010), as a disciplinary perspective it is shaped by an understanding of the broader political and economic structures of accumulation within a capitalist system. While Braverman's (1974) Marxist analysis of *Monopoly Capitalism* is a key intellectual anchor point for labour process contributions, much contemporary LPT analysis of voice is linked to Ramsay's (1977) 'cycles of control' thesis. In this, Ramsay argues that industrial participation or worker voice, at a macro level, is shaped by historical contingencies and power relations. In particular, when management's position of power and legitimacy is under threat from organised labour, employers offer more voice as a way to appease workers, only to renege or pull back on participation schemes when the threat to management authority has waned. However, Ramsay's (ibid.) thesis explaining voice vis-à-vis changes in broad conflict trends has been questioned as the cycle theory failed to predict newer 'waves of employee involvement' that emerged in the 1980s, along with more individualistic channels of voice and communication (see Ackers, 1992; Marchington et al., 1992).

Subsequent LPT debates picked up on these more individualistic voice practices – such as quality circles, team briefings and employee suggestions schemes – which emerged in tandem with declining union density and diminution of collective representative channels. Some of the later LPT contributions questioned the efficacy of newer voice development, in particular the potential for HRM and OB type arrangements to disguise issues of work intensification, with a shift in workforce responsibilities from management to the worker, adding to the latter's stress and work pressures (Thompson and Harley, 2007). Moreover, as Harley (this volume) articulates, LPT has added a particularly strong intellectual contribution that shaped debates on voice, engagement and worker participation with a unique critical flavour missing from other disciplinary approaches, especially as a corrective to the often unquestioning positivistic psychology of OB and some branches of HRM (Godard, 2014; Harley, 2015).

To summarise the key differences in disciplinary perspectives, we can safely say that in ER there is a concentration on the formal, structural and collective (i.e. representative) aspects of institutional voice. In LPT there is a critical realism that questions the upbeat and overly positive assumptions about alleged mutual gains or win-win outcomes for workers and employers from voice and engagement (Marks and Chillas, 2014). LPT is also more macro in its orientation, connecting institutions and workplace practices with broader socio-political patterns of capitalist accumulation that recognise struggle and contestation. Unlike OB research, there is also a strong sense that complaining (or dissent) is a vital part of voice – a countervailing power against managerial prerogative. For ER, voice is not firstly or primarily a pro-social behaviour. However, a criticism of LPT and ER is that they focus too heavily on voice as a form of dissatisfaction, with formalised structures seen as a necessary mechanism for employees to raise complaints and grievances (Barry and Wilkinson, 2016). Budd (2014) has pointed out this weakness, arguing that looking at voice as a form of dissatisfaction or conflict orientation tends to neglect the important role that voice plays in employee self-determination. For Budd (ibid.) voice needs to be linked to basic conceptualisations of the meaning of work, such that the desire for voice will be low if employees view work in negative or instrumental terms, and high where employees see work as part of their identity.

Limitations and possible integration

As we can see studies of voice have been heavily influenced by disciplinary traditions that have shaped core understandings of what is to be studied, with some disciplinary overlap and integration (Wilkinson et al., 2010, 2014). OB and HRM have accepted that there is a 'business case' for voice and are interested in how employee voice can enhance organisational performance. These studies appear to lack reference to the effectiveness of voice for employees, and assumptions about goal alignment do not greatly assist in evaluating whether management-led voice promotes employee interest in voicing. Research from ER and LPT raises an important distinction between opening up lines of communication on management's terms, voice leading to work intensification for employees and types of voice that actually allow employees to exert some influence over workplace decisions or engender a degree of silence. LPT and ER have, at times, the tendency to see voice as a potential countervailing check-and-balance against managerial power. In contrast, OB talks about voice being an extra-role, promotive behaviour. If voice is seen at all as challenging in OB terms, this tends to mean that employees offer suggestions so long as they lead to productivity enhancements, but not to challenge the underlying basis of management control.

On the other hand, ER researchers are keenly interested in the pluralistic value of voice. For them, voice reflects that employees have different interests to those of management, and is seen as a means to express employee interests as well as for employers to gain or maintain control over aspects of the work process. For ER, voice can be (and often is seen as) oppositional to management and organisational goals, rather than for the betterment of the organisation per se. As Kaufman notes (2015, p. 26), "central is the idea that employment relationships inevitably contain conflicts of interest among participants, and workers on moral and ethical grounds deserve voice to protect and promote their well-being".

From an ER standpoint, the OB conceptualisation of voice is excessively narrow, overly restrictive and biased towards management. Indeed Barry and Wilkinson (2016) labelled the OB conceptualisation of voice as being more accurately 'pro-management' rather than just pro-social. However, they also point out that ER could be similarly accused of being narrow in its interpretation of voice. So, just as OB has concentrated on the individual and relational aspects of voice, ER has been heavily focused on its structural and collective aspects. Moreover, there has been a view in ER that in the absence of a strong collective voice, employees are likely to be rendered powerless and silent. The implication here is that there is no voice without collective representation, when in fact silence may well be the result of a conscious decision to withhold voice, whether in a union or non-union setting (Cullinane and Donaghey, 2014).

Given what seems to be the gulf between these related disciplines, can there be an integrative view of voice that is accepted across ER, HRM, LPT and OB? Part of the difficulty of achieving integration is that in asking what the purpose of voicing is leads us into normative terrain, where disciplinary perspectives will lock voice scholars into very different viewpoints. As Barry and Wilkinson (2016) point out there is a strong unitarist view in OB, and to some extent HR, where what's good for the firm is seen as necessarily good for the worker. Here, voicing in a pro-social way for the betterment of the organisation or the improved performance of the work unit is not problematised. Also not questioned in OB research are fundamental desires on the part of employees and employers, such as whether employees actually want to contribute to organisational performance. As Marchington (2008) notes, whether in fact management actually want employees to be able to have a voice within the HR system is part of the debate. Brinsfield (2014, p. 128) raised exactly this point when he argued that OB researchers "need to thoughtfully question our paradigmatic assumptions around voice and silence, which may unwittingly constrain our thinking". Barry and Wilkinson (2016) also pointed to a larger problem with the OB voice conception – that it was gaining traction outside of OB, reaching into mainstream management journals, which meant that there was a danger that the OB conception was becoming *the* conception of voice (and thus, in its own way, being a form of integration). There seemed to be something perverse in the acceptance of a conception of voice for employees on terms determined by management interests (Donaghey et al., 2011).

If there is to be some integration it needs to be based on an acceptance that any conceptualisation of voice should incorporate the individual antecedents, relational attributes of actors and the broader institutional factors that are promotive or inhibitive of voice across multiple levels (e.g. transnational, national, intermediary, sectoral, organisational, work unit). As mentioned, many OB studies of voice do not consider the context around the act of voicing. The structural and systemic aspects of workplaces that promote climates of voice (or silence) are not well explored (Morrison and Milliken, 2000). The focus of OB studies is heavily weighted to the relationship between leader and member, and leadership style itself. Key questions interrogated in OB studies are how open to voice are leaders and do employees perceive leaders to be receptive to voice or do they fear retribution? These may well be important internalised reasons around a decision to voice or not, but too much is left to individual choice, without asking whether the presence or absence of voice owes more to broader institutions and factors beyond the organisational member. OB studies do not tend to identify wider contextual variables such as unemployment levels, labour laws or political/public policy objectives to encourage or discourage voice, and of course the presence or absence of workplace unions or other structures of employee representation that can promote voice. By contrast, ER studies can be seen as too heavily institutionalised and anchored in specific contextual settings. Here there has been a tendency to assume that anything less than the presence of an independent union isn't real voice. We know unionisation is declining and there are alternatives forms of indirect non-union employee representative (NER) voice as well as informal channels for workers to express concern (Cullinane et al., 2014; Marchington and Suter, 2013), but ER appears to have had an entrenched view of the superiority of union voice.

Studies that compare the effectiveness of voice systems in different institutional settings could be valuable in taking us past simplistic notions that equate the effectiveness of voice with individual attributes (as in OB) or the presence or absence of a particular structure of voice (as with ER). Doellgast (2008) examined voice practices in call centres in Germany and the US, comparing the institutional context of dual representation in Germany with unionised firms in the US. Her study emphasised that German practices were more aligned with the high-performance/high-involvement model, whereas US firms adopted management-led practices of reorganisation. The key difference in outcomes between similar firms in these two countries was the institutional support structures that gave workers, through works councils in Germany, rights to participate in decision-making. By comparison unions in the US were limited to enforcing job rules and so their influence did not extend to enabling worker participation in decision-making. In a comparative study of the impact of worker representative structures on voice outcomes in France and the UK, Marsden (2013) noted that the UK model tended to collectivise individual voice because of the close links between shop stewards and unions, whereas in France individual and collective voice more easily co-existed because of the institutional protection for works councils and the institutional separation of works councils and trade unions. This effectively meant that individual grievances could more easily be supported by management without the concern that they would necessarily spill over into matters of collective grievance or pay bargaining.

Table 16.1 Employee voice: theory, focus and philosophy

Theoretical strand	Indicative Voice Schemes	Voice Rationale	Form of Voice	Philosophy
HRM/HPWS	Focus groups; open door policy	Performance	Individual	Managerial/ unitarist: – Engender loyalty – Enhance performance
Political science	Workers on boards; joint consultation	Citizenship	Representative	Legalistic: – Democracy and rights-based
TCE	Dual (union and/or non-union) voice	Cost switching	Representative	Utilitarian: – Transaction efficacy
LPT	Collective bargaining; works councils; partnership;	Power & Control	Collective	Pluralist: – Power-sharing – Countervailing power
OB	Teamworking; sspeak-up programmes	Job design	Individuals and groups	Humanist/ unitarist: – Engagement; – Commitment;

Adapted from Wilkinson et al., 2014 p. 9

At the micro level a possible advancement to our understanding of the antecedents of voice is greater critical analysis of the motives that underlie decisions to voice or remain silent. While there is some limited acknowledgement within the OB literature of mixed motives (Van Dyne, Ang and Botero, 2003) there has not been much evidence of how those motives can be interpreted and disentangled. Employees might voice because they want to contribute to decision-making to enhance work unit and organisational effectiveness, but simultaneously they may wish to limit management control. Klaas, Olson-Buchanan and Ward (2012) note a scenario where employees voice in a pro-social manner to suggest that management formally assign work so as to improve efficiency, but to do so would limit the discretion of managers in allocating work and hence this voicing contains pro-social and power dimensions. Equally, individuals speaking up to suggest an improvement in a current process that might help others (i.e. be pro-social) might be primarily motived by a desire to create a positive impression of themselves for possible career advancement. As Barry and Wilkinson (2016) point out, the same act of voicing can be considered in OB definitional terms as both pro-social and not pro-social. The same logic can be applied to justice-oriented voice. An extreme example might be whistleblowing, which can be seen as loyalty to a firm if it is about exposing wrongdoing that would otherwise damage the organisation; however, if this wrongdoing is committed by management, it might be seen as an act of retribution or disloyalty.

Power and voice

Much of the preceding discussion has focused on the differences between the ER and OB views of voice. OB sees a world in which there are individuals choosing to voice (or to remain silent) to support and improve organisational decision-making. In the ER world there are workers who want voice to gain or maintain some control over organisational decisions, which they may well disagree with. As individuals, these employees are seen to either lack the power to exert an effective voice, or not seek to voice for fear that individual voice will lead to personal repercussions.

Given that ER sees employee voice as oppositional to management this raises issues of power and control. As Kaufman (2015) puts it, ER looks at the pie-sharing as well as pie-growing (which might be called the pro-social) aspects of voice. If pie-sharing starts to dominate the voice agenda – in other words, if employees want increased voice to leverage higher wages and better conditions – then this increases the cost of voice, and could provide a disincentive for management to supply or encourage it. Other factors could be important in this regard as well. Too much voice could lead to overload and thus complicate decision-making (Morrison and Milliken, 2003). Freeman and Lazear (1995) use a sporting analogy to convey the same point when they say that more time "huddling" (communicating) creates additional costs in that it slows down decision-making or, worse, can prevent management making a decision at a critical moment and lead to lost opportunities. In their analysis, for voice to be effective from a management perspective, the benefits of management obtaining voice must exceed the costs involved in the process and this would normally require workers to possess valuable information that managers could not otherwise obtain. This could be seen in economic terms as the transaction costs of voice (see Willman, this volume).

Another danger exists here for management. The provision of a limited voice could also give workers a greater appetite for voice, and lead them to seek stronger forms of voice if they remain unsatisfied with outcomes of voice that are delivered on management terms. A case study by Timur, Taras and Ponak (2011) showed that firms that had non-union collective voice structures became unionised in order to increase the power of workers so as to further their pre-existing claims. On the other hand, there is some evidence that collective and representative voice can improve performance compared with situations where collective voice is absent (Addison, 2005; Black and Lynch, 2001). In reviewing this literature, Harley (2014, p. 94) remained cautious as he noted that overall "there is a paucity of research on the role of collective voice, chiefly in the form of unions, in facilitating the introduction of HPWS and their capacity to deliver mutual gains."

In OB voice research there is less attention given to systematic issues of power. Hardy (1996) reminds us that a common problem with power is its negative perception. Power is often seen as that which 'A' holds over 'B', rather than the power to achieve something that comes when individuals act collectively. In the OB view of voice there is little need to consider power – for if A and B are both seeking to achieve the same goal then A does not need to use power to compel B to do anything. The OB view is that employees naturally want to voice in ways that benefit the organisation, and so power imbalance is not an issue. In their classic study of power, Bachrach and Baratz (1970) observed that power is not just that which is observed in open conflict over scarce resources: power is also used in non-decision making. The second face of power is the ability to keep issues (or voices) off the agenda. There are obvious implications for the OB view of voice. If management determines that permissible voice is that which is of benefit to the organisation, then issues that might bring workers into conflict with their supervisors or the organisation as a whole might be kept off the agenda (Cullinane and Donaghey, 2014, p. 403). If complaining is not deemed to be a legitimate form of voice, as per the Morrison (2011) definition, then grievance concerns of workers are off the voice table. Bachrach and Baratz (1970) discuss how decision-makers use power when they confine matters of debate to "safe issues". For example, managers may encourage speaking up if employees can suggest an improvement to a current process, but workers can be constrained or denied a voice when it comes to issues such as plant closure or redundancy. Royle's (1998) study described how management at McDonalds in Germany successfully circumvented the application of the European Works Council Directive so that voice would be confined to issues determined by the company.

In response to Bachrach and Baratz, Lukes (1974) advanced the notion that power relations can shape actor thinking concerning possible conflicts of interest. The third face of power is about the ability of a dominant hegemony to manipulate the preferences and interests of others, so that they do not perceive any conflict with the interests of those who hold power, nor do they see any alternative to the status quo. Hardy (1996, p. 8) identifies that system power "lies in the unconscious acceptance of the values, traditions, cultures and structures of a given institution and it captures all organisational members in its web".

The assumption that workers naturally want to voice in ways that benefit the organisation suggests a normative manipulation of employee interests and preferences consistent with Lukes'(1974) reasoning. The ER perspective suggests that employee voicing is aimed at maintaining or enhancing employee control over a work process, rather than improving the efficiency of that process. If employees are accustomed to performing a task in a certain way that gives them control over their work, or indeed gives their work greater meaning or dignity, then they would be highly unlikely to speak up to suggest a change that management would see as an improvement that streamlines the work process. Furthermore, if management suggested such a change it is likely that workers would speak up against the change, and seek to resist it if management sought to implement the change. In Roy's (1954) classic study of a machine shop the workers contrived to restrict output because they knew that if they worked more efficiently management would restructure pay rates so they would not be better off. Although the piece work payment system arguably worked against the notion of a HPWS, the point remains that workers perceived their interests to be opposed to those of management, which were to increase efficiency. The ER perspective seeks to capture this dynamic of power and control in understanding voice. Dundon et al. (2004) identified four manifestations of voice, one being collective representation, in which voice is a countervailing power to management and often occurs in this way through the agency of labour, whether unionised or not (Van den Broek and Dundon, 2012). Voice is a tool that employees can use to redress an inherent imbalance in power in the employment relationship. Voice provides capacity for involvement in and possible contestation of decision-making.

New directions and conclusion

The benefits of well-functioning voice systems appear profound. In a broad critique of management Alvesson and Spicer (2012) introduced the notion of stupidity management – decision-making that involves a lack of reflexivity and coherence, and leads to poor communicative processes. While on the one hand this type of unilateral managerial edict gives certainty in decision-making, the downside is that it marginalises critical or dissenting voices, which can reinforce conformity to current practices and in so doing embed stupidity. Functional stupidity stems from both an inability to question decision-making and a lack of accountability of managers to provide justifications for their decisions. Alvesson and Spicer (2012, p. 1200) claim that "Not requiring justifications allows practices to be accepted without any significant critical scrutiny or robust process of reason-giving… Refraining from asking for justification beyond managerial edict, tradition or fashion, is a key aspect of functional stupidity. It also results in the reproduction of problematic conditions and a shortage of what is sometimes referred to as 'voice' in the organisation."

Part of the issue seems to be that the perspectives on voice in OB are akin to ideal types and predicated on solving a problem for management. Thus, on the one hand, ER and LPT can be associated with voice as dissatisfaction and resistance, while some unitarist strands of HRM and OB view voice as a means to improve communication between goal-aligned parties so as to improve work processes and organisational performance. In their pure form all views provide only partial conceptualisations of a multifaceted phenomenon. The implication of stupidity management is that organisations need to seek out critical or dissenting voices as well as to create opportunities and find structures to support employees who wish to voice in ways that OB defines as pro-social. To that end ER and LPT offer the avenues for structural dissent to challenge a prevailing (managerial) status quo. Equally, there is good reason to suggest that assumptions that employees use voice to resist need greater nuancing. Courpasson, Dany and Clegg (2012) urge researchers to look at the effectiveness of resistance, and suggest that the ability to use resistance to achieve change depends on the skilfulness of resisters in identifying "objects of resistance" around which they can mobilise and influence management decision-making. These authors argue succinctly "that resistance can be better explained by what resisters do to achieve their ends rather than by seeing resistance as a fixed opposition between irreconcilable adversaries" (ibid., p. 801).

While the siloed nature of discipline-based research on voice means that the parties are in some ways poles apart, there is some evidence of interest in integration along the ER and LPT perspectives, in part due to the more critical employee-centric aspects of pluralistic nuances of HRM.

Acknowledgment

The authors would like to acknowledge the support of the Australian Research Council, DP 140100194.

References

Ackers, P., Marchington, M., Wilkinson, A. and Goodman, J. (1992). 'The use of cycles? Explaining employee involvement in the 1990s', *Industrial Relations Journal*, 23, pp. 268–283.

Addison, J.T. (2005). 'The Determinants of Firm Performance: Unions, Work Councils, and Employee Involvement/High Performance Work Practices', *Scottish Journal of Political Economy*, 52(3), pp. 406–450.

Alvesson, M. and Spicer, A. (2012). 'A Stupidity-Based Theory of Organizations', *Journal of Management Studies*, 49(7), pp. 1194–1220.

Bachrach, P. and Baratz, M.S. (1970). *Power and Poverty: Theory and Practice*. New York: Oxford University Press.

Barry, M., Wilkinson, A., Gollan, P. and Kalfa, S. (2014). Where are the Voices: New Directions in Voice and Engagement from around the Globe, in Wilkinson, A., Wood, G. and Deeg, R. (eds.) *The Oxford Handbook of Employment Relations: Comparative Employment Systems*. Oxford: Oxford University Press, pp. 522–540.

Barry, M. and Wilkinson, A. (2016). 'Pro-social or Pro-management? A Critique of the Conception of Employee Voice as a Pro-Social Behaviour within Organizational Behaviour', *British Journal of Industrial Relations*, 54(2), pp. 1–24.

Black, S.E. and Lynch, L.M. (2001). 'How to compete: the impact of workplace practices and information technology on productivity', *Review of Economics and Statistics*, 83(3), pp. 434–445.

Boxall, P. and Macky, K. (2014). 'High-involvement work processes, work intensification and employee well-being', *Work, Employment & Society*, 28(6), pp. 963–984.

Boxall, P. and Purcell, J. (2003). *Strategy and Human Resource Management*. Basingstoke: Palgrave Macmillan.

Braverman, H. (1974). *Labor and Monopoly Capital: The Degradation of Work in the Twentieth Century*. New York: Monthly Review Press.

Brinsfield, C. (2014). Employee voice and silence in organizational behaviour, in Wilkinson, A., Donaghey, J., Dundon, T. and Freeman, R.B. (eds.) *Handbook of Research on Employee Voice*. Cheltenham: Edward Elgar Publishing, pp. 114–131.

Budd, J.W. (2004). *Employment With a Human Face: Balancing Efficiency, Equity, and Voice.* Ithaca: Cornell University Press.

Budd, J. (2014). The future of employee voice, in Wilkinson, A., Donaghey, J., Dundon, T. and Freeman, R.B. (eds.) *Handbook of Research on Employee Voice.* Cheltenham: Edward Elgar Publishing, pp. 477–487.

Budd, J. and Zagelmeyer, S. (2010). Public policy and employee participation, in Wilkinson, A., Gollan, P.J., Marchington, M. and Lewin, D. (eds.) *The Oxford Handbook of Participation in Organizations.* Oxford: Oxford University Press, pp. 476–504.

Courpasson, D., Dany, F. and Clegg, S. (2012). 'Resisters at work: generating productive resistance in the workplace', *Organization Science*, 23(3), pp. 801–819.

Cullinane, N. and Donaghey, J. (2014). Employee silence, in Wilkinson, A. Donaghey, J., Dundon, T. and Freeman, R.B. (eds.) *Handbook of Research on Employee Voice.* Cheltenham: Edward Elgar Publishing, pp. 398–409.

Cullinane, N., Donaghey, J., Dundon, T., Hickland, E. and Dobbins, T. (2014). 'Regulating for mutual gains? Non-union employee representation and the Information and Consultation Directive', *The International Journal of Human Resource Management*, 25(6), pp. 810–828.

Doellgast, V. (2008). 'Collective Bargaining and High-Involvement Management in Comparative Perspective: Evidence from US and German Call Centers', *Industrial Relations: A Journal of Economy and Society*, 47(2), pp. 284–319.

Donaghey, J., Cullinane, N., Dundon, T. and Wilkinson, A. (2011). 'Reconceptualising employee silence problems and prognosis', *Work, Employment & Society*, 25(1), pp. 51–67.

Dundon, T., Wilkinson, A., Marchington, M. and Ackers, P. (2004). 'The meanings and purpose of employee voice', *The International Journal of Human Resource Management*, 15(6), pp. 1149–1170.

Dundon, T., Dobbins, T., Cullinane, N., Hickland, E. and Donaghey, J. (2014a). 'Employer occupation of regulatory space of the Employee Information and Consultation (I&C) Directive in liberal market economies', *Work, Employment & Society*, 28(1), pp. 21–39.

Dundon, T., Cullinane, N., Donaghey, J., Dobbins, T., Wilkinson, A. and Hickland, E. (2014b). 'Double-Breasting Voice Systems: an Assessment of Motives, Arrangements and Durability', *Human Relations*, 68(3), pp. 489–513.

Dundon, T., Cullinane, N. and Wilkinson, A. (2017). *A Very Short, Fairly Interesting and Reasonably Cheap Book About Studying Employment Relations.* London: Sage.

Foley, J. (2014). Industrial democracy, in Wilkinson, A., Donaghey, J., Dundon, T. and Freeman, R.B. (eds.) *Handbook of Research on Employee Voice.* Cheltenham: Edward Elgar Publishing, pp. 477–487.

Freeman, R. and Medoff, J. (1984). *What Do Unions Do?* New York: Basic Books.

Freeman, R.B. and Lazear, E.P. (1995). An econometric analysis of works councils, in Rogers, J. and Streeck, W. (eds.) *Works Councils – Consultation, Representation and Cooperation in Industrial Relations.* Chicago: Chicago University Press, pp. 27–52.

Freeman, R.B. and Rogers, J. (1999). *What Workers Want.* Ithaca: ILR Press.

Godard, J. (2004). 'A critical assessment of the high-performance paradigm', *British Journal of Industrial Relations*, 42(2), pp. 349–378.

Godard, J. (2014). 'The psychologisation of employment relations?' *Human Resource Management Journal*, 24(1), pp. 1–18.

Hall, P. and Soskice, D. (2001). *Varieties of Capitalism. The Institutional Foundations of Comparative Advantage.* Oxford: Oxford University Press.

Hardy, C. (1996). 'Understanding Power: Bringing about Strategic Change', *British Journal of Management*, 7(1), pp. 3–16.

Harley, B. (2014). High Performance work systems and employee voice, in Wilkinson, A., Donaghey, J., Dundon, T. and Freeman, R.B. (eds.) *Handbook of Research on Employee Voice.* Cheltenham: Edward Elgar Publishing, pp. 82–96.

Harley, B. (2015). 'The one best way? Scientific research on HRM and the threat to critical scholarship', *Human Resource Management Journal*, 25(4), pp. 399–407.

Heffernan, M. and Dundon, T. (2016). 'Cross-level effects of High-Performance Work Systems (HPWS) on employee well-being: the mediating role of organisational justice', *Human Resource Management Journal*, 26(2), pp. 211–231.

Hirschman, A.O. (1970). *Exit, Voice, and Loyalty: Responses to Decline in Firms, Organizations, and States.* Cambridge (MA): Harvard University Press.

Jaros, S. (2000). 'Labor Process Theory: A commentary on the debate', *International Studies of Management & Organization*, 30(4), pp. 25–39.

Kaufman, B. (2015). 'Theorising determinants of employee voice: an integrative model across disciplines and levels of analysis', *Human Resource Management Journal*, 25(1), pp. 19–40.

Kaufman, B.E. and Taras, D.G. (2010). Employee participation through non-union forms of employee representation, in Wilkinson, A., Gollan, P.J., Marchington, M. and Lewin, D. (eds.) *The Oxford Handbook of Participation in Organizations*. Oxford: Oxford University Press, pp. 258–285.

Klaas, B., Olson-Buchanan, J. and Ward, A-K. (2012). 'The determinants of alternative forms of workplace voice: an integrative perspective', *Journal of Management*, 38(1), pp. 314–345.

Kochan, T. and Osterman, P. (1994). *The Mutual Gains Enterprise: Forging a Winning Partnership Among Labor, Management, and Government*. Boston (MA): Harvard Business School Press.

Lukes, S. (1974). *Power: A Radical View*. London: Palgrave Macmillan.

Malos, S., Haynes, P. and Bowal, P. (2003). 'A Contingency Approach to the Employment Relationship: Form, Function and Effectiveness Implications', *Employee Responsibilities and Rights Journal*, 15(3), pp. 149–167.

Marchington, M. (2008). Employee voice systems, in Boxall, P., Purcell, J. and Wright, P. (eds.) *The Oxford Handbook of Human Resource Management*. Oxford: Oxford University Press, pp. 231–251.

Marchington, M. (2015a). 'Analysing the forces shaping employee involvement and participation (EIP) at organisation level in liberal market economies (LMEs)', *Human Resource Management Journal*, 25(1), pp. 1–18.

Marchington, M. (2015b). 'The role of institutional and intermediary forces in shaping patterns of employee involvement and participation (EIP) in Anglo-American countries', *The International Journal of Human Resource Management*, 26(20), pp. 2594–2616.

Marchington, M. and Dundon, T. (2017). 'The Challenges to Fair Voice', in D. Grimshaw, C. Fagan, G. Hebson and I. Travora (eds.), *Making Work More Equal*, Manchester University Press, pp. 90–107.

Marchington M., Goodman J., Wilkinson A. and Ackers, P. (1992). *New Developments in Employee Involvement. Employment Department Research Paper Series No 2*. HMSO, London.

Marchington, M. and Suter, J. (2013). 'Where Informality Really Matters: Patterns of Employee Involvement and Participation (EIP) in a Non-Union Firm', *Industrial Relations: A Journal of Economy and Society*, 52(S1), pp. 284–313.

Mares, I. (2003). 'The Sources of Business Interest in Social Insurance: Sectoral versus National Differences', *World Politics*, 55(2), pp. 229–258.

Marks, A. and Chillas, S. (2014). Labour process perspectives on employee voice, in Wilkinson, A., Donaghey, J., Dundon, T. and Freeman, R.B. (eds.) *Handbook of Research on Employee Voice*. Cheltenham: Edward Elgar Publishing, pp. 97–113.

Marsden, D. (2013). 'Individual voice in employment relationships: a comparison under different forms of workplace representation', *Industrial Relations: A Journal of Economy and Society*, 52(S1), pp. 221–258.

Morrison, E. (2011). 'Employee voice behavior: integration and directions for future research', *The Academy of Management Annals*, 5(1), pp. 373–412.

Morrison, E. (2014). 'Employee voice and silence', *Annual Review of Organizational Psychology and Organizational Behavior*, 1(1), pp. 173–197.

Morrison, E.W. and Milliken, F.J. (2000). 'Organizational silence: a barrier to change and development in a pluralistic world', *The Academy of Management Review*, 25(4), pp. 706–725.

Morrison, E. and Milliken, F. (2003). 'Speaking up, remaining silent: the dynamics of voice and silence in organizations', *Journal of Management Studies*, 40(6), pp. 1353–1358.

Mowbray, P.K., Wilkinson, A. and Tse, H.H. (2015). 'An integrative review of employee voice: identifying a common conceptualization and research agenda', *International Journal of Management Reviews*, 17(3), pp. 382–400.

Pohler, D.M. and Luchak, A.A. (2014). 'Balancing efficiency, equity and voice: the impact of unions and high involvement work practices on work outcomes', *Industrial & Labor Relations Review*, 67(4), pp. 1063–1095.

Ramsay, H. (1977). 'Cycles of Control: Worker Participation in Sociological and Historical Perspective', *Sociology*, 11(3), pp. 481–506.

Roy, D. (1954). 'Efficiency and "the fix": Informal intergroup relations in a piecework machine shop', *American Journal of Sociology*, 60(3), pp. 255–266.

Royle, T. (1998). 'Where's the beef? McDonalds and its European Works Council', *European Journal of Industrial Relations*, 5(3), pp. 327–347.

Thompson, P. and Harley, B. (2007). HRM and the Worker: Labour Process Perspectives, in Boxall, P., Purcell, J. and Wright, P. (eds.) *The Oxford Handbook of Human Resource Management.* Oxford: Oxford University Press, pp. 147–165.

Thompson, P. and Vincent, S. (2010). Labour process theory and critical realism, in Thompson, P. and Vincent, S. (eds.) *Working Life: Renewing Labour Process Analysis. Critical Perspectives on Work and Employment.* Basingstoke: Palgrave Macmillan, pp. 47–69.

Thompson, P. (2013). 'Financialization and the workplace: extending and applying the disconnected capitalism thesis', *Work, Employment & Society,* 27(3), pp. 472–488.

Timur, A., Taras, D. and Ponak, A. (2011). "Shopping for voice': do pre-existing non-union representation plans matter when employees unionize?' *British Journal of Industrial Relations,* 50(2), pp. 214–238.

Van den Broek, D. and Dundon, T. (2012), '(Still) Up to no Good: Reconfiguring the boundaries of worker resistance and misbehaviour in an increasingly unorganised world', *Relations Industrielles/Industrial Relations,* 67(1), pp. 97–121.

Van Dyne, L. and LePine, J.A. (1998). 'Helping and voice extra-role behaviors: evidence of construct and predictive validity', *The Academy of Management Journal,* 41(1), pp. 108–119.

Van Dyne, L., Ang, S. and Botero, I. C. (2003). 'Conceptualizing Employee Silence and Employee Voice as Multidimensional Constructs', *Journal of Management Studies,* 40(6), pp. 1359–1392.

Wilkinson, A. and Barry, M. (2016). 'Voices from across the divide: an IR perspective on employee voice', *German Journal of Human Resource Management,* 30(3–4), pp. 338–344.

Wilkinson, A., Gollan, P., Marchington, M. and Lewin, D. (2010). Conceptualising Employee Participation in Organisations, in Wilkinson, A., Gollan, P.J., Marchington, M. and Lewin, D. (eds.) *The Oxford Handbook of Participation in Organizations.* Oxford: Oxford University Press, pp. 3–25.

Wilkinson, A., Dundon, T. and Marchington, M. (2013). Employee Involvement and Voice, in Bach, S. and Edwards, M. (eds.) *Managing Human Resources: Human Resource Management in Transition.* Chichester: John Wiley & Sons Ltd, pp. 268–288.

Wilkinson, A., Dundon, T.J., Donaghey, J. and Freeman, R. (2014). Employee Voice: Charting New Terrain, in Wilkinson, A., Donaghey, J., Dundon, T. and Freeman, R.B. (eds.) *The Handbook of Research on Employee Voice.* Cheltenham: Edward Elgar Publishing, pp. 1–14.

Wilkinson, A., Redman, T. and Dundon, T. (2017). Human resource management: a contemporary perspective, in Wilkinson, A., Redman, T. and Dundon, T. (eds.) *Human Resource Management: Texts and Cases.* 5th edn. Pearson: London.

Wilkinson, A. (2015). Employee voice, in Wilkinson, A. and Johnstone, S. (eds.) *An Encyclopaedia of Human Resource Management.* Cheltenham: Edward Elgar.

17
KNOWNS AND UNKNOWNS IN THE STUDY OF WORKPLACE DISPUTE RESOLUTION

Towards an expanded research agenda

Alexander J.S. Colvin and Ariel C. Avgar

Introduction

Conflict is a pervasive and persistent feature of organisational life, with far-reaching implications for employer outcomes and employee well-being. As such, there is a great deal of potential value associated with institutionalised methods of dealing with workplace conflicts and disputes. The workplace dispute resolution landscape includes a wide array of vastly different organisational methods designed to deal with conflict. Dispute resolution scholars have provided a wealth of conceptual frameworks and empirical evidence on approaches to the resolution of organisational conflict. Nevertheless, alongside the knowledge generated by scholars across different disciplinary domains, there is much that is still unknown about workplace conflict resolution.

This chapter reviews central knowns and unknowns in the study of workplace conflict resolution. In doing so, we acknowledge the many advances made in this area of study while also pointing to research questions that, to date, have not been fully addressed or explored. With regards to knowns, the chapter reviews insights and empirical evidence from the study of conflict resolution in the unionised and non-union settings. This review summarises key knowns about unionised workplace grievance systems, the rise of alternative dispute resolution (ADR) and conflict management systems in the non-union setting, and the usage of and outcomes associated with these practices.

Alongside these important knowns, we also propose four areas of research that are still in need of conceptual and empirical development. First, we discuss the question of representation in conflict resolution. In the face of declining union density and the rise of individual employment rights regimes, there is still much that is not known about new models of providing employees with representation when making use of alternative methods to resolve conflict. Second, we maintain that there is also a need for additional research examining the organisational and individual outcomes associated with different conflict resolution methods. Evidence regarding the effects of different dispute resolution practices on a variety of firm and individual level outcomes is still lacking. Third, much of what we know about workplace dispute resolution is based on research conducted in the United States and Canada. We review the emerging body of comparative scholarship and highlight the need for additional research on other countries. Finally, almost all of the existing workplace dispute resolution research has been conducted in large organisations. We therefore call for additional conflict resolution research in small and entrepreneurial firms. Taken together, this review identifies key components of an expanded workplace dispute resolution research agenda.

Knowns in the study of workplace dispute resolution

Conflict resolution procedures in unionised workplaces

The effort to develop methods of resolving disputes has a long history in the field of labour and employment relations, dating back to some of the earliest public policy initiatives in the field. The initial impetus to develop dispute resolution mechanisms arose in the context of concerns about the negative impacts of rising industrial conflict in the late nineteenth and early twentieth centuries. As stronger union movements emerged in many countries, employer resistance to the new demands of organised labour produced a rise in the number, size and intensity of strikes, with correspondingly greater impacts of these disputes on the economy and society. In response, the experts of the day sought mechanisms that would provide alternative ways of resolving these conflicts, avoid their negative impacts and provide more rational, orderly ways of determining labour conditions.

A move towards using ADR methods to resolve labour disputes emerged in a number of countries around the same time. In New Zealand and Australia it took the form of the establishment of a system of public conciliation and arbitration of labour disputes (McCallum, 2007). Both countries established industrial relations (IR) commissions that would attempt to conciliate between the parties in the event of an industrial dispute. These commissions had the power to arbitrate the dispute in the event the parties were unable to reach a negotiated resolution. In North America, rising labour disputes in the early twentieth century also gave rise to experimentation with alternative mechanisms for resolving these disputes. In Canada, public policy put a strong emphasis on conciliation as a mechanism for resolving labour disputes (Taras and Walsworth, 2016). Meanwhile in the United States, public policy experimentation initially focused on the economically critical railway industry. This culminated in the 1926 passage of the Railway Labor Act, which established a National Mediation Board with authority to intervene in, and attempt to resolve, disputes in this industry.

Most of these early developments in dispute resolution focused on mechanisms for resolving interest disputes, where the parties were unable or unwilling to negotiate the terms of a collective agreement. By contrast, a major innovation in North American labour relations during the middle of the twentieth century was the widespread adoption of ADR mechanisms to resolve rights disputes concerning the implementation of collective agreements in the workplace. The system of labour arbitration that was developed represented one of the most distinctive and successful features of the Wagner Act model of labour relations adopted in the USA and Canada.

In the early part of the twentieth century, labour arbitration was used in certain American industries, notably in textiles, to resolve rights disputes where there was a claim that the provisions of a collective agreement were being violated. This use of labour arbitration to resolve rights disputes began to expand to other industries in the late 1930s and 1940s as unionisation increased rapidly in the United States. A key impetus to the spread of labour arbitration came during the Second World War, when wartime emergency labour legislation banned strike action and established a War Labor Board to administer labour relations during this period. The

War Labor Board encouraged unions and management to adopt labour arbitration provisions as part of their collective agreements as an alternative to strikes. By the late 1940s, labour arbitration procedures had been adopted in the vast majority of collective agreements as the mechanism for resolving disputes during the term of the collective agreement. The result was that in almost all cases, the strike weapon was confined to use in support of bargaining a new contract. This arrangement received the blessing and support of the US Supreme Court in its famous *Steelworkers Trilogy* of cases released on the same day in 1960. In these decisions, the court indicated that it would enforce labour arbitration provisions in collective agreements as a key component of industrial democracy in the workplace and the *quid pro quo* for the corresponding lack of strikes during the term of the contract clause.

In Canada, labour legislation of this era was patterned on the US Wagner Act model and unions and management similarly adopted labour arbitration as the mechanism for resolving rights disputes in the vast majority of collective agreements. Indeed, the trade-off of labour arbitration in return for the no-strike pledge became sufficiently entrenched in labour relations practice that Canadian labour laws require a provision to this effect to be incorporated into collective agreements (Taras and Walsworth, 2016).

If we look across union-represented workplaces in the United States and Canada today, we see a near universal adoption of a standard approach to conflict resolution. Collective agreements contain multi-step grievance procedures that provide for the resolution of rights disputes under the contract. These procedures begin with relatively informal attempts to resolve the grievance through discussion and negotiation, typically between a shop steward and a supervisor. In subsequent steps of the grievance procedure, successively high levels of union and management representatives review the grievance and attempt to negotiate a resolution to it. If these efforts are unsuccessful, the grievance is resolved through final and binding arbitration by a neutral labour arbitrator. There are some variations in the procedures. There may be three, four or five different steps. The specific individuals involved in each step of the grievance procedure will vary. Different time limits for each step will be used. But the striking feature is the similarity across the workplaces of the basic structure of the grievance procedures and the universality of labour arbitration as the final step of the procedure.

The stability of grievance procedures and labour arbitration in American workplaces is notable given the dramatic changes that have taken place in labour relations in recent decades. Union representation rates have declined steadily since the 1970s, with only 10.7 per cent of workers being members of unions in 2016 (Bureau of Labor Statistics, 2017). Strike rates and numbers of days lost due to industrial action have also declined dramatically over this same period (Katz, Kochan and Colvin, 2007). The nature of collective bargaining has also been transformed, with management increasingly taking the initiative to obtain concessions from unions in areas such as work rules, layoff protections and benefits. Yet throughout this period of major change in labour relations, workplace conflict resolution through grievance arbitration procedures has remained remarkably stable. What accounts for this relative stability in workplace conflict resolution? Although we do not have definitive research on this question, the best explanation appears to be the relative success of grievance procedures and labour arbitration as mechanisms for resolving workplace conflict and avoiding industrial action (Feuille, 1999). Both management and unions benefit from this system and so neither has an incentive to disrupt it.

This is not to suggest that there are no problems or weaknesses in the current system. The most commonly discussed problem is that of delay and cost in labour arbitration. It is common for a year or more to elapse before an arbitration hearing and decision can be obtained (Katz, Kochan and Colvin, 2007). Two major types of alternative procedures emerged as responses to concerns about the slowness and cost of labour arbitration. Expedited arbitration procedures attempt to speed up the process by establishing rules that include strict time limits, simplified hearing procedures and limited or no written reasons from the arbitrator. Meanwhile, grievance mediation is typically used as a step before labour arbitration and often involves a neutral body trying to mediate multiple cases on a single hearing day that is scheduled in advance, avoiding the scheduling complications that drive much of the delay in labour arbitration. Research on grievance mediation suggests that it is highly effective in resolving grievances at lower cost and with less delay than labour arbitration (Brett and Goldberg, 1983). Yet despite this success, Feuille (1999) has noted a paradox in that grievance mediation is still rarely used in comparison with the ubiquity of labour arbitration. The explanation he arrives at for this paradox is that despite concerns about delays in labour arbitration, the process of arbitration remains very robust in ensuring that the grievance will be resolved and the interests of the parties, particularly management, are protected. The result is that even as American labour relations in many respects is in an era of crisis with the precipitous decline of union strength, in the area of workplace conflict resolution, the grievance and labour arbitration procedures continue to be effective and successful in meeting the needs of the parties.

The rise of ADR in non-union organisations

Alongside research in the unionised setting, conflict resolution scholars have also documented one of the most fascinating and consequential workplace transformations over the past 35 years – the rise of alternative dispute resolution (ADR) practices in non-union firms. This research has contributed to a number of important knowns in the area of workplace dispute resolution. Beginning in the early 1980s, a growing proportion of non-union firms in the United States turned to a variety of internal dispute resolution techniques to address workplace conflict, thereby curtailing traditional approaches that rely primarily on managerial authority and litigation (for a review see Colvin, Klaas and Mahony, 2006; Lipsky, Seeber and Fincher 2003). These non-union firms began experimenting with a wide array of ADR procedures to address employment disputes within the boundaries of the organisation, such as peer review panels, mediation, arbitration and ombuds offices (Avgar, 2016; Colvin, 2003a; Colvin et al., 2006). The growing prevalence of and reliance on ADR represents an important reconceptualisation in the way non-union organisations approach and deal with workplace conflict and disputes, recognising that conflict is part of the fabric of organisational life (Avgar, 2015).

This dramatic restructuring did not go unnoticed by scholars interested in workplace dispute resolution. Researchers applying different disciplinary lenses, including IR, law and sociology, paid careful attention to this development, capturing the central contours of the practices being adopted and identifying the drivers at the heart of this important organisational transformation (Avgar et al., 2013; Bendersky, 2007; Colvin, 2003a; Eigen and Litwin, 2014; Ewing, 1989; Lewin, 1987; Lipsky and Avgar, 2008; Lipsky, Avgar and Lamare, 2014; McCabe, 1988; Westin and Feliu, 1988). This body of research has contributed a great deal of ADR-related knowledge. First, this scholarship has painted a detailed portrait of the rise of ADR and the nature of the various practices adopted by organisations. For example, Lipsky and colleagues (2003) studied usage patterns of different ADR practices, highlighting the widespread use of many of these within Fortune 1000 firms. Similarly, Colvin (2003a) documented the use of ADR within the telecommunications industry. What we know from this body of research is that ADR has gained a strong foothold within a sizeable proportion of large firms in the United States. We also know that the procedural characteristics of different ADR practices are extremely meaningful. ADR practices are often distinguished on the basis of their overarching procedural focus (Colvin et al., 2006). As such, scholars distinguish between interest-based processes, like mediation, where the neutral facilitates the parties' negotiation of a resolution based on their interests, and rights-based dispute resolution processes, like arbitration, where the neutral determines the merits of the parties' claims and demands (Avgar, 2015; Lipsky et al., 2003; Ury, Brett and Goldberg, 1988). Given these significant differences between processes, the adoption of different practices is likely to have very different dispute resolution consequences (Avgar, 2015).

A second dominant focus of ADR research is the factors that explain the diffusion of these practices in the non-union context. In particular, a great deal of attention has been given to the question of ADR adoption drivers (Avgar, 2016; Colvin et al., 2006; Lipsky et al., 2003). Why have a growing proportion of non-union firms decided to abandon their traditional approaches to managing workplace conflict and replace them with institutionalised internal mechanisms? What are the external and internal pressures that help to explain this workplace development? While there is some debate within the dispute resolution literature regarding the centrality and importance of different factors (Avgar, 2016), there is a broad agreement among scholars that the adoption of ADR practices is the product of a myriad of factors and pressures affecting different firms in different ways.

One of the ways scholars have conceptualised the factors that help to explain ADR adoption patterns is by distinguishing between external and internal pressures (Colvin et al., 2006). External pressures refers to forces operating outside the firm that increase the likelihood that the organisation will turn to some form of ADR. Internal factors refers to changes occurring inside organisations that contribute to the firm's decision to adopt and implement an ADR practice. Much of the early research examining workplace ADR focused on external and environmental pressures, with a particular focus on environmental threats that could, arguably, be defended against by using internal dispute resolution practices (see for example, Colvin 2003a, 2003b; for a similar discussion see Avgar, 2016).

Central among these external threats has been litigation. Early research highlighted litigation avoidance as a dominant driving force in the rise of non-union ADR (for a review see Colvin et al., 2006). Firms, according to this research, turned to ADR as a mechanism to buffer themselves from the external judicial system (Colvin, 2003a, 2003b). Increased employment regulation beginning in the 1960s paved the way for a dramatic increase in employment-related litigation. ADR can, therefore, be seen as an organisational defence against the growing role that the courts played in the adjudication of employment disputes (Lipsky et al., 2003). Scholars have debated the extent to which the use of ADR as an alternative to litigation represented a genuine effort to better address conflict within the boundaries of the firm or whether it served as a way of providing a symbolic response to a dramatic societal transformation (see for example Edelman, 1990; Sutton et al., 1994). Either way, litigation, or the efforts on the part of firms to minimise its reach, has been deemed an important factor for explaining the rise of ADR.

An additional external factor that has received a great deal of attention has been unionisation and collective bargaining. Unions have been shown to have two potential effects on the rise of non-union ADR. First, the decline of unions and collective bargaining in the United States has, among other things, meant the demise of one of the hallmarks of this labour-management relationship – the grievance system. Since the decline of unions does not mean an absence of workplace conflict, the disappearance of the grievance system from within the boundaries of many firms is likely to have left a conflict management vacuum (Avgar, 2016). In the absence of a union-based grievance system, some firms are likely to seek out ADR practices as a way to fill this conflict management vacuum. Second, scholars have demonstrated a link between firms' efforts to avoid unionisation and the use of ADR (see for example Colvin, 2003a). ADR can serve as a way to buffer the firm from potential unionisation activity by providing employees with a non-union form of voice as a way to pre-empt the establishment of unionised voice.

For example, in a study of telecommunications firms, Colvin found a relationship between the threat of unionisation and the adoption of peer review – a rights-based process that includes employee representatives on review panels established to resolve a given dispute. Interestingly, Colvin also found that the firm's threat of litigation was associated with the adoption of arbitration. In other words, firms are nuanced in their response to external pressures, adopting practices that are better suited to address the specific threat at hand. Alongside litigation and unionisation related pressures, scholars have also pointed to a number of other external pressures that have contributed to the rise of ADR, from increased market and competitive pressures to the effects of deregulation, globalisation and technological advances (Lipsky et al., 2003).

In addition to external pressures, ADR scholars have also documented a relationship between internal changes and pressures and the push toward new ways of dealing with conflict and disputes (Colvin et al., 2006). Most notably is the well-documented transformation of organisational work structures and arrangements beginning in the 1980s (Appelbaum and Batt, 1994; Kochan, Katz and McKersie, 1986). This transformation has taken on many forms over the past four decades, but is often associated with the organisational deployment of high-performance work systems (HPWS), which are characterised by an increase in frontline discretion empowerment, the use of teams and problem-solving groups, an emphasis on skills and training, and the alignment of compensation and employee incentives with this overall employment orientation (Appelbaum et al., 2000). These characteristics have clear and dramatic implications for both the manifestation of conflict and for the way it should be managed (Avgar, 2008). The collapsing of bureaucratic rules and hierarchical layers within organisations alongside the shift towards greater discretion and autonomy on the frontlines is likely to require new methods for dealing with conflict – methods that move away from relying on adversarial practices and managerial authority. As such, the rise of ADR can also be explained against the backdrop of this consequential organisational change and its implications for workplace conflict (Lipsky and Avgar, 2008).

A more recent approach to the study of ADR adoption drivers has explored the role that strategic choice plays in non-union firms (Avgar, 2016). Complementing research on the external and internal pressures discussed above, this research is beginning to examine the role that different organisational strategic orientations play in explaining the adoption of specific ADR practices (Avgar et al., 2013; Lipsky, Avgar and Lamare, 2014; Lipsky and Avgar, 2008). Building on Colvin's (2003a) study examining the adoption of peer review and arbitration, this research tests the argument that organisations adopt different ADR practices as a function of different strategic objectives.

Usage and outcomes

Dispute resolution procedures may formally exist on paper, but have little impact if they are not actually used by employees. How do employees use dispute resolution procedures? What outcomes does the use of dispute resolution procedures produce?

Early research in this area focused on trying to understand the process of grievance resolution and how the parties used the grievance procedure to further their interests in the workplace. A classic example of this type of study was James Kuhn's 1961 book *Bargaining in Grievance Settlement*. In a memorable chapter, Kuhn used the example of a single dispute, the "hot treads" grievance, to show how the grievance procedure served as the arena for the playing out of workplace labour relations conflict. Taken at face value, the hot treads grievance was a normal dispute about the application of a collective agreement to a workplace decision. However what Kuhn showed is that the workers were in fact using grievance filing activity as a strategy to exert pressure on management in support of a different set of concerns they had in the workplace that had festered and were less amenable to resolution through formal procedures. Although more than 50 years old now, Kuhn's study is a good example of research that brought together the often disparate perspectives of labour relations and organisational behaviour, providing insights for both fields.

In the 1970s and 1980s research on conflict resolution became increasingly quantitative in nature. For example, Lewin and Peterson's 1988 book, *The Modern Grievance Procedure*, provided detailed statistics on usage of grievance procedures in unionised workplaces across a range of different industries. Some of their findings confirmed conventional wisdom about grievance procedures, for example showing that most grievances were resolved at earlier stages in the process, with fewer grievances being appealed at each subsequent step. However their analysis also provided new insights into some limitations of these grievance procedures. In particular, they provided evidence indicating poor post-grievance outcomes for both grievance filers and supervisors who were complained against. These findings helped inspire a line of subsequent research investigating the issue of retaliation against grievance filers as a major problem in conflict resolution systems.

Studies of individual grievant work histories found that performance tended to deteriorate after grievances, even when compared with workers who had conflicts but did not file grievances (Boroff and Lewin, 1997). This suggested the existence of retaliation against users of grievance procedures and the idea that these procedures could be viewed as parts of systems of industrial discipline and punishment, challenging the exit-voice perspective, which suggests that the availability of voice mechanisms such as grievance procedures will produce positive outcomes of reduced exit behaviour (Freeman and Medoff, 1984). Subsequent research has added some further nuances to this story. At the individual level, research found that the negative effect of grievance filing may depend on the type of grievance filed, with negative impacts being limited to grievances related to personal actions of the supervisor and policy-related grievances having more neutral impacts (Olson-Buchanan and Boswell, 2002). In addition, while some of the earlier research suggested that more loyal employees would simply suffer in silence rather than engage in either voice through grievance filing or exit by quitting (Boroff and Lewin, 1997; Lewin and Peterson, 1999), subsequent work suggests that these more loyal employees are more likely to use informal methods to resolve problems in the workplace (Olson-Buchanan and Boswell, 2002). In addition, different relationships may exist at the organisational level as opposed to the individual level. While high grievance rates have been found to be associated with high quit rates at the organisational level, availability of grievance procedures may be associated with lower quit rates – albeit the evidence for this relationship is stronger for union grievance procedures (Rees, 1991) than for non-union procedures (Batt, Colvin and Keefe, 2002).

Another line of research that emerged in the 1980s looked at the relationship between grievance activity, other indicators of workplace labour relations and organisational performance. A series of studies found that high grievance rates were associated with negative indicators of the workplace labour relations climate, such as high absenteeism rates, and that workplaces with these conflictual patterns tended to have lower productivity and quality outputs (Cutcher-Gershenfeld, 1991; Ichniowski, 1986; Katz, Kochan and Weber, 1985; Norsworthy and Zabala, 1985). Research at the workplace level also found that grievance rates varied over time, increasing during periods when collective agreements came up for renegotiation or of heightened production pressure when management monitoring of workers increased (Kleiner, Nickelsburg and Pilarski, 1995).

More recent research on the use and outcomes of conflict resolution procedures has explored the impact of variation in types of non-union procedures. Research has found that use of procedures and employee success rates in challenging management decisions are higher where non-union grievance procedures included non-managerial decision-makers (e.g. peer review and arbitration) and increase with the extent of due process protections in procedures (Colvin, 2003b, 2013).

Recent research has also extended the earlier insights that conflict resolution activity is linked to the nature of the workplace labour relations climate and to the organisation of work. Studies in both unionised and non-union workplaces found evidence that grievance rates were lower in workplaces that adopted high-involvement work practices. These studies controlled for the type of conflict resolution procedure present in the workplace, suggesting that the reduction in grievance rates was a result of reduced levels of workplace conflict rather than a lack of availability of procedures to effectively express conflict. International evidence on this question is more mixed. In a study using the Canadian Workplace and Employee Survey (WES), Colvin (2003b) found high-involvement work practices being negatively associated with grievance rates in unionised workplaces but having no significant effect in non-union workplaces. By contrast, in another study using later iterations of the Canadian WES data, Pohler and Luchak (2014) find no significant relationship in unionised workplaces, but a positive relationship between high-involvement work practices and grievance rates in non-union workplaces, which they attribute to the effects of work intensification pressures.

Another line of recent research has looked at the outcomes of conflict resolution in terms of its impact on individual employee perceptual measures. Eigen and Litwin (2014) examined employee justice perceptions before and after the introduction of a new non-union grievance procedure that included mandatory arbitration. They found a paradox in that perceptions of interactional justice increased, but perceptions of procedural justice declined. They explained this in part as a result of successful efforts by lower-level managers to deal with conflicts informally in the workplace rather than letting the conflicts proceed through the formal grievance procedure, thereby resulting in positive perceptions of the informal justice interactions at the expense of the formal procedure.

The emergence of conflict management systems

A fourth clear known that stems from existing workplace conflict management research is the emergence of conflict management systems as an increasingly prevalent model within large American organisations. Traditional ADR research has, for the most part, focused on the adoption of a single practice or process. In the late 1980s and early 1990s, conflict management scholarship began exploring organisational use of multiple and complementary practices (Costantino and Merchant, 1996; Lipsky et al., 2003; Ury, Brett and Goldberg, 1988). Some organisations, researchers found, have moved beyond the deployment of a single dispute resolution practice or procedure and, instead, are making use of a system of practices that, at least in theory, are designed to provide a more integrative and comprehensive approach to resolving workplace conflict. A 1997 study found that approximately 17 per cent of Fortune 1000 firms in the United States made use of a conflict management systems approach (Lipsky et al., 2003). Survey research conducted in 2011 suggests that the proportion of Fortune 1000 firms utilising a conflict management system may have doubled and now stands at approximately 33 per cent (Lipsky et al., 2014).

Building on general systems theory, this conflict management research conceptualised conflict and the way it is dealt with as a system of interrelated parts (Costantino and Merchant, 1996; Lipsky et al., 2003). As such, this research points to the organisational advantages associated with an approach that views conflict management as a system of interrelated procedures that, together, are designed to deliver on an overarching goal or objective.

A systems approach to workplace conflict management is predicated on the argument that there are multiple different methods through which to deal with and address conflict. A systems approach maintains that given the multiple types of conflicts and disputes that are likely to arise within the boundaries of the firm, organisations should make use of an array of options to address them. Some conflicts may be best addressed using practices that focus on parties' interests while others may call for rights- or power-based options. The key is for organisations to implement a range of available procedures that can be deployed as needed. Writing in the late 1980s, Ury and colleagues advanced the argument that interest-based dispute resolution procedures are uniquely suited to deal with a variety of conflicts in a manner that is more likely to reduce transactional costs and to increase satisfaction (Ury et al., 1988). Nevertheless, despite this preference for interest-based options, Ury and colleagues also recognised the need to complement these procedures with those that rely on other means for resolving conflict, such as rights or power.

Conflict management systems also depart from the traditional ADR approach in terms of the level and stage at which organisations seek to address conflict. Conflict management scholars have distinguished between formal and informal manifestations of conflict (Lipsky et al., 2003). Disputes and lawsuits represent formal manifestations of conflict, while everyday tensions and disagreements represent its informal and often more prevalent expression. The rise of ADR, discussed above, represented a shift in many organisations from addressing conflict when it reached the very formal level of litigation to a model that attempted to deal with conflict when expressed as internal disputes (ibid.). The increased use of conflict management systems in organisations represents a second shift, reflecting an effort to address conflict at an informal level, when it is manifested as a lower-intensity tension or disagreement. This approach is consistent with existing literature on individual- and group-level conflict, which has identified functional and dysfunctional dimensions of conflict (Jehn, 1995, 1997). According to this research some forms of conflict can actually benefit the team or the organisation. For example, organisational behaviour scholars have pointed to the potential benefits associated with group-level conflict that focuses on work- or task-related issues (Amason and Schweiger, 1997; Simons and Peterson, 2000; van de Vliert and De Dreu, 1994). This research suggests that not all conflict within the organisation needs to be eradicated. Some forms of conflict should, instead, be managed. Nevertheless, once an organisational conflict has reached the level of a formal dispute it is less likely to yield team and organisational benefits. Conflict management systems, therefore, provide the organisation with more degrees of freedom in addressing conflict at the level at which potential benefits can be attained. As such, these systems provide organisations with the ability to be proactive in their management of conflict (Lipsky et al., 2003). Traditional ADR approaches, on the other hand, are designed to respond to conflict once it is expressed as a formal dispute, which constitutes a reactive approach.

Research conducted by David Lipsky, Ronald Seeber and Richard Fincher provides a well-developed and comprehensive analysis of the core characteristics of a conflict management system (ibid.). First, and building on the discussion above, conflict management systems tend to be broad in scope, both in terms of the types of conflict they are designed to address and the organisational members that are eligible to make use of their practices. Second, according to Lipsky and colleagues, a conflict management system should have multiple access points. In other words, organisational members should have a variety of different avenues through which to enter the system in an effort to address a conflict or dispute. Third, a conflict management system differs from a traditional ADR approach in its reliance on multiple conflict management options, including both interest- and rights-based options. Finally, given these features, a conflict management system should have adequate organisational support structures.

Finally, conflict management research has pointed to a link between conflict management systems and organisational strategy (Avgar, 2015, 2016; Lipsky et al., 2014; Lipsky and Avgar, 2008; Lipsky et al., 2003). While recent research has begun to provide empirical support for the argument that firms approach their deployment of conflict management practices and systems in a strategic manner (see for example Avgar et al., 2013; Lipsky et al., 2014), there is still a great deal that is unknown about the link between organisational strategy and conflict management strategy.

Unknowns in the study of workplace dispute resolution

Representation in conflict resolution

As our review has shown, there is an extensive body of employment relations (ER) research on conflict resolution focusing on different procedures for resolution of conflict. By contrast, much less attention in the field has been paid to issues of representation in conflict resolution. Some research on labour arbitration procedures has examined the impact of representation of the parties by attorneys on the outcomes of the procedure. For example, Block and Stieber (1987) found that both union and management sides had greater success in labour arbitration if they were represented by an attorney.

Systemic changes in recent years in the structure of ER suggest the need for new inquiries into the issue of representation in conflict resolution. Union decline has weakened a primary structure through which employees obtain representation in disputes with their employers. Individual employment rights have expanded to fill some of the vacuum created by the contraction of union representation. Yet while a statute can formally enact an individual employment right, this will mean little without some effective mechanism for enforcement of that right (Colvin, 2016). Effective enforcement of rights in turn depends on the employee being able to obtain representation from a knowledgeable and capable advocate. In the United States, this function has primarily been provided by private plaintiff attorneys who represent employees. For example, in the critical area of employment discrimination, fewer than two per cent of cases are prosecuted by the governmental Equal Employment Opportunity Commission, with the vast majority of the remainder brought by plaintiff attorneys on behalf of employees. Since most employees would be unable to pay the high hourly rates charged by attorneys, the majority of these cases are brought based on contingency fee arrangements under which the attorney receives a percentage (typically 30–40 per cent) of the damages if the employee wins the case but receives no fee if the employee loses (Gough, 2015).

Research on employment litigation indicates that the large majority of cases are brought with attorney representation, and that outcomes for employees are significantly better than for the employees who are self-represented (Neilsen, Nelson and Lancaster, 2010). There was some hope that the ADR procedures of arbitration and mediation would provide an accessible and effective mechanism for employees to pursue claims without attorney representation (Estreicher, 2001); however, subsequent research has found that self-representation only occurs in a minority of cases in arbitration, similar to the situation in litigation, and that self-represented employees obtain relatively poor outcomes in arbitration (Colvin, 2011; Colvin and Gough, 2015).

There has been a recent increase in interest in examining the role of representation in dispute resolution. A pair of recent studies of employment arbitration, examining cases administered by the American Arbitration Association (AAA) and by the Financial Industry Regulatory Authority (FINRA), looked at the role of attorney representation and found evidence suggesting that the repeat player advantage accruing to employers who participate in these procedures frequently is a result, in part, of their use of large employer-side law firms who are also repeat players in arbitration (Horton and Cann Chandrasekher, 2016; Lipsky, Lamare and Gupta, 2013). Relatedly, in a study of employment arbitration cases, Colvin and Pike (2014) found that employers were more likely than employees to be represented by attorneys who specialised in the employment law area and whose law firms had been involved in past arbitration cases, suggesting greater experience and expertise of representatives on the employer side.

While these studies indicate growing research interest in representation in dispute resolution, many issues and questions in this area remain in need of further investigation. One critical issue is the question of how to provide effective representation for employees with relatively small claims. The contingency fee mechanism works well for financing representation of employees with large claims, either due to high salary levels or particularly heinous employer conduct that is likely to be punished by a large jury award. But for an employee with a modest lost wages claim, the damages will not be large enough for a plaintiff attorney to justify financing the case through a contingency fee arrangement and the employee will be unlikely to be able to afford to pay hourly fees. One alternative may be a legal insurance type scheme, perhaps administered by labour unions for members. The trick with these schemes is to ensure that a high enough proportion of employees pay into them, given the reality that a dispute is a low probability event that most employees may assume will never happen to them. Traditional union representation solved the problem of financing representation through the membership dues mechanism; it is not clear yet what financing mechanism will be able to provide broad coverage in the individual rights world.

Another major issue in the area of representation is the question of how to provide representation in dispute resolution within the organisation. Most organisational dispute resolution procedures in non-union workplaces do not allow employees to have representatives at internal hearings or processes. Procedures more commonly allow attorney representation at arbitration if such a step is included and the case proceeds that far, but by the time a case gets to arbitration the employment relationship has typically been disrupted and almost all cases in employment arbitration involve termination situations (Colvin and Pike, 2014). Some internal procedures include involvement of fellow employees, notably peer review procedures, providing some degree of employee voice in the process (Colvin, 2003a). But this is only a partial form of employee representation, lacking a representative who advocates on behalf of the employee. Employers are reluctant to allow external advocates in non-union workplaces. There are some examples of organisations allowing a fellow employee to assist a complainant in processes like internal mediation, with indications that this type of internal representation can be surprisingly helpful (Colvin, 2004). However we lack systematic evidence of whether this can be effective on a broader scale and become institutionalised in the workplace. Going forward a major challenge for the viability of an individual employment rights-based ER system is how it will provide representation for employees that is broad in coverage and effective in the workplace.

Workplace conflict management and organisational and individual level outcomes

There is still much that is unknown about the ways in which organisational use of different dispute resolution practices influences and shapes employee attitudes and perceptions. There is also a need for additional research examining the relationship between these practices and a host of organisational performance measures. For example, while conflict management scholars have touted the many benefits associated with the internalisation of the resolution of conflict and disputes (see for example Costantino and Merchant, 1996; Ury et al., 1988), there is a wide range of outcomes that have, to date, not been empirically linked to the adoption and implementation of ADR or conflict management systems (for a similar argument see Roche and Teague, 2012b). While there are a host of outcomes that could be included in the study of ADR and conflict management systems, three categories of outcomes stand out in particular: a) organisational performance; b) individual attitudes, behaviours and perceptions; and c) workplace conflict.

There is still a great deal that we do not know about how ADR and conflict management systems affect organisations and their employees. At the organisational level, there is extremely limited evidence regarding the relationship between the adoption of different practices and measures of performance, such as productivity and profitability. In fact, one of the only studies to examine the relationship between conflict management systems and broad organisational outcomes finds limited evidence for a statistically significant relationship (Roche and Teague, 2012b). It is interesting to compare ADR and conflict management systems research to a related field of study – strategic human resource management (HRM). In the later 1980s and early 1990s HRM and IR scholars explored the relationship between work practices and firm performance (see for example Arthur, 1992, 1994; Huselid, 1995; McDuffie, 1995). This research demonstrated that the way in which work is organised has clear implications for central performance measures. Furthermore, this research also supported the notion that bundles of internally consistent practices have a more pronounced effect than individual practices (McDuffie, 1995).

Building on a similar logic, it is likely that the manner in which conflict is dealt with may also affect such outcomes. Different conflict management configurations may, therefore, provide organisations with a strategic advantage. Nevertheless, research questions about the relationship between conflict management practices and organisational outcomes have not been fully addressed. For example, is the adoption of non-union ADR practices associated with improved organisational performance? Furthermore, do different practices (interest-based versus rights-based) have different effects on organisational performance? Finally, given the increased prevalence of conflict management systems, do bundles of conflict management practices have a stronger effect on such outcomes than individual practices? The argument set forth by conflict management systems scholars is, in many ways, similar to the one advanced in the study of HRM systems, namely that bundles of integrated practices are likely to have a stronger effect on organisational performance than individual practices. While there is some empirical evidence supporting this complementarities argument (see most notably, Bendersky, 2007), to date, this proposition has received very little additional empirical support. Taken together, addressing these research questions would go a long way to advancing the state of organisational conflict management research.

In addition to organisational outcomes, conflict management research has been somewhat limited in terms of its examination of individual-level outcomes. Research in union and non-union settings has documented a link between grievance activity and some behavioural outcomes, such as turnover. In addition, we also know that grievance filing may have negative consequences in terms of real and perceived individual performance (Klass and DeNisi, 1989; Olson-Buchanan, 1996), and recent research has pointed to a relationship between conflict management systems and employee perceptions of justice (Eigen and Litwin, 2014). Nevertheless, there are at least two areas related to individual-level outcomes that are in need of additional research. First, evidence on the relationship between grievance activity and employee outcomes – turnover, performance and perceptions of justice – has, for the most part, not accounted for the nature of the procedure available to employees. Much of the existing research measures grievance filing but does not distinguish between different processes used in the grievance system. For example, do employees with access to mediation respond differently than employees who have access to arbitration? Second, there are a host of additional individual outcomes that have not been explored in the context of ADR and conflict management systems beyond turnover and job performance. Does access to and usage of union and non-union conflict management practices improve employee perceptions of the organisation? Do these practices increase expressions of goodwill and reciprocity? We know little about the extent to which different conflict management practices affect central workplace variables such as trust and organisational citizenship behaviour.

Finally, another outcome that has been surprisingly absent from the existing research on ADR and conflict management systems is conflict itself. This is largely a function of a disciplinary divide between scholars studying organisational conflict management and those studying the more micro expressions and perceptions of individual and group conflict (for a similar argument see Avgar and Colvin, 2016). Organisational behaviour scholars have amassed a great deal of evidence regarding different types of team-level conflict and their consequences for individual and performance outcomes (de Wit, Greer and Jehn, 2012). In addition, they have examined the role that individual and team conflict management styles play in affecting perceptions of conflict and associated outcomes (see for example Friedman et al., 2000). Nevertheless, there is no research that we are aware of that examines the relationship between organisational-level conflict management practices and individual- and team-level perceptions of conflict. Thus, we do not know whether the availability of ADR and conflict management practices affects employee perceptions of workplace conflict. Building on individual- and group-level conflict management research, we also do not know whether organizational-level conflict management practices moderate the relationship between group-level conflict and performance and individual-level outcomes. Addressing these questions requires scholars to establish bridges across different disciplinary boundaries, which, we believe, will add substantial knowledge regarding the link between organisational conflict management and the more micro manifestation of workplace conflict.

Comparative and international perspectives

Much of the existing research on alternative dispute resolution has emerged from the United States. To some degree this is a natural outgrowth of the American setting of intense employment litigation conflict and dramatically shrinking union representation. These factors have resulted in a hothouse of experimentation in alternative methods of resolving conflict in the employment arena and beyond. Methods such as transformative mediation, employment arbitration and a range of organisational ADR procedures such as peer review panels are innovations that have emerged from this environment of intense experimentation in the USA.

Although the USA has been an important source of research and insight in the ADR area, the American setting for much of this research also has limitations and some findings may not translate well to other national settings. One obvious unusual feature of the US system is its employment litigation system, involving relatively complex court procedures and dramatically larger damage awards than seen in other countries. Another important feature is its strongly institutionalised legal divide between unionised and non-union workplaces, making the prospects of unions providing any representation services in non-union workplaces improbable. The absence of these features in other national settings opens up the possibility of a range of different institutional arrangements undergirding employment dispute resolution.

While the existing dispute resolution research has had a heavily American slant to it, the last few years have seen the emergence of a new wave of international and comparative work in this area, which holds much promise of bringing new insights to the field. Some of the finest international work in this area has come out of Ireland, including a series of studies of conflict resolution conducted by Roche and Teague (2011, 2012a, 2012b). In a corrective to the primarily American-based literature on conflict management systems, they found that in Ireland adoption of conflict management systems was greater among local Irish firms than among multinational firms, many of which are American. Other recent work has provided insightful analyses of non-US examples such as the use of judicial mediation in UK employment tribunals (Urwin and Latreille, 2014) or the use of mediation and arbitration in New Zealand police bargaining disputes (McAndrew, 2014).

More systematic evidence of cross-national similarities and differences in conflict resolution are provided by the articles in a 2012 special issue of the *International Journal of Human Resource Management*, edited by Roche and Teague (2012a), and a set of international chapters in the *Oxford Handbook of Conflict Management in Organizations* (Roche, Teague and Colvin, 2014). The articles and chapters in these volumes cover conflict resolution in: Australia, China, France, Germany, Ireland, Japan, New Zealand, the UK and the US. A noteworthy feature of this work is that it is moving beyond the relatively homogenous Anglo-American countries to examine conflict resolution in continental European and East Asian countries. An example of the insights this extension of research perspective can bring is Benson's (2014) examination of community unions in Japan, which provide legal services to their members, illustrating an alternative potential structure for representation in dispute resolution. Future research could extend this type of work to include other regions and different national systems.

In addition to studies that use a range of different national settings, there has also been some recent work that engages in cross-national comparative analysis. A rare example of a cross-national survey research design is Colvin's (2006) study of how organisations in Canada and the US respond to pressure from their legal environments, which yielded the perhaps counter-intuitive finding that despite the lower level of substantive legal protections for employees in the US, American employers were more likely than their Canadian counterparts to have adopted internal ADR procedures due to concerns about the highly conflictual nature of American employment litigation. Looking more broadly across the six Anglo-American countries (Australia, New Zealand, Ireland, the UK, Canada and the USA), Colvin and Darbishire (2013) drew attention to the growing emphasis on individual employment rights across this grouping of countries, suggesting the importance of further research on dispute resolution in this area. Moving in this same direction, Currie and Teague (2016) examine how statutory dispute resolution agencies are developing new approaches to address individual employment rights disputes across the Anglo-American countries. Their work provides a useful contrast to the US-based research in that whereas in America private attorneys and employers have tended to be the main actors in recent innovations in employment dispute resolution, they show that in the other Anglo-American countries government agencies have played a larger and more innovative role. Going forward, comparative cross-national research designs hold particular promise for developing new theoretical and policy insights in the employment dispute resolution area.

Conflict management in entrepreneurial firms

An additional unknown in the study of organisational conflict management relates to small and entrepreneurial firms. Specifically, the vast majority of ADR and conflict management systems research has been conducted in large and established firms. Thus for example, Lipsky and colleagues' work on conflict management systems was based on quantitative and qualitative data conducted in US Fortune 1000 firms (Lipsky, Seeber and Fincher, 2003). More recently,

Lipsky and colleagues conducted a follow-up survey of US Fortune 1000 firms to assess changes in organisational adoption patterns. Colvin's (2003a) study, cited above, was conducted in large telecommunication firms in the USA.

The absence of sufficient research on organisational conflict management in small and entrepreneurial firms is noteworthy for a number of reasons. First, despite their size, these firms employ a large proportion of the workforce. As such, a substantial number of employees work under the conflict management arrangements put in place in such firms. Second, entrepreneurial firms have been playing an increasingly important role within the economies of both developed and developing countries (Carree et al., 2002; Naudé, 2010). To the extent that more effective ways of dealing with conflict can improve entrepreneurial firms' performance and survival rate – an open question empirically – conflict management research can contribute to entrepreneurship scholarship and practice. Finally, differences between traditional and entrepreneurial firms extend well beyond the issue of size. Entrepreneurial firms are characterised by high levels of uncertainty and ambiguity, substantial resource constraints and a host of workforce-related challenges, such as recruitment and retention (Cardon and Stevens, 2004; Heneman, Tansky and Camp, 2000; Taylor, 2006). As such, this serves as a fascinating context in which to advance conflict management theory. Do the established frameworks applied in large and traditional firms hold in the context of entrepreneurial firms? If not, what new frameworks help to explain the role that conflict and conflict management plays in this setting?

There are a number of research questions that are likely to be especially fruitful. First, from a descriptive standpoint, we know very little about what the conflict management landscape looks like within small and entrepreneurial firms. How do entrepreneurial firms address workplace conflict? Do they make use of informal methods of dealing with conflict? How do these compare with the methods used by large firms? Second, in light of their unique characteristics, entrepreneurial firms and their employees may experience different types of conflict and disputes. In other words, the very nature of conflict may be different in these firms. What does conflict look like in entrepreneurial firms? Finally, in the absence of empirical evidence regarding the actual expressions of conflict and the use of conflict management practices in entrepreneurial firms it is also difficult to assess consequences for key organisational and individual outcomes. Most notably in this context, what is the relationship between conflict and firm performance? Do different methods of dealing with conflict affect firm survival rates? Does the use of certain conflict management practices or methods alleviate some of the well-documented workforce challenges and constraints that entrepreneurial firms face? Are the traditional methods used to address conflict in large firms appropriate in entrepreneurial firms? Beginning to address these research questions would, we believe, go a long way to advancing both the study of organisational conflict management and of entrepreneurship.

Conclusion

Managing and resolving conflict is a central organisational activity. An impressive body of research has documented the varied ways in which firms do so in both the union and non-union settings. In the unionised context, we know a great deal about grievances and the procedures established through collective bargaining to resolve them. In the non-union setting, we know a great deal about the transformation that a growing proportion of firms have undergone in their approach to conflict and its management.

Nevertheless, as with any developing area of study, there are a number of important questions that have yet to be fully explored about these consequential developments and their implications for employees and their employers. We have outlined four key components of an expanded dispute resolution research agenda. First, as union representation continues to decline, this research agenda should, we argue, provide a careful assessment of the changing models of employee representation in conflict resolution. Second, building on the rich and in-depth research documenting the features and characteristics of different dispute resolution processes and systems, researchers should extend their focus to the wide array of potential outcomes associated with these practices. Third, we know a great deal about the changing dispute resolution landscape in the United States but there is a need for much more attention to the dispute resolution trends and developments in other counties. Finally, small and entrepreneurial firms are not immune to conflicts and disputes, yet we know very little about how these organisations deal with, resolve and manage conflict. It is important that we move beyond large and established firms and develop a research agenda that also includes small and entrepreneurial organisations. Addressing these important research questions will, we believe, serve to advance dispute resolution theory and practice in the years to come.

References

Amason, A.C. and Schweiger, D.M. (1997). The effect of conflict on strategic decision making effectiveness and organizational performance, in De Dreu, C.K.W. and van de Vliert, E. (eds.) *Using Conflict in Organizations*. London: Sage, pp. 101–105.

Appelbaum, E. and Batt, R. (1994). *The New American Workplace: Transforming Work Systems in the United States*. Ithaca: ILR Press.

Appelbaum, E., Bailey, T., Berg, P. and Kalleberg, A. (2000). *Manufacturing Advantage: The Effects of High Performance Work Systems on Plant Performance and Company Outcomes*. Ithaca: ILR Press.

Arthur, J.B. (1992). 'The link between business strategy and industrial relations systems in American steel minimills', *Industrial and Labor Relations Review*, 45(3), pp. 488–506.

Arthur, J.B. (1994). 'Effects of human resource systems on manufacturing performance and turnover', *Academy of Management Journal*, 37(3), pp. 670–687.

Avgar, A.C. (2015). Internal resolution of employment disputes, in Feliu, A., Outten, W., Drucker, J., Winograd, B. and Bloom, A. (eds.) *ADR in Employment*. Arlington: BNA Books.

Avgar, A.C. (2016). 'Treating conflict: the adoption of a conflict management system in a hospital setting', *Advances in Industrial and Labor Relations*, 22, pp. 211–246.

Avgar, A.C. and Colvin, A.J.S. (2016). Introduction, in Avgar, A.C. and Colvin, A.J.S. (eds.) *Conflict and its Management in Organizations: Integrating Insights across Disciplines*. Oxford: Taylor & Francis.

Avgar, A.C., Lamare, J.R., Lipsky, D.B. and Gupta, A. (2013). 'Unions and ADR: the relationship between labor unions and workplace dispute resolution in U.S. corporations', *Ohio State Journal on Dispute Resolution*, 28(1), pp. 63–106.

Batt, R., Colvin, A.J.S. and Keefe, J. (2002). 'Employee Voice, Human Resource Practices, and Quit Rates: Evidence from the Telecommunications Industry', *Industrial and Labor Relations Review*, 55(4), pp. 573–594.

Bendersky, C. (2007). 'Complementarities in organizational dispute resolution systems: how system characteristics affect individuals' conflict experiences', *Industrial and Labor Relations Review*, 60(2), pp. 204–224.

Benson, J. (2014). Conflict Resolution in Japan, in Roche, W.K., Teague, P. and Colvin, A.J.S. (eds.) *The Oxford Handbook of Conflict Management in Organizations*. Oxford: Oxford University Press, pp. 385–404.

Block, R.N. and Stieber, J. (1987). 'The Impact of Attorneys and Arbitrators on Arbitration Awards', *Industrial and Labor Relations Review*, 40(4), pp. 543–555.

Boroff, K.E. and Lewin, D. (1997). 'Loyalty, Voice, and Intent to Exit a Union Firm: A Conceptual and Empirical Analysis', *Industrial and Labor Relations Review*, 51(1), pp. 50–63.

Brett, J.M. and Goldberg, S.B. (1983). 'Grievance Mediation in the Coal Industry: A Field Experiment', *Industrial and Labor Relations Review*, 37(1), pp. 49–69.

Bureau of Labor Statistics (2017). *Union Members 2016*. (Press release). Available at: www.bls.gov/news. release/pdf/union2.pdf. (Accessed: 25 December 2017).

Cardon, M.S. and Stevens, C.E. (2004). 'Managing human resources in small organizations: what do we know?' *Human Resource Management Review*, 14(3), pp. 295–323.

Carree, M., van Stel, A., Thurik, R. and Wennekers, S. (2002). 'Economic Development and Business Ownership: An Analysis Using Data of 23 OECD Countries in the Period 1976–1996', *Small Business Economics*, 19(3), pp. 271–290.

Colvin, A.J.S. (2003a). 'Institutional Pressures, Human Resource Strategies, and the Rise of Nonunion Dispute Resolution Procedures,' *Industrial and Labor Relations Review*, 56(3), pp. 375–392.

Colvin, A.J.S. (2003b). 'The Dual Transformation of Workplace Dispute Resolution', *Industrial Relations*, 42(4), pp. 712–735.

Colvin, A.J.S. (2004). 'The Relationship between Employee Involvement and Workplace Dispute Resolution', *Relations Industrielles/Industrial Relations*, 59(4), pp. 681–704.

Colvin, A.J.S. (2006). 'Flexibility and fairness in liberal market economies: the comparative impact of the legal environment and high performance work systems', *British Journal of Industrial Relations*, 44(1), pp. 73–97.

Colvin, A.J.S. (2011). 'An Empirical Study of Employment Arbitration: Case Outcomes and Processes', *Journal of Empirical Legal Studies*, 8(1), pp. 1–23.

Colvin, A.J.S. (2013). 'Participation versus Procedures in Nonunion Dispute Resolution', *Industrial Relations*, 52(s1), pp. 221–258.

Colvin, A.J.S. (2016). 'Conflict and Employment Relations in the Individual Rights Era', *Advances in Industrial and Labor Relations*, 22, pp. 1–30.

Colvin, A.J.S. and Darbishire, O. (2013). 'Convergence in industrial relations institution: the emerging Anglo-American model?', *Industrial and Labor Relations Review*, 66(5), pp. 1047–1077.

Colvin, A.J.S. and Gough, M. (2015). 'Individual Employment Rights Arbitration in the United States: Actors and Outcomes', *ILR Review*, 68(5), pp. 1019–1042.

Colvin, A.J.S., Klaas, B. and Mahony, D. (2006). 'Research on alternative dispute resolution procedures', in Lewin, D. (ed.) *Contemporary Issues in Employment Relations*. Champaign: Labor and Employment Relations Association Series, pp. 103–147.

Colvin, A.J.S. and Pike, K. (2014). 'Saturns and Rickshaws Revisited: What Kind of Employment Arbitration System has Developed?' *Ohio State Journal on Dispute Resolution*, 29(1), pp. 59–83.

Costantino, C.A. and Merchant, C.S. (1996). *Designing Conflict Management Systems: A Guide to Creating Productive and Healthy Organizations*. San Francisco: Jossey-Bass.

Currie, D. and Teague, P. (2016). 'Economic Citizenship and Workplace Conflict in Anglo-American Industrial Relations Systems,' *British Journal of Industrial Relations*, 54(2), pp. 358–384.

Cutcher-Gershenfeld, J. (1991). 'The Impact on Economic Performance of a Transformation in Workplace Relations', *Industrial and Labor Relations Review*, 44(2), pp. 241–260.

de Wit, F.R., Greer, L.L. and Jehn, K.A. (2012). 'The paradox of intragroup conflict: a meta-analysis,' *Journal of Applied Psychology*, 97(2), pp. 360–390.

Edelman, L.B. (1990). 'Legal environments and organizational governance: the expansion of due process in the American workplace', *American Journal of Sociology*, 95(6), pp. 1401–1441.

Eigen, Z.J. and Litwin, A.S. (2014). 'Justice or Just Between Us? Empirical Evidence on the Trade-Off Between Procedural and Interactional Justice in Workplace Dispute Resolution', *ILR Review*, 67(1), pp. 171–201.

Estreicher, S. (2001). 'Saturns for Rickshaws: The Stakes in the Debate over Predispute Employment Arbitration Agreements', *Ohio State Journal on Dispute Resolution*, 16(3), pp. 559–570.

Ewing, D.W. (1989). *Justice on the Job: Resolving Grievances in the Nonunion Workplace*. Boston (MA): Harvard Business School Press.

Feuille, P. (1999). Grievance Mediation, in Eaton, A.E. and Keefe, J.H. (eds.) *Employment Dispute Resolution and Worker Rights in the Changing Workplace*. Champaign: Industrial Relations Research Association, pp. 187–217.

Freeman, R.V. and Medoff, J.L. (1984). *What Do Unions Do?* New York: Basic Books.

Friedman, R.A., Tidd, S.T., Currall, S.C. and Tsai, J.C. (2000). 'What goes around comes around: the impact of personal conflict style on work conflict and stress', *International Journal of Conflict Management*, 11(1), pp. 32–55.

Gough, M.D. (2015). *Employment Rights Enforcement: Forums, Actors, and Outcomes*. PhD Thesis, Cornell University.

Heneman, R.L., Tansky, J.W. and Camp, S.M. (2000). 'Human resource management practices in small and medium-sized enterprises: unanswered questions and future research perspectives', *Entrepreneurship Theory and Practice*, 25(1), pp. 11–26.

Horton, D.O. and Cann Chandrasekher, A. (2016). 'Employment Arbitration after the Revolution', *DePaul Law Review*, 65, pp. 457–496.

Huselid, M.A. (1995). 'The impact of human resource management practices on turnover, productivity, and corporate financial performance', *Academy of Management Journal*, 38(3), pp. 635–672.

Ichniowski, C. (1986). 'The Effects of Grievance Activity on Productivity', *Industrial and Labor Relations Review*, 40(1), pp. 75–89.

Jehn, K.A. (1995). 'A multi-method examination of the benefits and detriments of intragroup conflict', *Administrative Science Quarterly*, 40(2), pp. 256–282.

Jehn, K.A. (1997). 'A qualitative analysis of conflict types and dimensions in organizational groups', *Administrative Science Quarterly*, 42(3), pp. 530–557.

Katz, H.C., Kochan, T.A. and Colvin, A.J.S. (2007). *An Introduction to Collective Bargaining and Industrial Relations*. New York: McGraw-Hill Irwin.

Katz, H.C., Kochan, T.A. and Weber, M.R. (1985). 'Assessing the Effects of Industrial Relations and Quality of Work Life Efforts on Organizational Effectiveness', *Academy of Management Journal*, 28(3), pp. 509–527.

Klaas, B.S. and DeNisi, A.S. (1989). 'Managerial reactions to employee dissent: the impact of grievance activity on performance rating', *Academy of Management Journal*, 32(4), pp. 705–717.

Kleiner, M.M., Nickelsburg, G. and Pilarski, A. (1995). 'Monitoring Grievances, and Plant Performance', *Industrial Relations*, 34(2), pp. 169–189.

Kochan, T.A., Katz, H.C. and McKersie, R.B. (1986). *The Transformation of American Industrial Relations*. Ithaca: Cornell University Press.

Kuhn, J.W. (1961). *Bargaining in Grievance Settlement: The Power of Industrial Work Groups*. New York: Columbia University Press.

Lewin, D. (1987). 'Dispute resolution in the nonunion firm: a theoretical and empirical analysis', *Journal of Conflict Resolution*, 31(3), pp. 465–502.

Lewin, D. and Peterson, R.B. (1988). *The Modern Grievance Procedure in the United States: A Theoretical and Empirical Analysis*. Westport: Quorum.

Lewin, D. and Peterson, R.B. (1999). 'Behavioral Outcomes of Grievance Activity', *Industrial Relations*, 38(4), pp. 554–576.

Lipsky, D.B. and Avgar, A.C. (2008). 'Toward a strategic theory of workplace conflict management', *Ohio State Journal on Dispute Resolution*, 24(1), pp. 143–190.

Lipsky, D., Avgar, A.C. and Lamare, J.R. (2014). *The strategic underpinnings of conflict management practices in U.S. corporations: evidence from a new survey of Fortune 1000 companies*. Working paper.

Lipsky, D., Lamare, J.R. and Gupta, A. (2013). 'The Effect of Gender on Awards in Employment Arbitration Cases: The Experience in the Securities Industry', *Industrial Relations*, 52(S1), pp. 314–342.

Lipsky, D.B., Seeber, R.L. and Fincher, R.D. (2003). *Emerging Systems for Managing Workplace Conflict*. San Francisco: Jossey-Bass.

McAndrew, I. (2014). 'Med + Arb' in the New Zealand Police, in Roche, W.K., Teague, P. and Colvin, A.J.S. (eds.) *The Oxford Handbook of Conflict Management in Organizations*. Oxford: Oxford University Press, pp. 311–332.

McCabe, D.M. (1988). *Corporate Nonunion Complaint Procedures and Systems: A Strategic Human Resources Management Analysis*. New York: Praeger.

McCallum, R. (2007). 'Convergences and/or Divergences of Labor Law Systems: The View from Australia', *Comparative Labor Law and Policy Journal*. 28, pp. 455–467.

McDuffie, J.P. (1995). 'Human Resource bundles and manufacturing performance: organizational logic and flexible production systems in the world auto industry', *Industrial and Labor Relations Review*, 48(2), pp. 197–221.

Naudé, W. (2010). 'Entrepreneurship, developing countries, and development economics: new approaches and insights', *Small Business Economics*, 34(1), pp. 1–12.

Nielsen, L.B., Nelson, R.L. and Lancaster, R. (2010). 'Individual Justice or Collective Legal Mobilization? Employment Discrimination Litigation in the Post Civil Rights United States', *Journal of Empirical Legal Studies*, 7(2), pp. 175–201.

Norsworthy, J.R. and Zabala, C.A. (1985). 'Worker Attitudes, Worker Behavior, and Productivity in the U.S. Automobile Industry, 1959–76', *Industrial and Labor Relations Review*, 38(4), pp. 544–557.

Olson-Buchanan, J.B. (1996). 'Voicing discontent: what happens to the grievance filer after the grievance?' *Journal of Applied Psychology*, 81(1), pp. 52–63.

Olson-Buchanan, J.B. and Boswell, W.R. (2002). 'The Role of Employee Loyalty and Formality in Voicing Discontent', *Journal of Applied Psychology*, 87(6), pp. 1167–1174.

Pohler, D.M. and Luchak, A.A. (2014). 'Balancing Efficiency, Equity, and Voice: The Impact of Unions and High-Involvement Work Practices on Work Outcomes', *ILR Review*, 67(4), pp. 1063–1094.

Rees, D.I. (1991). 'Grievance Procedure Strength and Teacher Quits', *Industrial and Labor Relations Review*, 45(1), pp. 31–43.

Roche, W.K. and Teague, P. (2011). 'Firms and Innovative Conflict Management Systems in Ireland', *British Journal of Industrial Relations*, 49(3), pp. 436–459.

Roche, W.K. and Teague, P. (2012a). 'The Growing Importance of Workplace ADR', *International Journal of Human Resource Management*, 23(3–4), pp. 447–458.

Roche, W.K. and Teague, P. (2012b). 'Do Conflict Management Systems Matter?' *Human Resource Management*, 51(2), pp. 231–258.

Roche, W.K., Teague, P. and Colvin, A.J.S. (eds.) (2014). *The Oxford Handbook of Conflict Management in Organizations*. Oxford: Oxford University Press.

Simons, T. and Peterson, R. (2000). 'Task conflict and relationship conflict in top management teams: the pivotal role of intragroup trust', *Journal of Applied Psychology*, 85(1), pp. 653–663.

Sutton, J.R., Dobbin, F., Meyer, J.W. and Scott, W.R. (1994). 'The legalization of the workplace', *American Journal of Sociology*, 99(4), pp. 944–971.

Taras, D. and Walsworth, S. (2016). Employment Relations in Canada, in Bamber, G.J., Lansbury, R.D., Wailes, N. and Wright, C.F. (eds.) *International & Comparative Employment Relations: National Regulation, Global Changes*. Sydney: Allen & Unwin.

Taylor, S. (2006). 'Acquaintance, meritocracy and critical realism: researching recruitment and selection processes in smaller and growth organizations', *Human Resource Management Review*, 16(4), pp. 478–489.

Urwin, P. and Latreille, P.L. (2014). Experiences of Judicial Mediation in Employment Tribunals, in Roche, W.K., Teague, P. and Colvin, A.J.S. (eds.) *The Oxford Handbook of Conflict Management in Organizations*. Oxford: Oxford University Press, pp. 333–353.

Ury, W.L., Brett, J.M. and Goldberg, S.B. (1988). *Getting Disputes Resolved: Designing Systems to Cut the Costs of Conflict*. San Francisco: Jossey-Bass.

van de Vliert, E. and De Dreu, C.K.W. (1994). 'Optimizing performance by stimulating conflict', *International Journal of Conflict Management*, 5(3), pp. 211–222.

Westin, A.F. and Felieu, A.G. (1988). *Resolving Employment Disputes Without Litigation*. Washington, DC: Bureau of National Affairs.

18

A PACIFIED LABOUR?

The transformation of labour conflict

Lorenzo Frangi, Sung-Chul Noh and Robert Hebdon

Introduction

This chapter argues that a fundamental transformation of labour conflict is taking place due to the effects of globalisation on labour and work. These structural changes will require significant alterations to both theory and research on the topic. The traditional method of equating labour conflict with strikes has become increasingly inappropriate. Some emblematic cases presented in this chapter highlight that theory and focus must be broadened to include both the full range of collective and individual expressions.

Historically, labour resistance was an important engine of social change and economic progress for working people (Hyman, 1989). Known as industrial conflict it was defined broadly to include both individual (grievances, absenteeism, health and safety complaints, etc.) and collective (strikes, slowdowns, overtime bans, etc.) expressions (Feuille and Wheeler, 1981). However, labour conflict has been almost exclusively researched as collective employee mobilisation in the form of strikes (Kelly, 1998). Therefore, our challenge is to provide new insights that take into account contextual changes to understand and analyse labour conflict in this new era.

After a short section on the most important theoretical perspectives applied to study labour conflict, we examine the proposition that labour peace has triumphed over conflict. We document the decline in strikes, observe the willingness to strike in the working population and highlight three examples of new emerging forms of conflict. Next, research challenges flowing from our analysis will be identified. We conclude with a brief summary of our findings and an agenda for future research.

Two fundamental perspectives

There are two competing perspectives on labour conflict. The unitarist sees conflict as dysfunctional, with order and harmony being the natural state of affairs (Gall and Hebdon, 2008). Pluralist and Marxist scholars both view conflict as a natural event that flows from the structured antagonism inherent in the capitalist workplace (Edwards, 1986). They disagree, however, over the scope of this discontent and its ability to be resolved through collective bargaining. Marxists hold that the class conflict emanating from capitalism cannot be resolved through collective bargaining. Pluralists, on the other hand, believe that the institutions of collective bargaining and unions can restore the imbalance of power between labour and management.

Scholars taking a unitarist view on workplace conflict delineate between functional and dysfunctional forms of conflict (e.g. Jehn, 1997). They have proposed that although task conflict can be beneficial to organisational performance by stimulating creativity and innovation, relational conflict generally interferes with performance. Thus, much focus has been put on the HR practices to maximise the benefits of the former while minimising the detriments of the latter (DeChurch and Marks, 2001; Tjosvold, 2008). In this light, this view can be also labelled as the functionalist view on conflict.

This unitarist perspective is common within the managerialist paradigm and many economics and organisational behaviour (OB) scholars. Economists have almost exclusively studied strikes to the exclusion of other forms of conflict. Most economists consider strikes as irrational collective bargaining outcomes, avoidable with full information to the parties. However, the view of strikes as irrational has several limitations. There are very few micro studies that probe or test the irrationality assumption and models have been developed which argue that conflict is rational when information is asymmetric (Campolieti, Hebdon and Hyatt, 2005; Card, 1990). Management research in the field of OB has been primarily targeted to individual conflict (absenteeism, grievances, sabotage, turnover, etc.) and developing strategies to control it. While many management strategies have been proposed, more recent studies have highlighted that labour conflict is characterised by persistence, destructiveness and resistance, and is thus mostly intractable and difficult to eradicate (Coleman et al., 2007).

Theoretical perspectives such as pluralism and Marxism recognise that labour conflict is an inherent characteristic of employment relations (ER). Conflict is a persistent social dynamic involving an array of social groups with their distinct and differing interests (Gall and Hebdon, 2008). Situated in this perspective are mainly sociology and industrial relations (IR) scholars who assume that there is structured antagonism of interest between labour and capital. This hostility generates conflict in various forms, the most common of which are collective strikes and individual grievances (Edwards, 1986). For sociologists, conflict is not restricted to the wage-effort bargain but is seen in a wider societal context. Economic factors are less important than the ability of labour to act collectively to introduce social change. Thus, sociologists' research focus is not primarily on the collective bargaining economic outcome but rather on the impact of labour conflict on national politics and social dynamics (Brandl and Traxler, 2010; Jansen, 2014). Industrial relations researchers have also had a micro agenda, probing the individual factors that affect strikes and other forms of labour conflict (e.g. Van der Velden et al., 2007). A prolific literature thus emerged on strikes and grievances (see, for example, Hyman, 1989 on strikes and Lewin and Peterson, 1988 on grievances).

Thus, competing perspectives have contributed to a rich debate about the nature of labour conflict but at the same time fostered a disconnect between disciplines. Very little work has been done to integrate labour conflict theory (exceptions include: Godard, 1992; Hebdon, 2005; and Wheeler, 1985) with the result that there is no comprehensive theory. Theories about collective and individual expressions of labour conflict are still very independent and efforts to link them together have been limited. Moreover, theories about labour conflict are limited in their comprehensiveness because strikes have been the prevailing research focus. Theories about different forms of labour conflict such as individual and other non-strike expressions are underdeveloped (Ackroyd, 2012). Labour conflict may appear in many different forms apart from strikes – a particularly important notion given the decline in strikes. The lack of a comprehensive theoretical approach is probably the main reason why the decline of strikes is often misinterpreted as evidence of a general decline in labour conflict (Gall and Hebdon, 2008).

Reduction of structural opportunities and the withering away of strikes

There is a growing consensus about how global changes have dramatically reduced the structural conditions that allowed labour discontent to be organised and transformed into collective strikes (Kelly, 2015). First, in Western countries, due to the worldwide intensification of cost competition, manufacturing jobs have been offshored to developing countries. Companies also faced market volatility through continuous flexible productive (re)arrangements. Hence, the number of core employees in big firms shrank, several tasks were outsourced and the number of short-term contract employees boomed. These constant restructurings made job loss threat a daily reality. The Fordist blue-collar industrial army crumbled, together with its distinctive working-class solidarity and sub-culture; key factors in fostering collective strikes (Dixon, Roscigno and Hodson, 2004).

Second, many firms have implemented high-performance work systems. Tasks have been enriched with more autonomy and responsibility, collaboration became a major asset and possible tensions were promptly solved through conflict resolution techniques. These changes not only eradicated more alienating factors from work – sources of much employee discontent on which strikes flourished – but also stimulated employee identification with and loyalty to management (Godard, 2011). The employee perception of the "structural employer-employee antagonism" has been largely replaced by a unitary perception. Therefore strikes, perceived as the central weapon in labour's arsenal, might now be perceived as irrational actions (Godard, 2011; Hyman, 1989).

Finally, employee discontent has lost its most important channel to be organised and transformed into collective strikes – trade unions. Since the beginning of the 1980s unions have been facing a deep crisis. Union ability to organise employees and their discontent has atrophied (Gall and Allsop, 2015). Bargaining coverage suffered a major decline and unions have been frequently on the defensive (e.g. Bryson, Ebbinghaus and Visser, 2011). With this marginalisation of unions, ER have shifted from being bureaucratically protected and predictable to volatile, uncertain, complex and ambiguous (Roscigno, Hodson and Lopez, 2009) and a vicious cycle of union decline and strikes is in play (Kelly, 2015).

Given these structural conditions it is not astonishing that since the 1980s the decline of strikes has been steep and in some countries they have almost disappeared (Brandl and Traxler, 2010; Piazza, 2005). The few occurrences of strikes have been to defend the *status quo* against painful concessions and the odds of success have correspondingly declined. Employees have not only experienced the loss of the offensive influence of strikes but have also questioned the effectiveness of strikes in protecting past gains in wages and working conditions (Brym, Bauer and McIvor, 2013; Rosenfeld, 2014). Fatalism and acceptance of discontent seem to prevail among employees. Strikes have withered away and labour conflict is thus currently considered quiescent and pacified (Piazza, 2005; Shalev, 1992).

Has labour peace triumphed?

The general withering away of strikes seems to support this pacification perspective; however, the labour pacification thesis seems less convincing when a more comprehensive perspective is assumed and some recent evidence of traditional and emerging forms of labour conflict is taken into account (e.g. Brym et al., 2013). For the traditional forms of labour conflict, i.e. strikes, we specifically focus on some evidence of strike propensity in Western and non-Western countries, and on the unexpected willingness to strike expressed by many employees who never went on strike. Emerging forms of labour conflict will be the focus of a later section.

Some evidence of strike propensity. While in such liberal market economies as the US, UK, Australia and New Zealand labour conflict has been marginalised (Briggs, 2007), in Canada, another liberal country, labour tension erupted into strikes during the 2000s, especially in the public sector (Briskin, 2007). In the more coordinated European countries, strikes re-emerged in Belgium from 2000 (Martens amd Pulignano, 2008), especially in the public sector and among bank and insurance white-collar workers who demonstrated high militancy (Vandaele, 2007). Also, countries with a more corporatist tradition, such as Finland, Norway and Denmark, demonstrated a non-marginal rate of strikes during the 2000s (Kelly, 2015). In Denmark, for example, strike activity has remained reasonably stable since the seventies and it is thus considered an example of the withering away of social peace (Birke, 2007).

While workplace strikes have generally declined, interestingly strikes have been on the rise since the 1980s as political actions in western Europe (Hamann, Johnston and Kelly, 2013). General strikes against government increased from 21 in the 1980s, to 36 in the 1990s, to 39 between 2000 and 2009, and to 52 between 2010 and 2014 (Kelly, 2015). Unions have been able to organise the collective discontent against the implementation of neoliberal reforms aimed at the introduction of more flexible labour market arrangements and cutbacks in welfare provisions. The highest concentration of political strikes has been experienced in Italy, Spain, France and, especially, Greece (Hamman et al., 2012). These strikes reached high social visibility and have been populated by employees together with a wide range of people who shared a collective discontent towards neoliberal policies. For example, a political strike against the precarisation of first employment contracts for young employees was carried out in France in 2006 not only by unions but also by millions of students; the result was the defeat of the government (Bouquin, 2007).

Labour conflict is also present in many developing countries (see Gall, 2013). Unfortunately, major data constraints limit the possibility of a thorough longitudinal worldwide comparison and the debate has relied mainly on case studies. Three different perspectives have emerged as the most important in studying labour conflict in developing countries. First, while there are many data constraints, some scholars tried to develop a longitudinal study about strike activities in developing countries. The decreasing trend seems to also affect the already low strike level in developing countries (Wallace and O'Sullivan, 2006). Second, emphasis has been put on the fact that offshoring of manufacturing production to developing countries has created some of the structural conditions for the emergence of workplace strikes, such as the presence of a blue-collar army. Therefore, the possibility that strikes are 'migrating' from developed to developing countries has been sustained (Silver, 2003). National case studies seemed to support this perspective, such as the emergence of labour conflict in South Korea and Brazil during the 1980s (cf. Cho, 1985), although both South Korea and Brazil passed through a decline of strikes in the 1990s, and currently in Brazil strikes are mainly enacted by public white-collar employees (Boito and Marcelino, 2011). Also, important actions have been recorded in Argentina and South Africa (Dribbusch and Vandaele, 2007). Third, attention has been driven to the different nature and aim of labour action in some developing countries in comparison to the Western tradition. Studies of China and Vietnam demonstrated that wildcat strikes, high turnover and absenteeism are enacted several times as a challenge to law dispositions, not as a consequence of failed or slow negotiation but to support the possibility to have the right to bargaining, and to push from below changes into non-independent trade unions and authoritarian regimes (Anner and Liu, 2016; Chan, 2011). Regimes have thus been forced to provide some concessions in terms of employee rights (Elfstrom and Kuruvilla, 2014; Friedman and Lee, 2010).

Willingness to strike. In a general strike decline context, studying employee willingness to strike becomes a fundamental perspective. Indeed, employees who are willing to strike have not only to consider strikes as legitimate but also as effective actions to remedy discontent and tensions faced in their employment relations (Akkerman, Born and Torenvlied, 2013; Hyman, 1989; Martin and Sinclair, 2001). Willingness to strike is a necessary pre-condition for a strike (Su and Feng, 2013).

The unwillingness to engage in conflict by employees may depend on several factors (Godard, 2011; Hyman, 1989). First, since strikes are rare one may infer that willingness to strike has also withered away. Second, forces of globalisation put employee solidarity under stress and drive them to perceive strikes as irrational actions (Akkerman et al., 2013). Third, inexperience with strikes is the most common condition today and employees who never went on strike are more affected by feelings of inappropriateness, doubt and a sense of guilt about the possibility of engaging in a strike (Campolieti et al., 2005; Martin and Sinclair, 2001).

The scant research about willingness to strike has been exclusively focused around union members in a specific setting (e.g. industry, company, bargaining unit) or over a single bargaining issue (e.g. wages or working conditions) (Akkerman et al., 2013; Barling et al., 1992). Due to unions' organisational atrophy and the difficulty of organising workplace strikes, it is much more relevant to study strikes at a wider level to understand the perception of strike. In this perspective, 28.8 per cent of the Dutch population sample said they would be willing to join an economic strike if the issue was wage increases (Akkerman et al., 2013); 14.7 per cent gave a neutral response.[1] Frangi, Boodoo and Hebdon (2015) studied the willingness to strike in 13 OECD countries among employees who never went on strike; in this case strikes were generally defined as including both economic and political dimensions. The results are shown in Figure 18.1, below.

While variation across countries is large, at least one out of three employees who never went on strike are willing to strike. In western countries, where the withering away of strikes reduced

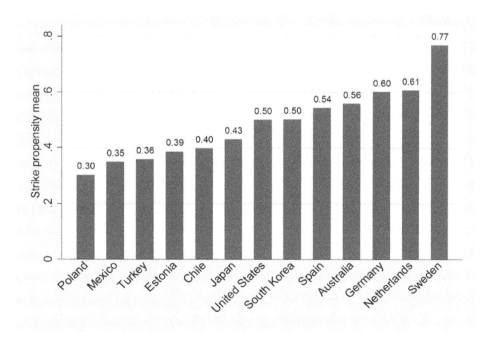

Figure 18.1 Willingness to strike in 13 OECD countries (World Values Survey, 2012–2014 wave)

labour conflict to a marginal action, more than one out of two employees who never went on strike are willing to strike (Japan being a partial exception). Notable is the case of the US. Considered as the fortress of the neoliberal model with one of the lowest union densities among Western countries, the US has an unexpectedly high level of 50 per cent being willing to strike. Multivariate analyses confirm that individual economic deprivation is a determinant of willingness to strike. However, progressive ideology, interest in politics and support of unions (in terms of membership but also as expression of confidence, see Frangi, Hennebert and Memoli, 2014; Frangi and Memoli, 2014; Frangi and Hennebert, 2015) are confirmed as stronger determinants. Moreover, employees living in countries that are wealthier and have higher levels of bargaining coordination have higher willingness to strike. Employees seem to be more willing to join strikes when conflict can help in fostering a more equal sharing of the richness produced through a bargaining system able to affect many employees.

The transformation of labour conflict

The occurrence of strikes to eradicate or at least diminish employee discontent is made significantly more difficult by structural changes introduced by globalisation. Alternative manifestations of labour conflict seem to emerge as increasingly more important (Kelly, 2015). We present three examples that highlight how labour conflict is passing through a process of fundamental transformation to assume forms substantially different from the traditional workplace strike. The first highlights the increased relevance of formal and informal individual conflict in the workplace; the second underlines how virtual individual actions outside the workplace can develop new forms of collectivity and conflict that transcend the boundaries of workplaces; and the third shows how the locus of conflict can shift from workplace to society.

Individualised forms of conflict: formal grievances and misbehaviour

Changes introduced to employment rights legislation have resulted in a lack of employee representation or voice in some workplaces. Unrepresented individual employees were left in many cases with no option but to pursue a personal grievance if they faced unfair treatment or dismissal, racial discrimination or harassment (Dix, Sisson and Forth, 2009). Furthermore, atrophied trade unions have tended to rely much more on the enforcement of statutory employment rights in order to defend employee rights (Dickens, 2002). This has led to, for example, a rising tide of claims to the Employment Tribunal over the past decades in the UK, as seen in Figure 18.2, below.

The trend shows a strong positive overall increase in grievances presented to the employment tribunal system until 2009. A record 236,100 applications were accepted during 2009–2010 amid the global financial crisis; this amounted to a 56 per cent increase over the previous year. The managerial response to the crisis in the form of downsizing, restructuring or other measures boosted overall levels of worker discontent and led to an increase in individual disputes. This immense volume of legal grievances led the UK government to change the law in July 2013 to charge a fee to file a tribunal claim, which accounts for the subsequent decreasing trend.[3] Alongside the growth in volume of individualised employment rights claims, the employment tribunal statistics also suggest a change in their composition. For instance, unfair dismissal, which had represented three quarters of employment tribunal claims in 1986, made up 31 per cent of the 218,100 claims in 2011–2012. Discrimination cases have formed a small, but growing proportion of the total cases, today representing jointly around 15 per cent of all applications.

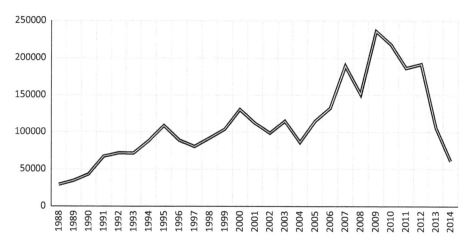

Figure 18.2 Employment tribunal claims in the UK, 1988–2014[2]

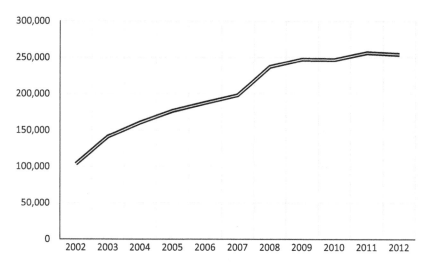

Figure 18.3 Trend in the number of cases of civil individual labour disputes in Japan[4]

The growing volume and changing nature of formalised individual disputes seen in the UK also appears in other developed countries. For instance, there were about 255,000 cases of consultation on civil individual labour disputes in Japan in 2012; the number has doubled over the past 10 years, as seen in Figure 18.3. Reflecting the workforce ageing faster than that of any other country, cases related to retirement accounted for the largest proportion with 18.3 per cent, followed by 'bullying/harassment' with 17.0 per cent, 'dismissal' with 16.9 per cent and 'worsened working conditions' with 11.2 per cent. The increase in costly tribunal claims has driven many enterprises to establish formal procedures, especially for cases of employee discipline and dismissals. It is illustrative that in 1971 only eight per cent of workplaces (with five or more employees) in the UK reported using formal procedures, whereas in 2011 89 per cent of workplaces had this procedure.

While grievances and employment tribunal cases are forms of individual-level conflicts formalised through legal systems or HRM practices, a large part of management-employee tensions and labour conflict remains unchannelled into these formal spheres and is thereby more difficult for management or unions to control (Collinson and Ackroyd, 2005). In particular, labour process theorists and industrial sociologists have highlighted everyday forms of resistance that have been rendered, in the unitarist perspective, merely antisocial, dysfunctional and counterproductive (Lawrence and Robinson, 2007). Most notably, in her case study on workplace conflict in an Irish call centre, Mulholland (2004) demonstrated that informal workplace resistance practices emerged among call centre workers as their union could not deal with issues such as work intensification, productivity and pay, and arbitrary management practices. The repertoire of resistance practices she identified included 'slammin", in which telesales workers pretend to be involved in the selling transaction to falsely meet the requirement of making a call every three minutes, as well as withdrawal of their emotional labour by simply following the sales script. Although these misbehaviours on the surface appear individualistic and fragmentary, the author suggests they could be seen as a covert and tacit form of collective resistance in that the telesales workers showed solidarity over such practices by supporting each other through empathy and sympathy. In a similar vein, Bain and Taylor (2000) show that misbehaviours which make the most of gaps in the system of electronic monitoring laid the groundwork for organising a union in one call centre in the UK. These studies suggest that it is important to explore the interaction between power and resistance that takes place within the informal terrain to fully understand conflict dynamics at work.

In particular, the introduction of advanced information systems has been blurring the boundary between informal and formal spheres of work, enhancing workers' autonomy and agency. Recent studies of new types of misbehaviour such as cyberslacking and cyberloafing show that workers' misbehaviour as a mode of resistance is a process under continuous evolution and innovation, adapting to the increasingly sophisticated managerial surveillance of work (Ivarsson and Larsson, 2011; Richards, 2007).

Online forms of conflict: clicktivism. Individual employees can voice discontent in their workplace through individual actions, but advances in information and communication technology have provided them with new opportunities to freely voice concerns outside the workplace and within a reconstituted form of collectivity. Through social media employees can connect with other like-minded individuals and groups and unite around specific issues and concerns, such as labour discontent, conditions and rights (Shirky, 2008). Social media platforms, while based on individual participation, allow the formation of new types of collectivity in the form of online communities. These collectivities differ from bureaucratic unions and party structures, as is explained next (Gerbaudo, 2012).

To take action all that is required is a simple click of support (*clicktivism*). In social media groups, participants do not have to face any entry or exit cost such as in unions, reducing the fear of being locked-in (Bryson, Gomez and Willman, 2010). Moreover, rather than statutes and bureaucratic structures as pivotal elements of their togetherness, they have easy-to-personalise action frames that allow for diverse interpretations (Bennett and Segerberg, 2013). Finally, the fear of possible retaliation, a major preventive element in the enactment of grievances and strikes, is not a constituent element in voicing discontent in cyberspace as it is in the workplace (Fitzgerald, Hardy and Lucio, 2012). However, the aim is similar to that of traditional forms of labour conflict: create solidarity among participants and take action to diminish or eradicate labour discontent.

Through a process of continuous peer production, participants boost their sense of togetherness and identification through the sharing and diffusion of content (Gerbaudo, 2012). While some critics have downgraded this action as a light form of engagement that has zero political or social impact (Morozov, 2011), most offer more positive views. For example, clicktivism may generate a shared sentiment of indignation, anger or pride; it could not only increase conscious-ness about labour-related causes, but also provide a sense of empowerment to participants that promotes a feeling of urgency to take action to change the *status quo* (Gerbaudo, 2012; Howard and Parks, 2012). Most active participants in social media groups mobilise, organise and pattern these online voices of discontent to transform them into actual conflict. Some of these actions have been online, such as email campaigns, petitions and even virtual sit-ins, but social media group mobilisation may also lead to important large-scale offline actions. Social media actions can become mobilisation accelerators transforming online discontent and tension into the real world (Gerbaudo, 2012; Panagiotopoulos and Barnett, 2015).

Social media activism has been fundamental, for example, in creating the powerful iden-tity of exploited low-wage workers in the Wal-Mart campaign that led to unexpected strikes. These actions were not the typical strikes contemplated in the Wagner act model (Wood, 2015). In the same way clicktivism has been fundamental to the Fight for $15 campaign. The movement has been backed by much online action in social media. Considering the many small and intermittent contributions to the cause of Fight for $15 on Twitter, Zhang, Frangi and Hebdon (2016) analysed the volume of tweets and re-tweets. As shown in Figure 18.4, until mid August 2015 levels of clicktivism were low, with the exception of a spike in late July. A period of much more intense clicktivism activity and increased emotional tension followed in August, September and especially October. This online conflict climaxed in a gigantic wave of online support and an actual strike on 10 November 2015 (when 41,274 Fightfor15 tweets were posted); the biggest strike yet for $15 per hour of many low-wage employees together with unions and supporters.

The potential of clicktivism resides in the strategic alliances that online communities allow to develop. For example, actions to improve labour rights can find the support of consumer and civil society organisations, together with many other individual sympathisers. The online community can amplify awareness of the labour issue to include people and organisations. Various institutional

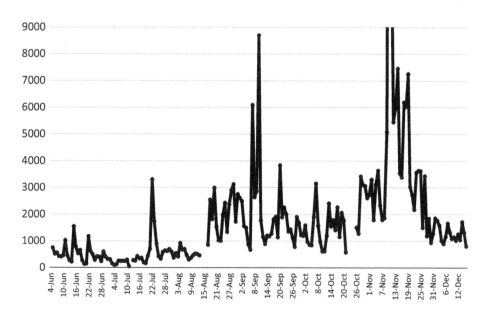

Figure 18.4   Volume of tweets relative to Fight for $15 (the highest spike has to be excluded for graphical reasons)

and mobilisation resources can find a strategic moment of coordination in the online community and become the main driver to organise several coordinated offline actions towards employers, public and private institutions, and governments (Evans, 2010). An outstanding example of the potential that this synergy can create is the case of the post-Rana Plaza mobilisation to push employers to respect fundamental labour rights (Reinecke and Donaghey, 2015).

Alternative collective forms of conflict: Fight for $15. Within industrialised nations, the US has experienced one of the most dramatic union density and bargaining coverage declines. Strikes in the US are limited by law (essentially the Wagner Act) to unionised workplaces (more than half of the employees must affiliate to unions to become unionised) and can be exclusively enacted to support collective bargaining. Hence union strikes dramatically declined. However, a new labour conflict form is taking shape, shifting the locus of conflict from workplace to society and having not only workers but a wider array of organisations and grass-roots supporters among the constituents.

Since the beginning of the 2000s, a large coalition comprised of unions, religious organisations, community groups, politicians and a large number of ordinary citizens has advocated for the right to have a living wage (Figart, 2004). After the 2008 economic and financial crisis this campaign lost momentum and seemed to disappear (Luce, 2015). However, it resurfaced with renewed vigour in November 2012. Working in non-unionised workplaces and so without the support of a union, fast-food employees conducted a one-day work stoppage in New York City, demanding a $15 per hour wage. Some non-unionised employees at Wal-Mart also withheld their labour on 'Black Friday' in 2012.[5] The movement mushroomed and quickly spread around the country. By late 2014 more than 190 US cities had been affected by a Fight for $15 strike. The wide sympathy and solidarity received by the Fight for $15 movement pressured politicians and firms to take action (Luce, 2015). By 2014 four cities approved a minimum salary of $15, and Chicago raised it to $13. GAP, McDonald's, Target and Wal-Mart raised their minimum wage close to $15 (Fraser, 2015). On 21 July 2015, the Los Angeles County Board of Supervisors voted to increase the minimum wage to $15 by 2020, and the day after, the Fast Food Wage Board appointed by the New York state governor announced plans to increase fast-food workers' wages. The movement achieved such significant power in society that in October 2015 President Obama hosted the first Worker Voice Summit at the White House. The movement's successes resulted in continued growth, with wide social support and solidarity. On 10 November 2015 Fight for $15 held a massive strike. Thousands of workers from Burger King, Wendy's, McDonald's, KFC and other restaurant chains joined home care, child care, grocery clerks and other low-wage workers and took to the streets in 270 cities across America. It was the largest strike ever in the battle for a $15-an-hour wage, producing excitement and a sense of empowerment among US lower-paid employees never before experienced. This enthusiasm crossed the border into Canada and a Fight for $15 campaign is also brewing there.

Unlike union workplace strikes, which have been targeted to support firm-specific requests during collective bargaining, Fight for $15 is taking the form of a social cause: a fair minimum wage for all low-wage workers (Luce, 2015). Fight for $15 conflict is characterised by fewer bureaucratic organisational structures in comparison with the one exclusively organised by unions, and participation is open to all people who would like to support the cause. Therefore, Fight for $15 is drawing on a much wider range of support than just unions and their supporters. The movement also takes advantage of a right to collective action found in the Wagner Act for non-union workers.

Research challenges

If one studies corporate power in the contemporary world of work and thinks of labour conflict purely in terms of Fordist clichés (essentially strikes), then the inevitable conclusion is that employee resistance is indeed quiescent. Even if overt and collective forms of resistance characteristic of Fordism may have been tempered, this by no means indicates that employers have finally succeeded in transforming the 'recalcitrant worker' into the supine, docile and biddable worker. Labour conflict has not disappeared. There are no signs that it will disappear soon since there is still enough discontent to fuel conflict. Employees are resilient and determined to find new ways of resisting.

It is evident, however, that labour conflict is undergoing a profound transformation in the way in which it is organised and expressed (Bélanger and Edwards, 2013). Increasing global and workplace constraints seem to stimulate employees to search for innovative forms to express and alleviate their labour discontent. Labour conflict has been compared to a balloon: if constraints reduce pressure on one part then there is expansion in another and the balloon assumes a new configuration (Sapsford and Turnbull, 1994).

New actors and new *loci* emerged as fundamental to labour conflict. White collars became protagonists of strikes in some western countries but the major change was the wider array of support that labour conflict achieved beyond just employees or unionised employees. This is evident in the larger coalitions in general strikes in Europe, in minimum wage campaigns in North America and in labour clicktivism in cyberspace, where social movements and individual sympathisers join forces to fight for a labour cause.

Labour conflict has also changed *locus*. For a long time strikes happened at the plant gate – now labour conflict seems more likely to be expressed in the individual intra-workplace space of production and in the extra-workplace space of tribunals for individual claims; squares and streets for larger social protest; and in the catalytic cyberspace where support for labour conflict is organised. To be able to analyse this transformation of labour conflict, scholars face major challenges far beyond their singular focus on the traditional union strike. We specifically focus on four pivotal challenges.

Theoretical challenges. The global decline of the mass production paradigm and economies rooted in managerialist ideology renders conventional theories inadequate for investigating how contemporary social forces have transformed workplaces. Many economic studies about labour conflict have provided important insights into strikes during their golden age and decline. While some determinants can still have some influence on the changing shape of labour conflict, economic theoretical contributions have more limited potential in tracing the environmental characteristics that allow specific forms of labour conflict to emerge. Due to bargaining coverage and union decline, the economic models that focus on incomplete information at the bargaining table are much less relevant. However, economic theories can substantially contribute to considering how different aspects of economic globalisation shape the forms that labour conflict assumes at national, firm and individual levels.

Thus, given the complexity introduced by the changing contours of labour conflict, economic theory alone is not sufficient to explain or understand this new world of conflict. More integrative approaches have to be considered to structure a more comprehensive theoretical approach to fully explore the new forms of labour conflict. Socio-psychological approaches have enriched the debate about strikes, but potential lies in the inclusion of other approaches, each one providing important insights in decoupling the complexity of innovative forms of labour conflict (Godard, 1992).

Since the locus of labour conflict is shifting progressively from workplace bargaining dynamics to socially open events where unions are no longer the only organiser, as in the case of political strikes or even more in Fight for $15, a promising direction for labour conflict research is to include social movement theory (Gahan and Pekarek, 2013; Martin, 2008). Social movement theory offers a useful conceptual vocabulary for understanding the new social structures wrought by transitory global production, volatile financial markets, and transnational collective action and governance. Among others, "resource mobilisation" and "political opportunities" frameworks seem promising (McCarthy and Zald, 2001). They can enhance our understanding about which internal resources are strategically mobilised and which structural opportunities allow for the emergence and expression of specific types of conflict. For instance, Rao, Morill and Zald (2000) build on these insights by demonstrating the role of collective action and social movements in the creation of new organisational forms and fields of practice.

Industrial and employment relations scholars have studied such institutional individual expressions of labour conflict as grievances, but we know little about more informal and covert individual forms. Alternatively, critical management studies and sociology of work have shed more light on deviant behaviours at work, analysing them through the lens of workplace intrinsic employer-employee antagonism (Mulholland, 2004). They unearthed a multitude of employee oppositional workplace practices directed at the organisation and line managers, ranging from resistance – such as that 'effort bargain' to get their work done with a minimum of effort – through misbehaviour (referring to self-conscious rule-breaking), to dissent in the form of linguistic or normative disagreement, the satirical mockery of managers and authority figures, absenteeism, work limitation, sabotage and theft to destructiveness (Collinson and Ackroyd, 2005). Moreover, this stream of research helps explain how specific forms of individualised resistance are related to particular types of managerial control (Fleming, 2007).

Finally, we need to recognise that social media play a pivotal role in condensing, organising and transforming labour discontent into conflict, such as in our analysis of Fight for $15 clicktivism on Twitter (Zhang et al., 2016). New media studies can therefore provide further insights, especially through the lens of framing emergence, definition, resonance and influence on enactment of conflict actions (Gahan and Pekarek, 2013; Gerbaudo, 2012). This approach can help identify the key leaders of labour conflict organisation, since this role is no longer the sole purview of trade unions.

Analytical challenges. The labour conflict literature has focused on analysing the volume of strikes, as the result of the three most important analytical dimensions (number of participants, duration, frequency) or other closely related dimensions (such as incidence per 1,000 employees). Other analytical dimensions have been identified but rarely empirically described and explained. For instance, labour conflict has been classified dichotomously as latent or manifest, unorganised or organised, individual or collective (Edwards, 1986; Hebdon and Noh, 2013). The individual and collective dichotomy, on the one hand, and unorganised and organised, on the other hand, have been frequently used as synonyms; unorganised conflict is seen as individual and organised conflict collective (Gall and Hebdon, 2008). However, individual actions can be the expression of a collective decision of reacting to discontent (see Bélanger and Edwards, 2013; Gall and Hebdon, 2008). Therefore, these two dimensions deserve to be treated separately.

The first analytical improvement that can provide more fine-grained insights into the study of the transformation of labour conflict is to abandon dichotomous classifications to instead consider a continuum scale between the two polarities previously traced (e.g. organised and unorganised) (Hebdon and Noh, 2013). The second and more substantial improvement is to consider a much wider range of analytical dimensions of labour conflict. The examples of new labour conflict forms presented above cannot be reduced to just a few dimensions. For instance, as in Fight for $15 the role of unions can no longer be taken for granted and their degree of involvement has to be analysed. Issues of conflict can affect a minimal number of workers, such as in the case of a plant-level strike, or a much wider population, such in the European political strikes. Moreover, conflict can be highly disruptive, such as in workplace strikes or much less so, for example in the case of individual court claims. Participants in the enactment of labour conflict can be just the concerned employees or a much larger array of people (other employees, non-employees and social movements), such as in the general political strikes or in the Fight for $15 case. Finally, labour conflict can be characterised by the different degree of respect of legal requirements.

While other dimensions can be added to the study of labour conflict, those discussed above appear to be of particular relevance. We therefore propose a spider-net analytical model to capture both traditional and emerging forms of labour conflict, shown in Figure 18.5. Figure 18.5a (solid line) represents a typical North American case of a four-day firm strike organised by unions in support of bargaining negotiations for the 60 employees of the bargaining unit. This

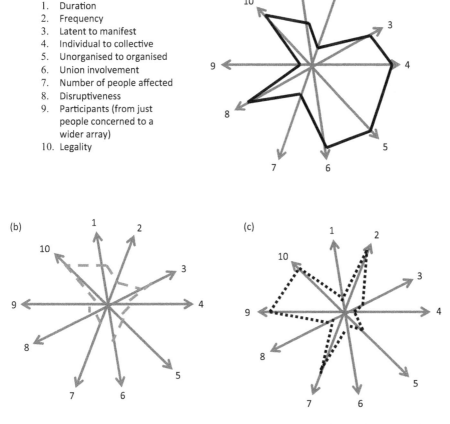

1. Duration
2. Frequency
3. Latent to manifest
4. Individual to collective
5. Unorganised to organised
6. Union involvement
7. Number of people affected
8. Disruptiveness
9. Participants (from just people concerned to a wider array)
10. Legality

Figure 18.5 Spider-net analytical model for traditional and emerging forms of labour conflict
    a Traditional workplace strike
    b Individual claim to court through union
    c Clicktivism

strike has been called respecting all legal conditions (legality). We assume that a strike happened four years before (medium-to-low frequency). Employees (people concerned) demonstrate outside the firm (manifest).

Figure 18.5b (dashed line) represents a case of an individual employee labour claim to a court for unpaid salary through a union legal service. This kind of conflict requires action to be taken once (open the case) and then be presented in court once (or few more times) (low duration and frequency). While it is a manifest action, it is much less visible to society than a workplace strike. Since it is an individual action it requires a minimum level of organisation. A union is involved to prepare the case but it is an involvement that requires much lower energy and efforts than a strike. This legal action has almost no disruptiveness consequences on production. Finally, Figure 18.5c (dotted line) represents a case of clicktivism for raising the minimum wage in the USA. Multiple times per day (frequency), an individual employee dedicates seconds for a click (duration) to endorse a labour cause in a social media group participated in by many individual sympathisers and social movements, some unions among them. The click action is in favour of raising the minimum wage for millions of US low-wage employees (number of people affected).

Methodological challenges. The most important methodological challenge to study labour conflict is data collection. Studies about strikes almost exclusively relied on national and ILO datasets. Comparative data suffer from lack of standardisation, specification (for example, strikes and lock-outs are not distinguished) and reliability issues but they are often the only available evidence (Lyddon, 2007). The data collection challenge becomes much more complex when we want to collect evidence about the different forms that labour conflict is assuming; however, merging different sources and co-construction strategies can help us to partially overcome this limitation.

In the case of more manifest, organised and collective forms of conflict, Elfstrom and Kuruvilla (2014) provided an excellent instrument to enhance data collection. First, official data have been compared and merged with newspapers, social media, blogs, and activist website articles and reports. Second, and most importantly, they developed a website where visitors are allowed to submit labour conflict events themselves.[6] Once uploaded, labour conflict reports are publicly accessible. A wide advertisement of a similar platform among scholars, trade unions, social movements and labour cause supporters would enhance labour conflict data collection. These collected data can be organised according to the analytical dimensions highlighted in the previous section. Bias is not excluded in the collection, but the fact that labour conflict reports have to be reinforced with links to relevant newspaper articles and/or photos, and that issues can be reported by anyone, partially limit this concern. The data collected will not be exhaustive of all manifest labour conflicts but there is potential to enhance our analyses.

The data collection challenge is even greater for more latent, individual and unorganised conflicts. In these cases, achieving a comprehensive picture is just utopia. We have to rely on a paleontological approach, searching for fragments of the phenomenon. Our fragments are small-scale surveys, in-depth interviews with privileged observers and employees, and participant observation. A major constraint to consolidating fragments is the variability of cases and the difficulty of standardisation. The advantage is that the information would be reported mostly by scholars. The possibility of establishing a shared databank of less manifest cases of labour conflict would be rich if researchers would describe the most important characteristics of the case and then try as much as possible to characterise the labour conflict fragment according to the dimensions presented in the previous section. The combining of fragments will improve our analyses and limited theories about labour conflict.

Geographical and temporal challenges. The few studies in employment relations that analyse labour conflict are almost exclusively Western-centred. The rare contributions to the international debate about labour conflict in non-Western countries demonstrated interesting evidence of labour effervescence, especially in countries that are experiencing an accelerated industrialisation and a wide array of blue-collar workers. However, except for these few contributions our general knowledge of labour conflict in non-Western countries remains sporadic and non-systematic. Expanding the geographical scope is therefore fundamental in labour conflict research to achieve more comprehensive insights.

The other challenge is temporal. Except for a few recent contributions (Akkerman et al., 2013; Frangi et al., 2015), the labour conflict literature is restricted to recollections on past actions. Labour conflict needs to be analysed in its potential form (e.g. strike propensity), especially to understand the type of actions employees will select and under what conditions. Moreover, mobilisation strategies can be developed using results from the analysis of conflict potential.

Conclusion and research agenda

The scholarly literature is trapped into viewing workplace strikes as the sole expression of labour conflict and this, in turn, leads to the fatalistic perspective of the withering away of strikes and hence all labour conflict. More recent evidence, however, demonstrates that labour conflict is persistent and able to resist the oppressive forces of the global economy. In a context of union atrophy, labour discontent may be expressed through non-institutionalised and innovative forms of conflict that are not captured by traditional approaches centred on union strikes. The major challenge for scholars is not only to capture and explain these forms of expression of labour conflict, but also to be able to link the different observed fragments of labour conflict to provide comprehensive theories.

Even if the labour conflict literature overcomes the challenges that we presented in this chapter, there are yet some unresolved issues that are key to understanding the transformation taking place. The first entails a rethinking of the traditional form of labour conflict, i.e. workplace strikes. It is proposed that the traditional workplace strike has followed manufacturing shifts from Western to developing countries (Bélanger and Edwards, 2013). While some cases have been studied, this proposition is still to be verified through a comprehensive approach. Another unsolved major point is the relationship between more manifest and collective forms of labour conflict, on the one side, and individual and more covert forms on the other (Hebdon and Noh, 2013). While some evidence seems to underline a possible trade-off, the relation remains to be empirically demonstrated. Finally, especially considering the emerging forms that labour conflict is assuming, it remains to be studied how individual, firm and national characteristics pattern the emergence of specific forms of labour conflict. In studying these three relationships in the ever-changing world of work we will fundamentally advance our knowledge of the infinity of worker resourcefulness in expressing discontent.

Notes

1 The authors wish to thank Prof. Agnes Akkerman for generously providing the results of her 2013 population survey.
2 *Each year stretches from 1 April to 31 March. Source from* House of Commons Research Paper *for 1988–2003 data* (http://researchbriefings.parliament.uk/ResearchBriefing/Summary/RP03-87), *the* Employment Tribunal Service annual reports for 2003–2010 *data* (http://webarchive.nationalarchives.gov.uk/20110207134805/http://www.employmenttribunals.gov.uk/Publications/annualReports.htm) *and the* Tribunals Service statistics for 2011–2014 (www.gov.uk/government/statistics?departments%5B%5D=ministry-of-justice&keywords=&topics%5B%5D=all&world_locations%5B%5D=all).

3 According to a TUC report, women and low-paid workers are being 'priced out' by the tribunal fees of up to £1,200. See www.tuc.org.uk/workplace-issues/employment-rights/tribunal-fees-have-been-%E2%80%9Chuge-victory%E2%80%9D-britain%E2%80%99s-worst-bosses

4 *Ministry of Health, Labour and Welfare Status on the Implementation of Individual Labour Dispute Resolution.*

5 These strikes were found to be legal by an NLRB decision dated 15 January, 2016. See www.nlrb.gov/news-outreach/news-story/nlrb-office-general-counsel-issues-complaint-against-walmart

6 The website is based on the free Ushahidi programme (www.ushahidi.com).

References

Ackroyd, S. (2012). Even more misbehavior: what has happened in the last twenty years, in *Advances in Industrial and Labor Relations*. Vol. 19. Bingley: Emerald Insight, pp. 1–28.

Akkerman, A., Born, M.J. and Torenvlied, R. (2013). 'Solidarity, Strikes, and Scabs: How Participation Norms Affect Union Members' Willingness to Strike', *Work and Occupations*, 40(3), pp. 250–280.

Anner, M. and Liu, X. (2016). 'Harmonious Unions and Rebellious Workers: A Study of Wildcat Strikes in Vietnam', *Industrial and Labor Relations Review*, 69(1), pp. 3–28.

Bain, P. and Taylor, P. (2000). "Entrapped by the 'electronic panopticon'? Worker resistance in the call centre', *New Technology, Work and Employment*, 15(1), pp. 2–18.

Barling, J., Clive F., Kelloway, E.K. and McElvie, L. (1992). 'Union loyalty and strike propensity', *Journal of Social Psychology*, 132(5), pp. 581–590.

Bélanger, J. and Edwards, P. (2013). Conflict and Contestation in the Contemporary World of Work: Theory and Perspectives, in Gall, G. (ed.) *New Forms and Expressions of Conflict at Work*. Basingstoke: Palgrave Macmillan, pp. 7–25.

Bennett, W.L. and Segerberg, A. (2013). *The Logic of Connective Action: Digital Media and the Personalization of Contentious Politics*. Cambridge (UK): Cambridge University Press.

Birke, P. (2007). The persistence of labour unrest: strikes in Denmark, 1969–2005, in van der Velden, S., Dribbusch, H., Lyddon, D. and Vandaele, K. (eds.) *Strikes Around the World, 1968–2005: Case-Studies of 15 Countries*. Amsterdam: Aksant, pp. 222–242.

Boito, A. and Marcelino, P. (2011). 'Decline in unionism? An analysis of the new wave of strikes in Brazil', *Latin American Perspectives*, 38(5), pp. 62–73.

Bouquin, S. (2007). Strong social eruptions and a weak tradition of collective bargaining, in van der Velden, S., Dribbusch, H., Lyddon, D. and Vandaele, K. (eds.) *Strikes Around the World, 1968–2005: Case-Studies of 15 Countries*. Amsterdam: Aksant, pp. 243–266.

Brandl, B. and Traxler, F. (2010). 'Labour conflicts: a cross-national analysis of economic and institutional determinants, 1971–2002', *European Sociological Review*, 26(5), pp. 519–540.

Briggs, C. (2007). Strikes and lockouts in the antipodes: neo-liberal convergence in Australia and New Zealand, in van der Velden, S., Dribbusch, H., Lyddon, D. and Vandaele, K. (eds.) *Strikes Around the World, 1968–2005: Case-Studies of 15 Countries*. Amsterdam: Aksant, pp. 173–195.

Briskin, L. (2007). Public sector militancy, feminization, and employer aggression, in van der Velden, S., Dribbusch, H., Lyddon, D. and Vandaele, K. (eds.) *Strikes Around the World, 1968–2005: Case-Studies of 15 Countries*. Amsterdam: Aksant, pp. 86–105.

Brym, R.J., Bauer, L.B. and McIvor, M. (2013). 'Is Industrial Unrest Reviving in Canada? Strike Duration in the Early Twenty-First Century', *Canadian Review of Sociology/Revue Canadienne de Sociologie*, 50(2), pp. 227–238.

Bryson, A., Gomez, R. and Willman, P. (2010). 'Online social networking and trade union membership: what the Facebook phenomenon truly means for labor organizers', *Labor History*, 51(1), pp. 41–53.

Bryson, A., Ebbinghaus, B. and Visser, J. (2011). 'Introduction: causes, consequences and cures of union decline', *European Journal of Industrial Relations*, 17(2), pp. 97–105.

Campolieti, M., Hebdon, R. and Hyatt, D. (2005). 'Strike incidence and strike duration: some new evidence from Ontario', *Industrial and Labor Relations Review*, 58(4), pp. 610–630.

Card, D. (1990). 'Strikes and Wages: A Test of an Asymmetric Information Model', *Quarterly Journal of Economics*, 105(3), pp. 625–659.

Chan, A. (2011). 'Strikes in China's export industries in comparative perspective', *The China Journal*, 65(January), pp. 27–51.

Cho, S.K. (1985). 'The Labor Process and Capital Mobility: The Limits of the New International Division of Labor', *Politics & Society*, 14(2), pp. 185–222.

Coleman, P.T., Vallacher, R., Nowak, A. and Bui-Wrzosinska, L. (2007). 'Intractable conflict as an attractor', *American Behavioral Scientist*, 50(11), pp. 1454–1475.

Collinson, D. and Ackroyd, S. (2005). Resistance, Misbehavior, and Dissent, in Ackroyd, S., Batt, R., Thompson, P. and Tolbert, P.S. (eds.) *The Oxford Handbook of Work and Organization*. Oxford: Oxford University Press, pp. 245–281.

DeChurch, L.A. and Marks, M.A. (2001). 'Maximizing the benefits of task conflict: the role of conflict management', *International Journal of Conflict Management*, 12(1), pp. 4–22.

Dickens, L. (2002). 'Individual statutory employment rights since 1997: constrained expansion', *Employee Relations*, 24(6), pp. 619–637.

Dix, G., Sisson, K. and Forth, J. (2009). Conflict at Work: The Changing Pattern of Disputes, in Brown, W., Bryson, A., Forth, J. and Whitfield, K. (eds.) *The Evolution of the Modern Workplace*. Cambridge (UK): Cambridge University Press, pp. 176–200.

Dixon, M., Roscigno, V.J. and Hodson, R. (2004). 'Unions, solidarity, and striking', *Social Forces*, 83(1), pp. 3–33.

Dribbusch, H. and Vandaele, K. (2007). Comprehending divergence in strike activity, in van der Velden, S., Dribbusch, H., Lyddon, D. and Vandaele, K. (eds.) *Strikes Around the World, 1968–2005: Case-Studies of 15 Countries*. Amsterdam: Aksant, pp 366–401.

Edwards, P.K. (1986). *Conflict at Work: A Materialist Analysis of Workplace Relations*. Oxford: B. Blackwell.

Elfstrom, M. and Kuruvilla, S. (2014). 'The changing nature of labor unrest in China', *Industrial and Labor Relations Review*, 67(2), pp. 453–480.

Evans, P. (2010). 'Is it labor's turn to globalize? Twenty-first century opportunities and strategic responses', *Global Labour Journal*, 1(3), pp. 352–378.

Feuille, P. and Wheeler, H.N. (1981). Will the Real Industrial Conflict Please Stand Up?, in *U.S. Industrial Relations 1950-1980: A Critical Assessment*. Madison: IRRA, pp. 255–291.

Figart, D.M. (2004). *Living Wage Movements: Global Perspectives*. London and New York: Routledge.

Fitzgerald, I., Hardy, J. and Lucio, M.M. (2012). 'The Internet, employment and Polish migrant workers: communication, activism and competition in the new organisational spaces', *New Technology, Work and Employment*, 27(2), pp. 93–105.

Fleming, P. (2007). 'Sexuality, Power and Resistance in the Workplace', *Organization Studies*, 28(2), pp. 239–256.

Frangi, L., Hennebert, M. and Memoli, V. (2014). 'Social Confidence in Unions: A US-Canada Comparison', *Canadian Review of Sociology/Revue Canadienne de Sociologie*, 51(2), pp. 170–188.

Frangi, L. and Memoli, V. (2014). 'Confidence in Brazilian Unions: a Longitudinal Analysis', *Latin American Perspectives*, 41(5), pp. 42–58.

Frangi, L. and Hennebert, M. (2015). 'Expressing Confidence in Unions in Quebec and the Other Canadian Provinces: Similarities and Contrasts in Findings', *Relations Industrielles/Industrial Relations*, 70(1), pp. 131–156.

Frangi, L., Boodoo, U.M. and Hebdon, R. (2015). *Strike propensity in 13 OECD countries*. Paper presented at the London School of Economics and Political Science.

Fraser, M. (2015). 'Franchise Fratricide and the Fight for $15', *New Labor Forum*, 24(3), pp. 95–98.

Friedman, E. and Lee, C.K. (2010). 'Remaking the world of Chinese labour: a 30-year retrospective', *British Journal of Industrial Relations*, 48(3), pp. 507–533.

Gahan, P. and Pekarek, A. (2013). 'Social movement theory, collective action frames and union theory: a critique and extension', *British Journal of Industrial Relations*, 51(4), pp. 754–776.

Gall, G. (2013). *New Forms and Expressions of Conflict at Work*. Basingstoke: Palgrave Macmillan.

Gall, G. and Allsop, D. (2015). 'Labor quiescence continued? Recent strike activity in Western Europe', *LERA 59th Annual Proceedings*, pp. 51–71.

Gall, G. and Hebdon, R. (2008). Industrial conflict, in Blyton, P., Heery, E., Bacon, N. and Fiorito, J. (eds.) *The SAGE Handbook of Employment Relations*. London: Sage, pp. 588–606.

Gerbaudo, P. (2012). *Tweets and the Streets: Social Media and Contemporary Activism*. London: Pluto Press.

Godard, J. (1992). 'Strikes as collective voice: a behavioral analysis of strike activity', *Industrial and Labor Relations Review*, 46(1), pp. 161–175.

Godard, J. (2011). 'What has happened to strikes?' *British Journal of Industrial Relations*, 49(2), pp. 282–305.

Hamann, K., Johnston, A. and Kelly, J. (2013). 'Unions against governments explaining general strikes in Western Europe, 1980–2006', *Comparative Political Studies*, 46(9), pp.1030–1057.

Hebdon, R. (2005). Toward a Theory of Workplace Conflict: The Case of U.S. Municipal Collective Bargaining, in *Advances in Industrial and Labor Relations*. Vol. 14. Bingley: Emerald Insight, pp. 35–67.

Hebdon, R. and Noh, S.C. (2013). A Theory of Workplace Conflict Development: From Grievances to Strikes, in Gall, G. (ed.) *New Forms and Expressions of Conflict at Work*. Basingstoke: Palgrave Macmillan, pp. 26–47.

Howard, P.N. and Parks, M.R. (2012). 'Social media and political change: capacity, constraint, and consequence', *Journal of Communication*, 62(2), pp. 359–362.

Hyman, R. (1989). *Strikes*. 4th edn. Glasgow: Macmillan Press.

Ivarsson, L. and Larsson, P. (2011). 'Personal internet usage at work: a source of recovery', *Journal of Workplace Rights*, 16(1), pp. 63–81.

Jansen, G. (2014). 'Effects of union organization on strike incidence in EU companies', *Industrial and Labor Relations Review*, 67(1), pp. 60–85.

Jehn, K.A. (1997). 'A qualitative analysis of conflict types and dimensions in organizational groups', *Administrative Science Quarterly*, 42(3), pp. 530–557.

Kelly, J. (1998). *Rethinking Industrial Relations: Mobilisation, Collectivism and Long Waves*. London: Routledge.

Kelly, J. (2015). 'Conflict: trends and forms of collective action', *Employee Relations*, 37(6), pp. 720–732.

Lawrence, T.B. and Robinson, S.L. (2007). 'Ain't misbehavin: workplace deviance as organizational resistance', *Journal of Management*, 33(3), pp. 378–394.

Lewin, D. and Peterson, R.B. (1988). *The Modern Grievance Procedure in the United States*. Westport: Quorum Books.

Luce, S. (2015). '$15 per Hour or Bust: an Appraisal of the Higher Wages Movement', in *New Labor Forum*, 24(2), pp. 72–79.

Lyddon, D. (2007). Strike Statistics and the Problem of International Comparison, in van der Velden, S., Dribbusch, H., Lyddon, D. and Vandaele, K. (eds.) *Strikes Around the World, 1968–2005: Case-Studies of 15 Countries*. Amsterdam: Aksant, pp. 24–40.

Martens, A. and Pulignano, V. (2008). 'Renewed trade union militancy in Belgium? An analysis based on expenditure from the Strike Fund (CWK/ACV) during the period 1974–2004', *Economic and Industrial Democracy*, 29(4), pp. 437–466.

Martin, A.W. (2008). 'Resources for success: social movements, strategic resource allocation, and union organizing outcomes', *Social Problems*, 55(4), pp. 501–524.

Martin, J.E. and Sinclair, R.R. (2001). 'A multiple motive perspective on strike propensities', *Journal of Organizational Behavior*, 22(4), pp. 387–407.

McCarthy, J.D. and Zald, M.N. (2001). The enduring vitality of the resource mobilization theory of social movements, in Turner, J.H. (ed.) *Handbook of Sociological Theory*. New York: Springer, pp. 533–565.

Morozov, E. (2011). *The Net Delusion: The Dark Side of Internet Freedom*. 1st edn. New York: Public Affairs.

Mulholland, K. (2004). 'Workplace resistance in an Irish call centre: slammin', scammin' smokin' an' leavin'', *Work, Employment & Society*, 18(4), pp. 709–724.

Panagiotopoulos, P. and Barnett, J. (2015). 'Social media in union communications: an international study with UNI global union affiliates', *British Journal of Industrial Relations*, 53(3), pp. 508–532.

Piazza, J.A. (2005). 'Globalizing quiescence: globalization, union density and strikes in 15 industrialized countries', *Economic and Industrial Democracy*, 26(2), pp. 289–314.

Rao, H., Morrill, C. and Zald, M.N. (2000). 'Power Plays: How Social Movements and Collective Action Create New Organizational Forms', *Research in Organizational Behavior*, 22, pp. 237–281.

Reinecke, J. and Donaghey, J. (2015). 'After Rana Plaza: building coalitional power for labour rights between unions and (consumption-based) social movement organisations', *Organization*, 22(5), pp. 720–740.

Richards, J. (2007). *Workers are doing it for themselves: examining creative employee application of Web 2.0 communication technology*. Paper presented at the *Work, Employment and Society (WES) Conference*, 12–14 September 2007, University of Aberdeen. Available at: https://pdfs.semanticscholar.org/165b/c2aa024 288507ba25da4ebfb3c387e1659a5.pdf.

Rosenfeld, J. (2014). *What Unions No Longer Do*. Cambridge (MA): Harvard University Press.

Roscigno, V.J., Hodson, R. and Lopez, S.H. (2009). 'Workplace Incivilities: The Role of Interest Conflicts, Social Closure and Organizational Chaos', *Work, Employment & Society*, 23(4), pp. 747–473.

Sapsford, D. and Turnbull, P. (1994). 'Strikes and industrial conflict in Britain's docks: balloons or icebergs?' *Oxford Bulletin of Economics and Statistics*, 56(3), pp. 249–265.

Shalev, M. (1992). The Resurgence of Labour Quiescence, in Regini, M. (ed.) *The Future of Labour Movements*. London: Sage, pp. 102–132.

Shirky, C. (2008). *Here Comes Everybody: The Power of Organizing Without Organizations*. London: Penguin.

Silver, B.J. (2003). *Forces of Labor: Workers' Movements and Globalization Since 1870*. Cambridge (UK): Cambridge University Press.

Su, Y. and Feng, S. (2013). 'Adapt or voice: class, Guanxi, and protest propensity in China', *The Journal of Asian Studies*, 72(1), pp. 45–67.

Tjosvold, D. (2008). 'The conflict-positive organization: it depends upon us', *Journal of Organizational Behavior*, 29(1), pp. 19–28.

van der Velden, S., Dribbusch H., Lyddon, D. and Vandaele, K. (2007). *Strikes Around the World, 1968–2005: Case-Studies of 15 Countries*. Askant: Amsterdam.

Vandaele, K. (2007). From the seventies strike wave to the first cyber-strike in the twenty-first century, in van der Velden, S., Dribbusch, H., Lyddon, D. and Vandaele, K. (eds.) *Strikes Around the World, 1968–2005: Case-Studies of 15 Countries*. Amsterdam: Aksant, pp. 196–205.

Wallace, J. and O'Sullivan, M. (2006). Contemporary strike trends since the 1980s: peering through the wrong end of a telescope, in Morley, M.J., Gunnigle, P. and Collings, D.G. (eds.) *Global Industrial Relations*. London and New York: Routledge.

Wheeler, H.N. (1985). *Industrial Conflict: An Integrative Theory*. Columbia: University of South Carolina Press.

Wood, A.J. (2015). 'Networks of injustice and worker mobilisation at Walmart', *Industrial Relations Journal*, 46(4), pp. 259–274.

Zhang, T., Frangi, L. and Hebdon, R. (2016). *An Alternative Voice through Online Activism: the Case of 'Fight for $15*. Paper presented at the LERA conference, Minneapolis.

PART IV

Broadening employment relations

19

EMPLOYMENT RELATIONS AND PRECARIOUS WORK

Chiara Benassi and Milena Tekeste

Introduction

Risky, uncertain and unstable working conditions have always affected part of the workforce, from the day labourers in agrarian societies to the guest workers in post-war industrialised European countries. The term 'precarious work', however, specifically refers to the growth of atypical, short-term, low-paid jobs in post-industrial economies since the seventies (Kalleberg, 2009). While the post-war manufacturing-based economies could provide relatively homogenous wages and working conditions to large segments of the workforce, high unemployment rates, the expansion of private sector jobs and the advancing neoliberal consensus paved the way to the precarisation of the employment relationship (Kalleberg, 2009; Ross, 2009).

The term 'precarious employment' has its origin in the French sociological literature of the late 1970s and was embraced particularly by scholars and activists in southern Europe (Barbier, 2002). While the term has limited use in the academic literature in other countries, the phenomenon of precarious work has been widely studied from different perspectives. Some scholars focused on precarious employment as work for remuneration characterised by uncertainty, low income and limited social benefits and statutory entitlements, and used this term as a synonym for 'atypical', 'non-standard' or 'bad' employment (Eichhorst and Marx, 2015; Houseman and Osawa, 2003; Kalleberg, 2011). Other scholars took broader definitions of precarious work, including also the social context and the welfare state (Laparra, Barbier and Darmon, 2004; Vosko, 2009). Vosko, for instance, argues that precarious employment is shaped by the relationship between employment status (i.e. self- or paid employment), form of employment (e.g. temporary or permanent, part-time or full-time), dimensions of labour market insecurity, as well as social context (e.g. occupation, industry and geography) and social location (e.g. gender, citizenship status). Departing from the concept of precarious work, scholars in the field of sociology used the term 'precariousness' to indicate the condition of insecurity and risk pervading contemporary societies. Precariousness derives from changes in the labour market and mode of production and is associated with social and political exclusion (Bourdieu, 1998; Standing, 2011).

This chapter will limit its focus to precarious work as a low-paid, unstable form of employment. Forms of precarious employment might include part-time and fixed-term employment, temporary agency work, contracted-out activities, posted labour, dependent self-employment and undocumented labour (Gumbrell-McCormick, 2011). The chapter illustrates the extent to which precarious work has spread in different countries and discusses the factors driving its growth. It then illustrates the impact of precarious work on employees, companies and society and the policy responses from governments, unions and international organisations. Finally, it critically discusses the theoretical frameworks traditionally used to explain the use of precarious work at the organisational level.

Precarious work – a cross-national overview

The growth of precarious work has affected most advanced political economies in the last 30 years. Figure 19.1 shows its diffusion among the workforce in different OECD countries, using as a proxy the rate of temporary contracts among the workforce. As we only considered fixed-term contracts due to data availability, informal employment relationships, permanent agency workers and freelancers are not included in the figure shown below, which therefore underestimates the phenomenon of precarious work.

Figure 19.1 shows that temporary work increased in most OECD countries from the 1980s, for instance in Austria, Belgium, France, Germany, Italy, Netherlands, Portugal, Spain and Sweden. In contrast, Denmark experienced a decrease in temporary work due to the labour market reforms during the nineties, which lowered the level of employment protection for permanent workers and therefore reduced employers' incentives to hire on temporary contracts. However, research suggests that in Denmark involuntary part-time work (not included here) is common and increasing, as it affected 15 per cent of the part-time workforce in 2011, which accounted for 25 per cent of the Danish workforce (Mailand and Larsen, 2011). In Japan and Spain, the rate of temporary contracts dropped in recent years, probably due to the economic crisis, which disproportionately affected fixed-term workers compared with permanent workers (Eichhorst, Escudero and Marx, 2010).

While the causes of the growth of non-standard work will be discussed in detail in the next section, it is worth discussing here the reasons for the cross-national variation in temporary

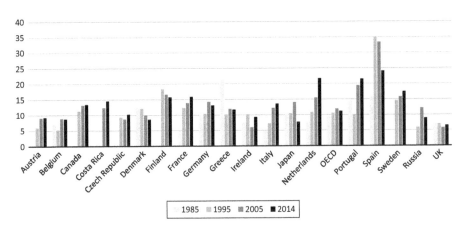

Figure 19.1 Temporary employment in selected OECD countries (1985–2014)
Only countries with three data points available were included in the chart. When data were not available for that year, the rate of temporary workers of the following or two years were used.
Source: OECD database.

work. The national economic context partly explains this variation, as countries characterised by relatively high unemployment rates such as southern European and Latin American[1] countries have indeed higher rates of temporary contracts. This is partly due to the limited choice workers have when labour market conditions are not favourable; on the other hand, it is also the result of government policies promoting part-time, fixed-term and agency contracts in order to stimulate employment growth (Heckman and Pagés, 2000; Houseman and Osawa, 2003).

The most important factors explaining cross-national variation in the size and type of precarious contracts are, however, national regulations and institutions of industrial relations (IR). Research in comparative political economy and in sociology found that employment protection is a key explanatory variable: countries with low dismissal protection for permanent workers have experienced slower and more limited growth of temporary contracts (e.g. UK, US) than countries with strict employment protection for permanent workers (e.g. Germany and Spain), where employers use precarious contracts in order to gain more flexibility in hiring and firing. Similarly, lower taxes and employers' contributions for non-standard contracts constitute an incentive for employers to use fixed-term, freelance or agency contracts (Houseman and Osawa, 2003). Particularly (but not exclusively) in developing countries, where the enforcement of labour legislation is lacking, employers hire cheap and flexible workers from the informal sector or use illegal migrant workers, as in the cases of India, Indonesia and Thailand (Hewison and Kalleberg, 2013).

Industrial relations research pointed out that institutions do not only provide incentive structures to employers' strategies and rather looked at how they affect workers' outcomes. The presence of encompassing institutions of collective bargaining, a relatively high minimum wage and high union density are crucial for workers' outcomes in terms of pay, benefits and working time (Gautiè and Schmitt, 2010). Focusing on low-end services, the Russell Sage Foundation project on low-wage work found that strong unions and strict legal regulation regarding contingent work limited the use of precarious work in services such as the catering and hotel industry, nursing, cleaning and retail in France, Denmark and the Netherlands, while lack of regulations, institutional loopholes and patchy representation allowed for low-pay employment in Germany, the UK and US (Appelbaum, 2010; Gautiè and Schmitt, 2010). The crucial role of institutions is visible also at national level, when looking at low pay data: according to the OECD (2015), in 2014 the countries characterised by lowest low-pay rates (between four and nine per cent) were Belgium, Denmark and Finland, which are traditionally characterised by inclusive labour market institutions and solidaristic workers' outcomes. In contrast, Canada, South Korea, the UK and the USA were characterised by the highest rates of low pay (over 20 per cent), which can be explained through fragmented collective bargaining institutions, low union density and deregulated labour markets.

The causes of (growing) precarious work

The growth of precarious work in advanced countries was explained through a wide range of factors. Some scholars pointed out supply-side factors such as the changing demographic composition of the workforce, which included more and more women and migrant workers (Kalleberg, 2012). Migrant workers represent a vulnerable segment of the workforce that would accept lower wages and working conditions; furthermore, the increase of women participating in the labour market was found to be partly responsible for the increase of non-standard work because they required a flexible work schedule (Gustafsson, Kejoh and Wetzels, 2003). Low unionisation rates among young workers and among workers in the expanding service sectors were also argued to contribute to the diffusion of precarious employment contracts (Heery and Abbott, 2000).

However, demand-side factors played the most determinant role. Technological change caused a decline of middle-range occupations, creating a polarised labour market between high-skill 'good' jobs and low-skill precarious jobs (Kalleberg, 2012). Occupational shifts took place also across sectors, as the economy in advanced countries shifted from manufacturing to services, which are more labour-intensive and characterised by lower productivity rates. This required companies to compress labour costs in the growing service industry (Iversen and Wren, 1998). Recent research pointed at the impact of 'financialisation' on employees' outcomes, as the increasing dependence of companies on financial markets forced them to focus on the short-term interests of their shareholders and made them more vulnerable to financial market volatility. This process had a negative impact on the job security of the incumbent workforce, leading more companies to downsize their workforce (Goyer, Clark and Bhankaraully, 2016). In order to compress labour costs and to react more flexibly to short-term downturns, companies have increasingly relied on staff agencies and external providers. This strategy allowed companies to reduce their headcount while benefitting from a cheap workforce often not covered by collective agreements and unions. Furthermore, the imperative to maximise profit pushed companies to shift their production to cheaper locations abroad, putting workers in advanced economies under increasing pressure to accept precarious working conditions (Batt and Appelbaum, 2013).

The growth of precarious work was also attributed to political dynamics at national level and at supranational level, which led to the deregulation of labour market institutions and IR. As growth rates of Western economies slowed down since the eighties and unemployment started rising at higher levels than in the past, the flexibilisation and deregulation of labour markets were promoted as job-creating policy instruments. They aimed at eliminating the existing labour market rigidities considered responsible for hindering economic growth (Kalleberg, 2009; Koch, 2013). In 1994 the Organization for Economic Cooperation and Development (OECD) published a famous strategic policy paper that is paradigmatic of the political consensus at the time. It asked national governments to adopt and implement the following measures (among others): to encourage flexible working time and part-time work; to allow fixed-term contracts; and to make wages more flexible by weakening sectoral bargaining and promoting company-level agreements (OECD, 1994). This shift towards a neoliberal consensus could hardly be counteracted by the labour movement, which had been declining across most advanced countries in terms of political influence and mobilisation potential (Kalleberg, 2009; Martin and Ross, 1999).

Between the 1990s and beginning of the 2000s several countries implemented reforms in order to flexibilise their labour market. For instance, in that period the national governments in Argentina, Peru, Japan, China, South Korea, Italy, Germany and France gradually deregulated the use of non-standard work (freelancers, agency work, fixed-term work and part-time work), lowering the employment and income protection for those workforce segments; as a result, precarious work started growing at the margins of the labour market (Heckman and Pagés, 2000; Palier and Thelen, 2010; Watanabe, 2015a).

Consequences of precarious work

The human resource literature on flexible employment pointed out the advantages for both companies and individuals. Companies employing short-term and cheap workers were argued to benefit from greater flexibility and cost savings (Lepak and Snell, 1999). Studies in the Silicon Valley IT industry and in the independent film-making industry also found that the increasing reliance on external labour markets and specialised figures for project-based contracts contribute to innovation (Saxenian, 1996). At the individual level, workers were argued to enjoy the freedom and autonomy of flexible working, suggesting that flexible employment is some-times the result of employees' free choice. These workers typically are knowledge workers, who have relatively high bargaining power in the employment relationship thanks to their sought-after skills and high employability (Marler, Woodard-Barringer and Milkovich, 2002).

In contrast, research on precarious employment – a term that has a negative connotation in itself – highlighted its negative consequences on the individual's psychological and physical well-being and on organisational performance, and the economic, social and political consequences for the wider society. This section will discuss the main research findings.

The individual and precarious work

Short-term and precarious contracts were found to have an impact on physical and psycho-logical well-being – which are often interrelated – of workers. Workers on fixed-term contracts, on agency contracts or employed by subcontractors were found more likely to experience physical injuries (from strain injuries to fatalities) at the workplace due to their limited work experience, the potential for errors and omissions in fragmented value chains, and lacking health and safety training for contingent workers (see Quinlan et al., 2000 for a review of the litera-ture). Furthermore, precarious workers experience higher rates of perceived job insecurity, which is associated with lower job satisfaction, psychological well-being and life satisfaction outside work. The negative association between temporary contracts and perceived job inse-curity held in different national and sectoral contexts, from public sector employees in the UK (Guest and Conway, 2000) to metal workers in a Belgian plant of a multinational corporation (Witte, 1999).

As a result of higher perceived job insecurity, fixed-term employees were found more likely to experience psychological distress, fatigue, exhaustion, stomach symptoms and increased sickness absence (Aronsson, Gustafsson and Dallner, 2002; Benavides et al., 2000). Along these lines, Warr (1994) included job insecurity as the most prominent stressor in temporary employment arrangements in his general framework for the study of work and mental health. Furthermore, Guest and Conway (2000) reported a negative association between temporary contracts and work–life balance, which could be linked to job dissatisfaction and greater stated intention to quit the organisation.

These findings can be mitigated by taking into consideration other factors that mediate the relationship between the type of contract and (perceived) job insecurity, health outcomes and level of satisfaction. For instance, Pearce (1998) pointed out that whether contingent employ-ment is the result of personal choice mediates the perceived level of job insecurity. Indeed, in their study of the relationship between type of contract, occupational choice and well-being among Swedish workers, Aronsson and Goransson (1999) found that being in the occupation of choice or not affects health outcomes more strongly than the permanent–temporary dimension. Finally, Quinlan, Mayhew and Bohle (2000) argued that lower levels of job satisfaction might also be explained through a lack of training and supervision, and limited access to information, which are associated with temporary contracts in most organisations, rather than exclusively to the limited duration of the employment relationship.

The organisation and precarious work

Existing research investigated the effect of precarious work on a company's competitiveness, finding either no significant effects on sales and value added per employee (Arvanitis, 2005) or a U-shape relationship indicating that a small amount of temporary work might be beneficial to a company's performance while high rates could undermine it (Nielen and Schiersch, 2014). Indeed, the employment of precarious workers was found to cause several coordination problems within an organisation, both between management and the workforce and also among workers themselves. Research suggested that organisations relying on fixed-term work arrangements find it difficult to maintain the clear mutual obligations and entitlements between the individual employee and the organisation that constitute the psychological contract (Rousseau, 1995). By comparing permanent and contingent workers, several scholars found that permanent employees reported significantly more obligations and inducements than their colleagues on a temporary contract *(relational psychological contract)* while contingent workers were more limited in their expectations and obligations *(transactional psychological contracts)* (Coyle-Shapiro and Kessler, 2002; Guest, 2004).

The non-fulfilment or violation of the psychological contract has implications for the organisation because it might lead to attitudinal and emotional responses such as lower employer trust (Robinson, 1996), job satisfaction (Robinson and Rousseau, 1994), organisational commitment (Coyle-Shapiro and Kessler, 2000), intentions to remain (Turnley and Feldman, 1999) and in-role and extra-role performance (Robinson, 1996). For instance, in a study conducted on 2,000 public sector employees on flexible and permanent contracts in the UK, Guest et al. (2000) found that employees on flexible contracts tended to show lower commitment, particularly if on agency contracts but also, albeit to a lower extent, on fixed-term contracts. Similarly, in their study of professional workers in two service firms in Singapore, Van Dyne and Ang (1998) found that contingent workers had lower levels of commitment to the organisation than their permanent co-workers because they could easily switch to a different employer.

As commitment levels affect performance and organisational citizenship behaviour (OCB), which refers to employees' voluntary actions and initiatives in support of the organisation, precarious employment can also be expected to be negatively correlated with the incidence of volunteering behaviour. Research findings confirm that workers on precarious contracts are less likely to engage in OCB while permanent employees engage in OCB independently from their perception of employer inducements and, thus, feel they cannot withdraw OCB contingent upon how the organisation is treating them (Coyle-Shapiro and Kessler, 2002; Van Dyne and Yang, 1998).

Finally, the presence of contingent workers at a workplace was found to impair cooperation and teamwork within the workforce, with negative consequences for organisational performance (Byoung-Hoon and Frenkel, 2004; Geary, 1992). For instance, in his study of three US electronic plants Geary found that the employment of temporary workers caused conflicts because these workers would be paid less and enjoyed fewer benefits. They perceived their status difference as unfair but, nevertheless, they would work overtime, avoid complaining and, overall, be easier to control. By so doing, they put permanent workers under pressure, causing further conflicts. Byoung-Hoon and Frenkel found that regular workers in a major South Korean auto company heavily discriminated against contingent workers for similar reasons and did not include them in their work 'community'.

Precarious work and society

The increase of precarious employment has significant implications for society as a whole. The most noticeable effect is the increase in inequality among the workforce. Low wage rates increased in many advanced political economies in the last two decades due to the growth of jobs that are no longer covered by labour market institutions and regulations (Gautiè and

Schmitt, 2010). Furthermore, the segmentation of the workforce exacerbated divisions along the dimensions of skills, age, gender and race. Young, low-skilled workers were found more likely to be employed on precarious contracts in Europe (Gebel and Giesecke, 2011), Asia (Inui, 2005) and North America (Kalleberg, Raell and Cassirer, 1997). Migrants and women are also disproportionately affected by precarious contracts in all countries (Fudge and Vosko, 2001). Migrants are particularly vulnerable due to their limited citizenship rights and increasingly tough migration restrictions, which pushed many into illegality, making them even more exploitable by employers (Anderson, 2010).

The growth of precarious work has increased the pressure on the welfare states of advanced political economies. First, employers' social security contributions are often lower for non-standard contracts, and low-paid workers also pay lower or no income taxes (Houseman and Osawa, 2003), with an overall negative impact on state revenues. Second, the welfare state needs to provide benefits and subsidies to workers earning below a certain threshold – the so-called working poor (Hartman, 2005). Third, employment precariousness contributes to declining fertility rates in advanced economies as economic security and home ownership – from which precarious workers are often excluded because they cannot apply for mortgages – are often preconditions for starting a family (Adserà, 2004; Lewchuk, Laflèche and Procyk, 2015).

The increase of precarious work was argued to be responsible for declining employee engagement in their workplace and in society. Evidence for this trend includes the lower union density rates among precarious workers compared with permanent workers. Figure 19.2 shows that there are cross-national differences in union density rates of workers in precarious working arrangements,[2] which vary from 1.1 per cent in the Czech Republic to 72.3 per cent in Iceland. However, it also shows that these workers present lower density rates in all countries covered, which include EU countries and some post-socialist countries, with gaps between the rates of permanent and temporary workers up to over 30 per cent as in the case of Norway.

The reasons for low membership rates lie in both the trade unions and the precarious workers themselves. On the one hand, trade unions developed when the Fordist model was dominant and their members typically are (male) workers on permanent full-time employment (Ebbinghaus, Göbel and Koos, 2009). Therefore, their ideologies and bargaining agendas were argued to be incompatible with the interests of precarious workers (Ebbinghaus, 2002) even though research showed that unions have started changing their structures and strategic repertoire, with mixed results (Benassi and Vlandas, 2015). On the other hand, precarious workers

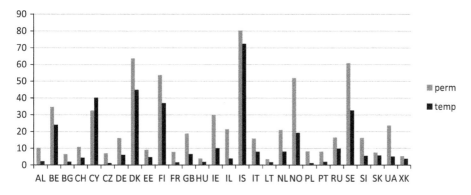

Figure 19.2 Union density of temporary and permanent workers (2012)
European Social Survey (2012), author's own calculations.

are difficult to organise because they do not develop an attachment to the company or even to the occupation or sector due to their high turnover rates. Furthermore, they are afraid of losing their job and therefore are reluctant to join the union and participate in workers' mobilisation initiatives and industrial action (Gumbrell-McCormick, 2011).

Finally, Standing (2011) argued that the increase in the precarious workforce has led to declining involvement in political activities, drastic falls in membership of political parties, declining turnouts at elections and a decrease in the percentage of young voters. This has dramatic consequences for society as apathetic and disengaged citizens are particularly vulnerable to political extremism.

Policy response to precarious work

The steady increase in precarious employment has alarmed national governments, unions and international organisations. In recent years, a wide range of policies have been introduced to control the phenomenon as well as to ensure decent standards of wages and working conditions for employees on precarious contracts.

In some countries national governments, supported by trade unions, have tried to partly (re) regulate the use of non-standard work contracts. In Bulgaria the legislator limited the use of successive fixed-term contracts while introducing more options for working time flexibility (Broughton, Biletta and Kullander, 2010). In New Zealand the use of zero hour contracts, by which employers do not have the obligation to provide any minimum working hours while the worker does not have to accept any work offered, has been banned since early 2016 (Roy, 2016). In China, the new Labour Contract Law in 2008 regulated the activities of labour-dispatching agencies, limiting them to specific sectors, clarifying their responsibilities towards employees and preventing them from subcontracting the same worker more than once (Lan, Pickles and Zhu, 2014).

Most of the regulatory efforts, however, were concentrated on raising the standards of wages, working conditions and social security of precarious workers. Most importantly, minimum wages were found to be effective in raising the wage floor for low-paid workers (Machin, Manning and Rahman, 2003) because they provide a minimum salary standard that cannot be amended by collective agreements or individual employment contracts (ILO, 2012). In some countries the introduction of minimum wage regulation can be dated back to the early nineteenth century, as governments introduced daily minimum wages for workers e.g. in Mexico, Canada and the US. In the last two decades, however, an increase in minimum wage regulations can be observed not only in Western countries such as the UK (1999) and Germany (2015) but also in developing/threshold countries such as Brazil (1994), South Africa (2003) and China (2004). Several national governments have also extended social security provisions to precarious workers, who had previously been excluded. For instance, in 2001 the Thai government extended the national social security scheme to workers employed in companies with fewer than 10 employees, who were in an informal employment relationship until then (Hewison and Tularak, 2013). Similarly, the Social Security Act passed by the Indian government in 2007 provided workers in the informal sector with social security benefits such as maternity leave, sick leave and pension, which are primarily funded by the state (Maiti, 2013).

Trade unions have also tried to regulate the use of non-standard work and to prevent the diffusion of low-paid contracts by following two main strategies. On the one hand, unions have tried to bargain quotas and other limitations to the use of non-standard work at company and sectoral levels. For instance, in German automotive companies workers' representatives bodies were found to bargain workplace agreements setting quotas for agency workers and temporary workers, and specifying the circumstances under which they can be employed (e.g. production peaks, replacement of workers on sick leave) (Benassi, 2013).

On the other hand, trade unions have initiated campaigns to recruit precarious workers and to bargain on their behalf for better wages and working conditions. In Japan, for instance, the national trade union confederation Rengo provided guidelines to industrial confederations and enterprise unions for organising part-time and agency workers, which were implemented to different extents and with mixed results (Watanabe, 2015b). Furthermore, precarious workers have sometimes set up their own unions. For instance, the Brazilian Ibitinga Needle Workers Union, which represents home-based garment workers, achieved a collective agreement in 2001 forcing employers to provide those workers with a labour card, granting them access to benefits; similarly, the Indian Self-Employed Women's Association bargained a minimum wage on a piece-rate basis for its members and has been fighting for access to social benefits (Tilly et al., 2013).

Parallel to the action of governments and unions, the International Labor Organization developed policy responses to address the challenges posed by growing precarious work. In addition to encouraging collective bargaining and governments' investments in economic and social policies aimed at sustainable economic growth, the ILO advocated the implementation and enforcement of 'older' conventions at national levels, such as the Labor Inspection Conventions approved between 1947 and 1969. More recently, the ILO passed Conventions addressing the difficult situation of specific groups of vulnerable workers such as the Private Employment Agency Convention (1997) and the Domestic Workers Convention (2011), which aim to ensure fundamental work rights to agency and domestic workers respectively (ILO, 2012).

Moving beyond the core-periphery model of the firm

In the 1970s and 1980s research in the field of sociology and ER started looking at the increasing segmentation of the workforce, and found that two different and complementary workforce segments can be distinguished in the labour market. On the one hand, internal or core labour markets are characterised by career ladders, pay scales, rules regarding work allocation and duty distribution; employees in internal labour markets have firm-specific skills and perform the core functions of the company. On the other hand, external or peripheral labour markets are characterised by low wages and volatile jobs, and employees perform low-end unskilled tasks. External labour markets serve as cost-reduction instruments and as a flexibility buffer to the core workforce in case of downward productivity cycles (Doeringer and Piore, 1971; Osterman, 1987).

Similarly, Atkinson (1984) suggested that companies require functional flexibility in their core, where permanent employees are multi-skilled and therefore able to perform various key tasks for the company. At their periphery, which is divided into subgroups (first and secondary peripheral groups, subcontracting and outsourcing), companies attempt to achieve numerical flexibility by employing workers on short-term contracts in order to quickly adapt the headcount to short-term market changes. Furthermore, companies increase their financial flexibility by compensating peripheral workers according to external market rates or through performance-related pay.

Findings from research conducted in organisations in different institutional and economic contexts are broadly consistent with core-periphery frameworks: non-standard contracts and low pay tend to affect workers with low and general skills, who perform tasks that are routinised and standardised. For instance, in their study of chemical production workers, IT professionals, teachers and housing benefits caseworkers in the UK, Grugulis, Vincent and Hebson (2003) found that workers under subcontractor or agency contracts were controlled more closely and had routinised tasks, with very negative consequences for their skill development. Similarly, Japanese firms in Hong Kong were found to subcontract low-level tasks to external providers they could easily get rid of in times of economic downturns (Wong, 2001). Furthermore, workers in cyclical and seasonal industries such as agriculture and tourism were found more likely to be on precarious contracts because companies need a buffer of workers to lay off when demand decreases (Kalleberg, Reynolds and Marsden, 2003).

The core-periphery frameworks, supported by the research findings above, suggest that there is a clear separation between standard workers in internal labour markets and precarious workers in external labour markets. It was also argued that core workers benefit from the presence of precarious workers, which protect them from market volatility and allow the company to be cost-competitive without cutting the salaries of permanent workers (Hassel, 2014). However, changes at the organisational level, together with the macro-level political and economic factors previously mentioned, contributed to a progressive blurring of the boundaries between core and periphery: among others, these include the erosion of Fordist bureaucracies and internal labour markets, which used to ensure stable and linear career paths (Cappelli, 1999); the increasing use of information technology to link the workers to the organisation (van der Wielen and Jackson, 1998); and the growth of project-based work (Hodgson, 2004). In their extensive study of new organisational forms in the UK, Marchington et al. (2005) argued that companies are increasingly characterised by flexible structures and are embedded in a dense network of contractors and suppliers. These new network structures have led to spanning responsibilities and decision-making across organisational boundaries while the workforce is increasingly fragmented rather than subdivided between core and periphery.

The evidence of blurring boundaries between core and periphery is so far based on qualitative evidence at the sectoral and workplace level. Precarious contracts, which are traditionally associated with low-skill jobs, were found to spread also in high-skill professions, including designers, journalists and teachers (Lee, 2012; McKinlay and Smith, 2009). For instance, in his study on the British independent industry Lee reported that "self-exploitation is rife, hours are long, the work is mostly de-unionised, and there is no clear demarcation between work and leisure time" (p. 481), highlighting the precariousness of (high-skilled) workers in creative industries. Furthermore, scholars found that precarious and permanent workers in the manufacturing industry perform similar tasks and work side-by-side in the same company such as in the case of Polaroid in the US (Lautsch, 2002) or in the direct production of a BMW plant in Leipzig (Benassi, 2013). Finally, rather than protecting core workers, researchers argued that a growing periphery can serve as a control instrument for managers. As core workers feel under pressure from the presence of a cheap workforce performing the same job tasks, they ultimately agree on work intensification and concessions in terms of salaries and working conditions (Doellgast, Sarmiento-Mirwaldt and Benassi, 2016; Reich, Gordon and Edwards, 1973).

Conclusions and future research

This chapter provided an overview of the diffusion of precarious work across advanced political economies, pointing out the role of labour market and industrial relations institutions for explaining cross-national variation. The drivers of the growth of precarious work as well as its consequences for individual workers, organisations and societies were then discussed, showing that precarious work bears negative consequences at both the micro and macro levels. The following section was dedicated to the challenges posed by the increase of precarious work to traditional analytical frameworks of labour market segmentation, as the division between core and peripheral workers has become increasingly blurred. The final section was dedicated to the policy responses from national governments, unions and the ILO to precarious work.

Given the shortcomings of existing theoretical frameworks for analysing the diffusion of precarious work and evidence of its negative impact on organisations, its diffusion, especially in skilled positions, calls for further investigation. In particular, we expect the following questions to challenge both practitioners and researchers in the following years: Under what conditions can companies profitably employ workers on precarious contracts? What adjustments in terms of work organisation and skill requirements can companies make in order to be able to efficiently employ precarious workers? To what extent do companies (still) need core workers?

Notes

1 Data for Latin American countries are not shown in the figure due to the limited availability of comparable data.
2 Here defined as workers without a contract or with a temporary contract.

References

Adserà, A. (2004). 'Changing fertility rates in developed countries: the impact of labor market institutions', *Journal of Population Economics*, 17(1), pp. 17–43.

Anderson, B. (2010). 'Migration, immigration controls and the fashioning of precarious workers', *Work, Employment & Society*, 24(2), pp. 300–317.

Appelbaum E. (2010). Institutions, Firms, and the Quality of Jobs in Low-Wage Labor Markets, in Gautié, J. and Schmitt, J. (eds). *Low Wage Work in the Wealthy World*. New York: Russell Sage Foundation, pp. 185–210.

Aronsson, G. and Göransson, S. (1999). 'Permanent employment but not in a preferred occupation: psychological and medical aspects, research implications', *Journal of Occupational Health Psychology*, 4(2), pp. 152–163.

Aronsson, G., Gustafsson, K. and Dallner, M. (2002). 'Work environment and health in different types of temporary jobs', *European Journal of Work and Organizational Psychology*, 11(2), pp. 151–175.

Arvanitis, S. (2005). 'Modes of Labor Flexibility at Firm Level: Are There Any Implications for Performance and Innovation? Evidence from the Swiss Economy', *Industrial & Corporate Change*, 14(6), pp. 993–1016.

Atkinson, J. (1984). 'Manpower strategies for flexible organizations', *Personnel Management*, 16(8), pp. 28–31.

Barbier, J.-C. (2002). *A Survey of the Use of the Term Précarité in French Economics and Sociology*. Document de Travail, No. 19. Paris: CNRS.

Batt, R. and Appelbaum, E. (2013). *The Impact of Financialization on Management and Employment Outcomes*. Kalamazoo: Upjohn Institute.

Benassi, C. (2013). *Political economy of labor market segmentation: agency work in the automotive industry*. ETUI Discussion Paper 2013.06. European Trade Union Institute. Available at: www.etui.org/content/download/11879/99183/file/13+WP+2013+06+Benassi+Political+economy+EN+Web+version.pdf.

Benassi, C. and Vlandas, T. (2015). 'Union inclusiveness and temporary agency workers: the role of power resources and union ideology', *European Journal of Industrial Relations*, 22(1), pp. 5–22.

Benavides, F.G., Benach, J., Diez-Roux, A.V. and Roman, C. (2000). 'How do types of employment relate to health indicators? Findings from the Second European Survey on Working Conditions', *Journal of Epidemiology and Community Health*, 54(7), pp. 494–501.

Bourdieu, P. (1998). *La précarité est aujourd'hui partout*. Contre-feux. Paris: Raison d'Agir, pp. 95–101.

Broughton, A., Biletta, I. and Kullander, M. (2010). 'Flexible forms of work: 'very atypical' contractual arrangements', *European Foundation for the Improvement of Living and Working Conditions*, EF/10/10/EN. Available at: www.eurofound.europa.eu/observatories/eurwork/comparative-information/flexible-forms-of-work-very-atypical-contractual-arrangements.

Byoung-Hoon, L. and Frenkel, S.J. (2004). 'Divided workers: social relations between contract and regular workers in a Korean auto company', *Work, Employment & Society*, 18(3), pp. 507–530.

Cappelli, P. (1999). 'Career Jobs Are Dead', *California Management Review*, 42(1), pp. 146–167.

Coyle-Shapiro, J.A-M. and Kessler, I. (2000). 'Consequences of the psychological contract for the employment relationship: a large scale survey', *Journal of Management Studies*, 37(7), pp. 903–930.

Coyle-Shapiro, J.A-M. and Kessler, I. (2002). 'Exploring reciprocity through the lens of the psychological contract: employee and employer perspectives', *European Journal of Work and Organizational Psychology*, 11(1), pp. 69–86.

Doellgast, V., Sarmiento-Mirwaldt, K. and Benassi, C. (2016). 'Contesting Firm Boundaries Institutions, Cost Structures, and the Politics of Externalization', *ILR Review*, 69(3), pp. 551–578.

Doeringer, P.J. and Piore, M. (1971). *Internal Labor Markets and Manpower Analysis*. Lexington: Heath Lexington Books.

Ebbinghaus, B. (2002). *Dinosaurier der Dienstleistungsgesellschaft? Der Mitgliederschwund deutscher Gewerkschaften im historischen und internationalen Vergleich*. MPIfG Working Paper 02/03. Cologne. Available at: www.mpifg.de/pu/workpap/wp02-3/wp02-3.html.

Ebbinghaus, B., Göbel, C. and Koos, S. (2009). Inklusions- und Exklusionsmechanismen gewerkschaftlicher Mitgliedschaft: Ein europäischer Vergleich, in: Stichweh, R. and Windolf, P. (eds.) *Inklusion und Exklusion: Analysen zur Sozialstruktur und Sozialen Ungleichheit*. Wiesbaden: VS Verlag.

Eichhorst, W., Escudero, V. and Marx, P. (2010). *The impact of the crisis on employment and the role of labor market institutions*. IZA Discussion Paper, No. 5320. Available at: http://ftp.iza.org/dp5320.pdf.

Eichhorst, W. and Marx, P. (2015). *Non-standard Employment in Post-industrial Labor Markets: An Occupational Perspective*. Cheltenham: Edward Elgar Publishing.

Fudge, J. and Vosko, L.F. (2001). Gender, segmentation and the standard employment relationship in Canadian labor law, legislation and policy', *Economic and Industrial Democracy*, 22(2), pp. 271–310.

Gautiè, J. and Schmitt, J. (2010). *Low-Wage Work in the Wealthy World*. New York: Russell Sage Foundation Publications.

Geary, J.F. (1992). 'Employment Flexibility and Human Resource Management: The Case of Three American Electronics Plants', *Work, Employment & Society*, 6(2), pp. 251–270.

Gebel, M. and Giesecke, J. (2011). 'Labor Market Flexibility and Inequality: The Changing Skill-Based Temporary Employment and Unemployment Risks in Europe', *Social Forces*, 90(1), pp. 17–39.

Goyer, M., Clark, I. and Bhankaraully, S. (2016). 'Necessary and sufficient factors in employee downsizing? A qualitative comparative analysis of lay-offs in France and the UK, 2008–2013', *Human Resource Management Journal*, 26(3), pp. 252–268.

Grugulis, I., Vincent, S. and Hebson, G. (2003). 'The rise of the 'network organization' and the decline of discretion', *Human Resource Management Journal*, 13(2), pp. 45–59.

Guest, D., Michie J., Sheehan M., Conway N. and Metochi M. (2000). *Effective People Management: Initial Findings of the Future of Work Study*. London: CIPD.

Guest, D. and Conway, N. (2000). *The Psychological Contract in the Public Sector*. CIPD Research Report. London: Chartered Institute of Personnel & Development.

Guest, D. (2004). 'Flexible employment contracts, the psychological contract and employee outcomes: an analysis and review of the evidence', *International Journal of Management Reviews*, 5(1), pp. 1–19.

Gumbrell-McCormick, R. (2011). 'European Trade Unions and 'Atypical' Workers', *Industrial Relations Journal*, 42(3), pp. 293–310.

Gustafsson, S., Kejoh, E. and Wetzels, C. (2003). Employment Choices and Pay Differences between Nonstandard and Standard Work in Britain, Germany, the Netherlands and Sweden, in Houseman, S. and Osawa, M. (eds.) *Nonstandard Work in Developed Economies: Causes and Consequences*. Kalamazoo: Upjohn Institute for Employment Research, pp. 215–266.

Hartman, Y. (2005). 'In Bed with the Enemy: Some Ideas on the Connections between Neoliberalism and the Welfare State', *Current Sociology*, 53(1), pp. 57–73.

Hassel, A. (2014). 'The Paradox of Liberalization – Understanding Dualism and the Recovery of the German Political Economy', *British Journal of Industrial Relations*, 52(1), pp. 57–81.

Heckman, J.J. and Pagés, C. (2000). *The cost of job security regulation: evidence from Latin American labor markets*. National Bureau of Economic Research working paper series no. 7773. Available at: www.nber.org/papers/w7773.

Heery, E. and Abbott, B. (2000). Trade unions and the insecure workforce, in Heery, E. and Salmon, J. (eds) *The Insecure Workforce*. London: Routledge, pp. 155–180.

Hewison, K. and Kalleberg, A.L. ('2013). 'Precarious Work and Flexibilization in South and Southeast Asia', *American Behavioral Scientist*, 57(3), pp. 271–288.

Hewison, K. and Tularak, W. (2013). 'Thailand and Precarious Work: An Assessment', *American Behavioral Scientist*, 57(4), pp. 444–467.

Hodgson, D.E. (2004). 'Project Work: The Legacy of Bureaucratic Control in the Post-Bureaucratic Organization', *Organization*, 11(1), pp. 81–100.

Houseman, S. and Osawa, M. (2003). Introduction, in Houseman, S. and Osawa, M. (eds.) *Nonstandard Work in Developed Economies: Causes and Consequences*. Michigan: W.E. Upjohn Institute for Employment Research, pp. 1–14.

ILO (2012). *From Precarious Work to Decent Work: Outcome Document to the Workers' Symposium on Policies and Regulations to Combat Precarious Employment*. Geneva: International Labour Organization, Bureau for Workers' Activities. Available at: www.ilo.org/wcmsp5/groups/public/@ed_dialogue/@actrav/documents/meetingdocument/wcms_179787.pdf.

Inui, A. (2005). 'Why freeter and NEET are misunderstood: recognizing the new precarious conditions of Japanese youth', *Social Work & Society*, 3(2), pp. 244–251.

Iversen, T. and Wren, A. (1998). 'Equality, employment, and budgetary restraint: the trilemma of the service economy', *World Politics*, 50(4), pp. 507–546.

Kalleberg, A.L., Rasell, E. and Cassirer, N. (1997). *Nonstandard Work, Substandard Jobs: Flexible Work Arrangements in the US*. Washington, DC: Economic Policy Institute.

Kalleberg, A.L., Reynolds, J. and Marsden, P.V. (2003). 'Externalizing Employment: Flexible Staffing Arrangements in US Organizations', *Social Science Research*, 32(4), pp. 525–552.

Kalleberg, A.L. (2009). 'Precarious Work, Insecure Workers: Employment Relations in Transition', *American Sociological Review*, 74(1), pp. 1–22.

Kalleberg, A.L. (2011). *Good Jobs, Bad Jobs: The Rise of Polarized and Precarious Employment Systems in the United States, 1970s to 2000s*. New York: Russell Sage Foundation Publications.

Kalleberg, A.L. (2012). 'Job Quality and Precarious Work: Clarifications, Controversies, and Challenges', *Work and Occupations*, 39(4), pp. 427–448.

Koch, M. (2013). Employment Standards in Transition: From Fordism to Finance-Driven Capitalism, in Koch, M. and Fritz, M. (eds.) *Non-Standard Employment in Europe: Paradigms, Prevalence and Policy Responses*. Basingstoke: Palgrave Macmillan, pp. 29–45.

Lan, T., Pickles, J. and Zhu, S. (2014). 'State Regulation, Economic Reform and Worker Rights: The Contingent Effects of China's Labour Contract Law', *Journal of Contemporary Asia*, 45(2), pp. 266–293.

Laparra, M., Barbier, J., Darmon, I. (2004). 'Managing labor market related risks in Europe: Policy implications', *Final Report ESOPE Project: Precarious Employment in Europe: A Comparative Study of Labor Market Related Risks in Flexible Economies*. Brussels: European Commission.

Lautsch, B.A. (2002). 'Uncovering and Explaining Variance in the Features and Outcomes of Contingent Work', *Industrial and Labor Relations Review*, 56(1), pp. 23–43.

Lee, D. (2012). 'The Ethics of Insecurity: Risk, Individualization and Value in British Independent Television Production', *Television & New Media*, 13(6), pp. 480–497.

Lepak, D.P. and Snell, S.A. (1999). 'The human resource architecture: toward a theory of human capital allocation and development', *Academy of Management Review*, 24(1), pp. 31–48.

Lewchuk, W., Laflèche, M. and Procyk, S. (2015). *The Precarity Penalty: The Impact of Employment Precarity on Individuals, Households and Communities – And What to do About it*. Southern Ontario: PEPSO.

Machin, S., Manning, A. and Rahman, L. (2003). 'Where the minimum wage bites hard: introduction of minimum wages to a low wage sector', *Journal of the European Economic Association*, 1(1), pp. 154–180.

Mailand, M. and Larsen, T.P. (2011). *Trade unions and precarious work*. Danish Country Report to the BARSORI-project, FAOS Research, paper 121. Available at: http://faos.ku.dk/pdf/forskningsnotater/forskningsnotater_2011/Forskningsnotat121.pdf.

Maiti, D. (2013). 'Precarious Work in India: Trends and Emerging Issues', *American Behavioral Scientist*, 57(4), pp. 507–530.

Marchington, M., Grimshaw, D., Rubery, J. and Willmott, H. (2005). *Fragmenting Work: Blurring Organizational Boundaries and Disordering Hierarchies*. Oxford University Press: Oxford.

Marler, J.H., Woodard-Barringer, M. and Milkovich, G.T. (2002). 'Boundaryless and traditional contingent employees: worlds apart', *Journal of Organizational Behavior*, 23(4), pp. 425–453.

Martin, A. and Ross, G. (1999). *The Brave New World of European Labor: European Trade Unions at the Millennium*. New York and Oxford: Berghahn Books.

McKinlay, A. and Smith, C. (2009). *Creative Labor: Working in the Creative Industries*. Basingstoke: Palgrave Macmillan.

Nielen, S. and Schiersch, A. (2014). 'Temporary Agency Work and Firm Competitiveness: Evidence from German Manufacturing Firms', *Industrial Relations: A Journal of Economy and Society*, 53(3), pp. 365–393.

OECD. (1994). *The OECD Jobs Study: Facts, Analysis, Strategies*. Paris: OECD.

OECD. (2015). Data. Available at: https://data.oecd.org/ (Accessed: 26 December 2017)

Osterman, P. (1987). 'Choice of employment systems in internal labor markets', *Industrial Relations: A Journal of Economy and Society*, 26(1), pp. 46–67.

Palier, B. and Thelen, K. (2010). 'Institutionalizing Dualism: Complementarities and Change in France and Germany', *Politics & Society*, 38(1), pp. 119–148.

Pearce, J. (1998). Job insecurity is important, but not for the reasons you might think: the example of contingent workers, in Cooper, C. and Rousseau, D.M. (eds.) *Trends in Organizational Behavior*. Series 5. Chichester: Wiley, pp. 31–46.

Quinlan, M., Mayhew, C. and Bohle, P. (2000). Contingent work: health and safety perspectives, in *Just in Time Employed – Organizational, Psychological and Medical Perspectives*. European Union Research Workshop. Dublin: National Institute of Working Life, pp. 1–55.

Reich, M., Gordon, D.M. and Edwards, R.C. (1973). 'A Theory of Labor Market Segmentation', *The American Economic Review*, 63(2), pp. 359–365.

Robinson, S.L. and Rousseau, D.M. (1994). 'Violating the psychological contract: not the exception but the norm', *Journal of Organizational Behaviour*, 15(3), pp. 245–259.

Robinson, S.L. (1996). 'Trust and breach of the psychological contract', *Administrative Science Quarterly*, 41(4), pp. 574–599.

Ross, A. (2009). *Nice Work If You Can Get It: Life and Labor in Precarious Times*. New York: NYU Press.

Rousseau, D. (1995). *Psychological Contracts in Organizations: Understanding Written and Unwritten Agreements*. California/London/New Delhi: Sage Publications.

Roy, E.A. (2016). Zero-hour contracts banned in New Zealand. *The Guardian*. (Online). 11 March. Available at: www.theguardian.com/world/2016/mar/11/zero-hour-contracts-banned-in-new-zealand. (Accessed: 26 December 2017).

Saxenian, A. (1996). Beyond boundaries: open labor markets and learning in Silicon Valley, in Arthur, M.B. and Rousseau, D.M. (eds.) *The Boundaryless Career: A New Employment Principle For a New Organizational Era*. Oxford and New York: Oxford University Press, pp. 23–39.

Standing, G. (2011). *The Precariat. The New Dangerous Class*. London: Bloomsbury Academic.

Tilly, C., Agarwala, R., Mosoetsa, S., Ngai, P., Salas, C. and Sheikh, H. (2013). *Informal Worker Organizing as a Strategy for Improving Subcontracted Work in the Textile and Apparel Industries of Brazil, South Africa, India and China*. UCLA: The Institute for Research on Labor and Employment.

Turnley, W. and Feldman, D. (1999). 'The impact of psychological contract violations on exit, voice, loyalty, and neglect', *Human Relations*, 52(7), pp. 895–922.

Van Dyne, L. and Ang, S. (1998). 'Organizational citizenship behavior of contingent workers in Singapore', *Academy of Management Journal*, 41(6), pp. 692–703.

Van der Wielen, J. and Jackson, P. (1998). *Teleworking: International Perspectives: From Telecommuting to the Virtual Organization*. London: Routledge.

Vosko, L.F. (2009). *Managing the Margins: Gender, Citizenship, and the International Regulation of Precarious Employment*. Oxford University Press: Oxford.

Warr, P. (1994). 'A conceptual framework for the study of work and mental health', *Work & Stress*, 8(2), pp. 84–97.

Watanabe, H.R. (2015a). 'Neoliberal reform for greater competitiveness: labor market deregulation in Japan and Italy', *Industrial Relations Journal*, 46(1), pp. 54–76.

Watanabe, H.R. (2015b). 'The Struggle for Revitalization by Japanese Labour Unions: Worker Organising after Labour-Market Deregulation', *Journal of Contemporary Asia*, 45(3), pp. 510–530.

Witte, H.D. (1999). 'Job insecurity and psychological well-being: review of the literature and exploration of some unresolved issues', *European Journal of Work and Organizational Psychology*, 8(2), pp. 155–177.

Wong, M. (2001). 'The strategic use of contingent workers in Hong Kong's economic upheaval', *Human Resource Management Journal*, 11(4), pp. 22–37.

20

GLOBALISATION AND WORK

Processes, practices and consequences

*Stephen Frenkel**

Introduction

Globalisation continued to transform societies between 2000 and 2015, the period with which we are concerned. However, anti-globalisation forces have been growing, encouraged by the 1997–1998 Asian financial crisis, the failure of the Doha round of trade negotiations in 2008, and the 2008–2009 global financial crisis (GFC). Project Washington Consensus, with its emphasis on market deregulation, privatisation and fiscal restraint, has been a major casualty, particularly in the light of China's sustained growth, which demonstrated the effectiveness of a state-guided market strategy. Meanwhile, sluggish economic growth and rising unemployment in developed countries, together with China's huge trade surplus, have encouraged leading economists to adopt a more qualified endorsement of globalisation. This attitude has hardened as income inequality has increased, although most economists attribute only between 10 to 15 per cent of growing US income inequality since the 1970s to globalisation (Rodrik, 2011, p. 55). In this chapter I explore the manner in which globalisation influences work, leading to an assessment of its impact, which remains highly controversial.

Before continuing, a few definitions are in order. Acknowledging that much economic activity is undertaken informally and is often unpaid, *work* refers to paid employment in the formal economy. Following Amoore (2002), *globalisation* comprises three aspects: project, process and practice. *Project* refers to the key organising principles of globalisation. However, a feature of the current period is that there is no project. No clear alternatives to the neoliberal Washington Consensus exist for countries based on private ownership, only questioning, contestation and experimentation (especially with new technology). *Process* refers to mechanisms pertaining to analytically distinct but interdependent and overlapping domains (e.g. migration is in the social domain with implications for labour markets in the economic domain). *Practice* denotes activity by individuals and collectivities, including corporations, in response to, and intended to shape policies relating to, globalisation. Practices are the content of processes that occur in different domains at varying levels of analysis. For example, at the macro (economy) level there is the process of unemployment created by the practice of reduced government expenditure, while at the micro (organisational) level there are employment status-generating processes comprising such practices as hiring of casuals and part-time workers. Global supply chains (GSCs) comprise cross-national organisation of economic activities to produce goods or services within a single firm and its subsidiaries or between firms. GSCs may therefore be fostered by foreign direct investment (FDI), or by contracting agreements between independent companies in different countries. A final clarification concerns the grouping of countries. The conventional distinction between developed (DVCs) and developing countries (DCs) is useful although on occasion finer categories are necessary, for example, advanced DCs are referred to as emerging countries.

The remainder of the chapter is organised as follows. In the first section I discuss the meaning of globalisation, arguing for a process-practice perspective. The second section examines empirical evidence pertaining to various processes, which in turn provides a basis for analysing the practices and consequences of globalisation. The third section reviews the employment effects of the open world economy, especially the transfer of work from the developed (DVCs) to developing countries (DCs), focusing first on manufacturing work and then on service and knowledge work. In the fourth section I explore how supplier participation in GSCs influences employment growth, workers' pay and conditions, and income inequality in countries affected by globalisation. The concluding section argues that the consequences of globalisation reflect variations in industry, occupation and national contexts. There have been winners and losers. Governments have largely failed to ensure that costs and benefits are shared equitably, leading to political opposition to economic globalisation. Assertions of national sovereignty will however be insufficient to address our most severe contemporary problems: climate change, migration and crime. These require global solutions. In time, these will be the catalysts that create global rules which will provide the foundation for global regulation.

Globalisation as a process in four domains

Viewed as a process, globalisation refers to four interdependent domains, which I consider in turn. These are the economy, technology, politics and society, each of which includes practices that are shaping the world's societies to a varying extent.

Economy

Several introductory observations provide the necessary context to the data presented below. Many DVCs have experienced a relative decline in manufacturing, which is reflected in a slowdown in capital accumulation as work has been offshored and manufacturing companies restructured to take advantage of profit-making through financial activity. In addition, in pursuit of shareholder value, profits have been distributed to shareholders and managers rather than re-invested (van der Zwan, 2014), a tendency that has contributed to growing income inequality as workers strive to maintain their living standards by accumulating private debt (details below). Meanwhile, as Table 20.1 shows, since 2000 and especially following the GFC, economic growth in DVCs and many DCs has slowed compared with the 1990s.

Table 20.1 shows that for both periods DVCs experienced lower growth than the DCs and in the recent period growth slowed further in the DVCs, while in the DCs some countries slowed slightly (China and Vietnam) while others accelerated (India and Indonesia). As we shall see (Figure 20.2), in both periods economic globalisation increased but faltered following the GFC of 2008–2009, suggesting that globalisation and economic growth are interrelated.

Considering economic growth from a global rather than national perspective and taking households as the unit of analysis, Corak (2016) summarises Milanovic's (2016) comprehensive analysis in an 'elephant curve', shown in Figure 20.1.

Table 20.1 Average GDP growth rates for selected developed and developing countries, 1990–2000 and 2000–2014

Country	1990–2000	2000–2014	Country	1990–2000	2000–2014
France	2.0	1.1	China	10.6	10.3
Germany	1.7	1.1	India	6.0	7.6
UK	3.0	1.4	Indonesia	4.2	5.5
USA	3.6	1.7	Vietnam	7.9	6.4

Source: World Bank Indicators (2014)

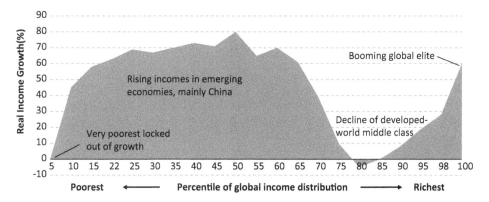

Figure 20.1   Global income growth, 1988–2008
Source: Corak, (2016) from data in Milanovic (2016)

According to Figure 20.1, in the period 1988–2008 persons occupying different positions in the global distribution of income had different experiences: the losers were the poorest five per cent, whose real income declined, and those in the 80th and 85th deciles residing mainly in DVCs. By contrast, persons occupying around the 25th to 70th deciles, located mainly in emerging economies like China and India, and the highest income earners resident mainly in DVCs, benefited from rising real income. These findings are consistent with the relatively weak growth of the DVCs compared with the DCs noted in Table 20.1.

Lacklustre economic performance by DVCs, especially in the past decade, has resulted in legitimacy problems for governments and corporations. This has been compounded by the huge costs incurred by leading DVCs as a result of their participation in conflicts in Afghanistan, Iraq, Syria and Libya, with little success. In the economy, the shareholder model of corporate governance has become suspect as reform has been restricted to legal changes designed to limit risk-taking and corporate irresponsibility in addition to corporate fines. These changes are probably insufficient to prevent the repetition of further crises and corporate malfeasance (Dobbin and Jung, 2010).

Regarding trade and investment, a key indicator of economic globalisation is the proportion of world production (gross domestic product, or GDP) accounted for by world trade. Figure 20.2 shows that since 1995 this ratio has been growing.

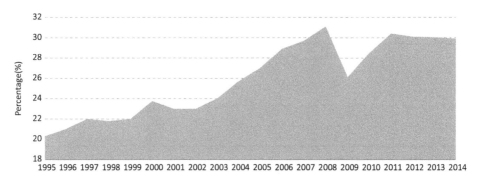

Figure 20.2 Ratio of trade in goods and commercial services to GDP, 1995–2014
Note: Trade to GDP ratio is estimated as total trade of goods and commercial services under BPM5 (exports + imports, balance of payments basis) divided by GDP, which is measured in nominal terms and with market exchange rates.
Source: World Trade Organization (WTO)

Figure 20.2 also highlights the impact of two financial crises – the Asian crisis of 1997–1998 was far less dramatic than the 2008–2009 GFC. Noteworthy too is the declining ratio since around 2011, indicating an inclination towards trade protection. According to WTO data, trade-protection measures are increasing more rapidly than at any time since 2009 (The Economist, 2016a, p. 24). This is further illustrated by current difficulties in obtaining ratification of major multilateral trade agreements aimed at promoting trade and investment. The Trans-Pacific Partnership (TPP) includes 11 nations but excludes the US is likely to be signed by the respective governments in early 2018 after ten years of secret negotiations, while the Transatlantic Trade and Investment Partnership (TTIP) between the US and the EU has yet to be signed after three years and 14 rounds of negotiation. Meanwhile, China, which is not a signatory to these agreements, is developing its own trade strategy based on reviving ancient Silk Road trade routes that includes huge infrastructure investments in countries stretching from eastern Europe through some of the Middle East and Africa and much of Asia and currently amounting to $980 million but projected to grow to $4 trillion (The Economist, 2016b, p. 53).

Regarding the distribution of trade between countries, two noteworthy points are first, trade between DVCs exceeds that between DCs and between DVCs and DCs, although trade between these two groups of countries has been growing relatively over time. Second, an important exception is China, whose trade with DVCs has grown significantly and is very large in relative terms. The expansion of trade more generally has been hampered by lack of progress on multilateral negotiations and time taken to negotiate regional multilateral agreements. Meanwhile, bilateral trade agreements have been filling the gap, particularly among Asian countries. In 1995 0.6 per cent of global exports were covered by these agreements; by 2012 coverage had increased to 5.5 per cent, with nearly a quarter of the extant 250 bilateral trade agreements containing labour standards provisions (ILO, 2013).

Thus far we have referred only to legal international trade. Illegal trading ranges from incontrovertible criminal activity to commercial activity involving some degree of illegality. The former includes trading in drugs, persons, animal products, counterfeiting and racketeering. The latter refers to activities such as transfer pricing, fake transactions and cybercrime. Estimates of illegal trading vary from 2.0 per cent to 4.3 per cent of world GDP (UNODC, 2011). Organised

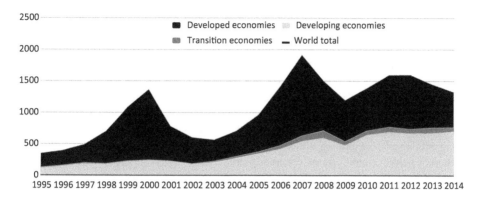

Figure 20.3 FDI inflows, global and by group of economies, 1995–2014 (US$ billions)
Source: UNCTAD

crime provides legally and morally indecent work to often desperate, destitute persons at huge human cost and suffering. In addition, it has destabilised institutions, replacing the rule of law with guns and violence, leading the UN Security Council to examine its implications in Afghanistan, the Democratic Republic of the Congo, Central America, Somalia and West Africa in relation to trafficking of arms, drugs, people and natural resources (UNODC, 2010). Most illicit money flows to and from DVCs and some emerging countries impose a significant impost on government expenditures by limiting expenditure on security and health.

Foreign investment. There are two main types: portfolio investment tends to attract short-term money and is more volatile and on average lower in value than FDI. However, as discussed later, these financial flows seeking higher returns have significant effects on income inequality within countries and limit what can be achieved through monetary policy. FDI, on the other hand, contributes directly to establishing and maintaining corporate subsidiaries in foreign countries that are usually implicated in GSCs and employ local labour. Figure 20.3 shows the growth of FDI by different types of economies over the past 20 years.

According to Figure 20.3, DVCs dominate FDI inflows, but the proportion of FDI into DCs has been rising, contributing more than half (55 per cent) of total FDI inflows in 2014. Much of this is accounted for by Asian countries, especially China (including Hong Kong), and to a smaller extent the South American countries of Brazil, Chile and Mexico. China was the leading recipient of FDI in 2013 and 2014, accounting for an estimated $430 billion, followed in second place by the US with $323 billion (UNCTAD).

Technology

Digital technology facilitates information and communication flows, and is increasingly penetrating the world as its cost declines. Between 2000 and 2015 the number of internet users grew from around five per cent to 43.4 per cent based on estimates of individual usage per 100 inhabitants/households (ITU, 2015). In 2015 there were 3.2 billion internet users, of which two billion were in DCs. Importantly, growth has been faster in DCs (including less developed countries (LDCs)) than DVCs: from approximately 0.1 billion in 2000 to 2.2 billion in 2015 (2,100 per cent increase), compared with DVCs where the corresponding increase was 0.3 billion to one billion over the same period (233 per cent increase). Nevertheless, the so-called digital divide persists: in 2015, 80 per cent of households in DVCs had internet access compared with 34 per cent in DCs and only seven per cent in LDCs. This disparity is mirrored in mobile broadband usage: 86.7 active subscriptions per 100 inhabitants in 2015 for DVCs, compared with 39.1 for DCs and 12.1 for LDCs. There is also a quality difference: DVCs generally enjoy much higher internet speeds than DCs (ibid.).

The growing connectivity provided by the internet and other digital technology (e.g. personal computers, mobile phones and associated software) has impacted firms and employees. Productivity has increased and connectivity between businesses and between firms and consumers, both within and across nations, has been strengthened. Examples include internet-based tendering, banking and shopping. Online intermediation, illustrated by eBay, Upwork, Uber and Airbnb, provides a new way of promoting and facilitating economic transactions. These exemplars of the 'share economy' are able to respond rapidly to immediate, customised consumer demand, which has implications for employment contracts, especially if these services are only lightly regulated.

Digitally enhanced productivity has limited the growth of both blue and white collar work by requiring less labour per unit of output and by offshoring to lower-cost countries. These processes are reducing labour's share of the economy as lower-priced investment goods substitute for labour in most economies (Karabarbounis and Neiman, 2013). Furthermore, future jobs appear to be threatened by the growth of artificial intelligence and robots. Currently, estimates of the job-reducing capability of these technologies in the US vary widely between nine per cent (Arntz, Gregory and Zierahn, 2016) and 45 per cent (Frey and Osborne, 2013) of total jobs within the next 10–20 years.

Digital technology has had significant political effects. Smartphones have enabled citizens to expose official brutality, share views and exercise political influence, either directly on the streets or mediated by tech-savvy NGOs (e.g. AVAAZ). Exposure of highly confidential, digitised state-restricted information by Wikileaks and Edward Snowden, amongst others, has embarrassed governments while revelations of tax avoidance highlighted in the Panama Papers have exposed wealthy individuals. All such activity has contributed to the fragile legitimacy of existing Western political-economic systems. However, the traffic has not been one-way: rising incidents of political violence and the threat of cyber war have encouraged states to introduce laws that allow for a high level of digital surveillance over citizens. Corporations too have been accumulating information, mainly through tracking of consumer internet-based activity coupled with big data analysis. The combination of state and corporate surveillance presents a future threat to democracy.

Politics

I have already drawn attention to the legitimacy problems faced by DVC governments and firms as globalisation fails to satisfy many people's expectations. This is in no small part a result of politicians' and mainstream media rhetoric extolling the virtues of lightly regulated, open economies. Right-wing, anti-immigration parties have been on the ascendant as populist politicians propagate the view that international trade, frequently referred to as globalisation, is a cause of persistently high unemployment and growing social inequality in DVCs. In this regard, European countries are likely to have converged with the US.[1] Comparative deprivation has been accentuated by restricted welfare expenditure in many DVCs; a problem shared with DCs that will in future be difficult to reverse because of ageing populations and tax competition between investment-seeking states (Razin and Sadka, 2005; Rudra, 2002).

China's ascendancy to the position of 'workshop of the world' is held as evidence in DVCs that globalisation is harmful. Detractors tend to ignore the benefits of lower consumer prices and the advantage for MNCs of a substantially large and growing market. US dominance has receded and EU unity has diminished against a backdrop of economic weakness of some member states (e.g. Greece and Portugal) and disunity in the face of immigration problems and UK withdrawal. More generally, ethnic or religious conflicts have fuelled arms proliferation, particularly in the Middle East and Central Africa. Rival political factions and criminal groups have asserted themselves in the spaces occupied by failing states (e.g. Libya, Guatemala, Somalia and South Sudan). State restrictions on civil rights in many DCs and the apparent ubiquity of corruption (stealing of public funds by politicians and tax evasion by wealthy individuals and organisations) have further undermined the legitimacy of many political systems (see Transparency International, 2015). This in turn has reduced investor confidence thereby perpetuating high unemployment, particularly among youth in many DCs. This has resulted in hopelessness and despair, making extreme politics more attractive (e.g. Islamic State) and international migration more likely. This sentiment, together with personal insecurity arising from violence and war, now poses a threat to social order and the customary dynamics of labour markets in Europe, as noted below.

Unions. The inability to regulate labour markets in DVCs also stems from worker weakness. In DVCs two related indicators of the decline in workers' power are the diminishing number of unionised workers as a proportion of the workforce (union density) and the low level of strikes. Available data (1980 to 2007) show that in most DVCs union density declined, but this varied substantially between countries. The Nordic social democracies fared best, experiencing only small decreases, while liberal market economies such as the US, the UK and Australia fared worst. In the middle were the coordinated market economies of Germany, France, Austria and the Netherlands (Schmitt and Mitukiewicz, 2011). Politics clearly mediates the impact of globalisation and technological change, both of which contribute to structural change (from manufacturing to service work) and flexible labour markets characterised by non-standard work contracts and the limited attraction unions have for young workers (The Economist, 2015).

Strikes. Strike volumes (number of working days lost through strikes per worker per year) have declined steadily in absolute terms in almost all European countries, a trend that appears to have been continuing in recent years in the majority of countries for which data are available. The only countries in which strike volume increased significantly are Denmark and France (European Commission, 2015). Bearing in mind the large-scale transfer of manufacturing work from DVCs to DCs, and the relatively high unemployment rates prevailing in DVCs, declining union density and strike volumes together signal that workers lack the necessary organisation and power to obtain concessions from employers and governments. With the exception of China, this statement also applies to industrialising Asian countries (Deyo, 2012) and most African and South American countries.

Society

Many societies – the US, Japan and China included – are ageing, making stronger economic growth necessary in order to support growing social health and pension benefits. There are also marked signs of division between young and old regarding social values. The former are less wedded to national symbols, preferring global icons (in music and dress) and enjoy different leisure pursuits, e.g. internet games. Politically, the young are less conservative in relation to government intervention, minority rights and immigration (Pew Research Center, 2010, pp. 63–68). Culturally, they rely more on social media than the mass media for information. Sharing text and images across short and long distances via digital devices has greatly added to personal and phone-based exchanges. In the many countries where war, social disorder, unemployment and lack of job opportunities offer little hope, exit appears to be the only option for young adults.

Earlier I noted workers' increased dependence on private debt as a means of improving living standards. Further details are as follows. In the UK between 2000 and 2007 household debt increased by 51 per cent, comprising 150 per cent of disposable income, while in the US, debt rose by 35 per cent, reaching 125 per cent of disposable income (Dobbs et al., 2015, pp. 6–7). Household debt in the form of subprime mortgages in the US was a key contributor to the GFC. Since 2007 those countries most affected by the GFC – the US, Ireland, Portugal and Spain – have reduced their household debt to income ratios. However, according to the same report (2015, p. 37), "In most advanced countries, household debt has continued to grow and in some cases reached much higher levels than the pre-crisis peaks in the US and the United Kingdom." In the Netherlands, Denmark and Norway, household debt now exceeds 200 per cent of income. In DCs, household debt is lower but growing rapidly. In China it has quadrupled. Seven countries have household debt that may be unsustainable: the Netherlands, South Korea, Canada, Sweden, Australia, Malaysia and Thailand (ibid, p. 8).

Migration. Over the past 15 years the average annual growth rate of international migrants worldwide was around two per cent a year, reaching 244 million in 2015, compared with 173 million in 2000. Over the same period, the share of migrants as a proportion of the world's population has remained stable at around three per cent. Most migrants originate from middle-income countries and live in Europe, Asia and the US (UN, 2016). Remittances, mainly to family, are an important consequence of migration. In 2015, worldwide remittance flows are estimated to have exceeded $601 billion. This is an underestimate for it excludes remittances via informal channels. Of that amount, DCs are estimated to receive about $441 billion, nearly three times the amount of official development assistance. In 2015, the top recipient countries of recorded remittances were India, China, the Philippines, Mexico and France. As a share of GDP, however, smaller countries such as Tajikistan (42 per cent), the Kyrgyz Republic (30 per cent), Nepal (29 per cent), Tonga (28 per cent) and Moldova (26 per cent) were the largest recipients. High-income countries – Saudi Arabia and the Gulf States, the US and Russia – are the main sources of remittances (World Bank, 2016a).

Recently, illegal migration and persons claiming refugee status have grown markedly. In 2015, the EU, with a population of some 500 million persons, admitted one million illegal migrants, many of whom claimed to have been refugees. As of September 2016 around 50,000 migrants remained stranded in Greece and Italy as negotiations regarding the sharing of migrants between EU countries remained deadlocked. In 2014, the total number of refugees worldwide was estimated at 19.5 million. Turkey became the largest refugee-hosting country worldwide, with 1.6 million refugees, followed by Pakistan (1.5 million), Lebanon (1.2 million) and Iran (1.0 million). More than half (53 per cent) of all refugees worldwide came from just three war-torn countries: Syria (3.9 million), Afghanistan (2.6 million) and Somalia (1.1 million) (The Economist, 2016c).

Globalisation's consequences for employment and work

Economic and technological globalisation have together facilitated intense product market competition in a world where consumers are price conscious and more sensitive to ethical issues (Williams, Bradley and Devadason, 2013, p. 52). Competition in financial markets is also strong as firms seek to continuously increase market capitalisation, which in part depends on achieving stronger control of GSCs, mainly by MNCs through direct control over overseas sub-sidiaries or indirectly via favourable contracts with independent suppliers based mainly in DCs. In summary, the logic of competition is overwhelming the competing logics of industrial peace and employment-income protection respectively (Frenkel and Kuruvilla, 2002). As noted above, high unemployment and limited worker power are not conducive to industrial conflict or mobilising sufficient political influence to satisfy demands for employment-income protection.

Multinational corporations: contribution to the global economy

As an institutional form, MNCs both reflect and foster globalisation, having grown exponen-tially in recent decades. In 1998, there were an estimated 63,459 MNCs that owned a total of 689,520 foreign affiliates. A decade later, 82,000 MNCs controlled around 810,000 foreign affiliates (UNCTAD, 2009). Persons employed in these affiliates rose substantially too, from approximately 21 million in 1990 to 72 million in 2012. Together, parent firms and their for-eign affiliates produce about 25 per cent of world GDP (UNCTAD, 2013). Most MNCs also participate in GSCs that include independent suppliers or buyers, so that their influence is more widespread than as indicated above. US MNCs continue to dominate, although Chinese com-panies now occupy second place ahead of firms headquartered in the EU. For example, of the 50 most highly valued firms, 31 are American, eight are Chinese and seven are European (The Economist, 2016d).

MNCs' relative size and technological expertise confers a competitive advantage. They tend to employ a higher proportion of skilled workers and invest more in maintaining their cor-porate and brand image, for their sensitivity to reputational damage increases as the brand is diffused across different countries. MNCs therefore tend to pay higher wages than comparable local firms but there is no evidence that working conditions are any better (OECD, 2008).[2] As we shall see, the positive pay effect does not include foreign suppliers to MNCs, despite higher productivity in these firms.

MNCs have been adept at avoiding taxation, so much so that this activity represents a major constraint on governments' ability to collect revenue. The problem of shifting taxation to low- or no-taxation jurisdictions has attracted government attention and been the subject of in-depth analysis with a view to changing the international tax regime (OECD, 2015). The OECD estimated that revenue losses from profit shifting amounts to between $100 billion and $240 billion annually, equivalent to 4–10 per cent of global revenues from corporate income tax. Given DCs greater reliance on such revenues, the impact on these countries is even greater. OECD governments have agreed to minimum standards in four areas: treaty shopping, country-by-country reporting, dispute resolution and harmful tax practices. However, implementation awaits the development of an inclusive and structured framework.

Multinationals, global supply chains and employment

Around 80 per cent of world trade arises from GSCs. This is particularly the case for DCs, whose share of world trade increased from 33 to 48 per cent between 2000 and 2012 (ILO, 2016, pp. 13–14). Over the period 2005–2010, participation in GSCs grew at an average annual rate of 4.5 per cent, with the EU having the highest participation rate (66 per cent) (ibid., p. 14). Increasing FDI outflows, mainly from emerging countries, have narrowed the gap between inward and outward FDI, indicating that firms based in emerging economies are increasingly establishing production facilities in other countries (ILO, 2016, p. 139).

The growth of GSCs has been accompanied by employment growth, by 53 per cent between 1995 and 2013 in 40 countries covering two-thirds of the global labour force, and reaching a total of 453 million persons in 2013 (ILO, 2016, p. 18). Most of this increase occurred prior to the GFC and is accounted for by emerging economies, particularly China. Since 2000, employment gains have been made in services, although in emerging countries manufacturing has continued to be more important. Overall, GSC-related jobs are estimated to represent around 20 per cent of total employment among the 40 countries analysed, compared with 16.4 per cent in 1995 (ILO, 2016, p. 132).

Although difficult to assess owing to a lack of comparable data, workers in GSCs do not appear to be better off than other workers. The growth in GSCs has been accompanied by the relatively faster growth of non-standard work such that among countries with available data (comprising 84 per cent of workers), around a quarter (26.4 per cent) are employed on a permanent contract, 13 per cent on a temporary or fixed-term contract and most of the remainder (60.7 per cent) work as self-employed or unpaid family workers. The incidence of non-standard work is much higher in DCs (around a third of workers) than DVCs (less than 10 per cent) (ILO, 2016, pp. 30–31). According to the ILO, (2016, p. 20) "participation in global supply chains does not seem to significantly impact workers' wages, although it is associated with higher productivity." Hours of work can be excessive, particularly in DCs where factories are required to flexibly respond to rapid changes in purchase orders by lead firms. Lacking power, workers in GSCs are typically unable to bargain for higher wages and improved conditions. However, some lead firms attempt to maintain standards and engage in various forms of upgrading that increase productivity and so permit improvements in workers' pay and conditions (ILO, 2016, pp. 27–37).

Globalisation, offshoring and other effects

Since the early 1990s manufacturing work has been mainly offshored from factories in DVCs to DCs (including emerging countries), mainly through the medium of GSCs. China and other Asian countries, including Vietnam, Malaysia, Indonesia and Thailand, have been prominent participants in this process. Following a general overview I will examine the employment, wage and income inequality effects of this in DVCs and DCs respectively.

Slow growth has adversely affected unemployment rates (see later) and employment growth in DVCs. As measured by the ILO's job gap method (i.e. comparing pre-crisis employment to population ratios with observed trends following the crisis) 61 million fewer people were employed in 2014 than there would have been had pre-crisis employment growth trends continued. This gap was most significant in DVCs, where employment growth since 2008 averaged only 0.1 per cent annually, compared with 0.9 per cent between 2000 and 2007 (ILO, 2016, p. 17). In 2014, DVCs accounted for 15.4 per cent of the global labour force and more than 37 per cent of the global jobs gap. This contrasts with the Asia-Pacific region, which accounted for 55.1 per cent of the global labour force but only 34 per cent of the world's jobs gap (ibid.). These gaps have contributed to a huge estimated loss in wages, equivalent to 1.2 per cent of world output in 2013, which has adversely impacted aggregate demand, unemployment, income inequality and poverty alleviation (ibid.).

Job loss and wage effects in developed countries

According to standard trade theory open economies would ensure that countries specialise in what they did best so that the gains from trade would benefit all. The transfer of low-skilled work from DVCs to DCs would enable the DVCs to achieve higher productivity and larger markets in complex goods and services. However, recently developed countries like Taiwan and South Korea have been successfully competing against major DVCs in higher-end markets, while DCs, especially China and India, are upgrading and beginning to challenge DVCs where the latter have been expected to retain a comparative advantage – hence a concern about jobless growth and the continued expansion of offshoring work. Blinder (2009, pp. 46–47, 61) has analysed the problem of 'offshoreable' jobs in the US, concluding that skill levels are irrelevant: what matters is whether a job is tradeable, i.e. can be undertaken in a foreign country. Assuming incremental technological progress and based on the 2004 distribution of occupations, Blinder concluded that around 26–29 per cent of US jobs were vulnerable over the next 10–20 years.

The threat to future jobs needs to be appreciated in the context of recent job losses. Between 1990 and 2014 US manufacturing declined from 15 per cent of total employment to slightly below 9 per cent. Almost all jobs created in the period 1990–2008 (for which data have been analysed) were in non-tradeable sectors, that is, jobs providing for domestic consumption. The only substantial job growth that occurred in tradeable jobs was at the highest end, including computer software engineers and applications personnel, systems analysts and administrators, and database managers, thereby adversely affecting income inequality. According to Spence (2011), changes in the employment structure are more attributable to economic globalisation than technological change. Further evidence comes from Autor, Dorn and Hanson (2013), who found that competition from Chinese imports accounted for 44 per cent of the decline in US manufacturing over 1990–2007. Furthermore, according to Autor and Hanson (2016), wages in local labour markets affected by Chinese competition have remained depressed, with high unemployment rates for at least a decade after Chinese competition commenced. Workers affected suffered higher rates of turnover and reduced lifetime income. At the national level, employment in the most import-exposed industries has fallen as expected, but offsetting employment gains in other industries have not yet materialised.

Much of the semi-skilled labour in advanced economies is now being absorbed in the non-tradeable services sector, such as in low-paid road transport and personal services (Park, Nayvar and Low, 2013). Growth in this type of work is often based on non-standard (agency employment, part-time, fixed period or self-employed) contracts, a characteristic partly attributable to the preferences of older workers, outsourcing of work, job restructuring arising from new technology and development of the flexible, 'share economy' referred to earlier (Katz and Krueger, 2016). Wood (2002) and Anderson, Tang and Wood (2006) show that the development of supply chains may have increased the wage gap between the majority of skilled workers and unskilled workers in DVCs, but also the wage gap between a small minority at the top of the income distribution and everyone else. This is because the initial effect of a decline in transport and co-operation costs is a widened gap in wages (or with rigid wages, in unemployment rates) between unskilled and all skilled workers in DVCs; by retaining the more skill-intensive activities, both highly and medium-skilled workers benefit. But as co-operation costs decline and firms in DCs upgrade their technological capacity, increasingly skill-intensive work is transferred so that the demand for medium-skilled workers in DVCs declines, so lowering the relative wage rate compared with the most highly skilled workers. Accordingly, Anderson et al. (2006) argue that beyond a certain point the wage gap between moderately skilled and unskilled workers may reduce rather than widen in DVCs. However, there is no evidence yet of this occurring.

Offshoring of service and knowledge work. Concern regarding offshoring has mainly centred on manufacturing work, but as noted above tradeable service and knowledge work is not immune from this process. Digital technology has made it possible to transfer many types of service work internationally, in effect increasing the relative size of the tradeable goods and services sectors in DVCs. A front runner in this development is India, whose business process engineering industry mainly serves the US market. Dossani and Kenney (2009) argue that offshored IT-enabled services have evolved from simple to complex processes, only limited by what can be engineered offshore and what is not legally or institutionally proscribed (p. 99). The authors note that DVC-based MNCs are relocating their global headquarters for service provision to India, making India an important competitor against DVCs. At the same time less complex call centre work has been shifting to the lower-cost Philippines.

Two examples of the transfer of more complex work from DVCs to India are in law and radiology. According to Kuruvilla and Ernesto (2016) the work of first- and second-year legal associate work has been increasingly transferred to India, where costs are around 20 per cent of those in the US. This is reducing the demand for young lawyers and changing the shape of US large law firm hierarchies from pyramids to diamonds, a development that is likely to be permanent. In the case of radiology, Yu and Levy (2010) showed that with regard to the transfer of diagnostic radiology work from the US, UK and Singapore to India, professional control over work was circumscribed mainly by the profession's relationship with the state, which determined both the level of offshoring and the amount of control radiologists had over the process. The authors caution against the assumption that countries like India can absorb this work. Local training institutions may not be able to cope with demand, and formal and informal training capacities complicate the picture regarding the number of individuals who will be qualified to supply these services. Furthermore, qualified workers may prefer to emigrate rather than remain in their home country.

Offshoring has disadvantages, including rising relative costs and distance from key markets. Some firms are therefore reconsidering their operations strategy, including inshoring of work that had previously been offshored. A recent OECD study found little evidence that as yet this process has had much effect: "Claims that reshoring will result in a large number of extra jobs at home are not supported; instead reshoring rather leads to additional capital investment in the home country but also in neighbouring countries. Because of these extra investments e.g. in robotics, the expectation is that reshored production will create only a limited number of additional jobs and that these jobs will increasingly be high-skilled." (De Backer et al., 2016, p. 4)

Job creation, wages and labour standards in developing countries

We have seen that the Asia-Pacific region had the lowest jobs gap, indicating that offshoring of work from DVCs to DCs has had a positive effect on employment, initially through the creation of a semi-skilled urban labour force (Grossman and Rossi-Hansberg, 2008). When the rural labour supply in DCs diminishes, labour markets tighten and wages are likely to rise. In DVCs and emerging countries there may be labour shortages in particular occupations. Unemployment data presented in Table 20.2 give some indication of labour markets according to region, time period and gender.

Table 20.2 shows that the regions that have attracted most offshored work – East Asia and Pacific, and South Asia – experienced lower unemployment rates than less successful DCs (Latin America, Caribbean and sub-Saharan Africa) and DVCs (Europe, Central Asia and North America) who were offshoring jobs. Furthermore, although world economic growth slowed after the GFC, average unemployment rates in East Asia and Pacific and South Asia remained relatively low and hardly increased for both males and females. This differed from other regions, where unemployment rates remained relatively high and increased between the two periods, the exception being North America where the unemployment rate remained high but stable for

Table 20.2 Average unemployment rate by gender, selected regions, 1990–1992 and 2011–2014

Country	Unemployment 1990–1992		Unemployment 2011–2014	
	Male %	*Female %*	*Male %*	*Female %*
East Asia and Pacific	4	5	4	4
South Asia	4	4	5	5
Latin America & Carib	6	5	8	8
Sub-Saharan Africa	8	7	10	9
Europe and Central Asia	8	9	9	9
North America	8	6	8	6

Source: World Bank (2016b)

both genders. In sum, these data suggest that economic globalisation was leading to a tightening of labour markets in the Asia-Pacific region with a tendency to improve wages, in contrast to other regions where subdued demand and a larger reservoir of agricultural labour were restricting wage rises or even depressing wage levels. However, MNCs were able to restrain wage increases by 'regime shopping' – switching production to subsidiaries or contract suppliers in countries with lower labour costs and less labour protection (Webster, Lambert and Bezuidenhout, 2008). On the other hand, some regions might have advantages that outweigh additional wage costs as indicated by pay rises in the southern provinces in China over the past decade.[3]

Labour standards. International labour standards refers to a limited set of rights and minimum levels of regulation articulated by the ILO and often referred to as 'core labour standards' (ADB-ILO, 2006). These include freedom of association and the right to collective bargaining; the elimination of forced and compulsory labour; abolition of child labour; elimination of discrimination in the workplace; and limits to excessive hours of work. These standards have been internationally endorsed by all DVC governments and many DC states and are supported by international guidelines, including the United Nations Global Compact and OECD Guidelines on MNCs. In addition, a growing number of international trade agreements include a social clause that refers to these standards (Ebert and Posthuma, 2011). Marginson (2016) notes that "considerable variation exists in the regulatory nature of these clauses, from more binding – either rewarding compliance with international labour standards (as under the EU GPS [General Preference System]) or punishing breaches of them (as under the US GPS) – to softer instruments such as promotion of good practice and mutual learning" (p.10). The EU is exceptional in regulating trade between member states through a treaty that includes a social dimension requiring institutionalised social dialogue within and across sectors, and information and consultation rights for workers employed in MNCs operating in the EU (ibid.).

Governments can be held accountable mainly by adverse publicity following alleged breaches of social clauses in trade agreements or failure to honour the terms of international framework agreements and conditions attached to financial packages provided by the IMF and EU. MNCs on the other hand are not legally obliged by international law to uphold labour standards outside of their home country. If strong unions are absent and states are unwilling or unable to enforce domestic labour laws, formal regulation is either non-existent or becomes privatised, created and implemented through multi-stakeholder initiatives (e.g. the Ethical Trading Initiative and International Standards Organization) (O'Rourke, 2006) or more frequently via codes of conduct initiated and implemented by lead firms (mainly MNCs) in GSCs.

Codes of conduct typically require that the MNC or lead firm's main suppliers are monitored regularly by the firm's officials and/or its agent. Sometimes there is provision for third-party monitoring, usually an NGO specialising in social auditing. There is a trend for codes to converge on content and for firms who supply several lead firms to accept the audit reports of other lead firms. There is also more formal collaboration by firms through codes agreed via employer organisations, for example, the Apparel Industry Code in the US and the Business Social Compliance Initiative code for European firms. These codes have reduced transaction costs through standardisation of norms and procedures; however, the private governance system suffers from several shortcomings, noted below, that have contributed to its problematic status as a form of regulation.

First, there is the difficulty of promoting common interests among the key parties (lead firms, suppliers, governments and workers) when each has competing internal and external conflicting interests (Locke, 2016). For example, lead firms aim to reduce unit costs but they are also mindful of maintaining corporate reputation; suppliers also prefer to keep costs down but they need to meet their code of conduct obligations to lead firms to maintain contract continuity. Second, standards enforcement generally applies only to tier-one suppliers. Sub-contractors further down the chain remain largely unregulated (see Labowitz and Baumann-Pauly, 2014). A third problem is that because lead firms prioritise cost-containment, they are reluctant to pay for some or all of the improvements that suppliers need to make in order to consistently maintain labour standards. Fourth, lead firms are often unwilling to invest in communication, monitoring and enforcement mechanisms that provide a credible threat to suppliers for avoiding or misreporting labour standards. Fifth, suppliers' values and attitudes towards workers do not encourage worker participation in job-related decisions and union representation. Sixth, there is no countervailing power in the factories: unions are either weak (Thailand, Cambodia and Bangladesh) or government controlled (China, Vietnam, Egypt) so that there is little opportunity to ensure that factory management abide by the code's standards. Finally, governments often lack the resources, capability or commitment to ensure that standards are maintained (Frenkel, Mamic and Greene, 2016).

These limitations do not mean that private governance of labour standards via codes gives no protection at all to workers. There are some cases where codes have succeeded (Egels-Zanden, 2014) and it is possible to identify conditions under which these are more likely to succeed – for example, where longer-term trust relations between the MNC and suppliers prevail and where MNCs and suppliers are committed to collaborating to improve productivity and workers' well-being (Frenkel and Scott, 2002; Locke, Qin and Brause, 2007). Potentially more important are instances of complementarity between public and private governance systems, although as Locke (2013) has shown regarding computer component suppliers to Hewlett-Packard in Mexico and the Czech Republic, public and private regulation may be substitutes rather than complements, depending on the national context and the specific issues being addressed.

Examples of public-private complementarity are highlighted in several studies. Amengual's (2010) comparative case study of firms in the Dominican Republic showed the development of complementary state-private regulation based on the advantages of each type of system. These reinforced each other, resulting in higher standards than would have been the case otherwise. Coslovsky and Locke (2013) studied the Coca-Cola sugar supply chain in Brazil, where private and public authorities pursued independent but parallel tracks. When combined, these resulted in improved labour standards. Posthuma (2014) showed that communications between private auditors and public labour inspectors in apparel value chains in Brazil reinforced one another, leading to a more effective administration of labour standards. In a study of regulations governing fixed-term contracts and minimum wage negotiations in the Indonesian garment industry as part of the ILO's Better Work programme, Amengual and Chirot (2016) found that

Table 20.3 Secondary household income Gini index of inequality by selected developed and developing countries

Country	Early 1990s	Late 2000s	% change	Country	Early 1990s	Late 2000s	% change
France	27.0	28.9	7.0	China	33.5	39.7	18.5
Germany	26.5	30.3	14.3	India	31.4	34.0	8.3
UK	32.8	36.5	11.3	Indonesia	34.9	37.6	7.7
USA	33.6	36.0	7.1	Vietnam	35.3	38.2	8.2

Source: UNDP, 2013: Annex 3B

Note: Secondary household income is household income consisting of different factor incomes (e.g. wages, sale of farm or home products etc.) in each household taking into account taxes and transfer payments arising from government policy. The Gini index or coefficient is a measure of statistical dispersion of the income distribution of a nation's residents according to household income. The lower the Gini index, the more equal the distribution of household income and vice versa. The actual year of data reporting in the early 1990s and late 2000s differs by country, depending on data availability.

complementarity between transnational and domestic regulations occurs when unions mobilise to influence state institutions, and when transnational regulators are supported in resolving ambiguities in formal rules in ways that require firms to engage with the regulating institutions.

Globalisation and income inequality in developed and developing countries

According to the UNDP (2013, p. 64), household income inequality shows a rising trend from the early 1990s to the late 2000s in most countries. Based on a sample of 116 countries, household income inequality as measured by the population-weighted average level of the Gini index increased by nine per cent for the group of high-income countries and by 11 per cent for low- and middle-income countries. Particular country differences are shown in Table 20.3.

Three comments can be made concerning the data in Table 20.3. First, the table shows that in all eight countries inequality increased between the two periods, albeit at different rates.[4] This suggests that governments were not doing enough to redistribute the benefits of globalisation to those adversely affected by structural change. Second, consistent with the notion that neoliberalism is stronger in the liberal market economies, income inequality is higher in the UK and USA than in France and Germany. Third, by the late 2000s, three of the four DCs – China, Indonesia and Vietnam (all relatively successful export-oriented industrialisers) – had the highest levels of income inequality, suggesting that high economic growth encouraged by globalisation is also associated with higher income inequality, although this need not be the case as governments have the capacity to redistribute income within certain limits.[5]

Growing income inequality within countries is also indicated by a declining share of income attributed to labour relative to capital in GDP, a finding applicable to many countries over the past two decades (ibid.). Various factors, including globalisation arising from trade and finance, technological change and domestic institutional variables, have been advanced as explanations. Of particular note is the role of financialisation. International capital flows associated with portfolio investment can cause volatility and exchange rate changes, which may lead to higher imports and lower demand for labour in DCs, including more non-standard and informal work arrangements and higher wage inequality in these countries. Expanded opportunities for international investment have meant that firms can invest in financial assets in addition to real assets overseas. Furthermore, an emphasis on increasing firms' share market price has encouraged management to seek short-term profits, limiting options that might improve workers' pay and working conditions (ibid.). A comprehensive international analysis by Stockhammer (2013) shows that in the case of DVCs, financialisation contributed 46 per cent of the fall in labour's share of GDP income shares, compared to 19 per cent attributed to trade globalisation and 10 per cent to technology. A further 25 per cent of the decline in labour's share arose from institutional variables: government consumption and union density. Regarding DCs, technology had a positive impact on the labour share, which probably reflects tightening in labour markets as labour surpluses turn to shortages, partly offsetting the negative effects of financialisation, trade-related globalisation and the shrinking of the welfare state. Similar to DVCs, financialisation was found to be the most important explanatory factor for labour's declining share of GDP. Unemployment has also had a strong negative impact, depressing wages and weakening workers' bargaining power.

Conclusion

In this chapter I have considered how globalisation has impacted work over the past 15 years. Inevitably, this has required selectivity, abstraction and simplification; however, a picture emerges that is both reasonably clear and challenging. I have shown that rather than constituting a project, globalisation comprises analytically distinct yet interrelated economic, technological, political and social processes and practices, which have led to intensified competition in product and financial markets. Global supply chains have been the principal institution through which MNCs have propagated economic globalisation. However, common processes do not necessarily lead to similar practices or convergent outcomes. Much depends on a country's industrial-occupational position in the world division of labour and how societies' unique regulatory systems have developed over time. In short, globalisation is disruptive, and because its many processes and practices comprise different ensembles of variable impact in different countries, its consequences for work and labour relations cannot be conceptualised in terms of simple concepts such as convergence and divergence. New theorising is required that links work and labour relations to globalisation's processes and practices via a changing international framework and societies characterised by different industrial-occupational architecture and specific types of labour market regulation.

Globalisation has spawned winners and losers. The winners in DVCs have been owners of capital, managers of larger enterprises and some highly skilled workers. In the DCs, it is capitalists, managers and workers in export-successful firms linked to GSCs and workers more generally who have benefited from economic growth. The losers have been routine manual and non-manual workers in the DVCs and managers and workers in DCs whose economies failed to compete successfully or remained largely outside the global economy. Regarding DVCs, tradeable jobs have been transferred, mainly to China and other Asian DCs, due to a power deficit manifested in the economy by high levels of unemployment, and politically by union weakness and traditional party-political ineffectiveness. Consequently, routine workers are accruing more personal debt and having to shoulder greater risk in order to maintain their current and future living standards and welfare requirements. This is in national contexts characterised by rising income inequality and controls over international labour mobility, conditions that also apply to rapidly growing DCs.

Globalisation's varying impact on particular sections of the workforce in different countries depends on regulatory regimes at international and national levels. We noted that global regulation is based on norms or what is often referred to as 'soft law', while the hard law of nation states ostensibly providing labour protection against exploitation is often ignored. Private governance of GSCs, the dominant form of global work regulation, was shown to be weak in DCs so that workers employed in factories generating export earnings in any particular country were no better off than their counterparts doing similar work; non-standard, precarious employment tended to prevail. In short, the returns on globalisation were accruing mainly to MNCs based in DVCs and to a lesser extent, local factory owners in competitive DCs. This consequence, together with that of increasing relative returns to capital and a minority of skilled workers in DVCs, reflects a bias in government policy towards the elites, that is, the pursuit of policies privileging free markets and budget restraint over market regulation and welfare spending. These are policies that protect the existing distribution of wealth and favour income generation for the few over income redistribution and employment-facilitating labour market policies for the majority. This conclusion implies that economic globalisation is not a malign force – indeed the evidence suggests otherwise – but rather, if the benefits and costs of globalisation are to be shared more widely, institutional conditions need to be changed. In short, a new globalisation project is required to temper the logic of competition with the logic of employment-income protection. This would require reform at the national and international levels, particularly stronger international regulation through democratic consent by national governments, increased commitment and enforcement of global rules by states and firms, and domestic policies that promote industrial specialisation and innovation and a wider sharing of the benefits and costs of globalisation.

At first sight the prospects of this occurring are slim: weak DVC governments and elites appear pre-occupied with conflicts and wars, domestic security and demands for re-settlement by refugees and immigrants. Resurgent nationalism and neoliberal opposition to Keynesian expansionism threaten to perpetuate slow growth and high unemployment. In many DCs, authoritarian governments and corruption provide little opportunity for change. At a deeper level however, elites acknowledge that current policies are failing and that change needs to be significant. This is reflected in the politics of many DVCs, where conventional candidates and policies have been rejected in favour of populist or radical alternatives. In DCs, social media discourses and the organisation of popular protests signal a huge appetite for change. Most importantly, some of the huge problems that we face – climate change, international terrorism, the migration crisis and crime and corruption – can only be addressed globally, hence the realisation that globalisation as a practice is a necessity rather than an option. Perhaps the most significant challenge will be to maintain a dynamic and open global order that accommodates the growing power of China while protecting the interests of countries perceived to be losing power or excluded from the world economy.

Notes

★ Thanks to Maria George for excellent research assistance.

1 According to a 2014 survey based on 48,643 adult respondents in 44 countries, Pew (2014, pp. 5–6) concluded that: "In developing economies, a median of 66 per cent say trade increases jobs and 55 per cent say it grows wages. In emerging markets, 52 per cent say global business ties create jobs and 45 per cent hold the view that it improves wages. Americans, on the other hand, are among the least likely to say trade creates jobs (17 per cent) or improves wages (17 per cent), exhibiting notably less faith in the benefits of trade than others in advanced economies."

2 Data relevant to arguments about trade effects comes from Riker (2015), who estimates that US export-intensive industries (i.e. those where exports accounted for more than ten per cent of total sales) paid more on average than other US industries and that the export earnings premium in 2014 was 16.3 per cent on average in manufacturing and 15.5 per cent on average in services. But higher earnings in manufacturing came at the cost of higher unemployment: US factories in 2016 produced 25 per cent more output than in 2009 but employed roughly the same number of employees.

3 Since the late 1990s labour shortages appeared and workers began to demand improvements in pay and conditions of work. New labour legislation was introduced beginning in 1994 and local governments have frequently raised minimum pay rates. In addition, strikes have increased, accompanied especially by demands for pay rises (Elfstrom and Kuruvilla, 2014). Consequently, pay rates have increased substantially in southern coastal regions contributing to continuing regional wage inequalities (Candelaria et al., 2013). In part, because of restrictions on union representation and collective bargaining unofficial strikes appeared to be the most effective way to speedily prosecute and settle collective industrial disputes (China Labour Bulletin, 2015).

4 As a recent World Bank report (2016c, pp. 85–88) suggests, measurements of inequality are sensitive to start and end dates. In this regard the Report notes that in the period 2008–2013 income inequality declined in more than twice the number of countries than it increased.

5 Although income inequality *within* countries has been increasing, *global* income inequality based on primary household income data (excluding taxes and transfers) has been decreasing. This is mainly because of the relatively strong growth of larger DCs such as China, Indonesia and India over the past 25 years compared with DVCs, whose primary household income inequality tends to be higher than for DCs (Milanovic, 2016; UNDP, 2013, Annex 3A).

References

ADB-ILO (Asian Development Bank-International Labour Organization) (2006). *Core Labour Standards Handbook*. Manila: ADB-ILO.

Amengual, M. (2010). 'Complementary Labor Regulation: The Uncoordinated Combination of State and Private Regulators in the Dominican Republic', *World Development*, 38(3), pp. 405–414.

Amengual, M. and Chirot, L. (2016). 'Reinforcing the State: Transnational and State Labor Regulation in Indonesia', *Industrial and Labor Relations Review*, 69(5), pp. 1056–1080.

Amoore, L. (2002). *Globalization Contested: An International Political Economy of Work*. Manchester (UK): Manchester University Press.

Anderson, E., Tang, P. and Wood, A. (2006). 'Globalisation, Co-operation Costs and Wage Inequalities', *Oxford Economic Papers*, 58(4), pp. 569–595.

Arntz, M., Gregory, T. and Zierahn, U. (2016). *The Risk of Automation for Jobs in OECD Countries: A Comparative Analysis*. OECD Social, Employment and Migration Working Papers, No. 189. Available at: http://dx.doi.org/10.1787/5jlz9h56dvq7-en.

Autor, D., Dorn, D. and Hanson, G. (2013). 'The China Syndrome: Local Labor Market Effects of Import Competition in the United States', *American Economic Review*, 103(6), pp. 2121–2168.

Autor, D. and Hanson, G. (2016). 'The China shock: learning from labour market adjustment to large changes in trade', *Annual Review of Economics*, 8(1), pp. 205–240.

Blinder, A. (2009), 'How many US jobs might be offshorable?', *World Economics*, 10(2), pp. 41–78.

Candelaria, C., Daly, M. and Hale, G. (2013). *Persistence of Regional Inequality in China*. Federal Reserve Bank of San Francisco Working Paper, no. 2013-06. Available at: www.frbsf.org/economic-research/publications/working-papers/2013/06/.

China Labour Bulletin (2015). *China's Labour Dispute Resolution System*. (Online). Available at: www.clb.org.hk/content/china%E2%80%99s-labour-dispute-resolution-system.

Corak, M. (2016). 'Worlds of Inequality: The winners and losers of globalization. Must it be this way?', *The American Prospect*, 27(2), pp. 101–103.

Coslovsky, S.V. and Locke, R. (2013). 'Parallel Paths to Enforcement: Private Compliance, Public Regulation, and Labor Standards in the Brazilian Sugar Sector', *Politics & Society*, 41(4), pp. 497–526.

De Backer, K., Menon, C., Desnoyers-James, I. and Moussiegt, L. (2016). *Reshoring: Myth or Reality?* OECD Science, Technology and Industry Working Paper, No. 27. Paris: OECD Publishing. Available at: www.nist.gov/sites/default/files/documents/mep/data/RESHORING_MYTH-OR-REALITY.pdf.

Deyo, F. (2012). *Reforming Asian Labor Systems: Economic Tensions and Worker Dissent*. Ithaca: Cornell University Press.

Dobbin, F. and Jung, J. (2010). 'The Misapplication of Mr. Michael Jensen: How Agency Theory Brought Down the Economy and Why it Might Again in Markets on Trial: The Economic Sociology of the U.S. Financial Crisis', *Part B Research in the Sociology of Organizations*, 30B, pp. 29–64.

Dobbs, R., Lund, S., Woetzel, J. and Mutafchieva, M. (2015). *Debt and (not much) Deleveraging*. McKinsey & Co. Available at: www.mckinsey.com/global-themes/employment-and-growth/debt-and-not-much-deleveraging.

Dossani, R. and Kenney, M (2009). 'Service Provision for the Global Economy: The Evolving Indian Experience', *Review Of Policy Research*, 26(1–2), pp. 77–104.

Ebert, F.C. and Posthuma, A. (2011). 'Labour provisions in trade arrangements: current trends and perspectives', *International Institute for Labour Studies*. Geneva: International Labour Organization.

Egels-Zandén, N. (2014). 'Revisiting supplier compliance with MNC codes of conduct: behind the scenes at Chinese toy suppliers', *Journal of Business Ethics*, 119(1), pp. 59–75.

Elfstrom, M. and Kuruvilla, S. (2014), 'The Changing Nature of Labor Unrest in China', *Industrial and Labor Relations Review*, 67(2), pp. 453–480.

European Commission (2015). *Industrial Relations in Europe, 2014*, Directorate-General for Employment, Social Affairs and Inclusion, Unit B.1. Available at: ec.europa.eu/social/BlobServlet?docId=13500&l angId=en.

Frenkel, S.J. and Kuruvilla, S. (2002). 'Logics of Action, Globalization and Changing Employment Relations in China, India, Malaysia, and the Philippines', *Industrial & Labor Relations Review*, 55(3), pp. 387–412.

Frenkel, S. J. and Scott, D. (2002). 'Compliance, Collaboration, and Codes of Labor Practice: The "Adidas" Connection', *California Management Review*, 45(1), pp. 29–49.

Frenkel, S.J., Mamic, I. and Greene, L. (2016). *Global Supply Chains in the Food Industry: Insights from the Asia-Pacific Region*. ILO working paper. Available at: www.ilo.org/asia/publications/WCMS_464077/lang--en/index.htm.

Frey, C.B. and Osborne, M.A. (2013). *'The Future of Employment: How Susceptible are Jobs to Computerization?' Technological Forecasting and Social Change*, 114, pp. 254–280.

Grossman, G.M. and Rossi-Hansberg, E.A. (2008). 'Trading Tasks: A Simple Theory of Offshoring', *American Economic Review*, 98(5), pp. 1978–1997.

International Labour Organization (ILO) (2013). *Social Dimensions of Free Trade Agreements*. Geneva: International Institute for Labour Studies.

International Labour Organization (ILO) (2016). *Decent Work in Global Supply Chains*. International Labour Conference, 105th Session, 2016. Geneva: International Labour Office. Available at: www.ilo. org/ilc/ILCSessions/105/reports/reports-to-the-conference/WCMS_468097/lang--en/index.htm.

International Telecoms Union (2015). *ICT Facts & Figures: The World in 2015*. Geneva: ICT Data and Statistics Division. Available at: www.itu.int/en/ITU-D/Statistics/Documents/facts/ICTFactsFigures2015.pdf.

Karabarbounis, L. and Neiman, B. (2013). *The Global Decline of the Labor Share*. National Bureau of Economic Research (NBER), Working Paper No. 19136. Available at: http://citeseerx.ist.psu.edu/viewdoc/download?doi=10.1.1.846.1802&rep=rep1&type=pdf.

Katz, L.F. and Krueger, A.B. (2016). *The Rise and Nature of Alternative Work Arrangements in the United States, 1995–2015*. National Bureau of Employment Research, Working Paper. Available at: https://scholar. harvard.edu/files/lkatz/files/katz_krueger_cws_resubmit_clean.pdf.

Kuruvilla, S. and Ernesto, E. (2016). 'From Pyramids to Diamonds: Legal Process Offshoring, Employment Systems, and Labor Markets for Lawyers in the United States and India', *Industrial and Labor Relations Review*, 69(2), pp. 1–24.

Labowitz, S. and Baumann-Pauly, D. (2014). *Business as Usual is Not an Option: Supply Chains after Rana Plaza.*, Center for Business and Human Rights, NYU Stern School of Business, New York University. Available at: www.stern.nyu.edu/sites/default/files/assets/documents/con_047408.pdf.

Locke, R.M. (2013). *The Promise and Limits of Private Power: Promoting Labor Standards in a Global Economy*. Cambridge (UK): Cambridge University Press.

Locke, R.M. (2016). We live in a world of global supply chains, in Baumann-Pauly, D. and Nolan, J. (eds.) *Business and Human Rights: From Principles to Practice*. Routledge: London, pp. 299–316.

Locke, R.M., Qin, F. and Brause, A. (2007). 'Does monitoring improve labor standards? Lessons from Nike,' *Industrial and Labor Relations Review*, 61(1), pp. 3–31.

Marginson, P. (2016). 'Governing Work and Employment Relations in an Internationalized Economy: The Institutional Challenge', *Industrial and Labor Relations Review*, 69(5), pp. 1033–1055.

Milanovic, B. (2016). *Global Inequality: A New Approach for the Age of Globalization*. Boston (MA): Harvard University Press.

OECD (2008). 'Do Multinationals Promote Better Pay and Working Conditions?' *OECD Employment Outlook*. Paris: OECD.

OECD (2015). *Policy Brief: Taxing Multinational Enterprises*. BEPS Update No. 3. Available at: www.oecd. org/ctp/policy-brief-beps-2015.pdf.

O'Rourke, D. (2006). 'Multi-stakeholder regulation: privatizing or socializing global labor standards?', *World Development*, 34(5), pp. 899–918.

Park, A., Nayvar, G. and Low, P. (2013). *Supply Chain Perspectives and Issues: A Literature Review*. Hong Kong/Geneva: Fung Global Institute and WTO. Available at: www.wto.org/english/res_e/booksp_e/aid4tradesupplychain13_e.pdf.

Pew Research Center (2010). *Millennials, A Portrait of Generation Next*. (Online). Available at: www.pewsocialtrends.org/files/2010/10/millennials-confident-connected-open-to-change.pdf.

Pew Research Center (2014). *Faith and Skepticism about Trade, Foreign Investment*. (Online). Available at: www.pewglobal.org/2014/09/16/faith-and-skepticism-about-trade-foreign-investment/.

Posthuma, A. (2014). 'Bridging the gap? Public and private regulation of labour standards in apparel value chains in Brazil', *Competition & Change*, 18(4), pp. 345–364.

Razin, A. and Sadka, E. (2005). *The Decline of the Welfare State: Demography and Globalization*. Boston (MA): MIT Press.

Riker, D. (2015). *Export-Intensive Industries Pay More on Average: An Update*. Washington, DC: Office of Economics Research, US Trade Commission, Note No. 2015-04A. Available at: www.usitc.gov/publications/332/ec201504a.pdf.

Rodrik, D. (2011). *The Globalization Paradox: Democracy and the Future of the World Economy*. New York: W.W. Norton & Co.

Rudra, N. (2002). 'Globalization and the Decline of the Welfare State in Less-Developed Countries', *International Organization*, 56(2), pp. 411–445.

Schmitt, J. and Mitukiewicz, A. (2011). *Politics Matter: Changes in Unionization Rates in Rich Countries, 1960–2010*. Washington, DC: Center for Economic & Policy Research.

Spence, M. (2011). 'The Impact of Globalization on Income and Employment: The Downside of Integrating Markets', *Foreign Affairs*, 90(4), pp. 28–41.

Stockhammer, E. (2013). *Why have wage shares fallen? A panel analysis of the determinants of functional income distribution*. Conditions of Work and Employment Series No. 35. Geneva: International Labour Organization.

Transparency International (2015). *Corruption Perceptions Index*. (Online). Available at: www.transparency.org/cpi2015.

The Economist (2015). 'Why Trade Unions are Declining', *The Economist*, September, pp. 19–20. Available at: www.economist.com/blogs/economist-explains/2015/09/economist-explains-19.

The Economist (2016a). 'Managing Chaos: how Brexit will affect growth in Britain, Europe and the wider world', *The Economist*, July, pp. 23–24. Available at: www.economist.com/news/briefing/21701539-how-brexit-will-affect-growth-britain-europe-and-wider-world-managing-chaos.

The Economist (2016b). 'Our bulldozers, our rules: China's foreign policy could reshape a good part of the world economy', *The Economist*, July, pp. 53–54. Available at: www.economist.com/news/china/21701505-chinas-foreign-policy-could-reshape-good-part-world-economy-our-bulldozers-our-rules.

The Economist (2016c). 'Europe's Migrant Crisis: Forming an Orderly Queue', *The Economist*, February, pp. 19–22. Available at: www.economist.com/news/briefing/21690066-europe-desperately-needs-control-wave-migrants-breaking-over-its-borders-how.

The Economist (2016d). 'Europe v America: From Clout to Rout', *The Economist*, July, pp. 57–58. Available at: www.economist.com/news/business/21701480-why-european-companies-have-become-fading-force-global-business-clout-rout.

United Nations (UN) (2016). *International Migration Report [Highlights]*. New York: United Nations.

United Nations Conference on Trade and Development (UNCTAD) (2009). *World Investment Report 2019: Transnational Corporations, Agricultural Production and Development*. New York: United Nations.

United Nations Conference on Trade and Development (UNCTAD) (2013). *World Investment Report: 2013: Global Value Chains: Investment and Trade for Development*. New York: United Nations.

United Nations Conference on Trade and Development (UNCTAD), FDI Statistics. Available at: www.unctad.org/fdistatistics (Accessed: 27 December 2017).

United Nations Development Programme (UNDP) (2013). *Humanity Divided: Confronting Inequality in Developing Countries*. New York: United Nations Development Programme for Development Policy.

United Nations Office on Drugs and Crime (UNODC) (2010). *The Globalization of Crime: A Transnational Organised Threat Assessment*. Vienna: United Nations Office on Drugs and Crime.

United Nations Office on Drugs and Crime (UNODC) (2011). *Estimating Illicit Financial Flows Resulting from Drug Trafficking and Other Transnational Organizational Crimes*. Vienna: United Nations Office on Drugs and Crime.

van der Zwan, N. (2014). 'Making sense of financialization', *Socio-Economic Review*, 12(1), pp. 99–129.

Webster E., Lambert, R. and Bezuidenhout, A. (2008). Grounding Globalization: Labour in the Age of Insecurity. Oxford: Blackwell.

Williams, S., Bradley, H. and Devadason, R. (2013). *Globalization and Work*. Cambridge (UK): Polity Press.

Wood, A. (2002). 'Globalisation and Wage Inequalities: A Synthesis of Three Theories', *Review of World Economics/Weltwirtschaftliches Archiv*, 138(1), pp. 54–82.

World Bank, (2016a). *Migration and Remittances, Factbook 2016*. 3rd edn. New York: World Bank. Available at: http://siteresources.worldbank.org/INTPROSPECTS/Resources/334934-1199807908806/4549025-1450455807487/Factbookpart1.pdf.

World Bank Indicators (2014). *The World Bank*. Available at: http://wdi.worldbank.org/table/4.1.

World Bank (2016b). *World Development Indicators: Unemployment*. (Online.) Available at: http://wdi.worldbank.org/table/2.5.

World Bank (2016c). *Taking on Inequality, Poverty & Shared Prosperity Series*. New York: World Bank. Available at: www.worldbank.org/en/publication/poverty-and-shared-prosperity.

World Trade Organization (WTO). *International Trade Statistics 2015*. Geneva: WTO. Available at: www.wto.org/english/res_e/statis_e/its2015_e/its15_toc_e.htm.

Yu, C-H. and Levy, F. (2010). 'Offshoring Professional Services: Institutions and Professional Control', *British Journal of Industrial Relations*, 48(4), pp. 758–783.

21

GLOBAL SUPPLY CHAINS AND EMPLOYMENT RELATIONS

Jimmy Donaghey and Juliane Reinecke

Introduction

When John Dunlop (1958) put forward his systems approach to IR in the 1950s, the system was relatively simple, with the relationship being one where the three main participants were unions, employers and government. This approach essentially envisaged production being carried out within the confines of the nation state and generally within one employer. However, as Frenkel outlines in this volume (Chapter 20), this model has come under pressure due to the twin forces of globalisation and technological development. As will be demonstrated, this has significant implications for the actors and processes of ER. While the sourcing of goods, components and raw materials is a long-standing practice going back many centuries, with the intensification of international trade and the liberalisation of product and capital markets, the volume and complexities of such activities have increased greatly. In particular, activities such as mass production now take place in countries other than those where the goods are consumed. This chapter will commence with a review of the three main debates on approaches to analysing ER in Global Supply Chains (GSCs); first, the global value chain and global production network approaches; second, one of analysing how ER in multinational corporations (MNCs) are regulated through private labour governance initiatives, with specific foci on international framework agreements and codes of conduct; and third, CSR approaches that cover labour issues. Bringing these three debates together the chapter will highlight that these approaches to different extents primarily focus on structures. This chapter will then highlight the implications these three approaches have for actors within GSCs. However, before outlining these, the chapter will provide a brief overview of supply chains and the organisational consequences of their existence.

What are global supply chains?

Global supply chains can be thought of as the interorganisational and intraorganisational linkages between the raw materials that go into production and the ultimate consumers of the goods (Donaghey, 2016). This is a broad definition that includes wholly owned subsidiaries and the external outsourcing of work though interorganisational linkages. For the purpose of this chapter, the focus will be placed on interorganisational linkages, i.e. supply chains will be taken as supply linkages between independent organisations that combine to finish a unified product or service for consumers. GSCs have become particularly important with the rise in techniques such as Just-in-Time, lean production and outsourcing to reduce the cost base of production or reduce inventories of raw materials and produce (Cohen and Mallik, 1997). While GSCs are often associated with manufacturing jobs, they also exist in service industries such as call centre type operations and data processing.

Globalisation and changing technologies have had significant effects on the ways in which many organisations operate in the modern economy. One of the most profound shifts has occurred in the area of the creation of supply chains to produce consumer goods. In an economic context, where brands are seeking to reduce both costs and their levels of risk, many consumer goods are produced through the outsourcing and sub-contracting of work. To reduce costs, brands have sought the production of mass-produced consumer goods in developing economies where labour costs are significantly lower than in developed economies. These arrangements are often in the form of outsourcing, where the end buyer company contracts out its production to organisations with which it has no relationship other than the actual purchasing contract. The consequences of the supply chain model can be found in three interrelated areas: economic, legal and risk.

Economic consequences: a key economic consequence of the emergence of GSCs has been the shift in production from developed to developing economies. Within this context, much mass, large-scale production has shifted to developing countries, where labour costs are a fraction of those in advanced and middle income countries. For these companies, cost competitiveness is gained from repetitive tasks being carried out by low-wage workers to produce cheap consumer goods for those in developed countries: in 2016, *The Guardian* newspaper in the UK reported that Lidl was launching a line of jeans that cost consumers just £5.99, with less than £0.02 being spent on labour costs per item (Chamberlain, 2016). In addition, changes in technology have led to corporations being able to coordinate production across multiple locations before bringing the various components together in a final assembly location. This is particularly the case in industries that produce relatively high-cost and complex products. For example, in the automotive sector, auto components are often sourced from multiple low-cost locations with the final assembly being carried out in developed economies. Where manufacturing has been retained in developed economies, the threat of relocation to lower-cost economies has played a central role in depressing wage settlements (Levy, 2005). The model has been central to the price of consumption being held down, and also has macro-economic consequences in that the shift in production is often viewed by developing economies as a mechanism through which fast inward investment can be achieved – yet it has consequences in real wage and (un)employment terms for developed economies. It is particularly attractive to governments in the developing world in the short term as demand for products from global brands can bring with it relatively stable volumes of demand.

Legal consequences: A key feature of the supply chain model in terms of its ER consequences is that the brands which market and sell the products often have no legal responsibility for the workers who produce their goods (Ruggie, 2007). Rather, the employer has such responsibility with the relationship to the brand being one of a commercial supply contract. This is not uncontested, however. For example, following the Ali Fashions fire in Pakistan, which killed at least 250 workers, three families sued the German retailer Kik on the basis that its dominant position in the factory meant it was a *de facto* employer. While the case was settled before a decision was made, in a preliminary decision, the court ruled in favour of the families and contrary to Kik's defence that it had no jurisdiction to hear the case. Similarly, though yet to be tested in court, arguments have been made that brands in supply chains can be thought of as 'joint employers', as defined by the National Labor Relations Board in the US (Galiatsos, 2015, p. 2094). That said, the general assumption is that the brand is not the employer in the case of supply chains.

Risk consequences: a key feature of the supply chain model is that it enables both suppliers and buyers to spread risk to varying degrees. For buyers, the model enables them to enter into short-term contracts with suppliers, often for relatively small amounts. This means that failure to deliver by one contractor can have an insignificant effect on the final supply of goods. In addition, where buyers source from multiple locations, the potential disruptive risk of political instability and the likes can be spread. For suppliers, the inverse case can be made. Suppliers are often wary of becoming dependent on one buyer as this can lead to becoming a price-taker. As such, by spreading orders across multiple buyers, the risk of being dominated by one buyer or facing peaks and troughs in demand can undergo smoothing. This approach does bring with it higher transaction costs for suppliers as it can mean conforming to different standards set by multiple buyer companies.

The governance of employment relations in supply chains

As outlined above, the Dunlopian approach to ER envisages a system where the actors are set within the legal framework of a particular jurisdiction (Dunlop, 1958). However, in the supply chain approach, the options for public regulation of GSCs are quite limited, though there have been a number of initiatives (Donaghey et al., 2014). First, at a very basic level, national governments have a variety of regulatory systems that have different foci in terms of how they govern business transactions, which makes compatibility of systems between governments difficult. Secondly, the issue of which system is used to enforce standards is problematic. As it stands, there is no effective transnational system for enforcing such decisions. The model most often cited is that of the Ruggie Framework, which of itself is dependent on private actors engaging in voluntary restraint (Ruggie, 2001, 2007). Thirdly, for many developing nations, attracting MNCs to source from their economy is viewed as a mechanism of developing economically. Thus governments often have incentives to keep standards low or not enforce their own laws to maintain competitiveness.

Early developments saw three main initiatives emerge aimed at establishing intergovernmental regulation of ER in multinationals. First, in 1976 the OECD published its *Guidelines for Multinational Enterprises*, which were revised in 2000 to include supply chains. This initiative was advisory with a complaints procedure but only applied within advanced industrialised countries. This was followed in 1977 by the *ILO Tripartite Declaration of Principles Concerning Multi-national Enterprises and Social Policy*, which again was only advisory in nature and like many other ILO initiatives lacked implementation in many countries. The year 2000 saw the UN launch its *Global Compact*, which like the two previous initiatives was advisory in nature but also introduced a system where organisations could actively sign up to the principles involved, though there was no meaningful sanction for failing to comply (Rasche, 2009). On the whole, these initiatives have all been viewed as lacking the teeth needed to develop meaningful regulation of the activities of MNCs. Compa (2008), for example, highlights the depth of the weaknesses of these three procedures in that it was not even possible to call complaints going through the internal processes 'complaints'.

The growth of private labour governance

With effectively no meaningful route for intergovernmental regulation of supply chains, paradoxically firms who base sourcing strategies on hyper-competitiveness end up developing regimes of private labour governance to fill the institutional void in these low-standard economies (Donaghey et al., 2014; Fransen, 2012). In essence, firms take decisions to source from low-cost and low-standard economies to avoid regulation. However, to protect themselves from reputational damage while keeping ownership over norms and standards, they end up devising their own forms of internal governance systems (Levy, Reinecke and Manning, 2016). Understanding how, why and when private labour governance emerges has become a major focus within literatures as diverse as international political economy, organisation studies-based CSR, ER and the labour process approach to the sociology of work. While not a pristine division, three literatures are relevant to the chapter, all of which shed some light but also to some extent fail to engage adequately with each other. The foundations of each of these approaches will now be examined in turn.

Global value chains and global production networks

Two competing terms are often used to describe the governance of GSCs, which have significant but indirect implications for ER literature: global value chains (GVC) and global production networks (GPN). The GVC approach emerged from the global commodity chain (GCC) approach. The stress in GCC was on commodities passing through multiple stages of ownership before meeting the ultimate consumer in a linear fashion. In GVC, this approach evolved to place an increased emphasis on the adding of value on the transfer of goods between stages in a linear fashion and how this value is created and captured. The GVC approach has been most associated with the work of Gary Gereffi (1994). The key debate in the area lies around the governance of GSCs, i.e. who controls the chain and what are the effects of this on workplace relations. Firms that have the most power are often referred to as '*lead firms*'. One of the key issues in the governance debate is where the lead firm sits within the GSC, and in particular, whether the supply chain is buyer driven or supplier driven. *Buyer-driven* supply chains are those where power lies close to the ultimate consumer; those firms who sell to consumers have the most leverage within the supply chain, generally because of low entry costs to compete for supply contracts from brands that have relatively established markets. The often cited example here is that of garment manufacturers where the end 'brand' exerts the most power. *Supplier-driven* supply chains are those where power is concentrated close to the raw material end (ibid.). In this scenario, power is concentrated in those companies that often control scarce and rare resources. An often-cited example here is that of mining or oil companies who have significant oligopolous influence over the entire supply chain. This framework essentially argues that within any given supply chain, there will be an actor who has the power to dominate the interactions of other actors in the chain.

A further development from this approach was provided by Gereffi, Humphrey and Sturgeon (2005), who developed five types of GVC categorisation: *market*, where at both ends of the value chain firms are fragmented with no significant concentration of power; *modular*, where producers make bespoke products for firms but in a short-term manner; *relational*, where non-market mechanisms link parties within the value chain in a close relationship; *captive* where small firms are dependent on large buyers or suppliers and this influences their practices; and finally *hierarchical*, where there is a direct control relationship between levels in the organisation, most often typified as being subsidiaries of a parent company they supply. However, this categorisation, while viewed as valuable in terms of inter-firm relationships, has a number of weaknesses associated with it in terms of its consequences for ER. GVCs are generally seen as being highly structurally determinant, with power travelling in a one-way direction from lead firms. Most significantly for this chapter, the GVC approach was criticised because it was overly focused on inter-firm power relations and not enough on the power relations between labour and capital (Newsome et al., 2015; Rainnie, Herod and McGrath-Champ, 2011). Secondly, the GVC approach has almost exclusively focused on brands placing downwards pressure on suppliers and workers. The key point in terms of ER from this approach is that different configurations have different implications for workers and labour conditions: there is a high level of variability between different GVCs in terms of their power relations. To date, much of the literature in this area has taken a structurally deterministic approach and as such issues around local agency often become lost in wider debates surrounding inter-firm power relations.

While much of this stream of research has focused on interorganisational relationships, there is a growing body of work that is beginning to explore the ER consequences of GSCs using the GVC approach as a conceptual lens. Riisgaard and Hammer (2011) highlight that while GVC structure constrained the ability of labour agency, labour agency also could have an effect on shaping GVC configurations. They highlight that features such as the 'driveness' of lead firms and other GVC factors play a key role in determining the nature of labour rights in the GVC. The GVC approach also underscores the arguments made by Lakhani, Kuruvilla and Avgar (2013), who use the five configurations of GVC as outlined by Gereffi et al. to build what they label as a "configurational" based framework for understanding ER across global networks. A key contribution made by Lakhani et al. is the focus they place on the effect of lead firms on elements of the employment relationship. They hypothesise that the closer the links between lead firms and suppliers, the greater the influence the lead firm will have on employment practices such as training.

An alternative but related concept to GVCs are global production networks (GPNs). The concept of GPNs was developed to take account of the much less linear structure than GVC theory allowed. In particular, it emphasises the interactions between the macro and micro levels within supply chains. The GPN approach developed from the work of economic geographers who argued that the GCC and GVC approaches were silent on issues of organising across space and the spatial relationships contained within production processes (Dicken, 2003; Henderson et al., 2002). Thus, the approach is favoured by those who argue that production is carried out through networks of relationships, with a stress on social relations in the production process. Levy (2008) sees GPNs as being a site for political contestation where actors can use resources and align with other actors in the network in various struggles. While initially being relatively ambivalent towards the role of labour, and particularly organised labour, the GPN framework has been developed in recent years to reintroduce the issue of labour (Cumbers, Nativel and Routledge, 2008; Newsome et al., 2015). For example, the labour process theory approach associated with the likes of Taylor, Newsome and Rainnie (2013) primarily focuses on the ways in which supply chains are used as mechanisms of worker control to exert negative pressures on workers, and assumes an alignment of employer and brand interests. Rainnie et al. (2011) highlight that the socio-political underpinnings of the GPN approach make it more inherently open to understanding the role of labour activism than the GVC approach. In particular, they highlight that the GPN approach provides a mechanism to "grasp the dialectics of global-local relations" (2011, p. 159).

Without doubt, the GPN approach has placed labour agency and associated actors such as unions and NGOs at the centre of its analysis. Yet the GPN approach is also not unproblematic. In particular, it can lead to a tendency to view power relations between firms as being directly transferrable to the employment relationship. While there is no doubt that these power relations can lead to increased downwards pressure on workers and their working conditions, our argument is that it is over-simplistic to make this leap. Rather, further investigation is necessary to understand the more nuanced nature of this relationship. Similarly, the approach by its very nature is focused on production processes and the social relations within them, and thus is viewed as somewhat privileging production relations over consumption relations and possibly failing to capture the full dynamics of the chain of production.

Employment relations literature on MNCs

While ER scholars do engage in debates about GVCs and GPNs, the more prevalent strand has emerged from scholars who are researching MNCs and the mechanisms used within them to regulate labour standards in both subsidiaries and their suppliers. Within this literature, a key focus has been placed on comparing international framework agreements (IFAs) with corporate codes of conduct (CoCs) as alternative tools used by MNCs in employment relations (Royle, 2011). These approaches emerged not to examine supply chains *per se* but to explain how MNCs governed ER in subsidiaries and in the wider supply chain. In general, a key feature of this approach has been to examine the democratic credentials of these different approaches (Donaghey and Reinecke, 2017).

IFAs are the closest example to a collective bargaining approach and are agreements that are generally concluded between MNCs and global union federations. IFAs essentially are about scaling the methods of collective bargaining to the level of the MNC. The first IFA was concluded in 1989 between Danone and the GUF the International Union of Food, Agricultural, Hotel, Restaurant, Catering, Tobacco and Allied Workers' Associations. The website *Global Unions* listed 113 IFAs in existence as of January 2017, mainly concentrated in multinationals of European origin. The content of IFAs can vary greatly: for example, whether they are procedural, substantive or a hybrid of both in their emphasis. Where they are procedurally based, the emphasis is generally on issues around the rights of workers to organise and take collective action in line with ILO Core Conventions. Those agreements that have more substantive comments generally are focused on establishing minimum floors of substantive conditions upon which local unions can build.

While they are often voluntary in nature, IFAs are subject to the associational power of the GUF in terms of their enforcement (Niforou, 2015). Due to the wide variety of countries covered by IFAs, they often take the form of procedural agreements where focus is placed on companies agreeing with the GUFs that the ILO fundamental rights are implemented throughout the company (Hammer, 2005). While there are some exceptions, the main focus of IFAs has been on those directly employed by the corporation and its subsidiaries rather than extending throughout the supply chain. In this circumstance, sub-contractors are often where conditions are the worst and in more need of meaningful labour governance mechanisms. This approach thus often has as its focus the management of relations within MNCs, rather than the actual effect of supply chain models.

In contrast to IFAs are corporate codes of conduct (CoC). CoCs are essentially corporate-driven codes that many MNCs expect their subsidiaries and suppliers to adhere to in order to maintain business. In terms of CoCs, the work of Locke is pertinent, though to some extent his assessment has shifted in recent years. Using the case of Nike, Locke and colleagues initially argued that CoCs can be useful in terms of shifting suppliers from a compliance-based approach to a commitment-based approach (Locke, Qin and Brause, 2007). CoCs are often wider in scope than IFAs, containing commitments to issues such as environmental standards as well, but are sometimes seen as voluntarism with a focus on protecting brand image. However, despite initial optimism about the potential of CoCs, Locke (2013) later took a more pessimistic stance and highlighted that as they mature, implementation can significantly weaken. Locke in particular highlights that when faced with the competing demands of purchasing/

procurement departments and CSR departments, the economic bottom line triumphs over social interests.

Within the ER approach, the focus has generally been placed on the extent to which these instruments have meaningful worker input into their design. In addition, this stream of research has focused on the factors that enable effective implementation of both these instruments. A number of studies have recently emerged that look at the issue of labour leverage (Niforou, 2015; Wright, 2016); Wright highlights how brands have become key targets in implementing governance initiatives. It is fair to say that this corpus of literature generally views IFAs as being qualitatively superior to CoCs but less quantitatively spread. In sum, this approach has brought forward useful insights into the adaptation of the ER approach to supply chain motions. However, there are weaknesses in terms of the lessons it draws for wider supply chains.

CSR approach

While the CSR literature focuses on labour rights challenges in global supply chains that are similar to those in ER literature, both endorse very distinct logics to global labour governance (Donaghey and Reinecke, 2017). The CSR approach to the regulation of labour within supply chains is one that views interventions by brands as taking action beyond their legal duty (Brammer, Jackson and Matten, 2012). As such, the action is discretionary and voluntary, underscored by an implicit assumption of multinationals generally acting in an altruistic manner. The CSR approach is built upon a vision of generating win–win–win situations between brands, their suppliers and workers within them with a heavy tone of a unitarist approach to ER. But corporations, subject to activist campaigns and media exposés, often make CSR commitments to reduce reputational risk emanating from poor labour conditions (Khan, Munir and Willmott, 2007; Wells, 2007). Critics of CSR have generally highlighted that such approaches are often little more than 'greenwashing', which seek to promote a positive image for brands with little proper engagement with suppliers or the workers within them (Banerjee, 2008, p. 64).

In recent years, a more critical approach to CSR has emerged in the shape of 'political CSR', which stresses the role brands play in developing private governance systems (Scherer and Palazzo, 2007, 2011). This approach views brands as stepping into institutional voids and providing regulatory activity where states have failed to do so. Central to this approach is that commercial contracts have adherence to labour standards during production as core features rather than them simply being contracts of supply and price. The CSR literature offers one explanation of why interests might diverge between brands and their suppliers: the role of reputation and brand image as a driver of CSR for consumer-facing organisations (den Hond and de Bakker, 2007). Reputational risk is an issue that has been prominent in the CSR/business ethics literature but not so much in ER (see Donaghey et al., 2014 for further discussion). A key feature of this literature is that corporate brands can become exposed to negative publicity, particularly from groups like NGOs, student activists and the like, over labour abuses in supplier firms. Yet what the actual effects of this are for ER and on ER actors is underdeveloped. This is partially because this approach covers a wide range of topics, including controversial issues such as labour and environmental standards but also issues such as corporate philanthropy (e.g. Czinkota, Kaufmann and Basile, 2014). Thus the focus is on the firm as an actor but not necessarily an ER actor (e.g. Amaeshi, Osuji and Nnodim, 2008).

Global supply chains have been a key focus of CSR policies of many MNCs, as they often present a paradox in that a company moves production to a country to take advantage of lower regulation but ends up regulating itself. Donaghey and colleagues (2014) outline that GSCs are often susceptible to consumer-led pressure over labour rights on lead firm brands rather than the direct use of labour power as brands often source from where workers have very limited power resources. While there is probably little doubt that protecting reputation is central to many Western brands in their CSR policies, scholars having examined these private governance regimes in more depth argue that identifying the presence of private regulation is insufficient. Rather, the stringency of such approaches is central, i.e. to what extent is there meaningful stakeholder input and monitoring of these initiatives, or whose interests do they serve (Fransen, 2012; Levy et al., 2016)? These more critical and nuanced approaches to the CSR private governance debate are important as they highlight that rather than treating all initiatives with a somewhat broad-brush approach, it is necessary to examine the nature of the participants in the private governance initiative and, within this, who controls the process. This focus on relations between NGOs, unions and brands builds significantly on previous work by the likes of O'Rourke (2003, 2006), Compa (2001, 2008) and others. However, despite this, the approach is rather muted on the relationship between brands, employers and workers. In particular, it is silent on the ways in which issues of variance of stringency are mediated by brand-employer relations. This is consistent with a wider problem of the CSR – narrow and political interpretations, where the CSR literature does not explore in detail the ER implications of CSR.

Employment relations in supply chains: understanding the changed role of actors

To date, as outlined above, the literature on GSCs and ER has generally been dominated by a focus on governance and structural features. In contrast, in the remainder of this chapter, a focus will be placed on using the existing research to outline the changed role of traditional ER actors as well as highlighting the roles that other non-traditional ER actors such as global brands and NGOs may play in ER in supply chains. Here, the previous approaches reviewed above become complementary in shedding light on the dynamics shaping the relations between different actors. The GVC approach is useful to understand interorganisational power relations between employers and brands. For instance, a key feature of this perspective is that power relations and linkages are multiplied compared with the standard employment relationship. In contrast, the ER literature is useful in understanding the relationship between unions, employers and the state. Finally, the CSR literature is helpful to understand the relationship between NGOs as engines of consumer voice and brands. Bringing these three approaches together while refocusing attention on actors can provide a fuller understanding of the implications of the supply chain model for ER.

Employers

As indicated above, employers generally form a key, if not the key, constituent of ER analysis (Kaufman, 2004). By employer what is meant here are the factories at the upstream ends of GSCs who employ the workers whose conditions are to be regulated. A point that has generally been overlooked is that in nearly all cases, legal duties and responsibilities are vested in the employer. A key weakness of all three approaches to supply chains outlined above is that none of them have as their central role the analysis of often the legal employers of the workers affected. Rather the focus has been placed on analysing the ways in which buyer firms influence the employment relationship: employers are viewed as rather passive recipients of the policies of brands within all three approaches as taken to date. This is problematic as it views these employers as relatively powerless and passive actors in the employment relationship. One notable exception is the recent work of Jenkins and Blyton (2017), who outline how supplier management in Indian garment manufacturers used issues around indebtedness as a mechanism to prevent social upgrading in garment supply chains.

More research is necessary into the extent to which employers navigate the constraints placed on them by buyer firms. As outlined early in the chapter, the employers, as supplier firms, are often servicing multiple buyers, each with their own particular private governance instruments. Yet, they do have agency in their own right. In addition, more focus needs to be placed on how they manage relationships with different suppliers. What is particularly important to take account of is that suppliers often supply multiple buyers, each of whom will have their own processes and policies. Understanding how employers manage these differing demands and how it translates into the management practices at the workplace is an area that to date is underdeveloped in research. Zhu and Morgan (2017) provide an interesting start to this approach, highlighting that in their research three employer responses to buyer constraints were evident: wholesale adaptation, where suppliers closely adopted practices dictated by buyers; ceremonial adaptation, where suppliers adopted policies in a way that visibly seemed to be in conformance with buyer-led practices but which beyond this was actually superficial in nature; and minimal adaptation, where the employer adopted a strategy of adjusting to the most minimal degree to buyer demands. What is particularly interesting in the context of this chapter is that Zhu and Morgan (ibid.) identify that managers exercised considerable autonomy in terms of responding to the demands of buyers. This list is not exhaustive and further more nuanced investigation of these approaches certainly would be welcomed.

Brands

Without doubt, the actor on whom most of the focus to date in supply chains has been placed has been that of brands/buyers. Without repeating in detail what has been said earlier in the chapter, a key difference between the existing approaches has been the analysis of the roles of brands. The GVC approach particularly highlights the influence of such actors on the entire system, often with rather negative implications. On the other hand, the CSR approach has a much more benevolent interpretation and focuses on the extent to which brands substitute for weak or failing states (Scherer and Palazzo, 2007, 2011). However, these significantly differing interpretations are symptomatic of the fact that brands themselves are being pulled in opposing directions. Despite their prominent position in research in the area, the question of how brands are to be understood is under conceptualised (Ruggie, 2017). Often they are examined as being sources of downwards pressures as in the GVC approach, or as potentially benevolent actors who help to develop probate labour standards for workers. Yet, understanding of this Janus-faced reality needs to be developed further.

An interesting start has been made by John Ruggie (ibid.), who argues that understanding brands as global institutions requires examining MNCs in terms of their power, authority and relative autonomy. In terms of power, Ruggie highlights three dimensions: instrumental power, which involves political activity by MNCs such as lobbying; structural power in terms of their ability to shift risk and set agendas; and discursive power, i.e. the ability of MNCs to frame public debate in their favour. Ruggie argues that authority involves the perceived right of MNCs to prescribe actions over their own subsidiaries and wider socio-economic actors. Finally, in terms of relative autonomy, Ruggie argues that MNCs exercise a relative autonomy from their owners and agents in terms of the exercise of their power and authority.

Unions

As outlined above, often those sourcing destinations at the upstream end of global supply chains feature immature system of ER, with few unions present and low labour power, such as in India (Jenkins and Blyton, 2017), Indonesia (Bartley and Egels-Zanden, 2015) and Bangladesh (Donaghey and Reinecke, 2017). In his often cited work, Erik-Olin Wright highlights two key sources of labour power in the form of structural power and associational power. Wright (2000, p. 962) defines structural power as "power that results simply from the location of workers within the economic system". This can be thought of as the ability of workers to threaten the consumption of goods. Associational is viewed as "the various forms of power that result from the formation of collective organisations of workers" (ibid.), i.e. trade unions, and at the supranational level global union federations. In essence, this focuses on the ability of groups of workers to act in support of each other through solidarity actions.

While the local unions in GSCs may be structurally weak, with locations being chosen because of low levels of worker organisation, key actors are GUFs who coordinate actions across countries. However, due to being organised at the sectoral level, it may mean that co-operation between global unions becomes necessary. The Bangladesh Accord is a recent example, where both IndustriAll (manufacturing workers) and UniGlobal (retail workers) are parties representing workers at opposite ends of the chain (Reinecke and Donaghey, 2015; Donaghey and Reinecke, 2017). However, coordination such as in this case is rare, and the nature of GUFs is such that coordinating activity can be difficult (Croucher and Cotton, 2009). Two interrelated structural issues represent challenges for GUFs. First, they are organised on a sectoral basis, thus even in the unlikely event that workers at both ends of the supply chain are unionised, unions at one end of the supply chain – for example, manufacturing unions – are likely to be in a different global union than those at the consumer end. Secondly, GUFs are organised on a broadly sectoral model without regard for the political, institutional and economic differences that Anner et al. (2006) highlight as being potential hurdles for international union cooperation.

In addition, leverage over actors is often most achieved by targeting the buyer firms rather than the actual employers. Wright (2016) argues that reputational risk amongst consumers is a lever that unions can utilise to improve labour standards in production networks. However, he goes on to argue that such leverage is not automatic but contingent on the different types of organisations and the markets within which they are embedded. Yet, it is not just about unions at the buyer end gaining leverage against buyers: in our research in Bangladesh, examples were found of workers specifically gathering evidence of who was sourcing from factories so that leverage could be applied to these. Thus, these issues need further examination by looking across entire supply chains to ascertain the ways in which unions may, or may not, leverage advantage against employers.

The state

By definition, GSCs involve bringing together actors and structures that operate across multiple countries. This creates potential conflicts of interests between states at different points as goods move from raw material to the consumer. There is a well-established literature from approaches such as the Varieties of Capitalism approach (Hall and Soskice, 2001) and the National Business Systems literature (Whitley, 1999) which shows that different institutional configurations have profound effects on the ways in which work is organised. Yet, the very nature of GSCs is such that brands may be sourcing from multiple different national business systems and suppliers may be selling to brands originating from multiple business systems. Anner (2015) highlights that in the producer states in the apparel sector, three mechanisms of labour control are exerted – state control, market despotism and employer repression – all of which entail different roles for the state. In state control, as in Vietnam or China, authoritarian states actively engage in repressing worker activism around labour rights issues. In market despotism, as in Bangladesh, the state plays a less active role in repression but actively works in concert with employers to maintain low standards through weak enforcement mechanisms and low social support. Finally, in employer repression as in Latin American countries like Honduras, the state plays a highly withdrawn role, to the extent that employers can carry out violence against labour activists with little fear of punishment. In many ways, the one governance route open is potentially the International Labour Organization; however, as Standing (2008) highlights, the ILO is poorly equipped to deal with the changes globalisation has brought and its ultimate sanction of naming and shaming can often have little to no effect.

For transnational issues involving brands based in one country and purchasing from other countries, the state lacks authoritative control beyond its borders and needs alternative strategies. What has emerged in some cases is a complementary 'division of labour' between private and public roles, whereby the state increasingly relies on non-state actors to deliver regulation, thereby leveraging businesses' economic power and transnational reach on the one hand and the moral authority of NGOs and civil society on the other hand. For instance, in the case of US conflict minerals legislation under the Dodd-Frank Act, the state did not ban the import of conflict minerals but instead mandated self-reporting that empowered NGOs and other civil society actors to act as watchdogs and hold corporations accountable (Reinecke and Ansari, 2016). The conflict minerals case illustrates how public and civil society actors played complementary roles in the emerging regulation mix involving polycentric governance regimes. In particular, the state can play a catalytic role by creating enabling conditions for private governance. Catalytic means that the state does not dictate or enforce behaviour, but can enable, entice and legitimise private governance. The state is less involved in 'first-order' governing to solve problems directly – instead, it can catalyse private actors to take on regulatory roles. In sum, private governance is thus not simply about a shift away from 'government' to 'governance' or from 'hard regulation' to 'soft regulation' (e.g. Locke, 2013). Instead, it involves both public and private actors with a shifting rather than a shrinking role of states.

NGOs

A central actor to emerge in transnational supply chain governance is the NGO. As outlined earlier in the chapter, in many countries where manufacturing has been relocated, workers lack both the structural and associational power to challenge their working conditions, but also governments often lack the political will to improve regulation. In this space, NGOs become an important actor for labour rights and may be based at any point in the supply chain (Bartley, 2007; Egels-Zandén, 2007, 2009, 2011). NGO leverage is often based heavily on corporate fear of consumer action rather than disruption of production, and this scenario provides a strong example of Hirschman's 'exit, voice and loyalty' approach (Donaghey et al., 2014; Reinecke and Donaghey, 2015). Hirschman (1970) highlighted that dissatisfied consumers had the option of remaining loyal to a brand, regardless of their thoughts; exiting to a different, competing product; or voicing their concerns in order to initiate change from the supplier. As such, NGOs often claim to speak for concerned consumers (Bartley, 2007) – though the extent to which they are actually concerned is far from certain. However, those who gain the most attention have been those who are best placed to challenge the practices of lead firms within a chain or network.

Yet, the role of such actors is not straightforward when compared to, for example, trade union representation in democratic societies (Reinecke and Donaghey, 2015). In addition, while sharing many substantive objectives, unions and NGOs do not always operate in a symbiotic relationship (Egels-Zandén, 2009). This is generally due to the differing underlying logics of membership of which each is composed. A key claim of unions as to their legitimacy is that their membership is a voluntarily coalition of workers who pursue an agenda to advance their material interests at work through a logic of industrial democracy (Donaghey and Reinecke, 2017). On the other hand, many NGOs are composed of people who wish to express solidarity with workers in poor conditions but who are not necessarily subject to such conditions themselves.

A key feature of the emerging picture in terms of ER governance in supply chains has been the role alliances of multiple actors, but particularly unions and NGOs, can play in governance. These alliances quite unsurprisingly include alliances between unions and labour rights NGOs but also more surprisingly alliances between MNCs, unions and labour rights NGOs. The relationship between unions and labour rights NGOs has to some extent been a difficult one: while both seek higher labour standards unions often question the democratic legitimacy of NGOs. On the other hand, NGOs often view the response of unions as slow and overly bureaucratic. A recent example of where there has been success is in the creation of the Bangladesh Accord for Building and Fire Safety (Donaghey and Reinecke, 2017; Reinecke and Donaghey, 2015). In this case, a legally binding and innovative agreement was reached between two GUFs and more than 200 consumer brands, with four NGOs as witness signatories, to cover an intense programme of improving worker safety in the Bangladesh garment sector. What was particularly important in this case in terms of alliances was that the strengths and weaknesses unions and NGOs had were complementary in nature: by having this complementarity it meant that turf wars were avoided. Similarly, neither unions nor the NGOs were particularly powerful and thus there was much to gain and little institutional cost to developing an alliance.

Conclusion

Global supply chains are a key feature of modern employment relations, particularly in manufacturing. To date, much attention has been focused on analysing governance structures and the implications of these structures for ER. What has emerged has been a number of groups of scholars who analyse such issues but often with little interaction between schools of thought. Greater conversations between approaches are to be welcomed as the tools identified can lead to a fuller understanding. The chapter also highlights that GSCs go beyond the traditional actors of employers, unions and the state and incorporate an increased range of actors, including NGOs and global brands, which require greater conceptualisation. The chapter highlights that these new actor configurations challenge existing frameworks of analysis of ER and are in need of further research from both conceptual and empirical perspectives.

References

Amaeshi, K.M., Osuji, O.K. and Nnodim, P. (2008). 'Corporate social responsibility in supply chains of global brands: a boundaryless responsibility? Clarifications, exceptions and implications', *Journal of Business Ethics*, 81(1), pp. 223–234.

Anner, M., Greer, I., Hauptmeier, M., Lillie, N. and Winchester, N. (2006). 'The industrial determinants of transnational solidarity: global interunion politics in three sectors', *European Journal of Industrial Relations*, 12(1), pp. 7–27.

Anner, M. (2015). 'Labor control regimes and worker resistance in global supply chains', *Labor History*, 56(3), pp. 292–307.

Banerjee, S.B. (2008). 'Necrocapitalism', *Organization Studies*, 29(12), pp. 1541–1563.

Bartley, T. (2007). 'Institutional Emergence in an Era of Globalization: The Rise of Transnational Private Regulation of Labor and Environmental Conditions', *American Journal of Sociology*, 113(2), pp. 297–351.

Bartley, T. and Egels-Zandén, N. (2015). 'Beyond decoupling: unions and the leveraging of corporate social responsibility in Indonesia', *Socio-Economic Review*, 14(2), pp. 231–255.

Brammer, S., Jackson, G. and Matten, D. (2012). 'Corporate Social Responsibility and Institutional Theory: New Perspectives on Private Governance', *Socio-Economic Review*, 10(1), pp. 3–28.

Chamberlain, G. (2016). How can Lidl sell jeans for £5.99? Easy … pay people 23p an hour to make them. *The Guardian*. (Online). 13 March. Available at: www.theguardian.com/business/2016/mar/13/lidl-jeans-bangladesh-worker-pay-23p-an-hour.

Cohen, M.A. and Mallik, S. (1997). 'Global supply chains: research and applications', *Production and Operations Management*, 6(3), pp. 193–210.

Compa, L. (2001). 'Trade unions, NGOs, and corporate codes of conduct', *International Union Rights*, 8(3), pp. 5–7.

Compa, L. (2008). 'Corporate social responsibility and workers' rights', *Comparative Labor Law & Policy Journal*, 30(1), p. 1.

Croucher, R. and Cotton, E. (2009). Global unions, global business, in *Global Union Federations and International Business*. London: Middlesex University Press.

Cumbers, A., Nativel, C. and Routledge, P. (2008). 'Labour agency and union positionalities in global production networks', *Journal of Economic Geography*, 8(3), pp. 369–387.

Czinkota, M., Kaufmann, H.R. and Basile, G. (2014). 'The relationship between legitimacy, reputation, sustainability and branding for companies and their supply chains', *Industrial Marketing Management*, 43(1), pp. 91–101.

den Hond, F. and de Bakker, F.G.A. (2007). 'Ideologically Motivated Activism: How Activist Groups Influence Corporate Social Change Activities', *Academy of Management Review*, 32(3), pp. 901–924.

Dicken, P. (2003). *Global Shift: Reshaping the Global Economic Map in the 21st Century*. London: Sage.

Donaghey, J. (2016). Global supply chains, in Wilkinson, A. and Johnstone, S. (eds.) *Encyclopaedia of Human Resource Management*. Cheltenham: Edward Elgar Publishing.

Donaghey, J., Reinecke, J., Niforou, C. and Lawson, B. (2014), 'From employment relations to consumption relations: balancing labor governance in global supply chains', *Human Resource Management*, 53(2), pp. 229–252.

Donaghey, J. and Reinecke, J. (2017). [Forthcoming]. 'When Industrial Democracy meets Corporate Social Responsibility – A Comparison of the Bangladesh Accord and Alliance as responses to the Rana Plaza disaster'. *British Journal of Industrial Relations*. (Online). Available at: doi:10.1111/bjir.12242

Dunlop, J.T. (1958). *Industrial Relations Systems*. Cambridge (MA): Harvard Business School.

Egels-Zandén, N. (2007). 'Suppliers' compliance with MNCs' codes of conduct: behind the scenes at Chinese toy suppliers', *Journal of Business Ethics*, 75(1), pp. 45–62.

Egels-Zandén, N. (2009). 'TNC motives for signing international framework agreements: a continuous bargaining model of stakeholder pressure', *Journal of Business Ethics*, 84(4), pp. 529–547.

Egels-Zandén, N. (2011). *Clean Clothes Campaign. Handbook of Transnational Governance: Institutions and Innovations*. Cambridge (MA): Polity, pp. 259–265.

Fransen, L. (2012). 'Multi-Stakeholder Governance and Voluntary Programme Interactions: Legitimation Politics in the Institutional Design of Corporate Social Responsibility', *Socio-Economic Review*, 10(1), pp. 163–192.

Galiatsos, C.B. (2015). 'Beyond Joint Employer Status: A New Analysis for Employers' Unfair Labor Practice Liability under the NLRA', *Boston University Law Review*, 95(6), pp. 2083–2116.

Gereffi, G. (1994). The organization of buyer-driven global commodity chains: how US retailers shape overseas production networks, in Gereffi, G. and Korseniewicz, M. (eds.) *Commodity Chains and Global Capitalism*. Westport: Praeger, pp. 95–122.

Gereffi, G., Humphrey, J. and Sturgeon, T. (2005). 'The governance of global value chains,' *Review of International Political Economy*, 12(1), pp. 78–104.

Hall, P.A. and Soskice, D. (eds.) (2001). *Varieties of Capitalism: The Institutional Foundations of Comparative Advantage*. Oxford: Oxford University Press.

Hammer, N. (2005). 'International Framework Agreements: global industrial relations between rights and bargaining', *Transfer: European Review of Labour and Research*, 11(4), pp. 511–530.

Henderson, J., Dicken, P., Hess, M., Coe, N. and Yeung, H.W.C. (2002). 'Global production networks and the analysis of economic development', *Review of International Political Economy*, 9(3), pp. 436–464.

Hirschman, A.O. (1970). *Exit, Voice, and Loyalty: Responses to Decline in Firms, Organizations, and States.* Vol. 25. Boston (MA): Harvard University Press.

Jenkins, J. and Blyton, P. (2017). 'In debt to the time-bank: the manipulation of working time in Indian garment factories and 'working dead horse'', *Work, Employment & Society*, 31(1), pp. 90–105.

Kaufman, B. (2004). Employment relations and the employment relations system: a guide to theorizing, in *Theoretical Perspectives on Work and the Employment Relationship*. Champaign: Industrial Relations Research Association, pp. 41–75.

Khan, F.R., Munir, K.A. and Willmott, H. (2007). 'A dark side of institutional entrepreneurship: soccer balls, child labour and postcolonial impoverishment', *Organization Studies*, 28(7), pp. 1055–1077.

Khan, F.R., Westwood, R. and Boje, D.M. (2010). 'I Feel Like a Foreign Agent': NGOs and Corporate Social Responsibility Interventions into Third World Child Labor', *Human Relations*, 63(9), pp. 1417–1438.

Lakhani, T., Kuruvilla, S. and Avgar, A. (2013). 'From the firm to the network: global value chains and employment relations theory', *British Journal of Industrial Relations*, 51(3), pp. 440–472.

Levy, D.L. (2005). 'Offshoring in the new global political economy', *Journal of Management Studies*, 42(3), pp. 685–693.

Levy, D.L. (2008). 'Political Contestation in Global Production Networks', *Academy of Management Review*, 33(4), pp. 943–963.

Levy, D., Reinecke, J. and Manning, S. (2016). 'The Political Dynamics of Sustainable Coffee: Contested Value Regimes and the Transformation of Sustainability', *Journal of Management Studies*, 53(3), pp. 364–401.

Locke, R.M., Qin, F. and Brause, A. (2007). 'Does monitoring improve labor standards? Lessons from Nike', *Industrial and Labour Relations Review*, 61(1), pp. 3–31.

Locke, R.M. (2013). *The Promise and Limits of Private Power: Promoting Labor Standards in a Global Economy.* New York: Cambridge University Press.

Newsome, K., Taylor, P., Bair, J. and Rainnie, A. (2015). *Putting Labour in its Place: Labour Process Analysis and Global Value Chains.* Basingstoke: Palgrave Macmillan.

Niforou, C. (2015). 'Labour leverage in global value chains: the role of interdependencies and multi-level dynamics', *Journal of Business Ethics*, 130(2), pp. 301–311.

O'Rourke, D. (2003). 'Outsourcing regulation: analyzing nongovernmental systems of labor standards and monitoring', *Policy Studies Journal*, 31(1), pp. 1–29.

O'Rourke, D. (2006). 'Multi-stakeholder regulation: privatizing or socializing global labor standards?' *World Development*, 34(5), pp. 899–918.

Rainnie, A., Herod, A. and McGrath-Champ, S. (2011). 'Review and positions: global production networks and labour', *Competition & Change*, 15(2), pp. 155–169.

Rasche, A. (2009). '"A Necessary Supplement": What the United Nations Global Compact Is and Is Not', *Business & Society*, 48(4), pp. 511–537.

Reinecke, J. and Ansari, S. (2016). 'Taming Wicked Problems: The Role of Framing in the Construction of Corporate Social Responsibility', *Journal of Management Studies*, 53(3), pp. 299–329.

Reinecke, J. and Donaghey, J. (2015). 'After Rana Plaza: Building Coalitional Power for Labour Rights Between Unions and (Consumption-Based) Social Movement Organisations', *Organization*, 22(5), pp. 720–740.

Riisgaard, L. and Hammer, N. (2011). 'Prospects for Labour in Global Value Chains: Labour Standards in the Cut Flower and Banana Industries', *British Journal of Industrial Relations*, 49(1), pp. 168–190.

Royle, T. (2011). Regulating Global Capital through Public and Private Codes: An Analysis of International Labour Standards and Corporate Voluntary Initiatives, in Wilkinson, A. and Barry, M. (eds.) *Comparative Employment Relations*, London: Sage.

Ruggie, J.G. (2001). 'Global_governance.net: the Global Compact as learning network', *Global Governance*, 7(4), pp. 371–378.

Ruggie, J.G. (2007). 'Business and human rights: the evolving international agenda', *The American Journal of International Law*, 101(4), pp. 819–840.

Ruggie, J.G. (2017). [Forthcoming]. 'Multinationals as global institution: power, authority and relative autonomy', *Regulation & Governance*. (Online). Available at: doi: 10.1111/rego.12154.

Scherer, A.G. and Palazzo, G. (2007). 'Toward a political conception of corporate responsibility: business and society seen from a Habermasian perspective', *Academy of Management Review*, 32(4), pp. 1096–1120.

Scherer, A.G. and Palazzo, G. (2011). 'The New Political Role of Business in a Globalized World: A Review of a New Perspective on CSR and its Implications for the Firm, Governance, and Democracy', *Journal of Management Studies*, 48(4), pp. 899–931.

Standing, G. (2008). 'The ILO: an agency for globalization?', *Development and Change*, 39(3), pp. 355–384.

Taylor, P., Newsome, K. and Rainnie, A. (2013). '"Putting labour in its place': global value chains and labour process analysis', *Competition and Change*, 17(1), pp. 1–6.

Wells, D. (2007). 'Too Weak for the Job: Corporate Codes of Conduct, Non-Governmental Organizations and the Regulation of International Labour Standards', *Global Social Policy*, 7(1), pp. 51–74.

Whitley, R. (1999). *Divergent Capitalisms: The Social Structuring and Change of Business Systems*. Oxford: Oxford University Press.

Wright, C.F. (2016). 'Leveraging Reputational Risk: Sustainable Sourcing Campaigns for Improving Labour Standards in Production Networks', *Journal of Business Ethics*, 137(1), pp. 195–221.

Wright, E.O. (2000). 'Working-class power, capitalist-class interests, and class compromise', *American Journal of Sociology*, 105(4), pp. 957–1002.

Zhu J. and Morgan, G. (2017). [Forthcoming]. 'Global supply chains, institutional constraints and firm level adaptations: a comparative study of Chinese service outsourcing firms', *Human Relations*. (Online). Available at: http://journals.sagepub.com/doi/10.1177/0018726717713830.

22

EMPLOYMENT RELATIONS IN THE INFORMAL SECTOR

Colin C. Williams

Introduction

Until now, the employment relations (ER) systems of countries have been differentiated by analysing the character of their formal economies, such as whether they are control, market or mixed economies (Arnold, 1996; Rohlf, 1998) or liberal or coordinated varieties of capitalism (Hall and Soskice, 2001). The starting point of this paper is that classifying ER systems by the character of their formal economies would be appropriate if most employment globally was in the formal economy. However, this is not the case. Some 60 per cent of the global workforce have their main employment in the informal sector (Jütting and Laiglesia, 2009), with many countries especially in the majority (third) world having more people employed in the informal sector than the formal sector (Dibben and Williams, 2012; ILO, 2013). Based on this recognition, recent years have witnessed the advocacy of new classificatory schemas of ER systems that recognise the prominence of the informal sector. The aim of this chapter is to highlight these developments and following this to discuss the future research issues.

To do this, the first section sets out the cross-national variations in the extent of the informal sector, along with the contrasting ways in which these cross-national variations have been explained and the findings of studies that have evaluated these competing explanations. This is then followed in the second section by an analysis of the cross-national variations in the nature of the informal sector. Just as studies of the extent of the informal sector have sought to evaluate the 'degrees of informalisation' of countries, this will reveal how the nature of the informal sector has been similarly evaluated. Increasingly, the tendency has been not simply to assess whether a job is either formal or informal but rather, to measure the degree to which a job is infused with informality. Again therefore, the degrees of informalisation approach used to evaluate the nature of the informal sector will be reviewed along with the contrasting ways in which the resultant cross-national variations in the nature of informality have been explained and the findings of studies evaluating these competing explanations. The third and final section then addresses future directions and issues for this field of enquiry. This will reveal not only the theoretical implications by highlighting the need to shift from a 'Varieties of Capitalism' approach to a 'diverse economies' approach when studying employment and work relations, but also how until now, much of the research on the informal sector so far as ER are concerned has concentrated on remunerated work in the informal sector. Little attention has been given to the plurality of work relations on the unpaid side such as non-remunerated internships.

Before commencing, however, the way in which the informal sector is conventionally defined must be reviewed. Reviewing the extensive literature on this subject, at least 45 different adjectives have been so far used, including 'hidden', 'shadow', 'unregistered', 'undeclared' and 'unregulated'. Nearly all describe what is absent, insufficient or missing relative to the formal sector. Despite the array of terms, a strong consensus exists regarding what is missing, insufficient or absent from the informal sector and it is that the activity is not declared to the state for tax, social security and labour law purposes when it should be declared, but is legal in all other respects (European Commission, 2007; OECD, 2012; Sepulveda and Syrett, 2007; Williams 2006). Consequently, if an activity possesses other absences or insufficiencies, such as that the good and/or service involved is illegal, then these are not considered part of the informal sector but instead 'criminal' activities. Of course, and as with all definitions, blurred edges exist, such as whether to include unpaid activity in this definition. Until now, the ER literature has largely included only activities that are remunerated when discussing the informal sector. Whether this should continue is an issue that will be returned to below, as will the issue of defining the informal sector more in terms of the social relations within which work is conducted rather than simply in terms of whether it is declared to the authorities.

The informalisation of employment relations

For much of the twentieth century, the belief was that the informal sector was a leftover from a past mode of production and gradually disappearing (Boeke, 1942; Geertz, 1963; Lewis, 1959). Since the turn of the millennium however, there has been widespread recognition of the persistence and extensiveness of the informal sector (Buehn and Schneider, 2012; ILO, 2002, 2011; Jütting and Laiglesia, 2009; OECD, 2012; Schneider, 2008, 2013; Williams, 2013, 2014a, 2015a, 2015d).

The 'degrees of informalisation' approach towards employment relations

How, therefore, might the persistence of the informal sector in economies be represented? One way forward is to adopt a 'degrees of informalisation' analytical framework that examines the proportion of paid employment in the informal sector. As Figure 22.1 displays, ER systems can be positioned on a continuum from wholly formal at one end to wholly informal at the other. In doing so, a global mapping of the pervasiveness of the informal sector can occur so as to reveal those global regions and countries in which formal employment is dominant and those in which the informal sector is to the fore.

Although this simple way of classifying the extent of informalisation enables all economies to be situated on this spectrum, great care is required in how their position is interpreted. In the past, a temporal sequencing was often overlaid onto such a spectrum in that a natural and inevitable temporal trajectory towards the left of the continuum was assumed, resulting in countries being placed in a hierarchical 'development queue', with the more formal ER systems of the west placed at the front of the development queue and viewed as more 'advanced', and the more

Wholly Formal	Quasi-Formal	Largely Formal	Mostly Formal	Semi-Formal	Semi-Informal	Mostly Informal	Largely Informal	Quasi-Informal	Wholly Informal
0	10	20	30	40	60	70	80	90	100

Figure 22.1 Typology of employment relations systems by the proportion of employment relations permeated by informality

informal ER systems of the third (majority) world depicted as at the back (Massey, 2005) and also as 'backwards' relative to their more formalised counterparts (Geertz, 1963; Lewis, 1959). However, the place any economy inhabits on this continuum does not necessarily represent normative superiority, but rather difference, and neither should a natural and inevitable temporal trajectory in a particular direction be assumed. If any lesson is to be learned from the past few decades, it is that different countries are moving in different directions along this continuum. Privileging formalisation as a universal process not only denies the lived practices but also excludes the possibility of alternative present and future trajectories.

To evaluate where countries sit on this spectrum, two options are available. Estimates of the cross-national variations in the proportion of employment in the informal sector can be produced using either direct surveys or indirect measurement methods that use proxy indicators or seek statistical traces of informality in macro-economic data collected for other purposes (OECD, 2002, 2012; Ram and Williams, 2008). Indirect methods can be divided into four broad techniques: those using individual non-monetary proxy indicators such as the number of very small enterprises (ILO, 2002) or electricity demand (e.g. Friedman et al., 2000); those employing individual monetary proxy indicators such as the level of cash deposits (Gutmann, 1977) or money transactions (Frey and Weck, 1983); income/expenditure discrepancies (Paglin, 1994); and those using multiple indirect proxy indicators (e.g. Schneider, 2013; Schneider and Williams, 2013). The problem with all of these methods is not only that they indeed use proxy indicators but also that data are often not available.

Here, therefore, one of the few direct surveys of cross-national variations in the proportion of employment in the informal sector is used. This is the International Labour Organization (ILO) dataset on 41 countries (ILO, 2011, 2012). Examining the findings, Table 22.1 reveals that the simple unweighted average is that the majority (53.9 per cent) of non-agricultural workers in these 41 emerging economies are in informal employment as their main job. However, a weighted average figure is here employed that takes into account the variable size of the workforce across countries. The resultant finding is that over one-third (34.4 per cent) of non-agricultural workers are in informal employment as their main job. Informal employment, therefore, is not some minor leftover of little importance.

However, there are marked regional variations. The weighted proportion of the non-agricultural workforce with their main job in the informal sector ranges from one in four

Table 22.1 Informal employment as percentage of total non-agricultural employment (unweighted and weighted): by global region

Global region	Percentage of non-agricultural workforce in informal employment, unweighted	Percentage of non-agricultural workforce in informal employment, weighted	Number of countries
East Asia & Pacific	44.1	44.0	5
Europe and Central Asia	17.0	26.8	5
Latin America & Caribbean	57.0	50.5	16
Middle East & North Africa	54.9	51.5	2
South Asia	74.7	82.6	3
Sub-Saharan Africa	59.4	53.2	10
All global regions	53.9	34.4	41

Source: derived from ILO (2012)

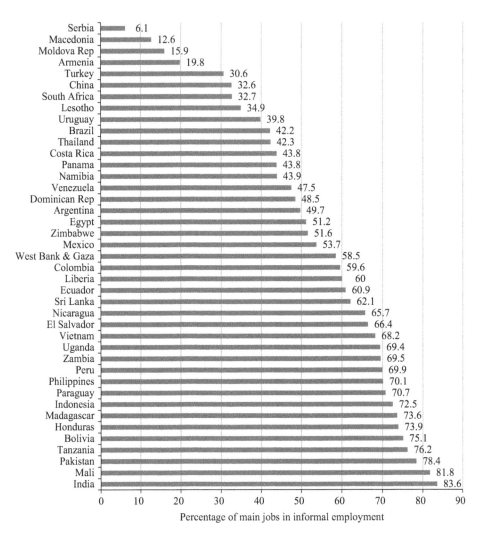

Figure 22.2 Informal employment as share of non-agricultural employment

(26.8 per cent) in Europe and Central Asia to more than four out of five (82.6 per cent) in South Asia. The permeation of the informal sector, therefore, is not evenly distributed across the globe. Moreover, there are also marked variations between countries within each global region. As Figure 22.2 displays, the proportion of the non-agricultural workforce with their main job in the informal sector ranges from 83.6 per cent in India to 6.1 per cent in Serbia. Indeed, in the majority of countries surveyed, namely 24 (59 per cent) of the 41 nations, over half of the non-agricultural workforce is in informal employment.

Explaining cross-national variations in the level of informal employment

Until now, three competing perspectives have sought to explain the cross-national variations in the level of informal employment.

Modernisation explanation. During the twentieth century, the informal sector was widely represented as a legacy of a pre-modern mode of production and viewed as fading as the modern formal sector became ever more hegemonic. Developing world countries in which informal employment is extensive are thus seen as portraying the characteristics of 'under-development' and even 'backwardness', whilst extensive formal sectors are viewed as representing 'advancement' and 'development' (Geertz, 1963; Gilbert, 1998; Lewis, 1959). The result is that the informal sector is seen as an expression of under-development (in the normative sense of a lack of 'progress') that will disappear with economic advancement and modernisation. Applying this to explaining the cross-national variations in the extent of informal employment, it can be suggested that in less developed economies, there will be a higher prevalence of informal employment.

Neoliberal explanation. Over the past few decades, nevertheless, not least due to the persistence and even expansion of informal employment globally, a range of competing explanations have emerged. For neoliberal commentators, informal employment is a rational economic decision voluntarily chosen by people and businesses as a result of high taxes, a corrupt public sector and too much state interference in the workings of the free market (e.g. Becker, 2004; De Soto, 1989, 2001; London and Hart, 2004; Nwabuzor, 2005). From this neoliberal perspective, therefore, informal employment will be higher in countries with higher taxes, public sector corruption and state interference in the workings of the free market.

Structuralist explanation. For structuralist scholars, the widespread existence and even expansion of informal employment is a direct by-product of the emergence of a deregulated open world economy (Castells and Portes, 1989; Gallin, 2001; Hudson, 2005; Slavnic, 2010). The ongoing functional integration of a unified global economic system is resulting in subcontracting and outsourcing becoming key vehicles for integrating informal employment into contemporary capitalism, resulting in further downward pressure on wages, the erosion of incomes and welfare provision, and the growth of yet more informal employment. From this structuralist perspective, in consequence, informal employment is a largely unregulated realm composed of low-paid and insecure work carried out under 'sweatshop-like' conditions as a survival tactic by marginalised populations excluded from employment in the formal economy (Castells and Portes, 1989; Davis, 2006; Gallin, 2001). In the new post-Fordist and post-socialist era, those engaged in informal employment are unwilling pawns cast into this sphere as a survival mechanism. From this perspective, therefore, informal employment will be more prevalent in those less developed countries with lower levels of state intervention to protect workers from poverty.

Evaluations of the competing explanations. In recent years, scholars have evaluated these competing explanations. The finding has been that no one explanation is universally valid. It has been contended, for example, that the structuralist explanation is valid when explaining informal employment in relatively deprived populations but the neoliberal perspective is more appropriate when explaining informality in relatively affluent populations (Evans, Syrett and Williams, 2006; Pfau-Effinger, 2009; Williams, 2004). Studies have similarly argued that the structuralist explanation is more valid when explaining women's necessity-driven informal employment and the neoliberal explanation for the voluntary exit rationales that characterise men's engagement (Franck, 2012; Grant, 2013; Williams, 2011). When examining cross-national variations in the scale of informal employment, meanwhile, it has been revealed using simple bivariate correlations that there is evidence to support the tenets of both the modernisation and structuralist perspectives but little or no evidence to support most of the tenets of the neoliberal perspective. This has been shown when examining the cross-national variations in the scale of the informal sector in the European Union (Williams, 2013, 2014b), post-Soviet countries (Williams, 2015b; Williams, Round and Rodgers, 2013), developing nations (Williams, 2015c) and Latin America (Williams and Youssef, 2014).

The outcome has been a call for a synthesis of the tenets of the modernisation and structuralist explanations in the form of a new 'neo-modernisation' explanation that explains lower levels of informal employment as being associated with economic development and state intervention in the form of higher tax rates and social transfers to protect workers from poverty. Future research will need to analyse whether this continues to be valid when multivariate regression analyses are conducted and other variables are introduced and held constant.

Nature of informality

Just as studies of the extent of the informal sector have sought to evaluate the 'degrees of informalisation' of countries, a similar process has started to occur with regard to the nature of the informal sector. Rather than simply depict paid employment as formal or informal, studies have increasingly sought to understand the degree to which a job is infused with informality. To achieve this, Figure 22.3 provides an analytical framework that captures how different forms of paid work are infused with informality to varying degrees. It also reveals how they each merge into one another by using overlapping circles with hatched lines to reveal a borderless continuum of, rather than separate, forms of paid employment relationship. The outcome is a representation of a seamless repertoire of paid employment relationships from purely formal at one end to purely informal at the other. Here, we briefly describe how this is the case before turning attention to their varying prevalence across countries.

Forms of paid employment relationship

Formal employment. Fully formal employment is here defined as paid work that is registered by the state for tax, social security and labour law purposes, and comes in an array of forms such as permanent or temporary, part-time or full-time, and waged employment or self-employment. Conventionally, moreover, three types of formal labour, namely in the private, public and third sectors, have been distinguished. However, given that private sector organisations are increasingly pursuing a triple bottom line, whilst public and third sector organisations are also pursuing profit (albeit in order to reinvest so as to achieve wider social and environmental objectives), an

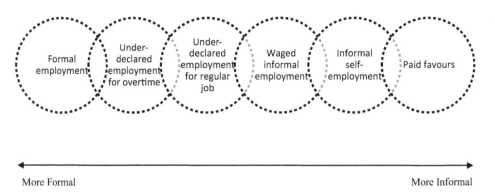

Figure 22.3 A typology of the repertoire of employment relations in contemporary societies

ongoing blurring of the boundaries between these three formal spheres is occurring. Formal employment, moreover, is not discrete.

Under-declared employment. In recent years, there has been recognition that not all formal employment is totally formal. Formal employees working for formal employers are sometimes paid two wages, an official declared wage and an additional unofficial undeclared ('envelope') wage (Meriküll and Staehr, 2010; Sedlenieks, 2003; Williams, 2009; Woolfson, 2007). Under-declared employment thus arises from fake employment contracts where the conditions in the formal written contract differ to that verbally agreed. Unless the employee agrees to these verbal conditions, then generally they do not get the job. Such conditions can include: firstly, the employee not taking their full statutory entitlement to annual leave; secondly, working longer hours than in their formal contract; and/or thirdly, undertaking different tasks and responsibilities to those specified in their formal contract (Williams and Horodnic, 2017). This verbal contract supersedes the formal written employment contract, constituting the unwritten 'psychological contract' regarding their conditions of employment (Rousseau, 1995). Such fake contracts can vary in the degree to which they differ from the formal contract, with envelope wages in some instances merely being paid for extra work or overtime, and in others the employee has a totally different contract and wage rate than is stated in the formal contract (Williams, 2009).

Informal waged employment. This refers to waged work not declared for tax, social security and labour law purposes. Similar diversity exists regarding informal waged employment. Such work ranges from work violating labour law such as 'false' or 'bogus' self-employment for one employer through to wholly informal waged employment without a formal contract and where there is not only labour law violations but also tax and social security non-compliance. This can be temporary or permanent employment, full-time or part-time and relatively low- or high-paid (Thörnquist, 2011).

Informal self-employment. Recent years have also seen growing recognition of the multifarious forms of informal self-employment, which is market-like own-account work conducted for financial gain. Besides 'bogus' self-employment, there are diverse forms of profit-motivated informal self-employment, ranging from the formal self-employed conducting various portions of their trade off the books (thus calling into question the notion that formal and informal enterprises are discrete and further blurring the formal/informal divide) to the wholly unregistered self-employed working entirely off the books (Webb et al., 2009).

Paid favours. Informal self-employment sometimes merges into the realm of paid favours (Larsen, 2013; Zelizer, 2011). There exists a continuum of informal own-account work ranging from various forms of profit-motivated self-employment (as discussed above), through social entrepreneurship in the informal sector (Gordin and Dedova, 2015) where the self-employed conduct work for less than market rates such as for the elderly, and own-account work conducted for and by kin living outside the household, friends, neighbours and acquaintances. Here, work relations significantly differ because this work is often conducted for redistributive and social rationales. There is also monetised family labour where paid work takes place for other family members within the household that is not declared to the state for tax, social security and labour law purposes when it should be declared, and market-like relations are absent despite money changing hands. As a general rule, the closer the social relations, the less market-like are the transactions, whilst the more distant the social relations the more market-like and profit-motivated is the employment relationship (White and Williams, 2010; Williams, 2004).

Evaluating the nature of informality

Given this multifarious repertoire of employment relationships, a way of classifying the nature of the informal sector in terms of the degree of informalisation is required. Table 22.2 proposes a classificatory schema. When more than half of the employment in the informal sector is waged (i.e. envelope-waged work and wholly undeclared waged employment), the economy is denoted as characterised by '*waged*' informalisation, which can be further sub-divided into '*under-declared waged-oriented*' informalisation when more than half of the informal waged work is envelope wages and '*undeclared waged*' informalisation when more than half the informal waged work is wholly informal. Meanwhile, when more than half of the employment in the informal sector is own-account work (i.e. informal self-employment and paid favours), the economy is denoted as characterised by '*own-account*' informalisation, again sub-divided into '*market-oriented own-account*' informalisation when more than half the own-account work is informal self-employment and '*solidarity-oriented own-account*' informalisation when more than half is in the form of paid favours.

A recent study uses this analytical framework to evaluate the cross-national variations in the nature of informality across the 27 member states of the European Union (Williams, 2014a). As Table 22.3 reveals, of the 8.6 per cent (one in 11) of the population in the EU reporting participation in the informal sector over the previous year in the 2007 Eurobarometer survey, nearly one-third (31.4 per cent) had received envelope wages from their formal employer, 14.4 per cent engaged in informal waged employment, 14.4 per cent in informal self-employment and 39.7 per cent in paid favours. The EU-27 as a whole can therefore be classified as an 'own-account' informal economy in that the majority (54.1 per cent) of informal work is own account work (i.e. self-employment and paid favours) and more particularly, it is a 'solidarity-oriented own-account' informal economy because the majority (73.3 per cent) of own-account informal work is paid favours.

Cross-national variations exist, however, in the nature of informality. While all 11 Nordic and western European member states are 'own-account' informal economies, 10 of the 16 southern and east-central European member states are 'waged' informal economies, and the remaining six are own-account informal economies, although the latter all have fairly substantial waged realms compared with Nordic and western European member states. Consequently, there is an

Table 22.2 Classification of the nature of informality in countries

Nature of informalisation	*Sub-types of informalisation*	*Degree of informalisation*
Waged (>50% of the informalisation of employment relations is in the waged realm)	'Under-declared wage-oriented' (>50% waged work is envelope wages) 'Undeclared wage-oriented' (>50% waged work is wholly undeclared waged work)	More formal relations in informal sector
Own-account (>50% of the informalisation of employment relations is in the own-account realm)	'Market-oriented own-account' (>50% own-account work is undeclared self-employment) 'Solidarity-oriented own-account' (>50% own-account work is paid favours)	More informal relations in informal sector

Source: derived from Williams (2014a)

Table 22.3 Nature of the informal sector in the EU-27: by type of informal work

Country	Informal waged		Informal own-account		Nature of the informal sector
	Envelope wages	Informal waged work	Informal self-employment	Paid favours	
EU27	*31.4*	*14.4*	*14.4*	*39.7*	*Solidarity-oriented own-account*
Nordic nations	11.0	13.0	11.3	64.7	Solidarity-oriented own-account
Finland	24.9	6.7	1.7	66.7	Solidarity-oriented own-account
Denmark	4.4	15.6	12.8	67.2	Solidarity-oriented own-account
Sweden	14.1	12.3	14.0	59.6	Solidarity-oriented own-account
Continental Europe	17.0	15.1	13.3	54.6	Solidarity-oriented own-account
Belgium	30.9	16.7	11.9	40.5	Solidarity-oriented own-account
UK	20.6	23.5	8.8	47.1	Solidarity-oriented own-account
Austria	26.3	12.7	13.9	48.1	Solidarity-oriented own-account
Germany	18.6	16.3	11.6	53.5	Solidarity-oriented own-account
Ireland	17.1	14.3	22.9	45.7	Solidarity-oriented own-account
Netherlands	7.4	17.6	14.7	60.3	Solidarity-oriented own-account
France	9.8	12.7	11.3	66.2	Solidarity-oriented own-account
Luxembourg	11.5	7.7	15.4	65.4	Solidarity-oriented own-account
East-Central Europe	41.2	13.7	16.9	28.2	Under-declared waged
Romania	73.5	3.7	5.9	16.9	Under-declared waged
Bulgaria	55.4	22.3	12.5	9.8	Under-declared waged
Poland	46.3	15.9	18.3	19.5	Under-declared waged
Hungary	31.7	23.1	16.8	28.4	Under-declared waged
Latvia	38.5	11.9	21.7	27.9	Under-declared waged
Lithuania	42.3	8.5	24.6	24.6	Under-declared waged
Slovakia	36.9	10.5	17.9	34.7	Solidarity-oriented own-account

(continued)

Table 22.3 (cont.)

Country	Informal waged		Informal own-account		Nature of the informal sector
	Envelope wages	Informal waged work	Informal self-employment	Paid favours	
Czech Republic	21.2	20.0	2.5	56.3	Solidarity-oriented own-account
Estonia	25.2	15.8	27.3	31.7	Solidarity-oriented own-account
Slovenia	27.4	11.3	9.7	51.6	Solidarity-oriented own-account
Southern Europe	35.6	18.0	20.1	26.3	Under-declared waged
Malta	22.2	66.7	11.1	0.0	Undeclared waged
Cyprus	72.7	0.0	9.1	18.2	Under-declared waged
Spain	40.5	17.0	17.0	25.5	Under-declared waged
Portugal	32.5	24.3	18.9	24.3	Under-declared waged
Italy	42.5	6.4	23.4	27.7	Solidarity-oriented own-account
Greece	18.6	20.9	25.6	34.9	Solidarity-oriented own-account

Source: Williams (2014a: Table 2)

east-to-west and south-to-north divide in the EU-27, with economies on the eastern/southern side being more waged informal economies and those on the western/Nordic side being own-account informal economies. Moreover, all waged informal economies are 'under-declared waged' informal economies, with the exception of Malta which is an 'undeclared waged' informal economy. All own-account informal economies, meanwhile, are 'solidarity-oriented own-account' informal economies. None are 'market-oriented own-account' informal economies.

Applying the above discussed modernisation, neoliberal and structuralist perspectives to explain these cross-national variations in the nature of informality in the EU, Williams (2014a) finds that more own-account informal sectors, similar to greater levels of informality, are significantly correlated with wealthier and more equal (as measured by the Gini-coefficient) countries, in which there is greater labour market intervention, higher levels of social protection and more effective redistribution via social transfers. What is now required is to evaluate whether similar findings are identified elsewhere.

Future directions and issues

Until now, research on the informal sector in the employment relations literature has concentrated almost entirely on paid work in the informal sector. Unpaid work has received little attention. To start to analyse such unpaid work, Figure 22.4 presents a typology that captures the various types of such work. This reveals how unpaid work, akin to paid work, can be positioned on a continuum from wholly formal to wholly informal. It also reveals how there is not a paid/

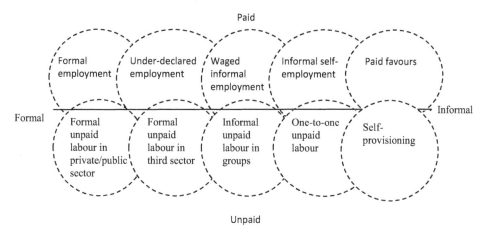

Figure 22.4 A typology of the diverse repertoire of work relations in contemporary societies

unpaid dualism, but rather a continuum from wholly non-monetised work practices, through work relations where there is gift exchange or in-kind labour, to wholly monetised practices. Here, each type of unpaid work is briefly discussed in order to reveal the need for more research.

In the private and public sectors, there appears to be a growing tendency towards using formal unpaid labour in the form of unpaid internships or, for example, one-week trials, with people doing this sometimes expecting paid employment at the end. Despite media reports increasingly calling attention to the labour rights and working conditions attached to unpaid (and paid) internships, little if any scholarly research has been undertaken. This is a significant gap that needs to be filled. In some instances, moreover, unpaid formal labour is not even a choice but a result of formal employers failing to pay their formal employees for protracted periods. Again, little research has been conducted (for an exception, see Shevchenko, 2009). Indeed, in Ukraine, Williams, Round and Rodgers (2013) find that 30 per cent of those who had started a new formal job over the prior 12 months had been asked to work on an unpaid trial basis, especially younger age groups. A significant minority had not been employed at the end, and respondents viewed this as a deliberate employer strategy to get 'free labour'. Further detailed research is required on this topic.

Formal unpaid labour is most extensively used in third sector organisations, however, where it is commonly termed 'formal volunteering', which is "giving help through groups, clubs or organisations to benefit other people or the environment" (Low et al., 2008, p. 11). Given the increasing tendency for formal employers to encourage their formal employees to conduct formal volunteering for other organisations as part of their job (Burchell and Cooke, 2013), this employment relationship – which is often overlooked – requires further research. In some instances moreover, unpaid labour for organisations can be 'off the radar', when help is provided to benefit other people or the environment but the required legal and regulatory formalities are not all fulfilled, such as when caring for children in a community-based group without the required licences to act as a child carer, or when running a sports team, community fund-raising or music event without the necessary licences to do so, perhaps based on the assumption that only those reimbursed need to conform to the laws and regulations. Until now, no research has been conducted on the prevalence of this form of labour relation.

Beyond these more organised forms of unpaid labour, the ER literature has seldom if ever examined more one-to-one forms of unpaid labour, perhaps based on the assumption that such work is unworthy of attention or beyond the scope of the study of ER. However, there are often employer/employee relationships, which can take various forms, ranging from individualised one-way giving (often termed 'informal volunteering') to two-way reciprocity. When reciprocity is involved, moreover, such unpaid endeavours often blur into paid favours since the reciprocity may take the form of either in-kind labour or gifts in lieu of payment. Indeed, financial gain can be present and usually more prominent when more distant social relations are involved, and redistributive and relationship-building purposes more prominent when conducted for and by closer social relations (Williams, 2004).

A final form of labour seldom if ever addressed by the ER literature is self-provisioning, which is unpaid work conducted by household members for themselves or for other members of their household. Again, however, such work can often take the form of an employment relationship, and there is also often a psychological contract between the parties involved. Indeed, it is perhaps rare in couple households that housework is today undertaken with no expectations of reciprocity between the parties involved and without regard for expectations of reciprocity (ibid.).

Besides these empirical gaps on unpaid work in the ER literature, there is also little discussion of the theoretical implications of identifying a diversity of ER. Until now, ER systems have been classified by the character of their formal economies, resulting in the identification of different 'Varieties of Capitalism'. The outcome is that the future is closed off to anything other than capitalist hegemony. Over the past decade, however, and beyond the ER literature, a loose coupling of post-development, post-colonial and post-structuralist scholars have begun to challenge this dominant belief that all economies can be depicted as contrasting varieties of capitalism (Escobar, 1995, 2001; Fuller, Jonas and Lee, 2010; Gibson-Graham, 1996, 2008a, 2008b, 2010; Jonas, 2010; Latouche, 1993; Lee, 2013; Leyshon, 2005; Leyshon, Lee and Williams, 2003; White and Williams, 2012, 2014; Williams, 2005). By re-imagining and re-visioning ER systems as being composed of heterogeneous work relations, the implications are two-fold. First, it is suggestive that there persist work relations that are not capitalist. Second, by locating non-capitalist work relations in the present, rather than the past, and not reducing them to a form or by-product of capitalism, this approach is engaged in the demonstrable construction and practice of alternatives to capitalism in the here and now. For Gibson-Graham, Cameron and Healy (2013), this re-reading is not simply about bringing minority practices to light. It is about de-centring capitalism from its pivotal position and bringing to the fore the existence of alternative work relations and futures beyond capitalist hegemony.

Conclusion

In sum, if this chapter encourages recognition among scholars of employment relations that there is work in the informal sector which is not some marginal or peripheral enclave but is the realm where the majority of jobs are located globally, then it will have achieved one of its main intentions. If this then leads more scholars to take seriously the study of the diversity of work relations in the informal sector, and to start to fill the significant theoretical and empirical gaps, then it will have achieved its broader intention.

References

Arnold, R.A. (1996). *Economics*. St Paul: West Publishing.
Becker, K.F. (2004). *The Informal Economy*. Stockholm: Swedish International Development Agency.
Boeke, J.H. (1942). *Economies and Economic Policy in Dual Societies*. Harlem: Tjeenk Willnik.
Buehn, A. and Schneider, F. (2012). 'Shadow economies around the world: novel insights, accepted knowledge and new estimates', *International Tax and Public Finance* 19(1), pp. 139–171.

Burchell, J. and Cook, J. (2013). 'Sleeping with the Enemy? Strategic Transformations in Business-NGO Relationships Through Stakeholder Dialogue', *Journal of Business Ethics*, 113(3), pp. 505–518.

Castells, M. and Portes, A. (1989). World underneath: the origins, dynamics and effects of the informal economy, in Portes, A., Castells, M. and Benton, L.A. (eds.) *The Informal Economy: Studies in Advanced and Less Developing Countries*. Baltimore: Johns Hopkins University Press, pp. 19–41.

Davis, M. (2006). *Planet of Slums*. London: Verso.

De Soto, H. (1989). *The Other Path*. London: Harper and Row.

De Soto, H. (2001). *The Mystery of Capital: Why Capitalism Triumphs in the West and Fails Everywhere Else*. London: Black Swan.

Dibben, P. and Williams, C.C. (2012). 'Varieties of capitalism and employment relations: informally dominated market economies', *Industrial Relations: a Review of Economy and Society*, 51(S1), pp. 563–582.

Escobar, A. (1995). *Encountering Development: The Making and Unmaking of the Third World*. Princeton: Princeton University Press.

Escobar, A. (2001). 'Culture sits in places: reflections of globalism and subaltern strategies of localization', *Political Geography*, 20(2), pp. 139–174.

European Commission (2007). *Stepping up the fight against undeclared work COM(2007) 628 final*. Brussels: European Commission.

Evans, M., Syrett, S. and Williams, C.C. (2006). *Informal Economic Activities and Deprived Neighbourhoods*. London: Department of Communities and Local Government.

Franck, A.K. (2012). 'Factors motivating women's informal micro-entrepreneurship: experiences from Penang, Malaysia', *International Journal of Gender and Entrepreneurship*, 4(1), pp. 65–78.

Frey, B.S. and Weck, H. (1983). 'What produces a hidden economy? an international cross-section analysis', *Southern Economic Journal*, 49(4), pp. 822–832.

Friedman, E., Johnson, S., Kaufmann, D. and Zoido, P. (2000). 'Dodging the grabbing hand: the determinants of unofficial activity in 69 countries', *Journal of Public Economics*, 76(3), pp. 459–493.

Fuller D., Jonas, A.E.G. and Lee, R. (2010). (eds.) *Interrogating Alterity: Alternative Economic and Political Spaces*. Aldershot: Ashgate.

Gallin, D. (2001). 'Propositions on trade unions and informal employment in time of globalisation', *Antipode*, 19(4), pp. 531–549.

Geertz, C. (1963). *Old Societies and New States: the Quest for Modernity in Asia and Africa*. Glencoe (IL): Free Press.

Gibson-Graham, J.K. (1996). *The End of Capitalism (As We Knew It)? A Feminist Critique of Political Economy*. Oxford: Blackwell.

Gibson-Graham, J.K. (2008a). 'Diverse economies: performative practices for "other worlds"', *Progress in Human Geography*, 32(5), pp. 613–632.

Gibson-Graham, J.K. (2008b). Poststructural interventions, in Sheppard, E. and Barnes, T.J. (eds.) *A Companion to Economic Geography*. Oxford: Blackwell, pp. 95–110.

Gibson-Graham, J.K. (2010). Forging post-development partnerships, in Pike, A., Rodriguez-Pose, A. and Tomaney, J. (eds.) *Handbook of Local and Regional Development*. London: Routledge, pp. 226–236.

Gibson-Graham J.K., Cameron, J. and Healy, S. (2013). *Take Back the Economy*. Minneapolis: University of Minnesota Press.

Gilbert, A. (1998). *The Latin American City*. London: Latin American Bureau.

Gordin, V. and Dedova, M. (2015). 'Social entrepreneurship in the informal economy: a case study of re-enactment festivals', *Journal of Enterprising Communities*, 9(1), pp. 6–16.

Grant, R. (2013). 'Gendered spaces of informal entrepreneurship in Soweto, South Africa', *Urban Geography*, 34(1), pp. 86–108.

Gutmann, P.M. (1977). 'The subterranean economy', *Financial Analysts Journal*, 34(11), pp. 26–27.

Hall, P.A. and Soskice, D. (2001). *Varieties of Capitalism: the Institutional Foundations of Comparative Advantage*. Oxford: Oxford University Press.

Hudson, R. (2005). *Economic Geographies: Circuits, Flows and Spaces*, London: Sage.

ILO (2002). *Decent work and the informal economy*. Geneva: International Labour Office.

ILO (2011). *Statistical update on employment in the informal economy*. Geneva: ILO Department of Statistics.

ILO (2012). *Statistical update on employment in the informal economy*. Geneva: ILO Department of Statistics.

ILO (2013). *Women and men in the informal economy: a statistical picture*. (Online). Available at: www.ilo.org/stat/Publications/WCMS_234413/lang--en/index.htm

Jonas, A.E.G. (2010). "Alternative" this, "alternative" that…: interrogating alterity and diversity, in Fuller, D., Jonas, A.E.G. and Lee, R. (eds.) *Interrogating Alterity: Alternative Economic and Political Spaces*. Aldershot: Ashgate, pp. 3–27.

Jütting, J.P. and Laiglesia, J.R. (2009). Employment, poverty reduction and development: what's new?, in Jütting, J.P. and Laiglesia, J.R. (eds.) *Is Informal Normal? Towards More and Better Jobs in Developing Countries*. Paris: OECD, pp. 42–65.

Larsen, L.B. (2013). 'Buy or barter? Illegal yet licit purchases of work in contemporary Sweden', *Focaal: Journal of Global and Historical Anthropology*, 66, pp. 75–87

Latouche, S. (1993). *In the Wake of Affluent Society: an Exploration of Post-development*. London: Zed.

Lee, R. (2013). The possibilities of economic difference? Social relations of value, space and economic geographies, in Zademach, H-M. and Hillebrand, S. (eds.) *Alternative Economies and Spaces: New Perspectives for a Sustainable Economy*. Bielefeld: Transcript Verlag, pp. 69–84.

Lewis, A. (1959). *The Theory of Economic Growth*. London: Allen and Unwin.

Leyshon, A. (2005). 'Introduction: diverse economies', *Antipode*, 37(5), pp. 856–862.

Leyshon, A., Lee, R. and Williams, C.C. (2003) (eds.) *Alternative Economic Spaces*. London: Sage.

London, T. and Hart, S.L. (2004). 'Reinventing strategies for emerging markets: beyond the transnational model', *Journal of International Business Studies*, 35(5), pp. 350–370.

Low, N., Butt, S., Ellis Paine, A. and Davis Smith, J. (2008). *Helping Out: a National Survey of Volunteering and Charitable Giving*. London: Office of the Third Sector.

Massey, D. (2005). *For Space*. London: Sage.

Meriküll, J. and Staehr, K. (2010). 'Unreported employment and envelope wages in mid-transition: comparing developments and causes in the Baltic countries', *Comparative Economic Studies*, 52(4), pp. 637–670.

Nwabuzor, A. (2005). 'Corruption and development: new initiatives in economic openness and strengthened rule of law', *Journal of Business Ethics*, 59(1/2), pp. 121–138.

OECD (2002). *Measuring the non-observed economy*. Paris: OECD.

OECD (2012). *Reducing opportunities for tax non-compliance in the underground economy*. Paris: OECD.

Paglin, M. (1994). 'The underground economy: new estimates from household income and expenditure surveys', *The Yale Law Journal*, 103(8), pp. 2239–2257.

Pfau-Effinger, B. (2009). 'Varieties of undeclared work in European societies', *British Journal of Industrial Relations*, 47(1), pp. 79–99.

Ram, M. and Williams, C.C. (2008). Making visible the hidden: researching off-the-books work, in Buchanan, D. and Bryson, A. (eds.) *Handbook of Organizational Research Methods*. London: Sage, pp. 120–144.

Rohlf, W.D. (1998). *Introduction to Economic Reasoning*. London: Addison-Wesley.

Rousseau, D.M. (1995). *Psychological Contracts in Organizations: Understanding Written and Unwritten Agreements*. Thousand Oaks: Sage.

Schneider, F. (2008). (ed.) *The Hidden Economy*. Cheltenham: Edward Elgar.

Schneider, F. (2013). Size and development of the shadow economy of 31 European and 5 other OECD countries from 2003 to 2013: a further decline. (Online). Available at: www.econ.jku.at/members/Schneider/files/publications/2013/ShadEcEurope31_Jan2013.pdf (Accessed: 29 December 2017).

Schneider, F. and Williams, C.C. (2013). *The Shadow Economy*. London: Institute of Economic Affairs.

Sedlenieks, K. (2003). Cash in an Envelope: Corruption and Tax Avoidance as an Economic Strategy in Contemporary Riga, in Arnstberg, K-O. and Boren, T. (eds.) *Everyday Economy in Russia, Poland and Latvia*. Stockholm: Almqvist and Wiksell, pp. 101–133.

Sepulveda, L. and Syrett, S. (2007). 'Out of the shadows? Formalisation approaches to informal economic activity', *Policy and Politics*, 35(1), pp. 87–104.

Shevchenko, O. (2009). *Crisis and the Everyday in Postsocialist Moscow*. Bloomington: Indiana University Press.

Slavnic, Z. (2010). 'Political economy of informalisation', *European Societies*, 12(1), pp. 3–23.

Thörnquist, A. (2011). False self-employment: a topical but old labour market problem, in Thörnquist, A. and Engtsrand, A.K. (eds.) *Precarious Employment in Perspective: Old and New Challenges to Working Conditions in Sweden*. Brussels: Peter Lang, pp. 100–120.

Webb, J.W., Tihanyi, L., Ireland, R.D. and Sirmon, D.G. (2009). 'You say illegal, I say legitimate: entrepreneurship in the informal economy', *Academy of Management Review*, 34(3), pp. 492–510.

White, R. and Williams, C.C. (2010). 'Re-thinking monetary exchange: some lessons from England', *Review of Social Economy*, 68(3), pp. 317–338.

White, R. and Williams, C.C. (2012). 'The pervasive nature of heterodox economic practices at a time of neoliberal crisis: towards a "post-neoliberal" anarchist future', *Antipode*, 44(5), pp. 1–20.

White, R. and Williams, C.C. (2014). 'Anarchist economic practices in a "capitalist" society: some implications for organisation and the future of work', *Ephemera: Theory and Politics in Organization*, 14(4), pp. 947–971.

Williams, C.C. (2004). *Cash-in-Hand Work: the Underground Sector and the Hidden Economy of Favours.* Basingstoke: Palgrave Macmillan.

Williams, C.C. (2005). *A Commodified World? Mapping the Limits of Capitalism.* London: Zed.

Williams, C.C. (2006). *The Hidden Enterprise Culture: Entrepreneurship in the Underground Economy.* Cheltenham: Edward Elgar.

Williams, C.C. (2009). 'Formal and informal employment in Europe: beyond dualistic representations', *European Urban and Regional Studies*, 16(2), pp. 147–159.

Williams, C.C. (2011). 'Reconceptualising men's and women's undeclared work: evidence from Europe', *Gender, Work & Organisation*, 18(4), pp. 415–437.

Williams, C.C. (2013). 'Evaluating cross-national variations in the extent and nature of informal employment in the European Union', *Industrial Relations Journal*, 44(5–6), pp. 479–494.

Williams, C.C. (2014a). 'Out of the shadows: a classification of economies by the size and character of their informal sector', *Work, Employment & Society*, 28(5), pp. 735–753.

Williams, C.C. (2014b). 'Explaining cross-national variations in the prevalence of envelope wages: some lessons from a 2013 Eurobarometer survey', *Industrial Relations Journal*, 45(6), pp. 524–542.

Williams, C.C. (2015a). 'Explaining cross-national variations in the scale of informal employment: an exploratory analysis of 41 less developed economies', *International Journal of Manpower*, 36(2), pp. 118–135.

Williams, C.C. (2015b). 'Evaluating cross-national variations in envelope wage payments in East-Central Europe', *Economic and Industrial Democracy: an International Journal*, 36(2), pp. 283–303.

Williams, C.C. (2015c). 'Tackling informal employment in developing and transition economies: a critical evaluation of the neo-liberal approach', *International Journal of Business and Globalisation*, 14(3), pp. 251–270.

Williams, C.C. (2015d). 'Out of the margins: classifying economies by the prevalence and character of employment in the informal economy', *International Labour Review*, 154(3), pp. 331–352.

Williams, C.C. and Horodnic, I. (2017). 'Evaluating the illegal employer practice of under-reporting employees' salaries', *British Journal of Industrial Relations*, 55(1), pp. 83–111.

Williams, C.C. and Youssef, Y. (2014). 'Classifying Latin American economies: a degrees of informalisation approach', *International Journal of Business Administration*, 5(3), pp. 73–85.

Williams, C.C., Round, J. and Rodgers, P. (2013). *The Role of Informal Economies in the Post-Soviet World: the End of Transition?* London: Routledge.

Woolfson, C. (2007). 'Pushing the envelope: the 'informalisation' of labour in post-communist new EU Member States', *Work, Employment & Society*, 21(3), pp. 551–564.

Zelizer, V. (2011). *Economic Lives: How Culture Shapes the Economy.* Princeton: Princeton University Press.

23

EMERGING ECONOMIES, FREEDOM OF ASSOCIATION AND COLLECTIVE BARGAINING FOR WOMEN WORKERS IN EXPORT-ORIENTED MANUFACTURING

Samanthi J. Gunawardana

Introduction

This chapter examines corporate-led governance of collective labour rights, such as the right to freedom of association and assembly (FOAA),[1] for women workers in global supply chains (GSCs). The workers who face the largest challenges in exercising their assembly and association rights are often migrant workers, women workers in general, supply chain workers, informal workers and domestic workers (United Nations General Assembly, 2016, p. 4). Many of these workers labour within or originate from emerging economies. Some may be migrant workers and located in the informal sector, as production sites in GSCs traverse conditions of formality and informality and include factories, small shops and households. Such production sites have proliferated under export-oriented industrialisation (EOI) development models pursued by emerging economy states in the latter half of the twentieth century.

Collective rights are enshrined in various international conventions. In addition to FOAA, they include the right to collective bargaining (CB)[2] and the right to strike (RTS).[3] When enforced, collective rights are examples of empowering enabling rights as they expand people's freedoms, opportunities and choices (Nussbaum, 2011; Sen, 1999) to strengthen agency and transform structures of constraint. In human rights law, so long as the exercise of these rights does not impinge upon the rights of others, they are approached as a fundamental precursor to social justice and equity.[4] For much of the twentieth century, many workers around the world have relied on collective rights to form collective associations such as trade unions. Trade unions and other associations have represented them in collective bargaining efforts with employers and the state, to enforce existing laws and transform institutions, structures, practices and policies that impact working conditions (Jaumotte and Osoria Buitron, 2015). Such collective action is commonly accepted to fortify economic, social and political agency in addressing power imbalances in the employment relationship. In other words, collective rights are designed to provide recourse in the face of power asymmetries.

Although labour rights are considered to be human rights (Gross and Compa, 2009), collective labour rights remain unenforced within many emerging economies (Mosley and Uno, 2007). EOI development models that have stressed the importance of labour market 'flexibility' in emerging economies, to attract foreign investment and spur local growth, have partly undermined collective rights. States pursuing EOI strategies have curtailed, suppressed or just not enforced collective labour rights as they viewed trade unions and collective bargaining as a source of inflexibility that would diminish competitive advantage in the global market (Deyo, 1989; Kuruvilla, 1996). Historically, this has occurred in response to development loan conditionalities determined by international financial institutions (IFIs) such as the International Monetary Fund (IMF) and World Bank. Under these programmes, collective rights have been treated as detrimental to economic growth prospects within a broader agenda of neoliberal inspired trade liberalisation and EOI strategies. Thus, even though the IMF has taken an interest in how collective trade union action can prevent widening wage inequality (Jaumotte and Osoria Buitron, 2015), and the World Bank has examined women's economic empowerment and collective action (Evans and Nambiar, 2013), neither has considered the importance of collective rights per se.

Collective rights provide a framework of necessary pre-conditions for economic empowerment, including women's economic empowerment. As multinational companies began to outsource their labour-intensive assembly operations to countries pursuing EOI, labour-intensive industries such as apparel and electronics recruited large numbers of women into manufacturing plants. Although the inclusion of women workers into waged labour is potentially empowering (Hancock et al., 2011; Lim, 1983), women faced disempowering gendered recruitment practices and exploitative labour conditions. Structural conditions combined with global and local gender norms and stereotypes curtailed the transformative possibility for women workers (Anner, 2011; Wright 2006).

As such, there is a strong gender component to the ongoing debate at the nexus of development, labour flexibility and collective rights, as women workers' capability to exercise assembly, collective bargaining and striking rights has been curtailed. Workers have been fired, blacklisted preventing further employment opportunity, or faced multiple forms of violence for engaging in collective action (Gunawardana, 2007; Madhok and Rai, 2012). Moreover, women face further challenges as the trade union movement has weakened globally during the rapid spread of export industries and inclusion of greater numbers of women workers in the late twentieth century, resulting in less coverage of workers by collective bargaining. Moreover, local male-dominated trade unions replicated gender inequalities in organisational structures, leadership and the type of issues they have bargained over.

As worker and activist protest intensified in the late twentieth century, large multinationals such as Nike and Apple became synonymous with unsustainable sweatshop practice. Many responded by embedding labour rights into voluntary governance mechanisms, such as monitoring and auditing supplier factory adherence to corporate codes of conduct and investing in 'value chain' upgrading of their supply chains (Barrientos, Gereffi and Rossi, 2011). Brand and reputation management is a fundamental element of increased investment in these ventures (Peck, 2010).

The issue is whether these mechanisms can help address power asymmetries by upholding collective labour rights. This chapter examines collective rights in corporate-led governance mechanisms in GSCs. In particular, it focuses on the experience of women workers and prospects for empowerment through the use of these mechanisms. The chapter is set out as follows. In the first section, the importance of collective rights for women workers in transforming the conditions of their employment is discussed. In the second section, the human rights framework for collective labour rights and their enactment under export-oriented manufacturing regimes is critically examined. Finally, two prominent mechanisms – monitoring and enforcement of corporate codes of conduct and value chain upgrading – are outlined and assessed using the literature. In conclusion, I sum up the key arguments in this chapter and summarise why working towards economic empowerment entails acknowledging political agency and fortifying collective rights.

Transformative collective rights and action and women workers in global supply chains

This section considers the relationship between collective rights and promoting transformative empowerment for women workers in supply chains. EOI opened up formal mass employment opportunities for women workers in 'unskilled and semi-skilled' positions (Elson and Pearson, 1980). Women were hired in the pursuit of gendered flexibility, as they were perceived as the embodiment of available, disposable and cheap labour (Wright, 2006) and assumed to possess natural (rather than learned) skills for manufacturing work, as well as docile dispositions that would pre-empt collective action and militancy (Caraway, 2007; Wright 2006). Free Trade Zone (FTZ) workplaces, in particular, are criticised for perpetuating gender-based discrimination and structural inequality in job opportunities and wages, curtailing democratic trade union activity, violating labour/human rights and exposing workers to violence, including sexual harassment, gender-based violence and stringent suppression of collective action including trade union membership (Anner, 2011; Gunawardana, 2014). Moreover, employment systems relied on depletive conditions (Gunawardana, 2016).

Although there is little consensus on the meaning of 'empowerment', feminist scholars emphasise the underlying process of the transformation of various power relationships, including disempowering gender relations, for individuals and groups (Batliwala, 2007; Kabeer, 1999; Rowlands, 1997; Sardenberg, 2008). A relational process, empowerment involves gaining greater access to more choices concerning their lives and the capabilities for exercising strategic forms of agency in relation to the larger structures of constraint that positioned them as subordinate to men (Wieringa, 1994).

This chapter argues that transforming the disempowering aspects of working conditions requires collective efforts to transform inherent power relationships (Batliwala, 2007; Cornwall and Anyidoho, 2010; Eyben and Napier-Moore, 2009; Kabeer, 1999). Moreover, collective action is a constitutive element of empowerment. It involves exercising and acquiring various forms of power: 'power over' (influence); 'power to' (decision-making/agency); 'power with' (collective power); and 'power within' (internal power) (Batliwala, 1994; Rowlands, 1997; Sen, 1999). Thus, what may be most empowering for women workers is the act of coming together, building alliances and movements, and mobilising together (Cornwall, 2016, p. 532). These empowering effects include "the solace of solidarity, the courage in collectivity, the sociality of shared struggle" and "respect and recognition" (ibid.).

This more expansive notion of empowerment is broader than the idea of inclusion and participation in employment, as reflected in recent UN documents on women's economic empowerment (Klugman and Tyson, 2016). According to these reports, the key to economic empowerment is therefore not only inclusion and participation in employment but the ability for women to "influence" transformation and the direction of that transformation. For export manufacturing workers, collectivisation can enable them to transform and impact the inherently unequal power dynamic within the employment relationship (Edwards, 2003).

The question about what form this collective action should take is important. As noted in the introduction, trade unions have been the dominant vehicle for exercising collective action around the world. However, male-dominated trade unions have been critiqued for historically excluding women and women's interests, which calls into question their empowerment potential for women workers. This literature points out that union leaders have typically been men; union structures reinforced patriarchy; did not reflect the interests of women; and historically excluded different types of workers, including women and migrants (Ford, 2013, Heery 2006). Women workers labour in sectors and occupations that are excluded from protective regulation on collective labour rights, including those engaging in the public sector, informal, domestic, migrant and agricultural work (Kabeer, Sudarshan and Milward, 2013).

Where unions did exist, collective agreements excluded issues pertinent to women owing to gendered assumptions about male breadwinner roles. In some countries such as Japan and South Korea, women responded by forming women-only unions as a challenge to male-dominated union structures that dismissed issues such as sexual harassment as a 'women's issue', not a workers' issue (Broadbent, 2007). Finally, trade union membership is not necessarily empowering, does not reflect women's interests even when union density is high, nor does it reflect the reality of women's collective action and empowerment. For example, in Cambodia unionisation has been maintained at about 60 per cent in the export apparel sector, with multiple unions often found in one factory, yet real wages declined between 2001 and 2013 (Arnold, 2017).

Over the past few decades, global unions have asserted that unlike in the past, they are perfectly positioned to take forward gender equality agendas. This is owing to their "…long-standing democratic structures and clear mandate to fight oppression and discrimination in the workplace", especially through collective bargaining processes (ICFTU, 2002, p. 29, in Franzway, 2017). Indeed, women activists have challenged the masculinised heteronormative politics of union movements to gain recognition of their interests and leadership positions and to influence policy (Franzway, 2017, pp. 61–63). Moreover, as trade union density has declined around the world in traditional sectors such as manufacturing, women now form the majority of members in unions, and the most unionised sectors are often the most feminised (see Ackers, 2015 for review).

Undeniably, collective rights enabling the formation of collectives such as trade unions have been instrumental in empowering women at work. Issues such as equal pay, family-friendly work, equity clauses, non-discrimination policies, prohibitions on sexual harassment, maternity leave, safe transport, flexible working arrangements and general work-family balance practice have been included in collective agreements (Dickens, 2000; Williamson and Baird, 2014). These clauses can help prevent deepening structural inequalities. Moreover strategies around 'gender equality bargaining', which emerged in the 1980s in formulating collective agreements, focused specifically on issues pertinent to women (Heery, 2006; Williamson and Baird, 2014, 155). More recently, unions have examined gender-based violence issues, including bargaining for inclusion of leave provisions for survivors of violence (Baird, McFerran and Wright, 2014) and raising awareness about the prevalence of violence against women in workplaces (Mackridge, 2017).

For workers in the global south working in export manufacturing factories, the number of entities advocating for women workers is vast and encompasses the local grassroots approaches, national-level fora and global advocacy. Local religious organisations, community-based organisations and legal centres operate alongside national-level workers centres and NGOs. Other transnational NGOs have stepped into labour relations as monitors (such as the US-based Fair Labour Association) and advocates (e.g. international NGOs) (Bronfrenbrenner, 2007; Fine, 2006; Ford, 2013). In conflict-affected contexts, human rights advocacy groups such as Amnesty International and Human Rights Watch have also taken up labour conditions, women and labour rights. Global initiatives such as the Ethical Trading Initiative, Fair Trade movement and Clean Clothes campaign involve a multitude of actors promoting labour standards through codes of conduct for employers.

Similar to the unions above, these organisations have advocated for issues pertaining to conditions in the workplace as well as outside. For example, the United Sisterhood Alliance in Cambodia presents an alternative explicitly self-expressed feminist intervention by focusing on women's interests at work as women and workers. The Alliance is made up of four groups, of which the Women's Information Centre (WIC) is one.[5] Their mission is to advocate and organise by providing a space for women to "work towards gender equality and equity" by promoting and supporting women's leadership to improve women worker's rights, rights to social services and social protection.

In summary, women's economic empowerment is reliant on the ability of workers to exercise collective association, assembly, agency and action. Restrictions can come from multiple sources, including from within collective associations such as trade unions, though these are still nonetheless useful for women workers pursuing improvements in their working conditions. However, a fundamental restriction workers face is the limitations on collective rights, including collective bargaining; these limitations are discussed in the following section.

Collective labour rights and development

Institutionalised processes of collective action and bargaining on working conditions emerge from histories of exploitation during the Industrial Revolution in the global north and colonisation in the global south from the eighteenth century onward. The economic structural changes during the Industrial Revolution in the United Kingdom, western Europe and the United States gave rise to exploitative working conditions, including poor wages, dangerous workplaces and long hours (Bender and Greenwald, 2003). The right to form collectives such as trade unions was banned under local laws and it was not until the late 1800s that unions were legalised in some western European countries. During the same period, the UK, France, Netherlands and the US were engaged in colonisation projects. Labour movements in Africa, Asia and Latin America collectivised to improve working conditions, including for workers in the Zambian copper fields, railway workers in West Africa (Cooper, 1996), urban workers in Indonesia (Ingleson, 2001) and plantation sector workers in Sri Lanka (Jayawardena, 1972). Limited association rights were endowed by colonial governments in some regions such as French West Africa (Cooper, 1996, p. 97). Labour movements subsequently played a major role in several independence movements (Jayawardena, 1972).

After the Second World War, several UN international human rights treaties and conventions in the liberal tradition of individual rights[6] were promulgated, including those involving work and labour. Within this framework, collective labour rights were articulated as providing the interlinking foundation for peace and economic and social justice as well as economic development in a liberal democratic environment (United Nations General Assembly, 2016). Thus it is not surprising that even today during periods of 'post-war' recovery and fragile state institution building, neoliberal economic policy packages that stress the primacy of the market are accompanied by programmes that seek to strengthen collective rights. For example, following the end of civil war in El Salvador (1980–1992) and Liberia (1980–2003), cessation of conflict in Nepal and the election of a democratic government in Cambodia (1993), the International Labour Organization (ILO) was a key institution advising states on regulatory reform and programmes. An aspect of these reforms is that they were designed to strengthen labour laws, including FOAA and CB, to improve economic growth (Marshall and Fenwick, 2016).

FOAA and CB are a key part of the ILO principles of social dialogue between employers and employees. They are enshrined in ILO Conventions 87 and 98, which are in turn listed as part of the ILO's eight fundamental conventions.[7] The Committee on Freedom of Association, set up in 1950, receives complaints regarding violations of freedom of association from employers and workers' organisations against states, regardless of whether the state has ratified the relevant conventions. Moreover, these rights are enshrined in other key international instruments as well,[8] including the Universal Declaration of Human Rights; the International Covenant on Civil and Political Rights; and the International Covenant on Economic, Social and Cultural Rights.[9] FOAA affirms people's right to work collectively towards common interests voluntarily, which is considered to be a foundational right within the international framework of human rights. While the right to FOAA applies to many contexts, such as peaceful protest or the right not to join a group such as a political party, when coupled with associated rights such as CB and RTS, these rights are essential enabling rights. They allow workers to gain leverage by organising themselves into collectives, resource those collectives (e.g. through membership fees) and appoint collective representatives to further their interests by negotiating (or 'bargaining') the terms of the employment relationship with both employers and the state.

As Fordist models of mass production came to dominate economic activities in the first half of the twentieth century, various national institutions emerged around the world to structure collective bargaining at industry, firm or national level (Kuruvilla and Venkataratnam, 1996). For many in the unionised sectors, collective bargaining helped to curb excessive wage competition, increase wages and decrease income gaps, distribute profit, improve working conditions including health and safety, uphold the dignity of workers and provide stability via the institutionalisation of industrial conflict (Hayter, 2011).

The impact of collective rights is dependent on states adopting, protecting and respecting these rights within their national governance systems. Even at the onset of their introduction, there was never an articulated consensus on state responsibilities as these rights limited employer action in capitalist production (Kang, 2012, p. 18). Although these collective labour rights were contested, Kang argues that they were widely adopted owing to the interests of powerful states in the global north and some workers organisations, post the two world wars, to secure democratic societies. Ethical concerns about human dignity, the link articulated about peace and security, the Bolshevik Revolution, concern about unfair trade practices and 'social dumping' precipitated the adoption of international labour rights and standards (ibid.).

This system of rights came to gain greater significance in the latter half of the twentieth century with the acceleration of global restructuring. On the one hand, collective labour rights came to be associated with inefficiencies that curtailed economic growth and competitiveness. This was particularly the case for states in the global south, where countries began to implement EOI strategies via development programmes such as structural adjustment programmes (SAPs) from the 1970s onwards. Before this, East Asian countries such as South Korea and Singapore embarked upon market and EOI models of growth in the 1960s. Their strategies were held up as models by the UN, World Bank and International Monetary Fund (IMF) to other countries in South Asia, Latin America and Africa, which were at the time focused on import-substitution policies. This latter group of countries were encouraged to pursue EOI growth models from the late 1970s onwards in waves of neoliberal-inspired reforms. SAPs were financed by loans from the World Bank and the IMF and influenced by neoliberal economic principles. Loan conditionalities emphasised the market while advising the retreat of the state. Emphasis was placed on trade liberalisation, attracting foreign direct investment (FDI), generating local employment and technology transfer (Safa, 2002).

EOI became the entry point into the world economy via integration into low-cost manufacturing activities along global supply chains, as multinational corporations outsourced their manufacturing activities (and at a later stage, their business processes such as payroll and accounting as well as their customer service operations). Globalised capital sought multiple forms of flexibility, including through access to 'flexible' labour markets and work arrangements that could be adjusted according to working time, location, worker and contract type, or through the restriction of labour rights (Tomei, 2000). Kuruvilla (1996) found that export firms tended to have dynamic, aggressive and flexible human resource management practices in countries such as Malaysia and the Philippines.

A common loan condition embedded in SAPs was labour market reform, including weakening of collective bargaining provisions and trade unions' role in the employment relationship. This included divesting workers of the right to organise or placing restrictions on exercising rights (Gopalakrishnan, 2007, p. 1). In pursuing export strategies, states played a key role in limiting collective labour rights, which was often reflective of the broader political regime, with more authoritarian governments pursuing more repressive actions (Cooney et al., 2002; Kuruvilla and Venkataratnam, 1996). The right to strike was often banned by deeming industries 'essential industries', with 'essential' being open to interpretation. The issues were compounded in countries experiencing conflicts. For example, Mosley and Uno (2007) found that the existence of civil conflict had a significant negative impact on collective labour rights in 90 developing nations between 1985 and 2002 – a period when neoliberal economic policies proliferated globally. In situations of conflict concerns about [military] security was used to enact emergency regulations and restrict labour mobility, expression and association as in the case of Sri Lanka (Biyanwila, 2010).

There are several examples of where the state actively intervened to curtail collective labour rights (Anner, 2011; De Stefano, 2017). Trade unions were banned in the Malaysian electronics industry until 1988. Before 1987, trade unions in South Korea were unable to bargain on wages. While some countries such as China, Pakistan and Nigeria imposed restrictions, others such as Bangladesh modified laws to curtail organising. FOAA was suppressed in the Dominican Republic so that union members were arrested for distributing information on their trade union. In Bangladesh, Nigeria and Pakistan, the RTS was curtailed under the law (Milberg and Amengual, 2008). Other factors such as the unavailability of state resources for law enforcement, particularly through factory inspections, have also contributed to violations of international standards (Anner, 2008). The issues on which workers could collectively bargain varied widely, from 'any issue' in India, to restrictive practices in Singapore on negotiation on transfers, promotion, work assignments and organisational restructuring (Kuruvilla and Venkataratnam, 1996).

The state also set up free trade zones (FTZs) and variants (export processing zones, maquiladoras, special economic zones) as entry points for manufacturing. FTZ-manufactured exports contributed significantly to national accounts in many smaller economies, in some cases as much as 80 per cent of export earnings in 2006 (Milberg and Amengual, 2008, pp. 7–10). Moreover, states such as China set up and managed economic zones outside of their borders (see Fei, 2017 for China's investments in Africa). FTZ employment systems have been consistently characterised as the epitome of flexibility. Workers rarely received a living wage, labour inspection practices were fragmented and trade unions were often restricted. Moreover, reports of excessive working hours, lax health and safety standards and greater work intensity were all reported (Milberg and Amengual, 2008, p. 2). Overall, employers denied unions entry to workplaces, and dismissed, suspended, transferred or blacklisted workers who tried to organise. Violence was used against workers who sought to organise, including murder (Gopalakrishnan,

2007). Where workers were able to join trade unions of their choosing, they faced union recognition restrictions, strike prohibition or refusal to bargain (ibid.).

Even where human rights are ratified, this has mixed results on the enforcement of collective rights. Scholars examining the relationship between ratifying international labour rights and state/employer action have found that ratification is not sufficient to uphold labour rights. A popular method has been to use Mosley and Uno's (2007) dataset, which captures collective workers' rights in GSCs between 1985 and 2002, including in export processing zones. Peksen and Blanton (2016) found a significant negative relationship between the number of ratified ILO conventions and the level of respect for general and collective worker rights across the globe. There is evidence that some states in Latin America used international rights as a cover for authoritarian tendencies on labour (Burgess, 2010). Caraway (2009) found that after Indonesia had ratified ILO conventions, employers violated labour laws by introducing more insecure contracts as they interpreted ratification as being symbolic only.

These findings may demonstrate what Susan Kang (2012, pp. 1–2) refers to as a paradox when it comes to collective labour rights during global restructuring: "public statements of support for trade union rights and their widespread violation". However, as Kang goes on to argue, collective labour rights can still influence state and employer behaviour by deploying the normative language of human rights and linking these rights to state interests. She asserts that in the right political contexts, states would change their labour laws to align with international standards if a labour dispute could be mutually understood as a human rights violation. This occurred when trade union rights were linked to state political or economic interests, or powerful judicial institutions were persuaded. Even then states did not necessarily enforce collective rights.

In summary, the importance of human rights and international labour conventions alongside local regulation in upholding collective rights has come to the forefront during an era of global restructuring. As noted, a key issue in the global economy is the violation of these rights within emerging economies, in the pursuit of liberalised export trade, investment and employment generation. In the next section, I examine the emergence of self-regulatory mechanisms promoted by corporations and their potential for upholding collective rights.

Corporate codes of conduct, social upgrading and collective rights

Collective rights are regulated not only via human rights conventions but via 'soft', self-regulating private and 'hard' externally regulated public modes of governance in global supply chains. In this section, I outline monitoring and auditing practices to enforce codes of conduct and value chain upgrading as two prominent self-regulatory ways in which collective rights may be applied to GSCs. These mechanisms often include the core labour conventions and human rights discussed above as the minimum standards to be adhered to.

Within the gamut of private regulation and global governance, self-regulating corporate codes of conduct are a prominent method deployed by non-state actors (Büthe and Mattli, 2011). Imposed by multinational firms on their GSCs, their enforcement requires monitoring systems ('social auditing') (Donaghey et al., 2014; Egels-Zandén and Merk, 2014). Codes of conduct are closely aligned to corporate social responsibility (CSR) regimes and have been characterised as 'soft' or voluntary self- regulation (Büthe and Mattli, 2011; Kuruvilla and Verma, 2006). They may apply to a single corporation and supply network, or several separate corporations may sign on to a global code of conduct (e.g. Worldwide Responsible Apparel Production, Fair Labour Association). Monitoring of these codes involves a variety of practices, including self-assessment, audits by a brand representative and audits by a third-party agency.

Privatised governance has flourished, with corporations playing a central role, whether it be the large multinational or the auditing and monitoring firm. They do not have the same powers of enforcement state institutions such as labour inspectorates can impose (Allain et al., 2013). Indeed, they do not have the same right of entry trade unions may have under labour legislation. As LeBaron et al. (2017) point out, private governance mechanisms involving profit-making audit firms are used to evaluate compliance with human rights laws and 'hard' national laws, and have become accepted by states and civil society as legitimate mechanisms to enforce labour standards. This results in regimes that reinforce neoliberal economic governance rather than overcome the deficiencies in global governance regimes (Le Baron et al., 2017, p. 4).

Two main findings from the literature are that those audit regimes are inadequate to capture non-compliance and that labour codes do not significantly improve collective labour rights (Anner, 2012; Barrientos and Smith, 2007; Bartley and Egels-Zandén 2015; Locke, 2013). Moreover, even though most CSR initiatives now include collective rights it is in a superficial manner in many cases (Egels-Zanden and Merk, 2014).

Anner's (2012) study is particularly instructive, as his conclusions are drawn from an original dataset based on 805 factory audits conducted by the Fair Labour Association over a seven-year period. He argues that as collective rights such as FOAA weaken corporate control by providing workers with a counter-voice and vehicle to alter power dynamics in the employment relationship, collective rights are not as closely monitored. Recognising that collective rights such as FOAA may be difficult to measure, Anner found that most non-compliance reports were in the areas of health and safety, wages, benefits and hours of work. Violations of FOAA made up the smallest number of reports in monitoring exercises. Examining the FLA's third party complaints mechanism (where complaints are proactively made), and the 19 complaints made in the same period, most complaints (32 per cent) were on issues of FOAA. For example, in a prominent case involving Russell Athletic's supply factory in Honduras, the FLA's monitoring reports regarding violations of FOAA indicated that there was no evidence of rights violation. An independent consultant, in contrast, discredited the original monitor's report, including how they had collected evidence. The FLA dismissed the revised report. A campaign was then instigated by student activists, who persuaded approximately 110 universities to cut their contracts with Russell owing to violation of worker's collective rights. As Esbenshade (2016) points out, the student campaign against Russell was successful not because of the FLA code, but because of the enforcement of licensing contractual obligations between universities and Russell.

The second approach is often inclusive of the above and designed to improve the entire supply chain. 'Up-grading' refers to moving to higher 'value-added activities in production' chains (e.g. moving from labour-intensive apparel manufacturing to including product design or improving logistics processes) and involves learning and acquiring new skills, implementing new technologies and increasing the benefits from participating in GSCs (Gereffi, 1999). Up-grading can occur in economic, social and environmental areas. Workers' conditions are included in 'social up-grading', which usually refers to job creation, skills development and improving terms and entitlements for workers as measured by various standards, and via the enforcement of rights. Workers are conceived of as 'social actors', and as such, the impact of social up-grading can extend to their families, with a strong correlation expressed between economic and social up-grading (Barrientos et al., 2011). As noted by Barrientos et al., the measurable standards are often the outcome of "complex bargaining processes, framed by the enabling [collective] rights of workers".

Social up-grading is tied directly to the ILO's Decent Work agenda (Barrientos and Smith, 2007). The agenda is concerned with: employment creation, skill development and enterprise development; social protection; standards and rights at work; and governance and social dialogue.

Recognition and enforcement of collective rights are incorporated specifically into standards, rights, governance and social dialogue. Moreover, the Decent Work agenda was integrated into the Millennium Development Goals. More recently, the Decent Work agenda formed the basis for Goal Number 8 of the Sustainable Development Goals (SDGs).

Critique of social up-grading is often linked to the critique of these broader agendas that point out the transformative limitations for workers. Selwyn (2013) and Mayer and Pickles (2014) argue that the co-option of the Decent Work agenda by IFIs (entities that previously categorised trade unions as market-unfriendly) has been wrought with contradictions between policy and benchmarking programmes, as well as relying on the non-existent enforcement mechanisms characteristic of ILO labour standards. Moreover, the Decent Work agenda fails to take into account deep-seated structural conditions that lead to poor-quality work. This includes class relations between labour and local/multinational capital. As Selwyn argues, this represents an institutionalised "discounting" of the "systemic exploitation of labour by capital" (Selwyn, 2011, p. 87). Notably, the Decent Work agenda fails to promote political mobilisation, limiting its transformative capacity (Mayer and Pickles, 2014; Selwyn, 2013). In other words, although some proponents do acknowledge that independent unions can contribute to social up-grading (Barrientos et al., 2011), the agenda underpinning social up-grading does little to empower workers as per definitions of empowerment found in the feminist literature.

The main drawback of both codes of conduct and social up-grading is not that they cannot affect long-term structural transformation, but that they are not designed to promote worker agency. Kabeer (2015, p. 11) points out that in labour-intensive supply chains such as apparel, footwear, toys, horticulture and electronics, where women are overwhelmingly employed, claims and demands are made on behalf of women workers. In particular, northern coalitions of unions, NGOs, religious organisations, rights activists, students and consumers have campaigned in northern consumption centres using advertising to 'reveal' the labour and labour conditions behind labels to consumers. This movement has in effect empowered consumers while only engaging with actual activists/workers on speaking tours. This results in reinforcing the image of the "passive victim of global capital". This point was raised in relation to women workers in GSCs by Siddiqi (2009), who asked whether "Bangladeshi factory workers need saving?" Her concern was with activist, feminist practice and anti-sweatshop movements that denied worker voices and agency through generalised and sensationalised representations of 'third-world women workers'.

Many of the key groups advocating for collective rights do not engage with organising workers or representing them directly. Thus, while the space for trade unions may have shrunk, other entities such as "alt-unions", "alt-labour" and "improvisational unionism" (Oswalt, 2016) now make representations about the interests and claims of workers even though they are not membership organisations. They have often de-emphasised unionisation, focusing instead on claims, lobbying, legal representation, protest, strikes and education (ibid.). Other groups, such as worker's centres (Fine, 2006), have taken on some of the traditional roles of unions while advocating for the enforcement of collective labour rights. Overall, NGOs do not have the same institutionalised access as trade unions to workplaces or international processes such as ILO tripartite processes. Moreover, some NGOs (e.g. CARE, Oxfam) often instigate issue-based campaigns concerning, for example, wages or sexual harassment, before consulting workers. As Egels-Zandén and Merk (2014) pointed out, workers are often "treated as passive objects of regulation", particularly in the design and implementation of codes of conduct.

Kabeer, Egels-Zandén and Merks and Siddiqi all ultimately draw attention to the importance of transformative agency enabled through collective rights (see also Gunawardana, 2011). This is vital to changing power asymmetries rather than enforcing the existing order. As research from Htun and Weldon (2012) demonstrated, autonomous association and organising contributed to changing power relations at a societal level, putting the needs of women on an equal footing with those of men.

Conclusion

This chapter has examined (a) the importance of collective labour rights for women working within export factories in global supply chains, and (b) the non-state voluntary corporate governance regimes that have emerged to regulate or improve working conditions, and their possibilities for upholding collective rights. Although women's empowerment is one of the reasons why EOI continues to be implemented in emerging economies (see, for example, Lopez-Acevedo and Robertson, 2016), it has been observed that although EOI generates employment for women workers, associated labour regimes may disempower them, including through weakened collective rights. Thus, the importance of human and labour rights in international labour conventions, alongside local regulation, has come to the forefront of discussion during an era of global restructuring. A key area of scholarly concern in the global economy has been the violation of these rights within emerging economies, in the pursuit of liberalised export trade, investment and employment generation.

The first section outlined how collective rights and action are a constitutive element of economic empowerment, as they enable a process of transformation. That is, addressing power asymmetries in employment does involve collective efforts to transform poor working conditions, including conditions particular to women; gender equality collective bargaining is one example discussed in this chapter. The second section outlined how collective rights are articulated in international conventions and human rights law and how they may be suppressed by states and corporations in pursuing EOI strategies.

Finally, the chapter outlined how self-regulatory mechanisms tend to uphold the weaknesses of the existing regimes rather than finding remedies. Importantly, this section concluded by observing that these mechanisms provided little space for worker inclusion in the design of auditing methods, or in some cases, of representing their interests accurately. In other words, they did little to address asymmetrical power, as, within the repertoire of global governance, codes of conduct and even social up-grading remain firmly rooted in the process of 'labour flexibilisation' – ensuring low-cost and pliable labour for multinational investment. As Phillips points out (2017, p. 14), multinationals themselves "push for the very 'gaps' in public governance that are necessary for their business model to thrive".

Notes

1 Although FOAA applies to employers and employees in the employment relationship (broadly conceived), this chapter will focus primarily on freedom of association as an enabling right for employees.
2 Article 2 of the ILO Convention 154 defines collective bargaining as a negotiation between an individual employer or a collective employer (including employer associations) and a workers' collective organisation on the following conditions: "(a) determining working conditions and terms of employment; and/or (b) regulating relations between employers and workers; and/or (c) regulating relations between employers or their organisations and a workers' organisation or workers' organisations".
3 Throughout the rest of the text, this trio will be referred to as 'collective rights' except when a right is referred to individually
4 For example, the Declaration of Philadelphia (1944) asserts that "lasting peace can be established only if it is based on social justice".
5 The three other groups are: the Women's Network for Unity, a union of sex workers; the Messenger Band, a group of former garment workers; and Social Action for Change-SAC, a group of activists who support the mobilisation and growth of grassroots democratic action in Cambodia.

6 While various political traditions have historically defined different elements of universal human rights, the interpretation of the right to association, assembly and collective bargaining came to be defined the liberal tradition of individual human rights (Ishay, 2007).

7 Fundamental worker's rights were declared at the 1995 Copenhagen World Summit for Social Development. Following this, the ILO adopted the Declaration of fundamental principles and rights at work in 1998.

8 I have not included here regional instruments e.g. European Union Convention on Human Rights.

9 Articles 20 and 23(4) of the Universal Declaration of Human Rights; Articles 2 (2), 2 (3) (a-c), 22 and 26 of the International Covenant on Civil and Political Rights; Article 8 of the International Covenant on Economic, Social and Cultural Rights. Other more recent conventions such as Convention 189 Domestic Workers Convention and the International Convention on the Protection of the Rights of All Migrant Workers and Members of Their Families also provide protection for association and assembly rights.

References

Ackers, P. (2015). Trade unions as professional associations, in Johnstone, S. and Ackers, P. (eds.) *Finding a Voice at Work? New Perspectives on Employment Relations*. Oxford: Oxford University Press, pp. 95–126.

Allain, J., Crane, A., LeBaron, G. and Behbahani, L. (2013). *Forced Labour's Business Models and Supply Chains*. Joseph Rowntree Foundation: London. Available at: www.jrf.org.uk/sites/default/files/jrf/migrated/files/forced-labour-business-full.pdf.

Anner, M. (2008). 'Meeting the challenges of industrial restructuring: labor reform and enforcement in Latin America', *Latin American Politics and Society*, 50(2), pp. 33–65.

Anner, M. (2012). 'Corporate social responsibility and freedom of association rights: the precarious quest for legitimacy and control in global supply chains', *Politics & Society*, 40(4), pp. 609–644.

Anner, M.S. (2011). *Solidarity Transformed: Labor Responses to Globalization and Crisis in Latin America*. Ithaca: Cornell University Press.

Arnold, D. (2017). 'Civil society, political society and politics of disorder in Cambodia', *Political Geography*, 60, pp. 23–33.

Baird, M., McFerran, L. and Wright, I. (2014). 'An equality bargaining breakthrough: paid domestic violence leave', *Journal of Industrial Relations*, 56(2), pp. 190–207.

Barrientos, S. and Smith, S. (2007). 'Do workers benefit from ethical trade? Assessing codes of labour practice in global production systems', *Third World Quarterly*, 28(4), pp. 713–729.

Barrientos, S., Gereffi, G. and Rossi, A. (2011). 'Economic and social upgrading in global production networks: a new paradigm for a changing world', *International Labour Review*, 150(3–4), pp. 319–340.

Bartley, T. and Egels-Zandén, N. (2015). 'Responsibility and neglect in global production networks: the uneven significance of codes of conduct in Indonesian factories', *Global Networks*, 15(S1), S21–S44.

Batliwala, S. (1994). The meaning of women's empowerment: new concepts from action, in Sen, G., Germain, A. and Chen, L.C. (eds.) *Population Policies Reconsidered: Health, Empowerment, and Rights*. Boston (MA): Harvard University Press.

Batliwala, S. (2007). 'Taking the power out of empowerment – an experiential account', *Development in Practice*, 17(4–5), pp. 557–565.

Bender, D.E. and Greenwald, R.A. (2003). *Sweatshop USA: The American Sweatshop in Historical and Global Perspective*. Abingdon and New York: Routledge.

Biyanwila, S.J. (2010). *The Labour Movement in the Global South: Trade Unions in Sri Lanka*. Oxford: Routledge.

Broadbent, K. (2007). 'Sisters organising in Japan and Korea: the development of women-only unions', *Industrial Relations Journal*, 38(3), pp. 229–251.

Bronfenbrenner, K. (2007). *Global Unions: Challenging Transnational Capital Through Cross-Border Campaigns (Frank W. Pierce Memorial Lectureship and Conference Series)*. Ithaca: Cornell University Press, pp. 78–88.

Burgess, K. (2010). 'Global pressures, national policies, and labor rights in Latin America', *Studies in Comparative International Development*, 45(2), pp. 198–224.

Büthe, T. and Mattli, W. (2011). *The New Global Rulers: The Privatization of Regulation in the World Economy*. Princeton: Princeton University Press.

Caraway, T.L. (2007). *Assembling Women: The Feminization of Global Manufacturing*. Ithaca: Cornell University Press.

Caraway, T.L. (2009). 'Labor rights in East Asia: Progress or regress?' *Journal of East Asian Studies*, 9(2), pp. 153–186.

Cooney, S., Lindsey, T., Mitchell, R. and Ying, Z. (eds.) (2002). *Law and Labour Market Regulation in East Asia.* London and New York: Routledge.

Cooper, F. (1996). *Decolonization and African Society: the Labor Question in French and British Africa.* Vol. 89. Cambridge (UK): Cambridge University Press.

Cornwall, A. (2016). 'Women's Empowerment: What Works?' *Journal of International Development*, 28(3), pp. 342–359.

Cornwall, A. and Anyidoho, N.A. (2010). 'Introduction: women's empowerment: contentions and contestations', *Development*, 53(2), pp. 144–149.

De Stefano, V. (2017). 'Non-Standard Work and Limits on Freedom of Association: A Human Rights-Based Approach', *Industrial Law Journal*, 46(2), pp. 185–207.

Deyo, F.C. (1989). *Beneath the Miracle: Labor Subordination in the New Asian Industrialism.* Berkeley: University of California Press.

Dickens, L. (2000). 'Promoting Gender Equality at Work – A Potential Role for Trade Union Action', *Journal of Interdisciplinary Gender Studies*, 5(2), pp. 27–45.

Donaghey, J., Reinecke, J., Niforou, C. and Lawson, B. (2014). 'From employment relations to consumption relations: balancing labor governance in global supply chains', *Human Resource Management*, 53(2), pp. 229–252.

Edwards, P. (ed.) (2003). *Industrial Relations: Theory and Practice.* Chichester: John Wiley & Sons.

Egels-Zandén, N. and Merk, J. (2014). 'Private regulation and trade union rights: why codes of conduct have limited impact on trade union rights', *Journal of Business Ethics*, 123(3), pp. 461–473.

Elson, D. and Pearson, R. (1980). *The Latest Phase of the Internationalisation of Capital and its Implications for Women in the Third World.* Falmer: University of Sussex Institute of Development Studies.

Esbenshade, J. (2016). Corporate Social Responsibility: Moving from Checklist Monitoring to Contractual Obligation?, in Appelbaum, R. and Lichtenstein, N. (eds.) *Achieving Workers' Rights in the Global Economy.* Ithaca: Cornell University Press.

Evans, A. and Nambiar, D. (2013). *Collective Action and Women's Agency: A Background Paper.* Women's Voice, Agency, & Participation Research Series 2013, No.4. Washington: World Bank. Available at: http://goo.gl/swyN5Z

Eyben, R. and Napier-Moore, R. (2009). 'Choosing words with care? Shifting meanings of women's empowerment in international development', *Third World Quarterly*, 30(2), pp. 285–300.

Fei, D. (2017). 'Worlding Developmentalism: China's Economic Zones Within and Beyond its Border', *Journal of International Development*, 29(6), pp.825–850.

Fine, J.R. (2006). *Worker Centers: Organizing Communities at the Edge of the Dream.* Ithaca: Cornell University Press.

Ford, M. (2013). Social Activism in Southeast Asia: An Introduction, in Ford, M. (ed.) *Social Activism in Southeast Asia.* London and New York: Routledge, pp. 1–21.

Franzway, S. (2017). The Changing Sexual Politics of Gender Regulation by Unions, in Peetz, D. and Murray, R. (eds.) *Women, Labor Segmentation and Regulation.* New York: Palgrave Macmillan, pp. 61–77.

Gereffi, G. (1999). 'International trade and industrial upgrading in the apparel commodity chain', *Journal of International Economics*, 48(1), pp. 37–70.

Gopalakrishnan, R. (2007). *Freedom of Association and Collective Bargaining in Export Processing Zones: Role of the ILO Supervisory Mechanisms* (No. 1). Geneva: International Labour Office.

Gross, J.A. and Compa, L.A. (2009). *Human Rights in Labor and Employment Relations: International and Domestic Perspectives.* Ithaca: Cornell University Press.

Gunawardana, S.J. (2007). Perseverance, struggle and organization in Sri Lanka's Export Processing Zones: 1978–2003, in Bronfenbrenner, K. (ed.) *Global Unions: Challenging Transnational Capital Through Cross-Border Campaigns (Frank W. Pierce Memorial Lectureship and Conference Series).* Ithaca: Cornell University Press, pp. 78–88.

Gunawardana, S. (2011). What does transnational labour organizing and solidarity mean for Sri Lankan Free Trade Zone women workers?, in Bieler, A. and Lindberg, I. (eds.) *Global Restructuring, Labour and the Challenges for Transnational Solidarity.* Abingdon and New York: Routledge, pp. 87–100.

Gunawardana, S.J. (2014). 'Reframing employee voice: a case study in Sri Lanka's export processing zones', *Work, Employment & Society*, 28(3), pp. 452–468.

Gunawardana, S.J. (2016). "To Finish, We Must Finish': Everyday Practices of Depletion in Sri Lankan Export-Processing Zones', *Globalizations*, 13(6), pp. 861–875.

Hancock, P., Middleton, S., Moore, J. and Edirisinghe, I. (2011). *Gender, status and empowerment: a study among women who work in Sri Lanka's Export Processing Zones (EPZs)*. Social Justice Research Centre, Edith Cowan University, Australia. Available at: https://goo.gl/l1qv4E

Hayter, S. (ed.) (2011). *The Role of Collective Bargaining in the Global Economy: Negotiating for Social Justice*. Cheltenham: Edward Elgar Publishing.

Heery, E. (2006). 'Equality bargaining: where, who, why?' *Gender, Work & Organization*, 13(6), pp. 522–542.

Htun, M. and Weldon, S.L. (2012). 'The civic origins of progressive policy change: combating violence against women in global perspective, 1975–2005', *American Political Science Review*, 106(03), pp. 548–569.

Ingleson, J. (2001). 'The legacy of colonial labour unions in Indonesia', *Australian Journal of Politics & History*, 47(1), pp. 85–100.

Jaumotte, M.F. and Osoria Buitran, C. (2015). *Inequality and Labor Market Institutions*. Washington, DC: International Monetary Fund.

Jayawardena, K. (1972). *The Rise of the Labor Movement in Ceylon*. Durham (NC): Duke University Press.

Kabeer, N. (1999). 'Resources, agency, achievements: reflections on the measurement of women's empowerment', *Development and Change*, 30(3), pp. 435–464.

Kabeer, N. (2015). *Women workers and the politics of claims-making in a globalizing economy* (No. 2015-13). UNRISD Working Paper. Available at: www.unrisd.org/80256B3C005BCCF9/(httpAuxPages)/AA7089E93E952A14C1257EB400562052/$file/Kabeer.pdf.

Kabeer, N., Sudarshan, R. and Milward, K. (eds.) (2013). *Organizing Women Workers in the Informal Economy: Beyond the Weapons of the Weak*. London: Zed Books.

Kang, S.L. (2012). *Human Rights and Labor Solidarity: Trade Unions in the Global Economy*. Philadelphia: University of Pennsylvania Press.

Klugman, J. and Tyson, L. (2016). *Leave No One Behind: A Call to Action For Gender Equality and Women's Economic Empowerment*. Secretariat, UN Secretary-General's High-Level Panel on Women's Economic Empowerment. Available at: https://cdn1.sph.harvard.edu/wp-content/uploads/sites/134/2017/06/For-Klugman-Ws-empowerment-HLP-WEE-Report-2016-09-Call-to-action-Overview-en.pdf.

Kuruvilla, S. (1996). 'Linkages between industrialization strategies and industrial relations/human resource policies: Singapore, Malaysia, the Philippines, and India', *ILR Review*, 49(4), pp. 635–657.

Kuruvilla, S. and Venkataratnam, C.S. (1996). *Economic development and industrial relations: the case of South and Southeast Asia*. [Online]. Available at: http://digitalcommons.ilr.cornell.edu/articles/1068.

Kuruvilla, S. and Verma, A. (2006). 'International labor standards, soft regulation, and national government roles', *Journal of Industrial Relations*, 48(1), pp. 41–58.

LeBaron, G., Crane, A., Allain, J. and Behbahani, L. (2017). 'Governance gaps in eradicating forced labor: from global to domestic supply chains', *Regulation and Governance*. (Online). Available at: http://dx.doi.org/10.1111/rego.12162.

Lim, L.Y. (1983). Capitalism, imperialism, and patriarchy: the dilemma of third-world women workers in multinational factories, in Nash, J.C. and Fernandez-Kelly, M.P. (1983). *Women, Men, and the International Division of Labor*. Albany: SUNY Press, pp. 70–91.

Locke, R.M. (2013). *The Promise and Limits of Private Power: Promoting Labor Standards in a Global Economy*. New York: Cambridge University Press.

Lopez-Acevedo, G. and Robertson, R. (eds.) (2016). *Stitches to Riches? Apparel Employment, Trade, and Economic Development in South Asia*. Washington, DC: World Bank Publications.

Mackridge, K. (2017). *Violence Against Women*. TUC. (Online). Available at: www.tuc.org.uk/blogs/un-international-day-elimination-violence-against-women-–-unions-must-be-part-solution

Madhok, S. and Rai, S.M. (2012). 'Agency, injury, and transgressive politics in neoliberal times', *Signs: Journal of Women in Culture and Society*, 37(3), pp. 645–669.

Marshall, S. and Fenwick, C. (2016). *Labour Regulation and Development. Socio-Legal Perspectives*. Cheltenham: Edward Elgar Publishing.

Mayer, F. and Pickles, J. (2014). Re-embedding the market: Global apparel value chains, governance and decent work, in *Towards Better Work*. London: Palgrave Macmillan, pp. 17–39.

Milberg, W. and Amengual, M. (2008). *Economic Development and Working Conditions in Export Processing Zones: A Survey of Trends*. Geneva: International Labour Office. Available at: http://citeseerx.ist.psu.edu/viewdoc/download?doi=10.1.1.490.1514&rep=rep1&type=pdf.

Mosley, L. and Uno, S. (2007). 'Racing to the bottom or climbing to the top? Economic globalization and collective labor rights', *Comparative Political Studies*, 40(8), pp. 923–948.

Nussbaum, M.C. (2011). *Creating Capabilities*. Cambridge (MA): Harvard University Press.

Oswalt, M.M. (2016). 'Improvisational unionism', *California Law Review*, 104(2), pp. 597–670.

Peck, J. (2010). *Constructions of Neoliberal Reason*. New York: Oxford University Press.

Peksen, D. and Blanton, R.G. (2016). 'The impact of ILO conventions on worker rights: Are empty promises worse than no promises?' *The Review of International Organizations*, 12(1), pp. 75–94.

Phillips, N. (2017). 'Power and inequality in the global political economy', *International Affairs*, 93(2), pp. 429–444.

Rowlands, J. (1997). *Questioning Empowerment: Working with Women in Honduras*. London: Oxfam.

Safa, H.I. (2002). 'Questioning globalization: gender and export processing in the Dominican Republic', *Contributions to Asian Studies*, 18(2–3), pp. 11–31.

Sardenberg, C. (2008). 'Liberal vs. Liberating Empowerment: a Latin American Feminist Perspective on conceptualising women's empowerment', *IDS Bulletin*, 39(6), pp. 18–27.

Selwyn, B. (2011). 'Beyond firm-centrism: re-integrating labour and capitalism into global commodity chain analysis', *Journal of Economic Geography*, 12(1), pp. 205–226.

Selwyn, B. (2013). 'Social upgrading and labour in global production networks: a critique and an alternative conception', *Competition & Change*, 17(1), pp. 75–90.

Sen, A. (1999). *Development as Freedom*. New York: Oxford University Press.

Siddiqi, D.M. (2009). 'Do Bangladeshi factory workers need saving? Sisterhood in the post-sweatshop era', *Feminist Review*, 91(1), pp. 154–174.

Tomei, M. (2000). *Home Work in Selected Latin American Countries: A Comparative Overview*. Working Paper No.1. Geneva: ILO. Available at: http://ilo.org/wcmsp5/groups/public/@ed_emp/@emp_ent/@ifp_seed/documents/publication/wcms_117733.pdf.

United Nations General Assembly (2016). *Report of the Special Rapporteur on the rights to freedom of peaceful assembly and of association, Maina Kiai*, 14 September 2016 A/71/150. Available at: http://freeassembly.net/wp-content/uploads/2016/10/A.71.385_E.pdf.

Wieringa, S. (1994). 'Women's interests and empowerment: gender planning reconsidered', *Development and Change*, 25(4), pp. 829–848.

Williamson, S. and Baird, M. (2014). 'Gender equality bargaining: developing theory and practice', *Journal of Industrial Relations*, 56(2), pp. 155–169.

Wright, M.W. (2006). *Disposable Women and Other Myths of Global Capitalism*. New York and London: Routledge.

24

EMPLOYMENT RELATIONS IN LATIN AMERICA

Mark Anner and Katiuscia Galhera[1]

Introduction

Latin America offers a vibrant example of complex and dynamic employment relations practices in the global economy. The region shares a common legacy of Iberian colonisation, civil law legal systems, state corporatism, commodity export dependency and labour market bifurcation with a very large informal economy. Employment relations practices have also been shaped by dramatic shifts between economic liberalism and protectionism, and authoritarian rule and democracy. All these factors encourage us to re-think dominant frameworks for studying ER in the global economy.

An employment framework for Latin America must also take into consideration contrasts. The region's largest economies – Brazil, Mexico and Argentina – have the strongest corporatist traditions, large domestic markets and relatively large labour unions. Central American and Caribbean countries have experienced more prolonged labour-repressive regimes and market economies built on highly competitive, low-cost exports such as apparel. The result has been relatively small and fragmented unions and authoritarian ER practices.

In general, Latin America as a region differs markedly from the pluralist ER regimes common in liberal market economies. But nor can it be considered a region of coordinated market economies with strong social actors. It is the state, rather than society, that has played the most dominant role in setting the strategic terms of labour-management interactions (Schmitter, 1974). As a result, a hierarchical market economy better represents the context for patterns of regional ER (Schneider, 2009).

This chapter seeks to explore ER practices in Latin America while developing an overarching framework for analysis. It examines general political, economic and legal trends that shape ER and examines the causes for diversity. In the sections that follow, we first outline our framework for studying ER in Latin America. Next, we explore how the economic context and labour market trends influence ER. In the third section, we examine the labour rights context in law and practice. The fourth and fifth sections review industrial relations (IR) and human resource management (HRM) practices in the region. The final section concludes.

A framework for studying employment relations in Latin America

When studying Latin America, there is a need to significantly modify employment relations frameworks that prioritise the strategic role of employers in shaping ER dynamics (Kochan, Katz and McKersie, 1994). Three factors make the study of Latin American ER significantly different than that of developed market economies, most especially the United States. First and foremost is Iberian colonisation, which left a legacy of ER built on civil law and economies highly dependent on exports and foreign direct investment (Bergquist, 1986). The second factor is the region's labour market context with its high levels of informality and other forms of labour market segmentation (ILO, 2015). The third factor is the political context, which has seen dramatic swings from state corporatism based on populist rule to highly labour-repressive dictatorships, and then to multi-party democracies (Drake, 1996). Finally, there are cultural factors that have shaped and, in turn, have been shaped by Latin America's history. These include collectivism, high power distance and strong risk aversion (Moran, Abramson and Moran, 2014).

A study of Latin America's contemporary ER practices begins with the region's history of colonisation and insertion into the world economy. In the 1500s, the Spanish and Portuguese forcibly brought the region into the world economy through the extraction of natural resources and export crops such as coffee (Bergquist, 1986). Class stratification deepened as European colonisers developed large landholdings with land expropriated from the indigenous population. Cash export crops such as sugar cane resulted in the dramatic growth of slavery, most notably in Brazil and the Caribbean (Salazar Vergara and Pinto, 1999; Zavala, 1990). Brazil took in more slaves from the transatlantic slave trade than any other country in the world, and, in 1886, was the last country in the western hemisphere to abolish slavery.

Over time, European descendants, known as *criollos* during Spanish colonisation, constituted rural oligarchies. The Spanish and the Portuguese also brought with them their legal systems. Following independence, lengthy labour codes based on this civil law tradition were established, and they determine in detail how unions are to be formed, when and over what subjects workers can bargain, how much vacation time and maternity leave are to be allotted to employees, etc. (Bronstein, 1995).

How Latin American nations inserted themselves into the global economy following Spanish and Portuguese colonisation had a profound effect on labour relations practices (Bergquist, 1986). Put simply, countries dependent on products that were conducive to centralised and stable employment and thus labour organising – such as bananas – would maintain relatively strong unions. In contrast, countries dependent on smallholdings and seasonal crops – such as coffee – would face a legacy of small and fragmented unionisation.

Nonetheless, economic legacies do not tell the entire story. Political dynamics and the role of the state also play a strong role in shaping current ER trends. In part, this is because labour abundance resulted in weak labour market bargaining power for workers. This pushed labour unions to target the state as opposed to employers in order to achieve their demands (Collier and Collier, 1991). Labour realised that national minimum wages and state-mandated social benefits could impact far more workers than attempts to organise and bargain workplace by workplace. During this period, labour also became a growing force in the electorate and politicians of a populist orientation – such as Juan Perón in Argentina, Getúlio Vargas in Brazil and Lázaro Cárdenas in Mexico – sought to incorporate labour into state institutions through a system of state corporatism (ibid.).

The Cold War saw the decline of populism and the rise of right-wing authoritarian regimes in the region. From Uruguay to Nicaragua, labour-repressive authoritarian leaders ruled Latin American states in the 1960s, 70s and 80s, often imprisoning labour leaders and prohibiting worker mobilisation (Drake, 1996). One cause for authoritarian rule was a state desire to control labour during periods of difficult economic reforms (O'Donnell, 1973). Geopolitics also played a role, especially after the Cuban revolution in 1959 when the US government supported authoritarian rulers in the region in order to prevent socialist regimes from taking power. In the process, the US often pursued efforts to weaken left-oriented unions while building moderate, pro-US labour groups in the region (Anner, 2011b).

In the 1980s and 1990s, democratisation and international pressure resulted in many pro-labour reforms, including laws that facilitated union formation (Cook, 2007). At the same time, market-oriented reforms created new competitive pressures that overpowered many of the pro-labour aspects of the legal reforms, contributing to union decline and fragmentation (Anner, 2008). The civil law system and the legacy of state corporatism meant that many formal sector workers continued to rely heavily on the state to determine wage and benefit levels, at the same time that the level of those benefits declined and labour markets became more flexible. Market-oriented reforms also increased the size of the informal sector, leaving millions of workers outside the purview of the formal labour relations regime and the protections, albeit limited, of state labour inspectorates (ILO, 2015).

The result is ER systems in Latin America that tend to be more state-centric than those in liberal market economies, and labour markets that are far more segmented than in developed market economies, not only between core and non-core workers, but also between formal and informal sector workers. Finally, the strong role of multinational corporations (MNCs), social clauses in trade arrangements and the imperatives of the International Monetary Fund (IMF) reflect influences that go beyond the national level. MNCs brought with them certain ER practices from their home countries at the same time as they sought to adapt to local culture (Elvira and Dávila, 2005). Social clauses in trade agreements resulted in important labour law reforms, especially in Latin America's smaller countries (Frundt, 1998). And IMF loan conditionality often resulted in increased labour market flexibility (Anner and Caraway, 2010).

These elements allow us to develop a framework for analysis that begins with the social actors: the state, employers and labour. But, unlike the case of coordinated market economies, in Latin America the state plays a more dominant role, which is why in our framework we place the state at the top of the social partners' triangular relationship. Second, to highlight the significant role of the informal sector, we suggest a bifurcated labour market, where the formal sector workers are protected by the state labour relations regime while a large segment of the workforce falls outside state protection. This ER regime exists within larger national political, economic and cultural contexts, which in turn exist within a broader international context shaped by foreign direct investment (MNCs), trade regimes and rules set by international financial institutions (IFIs). [See Figure 24.1.]

In the sections that follow, we will use this framework to examine contemporary ER practices in Latin America. We begin by exploring the economic and labour market context.

Economic and labour market context

Like much of the world, employment in Latin America has seen a shift from agriculture to industry[2] and then from industry to the service sector. Today, some 14 per cent of workers are employed in the agricultural sector, 22 per cent are in industry and 64 per cent are in services. Yet, within the region there are some significant variations. While less than one per cent of workers in Argentina is employed in agriculture, over 30 per cent of workers in Guatemala and Honduras still work in the sector. Argentina, Brazil, Chile and Mexico have the largest

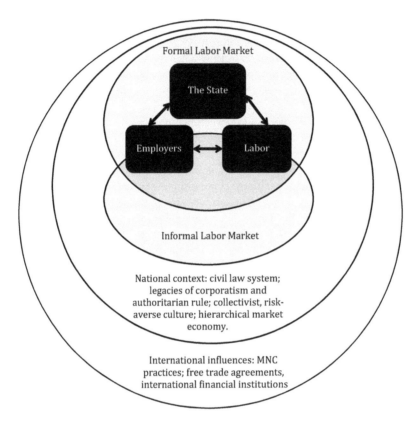

Figure 24.1   Framework for studying Latin American employment relations

share of their workers in industry in the region (over 22 per cent), compared with fewer than 17 per cent of workers in the Dominican Republic. And while over 70 per cent of workers in Argentina and Venezuela are employed in the service sector, less than 50 per cent of workers in Honduras are employed in that sector. [See Figure 24.2.]

Yet, even these differences hide deeper sources of labour market variation. For example, while Argentina and Honduras are both relatively strong in industry, Argentina's industrial employment includes high-end industrial sectors such as autos while Honduras' industry is based on low-end apparel assembly exports. And while the service sector is the dominant sector in terms of employment throughout the region, it is not the case that the service sector is unambiguously displacing jobs in industry across the region. In Central America, the Caribbean and Mexico, the per cent of the workforce employed in industry actually *increased* slightly from 1990 to 2005 (ECLAC, 2006).

The growth of employment in industry in these countries is a reflection of economic policies that have favoured export-oriented growth through light manufacturing. Under this model, producers assemble products under contract for major buyers such as Gap, Wal-Mart or Intel. In Mexico, auto parts assembly is also common. This model of export-oriented growth puts considerable downward pressure on wages and unionisation rates as a result of the segmentation of the workforce and increased competitive pressure on producers (Anner, 2011a).

This model of production varies greatly from the domestic market-oriented model of production known as *import substitution industrialisation* that dominated the region for much of

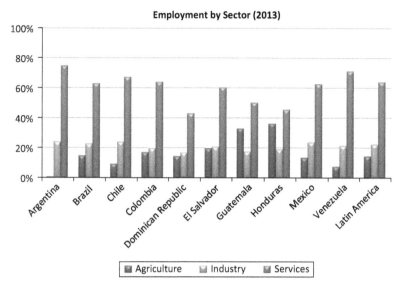

Employment by Sector (2013)

Source: World Development Indicators.

Figure 24.2   Employment by sector

the twentieth century. The protectionist regime, while it lasted, allowed for real wage growth and increased unionisation (Schamis, 1999). In the early twenty-first century, job tenure has tended to be more stable in high-end, domestic market-oriented sectors relative to low-end, hyper-competitive systems such as those based on apparel exports. The result is an important variation in ER practices. For example, the auto sector is characterised by high levels of unionisation and collective bargaining coverage with a large middle-aged male workforce, whereas the apparel export sector is characterised by low levels of unionisation, almost no collective bargaining coverage, authoritarian managerial styles and a predominance of young, female workers (Anner, 2011b).

The service sector in the region also varies in ER practices, ranging from public sector jobs with full benefits to informal sector domestic workers and street vendors. Indeed, perhaps the single greatest difference between Latin American ER practices and those in developed market economies is the high level of informality in Latin America. Informality is defined by the International Labour Organization (ILO) as, "economic activities that operate outside the formal reach of the law or those that, while operating within the formal reach of the law, are not subject to application or enforcement of the law in practice."[3] Some 47 per cent of workers in Latin America work in the informal sector. Approximately 59 per cent of workers in microenterprises (10 or fewer workers) are informal. Some 78 per cent of domestic workers and 82 per cent of 'own-account' workers (street vendors, etc.) are informal. [See Figure 24.3.]

The highest rates of informality can be found in Bolivia, Honduras and Paraguay, where over 70 per cent of workers are not covered by labour legislation. The majority of workers in Latin America under 25 years of age (55.7 per cent) are informal (ILO, 2015). We also find a higher participation of women in informal employment relative to men, such as among domestic workers and street vendors. In formal sector manufacturing jobs, women are more often employed in low-paid apparel assembly jobs. Thus, in exploring ER practices in Latin America,

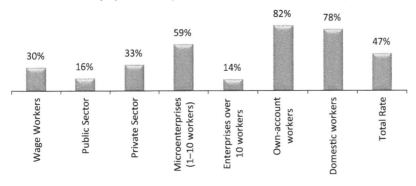

Source: ILO (2015)

Figure 24.3   Informal employment rate by sector in 14 Latin American countries (2015)
Source: ILO (2015)

an examination of labour and employment laws often only informs us about conditions for less than half of the workforce, excluding in particular young and female workers.

Finally, regional and international migration patterns influence economic and ER dynamics. Millions of Mexican, Central American and Caribbean migrants live in the United States and send billions in remittances back home, often helping workers in low-paid jobs in Latin America to pay their bills. That is, family remittances help to subsidise underpaid jobs. Regional migration is also high, with Nicaraguan agricultural workers in Costa Rica (Lee, 2010), Bolivian garment workers in Brazil (Veiga and Galhera, 2014) and Peruvian domestic workers in Chile (Staab and Hil Maher, 2006). The majority of these workers face poorly remunerated and exceptionally harsh and vulnerable working conditions.

Labour and employment laws

In the early part of the twentieth century, Latin American nations adopted their most important labour legislation to regulate employment and working conditions based on "a high degree of state intervention in collective labour relations" (Bronstein, 1995, p. 164). The goal was to control union formation while also limiting social conflict. Individual workers received important benefits and protections through state legislation in order to show, "the State was the guardian of the workers, not the unions" (ibid.). In the process, state officials decided when to grant unions recognition or when to deny it, how unions should select their leaders and who could or could not be a union leader. Unions were required to present regular membership rosters and financial reports to state authorities. Pro-labour governments could use these laws to build unions to their favour, while authoritarian regimes could use the same laws to curtail union formation and mobilisation (Drake, 1996).

Labour laws went through significant reforms in the 1990s and early 2000s as a result of democratisation and external pressure created by trade arrangements and international institutions (Frundt, 1998; Murillo and Schrank, 2005). In most cases, collective labour laws became more favourable to labour while individual labour laws became more flexible (Cook, 2007). Latin American governments 'flexibilised' their employment laws most significantly in the areas of hours of work, overtime, dismissals costs and employment contracts (ibid.). At the same time, several countries allowed for public sector unionisation and others reduced the number of workers needed to form a union at the enterprise level (Anner, 2008).

While some scholars focused on the reforms to laws, a growing body of research began to pay closer attention to enforcement. Some scholars, while acknowledging certain caveats, celebrated the 'Latin model' of labour inspection, because it "can reconcile regulation with economic flexibility and transform inspectors into the shock troops of a campaign for decent work" (Piore and Schrank, 2008, p. 1). This is because labour inspectors have the authority to weigh the costs and benefits of regulation at the firm level and can disseminate best practices (ibid.). Other scholars have noted that, absent pressure from civil society, labour inspectorates are often subject to political interference and lack resources (Amengual, 2014).

In the aftermath of the labour reforms, unionisation rates continued to decline in Latin America, especially in the private sector. This is because, whatever favourable legal aspects were provided by the reforms to labour, the adverse effects of market-oriented reforms on unions were greater (Anner, 2008). Second, often the reforms were not accompanied by corresponding reforms to labour inspectorates and other instruments of enforcement. While the number of labour inspectors did grow in many countries, they still proved insufficient to cover the hundreds of thousands of workplaces in the region. And, when labour and employment law violations were detected, the level of fines imposed on violators (sometimes no more than US$24) was not sufficiently dissuasive enough so as to prevent employers from committing further violations (Anner, 2008).

A database released in 2015 by the Center for Global Workers' Rights at Penn State University allows for a closer examination of these trends. The Labor Rights Indicators database (from here forward, 'LR Indicators') documents labour laws that violate ILO standards. The database codes violations of the right to form unions, bargaining collectively and strike by coding findings of the ILO supervisory mechanisms, US State Department Human Rights Reports, national legislation and International Trade Union Confederation (ITUC) annual surveys of human rights.[4] The database divides violations into 'violations in law' and 'violations in practice.' A violation in law is a case in which a labour law does not meet ILO standards, such as a prohibition on unionisation in export processing zones (EPZs). A violation in practice is a case where the law meets ILO standards, but in practice is systematically violated. This would be a case when there are no legal barriers to unionisation in EPZs, but the state fails to address a common employer practice of dismissing and blacklisting workers who try to unionise.

In terms of 'violations in law', what the database reveals is a significant number of violations in law of these core rights, with El Salvador and Honduras at the top of the list. [See Figure 24.4.] For example, in El Salvador, the law does not require employers to reinstate illegally dismissed workers, and it does not provide public sector workers with the right to collectively bargain and strike (LR Indicators). In Honduras, fines imposed on employers for acts of anti-union discrimination (such as firing a worker for union activity) range from approximately US$12 to a maximum of US$500 and are considered not to be "sufficiently dissuasive" by the ILO (LR Indicators).

In Brazil, a 2005 report found that local labour inspection offices often lacked computers, telephones, tables and chairs, which, according to the ILO, inhibited the ability of the labour inspectorate to carry out its duties (CEACR, 2005). Resources dedicated to enforcement increased significantly (by approximately 50 per cent) under the pro-labour government of Luiz Inácio Lula da Silva (Anner, 2008), but other limitations in the law remain in Brazil. For example, a collective bargaining agreement in Brazil can be declared null and void if it is found to conflict with the government's economic and financial policy, or the wage policy in force (LR Indicators).

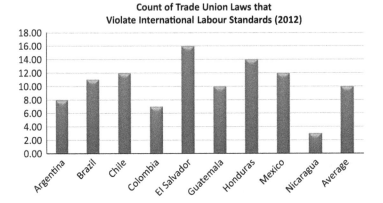

Figure 24.4 Count of trade union laws that violate international labour standards (2012)
Source: Authors' calculations based on the CGWR Labor Rights Indicators

In Guatemala, the existence of a union at the firm level does not mean that an employer has an obligation to bargain or even meet with the workers. Instead, the laws establish a much higher threshold for collective bargaining than for union formation, which results in the proliferation of small unions with no collective bargaining rights. Five countries in Latin America require between 60 and 75 per cent of the workforce to approve a strike action, which is also considered by the ILO to be an unreasonably high threshold. In addition, many countries have burdensome administrative steps that must be fulfilled before a strike can be authorised by the state (Anner, 2008).

In Mexico, violations of international labour standards are notable (La Botz, 1999). The ILO has consistently criticised Mexican labour law for its imposition of "trade union unity". Notably, the Federal Act on State Employees prohibits the co-existence of two or more unions in the same state agency (LR Indicators). Historically, this has allowed pro-government, monopoly union representation. Argentina, which has also been criticised for its system of monopoly representation, only recognises the right to strike for registered unions with official status, excluding, thereby, the right to strike of non-official unions (LR Indicators).

In sum, labour unions face considerable legal obstacles to exercise their rights to organise, bargain and strike in Latin America. However, in many ways it is not the law itself, but rather the failure to implement the law, that is the biggest obstacle to the functioning of labour unions in Latin America. We turn to this topic in the next section.

Labour laws in practice: unionisation and collective bargaining coverage

In Latin America, when assessing ER regimes, it is often necessary to examine labour standards in practice. Countries with relatively good laws may in fact have the worst record in terms of respect for those laws. This is certainly the case with Guatemala and Colombia. In both countries, the number of standards that are violated in practice is approximately three times the level of violations in law. These two cases represent the two most dangerous countries in the world to be a trade unionist. For many years, more unionists were killed in Colombia every year than the rest of the world combined. In 2011, of the 76 trade unionists murdered for union activity, 29 were Colombian and 10 were Guatemalans (ITUC, 2009). In recent years, killings of trade unionists were also recorded in Brazil, Panama, Peru and Venezuela.[5] On average, the Labour

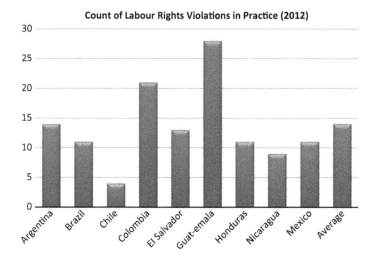

Figure 24.5   Count of labour rights violations in practice (2012)
Source: Authors' calculations based on the CGWR Labor Rights Indicators

Rights Indicators reveal that violations in practices are more prevalent than violations in laws, suggesting deficits in the area of state labour law enforcement mechanisms. [See Figure 24.5 for counts of labour rights violations in practice.]

While the killing of trade unionists is the most dramatic example of how trade union rights are violated in practice, more common practices include the manipulation of unions by employers and the government. The US Department of State's human rights report on Mexico observes, "The process for official government recognition of unions was politicized, and the government occasionally used the process to reward political allies or punish political opponents." (US Department of State, 2015, p. 33). The report continues:

> Protection (company-controlled) unions continued to be a problem in all sectors, and many observers noted working conditions of a majority of workers were under the control of those unrepresentative unions. Officially sanctioned "protection contracts" – formal agreements whereby the company creates an unrepresentative union in exchange for labor peace and other concessions – were common in all sectors and often prevented workers from fully exercising their labor rights as defined by law.
>
> *(US Department of State, 2015, pp. 33–34)*

The report concludes that these practices contributed to weak collective bargaining agreements and poor working conditions.

Patterns of violations also vary by sector. In sectors in which labour costs are more sensitive to competitive market pressures, such as the apparel export sectors that dominate manufacturing exports in Central America and much of the Caribbean, violations of national laws and international standards are particularly severe. Firing and then blacklisting workers who attempted to form unions in apparel export processing zones have been well documented in Honduras, Guatemala and El Salvador (Anner, 2011a; Delpech, 2015; US Department of State, 2009).

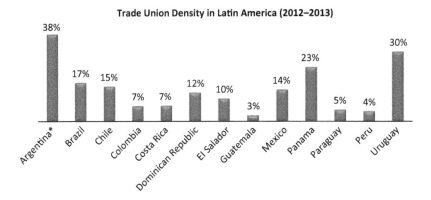

Source: ILOSTAT.
*Argentina figure is for 2008

Figure 24.6   Trade union density in Latin America (2012–2013)
*Argentina figure is for 2008
Source: ILOSTAT (www.ilo.org/ilostat)

The impact of these 'in law' and 'in practice' violations, as well as the general economic and political context outlined above, is significant variations in trade union density and collective bargaining coverage in the region. Trade union density rates indicate the number of union members who are employees as a percentage of the total number of employees.[6] What the data show are a group of countries with union density rates of 3–10 per cent (Colombia, Costa Rica, El Salvador, Guatemala, Paraguay and Peru). At the same time, there are several countries with relatively significant union density rates of full-time employees of 17–38 per cent (Argentina, Brazil, Panama, and Uruguay.) [See Figure 24.6.]

What accounts for this variation? At first blush, we see that levels and forms of economic development matter. Argentina, Brazil and Uruguay are all well above the Latin American mean in terms of GDP per capita and have a stronger economic foundation in heavy industry. In contrast, Guatemala, El Salvador and Paraguay have among the lowest GDPs per capita in the region and their manufacturing is more strongly based on low-end export assembly sectors. Mexico represents a mixed case of greater levels of economic development yet a high dependency on export assembly manufacturing. At the same time, an adverse labour relations regime in law and practice has inhibited independent unionisation, as we have seen above.

A further examination of law and practice trends reveals the importance of industry-level collective bargaining. The countries with the longest legacy of industry level bargaining – notably Argentina and Uruguay – have not only the highest union density rates, but also have among the highest collective bargaining coverage levels. Yet, Latin America is dominated by enterprise-level bargaining. Countries with enterprise bargaining, which fragments unions and weakens their leverage, tend to have the lowest union density rates as well as the lowest collective bargaining coverage rates. El Salvador, Honduras, Nicaragua, Panama, Paraguay and Peru all have collective bargaining coverage rates of below four per cent. Brazil's system of sub-national territorial unionism and bargaining agreement extension rules contributed to a high level of collective bargaining coverage there, with coverage of 42 per cent of employees. [See Table 24.1.]

Table 24.1 Collective bargaining coverage and level of bargaining

	Bargaining coverage rates of total employees	*Dominant collective bargaining level*
Argentina	27%	industry
Brazil	42%	municipality/occupational
Chile	13%	enterprise
Costa Rica	12%	enterprise★
El Salvador	3%	enterprise★
Honduras	3%	enterprise★
Mexico	9%	enterprise
Nicaragua	2%	enterprise
Panama	2%	industry
Paraguay	1%	enterprise
Peru	1%	enterprise
Uruguay	67%	industry
Venezuela	8%	enterprise

Source: International Labour Organization (2015). Trends in collective bargaining coverage: stability, erosion or decline? Available at: www.ilo.org/wcmsp5/groups/public/---ed_protect/---protrav/---travail/documents/publication/wcms_409422.pdf

★ assessment based on authors' interviews and research.

Human resource management practice

In the 1990s, as most Latin American governments carried out structural reforms through market deregulation, trade liberalisation and privatisation, the region became increasingly attractive to investment by MNCs. Foreign direct investment (FDI) grew from US$13 billion in 1991 to US$215 billion in 2014, a dramatic 17-fold increase. [See Figure 24.7.] This wave of FDI influenced human resource and ER practices in the region through the diffusion of MNC home-country HRM practices. And, through learning and other diffusion mechanisms, it influenced the practices of local corporations, too.

Diffusion of HRM practices through foreign investors and the practice of local business schools to promote North American HRM models indicate a degree of convergence in some HRM practices among Latin American countries (Elvira and Dávila, 2005; Sparrow, Schuler and Jackson, 1994). The similarities include promotion of employee participation mechanisms, managerial decentralisation and merit pay compensation schemes. Historically, Latin American corporations have put more emphasis on managing worker turnover and less emphasis on flexible work practices. At the same time, idiosyncratic factors in the region such as cultural, economic and historical processes shaped business management practices. What local managers realised is that the legitimacy of their practices could only be achieved by adapting to the unique cultural context (Elvira and Dávila, 2005; Schneider, 2009).

In general, countries in Latin America score high on the "power distance" dimension of Hofstede's dimensions of national culture.[7] This dimension measures the expectation that power in institutions is distributed unequally. The Latin American scores suggest a strong acceptance of hierarchy in society. Organisations tend to be centralised and very hierarchical with large wage differentials. Indeed, it has been argued that Latin America as a region represents hierarchical market economies (HMEs) as a specific 'variety of capitalism' (Schneider, 2009).

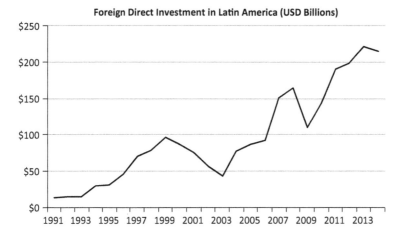

Foreign Direct Investment in Latin America (USD Billions)

Source: World Development Indicators.

Figure 24.7   Foreign direct investment in Latin America (US$ billions)
Source: World Development Indicators (http://databank.worldbank.org/data/reports.
aspx?source=world-development-indicators)

Schneider finds, "[W]hereas post-secondary or on-the-job training is more market-based in LMEs and more negotiated in CMEs, it is often unilaterally decided by firms or business associations in Latin America" (Schneider, 2009, p. 557). Hierarchy permeates ER in general, with few formal grievance procedures, limited worker voice outside unionised workplaces and numerous "top-down regulations issued by national governments and enforced by labour courts" (ibid.). In countries such as Mexico, high levels of paternalistic values prevail, which reinforce social relations and the social distance between superiors and subordinates (Martinez, 2005).

Latin American societies are also highly collectivist. In collectivist societies, individuals are tightly integrated into family and other groups. Members of the group usually share mutual support while emphasising loyalty. This can contribute to paternalistic ER practices and patterns in which older members of families are expected to bring younger members of families into their business.

A third dimension is uncertainty avoidance, which measures societies' tolerance for ambiguity. Latin American countries score high on this dimension, suggesting that many people prefer the status quo and rules-based systems where the results are clear and predictable. This cultural trait can find its roots in Latin American history, where dramatic changes in governments through coup d'états and periods of hyperinflation have left people in the region with a deep appreciation for stability. As a result, organisations and institutions tend to be bureaucratic and task-oriented.

Latin American Human Resources Management (HRM) scholars argue that based on the cultural aspects of Latin American societies, two common work values in the Latin America workplace are respect for authority and strong social relationships (Elvira and Dávila, 2005). This translates into a leadership style where managers and supervisors have the dual function of paying an employee's salary while safeguarding their personal needs, which reflects a sense of personal obligation to protect subordinates. As a result, family is sometimes used as a metaphor to describe organisations. These HRM scholars suggest that public criticism is often avoided as well as conflict with superiors because it can be interpreted as denigration, disobedience and insubordination.

Social relationships are also a key cultural aspect that shapes the organisational context. The development of personal relationships is promoted in organisations as a reflection of the cultural preference for collectivism. Personal contact is highly valued in Latin America. Managerial interactions and face-to-face communication strengthens centralisation while giving the sense of power proximity. Employees prefer cordial and affective relationships in the workplace. The emotional bond between supervisors and subordinates as well as between co-workers may create loyalty and trust (Elvira and Dávila, 2005).

Of course, these general traits are contingent and dynamic. During periods of authoritarian rule and economic crisis, Latin American workers have been remarkably militant in expressing their disapproval of leaders (Drake, 1996; Keck, 1989; Levenson-Estrada, 1994). Liberation theology and struggles for social justice have left a legacy of many social movements that question traditional hierarchies. Perhaps more so than any other region, Latin America labour unionists and worker activists have often aligned with other social movements –including student groups, women's organisations and faith-based communities – in their efforts to improve the living and working conditions of their members.

Conclusion

Latin America offers a mosaic of employment relations practices, from labour-repressive regimes in the export-processing zones of Central America, to the informal street vendors of Bolivia and the full-time production workers in German-transplant auto factories in Brazil. Variations in economic, political and ER legacies contribute to unionisation rates that vary from three per cent in Guatemala to 38 per cent in Argentina. Strong industrial unions in Uruguay bargain national agreements that cover 67 per cent of the workforce, while the fragmented enterprise unions of El Salvador negotiate collective bargaining agreements that cover only three per cent of formal sector workers.

Yet, within these variations, certain common traits emerge. The region shares a legacy of Iberian colonisation, state corporatism, authoritarian rule and democratic transition, and dramatic fluctuations between protective and free-market economic policies. As a result, common cultural and ER practices developed. A culture of collectivism, uncertainty avoidance and power distance reinforced the model of HMEs in which paternalistic ER practices prevail.

Latin America also remains a dynamic region. Decades of authoritarian rule were followed by democratisation and market-oriented reforms in the 1990s. Pro-labour reforms ensued, but these often failed to meet the challenges created by market liberalisation and enforcement was often weak. The early 2000s witnessed the rise of a moderate left in Latin America, with trade union presidents in Brazil and Bolivia. For a period of time, the decline in unionisation rates in some countries abated. But at the time of writing, economic boom is turning once again into crisis: the labour-oriented government in Argentina was voted out of power, voters denied Bolivia's labour-activist president a chance to run for a fourth term and the pro-labour government in Brazil lost power through a questioned impeachment process that not only removed the president, but also removed the pro-labour governing party. What this suggests is that employment relations practices in Latin America will continue to be dynamic and worthy of much future research.

Notes

1 The authors thank Denny Monteiro and João Gabriel Bounavita for their invaluable research assistance for this chapter. Katiuscia Galhera, while working on this project, benefited from a scholarship provided by CAPES Foundation, Ministry of Education of Brazil, Brasilia/DF – Brazil.

2 According to the World Development Indicators, 'industry' corresponds to ISIC divisions 10–45 and includes manufacturing (ISIC divisions 15–37). It comprises value added in mining, manufacturing, construction, electricity, water and gas.

3 ILO, 2015, "27 million Latin American and Caribbean Youth in the Informal Economy." Available at: www.ilo.org/wcmsp5/groups/public/---americas/---ro-lima/documents/publication/wcms_361990.pdf.

4 More information on the database and its methodology can be found here: http://labour-rights-indicators.la.psu.edu/ (Accessed: 3 January 2018).

5 Trade Union Rights in Law and Practice, http://labour-rights-indicators.la.psu.edu/ (Accessed: 3 January 2018).

6 For the purpose of this indicator in particular, trade union membership excludes union members who are not in paid employment, such as self-employed, unemployed and retired workers.

7 The Hofstede Centre, http://geert-hofstede.com/countries.html (Accessed: 3 January 2018).

References

Amengual, M. (2014). 'Pathways to enforcement: labor inspectors leveraging linkages with society in Argentina', *Industrial & Labor Relations Review*, 67(1), pp. 3–33.

Anner, M. (2008). 'Meeting the Challenges of Industrial Restructuring: Labor Reform and Enforcement in Latin America', *Latin American Politics and Society*, 50(2), pp. 33–65.

Anner, M. (2011a). 'The Impact of International Outsourcing on Unionization and Wages: Evidence from the Apparel Export Sector in Central America', *Industrial & Labor Relations Review*, 64(2), pp. 305–322.

Anner, M. (2011b). *Solidarity Transformed: Labor's Responses to Globalization and Crisis in Latin America*. Ithaca: ILR Press, an imprint of Cornell University Press.

Anner, M. and Caraway, T. (2010). 'International Institutions and Workers' Rights: Between Labor Standards and Market Flexibility', *Studies in Comparative International Development*, 45(May), pp. 151–169.

Bergquist, C.W. (1986). *Labor in Latin America: Comparative Essays on Chile, Argentina, Venezuela, and Colombia*. Stanford: Stanford University Press.

Bronstein, A.S. (1995). 'Societal Change and Industrial Relations in Latin America: Trends and Prospects', *International Labour Review*, 134(2), pp. 163–186.

CEACR (2005). 'Report of the Committee of Experts on the Application of Conventions and Recommendations.' (Online). Available at: www.ilo.org/public/english/standards/relm/ilc/ilc93/pdf/rep-iii-1a.pdf.

Collier, R.B. and Collier, D. (1991). *Shaping the Political Arena: Critical Junctures, the Labor Movement, and Regime Dynamics in Latin America*. Princeton: Princeton University Press.

Cook, M.L. (2007). *The Politics of Labor Reform in Latin America: Between Flexibility and Rights*. University Park: The Pennsylvania State University Press.

Delpech, Q. (2015). 'Concealed Repression: Labor Organizing Campaigns and Antiunion Practices in the Apparel Industry of Guatemala', *Mobilization*, 20(3), pp. 325–344.

Drake, P.W. (1996). *Labor Movements and Dictatorships: The Southern Cone in Comparative Perspective*. Baltimore: Johns Hopkins University Press.

ECLAC. (2006). *Social Panorama of Latin America 2005*. Santiago: Economic Commission for Latin America and the Caribbean. Available at: http://repositorio.cepal.org/bitstream/handle/11362/1224/1/S2005996_en.pdf.

Elvira, M. and Dávila, A. (2005). Culture and Human Resource Management in Latin America, in Elvira, M. and Dávila, A. (eds.) *Managing Human Resources in Latin America: An Agenda for International Leaders*. New York: Routledge, pp. 3–24.

Frundt, H.J. (1998). *Trade Conditions and Labor Rights: U.S. Initiatives, Dominican and Central American Responses*. Gainesville: University Press of Florida.

ILO. (2015). *Promoting Formal Employment Among Youth: Innovative Experiences in Latin America and the Caribbean*. Lima: ILO.

ITUC. (2009). *Annual Survey of Violations of Trade Union Rights 2009*. Brussels: International Trade Union Confederations.

Keck, M.E. (1989). The New Unionism in the Brazilian Transition, in Stepan, A. (ed.) *Democratizing Brazil: Problems of Transition and Consolidation*. New York: Oxford University Press, pp. 252–296.

Kochan, T.A., Katz, H.C. and McKersie, R.B. (1994). *The Transformation of American Industrial Relations*. Ithaca: ILR Press.

La Botz, D. (1999). *Mask of Democracy: Labor Suppression in Mexico Today*. Boston (MA): South End Press.

Lee, S.E. (2010). 'The Ties Made in the Harvest: Nicaraguan Farm-worker Networks in Costa Rica's Agricultural Exports', *Journal of Agrarian Change*, 10(4), pp. 510–536.

Levenson-Estrada, D. (1994). *Trade Unionists Against Terror: Guatemala City 1954–1985*. Chapel Hill: The University of North Carolina Press.

Martinez, P.G. (2005). Paternalism as a Positive Form of Leadership in the Latin American Context: Leader Benevolence, Decision-making Control and Human Resource Management Practices, in Elvira, M. and Dávila, A. (eds.) *Managing Human Resources in Latin America: An Agenda for International Leader*. New York: Routledge, pp. 73–95.

Moran, R.T., Abramson, N.R. and Moran, S.V. (2014). *Managing Cultural Differences*. New York: Routledge.

Murillo, M.V. and Schrank, A. (2005). 'With a Little Help from My Friends: Partisan Politics, Transnational Alliances, and Labor Rights in Latin America', *Comparative Political Studies*, 38(8), pp. 971–999.

O'Donnell, G.A. (1973). *Modernization and Bureaucratic-Authoritarianism: Studies in South American Politics*. Berkeley: Institute of International Studies University of California.

Piore, M. and Schrank, A. (2008). 'Toward Managed Flexibility: The Revival of Labour Inspection in the Latin World', *International Labour Review*, 147(1), pp. 1–23.

Salazar Vergara, G. and Pinto, J. (1999). *Historia Contemporánea de Chile: Actores, Identidad y Movimiento*. Santiago de Chile: LOM Ediciones.

Schamis, H.E. (1999). 'Distributional Coalitions and the Politics of Economic Reform in Latin America', *World Politics*, 51(2), pp. 236–268.

Schmitter, P.C. (1974). 'Still the Century of Corporatism?' *Review of Politics*, 36(1), pp. 85–121.

Schneider, B.R. (2009). 'Hierarchical Market Economies and Varieties of Capitalism in Latin America', *Journal of Latin American Studies*, 41(3), pp. 553–575.

Sparrow, P., Schuler, R.S. and Jackson, S.E. (1994). 'Convergence or Divergence: Human Resource Practices and Policies for Competitive Advantage Worldwide', *International Journal Of Human Resource Management*, 5(2), pp. 267–299.

Staab, S. and Hil Maher, K. (2006). 'The Dual Discourse About Peruvian Domestic Workers in Santiago de Chile: Class, Race, and a Nationalist Project', *Latin American Politics and Society*, 48(1), pp. 87–116.

US Department of State (2009). *2008 Human Rights Report: Honduras*. Washington, DC: US Department of State; Bureau of Democracy, Human Rights, and Labor.

US Department of State. (2015). *Mexico: Country Report on Human Rights Practices for 2014*. Washington, DC: US Department of State.

Veiga, J.P. and Galhera, K. (2014). Monitoring Precarious and Forced Labour in Brazil: Sweatshops in São Paulo from a Gender Perspective, in Blanpain, R., Wouters, J., Rayp, G., Beke, L. and Marx, A. (eds.) *Bulletin of Comparative Labour Relations*. Den Haag: Kluwer Law International, pp. 7–29.

Zavala, S. (1990). *La Encomiendo Indiana*. Madrid: Imprensa Helénica.

25

THE TRANSFORMATION OF EMPLOYMENT RELATIONS IN CONTEMPORARY CHINA[1]

Chris King-Chi Chan and Yunbing He

Introduction

It has been nearly four decades since the reform and open-door policy was introduced in China in 1978. Although China has remained an authoritarian state politically, its economy and society have experienced dramatic changes over this period. China is now the world's second largest economy in terms of GDP, with a workforce of 774.5 million in 2015 (National Bureau of Statistics of China, 2016). Statistics show remarkable changes in China's pattern of employment. In 1978, China's rural economy was dominant, with 71 per cent of the workforce in the primary sector, and only 17 per cent and 12 per cent in manufacturing and service industries, respectively. In 2000, the year before China joined the World Trade Organization (WTO), half of the workforce had shifted to non-agricultural sectors, with 22 per cent in manufacturing and 27 per cent in service industries. In 2015, service industries accounted for more than 42 per cent of total employment, whilst agriculture and manufacture represented about 28 per cent and 29 per cent, respectively. The contribution of the service industry to GDP (50.5 per cent) also surpassed that of manufacturing in 2015.

Alongside this process of industrialisation, it is important to note the phenomenon of rural-urban migration in past decades and its recent trends. Since the 1990s, millions of peasants have migrated from their hometowns to coastal cities in search of work, and the 'tidal wave of migrant workers' (*Min Gong Chao*) flooding train stations before and after the Spring Festival has become a familiar spectacle in China. This huge array of migrant workers forms a large reserve army in the labour market. In the private sector, the result has been an abundance of cheap labour and a prevalence of despotic management styles and bad working conditions. According to the National Bureau of Statistics, there were 277.5 million peasant migrant workers (*Nongmingong*) in 2015 (China Labour Bulletin, 2016). In general, migrant workers work in the city but hold a rural *Hukou* (household registration certificate). In the area of economic production, they are workers; however, they are not identified as urban citizens and do not have stable urban residences. In recent years, however, the *Hukou* policy has been relaxed. Migrant workers with better skills or qualifications are encouraged to apply for *Hukou* in the cities in which they work, and even without *Hukou*, migrant workers enjoy social rights in the workplace similar to those of their urban counterparts. For example, the Social Insurance Law that came into effect in 2011 granted uniform protection to both urban and migrant workers in five areas (medical, maternity, industrial injury, unemployment and pension insurance).

Forms of ownership in China have also shifted recently in favour of domestic private enterprises. Before 1978, outside of government institutions, all urban workers worked in state-owned enterprises (SOEs) or collectively owned enterprises (COEs). Foreign-direct investment (FDI) was introduced to China in the 1980s. Since the early 1990s, foreign-invested enterprises (FIEs) and joint ventures (JVs) have come to employ millions of migrant workers, especially in coastal cities. Although SOEs remain major players in the economy, the wave of privatisation in preparation for China's entry into the WTO led to millions of SOE workers losing their jobs. From 1990 to 2003, the number of industrial workers employed in SOEs declined from 43.64 million (68.4 per cent) to 13.34 million (36.3 per cent) (Lee, 2007). Meanwhile, private-owned enterprises (POEs), which were discouraged by the state during the early stages of reform, have expanded in recent years. In 2015, of 404 million employees in urban China, 62 million (15 per cent) were employed by SOEs, 130 million (32 per cent) by POEs (private enterprises and share-holding corporations) and 28 million (seven per cent) by FIEs (companies involving foreign capital or capital from Hong Kong, Macau or Taiwan).

While traditionally trade unions and collective bargaining are major domains of research in ER, the scenario in China is more complicated. First, independent trade unions are absent and official trade unions are more like state apparatus (Taylor and Li, 2007). Second, collective bargaining does not function well in the workplace (Clarke, Lee and Li, 2004). In fact, due to the historical divergence with the West, the term 'employment relations' is rarely used in Chinese scholarship. Most of the labour-related curricula in China are attached to the human resource management (HRM) school. But there are also a handful of labour relations experts who see labour and management as 'equal' parties in their analysis. They analyse the 'labour problem' from the perspective of law and state policy (e.g. Chang, 2004). The prominent work on Chinese labour outside China is influenced by two major schools. The first is the institutional analysis tradition in political sciences and IR that puts trade unions at the centre of enquiry (e.g. Chen, 2003; Clarke, Lee and Li, 2004). The second is the ethnographic approach in sociology and anthropology that focuses on the process of control and resistance in the workplace (e.g. Lee, 1998; Pun, 2005).

The rise of migrant workers' wildcat strikes and government's effort to rebalance and re-regulate workplace relations since 2008 (Lee, Brown and Wen, 2016) have created blooming opportunities for labour and employment studies in China. These recent researches are highly multidisciplinary and published in fields such as sociology, political sciences, management, development and China studies as well as labour and IR. Chinese scholars have generally called this group of scholarship labour studies (*laogong yanjiu*) or labour relations (*laodong guanxi*). When the term 'employment relations' is used, it refers to various issues such as wages, grievances and patterns of labour disputes in different types of firms (e.g. Cooke, 2008). Following this approach, in this paper we use the term 'employment relations' flexibly to refer to a wide range of literature concerning Chinese labour and workplace politics.

The next section offers a review of the changing political and economic contexts of ER in China. It is followed by an introduction to management practices in different kinds of enterprise. We then discuss two major issues in Chinese ER in the past two decades: industrial conflicts and trade unionism. In our conclusion, we summarise our main arguments and suggest directions for new research. As will be seen, there is no general form of ER in China. A specific historical context of a 'socialist' market economy has given rise to decentralisation (from central to local) and hybridisation (between different sectors, forms of ownerships and geographies) in labour relations (Lee, Brown and Wen, 2016; Friedman and Kuruvilla, 2015).

Political and economic contexts of employment relations[2]

This section will provide a historical review of the transformation of the political and economic contexts in China and its impact on employment. We show that the political atmosphere within the Chinese Communist Party (CCP), the policies of the central state and global economic conditions have shaped economic development and ER in China.

1949–1978: the socialist economy

The People's Republic of China closed its door to foreign countries and mainly developed domestic state-owned industries until 1978. Under the planned economy of state socialism, China attached great importance to heavy industry in urban areas. Meanwhile, it deliberately divided rural regions from urban regions. Peasants in rural areas were required to provide food for the entire population, whilst urban residents produced industrial goods in SOEs or COEs. The *Hukou* system was introduced in 1958 to control the inflow of migrants from rural areas to the cities. Under this system, migration was not possible without permission from the government. This policy stabilised the social order and achieved full employment in urban China. Factories adopted a *danwei* (work-unit) system. The *danwei* distributed almost all necessities required for the workers' daily lives (Perry, 1997), such as meals, clothing, housing, education and child care. The wage level was fixed according to the rank of the worker in the factory. Being a worker meant that one had an 'iron rice-bowl' (*tie fan wan*) (Kuruvilla, Lee and Gallagher, 2011). Although the wages were generally low, workers enjoyed many benefits, including planned housing allocation.

As in many other state socialist countries, the CCP directly led and established trade unions and party branches in each factory. All workers in SOEs and COEs in this period were trade union members. All trade unions had to be affiliated with the All-China Federation of Trade Unions (ACFTU), the only legal trade union centre in the country (Chen, 2003; Clarke, 2005). The ACFTU, according to its constitution, was under the leadership of the CCP. Workers were thus united in their *danwei* to develop their interests. A factory was also a community. After work, workers learned from and socialised with each other to build personal social networks.

1979–2000: global factories

In 1979, the economic reform was mainly carried out in rural areas. A market-oriented, household-based production contract system was introduced to replace the communes and production brigades. The export-oriented urban economic reform was firstly limited to four Special Economic Zones (SEZs). Two of these four SEZs, Shenzhen and Zhuhai, are in the Pearl River Delta (PRD) of Guangdong Province. Urban economic reform was not formally launched until 1984. Deng Xiaoping paid his first visit to the SEZs in January 1984 and highly praised the model of Shenzhen. In 1992, Deng again visited the southern SEZs and called for an acceleration of the reform process. A series of new policies was then put forward, as can be seen through the privatisation of small-sized SOEs, institutionalisation of the labour arbitration system in 1993 and announcement of the Labour Law in 1994.

The privatisation of SOEs resulted in millions of workers being laid off (Cooke, 2005; Lee, 2007). From 1996 to 2001, 26 million jobs were lost, equal to 40.5 per cent of manufacturing jobs (Jiang, 2004). In the late 1990s, state workers staged significant protests over the state's initiative to privatise SOEs or demanded pensions and proper compensation for lay-offs. However, as SOE workers failed to challenge the wave of privatisation and their numbers have declined, no such workplace conflicts have occurred in SOEs since the early 2000s. In contrast, strikes and other forms of protest have emerged amongst migrant workers, especially in the PRD.

The open-door policies also led to a rapid increase in FDI in China, which increased from US$4.7 billion in 1991 to US$11.3 billion in 1992 and US$26.0 billion in 1993 (National Bureau of Statistics of China, various years). China was well established as a 'global factory', with the PRD as its powerhouse. Major ethnographic research conducted in Hong Kong invested factories in the PRD (Lee, 1998; Pun, 2005) found that localism and sexism were used by management to maintain class domination and despotism, whilst women workers also used the resources of localism and gender to construct their identity as 'maiden workers' *(Dagongmei)*. Most FIEs did not have a trade union. Even when trade unions were established, they were 'paper unions' created merely to satisfy the requirements of the higher-level trade union. Workers had little knowledge about the existence of enterprise trade unions, and the unions were inactive.

2001–2011: harmonious labour relations?

Chinese ER have experienced further change in the new millennium. Politically, a series of socio-economic reforms was introduced in the name of building a 'harmonious society' after President Hu Jintao and Premier Wen Jiabao took office in 2002 (Hui and Chan, 2012). The CCP Central Committee and the State Council issued the 'No. 1 Document' entitled *'Opinions on Policies for Facilitating the Increase of Farmers' Income'* at the beginning of 2004. Social problems related to farmers, rural villages and agriculture (what are commonly called *san nong*) have since become of greater concern to the party-state. The 'No. 1 Document' stated that peasant workers had replaced state workers as the prime concern of the state's labour and welfare policies *(Renmin Wang,* 2003). Economically, the growth rate of FDI inflow increased from 0.94 per cent in 2000 to 14.9 per cent in 2001 and 12.4 per cent in 2002 (National Bureau of Statistics of China). Since 2003, China has surpassed the United States as the country with the greatest FDI inflow in the world. China's GDP also shocked the world, with an average annual growth rate of 10.5 per cent from 2001 to 2011 (National Bureau of Statistics of China, 2012).

The dramatic changes in the urban (rapid growth driven by export-oriented manufacturing) and rural economies (improvement in socio-economic conditions due to the new policy direction of the state) had given rise since 2003 to a new phenomenon – a shortage of labour (*mingonghuang*) – in stark contrast to the labour surplus (*mingongchao*) of the early 1990s. Within this context, rising waves of strikes have taken place in the PRD since 2004 (Chan, 2010; Chan and Hui, 2012). This unrest forced the government to increase the minimum wage and introduce three new labour laws. The Employment Promotion Law was intended to provide guidelines to local government at the county level to monitor employment agencies and facilitate the occupational and skill-based training of workers. The Labour Dispute Mediation and Arbitration Law simplified the legal procedure for mediation and arbitration and reduced the economic and time costs of workers. The Labour Contract Law has been regarded as the most important of the three. The law was intended to stabilise and regulate ER by making written contracts a legal obligation for employers. Workers were entitled to double pay if their employers did not sign a contract with them. After the workers completed two consecutive contracts or were employed for 10 continuous years, the employer was required to give them a permanent contract. Employers had to pay severance of one month's wages for each year of service if they wanted to dismiss a worker.

The global economic crisis in 2008 had a major effect on the Chinese economy. China's total exports in 2009 decreased by 16 per cent (National Bureau of Statistics of China, 2010).

Many factories in South China faced closure or bankruptcy, but the Chinese economy recovered quickly due to the government's huge investment in infrastructure and social spending. In 2010, the GDP growth rate returned to double digits (10.3 per cent) (*Global Times*, 2011). Concomitant with the economic revival was the re-emergence of labour shortages (*Chengdu Commercial Daily*, 2010). It was reported that a total of two million workers were needed in the PRD in early 2010. Against this background, a more significant wave of strikes led by Honda workers attracted global attention in June 2010 (Chan and Hui, 2012). These strikes gave impetus to the process of trade union reform, and the ACFTU began to promote a policy of wage bargaining and trade union direct election (Chan and Hui, 2014).

Since 2012: the economic slowdown

There was another turning point for ER in China in 2012 as President Xi Jinping took power. Unlike Hu-Wen's regime, which emphasised a harmonious society and adopted reformist social and labour policies, Xi's government has adopted a hard-line policy to pacify labour activism in the workplace and society. The growth of the Chinese economy has also slowed since 2012, with many factory closures and relocations. The GDP growth rate decreased from 10.1 per cent in 2011 to 8.1 per cent in 2012 and 6.7 per cent in 2016.

Most of these factories announced their relocation plans with minimal or no compensation to workers. In response, workers increasingly took collective action to defend their rights and interests. During this period, pension insurance became one of the main demands of migrant workers in strikes. This demand was encouraged by the Social Insurance Law, effective since 2011, and was also urgent because many migrant workers had reached retirement age or were nearing it. Some sought help from labour NGOs. One of the most successful cases was the Lide shoe factory case in Guangzhou in August 2014. Workers finally received compensation and social insurance before the factory's relocation with the help of the Panyu Migrant Workers Service Center (a labour NGO with much experience in helping workers since 1990s) (China Labor Bulletin, 2015). The strike at the Yueyuan shoe factory in Dongguan in April 2014 was the most influential strike concerning pension issues. More than 40,000 workers went on strike for more than 10 days, which gained much global attention. The strike ended with the company agreeing to pay the social insurance owed to the workers.

In the face of the economic slowdown, the state has lowered the standard of labour rights protection. For instance, Guangdong province announced in February 2017 that to lower operation costs of enterprises, the minimum wage now would be updated every three years rather than every two years (*Caixin Wang*, 2017). Thus, the minimum wage in 2017 would remain at the 2015 level. Labour protests became more and more common, with resulting police intervention and strikes that affected public order or urban traffic could be directly shut down. Workers' leaders have also risked arrest. One of the leaders of a strike in Shenzhen in 2013 was detained for 371 days. In addition to workers, labour NGOs have also been targeted by the government. At the end of 2015, the police arrested a dozen NGO leaders in Guangzhou and Foshan, and four have been charged with crimes.

During this period, the dramatic growth of the third sector in China also resulted in surging labour in the service industries. Workers' collective action in the service industries has accounted for 21 per cent of all collective action cases, surpassing the manufacturing industries for the first time in the third quarter of 2016, according to a report by the China Labour Bulletin (2016). In the following section, we will review how management practices in different forms of enterprises have changed in response to the political and economic context.

Changing management practices

Studies have shown that firms' management models are highly diverse (Child and Warner, 2003; Friedman and Kuruvilla, 2015). Here we will describe the changes in management practices in three types of firms: SOEs, JVs/MNCs and POEs/FIEs.

SOEs

Changes in management strategies and practices in SOEs are much slower than those in other types of enterprises, as a result of historical legacy, organisational inertia and continued government interference (Hassard et al., 2006). At the early stage of reform, the government experimented with a labour contract system and performance-related bonuses and awards to increase workers' motivation and productivity. The labour contract system was extended nationwide after a pilot experiment in the late 1980s. All new hires are required to sign a contract, and renewal is based on mutual agreement between employers and employees (Chan, Ngok and Phillips, 2008; Warner, 1996). A performance-based remuneration system was put into practice in almost all SOEs and other public sector organisations after restructuring in the 1990s (Warner, 1996). By then, few SOEs offered the former 'cradle to grave' social protection scheme, which was replaced by nationalised social insurance. Unemployment insurance was introduced in the late 1980s to protect workers as the 'iron rice-bowl' was phased out (Hassard, et al., 2006; Warner, 1996).

Despite the introduction of contract labour, however, Goodall and Warner (1997) found that in the late 1990s there was still an institutional and organisational continuity in 'iron rice-bowl' practices in both SOEs and JVs, mostly for employees with *bianzhi* (budgeted posts). This practice can still be found in SOEs nowadays, as formal workers cannot be easily removed from their *danwei* (work unit) unless they make serious mistakes. A CCP branch exists in all SOEs.[3] Nonetheless, there has also been a trend toward precarious labour in SOEs, which is to say the massive use of dispatch workers or agency labour. This prevailing trend mainly results from efforts to reduce social insurance and other labour costs, avoiding open-ended employment contracts and severance pay and gaining enhanced flexibility (Friedman and Kuruvilla, 2015). The use of dispatch workers is especially prevalent in SOEs in the petroleum, chemical, telecommunication, banking, airway and railway industries. Wang found that in some central state enterprises dispatch workers can comprise up to two thirds of the workforce (Wang, 2012). There is a large gap in working conditions and managerial control between dispatch workers and formal workers with *bianzhi*. In a study of the automobile industry, Zhang (2015) claimed this dualism was a 'lean-and-dual regime' that combines 'hegemonic' and 'despotic' elements in the labour regime. In many SOEs nowadays, the workforce is a mix of permanent workers, contract workers and dispatch (temporary) workers.

JVs and MNCs

For JVs and MNCs,[4] the central questions in management studies usually concern the influence of the foreign parent countries upon these companies. Scholars have argued that the sophisticated human resource (HR) systems of so-called blue-chip MNCs such as Nokia and Motorola were imported from Western practices and adapted to suit the Chinese context (Cooke, 2004). Cooke's case study of a large, wholly foreign-owned toy company in China shows that rather than following the earlier despotic Taylorist way of management or the imported blue-chip MNC pattern, the management practices of enterprises in China may come from several different sources: Western HR practical strategies from the parent country, good practices from SOEs and also perhaps some bad practices of private companies (ibid.). Goodall and Warner classified the HRM strategies of JVs into four types based on whether they are more inclined to traditional 'iron rice-bowl' HR practices or imported Western practices (Goodall and Warner, 1997).

Björkman and Lu (1999) also examine barriers or local constraints on exporting Western management practices to China, by exploring the impact of Chinese traditional culture on management in modern Chinese enterprises. To overcome difficulties and better suit the local environment, some MNCs use Western expatriate managers, who institute a relatively 'soft' labour regime with formalised management strategies and try to decentralise authority to middle management (Chan, 1998).

Other research has shown that Western HRM knowledge and practices greatly affect management practice in China. Regardless of the dominance of the Taylorist way of production in Chinese enterprises, the results of a questionnaire survey conducted by Yusuf, Gunasekaran and Dan (2007) indicate that there has been extensive adoption of total quality management (TQM) from MNCs. Cunningham's (2010) research on small and medium-sized enterprises (SMEs) in China also demonstrates a relative convergence with Western HRM practice, although strongly influenced by unique Chinese characteristics. He anticipates that HRM models that combine Eastern and Western characteristics are likely to emerge in the future (ibid.).

POEs and FIEs[5]

Management in POEs and FIEs favour a 'Taylorist' style, requiring a mass labour force for assembly-line production in the early period of economic reforms (Cooke, 2004). Back in the 1980s and 1990s, the unfinished process of legalisation, along with welcoming attitudes to foreign investment and aspiration toward economic development, gave birth to many small and medium-sized FIEs in South China. These are typically Hong Kong- or Taiwanese-owned labour-intensive factories that produce clothes, toys, shoes and so on, with women comprising the majority of workers. Because few legal controls are in place, the management style of these labour-intensive enterprises is often despotic and coercive (Chan, 2001; Lee, 1995; Pun, 2005). The majority of migrant workers in South China who work for FIEs are depicted as miserable and 'under assault' in the 'sweatshops' by Chan (2001), and Pun (2005) has argued that women workers suffer under triple oppressions – political, economic and socio-cultural.

Schlevogt (2001) has constructed a model of 'web-based Chinese management' to analyse management practices in POEs. This model centres on structural and contextual aspects of organisations, which can be further divided into four dimensions: centralisation and formalisation at the structural level and culture and size at the contextual level. His empirical study of more than 120 SOEs and POEs in Shanghai and Beijing shows a comparatively low degree of formalisation and greater centralised inclination in POEs than in SOEs; traditional culture, which emphasises respect for seniority and family loyalty, plays an important role in private companies and influences smaller POEs. This finding is backed up by Child and Warner (2003), who found that due to the influence of paternalistic culture, centrality is an obvious feature of most small and medium-sized private enterprises. Decision-making in most cases is personal and informal. For some bigger POEs, decisions may be made collectively by a more formal body or high-rank managers. Rank-and-file workers do not have the right to participate in decision-making in any case, even in decisions that concern their own welfare (ibid.).

Chinese cultural and institutional influence

Researchers have suggested that a management style with 'Chinese characteristics', influenced by Chinese culture and institutions, has emerged in China (Child and Warner, 2003; Cooke, 2004; Redding, 2002). According to Child and Warner (2003), culture mainly affects individual attitudes and behaviour, including interpersonal behaviour; institutions, however, have direct influence on the formal structures and rules. Child and Warner also suggest that cultural and institutional factors are interrelated. For instance, a hierarchical and collective orientation can be seen as the most distinctive feature of the historical Chinese institutional regime, which is based on the relational norms expounded by Confucius and traditional legal codes. Interpersonal communications and relationships in SOEs, and even the corporate cultures of some POEs and JVs, are also deeply influenced by the Chinese history of bureaucratic structure and culture.

Due to a long history of feudalism, a strong institutional influence still exists, and management in Chinese enterprises is thus characterised by top-down leadership and authority, with an emphasis on conformity, collectivism and dependence on the organisation (Child and Warner, 2003). In some small and medium-sized POEs, management is quite centred on the owner.

In terms of culture, Confucianism is widely acknowledged to have had a huge effect on management practices in China. For example, an emphasis on *guanxi* (trust and loyalty) is regarded as a Confucian HR practice (Chen, 2008). According to Rarick, the common characteristics of managerial practices in China – "centralised control, collectivism, harmony, authoritarian and paternalistic leadership, flexible strategies, family-staffed businesses, and strong organisational networks and business connections" – are all embedded in the wisdom and ideas of China's ancient philosophers, including Kongzi, Laozi, Sunzi and Mozi (Rarick, 2009).

Changes and trends

In the past decade, new developments have occurred in Chinese employment relations. For example, labour shortages, higher labour costs, frequent labour conflicts and newly enacted labour regulations have caused changes in enterprises' management strategies (Friedman and Kuruvilla, 2015). The previously mentioned strategy of using dispatch workers due to high labour prices has been adopted not only in SOEs, but also some large FIEs such as automobile factories (Zhang, 2015). The use of student and intern labour, which is not under the protection of the ER regulations such as the Labour Law and Labour Contract Law, has also become significant in many labour-intensive enterprises (Smith and Chan, 2015). Another approach has been to use a new kind of strategy – 'humanised management' – to replace the old despotic management style; according to Choi and Peng, it involves caring for the humanity of employees, advocating people-oriented managerial strategies and stressing the paternalistic nature of the relationship between employers and employees (Choi and Peng, 2015). However, the new management strategy has not changed the power relations in the workplace, and high profits are the necessary condition for successful implementation of this kind of paternalistic management, which may be hard to realise for enterprises at the bottom of the supply chain (ibid.).

Escalating industrial conflicts

Protests in SOEs

The most dramatic consequence of the restructuring of SOEs was a rise in the unemployment rate, which hit its peak in the history of PR China in the late 1990s (Lee, 2002). According to official statistics, the number of laid-off state workers increased rapidly, from three million in 1993 to 17.24 million in 1998 (Cai, 2002). During the 1990s, state workers (including those who had been laid off) engaged in thousands of protests.

Scholars have found a number of reasons or grievances that led to these protests. Chen (2000) has suggested that they were the result of 'subsistence crises'. The disorganised production development in China led to a despotic management style, which involves exploitation and the sacrifice of workers' material interests (Lee, 2002). The enterprise restructuring policy created armies of laid-off workers and many cases of 'illegal dismissal' and delayed or decreased pension payment (Hurst and O'Brien, 2002). Managerial corruption is usually an auxiliary grievance in SOE workers' strikes (Chen, 2000). In addition, a certain nostalgia for the days of state socialism, when workers were well cared for, also accounts for engagement in protests (Hurst and O'Brien, 2002). Chen (2000) describes the SOE protests as 'moral economy' protests, 'defensive' in nature and informed by the old ideology or morality rather than the rhetoric of rights under the new market economic system.

Addressing the challenge of state workers' protests, compensatory policies were introduced by the government. 'Re-employment' projects and social welfare programmes were initiated by the central government to help workers (Solinger, 2002). By the beginning of the new millennium, the wave of state workers' protests had waned, and scholarly attention gradually turned to the wildcat strikes of migrant workers in South China's FIEs.

Strikes in FIEs

As Hui (2017) reviews, researchers have distinguished between rights-based and interest-based protests of migrant workers in China (Chan, 2010; Chen and Tang, 2013). Rights-based strikes refer to those that demand employers fulfil workers' legal rights, while interest-based strikes are those where workers fight for employment conditions beyond the legal minimum. Similarly, researchers also categorise defensive and offensive strikes (Chan, 2014; Elfstrom and Kuruvilla, 2014). For defensive strikes, workers request employers to uphold the standards guaranteed by the legal system; for offensive strikes, workers proactively ask for benefits beyond the current legal protection. Using this analytical framework to examine the development of migrant workers' strike, scholars generally agree that labour protests in China have shifted from rights-based to interest-based (Butollo and ten Brink, 2012; Chan, 2010; Clarke and Pringle, 2009) and from defensive to offensive in the past two decades (Chan, 2014; Elfstrom and Kuruvilla, 2014).

In early 1990s, the wildcat strikes of migrant workers were claimed to be unorganised, spontaneous and cellular (Chen and Tang, 2013; Friedman and Lee, 2010; Lee, 1998, 2007). Since the Labour Law was introduced in 1994, many labour disputes had been absorbed into the legal channel. Migrant workers' resistance was usually against statutory violations committed by employers and aimed to gain legal rights protection covering for example unpaid wages, compensation for industrial injuries and overtime payments. The ideology of legalism strongly influenced migrant worker actions, which was part of the "rightful" popular protests in the country (Lee, 2007). In short, migrant workers have increasingly used labour laws as weapons to defend their interests and rights, which has led researchers to contend that a higher level of legal rights consciousness has developed among workers (Gallagher, 2006; Lee, 2007; Wong, 2011). However, some other scholars have argued that labour laws have in fact constrained migrant workers' ability to demand more than the legal minimum (Chan and Siu, 2012).

Chan's (2010) study on migrant workers' strikes in the PRD during 2004 and 2007 found that the pattern of protests shifted from demanding that employers follow labour laws concerning, for example, the minimum wage and overtime payment, to asking for conditions beyond legal standards, such as fair wages above the legal minimum rate and better working environments. Corresponding to this trend, it is argued a new working class is making itself in China while the power of the old working class (i.e. state workers) has been dismantled during the economic restructuring (Chan, 2010), and that the second generation of migrant workers is more vocal and motivated to take collective action to advance their interests compared with the older generation (Pun and Lu, 2010). Pun and Smith introduce the concept of "dormitory labour regimes" and suggest that worker dormitories have served as a platform for workers' solidarity building (Pun and Smith, 2007).

In 2010, a wave of strikes took place in China led by 1,800 workers in a Honda factory in Guangdong. Strikers at Honda demanded a monthly pay rise of 800 yuan, which was on top of the minimum wage, and the democratic reform of the workplace trade union. The strike attracted global attention and was regarded as one of the important examples of the interests-based strikes (Butollo and ten Brink, 2012; Chan and Hui, 2012; Chen and Tang, 2013). Therefore, scholars further contend that worker resistance is no longer restricted to the legal sphere; that legal actions are just one of the potential tools used by workers to advance their interests and rights; and both legal and non-legal means are deployed in parallel by the migrant workers during their protests (Chan, 2010; Leung and Pun, 2009).

The role of trade unions

The legacy of socialist trade unionism

The ACFTU is the only legitimate organisation representing Chinese workers. The dilemma of ACFTU has been conceptualised by Chen as a 'dualism identity': it sees itself not only as a labour organisation that represents workers' interests, but also a state instrument under the leadership of the Party (Chen, 2003). When there is no conflict between these double identities, the trade unions play their normal functions, such as organising recreational activities and initiating propaganda campaigns about good workers. But when tensions break out between the two identities, the ACFTU often finds itself in a dilemma. For example, during strikes, if workers' demands are rights-based, a trade union would usually support the workers and lead them to a judicial process; if these are interest-based labour strikes, the process usually involves a quadripartite interaction with the trade union functioning in a conciliation and mediation role (Chen, 2010). Taylor and Li (2007) argue that ACFTU is not a legitimate trade union because of its conflicted identity and its lack of autonomy or an electoral system for union leaders. They reject the possibility that Chinese trade unions can completely represent workers' interests, given the obvious absence of workers' involvement in the trade union organisation.

Nonetheless, workplace trade union elections have taken place in China from time to time. One recent example was after the Honda strike, when the Guangdong Provincial Federation of Trade Unions (GDFTU) initiated a pilot scheme for the 'democratic election' of workplace trade union leaders; in 2012, this project was also extended to Shenzhen (Hui and Chan, 2015). This is the first step towards a more democratic workplace trade union, even though there are still some obvious limitations. The election is only 'democratic' in a limited sense, as higher-level unions hold the legal power to influence the candidateship and appointment of trade union committee members. In addition, the workers' strike was the impetus of the direct union elections; because the workers' extra-union associational power is not sustained after the strike, trade union elections are easily transformed into indirect, non-democratic or quasi-democratic form by the state-capital alliance (ibid.). Scholars generally believe that 'direct election' would not lead to truly independent and democratic trade unions in China, without significant political changes in their relationship with the party-state (Chan and Hui, 2012; Pringle, 2011).

Some scholars have paid attention to local variations in the organisational patterns of trade unions. Liu (2010), based on intensive research between 2006 and 2008, identified different regional and industry-based patterns of union organisation and argued that the trade union in China is no longer a monolithic top-down organisation. Pringle (2011) articulated a similar idea, finding that some local trade unions better represent and protect workers' interests than others. He was also optimistic about the future of trade union reform, arguing that labour insurgency would put pressure on the ACFTU to improve its effectiveness in representing workers' interests. Chan et al. (2016) studied 12 FIEs in the PRD and found that the pressures from the ACFTU and the party-state were the most important factors that forced employers to accept the establishment of a trade union in their enterprise. Instead of suppression, employers used co-optation strategy to pre-empt confrontation with the union. However, Chan et al. also found that the co-opted unions have played positive welfare and communication roles in the workplace by organising social events and mediating in labour disputes, and these functions were welcomed by both employers and workers (ibid).

All these empirical researches support the idea that even though the Chinese economy has been highly integrated into global capitalism, the ACFTU and its subordinated organisations still function in the way of typical 'socialist' trade unionism. The union's representation role varies from case to case, but in general it is still under the influence of the management and the coordination of the party-state.

Collective bargaining

In 1994, in conjunction with the enactment of the Labour Law, the first Collective Contract Regulations came into effect, to regulate acts of collective consultation and the signing of collective contracts. By 2008, 69 per cent of trade union members were covered by collective contracts (Lee and Liu, 2011). The 2007 Labour Contract Law also includes six articles about collective contracts, setting out the right to ratify collective bargaining and the content and condition of collective bargaining (Kuruvilla and Liu, 2016). In 2011, the state instructed the trade union to strengthen its capability and its leading role in workplace collective bargaining (Ministry of Human Resources and Social Security, 2011). Kuruvilla and Zhang (2016) suggested that the government tried to direct collective bargaining into a legalistic and institutionalised channel to reduce industrial conflicts and rebalance the economy, although its efforts were not successful.

Rather than Western collective bargaining, the term 'collective consultation' is used in China. Usually the practice of collective consultation is just a formality, without significant bargaining between the trade union and company (Chan and Hui, 2014). Kuruvilla and Zhang have also found that the most frequent type of collective bargaining in China is 'template bargaining', in which the local trade union offers the enterprises a template collective contract to follow, without any interaction or collective bargaining involving the workers (Kuruvilla and Zhang, 2016; Kuruvilla and Liu, 2016). Clarke, Lee and Li (2004), in their examination of the development of a collective contract system in China, argue that this system is actually a means to secure 'harmonious labour relations' within the framework of workers' democratic participation in management, and also a continued integration of the trade union into management in the workplace. The collective contract system will become a real barrier to the development of a collective bargaining and IR system in China. However, Lee and Liu, based on quantitative analysis of the existing literature, argue that the organisational efforts of the ACFTU brought real changes to some extent. They contend that the workers' congresses and collective consultation are not only a formalistic and bureaucratic exercise but offer a channel for the collective voice of workers in the workplace (Lee and Liu, 2011).

As more radical collective actions have begun to take place in recent years, collective bargaining has gradually become an effective way for workers to advocate for their rights during strikes. Management was forced to bargain with representatives of the strikers, but the bargaining was usually just a one-off and no regular mechanism was established after the strikes. After 2010, to reduce the occurrence of strikes and in response to instruction by the party-state and higher-level trade union, local ACFTU branches actively intervened in some factories after strikes to facilitate the formation of a regular wage-bargaining mechanism, which has been conceptualised as 'party-state-led bargaining' by Chan and Hui (2014). Chan and Hui believe that 'worker-led bargaining' still has some way to go without rights to strike and organise in China. Chang and Brown (2013) also argue that the individual rights-based legal framework has hastened the development of collective labour relations and they call for legal reforms to strengthen workers' collective rights.

Despite the above mentioned limitations, researchers have found a positive impact of collective bargaining for workers. While enterprise-level collective bargaining takes place mostly in FIEs in South China, geographically based sectoral bargaining has also been encouraged by local governments for small and medium-sized POEs in East China. Lee, Brown and Wen's (2016) research on collective bargaining at both enterprise and sectoral levels found that the emerging collective bargaining practice had substantial impact on workers' wage and working conditions. New research on the automobile industry in Guangzhou has also found that worker-led collective bargaining does occur in some factories and successfully boosts workers' wages (Deng, 2017), although the bargaining mechanism has been only implemented in a small number of factories, and there is no sign that it will be extended to other regions or industries.

Conclusions

This chapter has reviewed the development of management, industrial conflicts and trade unionism in China since the reform, within a changing political and economic context. The Chinese government's efforts to integrate the country into the global economy since 1978 and its strategies to minimise the impact of the global recession since 2008 have defined the development of employment to a large extent. However, apart from structural and institutional factors, workers' agency is also an important factor in the analysis of these historical changes. Industrial conflict has been one of the major themes in Chinese employment studies in the past decade (Chan, 2010; Friedman, 2014; Zhang, 2015).

In this chapter, we have shown that the Chinese tradition and socialist legacy have continued to shape ER in China, as reflected in the innate authoritarian nature of Chinese ER. The continual influence of traditional 'iron rice-bowl' HR practices, an emphasis on the authority of superiors, the hierarchical corporate culture and the existence of Party committees in enterprises are all features of a hybrid socialist market regime. More importantly, the subordination of the ACFTU under the CCP and the 'dualism identity' of the workplace trade union have remained unchanged (Lee, Brown and Wen, 2016).

Nevertheless, Chinese employment relationships are not homogenous. There are many variations of management practices depending on the region, industry and form of ownership. Scholars have suggested that the ACFTU is not a monolithic organisation (Liu, 2010). Driven both by bottom-up pressure from workers and top-down policy from the party-state, the trade union has made efforts to reform itself, by introducing 'direct election' and collective bargaining, especially in the PRD and after 2010 (Chan and Hui, 2012, 2014; Chang and Brown, 2013). However, the impact and consequence of the reform remain controversial. In addition to traditional Chinese culture and the legacy of state socialism, Western HRM knowledge and practices have also deeply influenced Chinese management practice, especially in MNCs and JVs. All of these contribute to the decentralisation and hybridisation of ER (Lee, Brown and Wen, 2016; Friedman and Kuruvilla, 2015).

Industrial conflicts have also intensified in the past two decades. Whilst state workers' protests over industrial restructuring became less important in the early 2000s, their role was replaced by the migrant workers in FIEs. Since the late 2000s, migrant workers' strikes have shifted from being rights-based to being interests-based (Chan, 2010; Chang and Brown, 2013; Chen and Tang, 2013). Encouraged by the Social Insurance Law that came into effect in 2011, migrant workers have also raised the demand for pension protection since 2012 and created another form of conflict. The government has increasingly intervened in workplace relations. Although the new labour laws and regulations have been introduced to protect the interests of workers, strike leaders and independent labour organising by NGOs have been under more and more political pressure. This new development has gone beyond the conventional image of Chinese labour and ER – coercive management and docile woman workers in the production lines of the FIEs in South China – which were well studied in factory-based ethnography and documentary research conducted by labour sociologists in the 1990s (Chan, 2001; Lee, 1998; Pun, 2005).

Although migrant workers remain a major source of labour in urban China, *Hukou* has lost its importance in defining labour rights in the workplace. Statistics and observation show that a pattern of ER based in the service industry and dominated by domestic private businesses has gradually emerged. However, little empirical research has been conducted on POEs and the service sector. More empirical research in these areas in the future would be valuable.

Notes

1 The authors would like to thank the Research Grants Council (RGC) of Hong Kong (project no. CityU 140313; 11616115) and the City University of Hong Kong for financial support for their research.
2 This section has been partially drawn from several published works, such as Wang and Chan (2015); Chan (2010); and Hui and Chan (2012).
3 The new development is that other forms of enterprises, including POEs and FIEs, are also requested to establish a CCP branch (Chan et al., 2016).
4 JVs are collaborative enterprises between Chinese SOEs and foreign companies; MNCs are wholly foreign-owned companies. Although the direct investment of Western-based MNCs is also part of FIEs, their management style is somewhat different from supplier factories owned by Hong Kong, Taiwan, South Korean and other East Asian investors.
5 Research on management practice in POEs is rare. But according to our research experience the labour practice of POEs, usually SMEs, is similar to that of lower-end FIEs owned by East Asian businesses.

References

Björkman, I. and Lu, Y. (1999). 'The Management of Human Resources in Chinese-Western Joint Ventures', *Journal of World Business*, 34(3), pp. 306–324.

Butollo, F. and ten Brink, T. (2012). 'Challenging the Atomization of Discontent', *Critical Asian Studies in Comparative International Development*, 44(3), pp. 419–440.

Cai, Y. (2002). 'The Resistance of Chinese Laid-Off Workers in the Reform Period', *China Quarterly*, 170, pp. 327–344.

Caixin Wang. (2017). The minimum wage in Guangdong transformed to adjustment in every three years. [Guangdong zuidi gongzi biaozhun gaiwei "sannian yitiao"]. (Online). 4 March. Available at: http://china.caixin.com/2017-03-04/101062231.html.

Chan, A. (2001). *China's Workers Under Assault: The Exploitation and Abuse in a Globalizing Economy.* Armonk: M.E. Sharpe.

Chan, A. (1998). Labor Relations in Foreign-funded Ventures, Chinese Trade Unions, and the Prospects for Collective Bargaining, in O'Leary, G. (ed.) *Adjusting to Capitalism: Chinese Workers and the State.* Armonk: M.E. Sharpe, pp. 122–149.

Chan, A. and Siu. K. (2012). Chinese Migrant Workers: Factors Constraining the Emergence of Class Consciousness, in Carrillo, B. and Goodman, D.S.G. (eds.) *China's Peasants and Workers: Changing Class Identities.* Cheltenham: Edward Elgar.

Chan, A.W., Snape, E., Luo, M.S. and Zhai, Y.J. (2016). 'The Developing Role of Unions in China's Foreign-Invested Enterprises', *British Journal of Industrial Relations*, 55(3), pp. 602–625.

Chan, C.K.C. (2010). *The Challenge of Labour in China: Strike and the Changing Labour Regimes in Global Factories.* Routledge: New York.

Chan, C.K.C. (2014). 'Constrained Labour Agency and the Changing Regulatory Regime in China', *Development and Change*, 45(4), pp. 685–709.

Chan, C.K.C. and Hui, E.S.I. (2012). 'The Dynamics and Dilemma of Workplace Trade Union Reform in China: The Case of Honda Workers' Strike', *Journal of Industrial Relations*, 54(4), pp. 653–668.

Chan, C.K.C. and Hui, E.S.I. (2014). 'The Development of Collective Bargaining in China: From 'Collective Bargaining by Riot' to 'Party State-Led Wage Bargaining', *The China Quarterly*, 217, pp. 221–242.

Chan, K.W., Ngok, K.L. and Phillips, D. (2008). *Social Policy in China: Development and Well Being.* Bristol: The Policy Press.

Chang, K. (2004) *Lao Quan Lun: Dangdai Zhongguo Laodong Guanxi De Falu Tiaozheng Yanjiu* [The Theory of Workers' Rights: Research on the Legal Regulation of Labour Relations in Contemporary China]. Beijing: China Labour and Social Protection Press.

Chang, K. and Brown, W. (2013). 'The Transformation from Individual to Collective Labour Relations in China', *Industrial Relations Journal*, 44(2), pp. 102–121.

Chen, F. (2000). 'Subsistence Crises, Managerial Corruption and Labour Protests in China', *The China Journal*, 44, pp. 41–63.

Chen, F. (2003). 'Between the State and Labour: the Conflict of Chinese Trade Unions' Double Identity in Market Reform', *China Quarterly*, 178(Dec.), pp. 1006–1028.

Chen, F. (2010). 'Trade Unions and the Quadripartite Interactions in Strike Settlement in China', *The China Quarterly*, 201, pp. 104–124.

Chen, F. and Tang, M.X. (2013). 'Labor Conflicts in China: Typologies and Their Implications', *Asian Survey*, 53(3), pp. 559–583.

Chen, S.J. (2008). The Adoption of HR Strategies in a Confucian Context, in Lawler, J.J. and Hundley, G. (eds.) *The Global Diffusion of Human Resource Practices: Institutional and Cultural Limits.* Bingley: JAI Press, pp. 145–169.

Chengdu Commercial Daily (2010). Labour shortage in the Pearl River Delta is getting worse, 2 million workers are needed (zhusanjiao mingonghuang jiaju, quekou chao 200 wan). (Online). 22 February. Accessed 24 January 2018. Available at: http://news.163.com/10/0222/03/603J00JB000120GR.html.

Child, J. and Warner, M. (2003). Culture and Management in China, in Warner, M. (ed.) *Culture and Management in Asia.* London: Routledge Curzon, pp. 24– 47.

China Labor Bulletin (2015). The Lide shoe factory workers' campaign for relocation compensation. (Online). Available at: www.clb.org.hk/en/content/trying-hit-moving-target-lide-shoe-factory-workers%C3%A2%E2%82%AC%E2%84%A2-campaign-relocation-compensation.

China Labour Bulletin (2016). As China's economy shifts to services in Q3, so too does labour unrest. (Online). Available at: www.clb.org.hk/content/china%E2%80%99s-economy-shifts-services-q3-so-too-does-labour-unrest.

China Labour Bulletin (2016). Migrant workers and their children. [Online]. Available at: www.clb.org.hk/content/migrant-workers-and-their-children.

Choi, S.Y. and Peng, Y. (2015). 'Humanized Management? Capital and Migrant Labour in a Time of Labour Shortage in South China', *Human Relations*, 68(2), pp. 287–304.

Clarke, S. (2005). 'Post-Socialist Trade Unions: China and Russia', *Industrial Relations Journal*, 36(1), pp. 2–18.

Clarke, S., Lee, C.H. and Li, Q. (2004). 'Collective Consultation and Industrial Relations in China', *British Journal of Industrial Relations*, 42(2), pp. 235–254.

Clarke, S. and Pringle, T. (2009). 'Can Party-Led Trade Unions Represent Their Members?' *Post-Communist Economies*, 21(1), pp. 85–101.

Cooke, F.L. (2004). 'Foreign Firms in China: Modeling HRM in a Toy-Manufacturing Corporation', *Human Resource Management Journal*, 14(3), pp. 31–52.

Cooke, F.L. (2005). *HRM, Work and Employment in China*. London: Routledge.

Cooke, F.L. (2008). 'The Changing Dynamics of Employment Relations in China: An Evaluation of the Rising Level of Labour Disputes', *Journal of Industrial Relations*, 55(1), pp. 111–138.

Cunningham, L.X. (2010). 'Managing Human Resources in SMEs in a Transition Economy: Evidence from China', *The International Journal of Human Resource Management*, 21(12), pp. 2120–2141.

Deng, Y.X. (2017). *Labour protest and grassroots trade union reform: a study on the automobile industry in South China*. Unpublished PhD thesis, University of Hong Kong.

Elfstrom, M. and Kuruvilla, S. (2014). 'The Changing Nature of Labor Unrest in China', *Industrial and Labor Relations Review*, 67(2), pp. 453–480.

Friedman, E. (2014). *Insurgency Trap: Labor Politics in Postsocialist China*. Ithaca: Cornell University Press.

Friedman, E. and Kuruvilla, S. (2015). 'Experimentation and Decentralization in China's Labor Relations', *Human Relations*, 68(2), pp. 181–195.

Friedman, E. and Lee, C.K. (2010). 'Remaking the World of Chinese Labour: A 30-year Retrospective', *British Journal of Industrial Relations*, 48(3), pp. 507–533.

Gallagher, M.E. (2006). 'Mobilizing the Law in China: 'Informed Disenchantment' and the Development of Legal Consciousness', *Law and Society Review* 40(4), pp. 783–816.

Goodall, K. and Warner, M. (1997). 'Human Resources in Sino-Foreign Joint Ventures: Selected Case Studies in Shanghai, Compared with Beijing', *The International Journal of Human Resource Management*, 8(5), pp. 569–594.

Hassard, J., Morris, J., Sheehan, J. and Xiao, Y. (2006). 'Downsizing the Danwei: Chinese State-Enterprise Reform and the Surplus Labour Question', *The International Journal of Human Resource Management*, 17(8), pp. 1441–1455.

Hui, E.S.I. (2017). *Hegemonic Transformation: The State, Laws, and Labour Relations in Post-Socialist China*. New York: Palgrave Macmillan.

Hui, E.S.I. and Chan, C.K.C. (2012). 'The 'Harmonious Society' as a Hegemonic Project: Labour Conflicts and Changing Labour Policies in China', *Labour, Capital and Society*, 44(2), pp. 154–183.

Hui, E.S.I. and Chan, C.K.C. (2015). 'Beyond the Union-Centred Approach: A Critical Evaluation of Recent Trade Union Elections in China', *British Journal of Industrial Relations*, 53(3), pp. 601–627.

Hurst, W. and O'Brien, K.J. (2002). 'China's Contentious Pensioners', *The China Quarterly*, 170, pp. 345–360.

Jiang. X. (2004). *Woguo zhongchangqi shiye wenti yanjiu [Research on Medium- and Long-term Unemployment Problems in China]*. Beijing: China Renmin University Press.

Kuruvilla, S., Lee, C.K. and Gallagher, M. (eds.) (2011). *From Iron Rice Bowl to Informalization: Markets, Workers and the State in a Changing China*. Ithaca: Cornell University Press.

Kuruvilla, S. and Liu, M. (2016). 'The State, the Unions, and Collective Bargaining in China: The Good, the Bad, and the Ugly', *Comparative Labor Law & Policy Journal*, 38(2), pp. 187–210.

Kuruvilla, S. and Zhang, H. (2016). 'Labor Unrest and Incipient Collective Bargaining in China', *Management and Organization Review*, 12(1), pp. 159–187.

Lee, C.K. (1995). 'Engendering the Worlds of Labor: Women Workers, Labor Markets, and Production Politics in the South China Economic Miracle', *American Sociological Review*, 60(3), pp. 378–397.

Lee, C.K. (1998). *Gender and the South China Miracle: Two Worlds of Factory Women*. Berkeley: University of California Press.

Lee, C.K. (2002). 'From the Specter of Mao to the Spirit of the Law: Labor Insurgency in China', *Theory and Society*, 31(2), pp. 189–228.

Lee, C.K. (2007). *Against the Law: Labor Protests in China's Rustbelt and Sunbelt*. Berkeley: University of California Press.

Lee, C.H. and Liu, M. (2011). Collective Bargaining in Transition: Measuring the Effects of Collective Voice in China, in *The Role of Collective Bargaining in the Global Economy: Negotiating for Social Justice*. Geneva: International Labor Office, pp. 205–226.

Lee, C.H., Brown, W. and Wen, X.Y. (2016). 'What Sort of Collective Bargaining is Emerging in China?' *British Journal of Industrial Relations*, 54(1), pp. 214–236.

Leung, P.N. and Pun, N. (2009). 'The Radicalisation of the New Chinese Working Class: A Case Study of Collective Action in the Gemstone Industry', *Third World Quarterly*, 30(3), pp. 551–565.

Liu, M.W. (2010). 'Union Organizing in China: Still a Monolithic Labor Movement?' *ILR Review*, 64(1), pp. 30–52.

Ministry of Human Resources and Social Security (2011). Notice on Deepening the Promotion of Collective Contract System to Implement Rainbow Project. [guanyu shenru tuijin jiti hetong zhidu shishi caihong jihua de tongzhi]. Available at: www.mohrss.gov.cn/ldgxs/LDGXhetong/jtht/201107/t20110727_86307.htm.

National Bureau of Statistics of China (various years). *China Statistical Yearbook*. Beijing: China Statistics Press. Years 1996 onwards available online at: www.stats.gov.cn/english/statisticaldata/AnnualData/.

Perry, E.J. (1997). From Native Place to Workplace: Labor Origins and Outcomes of China's Danwei System, in Lü, X.B. and Perry, E.J. (eds.) *Danwei: Changing Chinese Workplace in Historical and Comparative Perspective*. New York: M.E. Sharpe, pp. 42–60.

Pringle, T. (2011). *Trade Unions in China: The Challenge of Labour Unrest*. New York: Routledge.

Pun, N. (2005). *Made in China: Women Factory Workers in a Global Workplace*. Durham (NC)/Hong Kong: Duke University Press/Hong Kong University Press.

Pun, N. and Lu, H. (2010). 'Unfinished Proletarianization: Self, Anger, and Class Action Among the Second Generation of Peasant-Workers in Present-Day China', *Modern China*, 36(5), pp. 493–519.

Pun, N. and Smith, C. (2007). 'Putting Transnational Labour Process in its Place: The Dormitory Labour Regime in Post-Socialist China', *Work, Employment & Society*, 21(1), pp. 27–45.

Rarick, C.A. (2009). 'The Historical Roots of Chinese Cultural Values and Managerial Practices', *Journal of International Business Research*, 8(2), p. 60.

Redding, G. (2002). 'The Capitalist Business System of China and Its Rationale', *Asia Pacific Journal of Management*, 19(2), pp. 221–249.

Renmin Wang (2003). Chinese Migrant Workers Can Now Join Trade Unions Amid Difficulties [Zhongguo nongmingong jiaru gonghui zai gannan zhong qibu]. (Online). 21 September. Available at: www.people.com.cn/GB/shizheng/1026/2099648.html.

Schlevogt, K.A. (2001). 'The Distinctive Structure of Chinese Private Enterprises: State Versus Private Sector', *Asia Pacific Business Review*, 7(3), pp. 1–33.

Smith, C. and Chan, J. (2015). 'Working for Two Bosses: Student Interns as Constrained Labour in China', *Human Relations*, 68(2), pp. 305–326.

Solinger, D.J. (2002). 'Labour Market Reform and the Plight of the Laid-Off Proletariat', *The China Quarterly*, 170, pp. 304–326.

Taylor, B. and Li, Q. (2007). 'Is the ACFTU a Union and Does It Matter?' *Journal of Industrial Relations*, 49(5), pp. 701–715.

Wang, S. (2012). 'On the causes of the overflowing of labor dispatch in state-owned enterprises. [Lun guoyou qiye laowu paiqian yonggong 'fanlan' chengyin]', *Journal of Educational Institute of Jilin Province*, 28(5), pp. 128–130.

Wang, T. and Chan, C.K.C. (2015). Changing Faces of Chinese Labour Regimes: Case Studies in Beijing and Shenzhen, in Wong, P.N. and Cheng, J. (eds.) *Global China: Internal and External Reaches*. Singapore: World Scientific, pp. 75–103.

Warner, M. (1996). 'Human Resources in the People's Republic of China: The 'Three Systems' Reforms', *Human Resource Management Journal*, 6(2), pp. 32–43.

Wong, L. (2011). 'Chinese Migrant Workers: Rights Attainment Deficits, Rights Consciousness and Personal Strategies', *China Quarterly*, 208, pp. 870–892.

Yusuf, Y., Gunasekaran, A. and Dan, G. (2007). 'Implementation of TQM in China and Organisation Performance: An Empirical Investigation', *Total Quality Management*, 18(5), pp. 509–530.

Zhang. L. (2015). *Inside China's Automobile Factories: The Politics of Labor and Worker Resistance*. New York: Cambridge University Press.

26

EMPLOYMENT RELATIONS IN AFRICA

Pauline Dibben and Geoffrey Wood

Introduction

There is a very extensive body of literature on the hard times experienced across many African states in the 1980s and 1990s, and the subsequent commodity-fuelled recovery. However, the bulk of this literature has been orientated toward examining the role of the state, investors, business and civil society. In contrast, the coverage of the effects of these changes on employees and how the employment relationship has been altered is much less extensive, with the predominant focus on individual country case studies. This chapter provides an overview of employment relations (ER) across the continent, but focuses on the relatively developed economies of southern Africa.

Due to formative institutional legacies, differences in natural resource endowments and state traditions, and physical and human infrastructures, there is much diversity, but at the same time there have been many common trends across the continent. Therefore, this chapter begins by reviewing: key similarities and differences in economic context, poverty and stability; institutional legacies; and industrial policy and structural adjustment. It then moves on to focus on various dimensions of union activity, covering: levels of union membership; different organisational types; transnational organisation; engagement with political parties and tripartite experiments; mobilisation; and representation of vulnerable workers.

Economic context, poverty and stability

Africa consists of around 54 countries, although the exact number is sometimes disputed. For example, within north Africa, Western Sahara, which enjoys substantial international recognition, was administered by Spain until 1976 but a large component is occupied and administered as an integral part of Morocco (BBC News, 2017), whilst the *de facto* state of Somaliland is largely unrecognised. Again, whilst different regions of Africa – southern, west and north– all have very distinct historical experiences and institutional legacies, some countries are difficult to locate within a particular category; for example, Sao Tome e Principe and Equatorial Guinea have much more in common with the Caribbean than much of continental Africa. In practical terms, this means that there are great disparities in institutional legacies, industrial development and the regulation of labour, as well as the relative role accorded to civil society.

In order to provide an indication of country differences, Table 26.1 below shows countries by region, approximate population figures and levels of human development (African Economic Outlook; see also, UNDP, 2017).

It can be seen from the table that the continent's population is very unevenly distributed. In some African countries, land is a very scarce resource. In others, labour is the scarcer commodity. This matters because in some countries it is relatively easy for peasants to opt out of the modern economy if need be and revert to subsistence-level agriculture (Mkandawire, 2002; Waters, 1992). In others, this is not a feasible option: the economically marginalised have little alternative other than precarious livings in urban slums. This makes for variation in the relative importance assigned to formal jobs, the relative bargaining position of employers and the stakes around retaining paid work.

There is also much diversity in levels of poverty across the continent. For example, according to World Bank data, the sub-Saharan region had a total population of around 973 million people in 2014 (World Bank, 2016a), and according to UNICEF-World Bank figures, there are high levels of poverty, with 49 per cent of children living in extreme poverty (The Guardian, 2016). There are high degrees of spatial inequality, with differences between rural and urban areas, and more generally, a lack of access to public services (Beegle et al., 2016). This is salient to the study of work and ER since those in absolute poverty are likely to concentrate on immediate issues of survival. In addition, accompanying absolute poverty is the high incidence of debilitating illnesses, which saps productivity in both the formal and informal sectors. Infrastructural shortfalls make it difficult for many informal sector operatives to move beyond the basic subsistence level.

Other important differences include whether the country is oil and gas producing and/ or centred on other mineral exports. As the literature on the resource curse alerts us, the oil and gas industry tends to crowd out investment in other areas (Robinson, Torvik and Verdier, 2006). Moreover, such countries tend to be associated with over-valued and volatile currencies, making it difficult for other areas of industry to compete. Finally, elites become accustomed to easy revenues, and neglect broader institutional building or development (ibid.). This means that the sectoral basis of formal ER can become quite narrow; there is a relative shortage of decent work in other areas of the national economy.

A further important distinction is the level of political and social instability within countries. Whilst a relatively small number of countries have managed to evade destructive internal conflicts (Zambia being a conspicuous example), in others social order remains more fragile. For example, Mozambique has enjoyed a degree of stability since the end of the civil war in the early 1990s, but in recent years there is some evidence of political violence, with reported attacks in 2015 and 2016 on key members of the opposition party, and similarly violent actions by the latter against government supporters (AllAfrica, 2016b). When confronted with political instability, employers are likely to adopt a particularly short-term view, and be reluctant to invest in assets that are not readily portable, be they physical plant or people.

Institutional legacies

Employment relations within Africa are still impacted by institutional legacies from colonial times. Historical institutionalist approaches suggest that formative historical events, taking place at relatively unusual times of crisis and rupture, exert long legacies (Sorge, 2005; Streeck and Thelen, 2005). A growing body of literature has sought to explore the effect of colonial legacies, and to some extent this has helped to explain the poor performance of many African countries. For example, in an influential account, Herbst (2014) argues that in much of Africa, labour was

Table 26.1 African countries: population and levels of human development

	Population (2014)(approx. millions unless otherwise shown)	Levels of Human Development (2014)
North Africa		
Algeria	40	High
Egypt	90	Medium
Libya	6	Low
Morocco	34	Medium
Tunisia	11	High
East Africa		
Burundi	11	Low
Comoros	770 (thousand)	Low
Djibouti	876 (thousand)	Low
Eritrea	5	Low
Ethiopia	100	Low
Kenya	45	Low
Madagascar	24	Low
Mauritius	1	High
Rwanda	11	Low
Seychelles	91 (thousand)	High
Somalia	11	Not available
South Sudan	12	Not available
Sudan	40	Low
Tanzania	52	Low
Uganda	38	Low
West Africa		
Benin	11	Low
Burkina Faso	18	Low
Cameroon	23	Low
Cabo Verde	514 (thousand)	Medium
Cote d'Ivoire	22	Low
Gambia	2	Low
Ghana	27	Medium
Guinea	12	Low
Guinea Bissau	2	Low
Liberia	4	Low
Mali	17	Low
Mauritania	4	Low
Niger	19	Low
Nigeria	178	Low
Senegal	15	Low
Sierra Leone	6	Low
Sao Tome e Principe	186 (thousand)	Medium
Togo	7	Low
Central Africa		
Angola (also Southern Africa)	24	Low
Burundi (also East Africa)	11	Low
Cameroon (also West Africa)	23	Low

Table 26.1 (cont.)

	Population (2014)(approx. millions unless otherwise shown)	Levels of Human Development (2014)
Central African Republic	5	Low
Chad	14	Low
Congo (Republic)	5	Medium
Congo (Democratic Republic)	75	Low
Equatorial Guinea	821 (thousand)	Medium
Gabon	2	Medium
Rwanda (also East Africa)	11	Low
Sao Tome e Principe (also West Africa)	186 (thousand)	Medium
Southern Africa		
Angola	24	Low
Botswana	2	Medium
Lesotho	2	Low
Malawi	17	Low
Mozambique	27	Low
Namibia	2	Medium
Republic of South Africa	54	Medium
Swaziland	1	Low
Tanzania (also East Africa)	52	Low
Zambia	16	Medium
Zimbabwe	15	Low

(*Source*: African Economic Outlook, 2015; AllAfrica.com, 2016a; World Bank, 2016c)

a scarcer commodity than land; this led to neglect of the building of private property rights, and a disproportionate amount of energy being devoted to the subjugation of labour, leaving a long legacy of weak property rights and dysfunctional labour markets. In contrast, La Porta et al. (2000) argue that variation in property rights stems from whether the colonial powers used civil or common law. In common law (formerly British) countries, property rights are much stronger than in (formerly French and Portuguese) civil law ones, leading to superior economic outcomes. Yet, the latter countries have more challenging physical geography and epidemiological rates than most of the British colonies, which were primarily concentrated in east and southern Africa, leading Acemoglu, Johnson and Robinson (2001) to argue that a major determining feature of the fortunes of African states was instead the extent to which there were significant attempts at European settlement. In west Africa, high incidences of tropical diseases meant that indirect rule was in place, with the interests of colonial powers being wholly predatory. This led to a lack of interest in building institutions, other than those of the most exploitative nature. In contrast, in southern and east Africa, there was more effort at building mini-Europes, replicating the institutions of the metropole to serve settler interests. The rule of law was stronger in such states, and the foundations were set for more broadly based and stable economic growth.

In his classic anti-colonial writings, Fanon (1967) argues that settler societies not only dispossessed, but also undermined the confidence of, the colonized, weakening capabilities both for self and community development; local elites were reduced to becoming parodies of the settler. Indeed, in some settings, settler societies were involved in the expropriation and subjugation of the indigenous population, while parallel security states and militarised police forces evaded the law (Dibben and Wood, 2013). These parallel security states have, in a number of instances, persisted into the post-colonial era, most spectacularly in Zimbabwe, but vestiges are visible even in relatively prosperous societies such as Kenya. This allows the authorities to act in ways that are legal or *de facto* unaccountable, with insufficient constitutional barriers to bring them to account, making for both weak property and worker rights.

Industrial policy and structural adjustment

On independence, many governments experimented with active industrial policies that initially seemed to be quite successful in promoting economic diversification and decent work, including the development of motor and/or clothing industries in countries such as Ghana, Nigeria, Kenya and Tanzania. Industrial policies were in many instances associated with ambitious socialist experiments, reflecting the complete discrediting of the ideologies of the dominant colonial powers. However, such experiments were often associated with neglect of the interests of the peasantry, which often constituted the majority of society (Mkandawire, 2002; Waters, 1992). The logical response of the latter was to further disengage from the state, making it very difficult to promote broad-based economic development (Hyden, 1981). Moreover, revenue flow from natural resources to support socialist development policies declined during the 1970s, leading to governments being unable to fulfil their commitments. The response was inevitably an abandonment of socialist experiments, even in those countries, such as Mozambique and Ethiopia, which had attempted to build fully fledged state socialism. The final collapse of socialist government experiments was hastened by the economic decline and breakup of the Soviet Union.

Increasing levels of debt forced governments to turn to the international financial institutions; emboldened by the rise of neoliberalism in the developed liberal market economies, the latter required radical structural adjustment policies as a price for debt relief. In practical terms, structural adjustment entailed the abandonment of active industrial policies, the lifting of protective tariffs, the de-regulation of labour markets and, often, cuts to expenditure on education and health care. This had the effect not only of undermining national skills development capabilities, resulting in less security of tenure, but also the wholesale closure of many industries across the continent, leading to massive formal sector job losses. For ER to take place, there has to be a recognisable employment relationship, and, in many instances, the latter increasingly became an event involving a diminishing proportion of the population. Structural adjustment also weakened the ability of governments to enforce the law. Even in relatively developed South Africa, recent research has indicated that a large number of small employers openly ignore the law and statutory collective bargaining agreements, while unions find it difficult to challenge non-compliance since workers are often in a very insecure position and, ultimately, the preservation of jobs is prioritised over worker rights (Bischoff and Wood, 2013).

Industrial policies have also been undermined by the rise of ultra-low cost producers in the Far East, notably China. These producers enjoyed a greater degree of regional government support, much lower input costs and easier access to bank financing, enabling many African markets to be flooded with goods that were, in some instances, priced at even less than the cost of the raw materials. This process was facilitated by the austerity-induced emasculation of state capabilities, making the process of illegal imports much easier. The industries that did survive were those that were the least portable. For example, as the content of both beer and soft drinks is mostly water, it is intrinsically much cheaper to produce them locally.

The 2000s saw a return to growth in many countries across the continent, buoyed up by a revival in primary commodities prices. In 2015, the GDP annual growth rate was 3.0 per cent for sub-Saharan Africa, compared with 1.5 per cent in 1961. However, this masks differences between countries. For example, while the growth rate in 2015 for Namibia, Mozambique and Tanzania was over five per cent, in Zambia it was 3.2 per cent and in South Africa 1.3 per cent (World Bank, 2016d). Moreover, in many contexts, it has been growth largely without jobs, with the bulk of revenue windfalls being captured by small local elites and offshore companies. Although physical infrastructure was improved, as a result of the need to service large mining and agricultural companies, social protection across the continent was generally weak; structural adjustment led to even the most basic public services in many highly impoverished African countries being subject to user fees. The response has been to fall back on extended peasant-based informal networks of support. Although this makes for a basic, low-level degree of redistribution and communitarian social protection, the operation of such networks brings negative consequences of its own, including placing great pressure on those with jobs (Wood and Haines, 2002). Demands can include financially supporting the wider family, incurring unsustainable levels of debt or being placed under great pressure to supplement livelihoods, if necessary by corrupt means (Hyden, 1981).

Union membership, density and mobilisation

Given the contextual circumstances and historical trends outlined above, trade unions within Africa have faced a series of challenges. For example, many unions have struggled to respond to restructuring, including the privatisation of industry and the consequent loss in members (Dibben and Wood, 2013; von Holdt, 2005). Data on membership of trade unions within African countries are not comprehensive. However, Table 26.2 below gives an indication of differences in membership levels by including figures from a survey conducted on behalf of the ILO in 2008–2009.

The table below shows much variation in density levels between countries, ranging from 70 per cent in Ghana to 12.9 per cent in Ethiopia, and proportionately small numbers of regular jobs.

Table 26.2 Trade union density rates in selected countries in Africa

Country	Year	Trade Union Density Rate	
		Proportion of wage and salaried earners	*Proportion of total employment*
Egypt	2007	26.1	16.1
Ethiopia	2007	12.9	1.0
Ghana	2006	70.0	
Kenya (private sector only)	2007	35.5	4.1
Malawi	2006	20.6	2.7
Mauritius	2007	28.2	14.8
Niger	2008		1.1
Sierra Leone	2008	46.8	3.6
South Africa	2008	39.8	24.9
Tanzania	2009	18.7	2.2
Uganda	2005		1.1

(*Source*: adapted from Hayter and Stoevska, 2011, p11)

A key feature of trade union power is the ability to mobilise members to take part in strike activity. Strike activity has grown in a few countries, most notably South Africa, since 2006. However, this has been accompanied by increasing levels of violence and intimidation; the Marikana Massacre in August 2012 resulted in the shooting of some 34 workers by police (Webster, 2015). One of the features of this occurrence was the preceding development of a breakaway union, the Association of Mineworkers and Construction Union (AMCU), from the National Union of Mineworkers (NUM). A further feature was the involvement of other actors such as NGOs. The protest here, as in other countries, should be seen not just in the context of worker rights, but also in relation to broader contextual features such as poverty and inequality (ibid.). Unions have, however, seen some success. For example, in Mozambique, 200 striking workers won concessions from the China Road and Bridge Corporation (CRBC), which had been contracted by the state-owned Maputo South Development Company to build a bridge in Maputo. The strikers had precarious contracts of only two months' duration, and won contracts for an indeterminate period. A previous strike at the same place had covered work contracts, the lack of protective equipment, racism, unjust dismissals, long working hours and no paid time off for illness or family emergencies. The Chinese company finally agreed to implement the agreement in full, including an eight-hour working day and paid overtime (AIM, 2015).

Employment relations and different organisational types

A feature of most African states (and, indeed, developing countries elsewhere) is a segmentation between large multinational and state firms and small and/or informal sector ones (Wood and Frynas, 2006; Wood et al., 2010). Wood and Frynas (2006) explain how in Kenya, Uganda and Tanzania, these distinctions partially coincide with relative insertion in the export economy; domestically orientated firms are mostly small or operating in the informal sector. Moreover, the larger firms are characterised by modern ER, often with a formal union presence and collective bargaining, even if the relative bargaining position of workers is weak. Such organisations are characterised by higher levels of regulatory scrutiny, and hence, are more inclined to adhere to labour law.

Multinational corporations (MNCs) represent a distinct category of firms in their own right. In many cases, their presence revolves around the exploitation of natural resources, but sometimes they need to reach and adapt to local consumer markets or harness existing capabilities. One of the most important examples of the latter two factors is the case of the global automotive majors in South Africa. Foreign MNCs in such areas of manufacturing have generally attracted a good reputation in terms of conditions of employment, investment in people, participative management techniques and a willingness to engage with unions. However, unionisation in the automotive industry in South Africa has faced challenges over time. Unions sought to achieve recognition and fight injustices, particularly when associated with racism (Baskin, 1991). But this led to splits between unions and growing industrial conflict (Von Holdt, 1990). In more recent times, workplace-based racism has been addressed by government policy and legislation such as the Employment Equity Act 1998 and the Broad-Based Black Economic Empowerment Act 2003, but differences in employment levels and promotion still remain (AllAfrica.com, 2014).

A more recent trend has been the growth in the number of multinationals from the developing world, and particularly the influx of Chinese multinationals. These companies have often tended to import labour, leading to a growing number of Chinese immigrants that have arguably displaced local workers from the relevant sector (Anshan, 2013). The growing number of Chinese firms and amount of Chinese investment in Africa has, more generally, caused much controversy, with acknowledgement of similarities in some work practices, but also concerns regarding the exploitation of resources (see, for example, Jackson, 2015; Wood and Horwitz, 2015). It should also be noted there has also been much inward investment from other countries, such as India (Horwitz and Budhwar, 2015). South African MNCs have, in many African countries, also attracted their share of controversy. Here, areas of concern include the relative willingness to make use of local suppliers (e.g. South African retailers), the dominant role of external managers (telecoms) and/or aggressive and anti-competitive market seeking behaviour (beverages) (Wood, 2015).

In smaller indigenous firms, ER are often patriarchal and authoritarian in nature. On the one hand, workers have weak employment rights and little or no union representation. Managerial authority is arbitrary (and often capricious), with employee voice mechanisms being weak or wholly absent. On the other hand, notions of paternalist obligation mean that firms often prioritise families of existing staff, and very low wages may be supplemented by loans or cash handouts in the event of family crisis, while training tends to be informal and on the job, on the 'learning with Nellie' principle (Wood et al., 2010). Within the lusophone countries, there is the phenomenon of the multinational small business, typically ethnically Portuguese owned, and formally or informally linked, controlled and capitalised by similar enterprises in the metropole. Although the HR techniques may be broadly similar to their local counterparts, the ability to access investment from abroad may make the firm more resilient, and provide the basis for more stable employment.

Another important feature is public sector work, since in many African countries governments represent the main source of formal employment. Moreover, public sector jobs can be regarded as more secure than those in the private sector, albeit that wages can be lower since the public sector may be characterised by fixed wages on the basis of seniority (Dibben and Wood, 2013). Jobs in the public sector have reduced over time, due to trends such as build-own-operate arrangements, public-private partnerships and the outright privatisation of state-owned enterprises. Privatisation in Africa was carried out relatively late compared with more developed countries, and often as the result of structural adjustment conditions from international organisations. In many cases, entities were privatised through dubious processes, with accusations of corruption (Dibben and Wood, 2013; Nwankwo and Richards, 2001; Pitcher, 2002). There have been mixed reviews of the outcomes of privatisation (see Josiah et al., 2010). It has resulted in certain efficiencies and positive changes for some groups of workers in terms of pay, training, promotion and the working environment (Boahen, 2016). However, in countries such as South Africa, Mozambique and Ghana, there is evidence to suggest that it has resulted in job losses and deleterious terms and conditions (Boahen, 2016; Bond, 2004; Dibben and Wood, 2013).

The weakening of the African state has meant that NGOs play an increasingly important role in many African countries in the provision of public services and local community betterment. They may also represent an important source of jobs, skills and capabilities, and an important resource for unions and other civil society actors. However, the track record of NGOs in Africa is mixed. There is a persistent tendency to favour highly visible capital projects, rather than the maintenance of any infrastructural investment or the enhancement of indigenous capabilities. Indeed, in commenting on Mozambique, it has been suggested that international aid has resulted in the 'recolonisation' of that country (Hanlon, 1991). With regard to ER, some NGOs have defaulted towards expatriate-orientated recruitment policies, with small closed communities of such workers constituting an insider labour market. Again, NGOs may be closed to local expertise and unwilling to entertain counter-arguments from communities. Many local and expatriate NGO workers are highly committed to the work they do, with many staff facing a wide range of risks for modest pay. Others are characterised by officials living, by local terms, lavish lifestyles in closed compounds that fit poorly with the modest social gains of their activities (Hancock, 1989). Another dimension of NGOs is their ability to work toward the improvement of society, and workers' rights in particular, through an intermediary or activist role, in cooperation with trade unions (Gallin, 2000). As explained in more detail in the later section on vulnerable workers, this co-operation has had some success in furthering the interests of those in insecure work (Dibben and Nadin, 2011).

Employer associations also have an important role to play in ER within Africa. Their main aim is to represent the interests of their member companies. This can involve lobbying government, providing advisory services to members, and bargaining with trade unions on terms and conditions within a bargaining unit or industry. In addition to operating at national level, they can also operate at regional level, as in the case of the East African Employers Organisation, which works on regional integration, and the free movement of labour, labour standards and skills development (East African Employers Organisation, 2016). As outlined below in more detail within the discussion of tripartism, employer organisations can also be represented, together with unions, in corporatist arrangements or some form of tripartism.

Transnational organisation of trade unions

Trade unions have sought to achieve influence through transnational activity. For example, the COSATU federation in South Africa sought to influence policy in Swaziland and Zimbabwe, but with limited effect, due to its inability to mobilise workers, but also due to a lack of support from, and the conflicting priorities of, the South African government (Wood, Dibben and Klerck, 2013). Further attempts have been made to collaborate internationally with unions outside of Africa through, for example, the Southern Initiative on Globalisation and Trade Union Rights (SIGTUR) (SIGTUR, 2016). Meanwhile, trade unions in Africa have also been involved in the International Trade Union Confederation (ITUC) and global union federations. The ITUC refers to itself as "the global voice of the world's working people", with a mission for "the promotion and defence of workers' rights and interests, through international co-operation between trade unions, global campaigning and advocacy within the major global institutions," taking action in relation to: trade union and human rights; economy, society and the workplace; equality and non-discrimination; and international solidarity. Within Africa, its regional organisation is the ITUC-AF, which works closely with the International Labour Organization and global union federations (ITUC, 2016a). One of the main GUFs in Africa is IndustriALL, which represents 50 million workers in 140 countries in the mining, energy and manufacturing sectors. It includes affiliates of former GUFs – the International Metalworkers' Federation (IMF), International Federation of Chemical, Energy, Mine and General Workers' Unions (ICEM) and International Textiles Garment and Leather Workers' Federation (ITGLWF) – and has affiliated organisations in 36 or more countries in Africa. In advancing worker rights, it includes a focus on global supply chains (IndustriALL, 2016). The GUFs have extended their reach, and have been successful in securing international framework agreements with multinationals on global minimum social standards. However, they have struggled to be effective, since these frameworks are normative instruments only, and they have suffered from a lack of resources (Muller, Platzer and Rub, 2010).

Engagement with political parties and tripartite experiments

Unions have historically played an important role in influencing government policy in Africa. In some instances, such as Zambia, Zimbabwe and Malawi, unions were at the forefront of struggles for democratisation, forging broad-based coalitions with civil society groupings. In other countries there was a strategic decision to move away from party politics, such as that made by the Ghana Trade Union Congress; however, this seems to have brought with it few gains, and arguably led to a lack of ability to prevent the government's embracing of neo-liberal reforms (Akwetey and Dorkenoo, 2010; Beckman and Sachikonye, 2010). In Nigeria, the union has a tradition of political involvement, and has also effectively mobilised workers to protest against both worker rights and social concerns, including petrol prices, and more recently, unions have stood in opposition to the structural reforms imposed by international institutions (Beckman and Sachikonye, 2010). In other countries, such as Mozambique, the unions have struggled to re-interpret their relationship with government. They are now operating in post-socialist countries, and have faced difficulties in adapting to the new environment (see, for example, Dibben and Wood, 2016). In others, such as South Africa, the union federation COSATU was instrumental in ending apartheid, but has struggled more recently to prevent the introduction of neoliberal reforms. Nevertheless, limited success has been achieved in forcing the government to adapt plans for privatisation in certain contexts (von Holdt, 2005).

In a number of southern African countries, including South Africa, Namibia and Mozambique, unions have been involved in tripartite experiments, associated with the move to democratisation. However, they have generally failed to achieve the gains that may have originally been anticipated. There are a number of reasons for this failure. Whilst a large proportion of big business was initially favourably inclined to such experiments in the interests of political stability and to secure their legitimacy, interest waned when post-democratic governments proved both stable and relatively business friendly. Moreover, employer organisations were never fully encompassing, and there was limited interest from small businesses and the informal sector in pursuing such arrangements (Dibben, Klerck and Wood, 2015). Not only did government support diminish given external pressures to pursue neoliberal policies, but also, the relative influence of intellectual proponents of tripartism declined, as ruling parties became increasingly dominated by political entrepreneurs (Daniel, Habib and Southall, 2003). Finally, unions were divided, with those in different sectors having radically different fortunes: while those in the public sector were relatively secure, those in manufacturing faced eroding memberships. More prosperous unions sought to reach their own deals with the major employers in their relevant sector. A number of prominent South African unions had to contend with radical breakaways, weakening their sense of purpose and membership base. This meant that they were less encompassing or unified organisations, making it harder to present a coherent bargaining position (Dibben, Klerck and Wood, 2015; Jauch, 2010).

Union representation of vulnerable and marginal categories of worker

Key issues for trade unions are equality and diversity. In African countries women still tend to work in more insecure positions than men, at least partly due to perceptions regarding their traditional roles, and religious or cultural reasons. Moreover, they have tended to lack effective representation within trade unions (Wood and Dibben, 2008). In addition, in many countries, workers have faced discrimination on disability, tribal, ethnic or racial grounds. In countries such as Mozambique, race was used to determine citizenship and worker rights in colonial times (O'Laughlin, 2000), and inequalities remain, while in South Africa, race was the defining feature of the apartheid regime. Contrary to the hopes of that nation, and government strategies aimed at broad-based black economic empowerment, racial discrimination has persisted, evidenced by employment figures on representation in senior level jobs (AllAfrica.com, 2014).

More generally, insecure and contingent work has been a characterising feature of African countries and emerging economies, with many workers forced to rely on labour brokers (Barrientos, 2013). A particularly vulnerable category of worker has been domestic workers. Unions have sought to protect these workers, and the ITUC has campaigned internationally alongside the International Domestic Workers Federation in order that they should be entitled to a minimum wage, social protection, regulation of working time and the right to one day off a week, while within Africa, Namibia has adopted labour reforms that extend rights to domestic workers, including paid maternity leave (ITUC, 2015).

Another major challenge for employment relations in Africa is the prevalence of the informal sector (see, for example, Dibben and Williams, 2012; Hayter and Stoevska, 2011; Webster, 2005). While in some countries informal sector employment is viewed as a phenomenon that needs to be eradicated, in others those working in the informal sector have received assistance from government in order to gradually move into the formal sector (Dibben, Wood and Williams, 2015). Informal sector workers often experience inferior terms and conditions and a lack of employment security due to the unregulated nature of the work, as well as the lack of ability to voice their concerns. Indeed, Webster has referred to the 'representational gap', whereby many workers are outside of formal sector work and beyond the scope of trade union remit (Webster, 2005). Although trade unions have tried to represent these workers, many attempts have failed, including the relatively recent attempt in South Africa by the Self Employed Women's Union (SEWU), which was set up in 1994 to represent women working in both rural and urban areas (ibid.). In contrast, in Mozambique, the OTM union federation has worked closely with ASSOTSI, the organisation representing the informal sector, and managed to persuade national and local government to view the informal sector more favourably (Dibben and Nadin, 2011). Meanwhile in Nigeria, the National Union of Textile, Garment and Tailoring Workers of Nigeria (NUTGTW) has sought to organise informal sector workers in the textile sector, using tailors as organisers. They provide educational programmes and provide loans at cheaper rates. This strategy has enabled it to increase the representation of women (Fredricks, 2015).

Conclusion

Employment relations in Africa have been characterised by radical and far-reaching changes, and the basis of the modern employment relationship has eroded across the continent since the 1980s. Structural adjustment policies saw the destruction of large numbers of regular jobs. The return to growth in the 2000s has not been matched with a commensurate increase in good work, and many Africans remain locked in informal and precarious livings. Although democratisation in the 1980s and 1990s may have given unions greater political autonomy and opportunities to organise, job losses mean that in many instances unions were reduced to a residual or firefighting role. Moreover, weakened state capabilities have led to frequent difficulties in enforcing labour law, whilst weak social protection makes the exit option less feasible. Given such challenging circumstances, it is difficult to conceive how better and more inclusive ER can be secured. However, key elements might include a greater investment in enforcement capabilities and developing viable strategies for the revival of industry, with some reform of protective tariffs. This may provide local industry with more time to prepare for ever-intensifying external competition. Finally, unions need to develop more effective strategies for union unity, and also formulate viable policy alternatives that serve to promote the interests of both core and more vulnerable workers as a basis for joint action with other civil society groupings and labour-orientated political parties.

References

Acemoglu, D., Johnson, S. and Robinson, J.A. (2001). 'The Colonial Origins of Comparative Development: An Empirical Investigation', *The American Economic Review*, 91(5), pp. 1369–1401.

African Economic Outlook (2015). Regional Development and Spatial Inclusion. (Online). Available at: http://www.africaneconomicoutlook.org/en/chapter/regional-development-and-spatial-inclusion.

Akwetey, E.O. and Dorkenoo, D. (2010). Disengagement from Party Politics: Achievements and Challenges for the Ghana Trades Union Congress, in Beckman, B., Buhlungu, S. and Sachikonye, L. (eds.) *Trade Unions and Party Politics: Labour Movements in Africa*. Cape Town: HSRC Press, pp. 39–58.

Communication Workers Union. (2014). *South Africa: CWU statement on the Telkom employment equity policy and plan*. (Press release). Available at: http://allafrica.com/stories/201407181557.html. (Accessed: 1 January 2018).

AllAfrica.com (2016a). *Countries*. (Online). Available at: http://allafrica.com/misc/sitemap/countries.html (Accessed 1 January 2018).

Hanlon, J. (2016b). Mozambique: Back to War – New Renamo Attacks On N1. *Mozambique News Reports and Clippings*. (Online). 14 February. Available at: http://allafrica.com/stories/201602140334.html. (Accessed: 1 January 2018).

Anshan, L. (2013). China's Africa Policy and the Chinese Immigrants in Africa, in Tan, C. (ed.) *Routledge Handbook of the Chinese Diaspora*. London: Routledge, pp. 59–70.

Barrientos, S. (2013). "Labour chains': analysing the role of labour contractors in global production networks', *Journal of Development Studies*, 49(8), pp. 1058–1071.

Baskin, J. (1991). *Striking Back – A History of Cosatu*. Johannesburg: Ravan.

Beckman, B. and Sachikonye, L. (2010). Introduction: trade unions and party politics in Africa, in Beckman, B., Buhlungu, S. and Sachikonye, L. (eds.) *Trade Unions and Party Politics: Labour Movements in Africa*. Cape Town: HSRC Press, pp. 1–22.

Beegle, K., Christiaensen, L., Dabalen, A. and Gaddis, I. (2016). *Poverty in a Rising Africa*. World Bank Group. Available at: www.un.org/africarenewal/sites/www.un.org.africarenewal/files/Poverty%20in%20a%20Rising%20Africa%20Overview.pdf.

Bischoff, C. and Wood, G. (2013). 'Selective informality: the self limiting growth choices of small business in South Africa', *International Labour Review*, 152(3–4), pp. 493–505.

Boahen, P.A. (2016). *Evaluating the Impact of New Public Management Reforms in Ghana: The Privatisation of Water*. Unpublished PhD thesis, University of Sheffield.

Bond, P. (2004). Contradictions confronting new public management in Johannesburg: the rise and fall of municipal water commercialisation, in Dibben, P., Wood, G. and Roper, I. (eds.) *Contesting Public Sector Reforms: Critical Perspectives, International Debates*. London: Palgrave Macmillan.

BBC News (2017). *Western Sahara Profile*. Available at: www.bbc.co.uk/news/world-africa-14115273. (Accessed: 1 January 2018).

Daniel, J., Habib, A. and Southall, R. (2003). *State of the Nation: South Africa, 2003–2004*. Cape Town: HSRC Press.

Dibben, P. and Nadin, S. (2011). 'Community Unionism in Africa: the case of Mozambique', *Industrial Relations/Relations Industrielles*, 66(1), pp. 54–73.

Dibben, P. and Williams, C. (2012). 'Varieties of Capitalism and Employment Relations: Informally Dominated Market Economies', *Industrial Relations: A Journal of Economy and Society*, 51(1), pp. 563–582.

Dibben, P. and Wood, G. (2013). Privatisation and employment relations in Africa: the case of Mozambique, in Newenham-Kahindi, A., Kamoche, K., Chizema, A. and Mellahi, K. (eds.) *Effective Management of People in Africa*. London: Palgrave Macmillan, pp. 72–96.

Dibben, P. and Wood, G. (2016). 'The legacies of coercion and the challenges of contingency: Mozambican unions in difficult times,' *Labor History*, 57(1), pp. 126–140.

Dibben, P., Wood, G. and Williams, C.C. (2015). 'Towards and against formalization: regulation and change in informal work in Mozambique', *International Labor Review*, 154(3), pp. 373–392.

Dibben, P., Klerck, G. and Wood, G. (2015). 'The Ending of Southern Africa's Tripartite Dream: The Cases of South Africa, Namibia and Mozambique', *Business History*, 57(3), pp. 461–483.

East African Employers Organisation (2016). *East African Employers Organisation*. Available at: www.eaeo.or.tz.

Fanon, F. (1967). *Black Skin, White Masks*. New York: Basic Books.

Fredricks, C. (2015). PROFILE: Nigerian unions get creative and organize informal workers. [Online]. Available at: www.industriall-union.org/profile-nigerian-unions-get-creative-and-organize-informal-workers.

Gallin, D. (2000). *Trade Unions and NGOs: A Necessary Partnership for Social Development*. United Nations Research Institute for Social Development. [Online]. Available at: www.unrisd.org/80256B3C 005BCCF9/search/5678DFBA8A99EEB780256B5E004C3737?OpenDocument.

Hancock, G. (1989). *The Lords of Poverty: The Power, Prestige, and Corruption of the International Aid Business*. New York: Atlantic Monthly Press.

Hanlon, J. (1991). *Mozambique: Who Calls the Shots?* Bloomington: Indiana Press.

Hayter, S. and Stoevska, V. (2011). *Social Dialogue Indicators: International Statistical Inquiry 2008–9*. Technical Brief. Geneva: International Labour Organisation. Available at: http://laborsta.ilo.org/applv8/data/TUM/TUD%20and%20CBC%20Technical%20Brief.pdf.

Herbst, J. (2014). *States and Power in Africa: Comparative Lessons in Authority and Control*. Princeton: Princeton University Press.

Horwitz, F. and Budhwar, F. (2015). Human Resource Management in Emerging Markets: An Introduction, in Horwitz, F. and Budhwar, P. (eds.) *Handbook of Human Resource Management in Emerging Markets*. Cheltenham: Edward Elgar Publishing.

Hyden, G. (1981). *No Shortcuts to Progress*. Nairobi: Heinemann.

IndustriALL (2016). About Us. Available at: www.industriall-union.org/about-us.

International Trade Union Confederation (ITUC) (2016a). About Us. Available at: www.ituc-csi.org/about-us.

ITUC (2015). The unstoppable domestic workers' movement: winning labour rights and protections for 15 million domestic workers. (Online). Available at: www.ituc-csi.org/the-unstoppable-domestic-workers?lang=en.

Jackson, T. (2015). Cross-cultural human resource issues in emerging markets, in Horwitz, F. and Budhwar, P. (eds.) *Handbook of Human Resource Management in Emerging Markets*. Cheltenham: Edward Elgar Publishing, pp. 42–67.

Jauch, H. (2003). *Trade Unions in South Africa*. Paper presented at Futures for Southern Africa Symposium, Windhoek, Namibia. Available at: www.sarpn.org/documents/d0000625/

Josiah, J., Burton, B., Gallhofer, S. and Haslam, J. (2010). 'Accounting for privatisation in Africa? Reflections from a critical interdisciplinary perspective', *Critical Perspectives on Accounting*, 21(5), pp. 374–389.

La Porta, R., Lopez de Silanes, F., Shleifer, A. and Vishny, R. (2000). 'Investor protection and corporate governance', *Journal of Financial Economics*, 58(1), pp. 3–27.

Mkandawire, T. (2002). 'The terrible toll of post-colonial 'rebel movements' in Africa: towards an explanation of the violence against the peasantry', *The Journal of Modern African Studies*, 40(2), pp. 181–215.

Mozambique News Agency (AIM). (2015). *Strikers Win Long Term Contracts*. No. 506. (Online). 6 May. Available at: www.poptel.org.uk/mozambique-news/newsletter/aim506.html#story7 (Accessed: 1 January 2018).

Muller, T., Platzer, H.-W. and Rub, S. (2010). *Global Union Federations and the Challenges of Globalisation*. Friedrich Ebert Stiftung. Available at: library.fes.de/pdf-files/id/ipa/07437.pdf.

Nwankwo, S. and Richards, D.C. (2001). 'Privatization – the myth of free market orthodoxy in sub-Saharan Africa', *International Journal of Public Sector Management*, 14(2), pp. 165–180.

O'Laughlin, B. (2000). 'Class and the customary: the ambiguous legacy of the indigenato in Mozambique', *African Affairs*, 99(394), pp. 5–42.

Pitcher, A. (2002). *Transforming Mozambique*. Cambridge (UK): Cambridge University Press.

Robinson, J.A., Torvik, R. and Verdier, T. (2006). 'Political foundations of the resource curse', *Journal of Development Economics*, 79(2), pp. 447–468.

Sorge, A. (2005). *The Global and the Local*. Oxford: Oxford University Press.

Southern Initiative on Globalisation and Trade Union Rights (SIGTUR). (2016). Network. Available at: www.sigtur.com/Network/. (Accessed: 1 January 2018)

Streeck, W. & Thelen, K. (2005). Introduction: institutional change in advanced political economies, in Streeck, W. & Thelen, K. (eds.) *Beyond Continuity*. Oxford: Oxford University Press, pp. 1–39.

The Guardian (2016). Nearly half all children in sub-Saharan Africa in extreme poverty, report warns. (Online). 5 October. Available at: www.theguardian.com/global-development/2016/oct/05/nearly-half-all-children-sub-saharan-africa-extreme-poverty-unicef-world-bank-report-warns.

UNDP (2017). United Nations Development Programme: Human Development Reports. Available at: http://hdr.undp.org/en/countries.

Von Holdt, K. (1990). 'Mercedes-Benz & NUMSA', *South African Labour Bulletin*, 16(4), pp. 15–26.

Von Holdt, K. (2005). 'Saving Government from Itself': Trade union engagement with the restructuring of Spoornet, in Webster, E. and von Holdt, K. (eds.) *Beyond the Apartheid Workplace: Studies in Transition*. Durban: University of KwaZulu-Natal Press, pp. 413–434.

Waters, T. (1992). 'A cultural analysis of the economy of affection and the uncaptured peasantry in Tanzania', *The Journal of Modern African Studies*, 30(1), pp. 163–175.

Webster, E. (2005). New forms of work and the representational gap: a Durban case study, in Webster, E. and von Holdt, K. (eds.) *Beyond the Apartheid Workplace: Studies in Transition*. Durban: University of KwaZulu-Natal Press, pp. 387–405.

Webster, E. (2015). 'The shifting boundaries of industrial relations: insights from South Africa', *International Labour Review*, 154(1), pp. 27–36.

Wood, G. (2015). South African multinationals in Africa: growth and controversy, in Demirbag, M. and Yeprak, A. (eds.) *Handbook of Emerging Market Multinational Corporations*. Cheltenham: Edward Elgar.

Wood, G., Dibben, P. and Klerck, G. (2013). 'The limits of transnational solidarity: The Congress of South African Trade Unions and the Swaziland and Zimbabwean crises', *Labor History*, 54(5), pp. 527–539.

Wood, G., Dibben, P., Stride, C. and Webster, E. (2010). 'HRM in Mozambique: homogenization, path dependence or segmented business system?' *Journal of World Business*, 46(1), pp. 31–41.

Wood, G. and Dibben, P. (2008). 'The Challenges Facing the South African Labour Movement: Mobilization of Diverse Constituencies in a Changing Political and Economic Context', *Industrial Relations/Relations Industrielles*, 63(4), pp. 671–693.

Wood, G. and Frynas, G. (2006). 'The institutional basis of economic failure: anatomy of the segmented business system', *Socio-Economic Review*, 4(2), pp. 239–277.

Wood, G. and Haines, R. (2002). 'Unemployment, marginalization and survival in Greater East London, South Africa', *Development Southern Africa*, 19, pp. 573–581.

Wood, G. and Horwitz, F. (2015). Theories and institutional approaches to HRM and ER in selected emerging markets, in Horwitz, F. and Budhwar, P. (eds.) *Handbook of Human Resource Management in Emerging Markets*. Cheltenham: Edward Elgar Publishing, pp. 19–41.

World Bank. (2015). *Southern Africa Confronts Rural Poverty*. http://web.worldbank.org/WBSITE/EXTERNAL/NEWS/0,contentMDK:20475321~pagePK:64257043~piPK:437376~theSitePK:4607,00.html.

World Bank. (2016a). *Data: Sub-Saharan Africa (developing only)*. Available at: http://data.worldbank.org/region/SSA.

World Bank. (2016c). *The World Bank in Africa*. Available at: www.worldbank.org/en/region/afr (Accessed: 1 January 2018).

World Bank (2016d). *GDP Growth (annual %)*. Available at: (Accessed: 1 January 2018).

27

INTERNATIONAL INSTITUTIONS AND SUPRANATIONAL INFLUENCE IN EMPLOYMENT RELATIONS[1]

Michel Goyer and Rocio Valdivielso del Real

Introduction

The governance of employment relations has been transformed in the last three decades under the pressures of globalisation (Beck, 2000; Berger, 2006; Goyer, Reinecke and Donaghey, 2014). The increased importance of trade, the multinationalisation of production chains and the mobility of capital across borders have not only shifted the balance of power at the workplace, but also significantly constrained the ability of governments to implement policies designed to protect workers from the disequilibrating consequences of unmediated market forces (Berger, 2000; Garrett, 1998; Garrett and Lange, 1991; Goyer, 2006; Marginson, 2016; Rodrick, 1997). The growing internationalisation of economic activities has increased the exit options of employers by preserving their ability to sell their products and services to local markets while being based in settings whose regulation is perceived to be more favourable to their interests, thereby creating fears of 'regime shopping' (Bognanno, Keane and Yang, 2005; Traxler, 1996; Traxler and Woitech, 2000). International competitive pressures threaten the distinctiveness of labour regimes and the distribution of resources in society.

This chapter analyses the role of international institutions in the governance of ER. In an anarchical world system, international institutions carry a Polanyian promise, namely to tame the excesses of competition so that economic globalisation can occur without threatening standards of living and working conditions (Polanyi, 1944, pp. 27–28; Ruggie, 1982). International institutions could enable countries, and their citizens, to secure at a supranational level what is increasingly difficult to achieve at the domestic level. This chapter illustrates how international/supranational institutions exert influence, or fail to do so, on the governance of ER across countries.

This chapter is divided into three sections. The first section presents an analytical overview of the origins and evolution of institutions. The discussion of the origins of institutional arrangements is characterised by two main approaches. A first approach conceptualises international institutions as the resulting efforts of countries to achieve joint gains through cooperation in an anarchical world system (Keohane, 1984; Milner, 2007; Stein, 1982). States aim to achieve collaboratively at the international level what they cannot secure on their own. A second approach highlights how institutional arrangements constitute the outcomes of conflict settlement across countries (Gourevitch, 1986; Hall, 1986; Roe, 2000). Institutional arrangements, national and supranational alike, require the support of important societal groups in order to influence outcomes. These two different approaches provide insights into the potential influence of international institutions on the governance of ER at the domestic level. Yet, and irrespective of whether institutions result from joint cooperation or conflict settlement, the evolution of the influence of institutions cannot be read back faithfully from the goals of their founders (Mahoney, 2000; Thelen, 2004). The impact of institutional arrangements on outcomes could change as a result of institutional drift, i.e. changing economic and social circumstances that lead to a change of scope of extant institutions, or the influence of institutions could change as the result of institutional layering, i.e. introduction of new institutional elements alongside existing ones (Thelen, 2003; see also Marginson, 2016; Streeck and Thelen, 2005).

The second section analyses the influence of supranational institutions in the European Union (EU). This section highlights the emergence of international institutional arrangements of ER in the advent of the financial crisis. It also illustrates why some institutional arrangements, most notably those associated with the provision of emergency funds (European Solidarity Mechanism) to debtor countries targeted by private bondholders, have proven more influential on the governance of ER than the (new) activism of the European Central Bank (Hall, 2012; Marginson, 2015; Meardi, 2014).

The third section discusses the modest influence of the International Labour Organization (ILO) on the governance of ER, across both a hard law regime (standard setting) and a soft law regime (general principles and involvement of representatives from civil society). The overall limited influence of the ILO not only reflects the presence of divergence among the key stakeholders (governments, employers and trade unions), but also the institutional settings that enable these actors to defend their interests against undesired policies (Baccaro and Mele, 2012; Standing, 2008).

International institutions and supranational influence: origins and evolution

An assessment of the influence of international institutions on the governance of employment relations at the domestic level requires an investigation of their origins and evolution. The analysis of the origins of international institutions highlights the aims of their founders. It illustrates whether international institutions were designed, in the first place, to influence the governance of ER at the domestic level. Yet, the functions performed by institutional arrangements could change over time in responses to changing external circumstances (Thelen, 2004), coalitional shifts (Gourevitch, 1986) or growing principal-agent gaps (Pierson, 1996). The causal variables accounting for institutional formation are different from the factors explaining institutional evolution (Mahoney, 2000; Thelen, 2003).

An important approach to the study of the origins of international institutions has been dominated by scholars emphasising the role of states/governments seeking to secure their preferences in an anarchical world system. In the field of international relations, scholars working under the loose label of 'modified structuralism' have emphasised that under certain restrictive conditions, often involving the failure of individual states to achieve Pareto-optimal outcomes on their own, international institutions will be introduced (Krasner, 1982). These international institutional arrangements – defined as norms, rules and decision-making procedures around which actor expectations converge – emerge out of the egoistic self-interest of national governments seeking to maximise their preferences in the context of a structurally anarchical world system (Keohane, 1982, 1984). Under this rational actor model whereby states seek to secure their preferences, scholars have made extensive use of notions of game theory to explain the formation of international institutions. For instance, Stein (1982) illustrates the relevance of the two most prominent games – namely prisoner's dilemma and the chicken game – to account for institutional creation. Under situations of prisoner's dilemma, states are facing a dilemma of common interests whereby unconstrained individual decision-making leads to Pareto-suboptimal outcomes. International institutions emerge as a cooperation mechanism to secure a Pareto-optimal outcome and, as a result, overcome the defeating self-rational decision to defect given that the choice of one actor is contingent upon the choice made by others. Under situations characterised by chicken game features, in contrast, states are facing a dilemma of common aversions whereby the aim is to avoid one (or several) outcome(s). International institutions emerge as a coordination mechanism to secure the avoidance of mutually undesired outcomes.

In the field of comparative politics, scholars working within the liberal intergovernmentalist frame have highlighted the importance of interstate bargaining in the process of international institutional creation (Garrett, 1993; Moravcsik, 1991, 1998; Schimmelfennig, 2015). International institutions emerge out of the convergence of interests among national governments around lowest common denominator bargaining. That is, international institutions reflect the convergence of interests among (usually) powerful states on specific issue areas where preferences converge. For instance, Moravcsik (1991) interprets the implementation of the Single European Act (SEA) in the then European Community as a convergence of interests in economic policy-making around the preferences of France, Germany and the United Kingdom around economic liberalisation on trade issues. Nothing else. In particular, the failure of redistributive Keynesianism under Mitterrand led to a refocus around economic liberalisation at the European level (Fioretos, 2011; Hall, 1986), but integration in other areas, such as greater employee rights at the supranational community level, desired by French policy-makers, was not possible due to the opposition of the UK government (Lange, 1993). The preferences of the governments of France, Germany and the UK did converge around the notion of market liberalisation, but not around the harmonisation of regulation of ER. This approach is particularly influential in terms of the overall absence of integration in the area of ER in the EU – at least until the great financial crisis. More specifically, the process of European integration has been characterised by 'negative' integration via market liberalisation rather than 'positive' integration via the development of a social model and the harmonisation of regulation of institutions of ER (Hoepner and Schaefer, 2012; Streeck, 1995).

Complementing the insights of the liberal intergovernmentalist approach, scholars working within a comparative historical-institutionalism political economy frame have emphasised how institutional arrangements at the domestic level constitute the outcomes of conflict settlement in historically specific settings (Campbell, 2004; Gourevitch, 1986; Hall, 1986). Domestic institutional arrangements shape the preferences of policy-makers that, in turn, shape the win-set of possible agreements in interstate bargaining (Putnam, 1988).

In contrast to the above theoretical perspectives, the neo-functionalist approach to economic integration (in the EU) conceptualises the process of institutional creation at the supranational level as the result of the character of the integration process itself (Schmitter, 1969, 2005). International institutions reflect an endogenous process whereby the ability to secure the gains of integration in one area requires further integration in other fields. For instance, the process of economic integration in the form of the removal of economic barriers to trade requires the integration of national currencies. Otherwise, currency devaluations could negate the benefits associated with the elimination of non-tariff barriers. Similarly, the proper functioning of a monetary union requires labour mobility across borders since traditional means of adjustment to economic shocks (currency devaluation and increase in money supply) have been removed (Eichengreen, 1991). The ultimate outcome is that states are increasingly losing formal competencies in legislative policy-making as the task of economic integration requires the transfer of powers to supranational institutions.

The above discussion, with the notable exception of the neo-functionalist approach, illustrates that the investigation of institutional creation at the international level reflects the self-rational behaviour of national states seeking to secure gains that they could not achieve on their own. Yet, the current functions performed by current institutions cannot be traced back in a faithful fashion to the goals of their founders (Thelen, 2003, 2004). The factors that account for the origins of institutions are different than those that explain institutional change (Mahoney, 2000). For a variety of reasons, scholars have emphasised the potential divorce between the original aims for institutional creation and the current functions performed by institutions.

Scholars working within the 'modified structuralism' framework highlight that international institutions constitute more than temporary arrangements that change with every shift in power or interests (Krasner, 1982). Institutions may outlive changes in the external environment in which they are embedded. Four factors drawn from game theory have been advanced to explain the potential separation between the initial aim of institutions and their current functions. First, international institutions embody elements of reciprocity whereby states may sacrifice short-term interests with the expectation that others will do so in the future even in the absence of formal legal constraints (Axelrod, 1984; Jervis, 1982). Second, institutional maintenance can become a desired objective in itself given the sunk costs of institutional building (Stein, 1982). Any shifts in interest do not translate faithfully into institutional change because they may be needed in the future. Third, international institutions are often nested in comprehensive agreements that cover several issues (Keohane, 1984). Potential short-term losses in one area are compensated by securing gains on other issues. Fourth, international institutions increase the provision of information on defectors, reduce transaction costs and enhance the credibility of commitments (Keohane, 1984; Koremenos, Lipson and Snidal, 2001; Milner, 2007). International institutions enable states to coordinate their activities and deal with enforcement issues. In other words, international institutions are valuable because they reduce uncertainties in a structurally anarchical world.

In the sub-field of historical institutionalism in comparative politics, scholars are increasingly focusing on the process of institutional (re)configuration over time – in contrast to the previous emphasis on seeking to illustrate how differences in (usually cross-national) institutional arrangements drive divergent outcomes – in order to explain potential gaps between the original aims of institutions and their current functions (Hall and Thelen, 2009; Thelen, 2003; Thelen and Mahoney, 2015). The full dismantling of extant institutional arrangements is not necessary for the current functioning of these institutions to differ from the aims of the original designers (Pierson, 1996; Thelen, 2004). Institutions are often resilient even in the face of enormous (external and endogenous) pressures. Instead, the transformation of the functions of extant institutional arrangements could occur through incremental innovation, namely through institutional drift and layering. The former refers to a situation whereby existing institutions fail to adapt to shifts in political/economic/social environments, thereby leading to an evolution of the functions they perform. Institutional drift constitutes an occurrence of disconnection with the new context in which institutions are embedded since they are ill suited to confront new sets of issues. The latter, in contrast, refers to the introduction of new institutions alongside, and not in place of, already exiting arrangements (Thelen, 2003). Institutional layering is politically easier to pursue in the context of vested interests (Pierson, 2015). As a result of layering, the influence of extant institutional arrangements is reduced given their interaction with new institutions.

Against the grain, Moravcsik (1991, 1998) stresses the ability of national governments to subject institutional evolution to tight control. In the context of the SEA, for instance, interstate bargaining among (powerful) states around the lowest common denominator, economic liberalisation, resulted in a major advancement of the process of European integration. Yet, states succeeded in protecting their national sovereignty by severely limiting power transfer. First, major decisions regarding the implementation of the SEA are decided by the Council of Ministers – not by the European Commission. Second, the use of qualified majority voting, whereby states could be outvoted, is strictly limited to issues of market liberalisation covered by the SEA. Other issues, such as institutional arrangements of labour market regulation, are still subject to unanimity, thereby enabling states to prevent unwanted transfers of power at the supranational institutional level. Thus, for the intergovernmentalist perspective, interstate bargaining among powerful countries not only takes place among the lowest common denominator characterised by the convergence of preferences – it also results in carefully circumscribed delegations of authority that prevent further erosion of national sovereignty.

In contrast, Pierson (1996), directly addressing the thesis put forward by Moravcsik, highlights the inability of states to fully predict instances of institutional drift and layering. Two factors are stressed. First, principal-agent infighting constitutes an inherent feature of the governance organisations – whether international institutions or domestic independent regulatory authorities (Kiewiet and McCubbins, 1991; Moe, 1990). Second, policy-makers, with their inevitable short-term preoccupations, will often discount the long-term consequences of their actions (Garrett and Lange, 1995). As a result, states are ill placed to deal with unintended consequences in the process of institutional evolution, with the outcome that while the formal structures of institutions might remain (largely) stable, their functions might change over time in a manner not anticipated by policy-makers.

International institutions and the governance of employment relations in the European Union

The impact of international institutions on the governance of the system of employment relations of EU member states was limited until the advent of the great financial crisis (Crouch, 1993; Lange, 1991). In particular, harmonisation of institutions and regulation of ER have proven to be conflictual issues among EU member states. The main factor accounting for this state of affairs is that (national) institutional arrangements reflect the varieties in outcomes of conflict settlement in historically specific settings across advanced capitalist economies (Gourevitch, 1986; Gourevitch and Shinn, 2005; Hall, 1986). The presence of institutional diversity across countries structures power relations – both at firm and national levels (Campbell, 2004; Whitley, 1999 – see also Goyer, 2011, pp. 1–51). For instance, variations in the institutions governing job security in the OECD shape managerial ability to determine who is recruited and laid off (Emmenegger, 2014). Restrictions placed on the managerial prerogative to dismiss workers shape the relationship between employers and employees and, in turn, place limits on the ability of top corporate executives to redistribute resources to other parties, such as shareholders (Roe, 2000).

The circumscribed prominence of supranational institutions in the area of ER in the EU thus reflected the distribution of legislative and regulatory powers (Lange, 1993; Streeck, 1995).

Under the legal provisions of the Treaty of Rome, the most important issues in ER – such as collective bargaining, right to strike/lockout and employment termination – were under national jurisdictions. The Maastricht Social Protocol, which the UK did not sign, marginally increased the influence of supranational institutions as some issues (health and safety of workers, information/consultation and equal treatment for men and women) became subject to qualified majority in the Council of Ministers; other issues (social security, co-determination and subsidies for job creation) became subject to unanimous voting in the Council of Ministers, while collective bargaining and the right to strike/lockout still remained under the legal prerogative of national governments.

As a result, the influence of supranational institutions on the governance of industrial relations (IR) remained limited in broadly two areas until the advent of the financial crisis that hit Eurozone countries hard (Marginson, 2005). First, the 1994 European Works Councils (EWCs) Directive stimulated the formation of information and consultation agreements in large European multinationals (Marginson and Sisson, 2004). These agreements focused around the issues of information rights of work councils, health and safety at work, and equal opportunity for women in the workplace. Second, cross-border bargaining coordination initiatives between Germany and its northern European trading partners around wage settlements took place in specific industrial sectors characterised by the presence of strong unions (Hancké, 2014; Johnston and Hancké, 2009). Coordination was motivated by a desire to link wage and productivity increases in order to avoid the problem of beggar-thy-neighbour, namely companies not translating productivity improvements into wage increases.

The global financial crisis (GFC), in contrast, witnessed an increase of supranational institutional innovation in the governance of ER in the EU (Clauwaert and Schoemann, 2012; Degryse, 2012). We contrast the prominence of supranational institutional innovation at two levels: countries that formally sought bailout packages (Hall, 2012, 2014; Marginson, 2015); and countries that were forced to comply with the demands of the European Central Bank (Meardi, 2014). We analyse them in turn.

International institutions of financial assistance: the case of the EU financial bailout packages

The first institutional innovation at the supranational level in the Eurozone is related to the financial assistance in the form of bailout packages for countries targeted by private bondholders. The allocation of the costs of adjustment to the debt crisis have been allocated in a disproportionate manner to debtor countries (Blyth, 2013; Crouch, 2014; Hall, 2012, 2014; Hyman, 2015). In the context of heightened pressures emanating from the bulk of Eurozone creditor countries and the Troika (ECB, European Commission and the International Monetary Fund), several debtor countries implemented extensive austerity measures and introduced important structural changes in their ER systems, mainly in the form of the liberalisation of employment termination and the decentralisation of collective bargaining (Degryse, 2012; Marginson, 2015). The scope for supranational influence has been particularly extensive in the case of debtor countries formally seeking a bailout package.

The provision of financial assistance in the first Greek financial rescue package took the form of two loans made conditional upon the introduction of budgetary cuts and austerity measures, namely a freeze on wages and pensions of public sector employees as well as an increase in the minimum retirement age (Clauwaert and Schoemann, 2012, p. 11; Koukiadaki and Kokkinou, 2016). In the sphere of IR, the Greek government, still under strong pressures from Germany and the Troika, reduced the minimum wage by 22 per cent and introduced lower threshold requirements for the dismissal of employees (Clauwaert and Schoemann, 2012, p. 13). In the area of collective bargaining, the Greek government was constrained to provide legal precedence to company-level over sectoral-based agreements and to facilitate the implementation of company agreements reached with non-unionised representatives (Marginson, 2015, pp. 102–108). Similarly, the provision of financial assistance to the Irish government was made conditional upon the imposition of austerity measures and the decentralisation of collective bargaining under strong pressures from major creditor countries and the Troika (Hickland and Dundon, 2016). The most prominent measures were the unilateral imposition of pay freezes on public sector employees and the substantial erosion of the multiple-employer collective bargaining framework in the wake of the withdrawal of government support (Hall, 2012, p. 363; Marginson, 2015). Finally, the imposition of strong elements of conditionality stood prominently in the design of the bailout package for Portugal (Tavora and Gonzalez, 2016). Pay freezes for civil servants were unilaterally introduced by the government, the extension provision of collective bargaining beyond the level of the firm was legally tightened, and the financial costs associated with collective redundancies were significantly reduced (Clauwaert and Schoemann, 2012, p. 32; Marginson, 2015). Thus, the provision of financial assistance in these three cases was made contingent upon important reforms in areas previously falling under the legal prerogative of national governments: collective bargaining and employment termination (Hall, 2012, 2014).

The responses of European policy-makers to the debt crisis has been impressive in terms of financial commitments designed to calm the turbulence in financial markets. As of July 2012, i.e. at the apex of the crisis, the provision of funding in the form of bailout packages to countries targeted by private bondholders amounted to slightly less than €600 billion (Degryse, 2012, p. 80).[2] Yet, these outcomes were far from being preordained since the EMU was explicitly established in the context of the absence of an institutionalised 'transfer union' characterised by formalised mechanisms by which member states and/or the ECB would be legally obligated to assist each other in times of financial difficulties (De Grauwe, 2013; Hall, 2012). The provision of financial assistance to Eurozone member states gripped by confidence problems from bondholders was not part of the legal purview enshrined in the Maastricht treaty. The institutional arrangements of the Maastricht Treaty were built around the notion of central bank independence as a disciplinary mechanism for inflationary prone countries; they were not designed to deal with sovereign debt concerns (Garrett, 1993).

Institutional innovation via the imposition of conditions on labour regulations in the case of the EU bailout packages and creation of the European Solidarity Mechanism (ESM) provides support for theoretical approaches that emphasise how international institutions reflect how countries seek to achieve joint gains that they could not achieve on their own. Consistent with a phenomenon of institutional drift, the institutional arrangements of the Maastricht Treaty were ill suited to tackle sovereign debt crises (De Grauwe, 2013). Therefore, the provision of financial assistance to countries targeted by private bondholders required the creation of a new institution, namely the ESM, a new supranational institution designed to assist Eurozone member states during periods of financial crisis. Consistent with a process of institutional layering, the new institutional arrangements were introduced alongside, not in place of, existing institutions (Marginson, 2016; see also Streeck and Thelen, 2005; Thelen, 2004). Yet the ESM also testifies to the importance of the distribution of the costs of adjustment (Hall, 2012).

An unexpected supranational actor: the European Central Bank

The second institutional innovation at the supranational level is associated with the role of the ECB (Bini Smaghi, 2013; Woodruff, 2016). The attempts at reforms of institutional arrangements of IR were not limited to countries that formally sought a financial bailout package. Through its intervention into secondary bond markets, the ECB was able to exert strong pressures on the Italian and Spanish governments (Meardi, 2014). In early 2010 – i.e. the first height of the European sovereign debt crisis – the secondary bond markets of debtor countries, including those of Italy and Spain, were characterised by anaemic trading in a context of uncertainty about the finances of Greece and of the piecemeal responses of EU policy-makers to financial turbulence (Blyth 2013, pp. 51–93). The ECB sought to lessen the herd behaviour of private bondholders by acting as lender of last resort on secondary bond markets via its Securities Market Programme (SMP). The ECB purchased important amounts of sovereign debt on the secondary markets during the existence of the SMP from May 2010 to December 2012: €13.6 billion in Irish bonds, €21.6 billion in Portuguese bonds, €30.8 billion in Greek bonds, €43.7 billion in Spanish bonds and €99.0 billion in Italian bonds. The aim was to reduce the borrowing costs for these countries in a context characterised by financial turbulence regarding whether private bondholders would have to accept losses on their holdings.

The intervention of the ECB came attached with stringent conditions for Italy and Spain. In the case of Italy, the ECB requested the introduction of budgetary cuts designed to reduce the size of its debt (Meardi, 2014). More specifically, the ECB identified the extensive, and expensive, system of sub-national institutions (provinces and towns) as ideal targets for budgetary cuts. In the sphere of IR, the ECB tied its purchase of Italian sovereign bonds to the liberalisation of employment protection based on the assumption that rigidities to dismiss workers result in the reluctance of employers to hire, thereby inhibiting growth (Bini Smaghi, 2013). In the case of Spain, the ECB, in alliance with the Bank of Spain, tied its intervention on the bond markets with the liberalisation of collective redundancies schemes for employees with open-ended contracts (Meardi, 2014). The aim was not only to facilitate the dismissal of employees, but also to reduce the importance of atypical work (fixed-term contracts and part-time work) in the Spanish economy. In both cases, the governor of the ECB did not hesitate to contact directly, albeit with the use of secret letters, the prime ministers of the two countries (Berlusconi and Zapatero) and, moreover, temporarily stopped its purchase of sovereign bonds as a strategic move to increase pressures (Bastasin, 2015).

Supranational institutional transformation and the governance of industrial relations: an empirical assessment

The above discussion of international institutional innovations in the governance of employment relations in the EU highlights both the importance of interstate bargaining and the prominence of the role of supranational actors (Caporaso and Rhodes, 2016). On the one hand, the management of the debt crisis involved hard bargaining, mainly – although not exclusively – between creditor and debtor countries over the design of bailout packages designed to provide funding to Eurozone countries targeted by private bondholders (Bastasin, 2015; Donnelly, 2014; Hall, 2012, 2014; Hyman, 2015). Although the EC took part in the negotiations, the key institutional features of the bailout rescue plans were primarily designed by the finance ministers of the Eurozone (ECOFIN). On the other hand, supranational actors played a key role in the introduction and implementation of new international institutions. The ECB, for instance, went well beyond its mandate of providing price stability (Meardi, 2014): through its intervention in secondary bond markets, the Frankfurt-based financial institution played a central role in crisis management and, arguably, has effectively become a lender of last resort – thereby functionally overcoming the prohibitions of the Maastricht Treaty on rescuing Eurozone member states in financial difficulties (Woodruff, 2016).

Yet, the constraining character of these international institutions on the governance of ER in Europe sharply differs. The (early) empirical evidence points to the unequally constraining character of these newly created international institutions. This divergence in the constraining character of institutions is measured by their impact on the economy. The institutional mechanisms associated with the EU bailout packages have involved major institutional reforms, which, at the time of writing, have not been reversed (Hall, 2012; Hermann, 2017). In the case of the third Greek bailout package, for example, financial assistance was provided under the strict condition that the Greek government committed itself not to reverse the liberalisation measures introduced since the beginning of the crisis. Moreover, the conditionality of the EU bailout packages, namely the imposition of austerity measures and the liberalisation of institutional arrangements of IR, has significantly influenced the adjustment process to the financial crisis in recipient countries. For instance, the decline in relative labour unit costs has been substantial for countries that formally received bailout packages (De Grauwe, 2013). The Greek economy experienced an important internal devaluation, i.e. reduction in prices and wages relative to other Eurozone members. From 2008 to 2012, its relative labour unit costs declined by 11 per cent. Similarly, relative unit labour costs declined by 23 per cent in Ireland between 2008 and 2012. By contrast, Italy experienced the lowest internal devaluation among countries targeted by private bondholders, with its relative unit labour costs declining by a mere 0.6 per cent between 2008 and 2012.

The involvement of the ECB, on the other hand, is characterised by mixed results regarding the influence of international institutions over the governance of ER. On the one hand, the transformation of IR in Spain has been profound since the GFC (Meardi, 2014). Under pressures from the ECB, the Zapatero government launched a series of reforms of labour markets in June 2010, characterised by a financial reduction in the cost of employee dismissals and the liberalisation of temporary work agencies in sectors where they were previously banned, most notably construction. Under the Rajoy government, further and more wide-ranging measures were introduced: the ability of employers to unilaterally introduce measures of internal flexibility (changes in job tasks and timetables), the introduction of a new one-year employment contract without employment security, and the reduction of compensation for dismissals from 45 to 20 days per year worked (ibid, p. 344).

The Italian case, on the other hand, is characterised by the lack of similarly corresponding adjustment. The first demand of the ECB focused on the issue of labour market flexibility. Compared with other advanced capitalist economies, Italy is characterised by the provision of relatively high employment protection as measured by the costs of firing new employees, size of severance payments, the length of notice requirements for the initiation of collective dismissal procedures, and the legal recourse of employees against collective dismissals (OECD, 2011). After initially agreeing to the principle of greater managerial freedom to dismiss employees, the Berlusconi government decided, after a severe defeat in the May 2011 local elections, to postpone all austerity measures and liberalisation of employment regulation policies until after the 2013 general election (Bastasin, 2015, pp. 255–282). The government of Mario Monti, while committed to extensive labour market flexibility, failed to secure sufficient support in parliament for a significant liberalisation of rules on employee dismissals. Instead, the Monti government was limited to modifying Article 18 of the Italian Labor Court (Culpepper, 2014). The new law allows labour judges to reinstate workers dismissed on *implausible economic grounds* in companies of 15 or more employees. Under the previous law, in contrast, employees could only be reinstated if they had been *wrongfully dismissed*.

The second request of the ECB focused on the introduction of budgetary cuts in the system of sub-national institutions (provinces and towns) of Italy. Instead, Italian governments focused primarily on raising revenues via taxes rather than cutting budgets (Bini Smaghi, 2013, pp. 123–129). As for the case of liberalisation of IR, the Berlusconi government approved, but decided to postpone, most austerity measures until after the 2013 national elections with the exception of pay freezes in the public sector (Bastasin, 2015, pp. 255–282). The last budget presented by Berlusconi, in September 2011, was heavily skewed toward tax revenues (73 per cent) at the expense of savings from budgetary cuts (27 per cent) in attempting to tackle burgeoning debt, thereby giving Italy the second highest tax level in the Eurozone area (ibid, p. 301). The (unelected) government of Mario Monti also found it easier to secure parliamentary support for raising taxes than for cutting spending. The most important sources of revenues were increases in highly regressive taxes, namely VAT, gasoline and residential taxes (Culpepper, 2014). Attempts to eliminate a level of state bureaucracy failed as a bill to cut the number of provinces and cities was not submitted for parliamentary approval before the general election of 2013. Thus, despite different sets of intentions, both Berlusconi and Monti found it easier to distribute the costs of adjustment among diffused voters rather than directly confront entrenched interest groups. This last statement should not suggest that the Monti government was completely powerless to control government expenditures: most notably, important changes to the pension system were introduced, such as steps toward a full defined-contribution system and the raising of the retirement age of women from 62 to 67 by 2018. However, these reforms were expected to generate savings in the future and, moreover, were not explicitly demanded by the ECB.

The above overview of the contrasting cases of Italy and Spain highlights the limits of the influence of the ECB despite its massive financial firepower. The inability of the ECB to impose a comprehensive overhaul of institutional arrangements of IR in Italy reflects the constraints associated with the environment in which the Frankfurt-based supranational bank operates. In particular, the decision of the German government and most of the creditor countries of the Eurozone to limit the size of the ESM at around €600 billion, despite repeated demands by the ECB for a bigger bailout fund, meant that the financing needs of large countries such as Italy and Spain could not be met in the form of bailout packages, thereby failing to reduce the risks of financial contagion (Bastasin, 2015, pp. 170–282). The lack of alternative sources of finance, in turn, imposed constraints on the credibility of the conditional character of ECB intervention (Wolf, 2014, pp. 45–88). While the firepower of the ECB is potentially extensive and well-suited to deal with the presence of uncertainties and herd behaviour of bondholders, the provision of unlimited, but conditional, support lacks credibility given the lack of financing alternatives. The ECB faces serious constraints in Italy in serving both as the lender of last resort and as the policy enforcer in the current context of the institutional architecture of Eurozone governance. In contrast, the heightened influence of the ECB in the Spanish context suggests the importance of the political orientation of the Rajoy government.

The International Labour Organization

The ILO was founded in 1919 as part of the peace settlement after the First World War and, perhaps more importantly, in the aftermath of the Bolshevik revolution. The motive of its founders was to counteract the appeal of socialism via the regulation of the excesses of untamed labour markets (Cox, 1973; Ryder, 2015). Its main role initially lied in the elaboration and supervision of international labour standards. The principal means used in its role as standard-setter are conventions and non-binding recommendations. Conventions are detailed legal provisions covering issues related to IR, labour-based social security and employment policy. If ratified by national governments, conventions become binding obligations. Recommendations, on the other hand, do not become part of the corpus of national law but simply constitute tools to guide policy-making at the domestic level. To be introduced, conventions and recommendations need a two-thirds majority at the annual meeting of the ILO followed by the obligation of member states to consider whether to adopt them.[3]

The effectiveness of the ILO as a standard-setter has been limited (Baccaro and Mele, 2012; Standing, 2008). Between 1960 and the late 1980s, an annual average of only two conventions have been adopted at the ILO annual meeting. The average number of countries, mostly located in the northern hemisphere, that have ratified them five years after their adoption at the ILO annual meeting is slightly less than 13 (Baccaro and Mele, 2012, p. 198). Moreover, the capacity of the ILO to monitor the implementation of ratified conventions and to design effective penalties has been limited (Meardi and Marginson, 2014; Niforou, 2012). Under the soft law strategy of naming and shaming – an interesting evolution from the rather rigid hard law strategy – the ILO seeks to condemn countries that have breached ratified conventions. Yet, national governments have refused to implement sanctions against fellow members. The influence of the ILO as a supranational institution of standard-setting has been fairly circumscribed.

Because of its overall modest record as a standard-setter, the ILO implemented a strategic change of orientation in the early 1990s (Ryder, 2015; Standing, 2008; see also Bartley, 2007). Interpreting the traditional standard-setting system as a form of hard law that directly limits the sovereignty of states, the ILO sought to move to a soft law regime in alliance with key partners in civil society.[4] Three features characterise the strategic re-orientation of the ILO (Baccaro and Mele, 2012). First, the emphasis is placed on the use of declarations of general, non-binding, principles that convey broad values. Second, the elaboration of these broad principles is inspired by civil society organisations and NGOs. Third, the ILO sought to develop a new role in the form of technical assistance for the assessment of the implementation of these broad principles via the development of quantitative indicators.

The success of this strategic re-orientation has been limited. Governments have vetoed proposals that would have provided ILO officials with added capacities to monitor the regulation of workplace conditions across countries (Standing, 2008). Key members of the senior staff of the ILO are still appointed on temporary contracts that, in turn, result in short-termism and limited professional/technical capacities. Moreover, government representatives have been overall suspicious of the involvement of representatives from civil society (Baccaro and Mele, 2012). Through the use of their voting power at the ILO annual meeting, they have successfully derailed activist attempts by top officials to open up the organisation to private monitoring schemes and to representatives of civil society.

The relatively modest influence of the ILO as a supranational institution suggests two theoretical insights. First, the membership of the ILO is composed of diverse groups with often opposing preferences. Two cleavages are prominent (Standing, 2008). The first one is the divergence of interests between employers' associations and labour unions, which severely restricts the room for manoeuvre of ILO officials. As a result, the discourse of the ILO is increasingly being framed around issues associated with new social movements, such as gender equality and environmental sustainability, rather than redistribution issues such as income inequalities (Ryder, 2015). The discourse of the ILO is also framed in broad and abstract terms in order to elicit widespread approval –such as the relatively modest theme of 'decent work' as the main promulgated objective for workplace conditions in the current era of globalisation (Standing, 2008, p. 370). The second cleavage is between advanced capitalist economies and transition/developing economies. The role of the ILO as standard-setter is circumscribed due to the different assessments of what those standards should be, namely a floor of working conditions or a ceiling (ibid, p. 367). Because of these two cleavages, it has been relatively complicated for ILO officials to orchestrate coordination among employers, unions and member countries in order to achieve a Pareto-optimal outcome. In the setting of game theory, the ILO is not plagued by problems of coordination associated with the prisoner's dilemma nor with the aversion of a common outcome reminiscent of the chicken game.

Second, the presence of divergence of preferences matters because of the institutional context of the ILO. Important streams in social sciences research have highlighted that the translation of the preferences of actors into desired outcomes is mediated by the institutional context in which they are embedded (Campbell, 2004; Garrett and Lange, 1995; Hall, 1986). Institutional arrangements shape the power of different stakeholders by offering disproportionate access to, and thus influence over, the decision-making process and its associated resources at hand. In the case of the ILO, its corporatist structure has enabled employers' associations, trade unions and member countries to block attempts by ILO officials to enact undesired policies (Baccaro and Mele, 2012; Ryder, 2015).[5] Institutional drift and layering have been limited by the relative ease through which key actors could express their divergence.

Conclusion

The internationalisation of economic activities in the form of cross-border capital flows, increased trade integration of goods and services, and the multinationalisation of production by transnational companies has seriously impeded the ability of governments to regulate employment relations at the national level (Berger, 2000; Garrett, 1998). Institutional innovation, or reconfiguration, is increasingly seen as necessary in order to achieve at the supranational level what has become elusive for national governments at the domestic level (Marginson, 2016).

The academic literature on institutions is both rich and insightful. Drawing from economics and game theory, a first group of scholars have investigated how the creation of institutions at the supranational level highlights the preferences of national governments to achieve joint gains via collaboration in an anarchical world (Keohane, 1984; Stein, 1982). Historical-institutionalist scholars, in contrast, stress how the process of institutional creation reflects the settlements of conflict across national settings that, in turn, serve as the basis of negotiations at the international level (Hall, 1986; Putnam, 1988; Roe, 2000). Yet, another stream of institutional analyses, often drawn from the historical-institutional group, illustrates how the influence of institutions could change over time in ways that differ from the goals of their founders (Mahoney, 2000; Thelen, 2004). Drawing from the concepts of institutional layering and drift, the impact of institutions on outcomes could change despite being structurally stable (Thelen, 2003).

Our case studies illustrate the range of outcomes associated with institutional analyses. The case of institutional innovation in the setting up of the ESM highlights the failure of the institutional arrangements of the Maastricht Treaty to tackle issues related to the financial crisis (De Grauwe, 2013; Garrett, 1993). Consistent with the concept of institutional drift, the Eurozone crisis highlights the inability of central bank independence to prevent countries from accumulating budget deficits and the inadequacies of the no-bailout clause in dealing with private bondholders and instabilities in financial markets. Consistent with the concept of institutional layering, the process of adjustment to the financial crisis did not involve the dismantling of existing institutional arrangements, a politically difficult process, but the introduction of new institutional arrangements on top of extant ones (Degryse, 2012; Marginson, 2015).

Yet, the emergence of institutional drift does not constitute a natural and automatic process. The case of the ILO illustrates how the structure of institutional design of supranational arrangements enables the original founders to maintain control over their operations (Baccaro and Mele, 2012; Standing, 2008). The procedural decision-making process of the ILO has enabled its key constituent parties to resist changes that would challenge their preferences despite a changing global economy. The case of the relatively modest influence of the ECB highlights the limits of attempting to develop a new institutional regime if support from key parties is missing. The absence of collaborationist co-conspirators in Italy limited the ability of the institutionally powerful ECB to impose its wills (Bastasin, 2015; Culpepper, 2014).

Notes

1 We thank Jimmy Donaghey for his insightful comments on this chapter.
2 Moreover, this commitment comes on top of the ECB purchasing massive amounts of government bonds in the secondary markets between May 2010 and December 2012: €13.6 billion in Irish bonds, €21.6 billion in Portuguese bonds, €30.8 billion in Greek bonds, €43.7 billion in Spanish bonds and €99.0 billion in Italian bonds (ECB, 2013). The ECB also provided more than €1,000 billion in the form of cheap loans to Eurozone banks between December 2011 and February 2012 (Degryse, 2012, p. 5).
3 The distribution of votes at the ILO annual meeting is as follows: unions and employers each hold a quarter of the votes while government representatives account for the remaining half.
4 For an analytical overview of hard law vs. soft law, see Abbott and Snidal, 2000).
5 See footnote three on the structure of voting system at the ILO.

References

Abbott, K. and Snidal, D. (2000). 'Hard and Soft Law in International Governance', *International Organization*, 54(3), pp. 421–456.
Axelrod, R. (1984). *The Evolution of Cooperation*. New York: Basic Books.
Baccaro, L. and Mele, V. (2012). 'Pathology of Path Dependency? The ILO and the Challenge of New Governance', *Industrial Labor Relations Review*, 65(2), pp. 195–224.
Bartley, T. (2007). 'Institutional emergence in an era of globalization: the rise of transnational private regulation of labor and environment conditions', *American Journal of Sociology*, 113(2), pp. 297–351.
Bastasin, C. (2015). *Saving Europe: Anatomy of a Dream*. Washington, DC: Brookings Institution Press.
Beck, U. (2000). *The Brave New World of Work*. Cambridge (UK): Polity Press.
Berger, S. (2000). 'Globalization and Politics', *Annual Review of Political Science*, 3, pp. 183–219.
Berger, S. (2006). *How We Compete: What Companies Around the World are Doing to Make it in Today's Global Economy*. New York: Doubleday.
Bini Smaghi, L. (2013). *Austerity: European Democracies Against the Wall*. Brussels: Centre for European Policy Studies.
Blyth, M. (2013). *Austerity: the History of a Dangerous Idea*. Oxford: Oxford University Press.
Bognanno, M., Keane, M. and Yang, D. (2005). 'The Influence of Wages and Industrial Relations Environments on the Production Locations of U.S. Multinational Corporations', *Industrial and Labor Relations Review*, 58(2), pp. 171–200.
Campbell, J. (2004). *Institutional Change and Globalization*. Princeton: Princeton University Press.
Caporaso, J. and Rhodes, M. (2016). Introduction, in Caporaso, J. and Rhodes, M. (eds.) *The Political and Economic Dynamics of the Eurozone Crisis*. Oxford: Oxford University Press, pp. 1–14.
Clauwaert, S. and Schoemann, I. (2012). *The crisis and national labour law: a mapping exercise*. ETUI working paper #2012/04. Brussels: ETUI.
Cox, R. W. (1973). ILO: limited monarchy, in Cox, R. W. and Jacobson, H. K. (eds.) *The Anatomy of Influence*. New Haven: Yale University Press, pp. 102–138.
Crouch, C. (1993). *Industrial Relations and European State Traditions*. Oxford: Clarendon Press.
Crouch, C. (2014). 'Introduction: Labour Markets and Social Policy after the Crisis', *Transfer*, 20(1), pp. 7–22.
Culpepper, P. (2014). 'The Political Economy of Unmediated Democracy: Italian Austerity under Mario Monti', *West European Politics*, 37(6), pp. 1264–1281.
De Grauwe, P. (2013). 'The Political Economy of the Euro', *Annual Review of Political Science*, 16, pp. 153–170.
Degryse, C. (2012). *The new European economic governance*. Working Paper 2012.14. Brussels: European Trade Union Institute.
Donnelly, S. (2014). 'Power Politics and the Undersupply of Financial Stability in Europe', *Review of International Political Economy*, 21(4), pp. 980–1005.

ECB (2013). *Details on securities holdings acquired under the Securities Markets Programme*. [Press release]. [Accessed: 10 January 2018]. Available at: www.ecb.europa.eu/press/pr/date/2013/html/pr130221_1.en.html.

Eichengreen, B. (1991). *Is Europe an optimum currency area?* Working paper no. 3579. Cambridge (MA): National Bureau of Economic Research. Available at: www.nber.org/papers/w3579.

Emmenegger, O. (2014). *The Power to Dismiss: Trade Unions and the Regulation of Job Security in Western Europe*. Oxford: Oxford University Press.

Fioretos, O. (2011). *Creative Reconstructions. Multilateralism and European Varieties of Capitalism After 1950*. Ithaca: Cornell University Press.

Garrett, G. (1993). 'The Politics of Maastricht', *Economics and Politics*, 5(2), pp. 105–123.

Garrett, G. (1998). 'Global Markets and National Politics: Collision Course or Virtuous Circle?' *International Organization*, 52(4), pp. 149–176.

Garrett, G. and Lange, P. (1991). 'Political Responses to Interdependence. What's 'Left' for the Left?' *International Organization*, 45(4), pp. 539–564.

Garrett, G. and Lange, P. (1995). 'Internationalization, Institutions and Political Change', *International Organization*, 49(4), pp. 627–655.

Gourevitch, P. (1986). *Politics in the Hard Times: Comparative Responses to International Economic Crises*. Ithaca: Cornell University Press.

Gourevitch, P. and Shinn, J. (2005). *Political Power and Corporate Control: The New Global Politics of Corporate Governance*. Princeton: Princeton University Press.

Goyer, M. (2006). 'Varieties of Institutional Investors and National Models of Capitalism', *Politics and Society*, 34(3), pp. 399–430.

Goyer, M. (2011). *Contingent Capital: Short-term Investors and the Evolution of Corporate Governance in France and Germany*. Oxford: Oxford University Press.

Goyer, M., Reinecke, J. and Donaghey, J. (2014). Globalization and labour market governance, in Wilkinson, A., Wood, G. and Deeg, R. (eds.) *The Oxford Handbook of Employment Relations*. Oxford: Oxford University Press, pp. 473–494.

Hall, P. (1986). *Governing the Economy: The Politics of State Intervention in Britain and France*. Oxford: Oxford University Press.

Hall, P. (2012). 'The Economics and Politics of the Euro Crisis', *German Politics*, 21(4), pp. 355–371.

Hall, P. (2014). 'Varieties of Capitalism and the Euro Crisis', *West European Politics*, 37(6), pp. 1223–1243.

Hall, P. and Thelen, K. (2009). 'Institutional Change in Varieties of Capitalism', *Socio-Economic Review*, 7(4), pp. 7–34.

Hancké, B. (2014). *Unions, Central Banks, and EMU*. Oxford: Oxford University Press.

Hermann, C. (2017). 'Crisis, Structural Reform and the Dismantling of the European Social Model(s)', *Economic and Industrial Democracy*, 38(1), pp. 51–68.

Hickland, E. and Dundon, T. (2016). 'The Shifting Contours of Collective Bargaining in Ireland', *European Journal of Industrial Relations*, 22(3), pp. 235–249.

Hoepner, M. and Schafer, A. (2012). 'Embeddedness and Regional Integration: Waiting for Polanyi in a Hayekian Setting', *International Organization*, 66(3), pp. 429–455.

Hyman, R. (2015). Austeritarianism in Europe: what options for resistance?, in Natali, D. and Vanhercke, B. (eds.) *Social Policy in the European Union: State of Play 2012*. Brussels: ETUI, pp. 99–126.

Jervis, R. (1982). 'Security regimes', *International Organization*, 36(2), pp. 357–378.

Johnston, A. and Hancké, B. (2009). 'Wage Inflation and Labour Unions in EMU', *Journal of European Public Policy*, 16(4), pp. 601–622.

Keohane, R. (1982). 'The Demand for International Regimes', *International Organization*, 36(2), pp. 325–355.

Keohane, R. (1984). *After Hegemony: Cooperation and Discord in the World Political Economy*. Princeton: Princeton University Press.

Kiewiet, D.R. and McCubbins, M.D. (1991). *The Logic of Delegation: Congressional Parties and the Appropriations Process*. Chicago: University of Chicago Press.

Koremenos, B., Lipson, C. and Snidal, D. (2001). 'The rational design of international institutions', *International Organization*, 55(4), pp. 761–799.

Koukiadaki, A. and Kokkinou, C. (2016). 'Deconstructing the Greek System of Industrial Relations', *European Journal of Industrial Relations*, 22(3), pp. 205–219.

Krasner, S. (1982). 'Structural Causes and Regime Consequences: Regimes as Intervening Variables', *International Organization*, 36(2), pp. 185–205.

Lange, P. (1993). 'Maastricht and the Social Protocol: Why did They do it?' *Politics and Society*, 21(1), pp. 5–36.

Mahoney, J. (2000). 'Path Dependence in Historical Sociology', *Theory and Society*, 29(4), pp. 507–548.

Marginson, P. (2005). 'Industrial Relations at the European Sector Level: The Weak Link?' *Economic and Industrial Democracy*, 26(4), pp. 511–540.

Marginson, P. (2015). 'Coordinated Bargaining in Europe: From Incremental Corrosion to Frontal Assault?' *European Journal of Industrial Relations*, 21(2), pp. 97–114.

Marginson, P. (2016). 'Governing Work and Employment Relations in an Internationalized Economy: The Institutional Challenge', *Industrial and Labor Relations Review*, 69(5), pp. 1033–1055.

Marginson, P. and Sisson, K. (2004). *European Integration and Industrial Relations*. London: Palgrave Macmillan.

Meardi, G. (2014). Employment relations under external pressure: Italian and Spanish reforms during the great recession, in Hauptmeier, M. and Vidal, M. (eds.) *Comparative Political Economy of Work*. London: Palgrave, pp. 332–350.

Meardi, G. and Marginson, P. (2014). 'Global Labour Governance: Potential and Limits of an Emerging Perspective', *Work, Employment & Society*, 28(4), pp. 651–662.

Milner, H. (2007). *Interests, Institutions and Information: Domestic Politics and International Relations*. Princeton: Princeton University Press.

Moe, T. (1990). The politics of structural choice: toward a theory of political bureaucracy, in Williamson, O.E. (ed.) *Organization Theory: From Chester Barnard to the Present and Beyond*. Oxford: Oxford University Press, pp. 116–153.

Moravcsik, A. (1991). 'Negotiating the Single European Act: National Interests and Conventional Statecraft in the European Community', *International Organization*, 45(1), pp. 19–56.

Moravcsik, A. (1998). *The Choice for Europe*. Ithaca: Cornell University Press.

Niforou, C. (2012). 'International Framework Agreements and Industrial Relations Governance', *British Journal of Industrial Relations*, 50(2), pp. 352–373.

OECD (2011). *OECD Employment Outlook 2011*. Paris: OECD.

Pierson, P. (1996). 'The Path to European Integration: A Historical Institutionalist Perspective', *Comparative Political Studies*, 29(2), pp. 123–163.

Pierson, P. (2015). Power and path dependence, in Mahoney, J. and Thelen, K. (eds.) *Advances in Comparative-Historical Analysis*. New York: Cambridge University Press, pp. 123–146.

Polanyi, K. (1944). *The Great Transformation*. New York: Farrar and Reinhardt.

Putnam, R. (1988). 'Diplomacy and Domestic Politics: The Logic of Two-level Games', *International Organization*, 42(3), pp. 427–460.

Rodrick, D. (1997). *Has Globalization Gone Too Far?* Washington, DC: Institute for International Economics.

Roe, M. (2000). 'Political Preconditions to Separating Ownership from Control', *Stanford Law Review*, 53(3), pp. 539–606.

Ruggie, J. (1982). 'International Regimes, Transactions and Change: Embedded Liberalism in the Postwar Economic Order', *International Organization*, 36(2), pp. 379–415.

Ryder, G. (2015). 'The International Labour Organization: The Next 100 Years', *Journal of Industrial Relations*, 57(5), pp. 748–757.

Schimmelfennig, F. (2015). 'Liberal Intergovernmentalism and the Euro Crisis', *Journal of European Public Policy*, 22(2), pp. 177–195.

Schmitter, P. (1969). 'Three neo-functional hypotheses about international integration', *International Organization*, 23(2), pp. 161–166.

Schmitter, P. (2005). 'Ernst B. Haas and the legacy of neofunctionalism', *Journal of European Public Policy*, 12(2), pp. 255–272.

Standing, G. (2008). 'The ILO: An Agency for Globalization?' *Development and Change*, 39(3) pp. 355–384.

Stein, A. (1982). 'Coordination and Collaboration: Regimes in an Anarchic World', *International Organization*, 36(2), pp. 299–324.

Streeck, W. (1995). 'Neo-Voluntarism: A New European Policy Regime', *European Law Journal*, 1(1), pp. 31–59.

Streeck, W. and Thelen, K. (2005). Introduction: institutional change in advanced political economies, in Streeck, W. and Thelen, K (eds.) *Beyond Continuity: Institutional Change in Advanced Political Economies*. Oxford: Oxford University Press.

Tavora, I. and Gonzalez, P. (2016). 'Labour Market Regulation and Collective Bargaining in Portugal during the Crisis', *European Journal of Industrial Relations*, 22(3), pp. 251–265.

Thelen, K. (2003). How institutions evolve: insights from comparative-historical analysis, in Mahoney, J. and Rueschemeyer, D. (eds.) *Comparative Historical Analysis in the Social Sciences*. New York: Cambridge University Press, pp. 208–240.

Thelen, K. (2004). *How Institutions Evolve. The Political Economy of Skills in Germany, Britain, the United States, and Japan*. New York: Cambridge University Press.

Thelen, K. and Mahoney, J. (2015). Comparative-historical analysis in contemporary political science, in Mahoney, J. and Thelen, K. (eds.) *Advances in Comparative-Historical Analysis*. New York: Cambridge University Press, pp. 3–26.

Traxler, F. (1996). 'Collective Bargaining and Industrial Change. A Case of Disorganization?' *European Sociological Review*, 12, pp. 271–287.

Traxler, F. and Woitech, B. (2000). 'Transnational Investment and National Labour Market Regimes: A Case of Regime Shopping?' *European Journal of Industrial Relations*, 6(2), pp. 141–159.

Whitley, R. (1999). *Divergent Capitalisms: The Social Structuring and Change of Business Systems*. Oxford: Oxford University Press.

Wolf, M. (2014). *The Shifts and the Shocks*. London: Allen and Lane Publishers.

Woodruff, D. (2016). 'Governing by Panic: The Politics of the Eurozone Crisis', *Politics and Society*, 44(1), pp. 81–116.

28

EMPLOYMENT RELATIONS, STAKEHOLDER THEORY AND BUSINESS ETHICS

Andrew Timming and Samuel Mansell

Introduction

In the light of the generally unequal relations of power between capital and labour (Offe and Wiesenthal, 1980), the employment relationship in a market-driven economy is inherently fraught with a myriad of inescapable ethical landmines. As a result, employment relations (ER), broadly conceived, cannot be fully understood in a moral vacuum. The question of whether (at least private sector) organisations have a responsibility beyond their fiduciary obligation to shareholders (Friedman, 1970; see also Mulligan, 1986) is at the very heart of what is commonly referred to today as stakeholder theory (Freeman, 1984; Mansell, 2013a; McWilliams and Siegel, 2001). Whilst the lion's share of the literature on corporate social responsibility (hereafter CSR) tends to conceptualise the main non-shareholding stakeholders as, for example, consumers (Sen and Bhattacharya, 2001), the environment (Lyon and Maxwell, 2008) or, perhaps more amorphously, 'society' (Pedersen, 2010), the focus of this chapter is on employees as organisational stakeholders. We explore this focus through two themes: first, we examine the ethics of child labour; and second, we examine whether employees have a right to participate in organisational decision-making.

Employees are often overlooked in the wider CSR literature (Young and Thyil, 2009), most of which overwhelmingly focuses on the impact of organisational decision-making on stakeholders that are largely external to the workplace. But this outward-looking focus is curious in the light of the fact that employees (which are, of course, *internal* to the firm) and consumers (which are, of course, *external* to the firm) can be viewed as one and the same, in the sense that employees are ultimately the key drivers of consumption in the economy (Cova and Dalli, 2009). In fact, one might argue that the question of how organisations treat employees is not independent of how they act towards society at large, since employees not only represent a sizeable proportion of society, but also act as consumers when they are not at work. In short, the purpose of this chapter is to draw some much-needed attention to the various ethical implications of viewing employees as stakeholders. It is in this light that the chapter makes an original contribution to the wider bodies of literature on business ethics, stakeholder theory and ER.

In the next two sections, the notions of power and exploitation are examined within the context of the employment relationship, with an emphasis on child labour in the developing world. The generally accepted supposition that management can leverage more power against employees than *vice versa* is arguably the source of all ethical questions within the employment relationship. After that, an overview of stakeholder theory is provided, with an emphasis on important scholars and debates and how they link back to employee participation in decision-making. The chapter then turns to the important question of whether ethical business practices (specifically with respect to employee participation) and firm performance can ever positively align. An agenda for future theoretical and empirical research in this area is then presented, followed by a brief conclusion.

Power and exploitation in the employment relationship

The study of ethics in the employment relationship starts, inevitably, with the study of power in the employment relationship, for it is through the exercise of power that behaviour often becomes unethical. Lammers et al. (2015) provide a useful overview of the literature on the relationship between power and morality. They argue that although power does not *necessarily* undermine morality (since power can also be used for good), it can and often does lead to disinhibition, which in turn promotes unethical behaviour. Pitesa and Thau (2013) also show, through experimental research, how power-holding can lead to self-serving behaviours, resulting in negative consequences for others. The logic here is that social relations based on the unequal distribution of power make possible corruption and the coercion of the less powerful on the part of the more powerful. Alternatively stated, where all parties have equal power (that is to say, no power) over one another, the scope for unethical behaviour is significantly reduced since there can be no material consequences. The problem with this position, of course, is that no social relationship, including in the spheres of work and employment, is ever characterised by a perfectly equal distribution of power.

Many social scientists draw from a Foucauldian perspective when analysing power (Foucault, 1995). Perhaps the most well known applications of Foucauldian power to the employment relationship are evident in Townley (1993, 1994). She conceptualises power as a form of disciplinary control that organisations and their agents leverage over workers. Looking at some of the key methods of human resource management (e.g. recruitment and selection, performance appraisal, job evaluation, etc.), she illustrates how the HR system aims to define work and correct deviation from behavioural and performance standards. In a similar vein, Pfeffer (1994) defines power as getting workers to do things that they otherwise would not do. It is easy to see the ethical implications inherent in this definition. The assumption is that workers often do not want to do what they are told, but they have no choice in the matter by virtue of the employment contract, whether written or implied.

Another key study of power in the employment relationship is offered up by Kelly (2000). In it, he investigates power not so much in the employer-employee relationship, but rather in the employer-union relationship, where unions are viewed as a countervailing force vis-à-vis management. He argues that "workers join unions in order to overcome their weakness as individuals in the employment relationship" (Kelly, 2000, p. 9). In other words, individual lack of power, which makes a worker vulnerable to managerial prerogative, can be re-balanced, at least to some extent, via the collective power of trade unions. Thompson's (1983) pioneering study of the labour process equally places an emphasis on the ways in which managers implement systems of control and surveillance, with the ultimate aim of circumventing trade union power and reasserting managerial authority over the workforce.

In short, there is, arguably, very little disagreement amongst ER scholars that employers, *ceteris paribus*, generally possess more power than employees or even unions. Organisations and workers are co-dependent from a certain point of view, but the former can, generally speaking, weather the withdrawal of labour much better than the latter can weather the withdrawal of livelihood. Because of this intrinsic imbalance of power in the employment relationship, workers are more susceptible to mistreatment, coercion and abuse at the hands of management. This is particularly the case in relation to child labour, a topic to which we now turn.

Business ethics and child labour

If employees are generally thought to be less powerful than employers, then it naturally follows that child labourers are arguably at the absolute bottom of the employment relations hierarchy in the light of their comparative vulnerabilities in the labour market. A common misperception is that child labour is just an historical blight staining the distant past (Humphries, 2013), but in its 2017 National Child Labour Survey, the International Labour Organization (2017) reports that some 168 million children are employed worldwide, 85 million of whom are engaged in what is deemed to be 'hazardous' work that poses a clear and present threat to their health and safety. It should not be at all surprising that the lion's share of these child labourers are employed in the least developed countries, where, on the whole, the legal regulation of employment is less extensive than in the developed world and, moreover, where cultural practices and economic hardships act in concert to encourage the employment of children. Even those so-called ethical companies that actively work to avoid the employment of child labourers on the front line of production often find that the raw materials they use to construct their products were ultimately sourced by young children (Zane, Irwin and Reczek, 2016).

The ethical debates surrounding child labour are well rehearsed (Hindman and Smith, 1999; Kolk and Van Tulder, 2004; Winstanley, Clark and Leeson, 2002), and yet there is still no consensus on the matter, a common outcome in ethical debates. Whilst very few scholars would argue that children (or indeed adults) should be subjected to dangerous working conditions, there is significantly more 'grey area' in relation to the employment of children in industries that pose a lower threat to health and safety. Although not an advocate of child labour, Sachs (2015) has controversially argued that sweatshops ought to be embraced and encouraged, rather than rejected on ethical grounds, based on the fact that they offer the kind of low-wage jobs that can be a useful stepping-stone toward greater levels of economic development and prosperity. A similar logic can, in theory, be extended to the employment of children. From a certain point of view, one could argue that paying children a wage that can be used to support their families and put food on the table is morally preferable to abject poverty, starvation and destitution. This moral position is predicated on the assumption that it is better to be exploited and employed than unemployed and starving, as it were. Such a position can be rightly situated within the consequentialist school of moral philosophy (Sinnott-Armstrong, 1992).

In contrast, a non-consequentialist approach to business ethics is less concerned with the relative morality of one scenario (exploited, but employed) vis-à-vis another (unemployed and starving) and more concerned with whether child labour is, in absolute terms, right or wrong. This approach is based in large part on the idea of the categorical imperative (Kant, 2012), which presupposes that the principles of morality are embedded in reason and can hold as universal laws. Right and wrong, in this light, are absolute, objective and immutable. From this perspective it could be argued, for example, that human beings, including children, have an inalienable right to the free development of their capabilities (cf. Sen, 1999; Nussbaum, 2007), and that this right is blatantly violated when children are employed, no matter what the material circumstances are. In similar vein, the starvation of unemployed children is also morally wrong, but neither scenario is juxtaposed vis-à-vis the other in relative terms, as is the case for consequentialist philosophers.

Our purpose in introducing this debate is not to advocate one position or the other, but rather to illustrate the complexity of such ethical issues. What is clear in this debate is that the employment relationship is characterised by an imbalance in the relations of power between capital and labour, and that this imbalance is even greater in the case of child labourers. The shades of the debate, however, become greyer when the question of right or wrong enters the equation. There are moral arguments in favour of, and against, child labour, and these may vary depending on whether one assumes a consequentialist or non-consequentialist philosophical approach to the topic. The conclusions one draws in relation to this question thus depend upon the ethical assumptions one brings to the debate. We now turn away from the ethics of child labour toward another key moral debate that has received, in our view, insufficient scholarly attention in the ER literature. To this end, in the next section, we ask whether employees have a moral right to participate in organisational decision-making.

The ethics of employee participation

Stakeholder theory and CSR are typically framed in opposition to Friedman's (1970) libertarian statement that "the only social responsibility of business is to increase its profits", and the corresponding implication that shareholders have a legitimate status in corporate governance superior to that of non-shareowning stakeholders. Normative versions of stakeholder theory, offering ethical accounts of the proper purpose of business, generally agree in placing the interests of non-shareowning stakeholders on at least an equal footing with those of shareholders. However, there is no consensus regarding the relative claims and status of different stakeholder groups (e.g. employees, customers, lenders, suppliers and communities). While the ethical imperative to create value for all stakeholders (Freeman, 2011) is regularly asserted, arguments in this literature that give ethical priority to employee participation in decision-making are relatively rare. This section of the chapter reviews the status of employees in ethical theories of stakeholder management and then considers the few explicit attempts that have been made to justify a central place for employees in corporate governance.

Employees as stakeholders

Freeman (1984, p. 46) famously defines a stakeholder of an organisation as "any group or individual who can affect or is affected by the achievement of an organisation's objectives". This definition potentially encompasses a broad range of stakeholder groups, including those who can hold adversarial relationships with the firm. It is also important to note that 'stakeholder' is employed here primarily in the context of the firm's strategy, rather than its ethical obligations (Freeman, 1984, p. 53). However, few stakeholder theorists today would draw a clear distinction between 'ethical' and 'strategic' objectives. Freeman et al. (2010, p. 29) argue that "executives must understand that business is fully situated in the realm of humanity [...] Stakeholders have names and faces and children [...] As such, matters of ethics are routine when one takes a 'managing for stakeholders' approach." For most contemporary stakeholder theorists, managing stakeholder relationships is seen intrinsically to be an ethical endeavour.

Concerning the status of employees in the 'managing for stakeholders' approach, Freeman, Harrison and Wicks (2007, p. 7) position customers, communities, suppliers and financiers alongside employees on a 'two-tier stakeholder map' consisting of 'primary' and 'secondary' stakeholders, the latter of which includes government, the media, special interest groups, competitors and consumer advocacy groups. Employees are among the former group, to whom "managers need to pay a special kind of attention" (Freeman et al., 2007, p. 6). Employees do not have superior ethical status within this group. In fact, Freeman (2010, p. 8) contends that managers should create value for *all* stakeholders without resorting to trade-offs: "From a managerial perspective, if managers look for trade-offs among stakeholders, then they will create trade-offs and they may never find the 'sweet spot' that signifies the joint interest of all key stakeholders."

In philosophical arguments for the stakeholder approach (see Mansell, 2013a, pp. 39–53 for an overview), employees are given a status equal to that of other stakeholder groups. For example, a prominent framework for establishing obligations to stakeholders draws on the 'social contract' method of John Rawls (1999). Rawls employed a famous thought experiment in which social institutions would be regulated by principles of justice that rational individuals choose when placed behind a 'veil of ignorance'. Behind this 'veil', no one would be aware of his or her personal characteristics or place in society. Therefore, to choose principles for themselves would be simultaneously to choose for all members of society. In an organisational context, Freeman and Evan (1990, p. 349) claim that the rules for establishing 'fair contracts' between stakeholders of a corporation should be decided by all stakeholders "behind a 'veil of ignorance', interpreted to mean that no one knows which particular stake he or she actually holds in the corporation". This application of Rawls's contractual argument implies "a basic equality among stakeholders in terms of their moral rights as these are realised in the firm" (Freeman, 1994, p. 415). Changes to the internal constitution of a company would, therefore, require the 'unanimous consent' of all stakeholders (Freeman, 1994, p. 416).

Another influential framework for normative stakeholder theory is that of Donaldson and Preston (1995). They appeal to theories of distributive justice to argue that a fair distribution of corporate wealth between all stakeholders can be established on the basis of "need, ability, effort, and mutual agreement" (p. 84). Although they acknowledge the 'stake' of long-term employees who have worked to build and maintain a successful business operation, employees are attributed no ethical priority in comparison with other stakeholder groups.

Employees have a more central role in work that explores the implications of 'incomplete contracts' between a firm and its stakeholders. Blair (1995) denies that shareholders are the only group to bear the 'residual risk' of investing in a corporation: "employees whose skills are specialised to the company will inevitably bear some of the risk associated with the enterprise, and this fact gives them a 'stake' in the company that is at risk in exactly the same way as the stake held by shareholders" (p. 238). It follows that "for many kinds of corporations, employees (and sometimes other major stakeholders) have as much claim to being owners of the corporation as do shareholders, and perhaps more so" (p. 239).

Similarly, Kaler (2009) establishes the relative standing of different stakeholder groups by employing a risk-based measure of their contribution to the economic functioning of a firm. He argues that in an 'optimally viable' version of stakeholder theory, employees would have "co-equal priority with shareholders" and "co-equal accountability rights with shareholders" (p. 304). By contrast, other non-shareowning stakeholders would have merely a 'minimal status'. Kaler (2009, p. 306) elaborates: "while employees are exposed to both financial and work-related risks, other non-shareholder stakeholders are (along with shareholders it should be said) only exposed to financial risk". Moreover, "not only are employees unique in being exposed to this extra level of risk but their exposure to financial risk is generally greater than that of other groupings" (p. 306).

Employee democracy and corporate governance

These arguments expound the ethical implications of the 'residual risk' and vulnerability of employees' firm-specific investments. However, a further step is required to justify placing employee interests at the centre of corporate governance with employees at all levels partici- pating in managerial decision-making – or at least able to hold managers to account and to re-balance the relations of power to some extent. Probably the most sophisticated argument in which this has been attempted (McMahon, 1994, 1995, 2007) conceives of the corporation as a *democracy* of employees that authorises management to act on its behalf. McMahon (1994) begins by observing the possibility for conflict between the moral obligations of employees and their obedience to management: "While the fact that one is being paid is a good moral reason for complying with a managerial directive ... it may conflict with other morally relevant con- siderations that count against compliance" (p. 6). He therefore asks what justifies managerial authority and demonstrates that it "is best regarded not as the authority of a principal over an agent but rather as authority that facilitates mutually beneficial cooperation among employees with divergent aims" (xiii).

McMahon's (1994) argument for employee democracy depends on the premise that those who have a right "to participate in a decision are not those who are affected by it but those whose actions are guided by it" (p. 12). This is a subtle point, which implies that "*if* corporate management is to be democratised, the group to whom corporate decision-makers should be accountable [...] is the employees. They are the people whose actions are guided by man- agerial directives" (p. 14). Managerial authority is, therefore, legitimate to the extent that it can be justified to employees "from the standpoint of reasons that apply to them" (p. 192). McMahon reasons that this justification cannot simply rest on the employees' promise (or con- tract) to obey management, because this obligation might be overridden at any time by stronger moral considerations (e.g. an employee's duty to disobey a managerial directive to commit fraud). McMahon adds that this will be "especially likely when, by acting collectively with other like-minded people, they can promote their conception of the moral good more effectively" (p. 241). However, "employees will also regard what happens when all of them comply with managerial directives only intermittently as undesirable, since opportunities for mutually bene- ficial cooperation will be missed" (p. 241). It follows that managerial authority should be seen from the standpoint of employees as *co-operation facilitating* authority.

But why does authority of this kind require employee democracy? McMahon (1994, p. 258) understands democracy as "the determination of the directive to be issued by a vote of the subjects", which he finds to be supported by the values of 'fairness' and 'welfare maximisation'. He writes: "Fairness supports democracy as a device for insuring that over time, each will get what he deems best about equally often [...] while welfare maximisation supports democracy as insuring that the directive issued is deemed best by more people than not" (p. 258). In this conception of authority, employees are not seen as agents of shareholders or senior manage- ment; instead, managers serve the employees "by enabling them to promote their conceptions of the moral good more effectively in their work" (p. 291). In his conclusion, McMahon calls for the "erosion of the power of managers chosen by non-democratic means, and a transfer of all ultimate managerial authority to democratically elected representatives of the employees" (p. 292).

A similar conclusion is reached through a less complex argument by Manville and Ober (2003), who champion the benefits of building a 'company of citizens' in which employees participate fully and democratically in the strategic direction of the company. Developing an analogy with the politics of classical Athens, they call for a "truly democratic system of manage- ment – one suited to the knowledge worker's need for and expectation of self-determination and self-government" (p. 48). Moreover, it is ultimately up to companies to provide a clear def- inition of 'formal citizenship' in their organisation and the "benefits, rights and responsibilities" that are part of it (p. 53).

To this end, employing the same analogy between business organisations and Greek city-states, Sison (2011) draws on Aristotle's (1996) *The Politics* to answer the question of who should count as a citizen of the 'corporate polis'. Sison (2011) advocates a 'civic republican' model of citizenship in which "every stakeholder-constituent is admonished to actively take part in the deliberation and execution of the corporate common good" (p. 5). Of the different stakeholders who might qualify as 'corporate citizens', "employees are the ones most closely integrated and identified with the corporation" (p. 7). However, he recalls Aristotle's argument that citizens practice *self-governance*: they govern their own affairs and do not rule on behalf of anyone else (p. 8). Sison is, therefore, led to the conclusion that shareholding employees, and in particular shareholding managers, best fit the Aristotelian conception of the corporate citizen: "That manager or employee and shareholder, agent and principal, governor and governed coincide in the same person is precisely the biggest advantage of workers over other stakeholder groups for civic republican corporate citizenship [...] In this sense, co-operatives, or business organisations that are run and controlled by their owners, would fit the definition of a self-governing corporate polity to perfection" (p. 8).

Employee participation as corporate citizenship

Arguments for employee democracy premised upon an identification of employees as 'corporate citizens', entailing greater employee participation in managerial decision-making, are a recurring theme (see Crane, Matten and Moon, 2008, pp. 88–122 for a critical overview of the literature characterising 'stakeholders as citizens'). Collins (1997) anticipates that organisational governance will come inevitably to mirror the advance of state-level democracy, leading to participatory management and the democratisation of organisations. Drawing an analogy between political, economic and organisational systems, he asks: "If people can be trusted to behave appropriately when granted political and economic liberty, why should they not be trusted to behave appropriately when granted liberty within organisations?" (p. 492). He then asks why civil liberties guaranteed for citizens – including freedom of speech, assembly, due process of law and privacy, among others – are generally denied in the workplace (p. 500). After an extensive comparison of 'organisational authoritarianism' with the progress of democratic ideals in the political sphere, he concludes that "the standard should be democratic organisations with a few authoritarian exceptions", rather than vice versa (p. 503).

Cludts (1999) also argues for employee participation at the level of company strategy and, in particular, in creating a 'shared value horizon'. The diversity of goals and values in all organisations means that "participation should be, at least partly, goal-oriented, and not only task-oriented" (p. 168). Cludts criticises managerial attempts "to secure the collective involvement of the workforce by communicating heavily their own objectives and strategic orientations" because it is difficult "for one to get involved with goals which one has no opportunity to influence" (p. 161). The point is that where corporate strategy is developed exclusively by senior management without the input of employees, the company's goals "are set in top-down, rational, utilitarian terms, thereby reducing everything to one sole criterion. As a result, nothing more than a rational, or calculative involvement can be expected from the subordinates, and neither groups nor individuals can be allowed to pursue their own goals [...] Since no commitment to any 'common good' is expected from the employee, they won't show any" (pp. 162–163). Cludts finally argues that conflict between corporate values and their personal values can be avoided only if employees participate actively in establishing a shared set of values; in other words, it "becomes necessary to create a *political culture* where a consensus could be developed about ethical issues" (p. 167).

A commonality in the preceding arguments is that employees should participate not only in deciding the *means* by which managerial directives might be implemented, but also in the setting of organisational *ends*. Berman and Van Buren III (2015) find a similar argument in Mary Parker Follett's writings on employee participation and integration. Follett viewed the role of management in its relation to workers as "one of shared control and non-coercive interaction for mutual benefit" (p. 46). She contrasted 'power-over' and 'power-with' such that: "the former was coercive control by managers exercised over workers (often with punitive effect), and the latter a jointly developed power between managers and workers in which power is exercised for mutual benefit" (p. 46).

While slightly different ethical vocabularies are employed in each attempt to prioritise the interests of employees in corporate governance, the concepts of participation, involvement, engagement, voice, democracy and citizenship have become standard frames of reference, especially amongst ER scholars. Timming (2015, p. 383) observes that the "distinction between these terms is, unfortunately, never clear, owing to the fact that researchers often use them interchangeably". However, he provides an important caveat: drawing on Aristotle's (1996) *The Politics*, it can be shown that corporate 'citizenship' (even in a 'participatory' sense) does not logically entail employee democracy. Contrary to Sison (2011, p. 4), who finds Aristotle's conception of citizenship best suited to a democracy, Timming (2015, p. 389) emphasises the 'elitist nature' of Aristotle's 'best regime'. In Aristotle's concept of the citizen, which is paradigmatic for much of the 'corporate citizenship' literature (e.g. Crane et al., 2008, pp. 7–10), the question of *which* employees can participate in organisational decision-making "boils down to whether or not the managerial *aristoi* judges a particular employee to possess what Aristotle (1996, pp. 65–68) refers to as 'excellence' [...] Only superior employees characterised by 'excellence' [...] are invited by the managerial *aristoi* to participate in decision-making" (Timming, 2015, p. 289). Timming goes on to argue that, for Aristotle, only employees with the 'best brains' could be considered citizens of the 'corporate polis': thus, the remaining workforce (e.g. the janitors and cashiers, etc.) are like the slaves and women of Aristotle's day, "denied a voice and made to be silent [...] due to their supposed lack of strategic insight" (p. 289).

Throughout this literature on the ethics of employee participation, a central theme is that the mere existence of managerial *power* over employees does not imply legitimate *authority*: power is therefore inherently questionable on ethical grounds (see Höpfl, 1999 for an elucidation of the different etymologies of 'power' and 'authority'). It is argued in this literature that legitimate managerial authority requires employee participation in the strategic direction and shared values of the organisation as a whole. Some have argued that this level of participation implies that employees have the power to hold managers to account through democratic procedures (see Collins, 1997; Manville and Ober, 2003; McMahon, 1994). Another widely held premise is that employees are distinctly vulnerable to firm-specific risk, relative to other stakeholder groups (Blair, 1995; Kaler, 2009). Employees can thus be said to have an ethical right to participate in managerial decision-making as a safeguard against the risk of unjust exploitation. In this sense, the argument in favour of workplace democracy is consequential: it is not seen as an end to be pursued for its own sake (whatever that might mean), but just to the extent that it offers protection to the interests of all employees.

The 'ideal' distribution of decision-making

At the heart of the discussion thus far is the idea that *politics* is central to the employment relationship. Political scientists and philosophers have concerned themselves with answering a fundamental question: what is the ideal distribution of decision-making within a state? This question can and should also be asked by employment relations researchers in the context of organisations conceptualised as political entities (Pfeffer, 1992). Thus, according to Timming (2016, p. 492):

> [W]orkplace democracy exists on a hypothetical continuum. On one end of the spectrum is the authoritarian organisation where all managerial decisions are made by the chief executive officer. In such an organisation, employees are simply expected to execute orders and follow directives. They have no 'say' over how to organise production. On the other end of the continuum is absolute worker control, where there is no distinction between managers and employees. In these types of organisations, the employees self-manage without any formal managerial structure. In practice, all organisations can be placed somewhere in between these two extremes, with some offering more and others less scope for employee participation in decision-making. The key political question centres around the *ideal* (emphasis ours) distribution of decision-making in organisations.

The dilemma here, it seems, centres primarily around the ambiguity surrounding the word 'ideal'. What might be an 'ideal' distribution of decision-making from the point of view of organisational performance and profitability may, it could be argued, be incompatible with an 'ideal' distribution of decision-making from the point of view of ethics and moral philosophy. Thus, whether an employee has a 'right' to participate in decision-making would ultimately need to be counter-balanced against the 'right' of an organisation (if such a thing exists) to demand employee compliance in exchange for wages paid.

For the sake of facilitating discussion on this dilemma, let us carry out a thought experiment in which we divide organisations into two types: low-voice and high-voice. Let us further recognise that these ideal types (Cahnman, 1965) are conceptual tools that allow us to make a complex reality more interpretable. Low-voice organisations can be defined as those in which decision-making authority is concentrated in the hands of management, whilst high-voice organisations are defined as those in which decision-making authority is more widely distributed throughout the workforce in the form of shared governance between managers and employees.

In the preceding section it was seen that for many business ethics scholars, low-voice organisations are morally problematic. It has been argued that employees are important stakeholders and, as such, they can make a legitimate moral claim to have some 'say' over organisational decision-making. But what about the business case against the low-voice model of governance? To answer this question, we must turn to the HRM literature. Wilkinson et al. (2004), among others, have argued persuasively that the delegation of decision-making authority to employees results in what they have called 'upward problem solving'. The assumption underlying this argument is that employees, by virtue of their position on the front line of production, possess valuable insight into the organisation that managers do not possess. Low-voice organisations fail to capitalise on this employee insight, thereby potentially weakening the never-ending quest to optimise production in the face of a constantly changing environment and market conditions.

By the same token, although the direct link between employee voice and financial performance has been elusive (Freeman and Kleiner, 2000), there is also a strong consensus amongst HRM scholars that participatory management yields a number of benefits for organisations. Appelbaum et al. (2000) argue persuasively that 'high-performance work systems', characterised by high levels of employee voice, pay significant dividends to organisations. Guthrie (2001) provides further evidence in corroboration of the link between employee participation in organisational decision-making and firm performance. Timming (2012) demonstrates that employee voice is positively associated with a number of desirable outcomes for an organisation, including higher job satisfaction, organisational commitment and trust in managers. In other words, it would appear that the moral case for employee voice, articulated in the preceding section, is not, at least in principle, wholly incompatible with the business case. Indeed, it would appear that they are aligned.

In summary, let us take stock of what can (and cannot) be said in conclusion. The arguments we have reviewed suggest that the low-voice model of governance, where decision-making is concentrated in the hands of management to the exclusion of employees, is ethically question-able *and* potentially bad for business. In a similar vein, the high-voice model of governance, where decision-making is shared more widely between managers and employees, has a number of ethical considerations in its favour and is also defensible on narrower economic grounds. However, these arguments cannot translate into unqualified support for employee voice because participation in decision-making can take on different permutations in terms of degree, level, scope and form (Marchington, 2005; Marchington and Wilkinson, 2005; Wilkinson et al., 2010). But they do suggest, at the very least, that ER researchers should keep an open mind when it comes to the compatibility between ethical management practices and the exigencies of organ-isational performance. The two are not diametrically opposed.

Discussion and future research agenda

This chapter opened with an analysis of power in the employment relationship. It was argued that the imbalance of power between employers and employees is the source of all ethical problems in the field of employment relations. The case of child labour was then presented from the point of view of business ethics. Child labour is an extreme manifestation of the power imbalance in the employment relationship and it was conceptualised from the perspec-tive of both consequentialist and non-consequentialist philosophy. The chapter then moved on to discuss stakeholder theory in the context of the ethics of employee participation in decision-making. It was argued that employees are important stakeholders that could potentially have a moral right to participation in organisational decisions that affect them. The argument concluded with a brief discussion of whether there is an 'ideal' distribution of decision-making in organisations.

When it comes to an agenda for future research on these topics, the proverbial sky is the limit. Whilst there is already a huge literature on CSR and stakeholder theory (Crane et al., 2008; Freeman, 1984, 1990, 1994; Freeman et al., 2007, 2010; McWilliams and Siegel, 2000; Freeman et al,; Freeman, 2010; Mansell, 2013a) and an equally huge literature on ER and employee voice (Dundon et al., 2004; Dundon and Rollinson, 2011; Marchington et al., 1994; Wilkinson, et al., 2004), very few studies have sought actively to marry the two fields. This chapter has provided a very tentative outline for such a marriage. It offers a framework for thinking seriously about the intersection of ER, stakeholder theory and business ethics.

In terms of taking research in this area forward, one potentially fruitful avenue would be to examine how specific moral philosophies relate to the idea of employee voice as a human right. This chapter provides a generalist philosophical overview of the topic, but it would be interesting to question further the application of different moral philosophies and theories in respect of employee participation in organisational decision-making. For example, what can Kantian ethics tell us about the right of employees to genuine workplace democracy? A Kantian perspective has already been applied to shareholding stakeholders (Mansell, 2013b), but this question has not often been explored from the perspective of employees. Similarly, can a Millian utilitarian perspective shine a new light on how ER researchers think about employee voice? From this perspective, perhaps voice can only be conceptualised as 'good' insofar as it leads to mutual benefits for both employees and employers. It has already been shown previously that ancient philosophies can add significant value to our contemporary understanding of ER (Timming, 2015), so more research along these lines is a welcome contribution.

Another potentially promising avenue for future research involves moving beyond thought experiments into the realm of empiricism. In short, we wish to call for methodological pluralism in the philosophical study of the employment relationship. It should not be surprising that most philosophical studies are non-empirical. However, the moral premises of philosophical debate about the claims of employees – and the practical context in which debates are thought significant – could be enriched by empirical research on employee participation in practice. For example, the 'ideal' distribution of decision-making, discussed above, is really an empirical question. To this end, statistical and experimental methods could be used to measure employee participation, and then qualitative follow up research could be conducted in order to capture employees' moral attitudes in respect of different variations in the distribution of decision-making. Qualitative research in this area could also entail interviews not only with employees, but also with managers, with regard to the question of whether workers *should* have a right to participate in decision-making. If so, there are additional questions surrounding whether *all* employees should have equal rights to participation, or if some have more rights than others. In short, the possibilities for empirical research along these lines are endless.

Finally, this chapter has provided a useful ethical framework for thinking about other topics in the wider ambit of ER. Although we focused on the ethics of child labour and employee participation in decision-making, there is any number of alternative employment-related topics that could be explored from a moral viewpoint. For example, future research could investigate the ethics of the living wage or employment discrimination on the basis of both protected and non-protected characteristics. There is certainly no shortage of ethical dilemmas in the study of ER.

Conclusion

In conclusion, this chapter has provided a comprehensive overview of the generally under-investigated intersection of employment relations, stakeholder theory and business ethics. Unlike most previous studies in CSR, this chapter places employees, thought of as stakeholders, at centre stage in the debate. We have examined critically the various ethical perspectives on employees as stakeholders, from child labour through to employee participation. We have also considered the important question of whether business ethics and firm performance, underpinned by employee participation in decision-making, align with one another. In the final analysis, we argue that this chapter has really only scratched the surface in terms of understanding the role of business ethics in ER. Future research, both conceptual and empirical, is needed to explore the arguments made in this chapter.

References

Appelbaum, E., Bailey, T., Berg, P. and Kalleberg, A. (2000). *Manufacturing Advantage: Why High-Performance Work Systems Pay Off*. Ithaca: Cornell University Press.

Aristotle (1996). *The Politics and the Constitution of Athens*. Everson, S. (ed.) Cambridge (UK): Cambridge University Press.

Blair, M. (1995). *Ownership and Control: Rethinking Corporate Governance for the Twenty-First Century.* Washington, DC: The Brookings Institution.

Berman, S. and Van Buren III, H. (2015). 'Mary Parker Follett, managerial responsibility, and the future of capitalism', *Futures*, 68, pp. 44–56.

Cahnman, W.J. (1965). 'Ideal Type Theory: Max Weber's Concept and Some of Its Derivations', *Sociological Quarterly*, 6(3), pp. 268–280.

Cludts, S. (1999). 'Organisation Theory and the Ethics of Participation', *Journal of Business Ethics*, 21(2–3), pp. 157–171.

Collins, D. (1997). 'The Ethical Superiority and Inevitability of Participatory Management as an Organisational System', *Organization Science*, 8(5), pp. 489–507.

Cova, B. and Dalli, D. (2009). 'Working consumers: the next step in marketing theory?' *Marketing Theory*, 9(3), pp. 315–339.

Crane, A., Matten, D. and Moon, J. (2008). *Corporations and Citizenship.* Cambridge (UK): Cambridge University Press.

Donaldson, T. and Preston, L. (1995). 'The stakeholder theory of the corporation: concepts, evidence, and implications', *Academy of Management Review*, 20(1), pp. 65–91.

Dundon, T. and Rollinson, D. (2011). *Understanding Employment Relations.* 2nd edn. London: McGraw-Hill.

Dundon, T., Wilkinson, A., Marchington, M. and Ackers, P. (2004). 'The meanings and purpose of employee voice', *International Journal of Human Resource Management*, 15(6), pp. 1149–1170.

Foucault, M. (1995). *Discipline & Punish: The Birth of the Prison.* New York: Random House.

Freeman, R.B. and Kleiner, M.M. (2000). 'Who benefits most from employee involvement: firms or workers?' *American Economic Review*, 90(2), pp. 219–223.

Freeman, R.E. (1984). *Strategic Management: A Stakeholder Approach.* London: Pitman.

Freeman, R.E. (1994). 'The politics of stakeholder theory: some future directions', *Business Ethics Quarterly*, 4(4), pp. 409–421.

Freeman, R.E. (2010). 'Managing for Stakeholders: Trade-offs or Value Creation?' *Journal of Business Ethics*, 96, pp. 7–9.

Freeman, R.E. and Evan, W. (1990). 'Corporate governance: a stakeholder interpretation', *Journal of Behavioural Economics*, 19(4), pp. 337–360.

Freeman, R.E., Harrison, J. and Wicks, A. (2007). *Managing for Stakeholders: Survival, Reputation, and Success.* New Haven: Yale University Press.

Freeman, R.E., Harrison, J., Wicks, A., Parmar, B. and de Colle, S. (2010). *Stakeholder Theory: The State of the Art.* Cambridge (UK): Cambridge University Press.

Friedman, M. (1970). 'The Social Responsibility of Business is to Increase its Profits', *New York Times Magazine*, 13 September, pp. 32–33.

Guthrie, J.P. (2001). 'High-involvement work practices, turnover, and productivity: evidence from New Zealand', *Academy of Management Journal*, 44(1), pp. 180–190.

Hindman, H.D. and Smith, C.G. (1999). 'Cross-Cultural Ethics and the Child Labor Problem', *Journal of Business Ethics*, 19(1), pp. 21–33.

Höpfl, H. (1999). 'Power, authority and legitimacy', *Human Resource Development International*, 2(3), pp. 217–234.

Humphries, J. (2013). 'Childhood and child labour in the British industrial revolution', *Economic History Review*, 66(2), pp. 395–418.

International Labour Organization (2017). Child Labour. Available at: www.ilo.org/global/publications/books/WCMS_575499/lang--en/index.htm.

Kaler, J. (2009). 'An Optimally Viable Version of Stakeholder Theory', *Journal of Business Ethics*, 86(3), pp. 297–312.

Kant, I. (2012). *Groundwork of the Metaphysics of Morals.* Cambridge (UK): Cambridge University Press.

Kelly, J. (2000). *Rethinking Industrial Relations: Mobilization, Collectivism and Long Waves.* London: Routledge.

Kolk, A. and Van Tulder, R. (2004). 'Ethics in international business: multinational approaches to child labor', *Journal of World Business*, 39(1), pp. 49–60.

Lammers, J., Galinsky, A.D., Dubois, D. and Rucker, D.D. (2015). 'Power and morality', *Current Opinion in Psychology*, 6, pp. 15–19.

Lyon, T.P. and Maxwell, J.W. (2008). 'Corporate Social Responsibility and the Environment: A Theoretical Perspective', *Review of Environmental Economics and Policy*, 2(2), pp. 240–260.

Mansell, S. (2013a). *Capitalism, Corporations and the Social Contract: A Critique of Stakeholder Theory.* Cambridge (UK): Cambridge University Press.

Mansell, S. (2013b). 'Shareholder Theory and Kant's 'Duty of Beneficence'', *Journal of Business Ethics*, 117(3), pp. 583–599.

Manville, B. and Ober, J. (2003). 'Beyond Empowerment: Building a Company of Citizens', *Harvard Business Review*, 81(1), pp. 48–53.

Marchington, M. (2005). Employee involvement: patterns and explanations, in Harley, B., Hyman, J. and Thompson, P. (eds.) *Participation and Democracy at Work*. Houndmills: Palgrave Macmillan.

Marchington, M., Wilkinson, A., Ackers, P. and Goodman, J. (1994). 'Understanding the meaning of participation: views from the workplace', *Human Relations*, 47(8), pp. 867–894.

Marchington, M. and Wilkinson, A. (2005). Direct participation and involvement, in Bach, S. (ed.) *Personnel Management in Britain*. Oxford: Blackwell.

McMahon, C. (1994). *Authority and Democracy: A General Theory of Government and Management*. Princeton: Princeton University Press.

McMahon, C. (1995). 'The political theory of organizations and business ethics', *Philosophy and Public Affairs*, 24(4), pp. 292–313.

McMahon, C. (2007). 'Comments On Hsieh, Moriarty and Oosterhout', *Journal of Business Ethics*, 71, pp. 371–379.

McWilliams, A. and Siegel, D. (2000). 'Corporate Social Responsibility and Firm Performance: Correlation or Misspecification?' *Strategic Management Journal*, 21(5), pp. 603–609.

McWilliams, A. and Siegel, D. (2001). 'Corporate Social Responsibility: A Theory of the Firm Perspective', *Academy of Management Review*, 26(1), pp. 117–127.

Mulligan, T. (1986). 'A critique of Milton Friedman's essay, "The Social Responsibility of Business is to Increase its Profits"', *Journal of Business Ethics*, 5(4), pp. 265–269.

Nussbaum, M. (2007). *Frontiers of Justice: Disability, Nationality, Species Membership*. Cambridge (MA): Harvard University Press.

Offe, C. and Wiesenthal, H. (1980). 'Two Logics of Collective Action: Theoretical Notes on Social Class and Organizational Form', *Political Power and Social Theory*, 1, pp. 67–115.

Pedersen, E.R. (2010). 'Modelling CSR: How Managers Understand the Responsibilities of Business Toward Society', *Journal of Business Ethics*, 91(2), pp. 155–166.

Pfeffer, J. (1994). *Managing with Power: Politics and Influence in Organizations*. Cambridge (MA): Harvard Business School Press.

Pfeffer, J. (1992). 'Understanding power in organizations', *California Management Review*, 34(2), pp. 29–50.

Pitesa, M. and Thau, S. (2013). 'Masters of the Universe: How Power and Accountability Influence Self-Serving Decisions Under Moral Hazard', *Journal of Applied Psychology*, 98(3), pp. 550–558.

Rawls, J. (1999). *A Theory of Justice*. Revised edn. Oxford: Oxford University Press.

Sachs, J. (2015). *The End of Poverty: Economic Possibilities for Our Time*. New York: Penguin.

Sen, A. (1999). *Development as Freedom*. Oxford: Oxford University Press.

Sen, S. and Bhattacharya, C.B. (2001). 'Does Doing Good Always Lead to Doing Better? Consumer reactions to corporate social responsibility', *Journal of Marketing Research*, 38(2), pp. 225–243.

Sinnott-Armstrong, W. (1992). 'An Argument for Consequentialism', *Philosophical Perspectives*, 6, pp. 399–421.

Sison, A. (2011). 'Aristotelian Citizenship and Corporate Citizenship: Who is a Citizen of the Corporate Polis?' *Journal of Business Ethics*, 100(1), pp. 3–9.

Thompson, P. (1983). *The Nature of Work: An Introduction to Debates on the Labour Process*. Houndmills: Macmillan.

Timming, A.R. (2012). 'Tracing the effects of employee involvement and participation on trust in managers: an analysis of covariance structures', *International Journal of International Human Resource Management*, 23(15), pp. 3243–3257.

Timming, A.R. (2015). 'The 'reach' of employee participation in decision-making: exploring the Aristotelian roots of workplace democracy', *Human Resource Management Journal*, 25(3), pp. 382–396.

Timming, A.R. (2016). Workplace Democracy, in Wilkinson, A. and Johnstone, S. (eds.) *Encyclopedia of Human Resource Management*. Cheltenham: Edward Elgar, pp. 492–493.

Townley, B. (1993). 'Foucault, Power/Knowledge, and its Relevance for Human Resource Management', *Academy of Management Review*, 18(3), pp. 518–545.

Townley, B. (1994). *Reframing Human Resource Management: Power, Ethics and the Subject at Work*. London: Sage.

Wilkinson, A., Dundon, T., Marchington, M. and Ackers, P. (2004). 'Changing patterns of employee voice: case studies from the UK and Republic of Ireland', *Journal of Industrial Relations*, 46(3), pp. 298–322.

Wilkinson, A., Gollan, P.J., Marchington, M. and Lewin, D. (2010). Conceptualizing employee participation in organizations, in Wilkinson, A., Gollan, P.J., Marchington, M. and Lewin, D. (eds.) *The Oxford Handbook of Participation in Organizations*. Oxford: Oxford University Press.

Winstanley, D., Clark, J. and Leeson, H. (2002). 'Approaches to child labour in the supply chain', *Business Ethics: A European Review*, 11(3), pp. 210–223.

Young, S. and Thyil, V. (2009). 'Governance, employees and CSR: integration is the key to unlocking value', *Asia Pacific Journal of Human Resources*, 47(2), pp. 167–185.

Zane, D., Irwin, J. and Reczek, R.W. (2016). Why Companies Are Blind to Child Labor. *Harvard Business Review*. (Online). Available at: https://hbr.org/2016/01/why-companies-are-blind-to-child-labor.

PART V

Contemporary reflections and future challenges

29

THE FINANCIAL MODEL OF THE FIRM, THE 'FUTURE OF WORK', AND EMPLOYMENT RELATIONS

Rose Batt

Employers just don't want to be employers anymore.
Generally, they will do anything possible to not hire a full-time employee

Steven Berkenfeld, Managing Director,
Investment Banking Division, Barclays April 12, 2016

Introduction

Concern over the 'future of work' in advanced economies has exploded in recent years. The concept is fuzzy enough to accommodate almost any change occurring in the world of work today. And many things *are* falling apart. Jobs are disappearing via offshoring or automation – creating greater competition for the remaining jobs and putting downward pressure on wages. The standard 40-hour work week has collapsed – replaced by overworked people or the under-employed holding multiple jobs. The dramatic growth in jobs that are contracted out or subject to contingent contracts has created unprecedented levels of precariousness and income insecurity. The Uberisation of the labour market has captured peoples' imagination – with workers connected directly to customers via online platforms operated by firms that deny they are employers even though they set prices and contractual terms. These trends affect not only low-wage workers in routine jobs but increasingly a broader swath of knowledge, professional and managerial workers.

For some, technology is driving these changes. Digitalisation and the logistics revolution allowed firms to establish global supply chains that shifted jobs in advanced economies to low-wage countries. Other new technologies automate and eliminate jobs on an unprecedented scale. For others, globalisation has 'forced' corporations to seek low-cost, flexible forms of labour to compete effectively. And some blame the millennials, who demand new forms of work, as a driving force behind this new world of work.

In this chapter, I try to make sense of the fundamental changes that are occurring in the world of work and employment relations (ER) and what they mean for researchers in the field of human resource (HR) studies and ER and, more generally, for policy-makers. I argue that under-lying the different dimensions of the new world of work is a fundamental change in the logic of capitalist organisation – from a managerial business model to a financial one. Globalisation is one dimension of this new order, but not its primary independent *cause*. New technologies are a powerful *tool* for the new order, and 'millennials' preferences are one of its justifications.

By beginning with a reconceptualisation of the firm and how corporations make money, we are more clearly able to scrutinise what the concept of the 'employment relationship' means in the current period, and in turn what kind of research our field should be pursuing. Using this lens, we can discount arguments that bosses are simply smarter, greedier or meaner than they were in the past – even though some may be. An analysis of the financial model of the firm points to why many employers don't *want* or *need* a relationship with employees in order to make money. For a large swath of activities, they simply need to contract for services rendered or buy technology, with labour already embedded as an input. This in turn suggests that a policy focus on the labour market alone – a strengthening or reform of labour and employment laws – is insufficient to achieve the kind of lasting reform needed to build sustainable economies that provide decent jobs and income security for the majority of working people. While many believe that the United States and UK are outliers in advancing the financial model of the firm, I argue that this model has diffused quite widely to 'coordinated economies' with institutions that historically constrained risky financial behaviour.

The financial model of the firm

In the non-financial sector, the primary institutional change in the last 30 years has been a shift from a managerial model of doing business to a financial model. Our strategic HR management and industrial relations (IR) scholarship has been premised on a managerial model, with the key assumption that value is created, extracted and distributed through the labour process – either unilaterally by management or through negotiations between labour and management representatives. The purpose of the firm is to produce goods and services as a means of profit-making and to reinvest retained earnings to improve productivity and profitability and expand market share. Managers rely on a productive and co-operative workforce to do this, with workers sharing in the gains from productivity growth.

The financial model of doing business, however, adopts a different logic for wealth creation and extraction, which is more immune to unions or social movements because the production of goods and services via the labour process is less central to the overall accumulation of capital. Firms increasingly make money via a range of financial activities that have little to do with producing goods or services. These activities include buying and selling companies or divisions of companies (mergers and acquisitions); selling off assets; making greater use of debt and other financial products to enhance profits; adopting fee-generating activities; manipulating stock share prices or engaging in share buybacks; and making greater use of tax avoidance and arbitrage. Hence, I use the term 'financial' because the model relies relatively more on capital accumulation via financial strategies than does the managerial model. Others use the term shareholder model because it is driven by shareholder interests and is designed to shift the relative distribution of retained earnings from workers to shareholders.

The most extreme form of the financial model is the leveraged buyout, as developed by takeover firms in the 1980s and perfected by private equity firms since then (Appelbaum and Batt, 2014; Gospel, Pendleton and Vitols, 2014). But the financial strategies of private equity firms have increasingly 'spilled over' into the broader economy and have been adopted by publicly traded corporations as well. One measure of the relative shift in public corporations' reliance on productive versus financial activities comes from Greta Krippner's work on financialisation. She measured financial activities in non-financial firms as the ratio of portfolio income (dividends, capital gains, interest payments) to corporate cash flow. She found that this ratio remained stable in the 1950s and 1960s at less than 10 per cent, rose to approximately 20 per cent by 1980 and 40 per cent by 1989, before falling off and then stabilising in 2000 at about 40 per cent (2011, p. 36). Another measure – the ratio of net acquisition of financial assets to tangible assets in non-financial firms – also supports the idea of a relative increase in reliance on financial activities, especially after 1980. The ratio was relatively stable at 40 per cent or less until 1980, and thereafter rose to about 100 per cent by 2000 (ibid., p. 39).

The financial model differs from the managerial model in that it is based on different assumptions about the nature of the corporation, the value of its assets and capital mobility. Under the managerial model, assets are relatively fixed resources used to produce goods and services, with retained earnings used to replenish those resources, expand the asset base of the firm and grow. The financial model, by contrast, views the corporation as a bundle of mobile assets to be bought and sold with the goal of increasing returns – often short or intermediate term – to shareholders. Capital is mobile and should seek out the best deal in the marketplace. Companies analyse the profitability of each business unit or line of production and keep only the most profitable ones (the ones it 'does best') – selling off those in product markets that are mature, less profitable or too competitive. In Albert Hirschman's terms (1970), they can simply exit. As CEO of General Electric in the early 1980s, Jack Welch pioneered this approach (Lowenstein, 2004, p. 55). Revenue from the sell-off of less profitable businesses are then returned to shareholders as dividends. This differs from the past, when investments in plant and equipment tied up capital in fixed investments, putting managers under pressure to innovate and turn around poor-performing businesses. They couldn't just exit.

Second, once capital investments are viewed as relatively liquid – to be bought and sold – rather than as fixed assets, the idea of labour as a quasi-fixed asset (Oi, 1962), or human capital as valuable and firm specific (Becker, 1964), also becomes less relevant to the firm's business and labour strategy. Because a firm's financial success depends relatively less on productive activities, its welfare is less intertwined with the welfare of employees. The decoupling of this inter-dependent relationship, due in part to the higher mobility of capital, unravels the incentives that the firm had under the managerial model to invest in the skills of labour and negotiate contracts to ensure labour's cooperation and peace.

Within each product or business function, firms also analyse the value chain in the production process to identify which pieces of the process are the most valuable and should be kept in house and which should be sold off. Value chain analysis has allowed firms to vertically dis-integrate their production systems, outsource activities to domestic contractors, or offshore activities to emerging market suppliers with lower wages and labour standards.

This process has been justified and promoted in the management literature via the 'core competency' argument – that firms should specialise in what they do best (Prahalad and Hamel, 1990) and spin off the rest to low-cost suppliers at home or abroad. Most of the literature attributes this strategy to heightened global competition and international labour arbitrage, rather than recognising that a primary driver is the financial model of the firm – that is, shareholder pressure to divest less profitable activities and return cash to them in the form of dividends. Thus, the research literature has paid considerably more attention to the labour implications of global supply chains than to the domestic equivalent of outsourcing within countries (Bernhardt et al., 2016). The European literature is somewhat more advanced than its US counterpart, but has focused heavily on public sector outsourcing and privatisation (Drahokloupil, 2015; Marchington et al., 2005).

Firms that follow a financial model are also more likely to engage in other types of asset sales – particularly selling off property or real estate assets to return cash to shareholders. Historically, companies in many industries – particularly in retail, restaurants, hotels, health care and other manufacturing and service businesses – owned their own property to hedge against downturns in the economy. During recessions, they could weather the storm because they didn't have to pay rent. When they did sell off property, they tended to use the cash to reinvest in and expand the business. Increasingly, however, activist shareholders such as hedge funds, or private equity firms that own portfolio companies, have demanded that companies sell assets to 'release the value' locked up in corporations. Companies are split into a property company and an operating company, the property is sold, and the operating company is forced to lease back the land or buildings it used to own – often at inflated prices. Proceeds from the sale are typically returned to shareholders as dividends, not reinvested in the company (Appelbaum and Batt, 2014).

In the summer of 2014, for example, hedge fund activists with a six per cent interest in Darden Restaurants – the largest restaurant chain owner in the world – demanded that the company sell off all of its properties and return the proceeds to shareholders. The company managed to hold on to most of its properties by making a deal to sell off one chain (Red Lobster) to a private equity firm. The firm immediately split the Red Lobster chain into two companies, sold off all 500 properties, and used that money to completely pay for the leveraged buyout it had just executed (Appelbaum, 2014a). Of course, ongoing net revenues at the restaurant chain were substantially reduced as the company now had to pay inflated rent on the property it previously owned. Thus, these asset sales make the operating companies much more vulnerable to financial distress and bankruptcy and, in turn, put pressure on managers to cut labour costs via layoffs or reductions in staffing, training or wages.

While activist investors primarily target US corporations, continental Europe has experienced a rise in activism, with 125 corporations targeted by activist funds between 2010 and 2015, according to Activist Investor (2015), a UK research and consulting firm that tracks shareholder activism. In addition, activist strategies have evolved to include not only pressure for board seats, but to change the direction of business strategy and other management decisions, such as outsourcing and the sale of property assets.

The financial model's effective implementation depends on aligning the interests of top management with those of shareholders through executive pay tied to stock options. This innovation grew rapidly in the 1980s, was embraced by US corporations after an influential 1990 *Harvard Business Review* (*HBR*) article by economists Jenson and Murphy (1990), and became institutionalised by the end of 1990s. This led to the dramatic rise in CEO-to-worker pay ratios in the following decades (Davis and Mishel, 2014). The practice also spread to Europe, where in 2014, the base salary for CEOs of the top 100 corporations was only 20–38 per cent of total pay in all countries but Italy and the Nordics (Towers Watson, 2015).

In 2016 – 26 years after the game-changing pay-for-performance article, *HBR* published an about-face – "Stop Paying Executives for Performance" (Cable and Vermeulen, 2016). That was because the cumulative research showed that pay-for-performance only works for routine tasks, not those involving creativity. It leads executives to focus excessively on stock price as the ultimate performance metric and is significantly associated with higher levels of shareholder lawsuits, lower product safety, and earnings manipulation. Research on earnings manipulation shows that since the 1990s, corporate stock buybacks have skyrocketed. A study of 91 per cent of the S&P 500 corporations between 2004 and 2013 found that the companies spent 51 per cent of their net income on buybacks and another 35 per cent on dividends – for an overall total of $5.7 trillion (Lazonick, 2014). The use of earnings for share buybacks and dividends crowds out investment in innovations – worker skills, technology, and research and development – that are required to compete effectively in 'knowledge-based' economies. Hence the excessive use of share buybacks has long-term negative spillover effects on the productive and innovative capabilities of firms and their ability to pay decent wages.

Tied to the greater use of retained earnings for stock buybacks is the higher use of bank loans to finance capital investments – with a resulting increase in the use of debt financing relative to equity financing. This strategy is attractive because the use of debt multiplies the return on assets; and it is even more attractive in countries such as the US where interest rates have been close to zero and the tax system allows interest on the debt to be deducted from corporate taxes. The greater relative use of debt lowers the tax burden of corporations, leading the general public to shoulder a larger share.

Buyout firms in the 1980s pioneered the use of high debt to goose their returns in leveraged buyouts of companies – a strategy that private equity firms continue to use. Private equity firms typically use about 70 per cent debt and 30 per cent equity when they purchase companies and take them private. By contrast, historically the typical public corporation had a debt/equity ratio of about 30/70 per cent. That, however, is changing, at least in the US where, according to one analyst, US public non-financial corporations are carrying debt equal to about 50 per cent of their net worth – far above historic levels. Those levels were below 20 per cent in the 1950s, 25 per cent in the mid-1980s, and below 40 per cent in 2007, prior to the Great Financial Crisis (Arends, 2014).

In sum, the shift towards a financial model of the firm has meant that corporate profitability draws on a much wider range of financial strategies than previously and that the corporation as an entity is viewed as temporal – a set of assets to be bought and sold – Lego pieces to be assembled and disassembled. Top management's commitment to the organisation has become more temporal, and it often views labour's contribution to the bottom line as more limited and equivalent to any other factor of production.

The financial firm and its implications for HR and employment relations

The shift to a financial model of the firm is not only driven by 'external' forces, such as shareholder activism, Wall Street analysts or global competition. Top managers have internalised the model as well. Whereas managers in the post-war period did recognise the need to maintain reciprocal relations with labour, by the 1980s they increasingly viewed labour as a commodity or just another factor of production. The careers and economic fortunes of executives were no longer tied to the long-term sustainability of the corporation but to the short-term success of stock prices. Their identities as individual shareholders trumped their identities as organisational leaders (Lazonick, 1992).

Perhaps equally important was a qualitative shift in management ideology. Peter Cappelli notes, "A fundamental change occurred in managerial ideology in the 1980s. Employers learned that they could treat employment just like any other contract, with penalties to pay for breaking it. And they didn't see any reason not to do so. They viewed this approach as perfectly ethical" (Cappelli, 2016). They moved away from a reciprocal model of employment commitment and pushed risk and uncertainty on to workers via the increased use of temporary agency contracting and part-time work. In the US, employers began to classify non-management workers as salaried and 'exempt' from overtime rules, or as independent contractors, even though they carried out the tasks of regular employees and were supervised as such. The new ideology legitimised the downsizing activities of firms in that period, which hit experienced managers and professionals as well as workers (Cappelli, 1999; Osterman, 1996).

To reduce legal liabilities, firms began to use professional employment organisations (PEOs) as the employer of record, with responsibility for compliance with payroll and tax obligations. They also embraced recruitment processing outsourcing (RPO), in which all responsibilities for recruitment and hiring are shifted to a service provider. Global RPO or HR outsourcing providers such as PONTOON Solutions (UK), Hudson RPO (US) and Alexander

Mann Solutions (UK) serve major multinational corporations around the globe. The goal, notes Cappelli, is to "… make labor supply like a faucet – turn it on only when you need it, then turn it off" (Cappelli, 2016). Steve Berkenfeld, a managing director in investment banking at Barclays, provides a similar assessment: "Now, investors view 'human resources' just like any other input… the goal is to minimise costs and maximise resource utilisation."[1] Based on this logic, it is a short leap to the idea that a 'relationship' with labour is no longer needed or desirable.

There are many reasons why employers don't want to – or don't need to – have a 'relationship' with employees any more. They can more easily assert managerial prerogative given the decline in institutional constraints and shift in the balance of power between capital and labour. They have a much broader range of management strategies and technological tools that they can mix and match to lower labour and other operational costs, eliminate legal liabilities, reduce managerial headaches, and shift risks and uncertainty to contractors or workers. For many tasks, direct labour is eliminated and embedded in powerful new technologies bought off the shelf. At the same time, new management philosophies and techniques – core competency philosophy and value chain analysis – have been central to decision-making and provide the justification and a step-by-step guide for outsourcing functions, and with them, the employment relationship. Core competency theory prescribes the segmentation of the workforce according to those who 'add value' and those who don't (Lepak and Snell, 1999). Workers with core competencies are kept in-house while non-core workers are viewed as a variable cost and outsourced. David Weil (2014) has described this as a 'fissuring' of the employment relationship. He also notes that the 'core' is shrinking. What is core versus non-core, however, is ambiguous, and managers often make decisions about what to keep in house and what to outsource not on the basis of an actual business analysis but on political pressure to reduce headcount: by reducing the denominator of the number of people employed, productivity and revenues per employee appear to be higher.

Outsourcing the employment relationship can take many contractual forms – including shifting work to outside contractors *off site*; shifting ownership to franchisees, who pay a royalty to the franchisor for use of the brand; or using temporary staffing firms, leasing firms or staff management companies to manage workers *on site* at the primary firm's locations. Each of these cases constitutes a form of inter-firm contracting that breaks the employment relationship between the primary firm and a worker, who is now hired, fired and managed by the contractor. In addition, employers may combine these *inter-firm service contracts* with alternative forms of *individual employment contracts* – such as freelancers, direct hire temps, on-call workers or on-demand platform workers. These strategies allow firms to drive down costs or improve performance by 'whipsawing' – pitting in-house workers against those employed by contractors, bidding down contract terms among subcontractors or creating competition between in-house workers, independent contractors and temporary employees. Our research on how employers use a mix of these forms of contracting and the implications for workforce management and ER is seriously undeveloped.

Outsourcing certain tasks or functions altogether allows employers to lower their exposure to market uncertainties. They reduce direct and indirect labour costs and shift rising health care and pension liabilities and lawsuits to contractors. As noted, by lowering headcount and reducing the denominator, revenues per employee go up. Companies with higher profits and lower labour costs have higher stock market valuations. Managers don't have to 'deal with' employee voice, diversity, discrimination, work-family balance, dual career problems, illness, absenteeism, scheduling and other time-consuming issues – in sum, they outsource HR management. The job of management is easier. Managing people is turned into managing a contractor – a function often handled by the procurement division of corporations. And with less labour and a smaller organisational footprint, companies reduce infrastructure and real estate costs as well.

This ideological turn has important ramifications for the field of strategic HR management as well as ER. The field of strategic HR management grew under the premise that the strategic management of human capital could add value to the firm (Dyer, 1984). Investments in firm-specific training could pay off by creating 'human resources' with unique knowledge and skills – providing a key point of leverage for sustainable competitive advantage (Barney, 1991). This argument drew on the seminal work of Gary Becker in *Human Capital* (1964), in which he posited that workers' knowledge and skills are valuable assets that firms can use to increase productivity. In this sense, labor is a 'quasi-fixed' factor of production (Oi, 1962), rather than a variable cost to be minimized. The field of strategic HR management grew under the premise that the strategic management of human assets could add value to the firm (Dyer, 1984). Investments in firm-specific training could pay off by creating 'human resources' with unique knowledge and skills – providing a key point of leverage for sustainable competitive advantage (Barney, 1991). Industrial relations scholars also embraced this view, with some hopeful that the two fields might converge around a common set of management principles that would support high firm performance and high-quality jobs (Kochan and Osterman, 1994).

Faced with a countervailing movement that promoted a financial model of the firm – and bolstered by powerful new technological tools and a management philosophy that justified a reduction in commitment to the employment relationship – that project of 'mutual gains' largely failed, at least for a large swath of working people.

The role of technology

Information and other advanced technologies have provided much more powerful tools now than in the past for employers who want to reduce their direct responsibilities for labour. To automate and eliminate labour, firms now may combine many new sophisticated technologies – numerically controlled machines, robotics, computerised inventory management systems, speech recognition, language translation, pattern recognition and online commerce, and self-driving vehicles (Brynjolffson and McAfee, 2011, 2016). These tools reshape the employment relationship in at least two important ways: at the level of the *organisation of production* (the allocation of parts of the production process or business functions within or across firms) and at the level of the *organisation of work* (the allocation of work tasks among workers and the labour content of those tasks).

At the level of production, digital technologies make it easier for firms to outsource particular parts of the value chain, such as assembly or distribution – or particular functions, such as accounting, payroll or legal services. While traditionally firms kept work in house in order to ensure control and coordination of processes, new information technologies facilitate virtual coordination and control via inter-firm data management systems used to monitor and enforce contractual obligations. As former employees become workers in contractor firms, the question of who is responsible for HR management across organisational boundaries has begun to receive some research attention (Marchington, Rubery and Grimshaw, 2011), but much more is needed. How does the primary (or client) firm ensure high levels of quality, alignment and coordination without also influencing or mandating certain HR standards of qualifications, training, performance management and pay? What inter-organisational tensions arise in this process, and who is ultimately responsible for employment liabilities in supply chains, particularly where power asymmetries exist and client firms establish the terms and conditions of service contracts?

This question has received considerable attention in the global supply chain literature, where parts of production are outsourced *and* sent off shore. Much less understood is the outsourcing of work to domestic contractors and suppliers, which probably is *more extensive* than offshore outsourcing because it can be applied to place-based activities in services ranging from janitorial and maintenance to logistics or health care.

The second use of technology – to automate and redesign workplace processes and the labour content of jobs – has received much more media attention. Researchers point not only to the consistent doubling of computing power that has driven changes in the IT industry (Ford, 2009), but more disruptive changes due to radical advances in artificial intelligence, machine learning, deep learning and robotics. Machine learning algorithms are at the heart of teaching robots how to navigate beyond the rules-based reasoning of computers. These changes turn 'machines as tools' into 'machines as workers,' leading to projected high rates of jobless-ness in advanced economies (Ford, 2015). Investment in robotics is accelerating, with venture capital investment, for example, doubling between 2014 and 2015, to $587 million (Waters and Bradshaw, 2016). At the extreme, technology consultants estimate that 45 per cent of the work tasks that people are currently paid to do could be automated using existing technologies, with potential to automate an additional 13 per cent of work activities (Chui, Manyika and Miremadi, 2015). Others argue that 'capable systems' are expanding the availability of expert knowledge to the general public in ways that fundamentally undermine the monopoly and control that professionals have had over knowledge in professional domains (Susskind and Susskind, 2015)

Research in HR management and ER will need to address how these changes affect the jobs that remain and how the transformation of work should be managed. Notably, although employers may believe they can simply automate away jobs to reduce labour costs and improve productivity, these reports emphasise that the process will be much more complicated and challenging for management. It will require companies to reorganise the labour process as the remaining tasks are recombined into new jobs. While there will be fewer jobs for a given set of activities, those that are left will be more complex and require higher-order skills or a reconfig-uration of skills. In addition, many low-wage jobs that are particularly resistant to automation – home health aides, janitors, maintenance workers or landscapers – will grow with the ageing of the population in advanced economies.

Similarly, research will need to address how new technologies change the jobs of man-agers. Data management and monitoring software reduce indirect labour costs by eliminating supervisors. This pattern was an important feature of the reorganisation of customer service and sales operations into mega-call centres in the 1990s, which lowered labour costs through econ-omies of scale and standardisation of processes and allowed the ratio of workers to supervisors to triple or quadruple. In the 2000s, these technologies spread to managerial and professional workers, whose productivity and specific location are now tracked and managed remotely and whose 'on-call' work hours are extended via email and mobile phone access. The performance management software industry now features a wide range of systems for continuous monitoring of workers' every move (Streigtfeld, 2015). These changes suggest an increase in the complexity and intensity of work for those managers and professionals who remain.

Digitalisation and the upgrading of communications infrastructure has also given companies a more viable option to use home-based workers or 'telework' – and thereby cut their real estate costs as well as management overheads. While enthusiasm about teleworking exploded in the 1990s and 2000s, only to be unrealised, now the fall in the price of transmissions technologies and the rise in the surveillance capabilities of IT may be leading to renewed experiments in technology-mediated home-based work. The question of how management will incorporate tele-workers into productive operations – and how compliance with labour and employment laws will be ensured – is a critical one yet to be addressed.

At the same time, corporations continue to use automation and new technologies to shift labour tasks to consumers – for example, via automated banking (ATM machines), automated airport check-in kiosks, on-line banking and travel reservations and the like. The new unpaid work of consumers as workers – aptly referred to as 'shadow work' by Lambert (2015) – also has implications for human resource management, as managers must 'manage' the interface between workers and consumers as workers.

In sum, new technologies arguably are having more profound effects on the organisation of production and the labour content of jobs than in the past. The range of options available for employers to reduce direct-hire employees and minimise the obligations that come with a 'standard' or traditional employment relationship is impressive. But employers' enthusiastic embrace of these options may underestimate the sticky legal and 'people' issues that accompany automation or alternative work arrangements – including labour conflicts, consumer backlash, privacy issues and liability issues. Amazon's use of an internal tool allowing any employee to anonymously report or criticise any other, for example, led to public repudiation for creating a workplace of fear and intimidation (Kantor and Streigtfeld, 2015). Our understanding of how these changes are occurring and their implications for HR management and ER is thin – and ripe for systematic research. Rubery and colleagues similarly note that there are many reasons why the enthusiastic embrace of 'flexible' labour and employment practices in the UK and Europe may backfire via lower productivity and higher social welfare costs (Rubery, Keizer and Grimshaw, 2016).

From employment relationships to contingent employment contracts

Beyond outsourcing and sub-contracting, employers have increasingly turned to hiring individual workers on a project or temporary basis. They may be called freelance workers, direct hire temporary workers, mini-jobbers, short-hour workers, on-call workers and the like. While independent contractors are often included here, they are in fact 'a firm' that may be a solo practice or have employees. What they have in common is that their employment contracts are 'contingent' and of uncertain duration. They are unlikely to have a 'relationship' with their employer – only a contract for services provided. In the US, the number of workers in these classifications is considerable, although substantially lower than those who work for outsourced or contractor firms; unfortunately national-level data do not provide accurate numbers. According to one study, workers in these types of 'alternative work arrangements' increased only marginally between 1995 and 2005, but from 10.1 per cent in 2005 to 15.8 per cent in 2015 – a 50 per cent increase (Katz and Krueger, 2016). Virtually all US net employment growth from 2006 to 2015 was in the form of what Katz and Krueger define as alternative work arrangements. In the European Union, the growth in temporary or contingent employment has actually exceeded that in the US because of employer efforts to avoid employment protection laws (that are limited in the US) or collective bargaining contracts (that cover less than eight per cent of the US private sector workforce).

Of particular controversy is the rise of 'on-demand' or 'gig' workers, who are linked to customers or clients directly via online platforms – the most well-known of which is Uber. Uber grew from zero workers in 2012 to an estimated 400,000–450,000 by January 2015 (Hall and Krueger, 2017). It is by far the most successful on-demand platform (Grubhub is a distant second), and represents roughly two-thirds of the on-demand market in the US. Overall, however, on-demand workers represent only 0.4 per cent of all US workers (ibid.), and the percentages in Europe are even lower. Some argue that the impact of this type of 'virtual service work' is particularly potent for higher skilled workers who find virtual work assignments via platforms such as Upwork.com (with eight million registered freelancers), witmart.com (with 13 million) and Mechanical Turk (with 500,000 workers).

Uber and other intermediary firms that operate online platforms insist that they are not employers because their technology simply facilitates a worker-consumer direct match. Critics argue that Uber sets the prices for fares, raises and lowers them at will, sets standards on cars and prohibits drivers from accepting tips. Workers have control over when they *won't* work, but not when they *will* – as they don't have control over the market and if they turn down too many customers, Uber can de-activate them from the list of drivers (Greenhouse, 2015).

On-demand contracting has spurred contentious debate in many countries, as well as law suits, labour mobilisations and a handful of experiments. In Europe, widespread public outcry led to Uber's retreat in major cities (Scott, 2016), while in June 2016, the European Commission issued a non-binding legal guidance to member states concerning business models that use collaborative platforms for the exchange of services. The guidance sets forth criteria (such as the level of control the platform exerts in setting prices, contractual terms and ownership of key assets) for determining whether an employment relationship exists between the platform and the worker (Dagnino, 2016). In the US, Uber and Lyft, the two leading on-demand ride services, have faced class-action lawsuits over misclassification of employees as independent contractors, as well as legislation in some cities (Seattle) asserting that Uber drivers are employees with the right to unionisation and collective bargaining.

Implications for the field of HR management and employment relations

What do these trends mean for scholars in the field of HR management and employment relations? The rise in the importance of financial strategies, the vertical disintegration of the firm, the ideological shift in management thinking and the enhanced capabilities of technology all pose serious challenges to the received wisdom in our academic fields. What kind of research is needed to assess the importance and implications of these trends for our theories and assumptions in strategic HR management and ER?

A first task is to overcome the siloed nature of our social science research. Management and labour scholars need to become more financially literate and incorporate financial analysis into our research. This means engaging in more interdisciplinary research with scholars in finance and economics – something that these fields would also benefit from so that they begin to pay attention to the organisational and employment implications of their theories. This kind of project might re-examine the assumptions about the nature of value creation and extraction and how that differs under a managerial versus a financial model of the firm. In the current economy, to what extent does value creation and extraction occur at the level of the workplace, as assumed under managerial capitalism, and to what extent is it the result of financial engineering and the rearrangement of claims among different owners of capital? In other words, what proportion of a firm's value creation depends on the effective management of people in the production of goods and services? Which people? And how does this vary across different industries or types of firms? Available evidence suggests that many large corporations and those owned by financial intermediaries such as private equity firms or hedge funds rely heavily on financial engineering strategies, but the extent of the diffusion of these practices across the economy and in smaller or entrepreneurial firms is poorly understood. Where do we find uneven penetration and why? And what can we learn from these examples?

The answers to these questions will help us understand whether strategic HR management is as important for firm performance as our theories say it is. If profits are increasingly based on financial engineering activities, then investing in human capital 'as a quasi-fixed asset' – and in turn the strategic role of the HR function – may be altered or diminished. Perhaps, strategic HR is now primarily relevant to manage the flow of the top 200 managers of the firm, or those in the finance and legal departments – but much less so for those in productive operations. Shedding light on these questions is also important for ER scholars to understand how the points of leverage for collective bargaining vary, depending on whether a firm relies heavily on productive versus financial activities and how it views the importance of its own workforce for value creation.

Second, how do financial strategies and the capital structure of the firm affect business strategies and HR policies? Again, teaming up with finance and economics scholars would be useful. Research on private equity-owned companies, for example, has shown that extensive use of debt financing and asset sales leads to financial distress more often than in less highly leveraged firms, thereby undermining long-term sustainability, and in turn, the economic security of the workforce. But debt financing is also needed for corporate growth and expansion. How much debt is too much? At what point do these financial strategies and the imperative to repay debt impinge on the decision-making scope of top management vis-à-vis innovative business and HR strategies? And what are the spillover effects on workers' jobs and pay?

The resource-based view of the firm, central to strategic HR theory, posits that firms can create sustainable competitive advantage by building human capital that is valuable, rare, socially complex and hard to imitate. This requires long time horizons. In this context, how does the financial model of the firm create *sustainable* competitive advantage, and if it does, what is the 'strategic' role of HR? To answer these questions, scholars will need to use more sophisticated methodologies with longitudinal data, longer time horizons and larger data sets.

Third, the theoretical explanations linking financial incentives and management decisions are poorly understood. How does the alignment of executive pay to stock price affect top management decisions about business and HR strategy and organisational restructuring? Under what conditions do HR managers play a strategic role or retain an independent scope of action that allows for longer time horizons, innovation or a consideration of broader stakeholder perspectives?

In the context of the sharp rise of pay-for-performance for managers, some research points to a concomitant rise in the callousness of managers' actions and behaviours. Desai, Brief and George (2009), for example, found that in firms with higher CEO-worker pay gaps, CEOs have enhanced perceptions of power and in turn, lower empathy and more likelihood of objectifying others. They found that the higher the compensation of a company's CEO, the "meaner" the ER practices. Again, interdisciplinary projects that bring together finance economists and micro and macro organisation scholars may shed greater light on the intersection between economic, sociological and psychological processes and inequality in organisations.

I have argued that the shift to the financial model of the firm also increases the likelihood that firms will make greater use of domestic outsourcing and inter-firm contracting. Our understanding of how the outsourcing of work affects HR strategies and the quality of workers' jobs and pay, however, is under-developed. A key empirical question is: How and why do HR strategies and ER differ in primary (client) versus contractor firms? Some argue that the vertical disintegration of the firm and the rise of contracting primarily create cost pressures that undermine the quality of jobs and wages because they open up new opportunities for whipsawing, shift jobs to job shops that operate on the margins of the law, shift risks to contractor firms that have greater demand volatility and fewer resources, and create obstacles for workers to take collective action or even know who their employer of record is (Doellgast and Greer, 2007; Weil, 2014). Others suggest that the outcomes are more contingent and depend on the level of specialisation and collaboration across networked firms and the extent of trust and balance of power in inter-firm relationships (Grimshaw, Willmott and Rubery, 2005).

The extensive use of outsourcing and contingent employment contracts also calls into question the assumptions of strategic HR management – that human capital or the management of people are critical differentiators for firm competitiveness and that firms need to invest in the skills and development of core employees to be profitable or successful. If it is a critical differentiator, which employees are 'core' and which are not? If parts of the production process are sent to contractors and managed by the procurement department of client firms, what role if any does the HR function play? To what extent do client firms exert influence or control over the HR policies of contractor firms or franchisees? And how do we measure the value of HR management in supplier firms as an input into client firms?

Related to this theme, I have reviewed some promising new research on innovative labour strategies that seeks to identify new forms of collective action and representation across organisational boundaries. What can we learn from these experiments to inform public policy? Given the institutional lag between labour and employment laws and IR systems on the one hand, and new networked forms of organisation on the other, what research is needed to build more effective labour market institutions responsive to new forms of production or 'the sharing economy'?

In addition, it is unlikely that labour market reforms alone will be sufficient to ensure employment and income security for working populations in advanced economies. A comparative research volume on private equity, hedge funds and sovereign wealth funds, for example, found that IR systems in Europe were somewhat effective in limiting the negative impact of these intermediaries on workers' jobs and pay, through mechanisms such as co-determination and union power. But financial regulations in Europe were not because they did not anticipate financial activities such as the high use of debt and asset sales that undermine company stability (Gospel, Pendleton and Vitols, 2014). Thus scholars need to pay closer attention to how capital market rules shape firm behaviour and HR management strategies, again highlighting the need for collaborative research between finance, management and labour relations scholars.

Finally, these changes in the real world of work suggest the need for a major overhaul of management education. Currently, most business schools rely heavily on function-based classes (finance, marketing, accounting) in siloed departments and tenure faculty based on discipline-based articles. Firms face real world problems that require leaders with interdisciplinary training – people who can understand the links between finance capital, strategy, HR management and ER. They need a clear understanding of how national and international institutions face off with business strategy and management. At the same time, labour relations scholars need to 'study up' – gaining a much clearer understanding of how capital markets and financial intermediaries affect corporate decisions and in turn, the degrees of leverage available for collective representation across networked and technology-mediated organisations.

Conclusion

In this chapter, I have argued that the fundamental shift in the business model of the firm – from a managerial to a financial one – is central to explaining how and why the management and employment relations of companies has changed and why the quality of jobs and pay has deteriorated for many working people. The shift has allowed top managers to realise that their fortunes depend much less on the co-operation of productive labour, which in turn has led them to change their approach to HR management and ER and to return a higher proportion of retained earnings to themselves and their shareholders – often at the expense of working people. Armed with new disruptive technologies that automate and eliminate work or facilitate its shift to tiers of contractors, employers appear to have reduced their commitment to labour as a 'valuable human resource' or have sought to exit the employment relationship all together. And in the context of a global labour market that doubles the ratio of labour to capital, labour's bargaining power has waned.

Our role as social scientists in this historic period is to *go to the field* and carefully examine what is occurring in the management of organisations. We need to document the overall trends; the variation in those trends across occupations, industries and countries; and the winners and losers in the process. We need to clearly articulate the causal mechanisms linking changes in the ownership structures of companies and their business models to the management of work and employment relations and outcomes for differentially situated workers. And we need to use careful evidence-based research to inform public policy and create innovative institutions that effectively respond to the rapid changes taking place in the world of work.

Note

1 Personal interview, 12 April, 2016.

References

Activist Investor. (2015). 'Activism by the Numbers', *Activist Investor*, 4(11), p. 8.

Appelbaum, E. (2014a). 'Why Private Equity Investors Can't Save Red Lobster'. *Fortune Magazine*. [Online]. 30 June. Available at: http://fortune.com/2014/06/30/why-private-equity-investors-cant-save-red-lobster/

Appelbaum, E. and Batt, R. (2014). *Private Equity at Work: When Wall Street Manages Main Street*. New York: Russell Sage Foundation.

Arends, B. (2014). 'Watch out for the corporate debt bomb'. *MarketWatch*. (Online). Available at: www.marketwatch.com/story/watch-out-for-the-corporate-debt-bomb-2014-08-04.

Barney, J.B. (1991). 'Firm resources and sustained competitive advantage', *Journal of Management*, 17, pp. 99–120.

Becker, G. (1964). *Human Capital: A Theoretical and Empirical Analysis, With Special Reference to Education*. Chicago: University of Chicago Press.

Bernhardt, A., Batt, R., Houseman, S. and Appelbaum, E. (2016). *Domestic Outsourcing in the US: A Research Agenda to Assess Trends and Effects on Job Quality*. Upjohn Institute Working Paper 16-253. W.E. Upjohn Institute for Employment Research. Available at: https://doi.org/10.17848/wp16-253.

Brynjolfsson, E. and McAfee, A. (2011). *Race Against the Machine: How the Digital Revolution is Accelerating Innovation, Driving Productivity, and Irreversibly Transforming Employment and the Economy*. Cambridge (MA): MIT Center for Digital Business.

Brynjolfsson, E. and McAfee, A. (2016). *The Second Machine Age: Work, Progress, and Prosperity in a Time of Brilliant Technologies*. New York: W.W. Norton & Company, Inc.

Cable, D. and Vermeulen, F. (2016). 'Stop Paying Executives for Performance'. *Harvard Business Review*. (Online). 23 February. Available at: https://hbr.org/2016/02/stop-paying-executives-for-performance

Cappelli, P. (1999). *The New Deal at Work: Managing the Market-Driven Workforce*. Boston (MA): Harvard Business School Press.

Cappelli, P. (2016). *Trends in Alternative Work and the Power of Ideas*. Presentation, Russell Sage Foundation Workshop, 'Non-Standard Work: How Do We Measure It and What Is Its Impact On Workers, Workplaces And The Economy?' 1 April, New York.

Chui, M., Manyika, J. and Miremadi, M. (2015). 'Four fundamentals of workplace automation'. *McKinsey Quarterly*. (Online). November. Available at: www.mckinsey.com/insights/business_technology/four_fundamentals_of_workplace_automation?cid=other-eml-nsl-mip-mck-oth-1512.

Dagnino, E. (2016). *Work in the Sharing Economy. The Position of the EU Commission*. Adapt and CIETT (International Confederation of Private Employment Agencies). 26 June.

Davis, A. and Mishel, L. (2014). *CEO Pay Continues to Rise as Typical Workers Are Paid Less*. Issue Brief 380. Washington, DC: Economic Policy Institute.

Desai, S.D., Brief, A.P. and George, J. (2009). Meaner managers: a consequence of income inequality, in Kramer, R., Bazerman, M. and Tenbrunsel, A. (eds.) *Social Decision Making: Social Dilemmas, Social Values, and Ethical Judgments*. New York: Taylor & Francis, pp. 315–334.

Doellgast, V. and Greer, I. (2007). 'Vertical Disintegration and the Disorganization of German Industrial Relations', *British Journal of Industrial Relations*, 45(1), pp. 55–76.

Drahokoupil, J. (ed.) (2015). *The Outsourcing Challenge: Organizing Workers across Fragmented Production Chains.* Brussels: ETUI.

Dyer, L. (1984). Strategic human resources management and planning, in Ferris, G.F. (ed.) *Research in Personnel and Human Resources Management.* Greenwich (CT): JAI Press.

Ford, M. (2009). *The Lights in the Tunnel: Automation, Accelerating Technology, and the Economy of the Future.* New York: Basic Books.

Ford, M. (2015). *The Rise of the Robots: Technology and the Threat of a Jobless Future.* New York: Basic Books.

Gospel, H., Pendleton, A. and Vitols, S. (eds.) (2014). *Financialisation, New Investment Funds, and Labour: An International Comparison.* Oxford: Oxford University Press.

Greenhouse, S. (2015). Uber: on the road to nowhere. Uber drivers are getting creative in their fight for basic workplace rights. *The American Prospect.* (Online). 7 December. Available at: http://prospect.org/article/road-nowhere-3.

Grimshaw, D., Willmott, H. and Rubery, J. (2005). Inter-organizational Networks: Trust, Power, and the Employment Relationship, in Marchington, M., Grimshaw, D., Rubery, J. and Willmott, H. (eds.) *Fragmenting Work: Blurring Organizational Boundaries and Disordering Hierarchies.* Oxford: Oxford University Press, pp. 63–88.

Hall, J.V. and Krueger, A.B. (2017). [Forthcoming]. 'An Analysis of the Labor Market for Uber's Driver-Partners in the United States', *Industrial and Labor Relations Review.* (Online). Available at: http://journals.sagepub.com/doi/abs/10.1177/0019793917717222.

Hirschman, A. (1970). *Exit, Voice and Loyalty.* Cambridge (MA): Harvard University Press.

Jensen, M.C. and Murphy, K.J. (1990). 'CEO Incentives – It's Not How Much You Pay But How', *Harvard Business Review*, 68(3), pp. 138–153.

Katz, L. and Krueger, A.B. (2016). *The Rise and Nature of Alternative Work Arrangements in the United States, 1995–2015.* Working Paper. Available at: https://scholar.harvard.edu/files/lkatz/files/katz_krueger_cws_v3.pdf.

Kantor, J. and Streitfeld, D. (2015). 'Inside Amazon: Wrestling Big Ideas in a Bruising Workplace'. *New York Times.* (Online). 15 August. Available at: www.nytimes.com/2015/08/16/technology/inside-amazon-wrestling-big-ideas-in-a-bruising-workplace.html?ref=business&_r=1.

Kochan, T. and Osterman, P. (1994). *The Mutual Gains Enterprise: Forging a Winning Partnership among Labor, Management, and Government.* Cambridge (MA): Harvard Business School Press.

Krippner, G. (2011). *Capitalizing on Crisis: the Political Origins of the Rise of Finance.* Cambridge (MA): Harvard University Press.

Lambert, C. (2015). *Shadow Work: The Unpaid, Unseen Jobs That Fill Your Day.* New York: Counterpoint.

Lazonick, W. (1992). 'Controlling the Market for Corporate Control: The Historical Significance of Managerial Capitalism', *Industrial and Corporate Change*, 1(3), pp. 445–488.

Lazonick, W. (2014). 'Profits without prosperity', *Harvard Business Review*, September, pp. 3–11.

Lepak, D. and Snell, S. (1999). 'The Human Resource Architecture: Toward a Theory of Human Capital Allocation and Development', *Academy of Management Review*, 24(1), pp. 31–48.

Lowenstein, R. (2004). *Origins of the Crash: The Great Bubble and its Undoing.* London: Penguin.

Marchington, M., Grimshaw, D., Rubery, J. and Willmott, H. (eds.) 2005. *Fragmenting Work: Blurring Organizational Boundaries and Disordering Hierarchies.* Oxford: Oxford University Press.

Marchington, M., Rubery, J. and Grimshaw, D. (2011). 'Alignment, Integration, and Consistency In HRM across Multi-Employer Networks', *Human Resource Management*, 50(3), pp. 313–339.

Oi, W. (1962). 'Labor as a Quasi-Fixed Factor', *Journal of Political Economy*, 70, pp. 538–555.

Osterman, P. (ed.) (1996). *Broken Ladders: Managerial Careers in the New Economy.* Oxford: Oxford University Press.

Prahalad, C.K. and Hamel, G. (1990). 'The Core Competencies of the Corporation', *Harvard Business Review*, 68(3), pp. 79–91.

Rubery, J., Keizer, A. and Grimshaw, D. (2016). 'Flexibility bites back: the multiple and hidden costs of flexible employment policies', *Human Resource Management Journal*, 26(3), pp. 235–251.

Scott, M. (2016). 'Uber's No-Holds-Barred Expansion Strategy Fizzles in Germany'. *New York Times.* (Online). 3 January. Available at: www.nytimes.com/2016/01/04/technology/ubers-no-holds-barred-expansion-strategy-fizzles-in-germany.html?_r=0.

Streigtfeld, D. (2015). 'Data-Crunching Is Coming to Help Your Boss Manage Your Time'. *New York Times.* (Online). 17 August. Available at: www.nytimes.com/2015/08/18/technology/data-crunching-is-coming-to-help-your-boss-manage-your-time.html.

Susskind, R. and Susskind, D. (2015). *The Future of the Professions: How Technology Will Transform the Work of Human Experts*. Oxford: Oxford University Press.

Towers Watson (2015). *CEO pay in the Eurotop100: Insights on similarities and differences in CEO pay across Europe*. [Online]. October. Available at: www.towerswatson.com/en/Insights/IC-Types/Survey-Research-Results/2015/10/CEO-pay-in-the-Eurotop-100.

Waters, R. and Bradshaw, T. (2016). 'Rise of the robots is sparking an investment boom'. *Financial Times*. (Online). 3 May. Available at: www.ft.com/content/5a352264-0e26-11e6-ad80-67655613c2d6.

Weil, D. (2014). *The. Fissured Workplace*. Cambridge (MA): Harvard University Press.

INDEX